C000170894

THE PLAYS OF EURIPIDES

SELECTED FRAGMENTARY PLAYS: II

General Editor

Professor Christopher Collard

ARIS & PHILLIPS CLASSICAL TEXTS

EURIPIDES

Selected Fragmentary Plays

with Introductions, Translations and Commentaries

by

C. Collard, M. J. Cropp and J. Gibert

Volume II

*Philoctetes, Alexandros (with Palamedes and Sisyphus),
Oedipus, Andromeda, Hypsipyle, Antiope, Archelaus*

Aris & Phillips is an imprint of
Oxbow Books, Park End Place, Oxford OX1 1HN

© C. Collard, M. J. Cropp & J. Gibert 2004. All rights reserved.
No part of this publication may be reproduced or stored in a retrieval
system or transmitted in any form or by any means including
photocopying without the prior permission of the publishers in writing.

ISBN 0-85668-620-4 cloth
ISBN 0-85668-621-2 paper

A CIP record for this book is available from the British Library.

Printed and bound by Antony Rowe Ltd, Chippenham

To the memory of

Kevin Hargreaves Lee

CONTENTS OF VOLUME TWO

GENERAL EDITOR'S FOREWORD

In the volumes of this Series which offer the complete plays I have begun my Foreword with the argument that Euripides' remarkable variety of subjects, ideas and methods challenges each new generation of readers, and audiences, to a fresh appraisal. The complete plays, eighteen in number, are challenge enough, but there are nearly as many fragmentary plays which it is possible to reconstruct in outline and which increase and diversify the challenge still more. The Preface and General Introduction to *Selected Fragmentary Plays I* (1995) asserted the great interest of these plays in their own right, and described the ways in which they illuminate the complete plays while depending on them for their own illumination.

While the two volumes are in the general style of the Aris & Phillips Classical Texts, the fragmentary material on which they draw has sometimes to be presented and discussed on a fuller scale, and is offered to a rather wider readership. Not just school, college or university students and their teachers but also professional scholars will, we hope, be served by these two volumes. For each play there is an editor's introduction which attempts reconstruction and appreciation, discussing context, plot, poetic resources and meaning. The Greek text is faced by an English prose translation – for many of the plays the first complete such translation to be published. The commentaries privilege interpretation and appreciation as far as possible over philological discussion; but the needs of fragmentary texts make the latter inseparable from the former.

The content and nature of the two volumes explain the omission of the General Introduction to the Series and the General Bibliography which are found in other volumes. Instead, a General Introduction to the fragmentary tragedies is offered in Volume I, including a section which reviews the special features and problems of these plays; and in each volume there is a Bibliography listing frequently cited studies and editions, as well as a select Bibliography for each play.

Oxford   Christopher Collard

PREFACE

We have been pleased by the welcome given to the first volume of *Euripides: Selected Fragmentary Plays*. All reviewers thought we had achieved our main objectives, to increase accessibility to these fragmentary plays for specialists and non-specialists alike, and to 'encourage attention to some fascinating texts which are often of considerable importance to the critical appreciation of the poet' (Vol. I, Preface, p. vii). We have noted the following reviews:

JACT Review 20 (1996), 13–14 (R. Shone); *Greece & Rome* 42 (1996), 227 (S. Halliwell); *L'Antiquité Classique* 65 (1996), 269–70 (H. Van Looy); *Bryn Mawr Classical Review* 8 (1997), 207–9 (S. Goldberg); *Mnemosyne* 50 (1997), 246–50 (M. A. Harder); *Phoenix* 51 (1997), 226–7 (R. Scodel); *Prudentia* 29 (1997), 60–4 (J. Davidson); *Revue de Philologie* 71 (1997), 297–8 (F. Jouan); *Classical Review* 48 (1998), 474–5 (S. Ireland); *Echos du Monde Classique/Classical Views* 18 (1999), 403–11 (J. R. Porter); *Faventia* 23 (2001), 138–9 (R. Torné Teixidó).

The contents of this second volume are as promised in the first. The plays appear in known or likely chronological order. We include brief Addenda and Corrigenda to Volume I, and an Index to both volumes.

Since the first volume appeared in 1995, F. Jouan and H. Van Looy have not only begun but finished their Budé edition of the fragmentary plays and unassigned fragments, in four volumes (1998–2003), and have published a number of incidental papers. We commend their achievement as well as their speed, and we record with regret the death of H. Van Looy soon after the last volume was published; his earliest work on the fragments (see our Vol. 1 p. 4 n. 3 and p. 13) was very important as a starting-point and encouragement to others. Like ourselves, Jouan and Van Looy benefited from the generous help of Richard Kannicht, whose *Euripides* in *TrGF* is complete and may well have appeared sooner than this volume. Mere congratulations to Professor Kannicht will be insufficient to recognize the profound and exact scholarship which has attended his work, and countless preparatory and separate studies, over more than thirty years. It is already evident that much closer attention is being given to Euripides' fragmentary plays than ever before.

Our working methods have been as in Volume I. Each of us took the first and final responsibility for individual plays, as indicated on the contents-page. All three of us have however read and annotated one another's drafts, and for one memorable week in Oxford in August 2002 we were able to discuss a large part of the volume as a team.

We dedicate this volume to the memory of Kevin Lee, a fine Euripidean and an even finer colleague and friend. These qualities were amply displayed and appreciated at the 1999 Banff Euripides Conference which he and Martin Cropp organized; together with David Sansone they saw the collected papers into print as *Euripides and Tragic Theatre in the Late Fifth Century*, published as *Illinois Classical Studies* 24/25 (1999–2000), a book similarly dedicated to the memory of a wonderfully sympathetic Euripidean and spirit, Desmond Conacher, who was the *éminence* of the Banff Conference.

Kevin Lee was to have undertaken *Philoctetes* and *Alexandros* (together with *Palamedes* and *Sisyphus*) for our second volume. He had made a beginning on them, and we have drawn upon his notes where practicable, acknowledging them with his initials. Christopher Collard and Martin Cropp were very pleased to have persuaded John Gibert to take Kevin's place, and in consequence we reallocated some of the plays. The change in our team, and also some unexpectedly long deflections of all three of us towards other work and duties, have caused this second volume to appear much later than we had hoped.

In working on the fragments we have been more than usually conscious of a debt to our predecessors, especially those who have edited and commented in recent years on plays presented in this volume. In addition to Richard Kannicht and the Budé editors, these include Godfrey Bond, Walter Cockle, James Diggle, Annette Harder, Jean Kambitsis, Rainer Klimek-Winter, and Carl Werner Müller. We are also grateful once more to colleagues and friends who have encouraged and assisted us in various ways or offered valuable comments on our first volume: Colin Austin, Walter Cockle, James Diggle, Pat Easterling, Wolfgang Luppe, Jim Neville, Doug Olson, John Porter, and Scott Scullion.

As before, preparation of the final copy was undertaken by Martin Cropp, who thanks Jason McClure and Paul Harms for their assistance with copy-editing and indexing. He also wishes to acknowledge the support of a Center for Hellenic Studies Summer Scholarship (1999), a University of Calgary Research Grant (1997–2000), and a University of Calgary Sabbatical Research Fellowship (Fall 2000).

We conclude this Preface by expressing our gratitude to Adrian and Lucinda Phillips of Aris and Phillips, who supported and published our first volume with particular enthusiasm, and with warm thanks to David Brown of Oxbow Books, who has taken over their imprint and was willing to accept a book bigger than we had at first expected to produce.

August 2004   Christopher Collard (Oxford)
                                                              Martin Cropp (Calgary)
                                                              John Gibert (Boulder)

FORM AND CONTENT OF THIS EDITION

We present each play as follows: *First*, a summary Bibliography arranged under Texts and Testimonia, Myth (sources and analytic discussions), Illustrations (vase-paintings, sculpture etc.), and Main Scholarly Discussions. *Second*, an Introduction discussing Reconstruction of the plot (including the fitting of the fragments into an outline, and the use of *testimonia* and illustrations), the Myth and its history, Themes and Characters, Staging, Date, and Other Dramatizations and Later Influence. *Third*, Greek text with a critical apparatus in English (sometimes continued on the facing page), and facing this an English prose translation. *Fourth*, a Commentary in which lemmata are taken from the English translation. Text-critical discussion is where possible segregated within square brackets, normally at the end of line-numbered sections.

The plays are printed in approximate chronological order. In Volume II the fragments are presented with the numbering of the new *Tragicorum Graecorum Fragmenta (TrGF)*, which follows for the most part the numbering of Nauck-Snell; we are extremely grateful to Professor Kannicht for making his numbering of the fragments available to us before his own volume is published. The numerical order of *TrGF* is also maintained, except in a few cases where considerations of reconstruction required a change (such changes are indicated by cross-references in Text and Translation). *TrGF* fragment-numbers identical with Nauck's or Snell's numbers are given in the Greek Text and Translation as (e.g.) **42**; those not present in Nauck or Snell are given as (e.g.) **41a (– N)**, and those present in Nauck or Snell but renumbered in *TrGF* are given as (e.g.) **43 (46 N)**, **62f (935 N, 42a N-Sn)**, etc. All cross-references use the *TrGF* number only (e.g. *Alex.* F 62f). We have discontinued the use of Mette's numbers, which were used in Volume I in a few cases where alternative numbers were not available. Fragment-numbers of other important editions, if different from *TrGF*, are give in the Apparatus; these include the complete Budé edition and the collections of C. Austin in *Nova Fragmenta Euripidea* (1968: = 'A' in the Apparatus) and J. Diggle in *Tragicorum Graecorum Fragmenta Selecta* (1998: = 'D'), as well as individual editions designated by editor's name or an obvious abbreviation. Details of the first publications and other important editions of papyrus-fragments are given in the play-bibliographies and/or the Apparatus for the relevant fragment.

Spans of papyrus text with no intelligible content are presented as succinctly as possible, often with a bare English description, e.g. 'remains of three lines'.

The Greek Text uses the following editorial signals:

[ ]   in papyrus texts enclose supplements of textual matter conjectured to have stood there before physical loss;

⌊ ⌋   enclose matter deficient in a papyrus but extant elsewhere, usually in a book-fragment;

α (etc.) Subscript dots accompany letters uncertainly read in a papyrus. Under a blank space a dot stands for one letter reckoned to be missing;

| indicates a line-end in a papyrus where the printed colometry differs;

< > in texts other than papyrus enclose supplements of matter which the text did not contain but which Euripides is conjectured to have written; such brackets may contain three dots to indicate a brief loss which cannot be filled with confidence, or may be left empty to indicate a more extensive loss;

{ } in both papyrus and other texts enclose matter which stood in those texts but is judged inauthentic;

† † *Obeli* ('daggers') enclose matter judged incurably corrupt;

( ) enclose *(a)* speaker-identifications not supplied in the sources, or *(b)* parentheses within the text;

—   A *paragraphus* at the left margin of the Greek text or Translation denotes an unidentified speaker;

— ‿ x The symbols for 'long', 'short' and 'indifferent' *(anceps)* syllable-length are occasionally used within the Greek text to indicate the rhythm of missing words.

The English Translation reproduces < >, { }, † † and ( ) as closely as possible from the Greek text, except that < > enclose translations of *all* conjectured supplements. In addition, all words judged uncertain and all supplements are italicized. Where possible, text-fragments are accompanied in the Translation by an indication of their probable location in the play. Line-numbers inserted into the Translation indicate as nearly as possible the end of the corresponding Greek verse-line.

    The critical Apparatus contains only information essential to understanding the problems of identifying, constituting and interpreting primary texts or book-fragments (which are often physically damaged or deficient, or otherwise corrupt and uncertain). Only the principal text-sources are named. Most matters of orthography, word-division, accentuation and punctuation are omitted, and obvious corrections of obvious minor errors are not recorded. Editorial conjectures are mentioned in the Apparatus only if judged worthy of discussion in the Commentary.

BIBLIOGRAPHY AND ABBREVIATIONS

This list identifies all items cited in abbreviated form in Volume II, except (i) those whose full details are given in the bibliographies for individual plays, and (ii) most ancient works (which are cited from current standard editions with editor's name added where needed). Abbreviated citations are by author's name, or author's name and abbreviated title, except where indicated in square brackets before an entry.

(a) Modern studies and reference-works

Aélion, R. *Euripide héritier d'Eschyle*. 2 vols. Paris, 1983.

Aélion, R. *Quelques grands mythes héroiques dans l'oeuvre d'Euripide*. Paris, 1986.

Burkert, W. *Greek Religion*, transl. J. Raffan. Oxford, 1985.

Carpenter, T. H. and C. A. Faraone (eds.). *Masks of Dionysus*. Ithaca, 1993.

Chantraine, P. *Dictionnaire étymologique de la langue grecque*. 4 vols. in 5. Paris, 1968–1980. Reprinted with Supplément, 1999.

Cropp, M. and G. Fick. *Resolutions and Chronology in Euripides: the Fragmentary Tragedies*. London, 1985 (*BICS* Suppl. 43).

Csapo, E. and M. Miller, eds. *Poetry, Theory, Praxis: the Social Life of Myth, Word and Image in Ancient Greece. Essays in honour of W. J. Slater*. Oxford, 2003.

Csapo, E. and W. J. Slater. *The Context of Ancient Drama*. Ann Arbor, 1995.

Denniston, J. D. *The Greek Particles*, 2nd ed. by K. J. Dover. Oxford, 1954.

Diggle, J. *Euripidea*. Oxford, 1994.

Diggle, J. *Studies on the Text of Euripides*. Oxford, 1981.

Flashar, H. *Inszenierung der Antike: das griechische Drama auf der Bühne der Neuzeit 1585–1990*. Munich, 1991.

Gantz, T. *Early Greek Myth: a Guide to Literary and Artistic Sources*. Baltimore, 1993.

Green, J. R. *Theatre in Ancient Greek Society*. London, 1994.

Hofmann, H. and A. Harder, eds. *Fragmenta Dramatica*. Göttingen, 1991.

Hose, M. *Drama und Gesellschaft: Studien zur dramatischen Produktion in Athen am Ende des 5. Jahrhunderts*. Stuttgart, 1995 (*Drama* Beiheft 3).

Huys, M. *The Tale of the Hero who was Exposed at Birth in Euripidean Tragedy: a Study of Motifs*. Leuven, 1995.

Jong, I. J. F de. *Narrative in Drama: the Art of the Euripidean Messenger-speech*. Leiden, 1991 (*Mnemosyne* Suppl. 116).

Jouan, F. *Euripide et les légendes des chants cypriens*. Paris, 1966.

[KG] Kühner, R. *Ausführliche Grammatik der griechischen Sprache*, 2er Teil, rev. B. Gerth. Hanover, 1898–1904.

[*LIMC*] *Lexicon Iconographicum Mythologiae Classicae.* 9 vols. in 18. Zurich, 1981–1999.

[LSJ] Liddell, H. G. and R. Scott, *A Greek–English Lexicon.* with *Supplement.* 9th ed. rev. H. Stuart-Jones etc. Oxford, 1968.

[LSJ Rev.Supp.] Liddell, H. G. and R. Scott, *Greek–English Lexicon Revised Supplement,* ed. P. G. W. Glare. Oxford, 1996.

Mastronarde, D. J. *Contact and Discontinuity: Some Conventions of Speech and Action on the Greek Stage.* Berkeley, 1979 (University of California Publications in Classical Studies, 21).

[*Neue Pauly*] *Der Neue Pauly: Enzyklopädie der Antike.* Numerous vols. Stuttgart, 1996–2003. (An English translation is being published as *Brill's New Pauly.*)

[*OCD*] *The Oxford Classical Dictionary.* Oxford, 1996[3].

[*OGCMA*] *The Oxford Guide to Classical Mythology in the Arts, 1300–1990s.* 2 vols. Oxford, 1993.

Parker, R. *Miasma.* Oxford, 1983.

Powell, J. U., ed. *New Chapters in the History of Greek Literature, Third Series.* Oxford, 1933.

Preller, L. and C. Robert, *Griechische Mythologie.* 2 vols. in 4. Berlin, 1894[1]–1921[4].

Rau, P. *Paratragodia: Untersuchung einer komischen Form des Aristophanes.* Munich, 1967 (*Zetemata* 45).

[*RE*] *Real-Encyclopädie der classischen Altertumswissenschaft.* Numerous vols. Stuttgart and Munich, 1893–1980.

Rossum-Steenbeek, M. van *Greek Readers' Digests: Studies on a Selection of Subliterary Papyri.* Leiden, 1998 (*Mnemosyne* Suppl. 175).

Schmid, W. *Geschichte der griechischen Literatur,* III. Munich, 1940.

Séchan, L. *Études sur la tragédie grecque dans ses rapports avec la céramique.* Paris, 1926.

Stinton, T. C. W. *Collected Papers on Greek Tragedy.* Oxford, 1990.

Trendall, A. D. and T. B. L. Webster. *Illustrations of Greek Drama.* London, 1971.

Webster, T. B. L. *Monuments Illustrating Tragedy and Satyr-Play.* London, 1967[2] (*BICS* Suppl. 20).

Webster, T. B. L. *The Tragedies of Euripides.* London, 1967.

Wilamowitz-Moellendorff, U. von. *Kleine Schriften.* 6 vols. in 7. Berlin, 1935–72.

(b) Editions of ancient texts

[A/Austin] = *NFE* below.

[Apollod.] Ps.-Apollodorus, *The Library*, ed. and trans. J. G. Frazer. London and Cambridge, Mass., 1921 (Loeb Classical Library).

[von Arnim] H. von Arnim. *Supplementum Euripideum*. Bonn, 1913.

[ed. Budé] F. Jouan and H. van Looy, *Euripide: Tome VIII, Fragments*, in 4 parts. Paris, 1998–2003.

[CGFP] C. Austin, *Comicorum Graecorum Fragmenta in Papyris Reperta*. Berlin, 1973.

[D] = *TrGFS* below.

[DK] H. Diels, W. Kranz, *Die Fragmente der Vorsokratiker*. Berlin, 1951–2[6].

[EGF] M. Davies, *Epicorum Graecorum Fragmenta*. Göttingen, 1988.

[FGH] F. Jacoby, *Die Fragmente der griechischen Historiker*. Berlin, 1923–58.

[Hygin. Fab.] *Hygini Fabulae*, ed. P. K. Marshall. Munich, 2002[2].

[IEG] M. L. West, *Iambi et Elegi Graeci*. Oxford, 1989–91[2].

[N/Nauck] A. Nauck, *Tragicorum Graecorum Fragmenta*. Leipzig, 1889[2]. Repr. with Supplement by B. Snell, Hildesheim, 1964.

Mastronarde, D. J. *Euripides: Phoenissae*. Cambridge, 1994.

[M/Mette] H. J. Mette, *Euripides: die Bruchstücke*. *Lustrum* 23/4 (1982); 25 (1983), 5–14; 27 (1985), 23–6.

[NFE] C. Austin, *Nova Fragmenta Euripidea in Papyris Reperta*. Berlin, 1968.

[PCG] R. Kassel, C. Austin, *Poetae Comici Graeci*. 8 vols. in 10. Berlin, 1983—.

[PMG] D. L. Page, *Poetae Melici Graeci*. Oxford, 1962.

[PMGF] M. Davies, *Poetarum Melicorum Graecorum Fragmenta*. Oxford, 1991—.

[Page, *GLP*] D. L. Page, *Select Papyri, III: Literary Papyri, Poetry*. London and Cambridge, Mass., 1941 (Loeb Classical Library).

[Stob.] C. Wachsmuth, O. Hense, *Ioannis Stobaei Anthologiae*. Berlin, 1884–1923.

[TrGF] *Tragicorum Graecorum Fragmenta*. 5 vols. Göttingen: I. *Poetae Minores*, ed. B. Snell (1971, rev. R. Kannicht, 1986); II. *Adespota*, ed. R. Kannicht, B. Snell (1981); III. Aeschylus, ed. S. Radt (1985); IV. Sophocles, ed. S. Radt (1977, 1999[2]); V. Euripides, ed. R. Kannicht, forthcoming. (All *TrGF* volumes continue Nauck's numbering of the fragments, except that Vol. IV continues that of A. C. Pearson, *The Fragments of Sophocles*, Cambridge, 1917.)

[TrGFS] Diggle, J. *Tragicorum Graecorum Fragmenta Selecta*. Oxford, 1998.

(c) Titles of Euripides' Plays (* = *fragmentary play*)

Alc. Alcestis   **Alcm.Cor**. *Alcmaeon in Corinth*   **Alcm.Ps**. *Alcmaeon in Psophis*
Alcmaeon *Alcm.Cor*. or *Alcm.Ps*. (assignment uncertain)   **And**. Andromache
Androm. *Andromeda*   **Antig**. *Antigone*   **Arch**. *Archelaus*   **Bacc**. Bacchae
Bell. *Bellerophon*   **Chrys**. *Chrysippus*   **Cresph**. *Cresphontes*   **Cret**. *Cretans*
Cret.W. *Cretan Women*   **Cyc**. Cyclops   **El**. Electra   **Erec**. *Erectheus*   **Hec**. Hecuba
Hel. Helen   **Hcld**. Heraclidae (Children of Heracles)   **HF** Heracles (= Hercules
Furens: Hercules Mad)   **Hipp**. Hippolytus Stephanephoros (Garlanded Hippolytus)
Hipp.Cal. *Hippolytus Calyptomenos (Hippolytus Veiling Himself)*   **Hyps**. *Hypsipyle*
IA Iphigenia at Aulis   **IT** Iphigenia in Tauris   **Med**. Medea   **Mel.D**. *Melanippe
Desmotis (Captive Melanippe)*   **Mel.S**. *Melanippe Sophê (Wise Melanippe)*
Mel. *Mel.D*. or *Mel.S*. (assignment uncertain)   **Oed**. *Oedipus*   **Or**. Orestes
Palam. *Palamedes*   **Pha**. *Phaethon*   **Phil**. *Philoctetes*   **Pho**. Phoenissae
(Phoenician Women)   **Pir**. *Pirithous* (not certainly Euripidean)   **Prot**. *Protesilaus*
Rhad. *Rhadamanthys* (not certainly Euripidean)   **Rhes**. Rhesus (spurious)
Sthen. *Stheneboea*   **Supp**. Suppliant Women   **Tel**. *Telephus*   **Tem**. *Temenus*
Temenid. *Temenidae (Children of Temenus)*   **Tro**. Trojan Women.

The titles of *Ion* and of all other fragmentary plays, including *Tennes* (not certainly
Euripidean) and the two *Phrixus*-plays *(A and B)*, are given in full.

PHILOCTETES

Texts, testimonia. P. Oxy. 2455 fr. 17 cols. xviii–xix (Hypothesis: = *TrGF* T iiia); Aristophanes of Byzantium, Hypothesis to *Medea* (= T ii); Dio of Prusa ('Chrysostom'), *Orations* 52 and 59; *TrGF* F 787–803, T i–v. G. Avezzù, *Il ferimento e il rito. La storia di Filottete sulla scena attica* (Bari, 1988), 124–45 (texts and *testimonia* in Italian tr., with notes); C. W. Müller, *Euripides. Philoktet* (Berlin, New York, 2000; together with Müller's *Philoktet. Beiträge* [Stuttgart and Leipzig, 1997], this edition is a study of the play on the largest possible scale); F. Jouan in ed. Budé VIII.3 (2002), 269–312.

Myth. Hom. *Il.* 2.718–25; *Cypria* in Proclus' Summary (*EGF* p. 32.64–6); *Little Iliad* in Proclus' Summary (*EGF* p. 52.6–9); Aeschylus, *Philoctetes* F 249–57; Pind. *Isthm.* 1.50–5; Bacchyl. F 7; Sophocles, *Philoctetes* (extant) and *Philoctetes in Troy* F 697–703; Accius, *Philocteta* F 1–22 Ribbeck; Apollod. *Epit.* 3.26–7, 5.8; Hyginus, *Fab.* 102.2–3; Quintus of Smyrna, *Posthomerica* 9.327–546, 10.167–241. Preller-Robert III.2.1207–18; *RE* XIX.2 (1938), 2500–9 ('Philoktetes': K. Fiehn); Gantz 589–90, 635–9; Müller (ed.) 25–64; R. Scanzo, *Maia* 55 (2003), 481–500.

Illustrations. O. Mandel, *Philoctetes and the Fall of Troy* (Lincoln, Nebraska, 1981), Pls. 1–20, Figs. 1–4; *LIMC* VII.1 (1994), 376–85 and Nos. 1–78 ('Philoktetes': M. Pipili), with Pls. in VII.2.321–6; E. Simon in H. Cancik (ed.), *Geschichte-Tradition-Reflexion. Festschrift M. Hengel* (Tübingen, 1996), II.15–39 with Pls. 1–11; Müller, *Beiträge*, 318–9 with Pls. 1–30, and ed., 459 with Figs. 1–8 (D. Fontannaz, *AK* 43 (2000), 53–69 adds little to the above).

Main discussions (almost all reconstructions and discussions are summarized by Müller (ed.), 83–124). N. Wecklein, *SBAW* 1888 I.127–39; R. Jebb, Sophocles: *Philoctetes* (Cambridge, 1890), ix–xix; W.-H. Friedrich, *Hermes* 76 (1941), 120–8 and *Philologus* 94 (1941), 157–64; Jouan, *Euripide et les légendes des chants cypriens* (1966), 308–17; Webster, *Euripides* (1967), 57–61, cf. *Sophocles: Philoctetes* (Cambridge, 1970), 3–5; W. M. Calder III, in O. Mørkholm, N. M. Waggoner (eds.), *Greek Numismatics: Essays...M. Thompson* (Wetteren, 1979), 53–62; M. T. Luzzatto, *Prometheus* 9 (1983), 199–220; Avezzù (above; cf. Müller 118–20); S. D. Olson, *Hesperia* 60 (1991), 269–83; Müller, *RhM* 137 (1992), 104–34 = *Beiträge* 11–42 (cf. Müller (ed.) 121–3).

Preliminary note. The extensive evidence from Dio's two *Orations* is presented in translation alone; it is categorized and printed in *TrGF* as both *testimonia* and frag-ments; here, *Or.* 52 stands in summary in an Appendix after the Introduction, *Or.* 59 appears with the text-fragments. Kevin Lee had drafted some paragraphs on the play before his death; our debt to them is recorded where practicable with his initials (K.H.L.). Only major features and problems are treated in the following Introduction.

A fragmentary play of particular interest, for which the secondary evidence is distinctive: not only does the later Sophoclean drama upon the same mythic episode survive, but there is a mainly literary comparison of both plays, and of Aeschylus' earlier but now very fragmentary *Philoctetes*, by the 1st–2nd century rhetorician and critic Dio of Prusa (*Oration* 52). Dio says he read and compared the three plays one day when he was ill (like Philoctetes); he deals with them in chronological order, giving most room to Aeschylus and Euripides but the highest praise to Sophocles. Also there is Dio's summary paraphrase of the play's prologue-speech and an early scene or even complete episode (*Oration* 59). It is frustrating that such rich secondary evidence supplements only a very few scraps of Euripides' poetic text itself (totalling as few as 40 lines). The one recent addition to this long-known material is a fragmentary 'narrative hypothesis' (P. Oxy. 2455, 1962), but it gives hardly any fresh help.

Myth. The most poignant episode in Philoctetes' story is that dramatized in the tragedies which Dio 52 compares; and it is the one upon which ancient writers and artists naturally concentrated. Its core is already there in Epic: Homer, *Iliad* 2.718–25 records the bowman's skill which made Philoctetes so formidable (but his possession of Heracles' bow is not mentioned), and the snake-bite he suffered which was so noisome that his fellow Greeks at Troy marooned him on Lemnos; and Homer says that 'the Greeks were destined soon to recall him to mind'. The bite and his abandonment were also in the *Cypria*, according to Proclus' Summary; the *Little Iliad* in Proclus' Summary gives more detail: Odysseus' capture of the Trojan seer Helenus, who prophesied about the capture of Troy, stating or implying that it would fall only through the use of Heracles' bow (this provides the theme for all three tragedians); Philoctetes' recovery from Lemnos by Diomedes; his healing from the bite by the Greeks' surgeon at Troy, Machaon; his killing of Paris. In 470 B.C. Pindar, *Pyth.* 1.50–5 recounted his recovery from Lemnos by unnamed heroes, saying that it was his 'fate' to go to Troy though sick in body; Bacchylides may already have composed his dithyramb about him (F 7). Aeschylus' tragedy was very close in date to both Pindar and Bacchylides, and very probably earlier. Perhaps the first dramatization, it is much more fragmentary even than Euripides' play, but it does seem, from Dio's descriptions in 52, that Aeschylus introduced to the myth the tragic and ironic conflict when Odysseus, the Greek most responsible for banishing Philoctetes, is the one sent to recover him. Some details in Sophocles cannot certainly be attributed to the myth as known to Euripides, whose play was twenty years earlier (see below, *Reconstruction*). Lastly, mythographers seem to agree upon the place of the bite (the homonymous island of the nymph-goddess Chryse near Lemnos), but differ about its cause, e.g. her anger at his rejection of her love (Schol. S. *Phil.* 194) or the anger of the goddess Hera for his help to Heracles (Apollod. *Epit.* 3.26, Hygin. *Fab.* 102.1). Odysseus' capture of

Helenus is merely stated (E. *Phil.* Hypoth. 11) or attributed to his initiative (S. *Phil.* 606–9). The promise of healing has varying importance in Philoctetes' leaving Lemnos, either as men's inducement (S. *Phil.* 1333–4 etc.) or as divine prediction (S. *Phil.* 1437–8). It is very frustrating that secondary sources throw no clear light for Euripides upon the 'forcible persuasion' of Philoctetes to leave Lemnos which Dio 52.2 attributes to all three tragedians. Vase-paintings from the 5th century are few and depict only general scenes from the myth (see *Illustrations*). The scrappy fragments of Accius' *Philocteta*, a play said by Cicero to derive from Euripides, fill out neither the play nor the myth in any certain detail (the strongest assertion was by Friedrich, *Hermes* [1941]).

Philoctetes' success at Troy and further adventures (he had as difficult a Return Home (*Nostos*) as the other Greeks, in fact being driven to S. Italy) are told by mythographers such as Apollodorus, Hyginus, and chiefly in the much later poetic account of Quintus of Smyrna (5th C. A.D.), who relied no doubt upon the earlier Epic tradition lost to us.

Reconstruction. The scene is Lemnos; the stage-back with its central door represents Philoctetes' cave-dwelling (see *Staging* below). Thanks to Dio 59, the play's beginning is clear in outline, if not in arrangement. Odysseus enters, coming unaccompanied from his ship; in his prologue-speech he debates with himself why, when he has risked so much before, he has undertaken yet another dangerous task; the answer is, it is man's irresistible desire for fame (summaries in **F 787–789**, then separately **F 789a, 787, 788, 789**). Odysseus is to recover Heracles' invincible bow and its owner Philoctetes, which prophecy has revealed will alone defeat Troy (Dio in **F 789b(2).2**; cf. Dio 52.14 and Hygin. 102.3). Then he braces himself to confront Philoctetes and persuade him into returning, for his exile was largely at Odysseus' own initiative (**F 789b(2).3**, cf. S. *Phil.* 1005ff.); but he has a promise from his guardian the goddess Athena to keep him safe against Philoctetes' vengeance, for she has transformed him and made him unrecognizable (also F 789b(2).3, cf. Dio 52.5, 13, who must be thinking of Athena's help to Odysseus in the *Odyssey*). Odysseus knows too that the Trojans will attempt to win Philoctetes to their side, in fear of Helenus' prophecy (**F 789b(2).4**, cf. Hypoth. 9–10 and Dio 52.13).

Dio in 59 moves from paraphrase of Odysseus' prologue-soliloquy (F 789b(2)) straight to Odysseus' exclamation at the approaching Philoctetes' wretched appearance (**F 789d(5)**, cf. 11; cf. Ar. *Acharnians* 423–4, Euripides speaking, 'Whatever sort of ragged clothes is the man asking for? Are you talking about Philoctetes the beggar?', and Schol. RLh 424 Wilson 'Euripides brings on Philoctetes in poverty on Lemnos' [= T iva]). Dio does not say whether Philoctetes enters from his cave or is returning to it. Whether his exchange with Odysseus (**F 789d(5)–(11)**) precedes or (less likely) directly follows the parodos, at its end the unrecognized Odysseus deceives Philoctetes into sympathy by asserting falsely that he too has been insulted and betrayed by the Greeks (F 789d(8)). The two prepare to enter the cave, with Philoctetes warning Odysseus of the poverty and squalor he must tolerate as his guest (**F 789d(10)–(11), F 790, **790a**, and perhaps **792**, mention of his original wound).

Almost all reconstructors see the exchange in F 789d as an extension of the prologue-scene, so that Philoctetes is already present to hear the Chorus apologize when they enter in the parodos (Dio 52.7 in **F 789c**). This arrangement is a reasonable inference from Dio, but it is not an inescapable one. First, Dio is not recounting the play's course in full, he is interested chiefly in the ethical portraits of Odysseus and Philoctetes; he almost certainly omits the background narrative which is a constant feature of Euripidean prologue-speeches and may have made some reference to Diomedes (K.H.L.: see below). Second, Dio may only be noting the Chorus's explanation of its coming, in contrast with Aeschylus who gives it no motive at all; the Chorus may well 'reconnoitre' the area near the cave before calling Philoctetes out (K.H.L.), or before he approaches; and Odysseus may be an unseen observer, like Orestes at the start of Aeschylus' *Choephori*. A sequence of prologue-speech, parodos and first episode beginning with Philoctetes' entry and exchange with Odysseus is possible. Müller himself (ed. 67, 122) thinks that Dio in 59.5–11 (**F 789d**) is paraphrasing the second episode; he argues that the much delayed entry of Philoctetes would create exceptional tension.

Dio in 52.8 names an individual Lemnian, the shepherd Actor, who alone so far has visited and helped Philoctetes (cf. Hygin. *Fab.* 102.2, 'a shepherd of King Actor named Iphimachus the son of Dolopion sustained (Philoctetes) when marooned...on Lemnos...'). Actor's appearance is certain to have followed the first exchange of Odysseus and Philoctetes and came probably in the first episode, after the Chorus' entry and apology for not visiting Philoctetes (Dio 52.7 = F 789c; **F 792a** is less likely here than in the second or third stasimon). Thus Euripides would maintain a focus of sympathy; Actor may even have interrupted and stopped the entry to the cave. Reconstructors give him the role of warning Philoctetes that the Trojans are about to approach him; later in the play he may have aided or encouraged Philoctetes further (see below); but after his warning he must either enter the cave himself or leave by a side, for the actor playing him is needed for the Trojan representative in the next episode.

Thus far Dio, supported by some separately transmitted fragments; the rest is inference or conjecture from the few remaining fragments, some slight further secondary evidence, and possible reflections in art.

First, what we are told in Dio 52 of Aeschylus' play permits little positive inference for Euripides (above, *Myth*). Dio emphasizes features of Aeschylus absent

from, or in contrast with, Euripides: Aeschylus' archaic directness in plot, characterization and language (52.4, 15); no disguise of Odysseus by Athena (5–6); no
apologetic Chorus but one ignorant of Philoctetes altogether, with his story needing
to be told them (7–9); plain rather than devious falsehood in Odysseus' story for
Philoctetes (10); no invented occasion for rhetorical exchanges such as Euripides
contrives with the embassy of the Trojans (11–14). The fragments of Aeschylus
themselves help even less, for almost all evoke Philoctetes' physical agony and
isolation, in his own words.[1] Second, no reconstruction should be influenced too
much by Sophocles' play, in which, for all its loose similarity of plot (Dio 52.2) and
some comparable details, much is very different. In particular, it is Philoctetes who is
entirely isolated, on an uninhabited Lemnos, while his would-be captor, the
impressionable Neoptolemus, is instructed directly by Odysseus and indirectly by his
emissary the Merchant, and accompanied by a sympathetic chorus of fellow Greeks;
this reorientation of scene and persons shifts the play's moral issues completely, to
the personal as much as the 'political'. In Euripides Odysseus is the near-isolated
figure ('Euripides rests everything upon him', Schol. S. *Phil.* 1 in F 787–789 (3)) –
except for the presence of Diomedes, whose active role is unclear (see below);
Philoctetes has the sympathy of both Chorus and Actor, and both he and Odysseus
face a rival approach from the Trojans for his help.

The centre and end of the play can be guessed in their probable content. At
the start probably of the second episode the Trojan embassy comes, trying to
recruit both hero and bow; **F 794** may belong to their leader's major speech of
inducement.[2] The episode was developed as a 'formal debate', an *agon*, beginning between a Trojan representative and Philoctetes alone; some, e.g. Wecklein
and Webster, have speculated that the Trojan speaker was Paris himself.[3] Odysseus is at first silent but later breaks in purely as a 'Greek', shifting the pressure
upon Philoctetes deliberately towards 'patriotism' (**F 796,** perhaps before his
795; see the Volterra urn, (1) in *Illustrations* below). Odysseus would not have
revealed his true identity at this point, for that would have tipped Philoctetes
towards the Trojans; more importantly, it would have destroyed the integrity of
the debate, its concentration on moral and political issues. In fact, Philoctetes

---

[1] For reconstructions of the play, with bibliography, see Müller (ed.) 38–64, Jouan
(ed. Budé) 272–7; also Jouan, *REG* 115 (2002), 409–16, suggesting that Dio may
have had Aeschylus in front of him in composing his 'Trojan' *Oration* 11.

[2] The embassy was almost certainly Euripides' invention, including too the Trojans'
knowledge of Helenus' prophecy (Dio 52.13 and 59.4 in F 789b, cf. F 795): K.H.L.

[3] The one, insecure indication for this lies in Acc. *Phil.* F 17–18, which have
references to Trojan mildness and either a direct address of Paris or, more probably, an
apostrophe of him; cf. Müller, *Beiträge* 116f.

resisted both the Trojans and Odysseus, no doubt in a stubborn sense of vindication (not unlike his final obduracy at S. *Phil.* 1397ff.).

The Trojan's departure heralded the end of, or indeed closed, the episode, and would be marked by a full stasimon. Philoctetes' rejection of the Trojans was a turning-point for Odysseus: encouraging because one anticipated threat to his success had gone away (ironically, through Philoctetes himself), discouraging because it showed how stubborn Philoctetes was, and how persuasion alone (F 789b(2).3) would not be enough: he would have to use guile, to dispossess Philoctetes of his bow, so that he would then be helpless to resist, and might perhaps be removed physically. Dio 52.14 states that Euripides has Diomedes in the play, 'just like Homer'; but *Iliad* 2.718–25 does not mention Diomedes, and Dio may be remembering rather the *Little Iliad* (see under *Myth*), or the joint night-raid of Odysseus and Diomedes in *Iliad* 10.242ff. We do not know whether Diomedes' arrival was part of a deception already prepared with Odysseus (below), but his appearance would have made dramatic sense immediately or soon after the Trojans withdrew, and in a third episode; indeed it may have been a complete surprise to the audience, unmentioned by Odysseus even in his prologue-speech and forcing a turn in the action like the arrival of Aegeus in *Medea* (K.H.L.). The stress of rejecting the Trojans probably led at once to Philoctetes' suffering a seizure of pain from his old wound, or Diomedes' entry may have precipitated it when Philoctetes recognized him; perhaps **F 792** expressing his ulcer's pain came here and not earlier, soon followed by the Chorus' despairing sympathy in **F 792a**? (In his first scene with Odysseus, at F 789d(11), his words 'I'm not pleasant to be with, when the agony strikes' are in general taken as Euripides' warning to the spectators that such a seizure lies ahead.) Philoctetes' consequent incapacitation, even unconsciousness, gave the opportunity to take the bow (Dio 52.2; seized by pain in Sophocles, he himself hands it to Neoptolemus for safekeeping, *Phil.* 763ff.; at 973ff. he requires its return just before Odysseus enters to demand it from Neoptolemus). Euripides' Odysseus may have had a scheme to steal or snatch the bow while Philoctetes was distracted in some way, perhaps in response to a false offer from Diomedes to take both himself and the still unrecognized Odysseus to Greece (compare the manoeuvring in S. *Phil.* 526–627 in the scene with the Merchant); but the paroxysm of pain made such a scheme suddenly quite easy (contrast Neoptolemus' indecision at S. *Phil.* 839ff). We do not know when Odysseus revealed his true identity, but, again, that would make best dramatic sense only after he had dispossessed Philoctetes of the bow.

An acceptable way from these uncertainties was Wecklein's suggestion (cf. Luzzatto, Müller (ed.) 116, Jouan 294): Diomedes' prearranged and false promise of transport to Greece leads to Odysseus' taking Philoctetes inside the cave, to prepare for departure; one way or another Diomedes himself goes in, or goes to the rear entrance (i.e. out by the side of the *orchêstra*, to behind the stage-back: see *Staging*); Philoctetes' paroxysm occurs inside the cave, permitting, first, Diomedes to snatch the bow, which he immediately brings outside, and, second, when Philoctetes recovers, Odysseus to come out after revealing his true identity to him and – most important theatrically – changing his mask off-stage. Even so, it must remain conjectural whether Philoctetes' paroxysm was first narrated in a full 'report', or surrogate messenger-speech, by Diomedes or, as some think, by Actor who had remained in the cave after his earlier entry to help Philoctetes. Some reconstructors, e.g. Luzzatto, Avezzù, Olson, are anxious to create a substantial role for Actor, beyond his warning of the Trojans' approach; but if Actor narrated, what did Diomedes do – remain mute? That would be strange if he had already had a speaking part, although in *Antiope* Zethus becomes mute after his important debate with Amphion, and Thoas is mute in the final scene of *Hypsipyle*. It would make a typically fluid Euripidean sequence for a long third episode to encompass Diomedes' arrival, the excitement of Philoctetes' paroxysm, his entry to the cave with Odysseus and Diomedes, some brief scene-dividing lyrics from the Chorus, and then the 'report'.

In the end Philoctetes was overcome by 'forcible persuasion': this is the phrase which Dio 52.2 applies to all the three tragedians' plays, adding that persuasion was irresistible 'since he had been deprived of the weapons which provided him with subsistence on the island' (cf. S. *Phil.* 1089ff.). It is most probable that after the bow had been taken from him, Philoctetes was subjected to further altercation in order to secure his willing departure. Whether Euripides mounted this exchange as a second 'formal debate' is not to be known, but it is likely (note Dio's commendation of his skill in this play in contriving opposed arguments, 52.13; most reconstructors suppose it). **F 798, 799** and perhaps **799a** would seem to belong better in such a second exchange than in the first involving also the Trojans; **F 800** best suits a comment made by the Chorus either to punctuate the exchanges or after the gods' provision for Philoctetes is at last set to be fulfilled. There may have been a threat of violence, particularly if Diomedes was still there (Odysseus uses violence briefly against Philoctetes at S. *Phil.* 1003ff.); or Odysseus may have applied overwhelming moral pressure, using some of the arguments from service and reward which he pondered in his prologue. It is frustrating that Hypoth. 21 has lost any details of the 'compulsion' used.

Recent reconstructors (e.g. Olson 277, Jouan 296 n. 60) have moved away from suggesting a god's final intervention; Calder and once Luppe (1983: see Hypoth. apparatus) had suggested Athena because of her direction and disguise of Odysseus (F 789b(2).3, cf. Hypoth. 16), and it is tempting to think of Euripides anticipating Sophocles when Heracles intervenes to deal with Philoctetes' much greater obduracy (S. *Phil.* 1387ff.). Whatever the truth, Philoctetes' final exit would have been reluctant; perhaps Odysseus, perhaps Diomedes too, perhaps Actor, helped him physically from the audience's view, to prevent a return of pain: cf. Acc. *Phil.* F 21, which speaks of moving Philoctetes from Lemnos in a way not aggravating his wound (see *Illustrations*, 3 and 4).

F 797 is the one fragment particularly hard to locate; it appears to come from a three-person scene, with two opponents and a third for whose approval they are competing. Lines 1–2 say that the opponent has already damaged the speaker's argument, either by anticipation or by a candid admission of his own fault (there is textual uncertainty: see Comm.); the speaker is not known. The three-way 'Trojan' scene suggests itself; for if the fragment is located at play-end, and spoken by Philoctetes, after Odysseus has spoken first, it is hard to think whose judgement matters, or can change the now inevitable outcome. Perhaps the words address the Chorus, for they are Lemnians, not Greeks, and may need to have their feelings accommodated (cf. F 800), given their earlier guilt over Philoctetes' suffering, no less than the theatre-audience.

Of the remaining fragments, F 801–3 are lexicographic and cannot be placed, and *801a probably does not belong at all.

Other proposed ascriptions. F 870 N (tentatively assigned by Müller (ed.) 446; om. Budé, *TrGF*) 'a serpent's look, blood in its eyes', possibly a recollection of the snake-bite.   Adesp. F 10 (= F 18 Müller, om. Avezzù, Budé, *TrGF*) 'What bride, what young maiden would accept you? You are in a fine state for marrying, you wretch!', Odysseus supposedly bullying Philoctetes if he does not come back to Troy for his wound to be healed (ascribed by Musgrave).   Adesp. F 579 (= F 10 Avezzù, F 7 Müller, om. Budé, *TrGF*) 'You have come in your weakness to <us?> who are weak', Philoctetes supposedly responding to Odysseus' deception (ascribed by Musgrave).   Also, from *Cyc.* 103–4 the adj. 'sly' used of Odysseus, ascribed by Müller on the strength of Dio 52.5 (F 24, om. Budé, *TrGF*), and *Cyc.* 706–7 the words 'through this tunnel-cave' used of the Cyclops' cave, ascribed by Müller (F 5, om. Budé, *TrGF*) comparing S. *Phil.* 16 'cave with two mouths'.   Scholars in the 19th century reconstructed iambic dialogue trimeters from Dio 59 (see Nauck p. 616; nos. 1107–13, 1114c Mette; F 4–9, 13 Avezzù; om. Budé [but see the apparatus there on pp. 283–6] and *TrGF* [but see the apparatus there on F 789d. 12, 15, 17, 23–4, 34, 60]).

Illustrations. Almost all eighty or so works listed in *LIMC* have no sure bearing on any individual tragedy; Simon (1996) exemplifies the most recent diffident speculation. The earliest Attic vase-paintings are from about 460 B.C. onwards, probably therefore later than Aeschylus' shaping of the dramatic myth (above); but like almost all subsequent works of art they imagine Philoctetes either at the scene of the snake-bite or in his wretched isolation on Lemnos. A few later ones depict the Greek embassy to recall him or the theft of the bow; very few show him being healed or fighting again at Troy. Two or three are however regularly adduced in loose illustration of Euripides' play, or to confirm suggested reconstruction:

(1) an alabaster urn of the mid–2nd C. B.C. from Volterra (*LIMC* no. 57 = 'Alexandros' no. 102; Müller (ed.) fig. 5 and *Beiträge* Pl. 5a–b); it shows Philoctetes with bow and arrows in hand, in front of his cave, emerging(?) to confront (right) two Trojans, one wearing a Phrygian cap, the other carrying a shield; on the left is (presumably) Odysseus with a younger man eavesdropping (this would be Diomedes in Euripides, following the *Little Iliad*);

(2) a silver cup of the 1st C. B.C. or A.D., now in Copenhagen, the so-called 'Hoby' cup (*LIMC* No. 69; Schefold-Jung, *Die Sagen von den Argonauten* (1989), 270 with Pls. 242–3; Müller (ed.) fig. 7 and *Beiträge* Pls. 12–14, with full discussion on pp. 133–76 of its Roman provenience): in one of two scenes a seated Odysseus is sliding the (stolen) bow behind him to a crouching figure (Diomedes?), away from Philoctetes who sits but leans on a staff, perhaps during or after his wound's attack, while on the right a man eviscerates a large hanging fowl (symbolizing the Lemnian wilderness: Actor?). The other scene on this cup (*LIMC* No. 74; Müller (ed.) fig. 1 and *Beiträge* Pls. 15–16) shows Philoctetes being healed by a physician—Machaon?—at Troy, cf. *Little Iliad* in *Myth* above;

(3) an undated Etruscan intaglio (*LIMC* No. 71; Müller, *Beiträge* Pl. 30a) showing a man in travelling clothes helping an obviously lame one; most interpreters refer this to the Philoctetes-story, but it may be 'beyond the play';

(4) certainly 'beyond the play': a lost Roman sarcophagus of the 2nd C. A.D., once in Florence (*LIMC* No. 70/67; Müller (ed.) fig. 8 and *Beiträge* Pl. 25), showing Philoctetes riding in a cart while Odysseus carries his bow and arrows.

Themes and characters. Credible incident, character and their effective expression in words were prime interests of Dio in his comparison of the three tragedians: see especially 52.11–14 on Euripides' distinctive rhetorical quality in opposed arguments; on the clarity and realism of his language, especially in dramatizing plausible incident and iambic dialogue. Dio says that the iambics contain much to benefit the reader (11) and the lyrics have much to encourage virtue (14, 17): note 'reader': this is an educational rhetorician writing, not a theatre-goer. The fragments themselves are too few and thin to prove these judgements in detail; but we have Odysseus in his prologue analysing his own behaviour with convincing realism (F 787–789), and he gives matter-of-factly the background to his dangerous undertaking (F 789b); in his first scene with Philoctetes (F 789d) his language shifts between alarm (5, 7), deceit (6–8, 10) and callous ingratiation (10). Euripides matches these qualities with a Philoctetes who is naturally embittered (against the unrecognized Odysseus in particular, 6–9), but also credibly sympathetic towards a feigned plight like his own (11). Possibly Actor helped to illustrate the interplay between the two heroes, from the view-point of the 'ordinary man', as the Nurse and Tutor fill out the conflict between Medea and Jason in *Medea* (K.H.L.). Contrasts in attitude clearly made for effective argumentation, in one if not two 'formal debates', and for much exercise of 'persuasion' by Odysseus: see Dio in 52.11, 14, and in F 789b(2).3.

It does seem as if Euripides – like Sophocles after him, certainly, and possibly Aeschylus before him – used the singular predicament of Philoctetes as proving-ground for his own and his visitors' moral character. If Sophocles' Neoptolemus is impressionable, his Odysseus is hard and unscrupulous enough; so, when Dio states (52.16) that Sophocles' Odysseus is 'much gentler and franker' than Euripides', it is a surprise to us, but such a view fits perhaps his callousness in Euripides.[4] His manipulation of Philoctetes through the story of Palamedes is particularly effective (F 789d(8)), for both helped the Greeks and both were betrayed, and the real Odysseus ruined them (K.H.L. compared Achilles in S. *Phil.* 343ff. as Neoptolemus' hold upon Philoctetes, and noted Friedrich's argument in *Philologus* (1941) that Virgil adapted the Palamedes-story from Euripides for the deceiver Sinon in *Aen.* 2.81ff.). Odysseus is opportunist in rejecting the very power of prophecy which has brought himself to Lemnos (F 795). Analogies for the obstinate and potentially self-destructive Philoctetes are Heracles in *Heracles* (lines 1241–1310) and perhaps Bellerophon (see our Vol.1, p. 101). Jouan (2002) 298 describes Philoctetes as an example of archaic heroism overcome only through the contrivances of the morally inferior Odysseus; similarly Müller (ed.) 70, who finds the play-end typically Euripidean in frustrating the audience's sympathy for Philoctetes when he is removed forcibly rather than willingly.

Dio 52.11 and 14 uses the Greek word πολιτικός, 'political', to describe a distinctive feature of the play, its reflection of realities in everyday home and city life (Müller [ed.] 69 n. 18, 266 urges the translation 'plain, everyday, real' rather than 'political'). Odysseus' prologue shows him weighing up the pressures upon an able man to serve the common good (F 787–789b and 789d(9)), especially the ambition (cf. F 788, 798) which overcomes any inclination to rest upon one's laurels and enjoy the benefits won by others, in anonymous inactivity (ἀπραγμοσύνη: Dio 52.12, F 787.1–2; cf. Comm. on *Antiope* F 193; the conflict between patriotism and its rejection is fully discussed by Müller,

---

[4] For the generally 'villainous' Odysseus of Tragedy see N. Worman, *Helios* 26 (1999), 35–68.

Beiträge 11–42). Olson 280–3 sees Odysseus' behaviour as typical of 'a successful popular politician in the Athenian imperial government' (280) of the later 5th century, driven by φιλοτιμία, 'desire for public honour'.[5] It is ironic that Philoctetes abuses the unrecognized Odysseus for destroying the public-spirited Palamedes (F 789d(8)–(9)).

Do the gods have any significance in this play? Athena as final 'god' is now generally discounted (above). Other than in commonplace allusions (e.g. F 794 on their 'human' interest in profit, F 800 on their ultimate power), the limited evidence shows them impinging on the action in only two respects. First, the prophecy of Helenus is prominent enough in Dio 59.2 (F 787–789) and Hypoth. 9–13, but we do not know how it was presented, or how frequently, in the play, except in the context of F 795 (above; in Sophocles it is progressively revealed). Second, Athena apparently helps Odysseus spontaneously (F 789b(2).3, cf. 789d(5)); Müller (ed.) 69 observes that this happens without moral justification, and that Odysseus operates entirely from personal and political ambition. In this (possible) lack of reason for the divine, *Philoctetes* may share something with its companion play of 431 B.C., *Medea* (in which the significance of the gods is variously minimized or counter-asserted by critics); there is nothing in the nearly twenty fragments of the other companion tragedy *Dictys* to indicate a significant role for the gods there either. Lack of hard evidence makes the drawing of any connection mere speculation; even in the Trojan tetralogy of 415, where there is more evidence to provoke it, inconclusiveness is wise (see on *Alexandros*, p. 48 with n. 10).

Staging. The central stage-door represented Philoctetes' cave on Lemnos, as in Sophocles; cf. the Herdsman's cave in *Antiope* (p. 268) and the Cyclops' cave in *Cyclops* (706–7). Müller (*RhM* 134 [1991], 262–75 = *Beiträge* 98–111) uses this second example to argue that a similar 'tunnel-cave', one with a second entrance at the back, i.e. off-stage, was implicit in *Philoctetes*, so that Diomedes might enter it there to assist in the seizure of the bow from a Philoctetes unconscious from pain (above, *Reconstruction*). The cave would also credibly house Odysseus' change of mask as Athena's disguise leaves him. Philoctetes was dressed in animal-skins and rags, as Dio describes (F 789d(5), (11)). No doubt Heracles' bow focused the spectators' gaze, as in Sophocles and perhaps Aeschylus.

---

[5] For pride in this aspiration see especially Alcibiades' words in Thuc. 6.16.1–4, Mantitheus' in Lysias 16.20–1, cf. 25.12–13: on the whole phenomenon, Stockert on *IA* 22 and D. Whitehead, *C & M* 34 (1983), 55–74.

Date. 431 B.C., together with *Medea, Dictys* and (satyric) *Theristae* ('Harvesters'). Euripides came third after Euphorion and Sophocles (Hypoth. *Medea*).

Other dramatizations; influence. It is not known whether Sophocles' *Philoctetes at Troy* (see bibl., *Myth*) preceded or followed his extant *Philoctetes* of the year 409. We have a mere title and one fragment, respectively, for Euripides' contemporaries Philocles (*TrGF* I 24 T 1) and Achaeus (20 F 37). Tragedians of the 4th century liked the myth: there are scraps of plays by Theodectas (72 F 5b: the snake bites Philoctetes' hand) and unknowns (*TrGF* II adesp. F 10, 579, 654: see *Other proposed ascriptions*). Comedy burlesqued the story both before Euripides (Epicharmus F 131–2 *PCG*) and after (Antiphanes F 217 and Strattis F 44–5 *PCG*). Several fragments survive from the 2nd C. B.C. Roman tragedian Accius' *Philocteta* (see bibl., *Myth*) but, as always, his debt to Greek models cannot be established in detail (see Müller, *Beiträge* 260–84); the story stands in e.g. Ovid, *Met.* 13.45–62, 313–39 (Müller 285–305). For the myth throughout antiquity see Müller (ed.) 72–83; for later antiquity see Mandel (bibl. above) reviewed and supplemented by G. Avezzù, *MD* 19 (1987), 131–42; Mandel 121–250 includes translations of modern plays by Gide, himself and H. Müller (for this last adaptation, often performed in Germany since 1968, see Flashar, *Inszenierung* 141–3). Also: E. Wilson, *The Wound and the Bow* (Cambridge, Mass., 1941); *OGCMA* 2.892–5 records poetic and prose-adaptations from the early Middle Ages, graphic and plastic arts, music, opera, television.

Appendix
Evidence for the play's content and nature from Dio, Or. 52

52.2. ...(the tragedies of) Aeschylus, Sophocles and Euripides all concern the same plot, namely the theft or (it should be called) seizure of Philoctetes' bow, except that Philoctetes has it taken from him by Odysseus and is himself led off to Troy, for the most part unwillingly (Dio mss., Kannicht: 'willingly' Welcker, von Arnim) but in some degree through forcible persuasion, since he had been deprived of the weapons which provided him with subsistence on the island as well as courage in such bodily affliction, and at the same time renown (T iiib) ...

5. ...Aeschylus did not need to have Athena transform Odysseus so that he should not be recognized by Philoctetes for the man he was, in the way that Homer did, followed by Euripides (part of T ivc (a), cf. 13 below) ...

6–7. (Differences between Aeschylus and Euripides in their treatment of Odysseus and Chorus: see F 789c)

8. Next it was wholly impossible that no Lemnians had either approached Philoctetes or had any concern for him, for, I think, he would not have survived the ten years without getting some help; but it is reasonable (to think of) his getting it infrequently and in no great quantity, with no one choosing to receive him in his house and

to tend his wound because it was intolerable. At any rate, Euripides himself brings on stage Actor, one of the Lemnians, who approaches Philoctetes as an acquaintance he has often met (T ivb).

11. Euripides' intelligence and care with every detail, neither to permit anything incredible and careless nor to employ simply incidents, but every power of language – these are as it were the opposite of Aeschylus (a word may be missing in Dio, e.g. 'Aeschylus' <simplicity>' Reiske, 'Aeschylus' <poetry>' Müller), being very political and rhetorical and capable of giving the greatest benefit to readers (part of T v, cf. 14 below) . . . Odysseus (speaking the prologue and) turning over with himself political considerations in general but primarily in doubt on his own account, in case he may appear clever to most people and superior in intelligence, but actually be the opposite. (12) This is because, although it is possible for him to live without stress and excessive activity, he is constantly involved in affairs and dangers willingly (cf. F 787.1–2); and he says that the cause of this is the ambition in able and well-born men, because in their desire for a good reputation and universal fame they willingly undertake the greatest and most difficult tasks (cf. F 789b(2).4).

12 (end). Then (Odysseus) reveals the play's plot clearly and in precise detail, and why he has come to Lemnos (= F 789b(1)).

13. ...(Odysseus) says he has been transformed by Athena so as not to be recognized by Philoctetes when he meets him, in this imitating Homer (part of T ivc(a), cf. 5 above) . . . (Odysseus) says that an embassy from the Trojans is about to come to Philoctetes, to beg him to put himself and his weapons at Troy's disposal, with its throne as reward; (Euripides) adds variety to the play and invents occasions for debates, where in handling opposed positions he shows himself most resourceful and incomparably able (T ivc(b), cf. F 789b.194–6).

14. Euripides has Odysseus come not on his own but with Diomedes, just like Homer (T ivc(c), cf. 5 above) . . . In sum, as I said, throughout the play (Euripides) displays the greatest intelligence and credibility in the incidents, and an irresistible and astonishing power in the speeches; the iambic parts are clear, natural and politically realistic, and the lyrics afford not only pleasure but a great incentive to virtue (part of T v, cf. 11 above, 17 below).

15. ...(Sophocles), unlike Aeschylus and Euripides with their chorus of Lemnian inhabitants, has composed his from those who sailed with Odysseus and Neoptolemus on their ship (T iv).

16. ...(Sophocles) has made the character of Odysseus much gentler and franker than Euripides (T iv(a)).

17. ...(Sophocles') lyrics do not have much that is sententious or an incentive to virtue like those of Euripides (part of T iv d, cf. 14 above)...

ΦΙΛΟΚΤΗΤΗΣ

T iiia (–N) Hypothesis P. Oxy. 2455 fr. 17

*about 7 lines missing from the top of col. xviii; line 1 has traces of
only 2 letters at the start*

ρα[. . .]σας Φιλοκτ[ή]τ̣[8–9 letters]ο̣ι̣   2
λευ . . . ς ἐν τοῖς τ[ό]ποις [ἐν οἷς ἐδ]η-
χθη· περιαλγῆ δ᾽ α[ὐτὸν γενόμ]ενον
ἐπὶ τὴν παρακειμένην Λ[ῆ]μνον δια-   5
κομ̣[ίσ]αντες εἴασαν· ὁ δ[ὲ] τὸν δεκαετῆ
χρό[ν]ον διέζησεν ἀτυχῶν, ὡς ἂν βίον
ἔχ[ων] τὸν ἔλεον τῶν ἐντυγχαν[ό]ντων·
ἔ[π]ε[ι]τα καὶ ῞Ελενος εἶπεν τοῖς Τρωσὶ τοῖ[ς
῾Ηρακλέο[υς] τόξοις ἀσφαλίσασθα[ι] τὴν πό-   10
λιν, καὶ λ[η]φθεὶς δ᾽ αἰχμάλωτος τὴν αὐ-
τὴν ποιεῖσθ]αι συμμαχ[ί]α[ν] . [. . . (.)]ισεν
9–10 *letters*]τὸν Φιλοκτ[ήτ-
7 *letters*] Ὀδυσσεὺς εκ[
7 *letters*]τείλατο μὲν ἐμφ[15
7 *letters*] Ἀθηνᾶς βου[λ-
remnants of lines 17–18;
about 13 lines missing at top of col. xix, then:
remnants of line 19

]ην ἀσφάλει-   20
αν ἀναγκάζει[ν εἰς τὴν ν]αῦν συνακ[ο]λουθεῖν.

T iiia Hypothesis P. Oxy. 2455 fr. 17 col. xviii and part of col. xix (lines 246–66) ed. Turner
(1962, without Plate) (= P here); re-ed. Austin, *NFE* no. 28, p. 100; van Rossum-Steenbeek
223–4; Müller (ed.) 144–6 (= H 2); Jouan, ed. Budé 279–81, Kannicht, *TrGF* T iiia; re-ed.
and discussed by W. Luppe, *Anagennesis* 3 (1983), 187–200 with Pl. iv, and *WJb* 19 (1993),
47–53, defending his earlier reconstruction against C. W. Müller, *ZPE* 98 (1993), 19–24 =
Beiträge 43–51. Readings are those of ed. pr. unless stated.   2 beg. Kannicht]εας or
]σας ed. pr. (ἐ)|θερά[πευ]σαν Φιλοκτ[ή]τ[ην Luppe (]σαν doubted by Kannicht) ἱερὰ
[ποιή]σας Müller ([θύ]σας Kannicht)   Φιλοκτ[ή]τ[ου συμβ]ου|λεύοντος Luppe
(συμ- or ἐπιβουλεύσαντες or -τος ed. pr.)   end: 'or]ου' ed. pr.   3 beg. Kannicht

14

PHILOCTETES

T iiia Hypothesis

(an uncertain number of lines missing from the start)

... Philoctetes ...[2] ... in the place <*in which*> he was bitten. In his extremity of pain they took him across to nearby Lemnos[5] and left him. He lived miserably for the period of ten years, as would one who had as his livelihood the pity of those who encountered him. Then Helenus both told the Trojans to secure their city with the aid of Heracles' bow,[10] and when taken prisoner ... (the Greeks) <*to make*> the same alliance ... Philoctetes ... Odysseus ...[15] ... Athena's (counsel?) ... *(remnants of 3 lines surround about 15 missing lines)* ... safety,[20] (to) compel (Philoctetes) to accompany him <*on board the*> ship.

λευσ [.]ες ed. pr.   3–4 ἐδ]ηι|χθηι· περιαλγηι P   6 ιασαν P   end -τηι P
8 ἔλαιον P   9 Kannicht after [ἐπ]ε[ι]τα ed. pr.   12 towards end]π[rather than]ε[(ed. pr.) Kannicht, whence π[αρέπ]εισεν Müller (too long?) ἔ[πε]ισεν or even ἐ[θέσπ]ισεν ed. pr.   13 τοὺς ῞Ελληνας] τὸν Φιλοκτ[ήτην ed. pr.   15 ἐνε]τείλατο ed. pr. ἐσ]τείλατο Müller   μὲν above line P   21 ἀναγκάζει[ν εἰς τὴν ν]αῦν Luppe ἀναγκάζει [πρὸς τὴν ν]αῦν ed. pr.   end -θειν above line P   A paragraphus marks the end of the hypothesis; line 22 begins that for *Phrixus B*.

787–789 *(a composite entry in TrGF: the individual F 787–789b follow 789a)*

General evidence for Odysseus' prologue-speech:

(1) Dio 52.11–12. A summary of Odysseus' internal debate; fuller in:

(2) Dio 59.1 *(Odysseus speaking)*. I am afraid the allies may prove wrong in their opinion that I am indeed the best and cleverest of the Greeks. And yet what kind of cleverness and wisdom is it exactly, which compels someone to work more than others for the common safety and victory (cf. F 789d(9) below), when he may pass as one of the crowd and have no less of these *(continued opposite)*

789a (793 N)

(ΟΔΥΣΣΕΥΣ) μακάριος ὅστις εὐτυχῶν οἴκοι μένει·
ἐν γῆι δ' ὁ φόρτος, κοὐ πάλιν ναυτίλλεται.

787 'Οδ. πῶς δ' ἂν φρονοίην, ὧι παρῆν ἀπραγμόνως
ἐν τοῖσι πολλοῖς ἠριθμημένωι στρατοῦ
ἴσον μετασχεῖν τῶι σοφωτάτωι τύχης;

788 'Οδ. οὐδὲν γὰρ οὕτω γαῦρον ὡς ἀνὴρ ἔφυ·
τοὺς γὰρ περισσοὺς καί τι πράσσοντας πλέον
τιμῶμεν ἄνδρας τ' ἐν πόλει νομίζομεν.

789 'Οδ. ὀκνῶν δὲ μόχθων τῶν πρὶν ἐκχέαι χάριν
καὶ τοὺς παρόντας οὐκ ἀπωθοῦμαι πόνους.

789a *See before F 787*

787–789 ((1) = H 4, T 2, P 2–3 Müller; ed. Budé 287 n. 40 (transl.); (2) = P 1, 4–5 Müller; ed. Budé 283, 287 (transl.); (3) = T 1 Müller; transl. from Schol. Soph. *Phil.* 1 p. 350 Papageorgiou) **789a** (1 Müller, 1 Budé) Stob. 4.17.18, attrib. Eur. *Phil.* 1 Stob. 3.39.13, attrib. Eur. *Phil.*, Clem. Alex. *Strom.* 6.2.7.6, attrib. Eur.; versions of the axiom in 1 occur in e.g. Aesch. F 317 (quoted and attrib. Aesch. by Clem. but to Soph. at Stob. 3.39.14), Men. F 82 *PCG*, adesp. F *140 *PCG* 2 attrib. to Comedy by Gomperz; the whole fr. appears as adesp. F *687 *PCG*. Located in the prologue before F 787 by Müller. Lacuna between 1 and 2 some scholars 2 κοὐ πάλιν Gesner καὶ πάλιν Stob., Clem. καὶ πόλιν Schott and (with ἐν γῆι θ') West **787** (2 Müller, 2 Budé) Plut. *Mor.* 544c, together with F 789, unattrib. 1–3 μετασχεῖν Aristot. *EN* 1142a1, attrib. Eur., together with F 788.2; paraphrased by Dio

16

things than the best men (cf. F 787 below)? Yet it is perhaps difficult to find a thing as proud and ambitious as man naturally is; for we admire almost all those who are prominent and dare to aim for more, and consider them real men (cf. F 788 below). (2) This ambition has led me too into very many troubles and a life of toil beyond anyone's whatever, always accepting some fresh danger, in reluctance to destroy my fame from previous ones (cf. F 789b(2).4).

(3) Schol. Soph. *Phil.* 1. Odysseus speaks the prologue in Sophocles just as in Euripides, but with the difference that Euripides rests everything upon Odysseus...

The next five fragments are all from Odysseus' prologue-speech:

789a (*Odysseus*) Blest the man who stays at home in good fortune!
With his cargo on land he does not go to sea again.

787 *Od.* How would I be sensible, when I could be inactive
and numbered among the army's masses, with a share
in success equal to the cleverest men?

788 *Od.* Nothing is so vainglorious by nature as a man: for
we honour those who go beyond the ordinary and
seek more success, and consider them as real men in
the city.

789 *Od.* From reluctance to waste the gratitude for past
labours I do not reject these present tasks either.

789a *See before F 787*

59.1 in F 787–789 (2)   2 ἠριθμημένωι Ar. most mss., Plut. -μένον Ar. one ms.   3 ἴσον Ar. two mss., Plut. ἴσων, ἴσου, ἴσω variously in other Ar. mss.   **788** (3 Müller, 3 Budé) paraphrased by Dio 59.1 in F 787–789 (2)   1 Dio 52.12 and Schol. Ar. *Frogs* 282, attrib. Eur. *Phil.*; expanded in Plut. *Mor.* 779d, unattrib.; Hesych γ 214 Latte has γαῦρος, attrib. Eur. *Phil.*   2 see Ar. *EN* 1142a1 in App. to F 787   2–3 Stob. 3.29.15, attrib. (Eur.) *Phil.*, joined without new lemma to F 789.1   **789** (4 Müller, 4 Budé) Plur. *Mor.* 544c, unattrib.: see App. to F 787   1 Stob. 3.29.16, implicitly attrib. Eur. *Phil.*: see App. to F 788   2–3 paraphrased by Dio 59.2 in F 787–789 (2)   1 ὀκνῶν Heath, from Dio ὀκνῶ Plut., Stob. 2 παρόντας Plut. ms. D πράττοντας all other mss.

17

EURIPIDES

789b *Evidence for the later part of Odysseus' prologue speech:*

(1) Dio 52.12. Odysseus reveals the play's plot...and why he has come to Lemnos; fuller in:

(2) Dio 59.2–4 (*paraphrase of Odysseus' words*). '...so now I have come here to Lemnos on an altogether dangerous and difficult task, to fetch Philoctetes and the bow of Heracles for the allies. This is because Priam's son Helenus, the most skilled of the Phrygians in prophecy, revealed when he happened to have been taken prisoner, that Troy would never be captured without them. (3) Now I did not give the Greek princes my consent to this task, for I know the man's hostility: I was myself the cause of his being left behind when he happened to get a severe and incurable bite from a viper. So I was thinking that I certainly wouldn't find the kind of persuasion which would ever make him gentle towards me; rather, I thought, I should be killed by him at once. Later, however, when Athena had exhorted me in my sleep, as is her custom, to go and get the man confidently, because, she said, she would alter my appearance and voice, so that I might meet him unrecognized – well, this is how I had the confidence to come. (4) I learn that envoys from the Phrygians too have been secretly despatched to see if they can somehow persuade Philoctetes with gifts and also on account of his hostility to us, and to bring him and the bow back to Troy. With such a prize at stake, how should any man not be eager? For if one fails in this task, all previous achievements seem to have been empty effort.'

789c *Evidence for the parodos of the Chorus:*

Dio 52.7 (*Chorus of Lemnian men*)...(Euripides has made them) apologizing at once for their previous lack of concern, namely that during so many years they have neither approached Philoctetes nor helped him in any way.

789d *Dio 59.5–11: paraphrase of a complete scene, either at the end of the prologue-scene or at the start of Episode 1. Philoctetes slowly makes his initial entry; he does not recognize the transformed Odysseus:*

(5) Odysseus. Oh! The man approaches! Here he is himself, the son of Poias, his plight quite obvious, advancing with difficulty and in pain. What a miserable and dreadful sight he is, like this: his appearance is frightening because of his affliction, and his garb unnatural; hides of wild beasts cover him.

Now, mistress Athena, defend me! and show that your promise of my safety was not empty!

789b ((*1*) = H 4, P 6, Müller; (2) = P 6 and 8, T 20 Müller; ed. Budé 283–4, 287–8) *(2)* 'taken prisoner': wording as in Hypoth. 11   **789c** (H 4, P 9 Müller; ed. Budé p. 292 n. 45 (transl.))   **789d** (= P 10–14 Müller; pp. 284–6, 288–90 Budé)   *(5)* '...sight he is, like this: his appearance' Dio mss. '...sight he is! Like this, his appearance etc.' Wilamowitz, von Arnim   *(6)* end: 'as <friend and> no stranger' Müller

PHILOCTETES

(6) Philoctetes. What is it you want, whoever you are, or what bold purpose did you have in coming to this bare dwelling – is it for plunder or to spy on my miserable lot?

Od. You see no aggressor, I assure you.

Phil. I swear, you've no previous habit of coming here.

Od. No, no habit; but I wish that my coming even now is timely.

Phil. There seems a great lack of reason for your journey here, in what you say.

Od. Well, you are to know that I do not come without cause and will be revealed as no stranger to yourself.

(7) Phil. Where from, please? It's reasonable I should know this first.

Od. I'm a Greek, then, from those who sailed against Troy.

Phil. Where from? Say it again, so I may know more certainly.

Od. You hear it a second time, then: I say that I am a Greek who campaigned against Troy.

Phil. A fine thing indeed to say you are my friend, when you've shown yourself one of the Greeks, my worst enemies! You'll pay penalty this very instant for their injustice to me.

Od. In the gods' name, I beg you, hold back from shooting that arrow!

Phil. Impossible, if you really are a Greek, for you not to lose your life this day!

(8) Od. But I've suffered such things at their hands as would justly make me your friend but their enemy.

Phil. And what is it you have suffered which is so hard?

Od. Odysseus drove me out of the army into exile.

Phil. And what did you do to deserve this penalty?

Od. I think you know Palamedes, the son of Nauplius?

Phil. Yes, of course: he was no ordinary companion on the voyage, and of no little value to either army or commanders.

Od. Such indeed was the man destroyed by that common bane of the Greeks.

Phil. Did he overcome Palamedes openly in a fight or through some trick?

Od. He charged him with betraying the army to Priam's Trojans.

Phil. Did that match the truth or did Palamedes suffer lying accusations?

Od. How could anything whatever of Odysseus' actions be just?

(9) Phil. No holding back in you, Odysseus, from anything of the harshest, you most villainous of men in word and deed! What a man you've once again destroyed in Palamedes, who was no less useful to the allies than you actually were, I think, yourself, inventing and concerting the most excellent and clever things! It was just like this, quite certainly, that you got rid of myself too, now

19

fallen into this plight for the sake of general safety and victory, because I showed them Chryse's altar where they were to sacrifice to overcome their enemies; and unless they did, their campaign was lost.

But what have Palamedes' fortunes to do with you?

(10) Od. You are to know that the evil business reached to all Palamedes' friends, and that all have lost their lives except any capable of escape. That's why I myself reached safety here, sailing across alone last night. So I am almost in as great a need as you stand yourself. If then you have any means of it, join eagerly in getting me a voyage home: you will have done me a good deed and at the same time you will be sending home to your own people a messenger of the troubles which attend you. *(continued opposite)*

790 ΦΙΛΟΚΤΗΤΗΣ δύσμορφα μέντοι τἄνδον εἰσιδεῖν, ξένε.

**790a (adesp. 389 N)

(Φι.) οὐκ ἔστ' ἐν ἄντροις λευκός, ὦ ξέν', ἄργυρος.

791 N = *792a*

792 Φι. φαγέδαιναν ἥ μου σάρκα θοινᾶται ποδός.

792a (791 N)

ΧΟΡΟΣ ἅλις, ὦ βιοτά· πέραινε,
πρίν τινα συντυχίαν
ἢ κτεάτεσσιν ἐμοῖς ἢ σώματι τῶιδε γενέσθαι.

793 N = *789a*

(11) end: 'full <*of blood*> Bothe <*of pus*> Hermann   **790** (9 Müller, 5 Budé) Plut. *Mor.* 521a, unattrib.; the paraphrase in Dio 59.11 (F 789d) was recognized by D. Canter ****790a** (8 Müller, *6 Budé) Plut. *Mor.* 533a, unattrib.; assigned to *Phil.* by Hilberg, noting Dio 59.6 (F 789d(6)) (Od.) 'coming to this bare dwelling...for plunder ...?', and 59.11 (F 789d (11)) (Phil.) 'without resources etc.'   **792** (10 Müller, 8 Budé) Ar. *Poet.* 1458b19ff. attributes 'the same verse' to Aesch. *Phil.* (F 253) and, with change of only one word, to Eur., citing both versions.   φαγέδαιναν S. Butler φαγάδαινα Ar. ms. B, with loss of final letter (-ν? Kassel) φαγάδενα, φαγέδαινα other mss.   φαγέδαινά <γ'> Barnes

20

(11) Phil. You poor wretch, you have come to another of your own kind for an ally, himself thrown upon this shore without resources and deprived of friends, meanly and hardly with this bow getting both food and clothing, as you see. The clothing I had before, time has ruined. Yet if you will be willing to share this life here with me, until other safety falls your way from somewhere, I won't begrudge you. The sights inside are hard to take, though, stranger, truly they are [cf. F 790] – bandages full <of...> and other tokens of my affliction; and I'm not pleasant myself to be with, when the agony strikes. And yet much of my affliction has become lighter with time, while at the start it was in no way bearable.

The next three fragments seem to continue this same scene:

790   PHILOCTETES
The things inside, however, are an ugly sight, stranger.

Philoctetes prepares Odysseus for the grim conditions he will have to share.

**790a   *(Phil.)* There is no pale silver in the cave, stranger.

Continuing the warning to Odysseus?

791 N = *792a*

792   *Phil.* An ulcer which feasts on my foot's flesh.

Possibly from this same scene, but not confidently located

792a   CHORUS Life, enough! Make an end, before any mishap comes to my property and my own self here.

From the parodos or first stasimon, as the Chorus realise the full horror of Philoctetes' misery.

793 N = *789a*

φαγέδαιν' ἀεί μου Nauck   θοινᾶται Eur. ἐσθίει Aesch.   **792a** (6 Müller, 7 Budé) Stob. 4.52.29, attrib. Eur. *Phil.* ms. A, Eur. alone ms. S; assigned to 'Cho(rus)' in ms. S 1 ἅλις ms. S μόλις ms. A

EURIPIDES

794   (ΤΡΩΣ) ὁρᾶτε δ' ὡς κἀν θεοῖσι κερδαίνειν καλόν,
θαυμάζεται δ' ὁ πλεῖστον ἐν ναοῖς ἔχων
χρυσόν· τί δῆτα καὶ σὲ κωλύει ⟨λαβεῖν⟩
κέρδος, παρόν γε, κἀξομοιοῦσθαι θεοῖς;

795   ('Οδ.?) τί δῆτα θάκοις μαντικοῖς ἐνήμενοι
σαφῶς διόμνυσθ' εἰδέναι τὰ δαιμόνων,
οἱ τῶνδε χειρώνακτες ἄνθρωποι λόγων;
ὅστις γὰρ αὐχεῖ θεῶν ἐπίστασθαι πέρι,
οὐδέν τι μᾶλλον οἶδεν ἢ πείθειν λέγων.

796   ('Οδ.) ὑπέρ γε μέντοι παντὸς Ἑλλήνων στρατοῦ
αἰσχρὸν σιωπᾶν, βαρβάρους δ' ἐᾶν λέγειν.

797   λέξω δ' ἐγώ, κἄν μου διαφθείρας δοκῆι
λόγους ὑποφθὰς αὐτὸς ἠδικηκέναι·
ἀλλ' ἐξ ἐμοῦ γὰρ τἀμὰ †μαθήσηι† κλυών,
ὁ δ' αὐτὸς αὐτὸν †ἐμφανιεῖ† σοι λέγων.

798   ('Οδ.?) πατρὶς καλῶς πράσσουσα τὸν τυχόντ' ἀεὶ
μείζω τίθησι, δυστυχοῦσα δ' ἀσθενῆ.

794 (15 Müller, 9 Budé) [Justin Martyr], *On Monarchy* 5.8, attrib. 'the tragedian in *Phil.* ' in a Euripidean sequence; assigned to 'Trojan legates' by Valckenaer   1 ὁρᾶις γ' ὅπως Valckenaer ὅρα γ' ὅπως Welcker   3 ⟨λαβεῖν⟩ (e.g.) Sylburg   4 comma after γε Barnes   **795** (14 Müller, 11 Budé) Stob. 2.1.2, attrib. Eur. *Phil.* mss. FP, Eur. alone ms. L; assigned to Odysseus by e.g. Calder, to Philoctetes by Olson.   1 θάκοις Dindorf θώκοις Stob.   μαντικοῖς Nauck ἀργικοῖς Stob. ἀρχικοῖς Valckenaer ἀργυροῖς Ellis 1–3 punct. as question Stob., then perhaps ὦ for οἱ Kannicht; lacuna after 3 Müller 5 ἢ πείθειν Musgrave ἢ πείθει Stob. (κ)εἰ πείθει Munro   **796** (13 Müller, 10 Budé) Plut. *Mor.* 1108b, unattrib. 2 transl. Cicero, *De Oratore* 3.141 'about Philoctetes', with the substitution for *barbaros* of *Isocratem* attrib. to Aristotle; cf. (in Greek) Philod. *Rhet.* 36.3–5 (II p. 50 Sudhaus) and 40.5–7 (p. 55 Sudhaus); also transl. Quintilian, *Inst.Or.* 3.1.14, attrib. *Phil.* 2 first attrib. Eur. *Phil.* by D. Canter; the whole fr. reconstructed by Grotius (with βαρβάρους for Cicero's *barbaros*) and by Musgrave from Plut.; assigned to Od. by Valckenaer   **797** (16 Müller, 12 Budé) Anaximenes, *Ars Rhet.* 18.15 p. 49 Fuhrmann (= [Aristot.] *Rhet. ad Alex.* 1433b10ff.), discussing the rhetorical technique of anticipation, attrib. Eur. *Phil.*; TrGF cites a Latin transl. in ms. Vat. 2995 (14th C.) ed. M. Grabmann, *SBAW* 1931–2 no. 4, 26ff.   1 διαφθεῖραι Munro   2 ὑποφθὰς Weil, cf. *praeveniens* 'anticipating' ms. Vat. ὑποστὰς Anax.   3 †μαθήσηι† is unmetrical; cf. *addisces* 'you

22

PHILOCTETES

The next three fragments are from the episode between a Trojan envoy, Philoctetes and the still disguised Odysseus:

794   (A TROJAN) You see how making profit is honoured even among the gods, and that the one who has most gold in his temples is admired. What then prevents you too <*from taking*> profit when it is quite open to you, and making yourself like the gods?

A Trojan envoy tries to win Philoctetes as ally.

795   (Od.?) Why then, seated on your seers' thrones, do you solemnly swear to sure knowledge of the gods' will, you people who are pastmasters of these sayings? – for anyone who claims to know about the gods, knows no more than how to persuade with words.

A duplicitous attack on seers by Odysseus.

796   (Od.) When it is on the whole Greek army's behalf, however, it is shameful to keep silent while allowing barbarians to speak.

Odysseus will try to thwart the Trojan inducements to Philoctetes.

797   I'll speak myself, even if he seems to have cheated in destroying my argument by anticipation; you'll hear and †learn† my case from myself, and he †will make himself clear† to you in his own words.

Speaker and context uncertain; perhaps Odysseus in the scene with the Trojan and Philoctetes

The next two fragments may come from the same or a later scene:

798   (Od.?) His country's prosperity makes the successful man greater, but its misfortunes weaken him.

Odysseus tries to persuade Philoctetes to rejoin the Greeks.

shall learn' ms. Vat. τἄμ' ἐπιστήσηι Pflugk τἀμὰ πάντ' εἴσηι Meineke   κλυών Mette   κλύων Anax.   4 †ἐμφανιεῖ† is unmetrical; cf. *demonstrabit* 'he will reveal' ms. Vat. ἐμφανίζει Heath ἐμφανῆ (Musgrave) θήσει Jacobs   **798** (17 Müller, 13 Budé) Stob. 3.40.1, attrib. Eur. *Phil.*; assigned to Od. by Welcker   1 τὸν τυχόντ' Matthiae   τὸν εὐτυχοῦντ' Stob.   2 δυστυχοῦσα Stob. ms. Paris 1985 acc. to Gaisford   δυστυχοῦντα Stob. other mss.

EURIPIDES

799   ('Οδ.) ὥσπερ δὲ θνητὸν καὶ τὸ σῶμ' ἡμῶν ἔφυ,
             οὕτω προσήκει μηδὲ τὴν ὀργὴν ἔχειν
             ἀθάνατον ὅστις σωφρονεῖν ἐπίσταται.

799a   (Φιλ.) ἀνδρὸς κακῶς πράσσοντος ἐκποδὼν φίλοι.

800   (Χο.?) φεῦ·
             μηδέν ποτ' εἴην ἄλλο πλὴν θεοῖς φίλος,
             ὡς πᾶν τελοῦσι, κἂν βραδύνωσιν, χρόνωι.

Unplaced Fragments

801   ἀπέπνευσεν αἰῶνα

802   αἱρεῖς

803   ἀκριβές

Uncertain Fragment

*801a   βέβληκ' Ἀχιλλεὺς δύο κύβω καὶ τέτταρα

799 (19 Müller, 14 Budé) Stob. 3.20.17, attrib. Eur. *Phil.*; generally assigned to Od.; letters from 1–2 seem to be preserved in Men. *Monost.* Pap. XIX.5–6 Jaekel (= *CGFP* F *305a Austin); paraphrased at Dion. Hal. *Ant.Rom.* 5.4.3 and Phalaris, *Epist.* 51 p. 420 Hercher 799a (20 Müller, 15 Budé) Schol. Eur. *Pho.* 402, attrib. (Eur.) *Phil.*; Schol. *And.* 975 and Schol. Soph. *El.* 188, unattrib.; cf. Men. *Monost.* 34 Jaekel etc.; assigned to Phil. by Wecklein. Variants of this proverb occur at Aristid. *Or.* 1.60 and 20.18, attrib. Soph. (F 667 N = 733 Pearson; excluded from *TrGF* IV).   800 (21 Müller, 16 Budé) Orion V.4 Haffner, attrib. Eur. *Phil.*; Orion, *Appendix Eur.* 1 Haffner, unattrib.; assigned to Chorus by most editors 1–2 Suidas μ 875 Adler, unattrib.   φεῦ | μηδέν ποτ' Nauck   φεῦ· μήποτ' Orion (both places) μηδέν ποτ' Suidas   2 θεοῖς Orion V.4 and perhaps *Appendix* (damaged) θεῶι Suidas   3 πᾶν τελοῦσι Nauck πάντ' ἔχωσι Orion (both) πᾶν τεχνῶνται West in *TrGF* comma after βραδύνωσιν Wecklein   801(12 Müller, 17 Budé) Hesych. α 2216 Latte,

799 *(Od.)* Just as our body too naturally dies, so it befits the man who knows good sense not to keep his anger undying either.

Odysseus tries to end Philoctetes' rancour against the Greeks.

Possibly from the same scene as the previous two fragments:

799a *(Phil.)* When a man does badly, friends get out of his way.

Philoctetes perhaps defending his stubborn self-dependence in the light of his experience on Lemnos.

Probably from the play's final scene:

800 *(Cho.?)* Oh! I wish I may never be anything other than dear to the gods, because even if they are slow, in time they fulfil everything.

The Chorus(?) witnesses Philoctetes' forcible capitulation at last to his destiny.

Unplaced Fragments

801   He breathed his life away.

802   you understand (*or* 'mean' *or* 'suppose')

803   point (*or* 'peak')

Uncertain Fragment

*801a   Achilles has thrown two ones and a four.

attrib. Eur. *Phil.*   **802** (22 Müller, 18 Budé) Hesych. α 2068 Latte, attrib. Eur. *Phil.* = (all unattrib.) *Synag.* p. 359.22 Bekker, Photius α 689 Theodoridis, Suidas αι 300 Adler (II.178.28)   αἱρεῖ[ς] i.e. αἱρῆι some eds.   **803** (23 Müller, 19 Budé) Hesych. α 2569 Latter, atrib. Eur. *Phil.*   ***801a** (T 30 Müller, – Budé) Ar. *Frogs* 1400, where it is probably a pastiche of Euripides; scholia there, citing other ancient authorities, could not identify the verse, ascribing it to *Telephus* (see our Vol. 1, p. 21), *Phil.* or *IA,* or naming no author.

25

Commentary on *Philoctetes*

T iiia Hypothesis. Of the 'narrative' kind (Vol. 1, p. 2). Lost from its start are the play's first line and much of its remoter background, which ended in lines 1–8; then comes the immediate background (9–15). From the action itself there survive only Athena's disguise of Odysseus (16: F 789b(2).3) and Philoctetes' involuntary departure with him (20–21: Dio 52.2).

Note. Some details in the two hypotheses to Soph. *Phil.* (*Sophocles OCT* ed. Pearson, not in Lloyd-Jones and Wilson) may be muddled with Euripides' play, i.e. Hypoth. I.10 Odysseus is sent apparently on his own to fetch Philoctetes and his bow (but what of Diomedes?), and II.12–13 the Greeks' seer Calchas directs them to capture the Trojans' seer Helenus (see on Eur. *Phil.* Hypoth. 11 below).

2. ['*<tended>* **Philoctetes**' Luppe: that is, the Greeks tended him immediately after the snake-bite, including almost certainly Machaon, their field-surgeon at Troy (Hom. *Il.* 11.512–5 etc.). Kannicht however doubts a 3rd Plural Aorist form in P. Oxy; of the alternative supplements in 2–3 by Müller and Kannicht, both giving '*<(Agamemnon) making sacrifice>*', Kannicht's seems too short for the space. Across 2–3 forms of συμ- or ἐπιβουλεύω have been supplemented, e.g. '*<on the advice of>* Philoctetes' Luppe.]

3. the place *<in which>* **he was bitten**: the island near Lemnos named for Chryse, a Thracian nymph or goddess (S. *Phil.* 194), where Philoctetes had told the Greeks 'they were to sacrifice to overcome their enemies', F 789d(9); **place** is an allusive Plural in the Greek. The island of Chryse was much visited because of the Philoctetes legend; it was however overwhelmed by the sea shortly before the 2nd C. A.D. geographer Pausanias described it (Paus. 8.33.4); the earlier Epic account located the incident on the island of Tenedos, a little nearer Troy (*Cypria* [Proclus] 64–6, Ar. *Poet.* 1459b5). **his extremity of pain**: cf. F 792, Acc. *Phil.* F 12.

6–7. for...ten years: cf. S. *Phil.* 311–3, Acc. *Phil.* F 15; that is, during most of the war. Achilles' death in the tenth year threatened defeat for the Greeks and prompted their recovery of Philoctetes after learning Helenus' oracle (9–11).

8. those who encountered him: S. *Phil.* 305–10. Eur. has Actor the Lemnian as his only regular visitor (Dio 52.8, cf. Introd., *Reconstruction*). **as would one who**: ὡς ἄν with potential participle ('as you'd expect with'), e.g. Xen. *Anab.* 1.1.10, 5.2.8; KG I. 242.

9. Helenus: the Trojan seer, cf. F 789b(2), S. *Phil.* 604ff. Apollod. *Epit.* 5.8 attributes a similar prophecy to the Greeks' own seer Calchas (see next note).

11. taken prisoner: cf. F 789b(2); apparently by accident, but at S. *Phil.* 608 kidnapped by Odysseus on the advice of Calchas (S. *Phil.* Hypoth. II, cited above); cf. Quint. Smyrn. 9.315–32.

12–13. ['(Helenus) *<persuaded (the Greeks)>*' (ed. pr.) seems the best supplement in sense and length; '*<pronounced that (the Greeks) should make>*' (also ed. pr.)

26

and '<persuaded (the Greeks) to change their decision>' (Müller, with further supplementation); both seem too lengthy.]

15. Athena's (counsel?): given to Odysseus in his sleep, with the promise to keep him safe by transformation, F 789b(3), 789d(5); see next note. ['**Odysseus** <ordered>' ed. pr., but Müller objects that Odysseus could not order, only recommend; so he suggested '<set sail>', i.e. to Lemnos.]

20. safety: usually understood to be that promised to Philoctetes by Odysseus, or perhaps Diomedes (see Introd., *Reconstruction*); cf. Neoptolemus to Philoctetes at Soph. *Phil.* 1391; but Müller thinks of Odysseus' own safety once he has obtained the bow, cf. F 789b(2).2 'dangerous task', 789d(5) Athena's promise of safety.

21. (to) compel: 'forcible persuasion', Dio 52.2, cf. Introd., *Reconstruction*, at end. [The Infin. is controlled from the defective line 20; ed. pr. gives 'compel' Indicative, but Luppe and Kannicht note that narrative Present tenses are foreign to 'narrative hypotheses'.]

787–789 (1)–(2). Dio's general remarks here on Odysseus' political ambition are discussed in the Introd., *Themes*; cf. Pl. *Rep.* 620c–d (= T 3 Müller) where the soul of Odysseus recovers from ambition and, remembering its past toils, seeks a life of political inactivity. *(3)*. **Euripides rests everything upon Odysseus**: see Introd., *Reconstruction*.

789a. Almost certainly the play's opening lines (so located first by Müller); axiomatic statements begin also *Hcld.*, *Or.*, *Sthen.* (F 661). **Blest the man who:** a near-formula, e.g. *Arch.* F 256.1 (see note there), F 1057.1; cf. on *Antiope*, Uncertain Fragment F 910.1. Such an idea was probably proverbial; Müller compares Philemon F 51 *PCG*, amazement that a man home from the sea should set sail again; cf. Hor. *Odes* 1.1.15–18. Translation, coherence of thought and integrity of text are much disputed, however. [In 2 Gesner's κοὐ is printed as the easiest solution, lit. 'and his cargo is on land and he does not go to sea again'; after this general truth, Odysseus will continue with a rueful exception of his own case, F 787–789b. Stobaeus' καὶ (4.17.18) is defended as 'and yet', the generaliz-ation in line 1 being contradicted by the reality in line 2 (but this usage is colloquial: Denniston, *GP* 292); or καὶ is merely 'and', and 2 expands 1 not quite logically, '...his voyage is back home' (i.e., it is assured). καὶ with Schott's πόλιν gives 'and the city is what he sails'; ναυτίλλομαι is then uniquely meta-phorical, but (West) like ναυκληρέω at A. *Sept.* 652. Lastly, Stob.'s Ch. 4.17 (*On seafaring*) is the only source citing both verses, while his Chapter 3.39 (*On one's native country*) cites only the first, and this axiomatic line appears singly if varied in many other sources (see App.); so Gomperz supposed loss of a lemma between the verses in Stob. 4.17 (cf. e.g. Comm. on *Antiope* F 215), the second verse deriving from Comedy (*PCG* treats the whole couplet as Comic).]

787. inactive: that is, politically; the word ἀπράγμων was a significant concept in Athenian democracy, e.g. Thuc. 2.40.2, Antiphon 3.2.1, cf. Dunbar on Ar. *Birds*

44: see also on *Antiope* F 183.2, 193.　　**numbered among:** a very loose metaphor, *Hel.* 729, *Supp.* 969, *Hyps.* F 757.830.　　[In 2 the variant ἠριθμημένον is an Accus. drawn to the natural Subject case of the infin.; cf. e.g. *Hec.* 541, *Med.* 815.]　　For the implicit contrast in **among the army's masses...cleverest** Müller compares *El.* 382 'found to be the best among the masses'. Yet in F 787–789 (2) Odysseus knows that the Greeks do regard him as both 'the best and cleverest', ἄριστος καὶ σοφώτατος, cf. S. *Phil.* 119; the adjectives are coupled at e.g. Hdt. 8.110.3, of the wily Themistocles.

788. vainglorious: cf. *Alex.* F 61b.8, *Bell.* F 285.11 etc.　　**is...by nature:** the full meaning of the verb ἔφυ, shown by Dio's paraphrase 'as man naturally is' (59.1 in F 787–789 (2)).
2. go beyond the ordinary: the adj. περισσός seems to have its pejorative meaning here, as at e.g. *Hipp.* 445, F 924.2 and especially S. *Ant.* 68 περισσὰ πράσσειν, this last of the politically over-active man, the πολυπράγμων. This is also the implication of the words **seek more success**, for τι πράσσοντας πλέον, paraphrased by Dio as 'daring to aim for more', can be heard as a synonym for πολυπράγμονας, those who push themselves forward and 'interfere'. For the complex of associated values in Athens see on *Antiope* F 193; Olson 279–83; cf. Introd., *Themes*. The neutral translations 'who are exceptional and have more success' miss the point.
3. real men; bare ἀνήρ as e.g. *El.* 693, S. *Aj.* 77; LSJ ἀνήρ IV.

789. waste: lit. 'pour out, away', metaphorical of prosperity A. *Pers.* 826 etc. **gratitude:** reward through recognition, 'fame' in Dio's paraphrase (59.2 in F 787–789 (2)); cf. 'vainglorious' in F 788.1.　　[**From reluctance:** the participle, not the Indicative, is correct because syntax requires it before adverbial καὶ **either** in 2.]

789b(2). Helenus...most skilled...in prophecy: so too in S. *Phil.* 1338, cf. 604ff.
(3). this task: that mentioned in §2.　　**left behind:** self-excusatory, milder than 'abandoned'.　　**bite from a viper:** see F 789d(9) for the place, Chryse's island (Introd., *Myth*), and for Odysseus' subsequent action against Philoctetes. **persuasion:** Dio 52.13–14 notes the accomplished rhetorical writing of Euripides in the play; see Introd., *Themes*.　　**I should be killed by him:** Odysseus' fear at S. *Phil.* 75–6, at a similar stage of his planning.　　**Athena:** Odysseus later appeals to her for safety at F 789d(5).　　**unrecognized:** as transpires, F 789d(6), where Philoctetes says to Odysseus 'whoever you are'; cf. Dio 52.13.
(4). envoys from the Phrygians: also Dio 52.13, F 794 below.　　**how...not be eager:** cf. 'ambition' Dio 52.12 and F 787–789 (2).2.

789c. *Lemnian men*: providing the Chorus also in Aeschylus (Dio 52.6), unlike
in Sophocles, where they are from Neoptolemus' crew (S. *Phil.* 135): see Introd.,
Reconstruction.   **apologizing at once**: concern for the hero(ine) is the
Euripidean chorus's regular explanation for its arrival, e.g. *Alc.* (esp. 108ff.), *Med.*
136ff.; but the feelings here may have been in a vacuum, for Philoctetes has yet to
appear (F 789d(5)) – like the heroines in *Alcestis* and *Medea*.   **neither
approached nor helped**: so also Dio 52.8 – but the individual Lemnian Actor
had done so occasionally: see Introd., *Reconstruction*.

789d(5). **advancing...in pain**: cf. S. *Phil.* 163ff., 289ff.   **like this**:
emphatic postponement to sentence-end of the Greek adverb which qualifies both
miserable and **dreadful**; Müller compares *Hcld.* 413, S. *Phil.* 486f.
[Wilamowitz's repunctuation involves further unlikely changes to Greek word-
order].   **garb unnatural etc.**: he has 'tattered clothes' in paratragedy at Ar.
Ach. 423–4 (with Schol.: T ivb), cf. Telephus' rags *Ach.* 407ff (our Vol. 1 p. 24,
cf. *Tel.* F 697 etc.). Sophocles has Philoctetes' ragged clothing (*Phil.* 274)
supplemented by occasional visitors' gifts (319; cf. our Hypoth. 8); Acc. *Phil.* F 5
gives him clothes woven of birds' feathers.   **promise of my safety**: cf.
Athena in F 789b(2).3.
(6). **whoever you are, or what bold purpose etc.**: cf. Acc. *Phil.* F 13.
bare dwelling: στέγη, his cave (cf. S. *Phil.* 16 etc., and the Herdsman's cave at
Antiope F 223.19 etc.).   **for plunder**: compare the Cyclops' fear of Odysseus
and his men at *Cyc.* 252–3 (based on Hom. *Od.* 9.252–5); cf. F **790a below.   **to
spy on my miserable lot**: cf. Prometheus' accusation of the 'visiting' Chorus
at *PV* 118.   [End: Müller based his supplement 'as <friend and> no stranger'
upon §7 below, 'A fine thing...to say you are my friend'; but 'as no stranger' is
enough to explain 'not...without cause'.]
(7). **hold back...that arrow**: similarly Neoptolemus to Philoctetes at S. *Phil.*
1300, when he has restored the bow to him, and he hopes for revenge.
(8). **I've suffered such things etc.**: cf. Neoptolemus' false tale of his
maltreatment by the Greeks, S. *Phil.* 319ff.   **Palamedes**: for his story see on
Palamedes, p. 93 below.   **that common bane of the Greeks**: Ajax calls
Odysseus his 'bane' (λυμεών), S. *Aj.* 573; Müller compares Tzetzes, *Posthomerica*
297 'bane of the heroes, a detestation to the best men'.
(9). **No holding back in you, etc.**: in the Greek, Dio reproduces the
participial Vocative of the high Tragic style; cf. *Hyps.* F 757.853, Collard on *Hec.*
1000.   **most villainous...in word**: Odysseus' unscrupulous and devious
rhetoric is a cliché of Tragedy: S. *Phil.* 407–8, cf. e.g. *Tro.* 284–8, *Hec.* 132–3
with Collard's n. Philoctetes is of course unaware that it is being used against him
now. Earlier, at F 789 b (2) §3, Odysseus doubts his powers of persuasion.
general safety and victory: as F 787–789 (2).1.   **I showed them
Chryse's altar**: where he was bitten, Hypoth. 3 and n., F 789b(2).3; cf. Introd.,
Myth.

(10). **sailing across alone**; part of Odysseus' deceit, for Diomedes came with him and later gives his physical if not verbal support: see Introd., *Reconstruction*. **you will be sending home, etc.**: Odysseus' deception of Philoctetes is more cautious than Neoptolemus' feigned departure without him at S. *Phil.* 461ff. In Sophocles too, Philoctetes' messages home entrusted to earlier visitors have been unavailing, 494–6.

(11). **thrown upon this shore...deprived of friends**: S. *Phil.* 1017–18. **with this bow getting both food etc.**: Dio 52.2, S. *Phil.* 285–92. **the clothing I had before**: see on *(5)* above. Acc. *Phil.* F 3–12 and 15 describe Philoctetes' miserable existence on Lemnos. **The sights inside...bandages etc.**: S. *Phil.* 38–9 'rags full of a heavy discharge', cf. 7 [hence the supplements in Dio: 'full of blood, pus', Bothe, Hermann]. **I'm not pleasant myself to be with**: so Philoctetes at S. *Phil.* 473, 890–1, 900, cf. Acc. *Phil.* F 14. Cf. *Or.* 792 'it's difficult to touch a diseased person'.

790. Plutarch cites this line to illustrate the ill manners of looking nosily through a neighbour's door at unpleasant sights within. **ugly:** the adj. δύσμορφος, used of Menelaus' rags at *Hel.* 1204; cf. S. *Phil.* 38–9 (previous n.).

790a. Plutarch cites the line as an appropriately brusque deflection of a would-be sponger. The idea and formulation are no doubt proverbial. **pale silver: the adj. is ornamental: cf. *Oed.* F 542.1.

792. Located early in the play and usually in this same scene by most eds., but immediately before Philoctetes' later paroxysm by others. 'Eating' describes Philoctetes' ulcer also at S. *Phil.* 7 (our 'rodent') and is the medical metaphor (see e.g. LSJ ἐσθίω 2 and in general J. Jouanna, *Métis* 3 [1988], 353–9); of leprosy at A. *Cho.* 281. For the agony of the bite-wound see Hypoth. 3. Aristotle cites the verse to illustrate the difference in stylistic level between standard 'eat' (commoner in Aeschylus and Comedy) and metaphorical **feasts on** (commoner in Euripides; cf. on *Andromeda* F 145).

792a. **enough!:** ἅλις, abrupt and perhaps colloquial, *Hel.* 1581, S. *Aj.* 1402 [μόλις 'with difficulty' in Stob. ms. A is merely a copying error]. **my own self here:** lit. 'this body', a regular periphrasis, cf. *Alc.* 636, *And.* 315 etc.
　　METRE. A paroemiac (anapaest + syncopated iambus) seems to be followed by two dactylic verses, hemiepes and hexameter (so Kannicht).

794. The Trojans approach Philoctetes, in consequence of their seer Helenus' prophecy (Hypoth. 9–11, cf. F 789b(2).4). Acc. *Phil.* F 17–18 may indicate the participation of the Trojan Paris himself: see Introd., *Reconstruction*.
1. You see: Plural, i.e. both Philoctetes and Odysseus; the latter's disguise is not yet broken to either of the two other parties to the debate. Probably Indicative like e.g. *Ion* 1090, *IA* 1259, not Imperative (unless the Plural is a general appeal like

Hipp. 943, *Bell.* F 286.4). [The Singulars in Valckenaer's 'You see how...' and Welcker's 'See though how...' confine the appeal to Philoctetes (Sing. 'you' in line 3). The restriction would be more likely if Euripides were making a pun upon his name, lit. 'Lover of Possessions'; for such play on names cf. Pentheus 'Man of Sorrow' *Bacc.* 367, Atreus 'Fearless' *IA* 321, Thoas 'Swift' *IT* 32; also on *Antiope* F 181.]   **making profit is honoured even among gods:** the idea possibly at A. *Cho.* 255–6.

METRE: θεοῖσι scans as two syllables (synizesis), cf. F 795.4.

2. most gold in his temples: men had made Apollo's Delphic temple the richest (*And.* 1092–3, *IT* 1275 etc.; Hdt. 1.14.1, Paus. 1.9.3 etc.). Euripides is perhaps anticipating Odysseus' attack on seers, servants of Apollo, in F 795.

3. What then...: τί δῆτα regularly introduces a counter-assertion or expostulation, like F 795.1 'Why then...?', *Hec.* 814 etc.: Denniston, *GP* 270 (2).   [**<*from taking*>:** Sylburg's is the easiest supplement in sense, and most easily explains the omission as haplography in ΚΩΛΥΕΙΛΑΒΕΙΝ.]

4. quite open to you: by acquiring Trojan wealth and power (Dio 52.13 = T ivc(b)); 'quite' translates the emphatic particle γε.   **making yourself like the gods:** the highest measure of well-being, registered e.g. in the adj. 'blest', (F 789a); 'equal to the gods' is a regular self-description by Trojans, e.g. *Tro.* 1169, *Hec.* 356. For such mortal aspiration see Barrett on *Hipp.* 459–61.   [The line without Barnes' second comma means 'since this way you may indeed also become like the gods'.]

795. Odysseus shows his duplicity by devaluing Helenus' prophecy while himself acting in its light, F 789b(2).2. Both text and interpretation of this fragment are insecure.

1. Why then...: see on F 794.3.   **seers' thrones:** a regular picture, *Bacc.* 347, *Ion* 909, *IT* 1254 etc.   [Nauck's **seers'** restores a typically clear headline to a Euripidean denunciation. Stob.'s adj. 'lazy' is incongruous (and a non-existent word); Valckenaer's 'ruling' gives seers a 'rule' they nowhere possessed; Ellis's 'silver' inappropriately introduces seers' venality (e.g. S. *OT* 388–9).]

2. solemnly swear: the Greek compound verb is redolent of the law-court, Antiphon 1.28 etc.

3. pastmasters: lit. 'hand-lords', shown to be contemptuous by its coupling as adj. with colloquial ἄνθρωποι **people;** for this idiom cf. Ar. *Birds* 983, *Frogs* 837. For the metaphor in -άνακτες 'lords' cf. esp. *And.* 447 ψευδῶν ἄνακτες 'lords of lies'; the compound χειροτέχνης 'hand-craftsman' occurs at S. *Trach.* 1000 (of a surgeon, but not contemptuous).   [**3. you people who (etc.):** for the Greek phrase defining the unexpressed subject of a 2nd Person verb see KG I.602 n. 2; Kannicht's 'O you pastmasters' in 3 would ease the definition. Some editors punctuate 3 as a self-contained statement ('Men are pastmasters, etc.') or question; both give less logical preparation for 4–5; so Müller wondered whether text has been lost.]

4-5. The sense is well explained by Müller (advocating Musgrave's πείθειν **how to persuade**): a typical seer only **claims** **to know** when he does not, so that his credibility **with words** is false; **words** echoes 3 **sayings** [Stob's πείθει gives 'knows no more about the gods than he is (un)persuasive with words']. Cf. e.g. *IT* 574 'not foolish but persuaded by the words of seers' and Euripides' extended attack upon seers at *Hel.* 744-60, with Cropp's n. on *El.* 399-400; for attacks on false rhetoric see *Antiope* F 206 and n.	**claims:** the verb αὐχέω seems here to connote spoken confidence, if not quite boasting, continuing 'solemnly swear' in 2: for this rare sense cf. *And.* 311 after 245, 253ff.; the verb normally denotes mental confidence, not voiced (so Fraenkel on *Ag.* 1497; Barrett on *Hipp.* 952 confines it to this meaning).

796. the whole Greek army: Odysseus rests upon this ultimate authority, as in S. *Phil.* 1243, 1257 etc., just like the uncomfortable Talthybius at *Hec.* 538 etc. and Agamemnon at *Hec.* 858, 860 etc.	**shameful to keep silent:** Odysseus' outburst is like that of Telephus at *Tel.* F 706 though facing imminent violence when possessed of a 'just counter-argument'; cf. *Dictys* F 334.4-5, silence in front of 'inferior persons'; F 883 'shameful to speak and heavy to keep silent'. The line, supposedly adapted by Aristotle to discomfort his rival Isocrates, became a tag, deployed through its first two words alone (Cic. *Ep. Att.* 6.8.5).	**barbarians:** just non-Greeks, not savages: for this common use see e.g. *Tro.* 933 (a Trojan speaking), 1021; *IT* 1170 with Cropp's n.

797. For the difficulty in locating this fragment see Introd., *Reconstruction* at end.
1-2. by anticipation: Kannicht cites *IT* 669 'You've anticipated me a little, but in your anticipation you're saying the same'. Such rhetorical undermining is common in Euripidean confrontations, e.g. *Supp.* 184-5, *Or.* 665.	[Weil's conjecture ὑποφθὰς giving this sense suits Anaximenes' context exactly and is supported by the medieval Latin translation; but the compound verb is not otherwise known in Tragedy. Munro's διαφθεῖραι accommodates the transmitted ὑποστὰς, 'even if he seems to have destroyed my argument by admitting that he has himself done wrong'.]
3-4. hear: the Aor. participle (Mette), not the Pres., is the Tragic idiom: see M. L. West, *BICS* 31 (1984), 176.	[Two bad metrical faults in successive lines are remarkable. Any correction of the first must give the sense 'hear and learn', so apt to the context (unlike in 2, the medieval Latin translation here and in 4 only confirms the Greek ms. of that date); and a Fut. verb is needed in 4 to match that of 3; likewise, the emphatic distinction in 3 and 4 between 'me' and 'him' must be retained. So, in 3, e.g. 'you'll understand my case' (Pflugk) and 'you'll know all my case' (Meineke). In 4 Musgrave and Jacobs give the same, correct meaning as in the obelized translation; less good is Heath's Pres. tense 'makes clear'. Full discussion by Jouan 306 n. 76.]

798. More plausibly assigned to a final scene between Odysseus and Philoctetes (Müller, Jouan) than to that between these two and the Trojan (Calder, Webster); Odysseus is no doubt offering Philoctetes the glory promised in Helenus' prophecy. Two translations appear possible: (1) that printed, in which the verb in the idiom (ὁ) τυχών means 'the successful person (or thing)', as e.g. *Hec.* 819, *Pho.* 765, and the idea is comparable with *Supp.* 897–8 'a successful city rejoices but takes ill success hard', cf. *El.* 1077–8; and (2) that in which (ὁ) τυχών means 'the chance person (or thing)' like F 1041.2 ἡ πρόφασις τυχοῦσα 'the chance reason' (cf. LSJ I.A.2b); for the idea contrast Thuc. 2.60.2 'an entire city conducting itself soundly helps its private citizens (i.e. the 'chance' persons) more than if it prospers in individuals but fails collectively', cf. 6.9.2.   [Stob. 3.40 is a chapter about *A foreign country*, so that Hense wonders whether this quotation belongs rather to chapter 39 *On one's home country* (cf. F 789a and n.) and once accompanied lemmata nos. 1–4 there or followed nos. 5–10, two sets of Euripidean fragments arranged alphabetically by play-title.]

799. For advice to Philoctetes to relent cf. Neoptolemus at S. *Phil.* 1387. At Quint. Smyrn. 9.520–2 a markedly more amenable Philoctetes himself is made to deprecate undying anger. Cf. adesp. F 79 'Do not as a mortal maintain undying anger'; the sentiment resembles 'humanity is mortal and should not think immortal thoughts' (Epicharmus 23 B 20 DK).

799a. Philoctetes at play-end, perhaps, when the Chorus shows stronger sympathy (F 800?), rather than in his first meeting with Odysseus; the line may come from stichomythia (Müller). The thought is a commonplace (see the App.), e.g. *El.* 605, *HF* 559 in Eur.

800. For the location of the fragment see Introd., *Myth.*   [Nauck's corrections in 1–2 bring the expression into line with Euripides' common usage in which the interjection φεῦ stands outside the iambic line and μηδέν rather than μήποτε occurs with ἄλλο πλήν: cf. *Aeolus* F 25 etc. Suidas glosses lines 1–2 with 'as long as I am reckoned in his province and power', but these words are not certainly a paraphrase of a further line lost from the fragment]
3. fulfil: supremely the verb of divine action, e.g. *Alc.* 1161 etc., cf. Zeus the Fulfiller in A. *Ag.* 973 etc. The gods are **slow**, *Ion* 1615, *Bacc.* 882–4 (Justice, *Antiope* F 223.57). [So Wecklein's comma is correct in 3; Orion's reading there is merely a copyist's slip. West's '(the gods) devise everything' has a parallel at S. *Aj.* 86 πᾶν θεοῦ τεχνωμένου, but there the goddess Athena 'engineers' a disaster; here the sentiment is general, and pious.]

801. breathed his life away: not a reference to Philoctetes in a coma after his paroxysm, but perhaps to Palamedes whose death Odysseus plotted (F 789d(8), cf. *Palamedes*, p. 93) or even to Achilles, whose death at Paris' hands made the crisis requiring Philoctetes' return. Hesychius glosses αἰών, lit. 'lifetime', with the meaning 'life, life-spirit' (ψυχή), an Epic usage, e.g. Hom. *Il.* 22.58, *Od.* 5.160, cf. *Bacc.* 92 'left life'. For the verb cf. esp. Pind. *Isthm.* 7.34 ἡλικίαν 'breathed away his youth', i.e. 'died young'.

802. The lexicographers gloss the word αἱρεῖς with δοξάζεις, ἡγῆι 'you suppose, consider', but the nearest comparable meaning certainly attested for αἱρέω is 'comprehend, understand', a Platonic usage (LSJ A.III), coupled with λαμβάνω 'take, grasp' at *Phileb.* 17e. Editors have therefore wondered if the gloss with a 2nd Person form points to Middle αἱρεῖ or αἱρῆι, which nears 'think' through 'choose a belief', a later Greek usage (but cf. Pl. *Phaedr.* 256c).

803. The word **point** is either adj. or noun in Hesychius, glossed with similarly ambiguous 'top'. Both Greek words share the root ἀκρ-, but ἀκριβής is usually 'precise, exact'. *Tro.* 901 has οὐκ εἰς ἀκριβὲς ἦλθεν, where the adj. is used as noun without article, and the sense appears to be 'it did not come to a head', of a vote needing to be exactly counted; cf. perhaps *Antiope* F 206.3.

*801a. The verse is hardly authentic. It is difficult to imagine a context on Lemnos for a report, in a primary tense, of the now dead Achilles dicing (but the lyric *IA* 195–8 describe Palamedes (cf. F 799a above) playing a board-game at Aulis). **two ones and a four:** a very poor throw, three sixes being the best (A. *Ag.* 33): see Dover on *Frogs* 1400 (who thinks that the scholia could not identify the verse because it is pastiche and only the first two words may be Euripidean).

ALEXANDROS

Texts, Testimonia. P. Oxy. 3650 col. i (= *TrGF* T iii, Hypothesis) ed. R. A. Coles, *BICS* Suppl. 32 (1974) and *Oxyrhynchus Papyri* Vol. 52 (1984), 13–19; *TrGF* F 41a–63 including P. Strasb. 2342–4 ed. W. Crönert, *NGG* 1922, 1–17, re-ed. C. Lefke, *De Euripidis Alexandro* (diss. Münster, 1936), B. Snell, *Euripides Alexandros (etc.)* (Berlin, 1937: *Hermes* Einzelschr. 5), 1-68, Coles 38–58 (parts). Page, *GLP* 54–61; Diggle, *TrGFS* 80–4 (Hypoth. and parts of P. Strasb.); F. Jouan, ed. Budé VIII.1 (1998), 39–76.

Ennius, *Alexander*: H. Jocelyn *The Tragedies of Ennius* (Cambridge, 1967), 75–81 with Comm. 202–34.

Myth. Cypria? (below, p. 43); Pind. F 52i(A).14–25; Soph. *Alexandros* (*TrGF* IV F 91a–99); Eur. *Andr.* 293-300 with Schol. 293 (= T ivb(3)), *Tro.* 597, 919–22 (= T iva); Asclepiades *FGH* 12 F 12 (= Schol. Hom. *Il.* 3.325); Dio Chrys. *Or.* 15.10 (= T ivc); Apollod. 3.12.5 (= T ivb(1)); Hygin. *Fab.* 91 (= T ivb(2)), 273.12; Mythogr. Vat. 2.197; Servius on Verg. *Aen.* 7.320; Dict. Cret. 3.26; Tzetzes on Lycophr. *Alex.* 138. C. Robert, *Bild und Lied* (Berlin, 1881), 233–9; Preller-Robert II.3, 979–82; Kuiper (below); Lefke (above), 5–24, 103–5; Snell (above), 56–65; *RE* XVIII.2 (1949), 1484–1536 ('Paris': E. Wüst); T. C. W. Stinton, *Euripides and the Judgement of Paris* (London, 1965: repr. in *Coll. Papers*, Oxford, 1990); Jouan, *Eur. et les légendes* (1966), 135–8, and ed. Budé 39–42; *LIMC* (below); Huys, *Tale* (see contents-list); *Neue Pauly* 9 (2000), 334–6 ('Paris': M. Stoevesandt).

Illustrations (cf. *TrGF* T ivd). J. Davreux, *La légende de la prophétesse Cassandre* (Liège, 1942), 108–17 with Figs. 7–21; Webster, *Monuments*[2] 154 and *Euripides* (1967), 172–4; Coles 26, 30-2; *LIMC* I.1.494–7, 500–5, 523, 526–8 with I.2.380–3 ('Alexandros': R. Hampe, I. Krauskopf, 1981).

Main discussions. K. Kuiper, *Mnem.* 48 (1920), 207–21; Crönert (above); G. Murray in *Mélanges Glotz* (1932) II.645–56 = *Greek Studies* (Oxford, 1946), 127–4); Lefke (above); Snell (above); A. W. Pickard-Cambridge in Powell, *New Chapters* III.137–42; Schmid 475–6; Davreux (above) 37–41; F. Scheidweiler, *Philologus* 97 (1948), 321–35; L. Strzelecki, *Trav. Soc. Sc. et Lett. Wroclaw* 33 (1949), 5–25; B. Menegazzi, *Dioniso* 14 (1951), 172–97; A. Pertusi, *Dioniso* 15 (1952), 251–73; D. Lanza, *SIFC* 34 (1963), 230–45; J. Hanson, *Hermes* 92 (1964), 171–81; H. J. Mette, *Lustrum* 9 (1964), 69–72; Stinton (above), 64–71; Jouan, *Eur. et les légendes* (1966), 113–42; Webster, *Euripides* (1967), 165–74; D. J. Conacher, *Euripidean Drama* (Toronto, 1967), 127–32; G. Koniaris, *HSCP* 77 (1973), 85–124; Coles (above), and reviews by J. M. Bremer, *Mnem.* 28 (1975), 308–12, R. Hamilton, *AJP* 97 (1976), 65–70, F. Jouan, *Gnomon* 48 (1976), 808–10; W. Luppe, *Philologus* 120 (1976), 12–20; R. Scodel, *The Trojan Trilogy of Euripides* (Göttingen, 1980), 20–42, 68–121, 138–42; D. Kovacs, *HSCP* 88 (1984), 47–70; M. Huys, *ZPE* 62 (1986), 9–36 and *Tale* (above); Hose, *Drama und Gesellschaft* 36–45; S. Timpanaro, *RFIC* 124 (1996), 5–70 (important for both Euripides and Ennius); Jouan in ed. Budé 39–59.

Alexandros was the first play of the 'Trojan trilogy' which Euripides produced in 415 B.C. (see *Date* below), the second and third plays being *Palamedes* and the extant *Trojan Women*. The fragments of *Palamedes* are presented here in Appendix Two (pp. 92–103), and the question of the coherence of the trilogy is briefly discussed under *Themes and Characters* below.

Reconstruction. Earlier reconstructions relied mainly on some twenty book-fragments (almost all sentials), a dozen book-fragments from the prologue, messenger-scene and Cassandra-scene of Ennius' *Alexander*, and a narrative summary in Hygin. *Fab.* 91. Apollodorus tells the story of Hecuba's dream and Paris's exposure and early life, but adds only that later 'he discovered his parents'. It is generally accepted that Ennius' play was a version of Euripides', albeit with stylistic adaptations and reworkings of detail for a Roman audience, especially since in quoting Ennius F 20 Varro refers to his 'imitating' Euripides and makes a direct comparison between the Latin and Greek texts.[1] The status of Hyginus' summary was and is uncertain, but until the publication of the Hypothesis nothing told decisively against its being derived from Euripides. Its essentials are that Paris, exposed at birth because of Hecuba's portentous dream and reared by herdsmen, went to Troy to compete in funeral games set up by Priam in his memory, in order to win back a favourite bull which the king's servants had commandeered as a prize; after winning all the events he was attacked by Deiphobus and took refuge at an altar of Zeus Herkeios, but was identified by Cassandra and so accepted by Priam into the royal family. The Strasbourg papyrus fragments (now F 46, 46a, 61d, 62a–e, 62k) were worked into this outline rather sketchily by their editor (Crönert, 1922). The same materials were re-studied by Lefke (1936), and more influentially by Snell (1937).

Snell's reconstruction became the basis of discussion until in 1974 Coles published an almost complete papyrus hypothesis (see pp. 50–1) in which Paris does not enter the games to retrieve his bull but rather is arraigned before Priam by his fellow-herdsmen because of his arrogant behaviour towards them, and defends himself so effectively that he is allowed to enter the games (no particular motive for his doing so is stated), and wins several events; Deiphobus and his companions are enraged and persuade Hecuba to kill him, but Cassandra recognizes him and prophesies about the future, Hecuba's assault is stayed, and Paris's foster-father is compelled to reveal the truth about him. This differs substantially from Hyginus and raises the question whether Hyginus' summary is fundamentally Euripidean but contaminated, or derives from a different original such as Sophocles' *Alexandros* (see further below, *Myth*). In addition to

---

[1]   Strzelecki's argument that some passages in the Cassandra-scene of Seneca's *Agamemnon* are directly derived from Eur. and Enn. *Alex.* is based on a misunderstanding of Sen. *Ag.* 730–3 (on which see R. Tarrant's commentary).

publishing the Hypothesis, Coles re-examined the Strasbourg fragments and noted that P. Strasb. 2343 (= F 6 Crönert, F 43.1–10, 36–105 Snell) had been wrongly assembled and should be separated into what are now F 62b and F 62d; also these two fragments along with F 62a and 62c (P. Strasb. 2342.2–3) could be placed fairly close together, perhaps even as successive columns, so as to represent a single dramatic sequence.

The outline of the play that now emerges still presents numerous problems and gaps. The prologue-speech is probably reflected in Hypoth. 4–12 which mentions Hecuba's dream and its interpretation (cf. Enn. F 18), the attempted exposure of the baby, his rearing and naming as Paris by a herdsman, and Hecuba's grief and the establishment of the memorial games, all twenty years previously (cf. **F 42**). Hyginus differs only slightly, having the baby exposed out of pity by servants charged by Priam to kill him and then rescued by herdsmen (who might not, then, know his origin; the brief and damaged wording of the Hypothesis is unclear on this point). The speech probably went on to explain how Paris exhibited extraordinary qualities as he grew up (cf. Hypoth. 13–14) and acquired the name Alexandros ('Protector': cf. **F 42d** with Comm., Enn. F 20). The prologue-speaker is unknown, but it probably needed to be someone who knew about the baby's survival and upbringing. Hecuba and Priam are thus eliminated, and Cassandra is inappropriate since she does not have objective knowledge and her prophetic knowledge needs to be revealed with full dramatic impact later (cf. Scodel 23). The foster-father is favoured by Scodel and others (e.g. Huys, *Tale* 318–9; Di Giuseppe cited below, p. 72), but there is no apparent reason for him to be at the royal palace at the beginning of the play, and the Hypothesis suggests (against some earlier reconstructions) that he did no more than confirm Paris's identity at the end. The choice then is narrowed to gods. Aphrodite has been much favoured (recently Kovacs 64–6, Timpanaro 9–10), and Apollo occasionally (Stinton 71–2), but Kevin Lee noted that a minor god less involved in the fate of Troy, such as Hermes, would have been better placed to give the appropriate information and some (carefully limited) indications about how the plot would unfold. The prologue of *Ion* is suggestive, though obviously not decisive, in favour of this (cf. also on *Oedipus*, p. 108).

How the prologue and parodos proceeded is uncertain. Four fragments are concerned with the consolation of Hecuba's grief over her long-lost child (cf. Hypoth. 7–10), one in anapaests (**F 43**) and three in iambics (**F 44–46**), the last a dialogue which mentions Priam (so he is not a speaker) and seems to end with the announcement of a character's entrance. The most economical interpretation (reflected in Kannicht's re-numbering of these fragments) is that Hecuba lamented, perhaps first in a monody, and the Chorus consoled her first in an amoibaic parodos and then in a short iambic dialogue with the Chorus-leader speaking (cf. F 43–46 n.). If this is right, there is no trace of any dialogue-scene before the parodos, and the pattern is like that of *Hecuba* and *Ion*, or (without monody) *Bacchae*, which have prologue-speeches by Polydorus' ghost, Hermes and Dionysus respectively. There is no hard evidence for the identity of the Chorus, and cases have been made for both Trojan elders and women friendly to Hecuba. As Hanson (176) argued, it would be surprising if a character so central to the play and its intrigue as Hecuba were not accompanied by a female chorus, as are Medea, Andromache, Hecuba in *Hec.*, Electra, Iphigenia, Helen, Creusa in *Ion*, Hypsipyle, and Melanippe in *Mel.D.* The choruses of *Alexandros* and *Trojan Women* may have had much in common.

Wilamowitz's supplements on F 46.11–12 provide the only indication that Cassandra appeared in an early scene, whereas the Hypothesis and Hyginus mention only her intervention at the end. The supplements obviously need to be treated with caution, but the papyrus remnants do seem to imply the noticing of a child of Hecuba's in some connection with a shrine, and Cassandra is the obvious candidate. Snell (26–33) inferred that Cassandra delivered her prophecies in the first episode rather than towards the end of the play. But the Hypothesis now contradicts this, and it was always unlikely that her prophecies about Paris should have been delivered before his first appearance in the play, and before any other character could know who she was talking about.[2] If Cassandra did appear in this early scene, it was presumably in a sane dialogue with Hecuba which in some way prepared for her later mad entry. It might have included one or two fragments spoken in her uninspired voice, which are here assigned to the prophetic scene (F **62g, Enn. F 17.34–40).

Also tentatively placed is **F 46a**, which appears to have Priam discussing arrangements for the games, perhaps as he sets out for them. If so, his departure may have been interrupted by the arrival of the secondary chorus of herdsmen (known for this play from Schol. *Hipp.* 58 = **T v**) bringing Paris to Priam with their complaints (Hypoth. 16). Hypoth. 17–21 states that Paris now refuted his accusers and Priam made his (surprising) decision to admit the slave-herdsman to the games. This implies a debate-scene (despite the scepticism of Kovacs 47–54), and this scene can accommodate most if not all of the argumentative fragments **F 48–61** in which someone condemns slaves in general and the ambitious slave Paris in particular, Paris defends himself against the injustice of a rich and rhetorically trained opponent, and Priam decides to give him an opportunity to prove his worth. A stasimon including **F 61b–c**, reflecting on the true nature of virtue, will have followed. (For details of this sequence see the

---

[2] This was already denied by e.g. Schmid 475–6 n. 11, Strzelecki 22–5. Others allowed for prophecies or forebodings both early and late (Scheidweiler 323–7, Stinton 67–9).

Comm.; all of these and some other fragments had previously been connected with a debate *after* the games over Paris's entitlement to the prizes.) But such a summary leaves several questions open: what use was made of the secondary chorus, what particular offence was Paris accused of, why did he want to enter the games, and who resisted his admission? The secondary chorus's role must in fact have been quite limited, as seems usual in Euripides (cf. Lanza 237–44); the herdsmen probably sang their complaints, perhaps with interjections from Paris, as they brought him in, but they could not have continued to speak as a group through the entire scene, and none of the fragments is assignable to this chorus. As for Paris's offence, one solution has been to combine the explanations of the Hypothesis and of Hyginus in a rather awkward compromise: Paris arrogantly resisted the seizure of his bull, was arrested by his more servile fellows, and used the occasion to persuade Priam to let him enter the games so that he could get the bull back (Coles 24–5). But the bull motif is almost at cross-purposes with the motif of Paris's arrogance and urge to prove himself (cf. Scodel 29), and it may be better to exclude it altogether and conclude that Hyginus's summary is either contaminated at this point or irrelevant (cf. below, *Myth*). Perhaps Paris was simply arrested for his high-handed and violent behaviour towards his fellows, and demanded entry to the games to prove his worth. As for the opponent, it seems unlikely that the Chorus-leader or an incidental character otherwise unattested would have carried the burden of such an important argument. Deiphobus has seemed likely in view of his later hostility, but there is a difficulty in ascribing F 48 to a son of Priam, and this fragment is much more likely to belong to the main debate-speaker than to the Chorus-leader (see the Comm. on these points). Hecuba has not been much considered as a possible opponent since (1) Paris seems to refer to a male speaker in F 56.3 (but this may only be because he is generalizing), (2) nothing in the debate-fragments clearly suggests a female speaker, and (3) one way of allocating roles to actors gives the roles of both Priam and Hecuba to the same actor (but this is by no means inevitable: see below, *Staging*). Hecuba would however be an appropriate speaker insofar as she is featured both at the outset and in all that follows the games. If it was she who resisted the idea of a slave being involved in her dead son's commemoration and competing with her living sons, this would link well with it being she who received the report of the games and managed the plot against Paris. She would then be consistently the play's focal figure, as are other Euripidean heroines such as Hecuba in both *Hecuba* and *Trojan Women*, Electra in *Electra*, and Creusa in *Ion*. The problem cannot be solved with certainty, however, and it is difficult to sketch with confidence this episode's progression from the dispute with the herdsmen to the dispute over admission to the games.

The shape of the next episode is given by **F 61d** and **F 62a–d** (as arranged by Coles) with Hypoth. 21–5. A messenger arrives from the games and reports Paris's successes to Hecuba in a speech (perhaps including **F 61a** and **F 54**: see Comm. on these; some details in Enn. F 19, 24, 22 Sn, 22, 23). Then, perhaps without an intervening stasimon (cf. Huys 1986, 11–12), Deiphobus and Hector enter engaged in a heated argument about what Deiphobus sees as an insufferable humiliation. If **F 62a** and **F 62b** are from adjacent columns, their discussion continued for some 60–70 lines. Hecuba then intervened (F 62b.39), and Hector probably left, for **F 62d col. ii** gives us, perhaps in the next column but one, Hecuba and Deiphobus plotting their attack on Paris. **F 62d col. i** and **F 62c** probably have intervening bits of their dialogue, and **F 62d col. iii** seems to give the beginning of the following action with the Chorus reflecting briefly on Paris's expected downfall and then an arrival of someone looking for Priam and Hecuba; this may be Paris himself (see Comm. on F 62d col. iii).

The details of the plot against Paris and the roles of Hecuba and Deiphobus in it are unclear. Hypoth. 24–5 and 29 has Hecuba persuaded by Deiphobus and his companions to kill Paris, and actually attempting to do so, while F 62d.24–33 seems to have them planning to lure Paris to the palace from his celebrations in the city so that Hecuba can kill him, possibly with assistance from Deiphobus (see Comm. on these lines). Hecuba could hardly have undertaken to kill Paris single-handed; more likely (as Huys 1986 argues in detail) she took the lead in forming the plan and meant to strike the death-blow after Paris had been overpowered by Deiphobus and/or his men. The three-actor rule makes it difficult to put Deiphobus himself on stage during the final scenes, but his involvement seems to be implied by the plotting and the later iconography (below, p. 45). All of this raises the question why Hecuba should want to murder the young herdsman, especially when Hector is undisturbed by his successes (cf. Scodel 33); she needs a motive comparable with those of Merope (who thought that the disguised Cresphontes had murdered her son) or Creusa (who thought that Ion was Xuthus' bastard son). A speculative answer is that she saw Paris as a rival to her own sons, or even suspected he might be a bastard son of Priam and favoured by him (as suggested perhaps in the debate-scene and the messenger's report: cf. especially F 62c with Scodel 32–4, Huys 1986, 20–2). Huys' suggestion that Hecuba had to be persuaded to share Deiphobus' extreme hostility (cf. F 62b.39–42) is doubted by Timpanaro 46.

Even with the help of the Hypothesis it remains unclear how the attack, Cassandra's intervention, the crisis at the altar, the recognition, and the foster-father's revelations were organized dramatically, and with the use of only three actors. Presumably Hecuba and Paris were on stage continuously at least from the point when Paris took refuge at the altar, and only one speaking character could then be on stage with them, with time needed for successive characters' costume-changes. Hypoth. 25–32 states that Paris arrived, Cassandra in a mantic fit recognized him and made prophecies, Hecuba was prevented from killing him, and the foster-father was compelled to admit the truth. Hyginus might or might not be compatible with this: Deiphobus makes an attack (no mention of a plan or of Hecuba), Paris flees to the altar of Zeus Herkeios (unmentioned in the Hypothesis), Cassandra is inspired and identifies him, and Priam accepts him into the royal family. The fragments provide traces of Cassandra's entry and prophecies in **F 62e–h** and Enn. F 17, 25, 26 (though **F **62g** and Enn. F 17.34–40 might belong in her earlier scene: see above, p. 38). After this we have only Paris's despairing cry (**F 62i**) and the Chorus-leader's comment on the recognition (**F 62**). Later representations show the attack on Paris at the altar, but their relevance is difficult to establish precisely (see below, *Illustrations*). Scodel (35–8) suggests that Cassandra in fact arrived first, and delivered her prophecies while Paris arrived and entered the palace peacefully; he then emerged from the palace, was attacked by Hecuba, and took refuge at the altar until the herdsman intervened (perhaps spontaneously, or summoned earlier by Priam). On the other hand, Jouan (1998, 53–7) has Paris chased in by Deiphobus or his men and fleeing to the altar, Cassandra intervening with her prophecy, Hecuba's attack interrupted (by Cassandra and/or something said by Paris), and the herdsman then arriving. On yet another view the Cassandra-scene occurred *after* the crisis had passed and the recognition was complete (e.g. Hartung, Jouan 1966, 130–5; Timpanaro 47–9; for further less coherent schemes see e.g. Coles 29, Kovacs 54–64, Hose 39–41). A minimal interpretation of the essential evidence might be that Paris arrived at the palace of his own accord (Hypoth. 25–6; F 62d.51–5?), was confronted by Hecuba with Deiphobus and/or some palace servants, and fled to the altar; Cassandra intervened with her prophetic warnings (Hypoth. 27–8), Hecuba was restrained (Hypoth. 29–30), and the herdsman intervened (or was brought in) to save Paris by identifying him (Hypoth. 30–2), like the Delphic priestess intervening in Ion's attack on Creusa in *Ion*. Recognition proofs are possible but not needed (they appear only in a few Latin sources starting with Ov. *Her.* 15.90). It is hard to find any room in this for Priam, or to be sure about the exact context and effect of Cassandra's intervention. A more complete text would probably yield some surprises.

Many reconstructions include the intervention of a god (usually Aphrodite as in Etruscan art) along with Eur. F 1082, 'Zeus the father planned these things, wanting evil to come upon the Trojans and sorrow upon the Greeks' (cf. Snell 52–6 with n. 3, Jouan [1998], F 40 with p. 57 and n. 38). The fragment must however be excluded, for a plain statement to the Trojans about their disastrous future would destroy the impact of Cassandra's unbelieved warnings, which convey information of a kind given by gods – and therefore believed – in other plays. Snell suggested that Aphrodite spoke to the audience after the final exit of the Trojan characters, but this would be unparalleled and in any case overlooks the continued presence of the Chorus. Scheidweiler (334) has Cassandra prophesying to the Chorus and rousing them against Paris until Aphrodite intervenes, and Coles (30–2) sketches a continuation in which Cassandra and Deiphobus try to kill Paris, and the goddess intervenes to prevent them. But Coles accepts that the presence of a goddess in depictions of the altar-scene does not prove that she appeared in the play, and concludes that such a continuation 'so far as the literary evidence is concerned...can happily be discarded'. A role for Aphrodite in the story *before* the Judgement of Paris (see *Myth* below) is in any case unlikely. Lanza (232–5), Scodel (39–40) and Timpanaro (66–8) have argued persuasively against a divine intervention.

Other proposed ascriptions. A few sententious Euripidean fragments have been assigned to the debate-scene because of a general similarity of topics: **F 958** 'What slave does not think of death?' (Hartung); **F 976** 'The children of slaves are socially undisciplined', (Welcker, Hartung; Snell F 30*, pp. 39–40 n. 5; Budé F *12); **F 1068** 'No one can educate boys so well as to change their nature from bad to good' (Welcker, Hartung; Snell F 31*, pp. 39–40 n. 5). Similarly Hartung related **F 960** (Snell F incert. 63), choral lines on work, wealth and virtue, to the following stasimon (F 61b–c).   Two tragic adespota may well come from Sophocles' or Euripides' *Alexandros,* and more likely Euripides' since it was more widely quoted: **adesp. F 286** 'How like Priam's sons is this herdsman!', assigned to Priam on Paris's first arrival by Hartung, to the Chorus-leader at that point by Snell (F 25* with p. 39) and others (Budé F *7, cf. Huys 1986, 35), to Hecuba beginning to recognize Paris by Wilamowitz in Crönert 16 n. 1 (cf. Webster 172), and attractively to the messenger-speech as a comment from games-spectators by Murray; from this speech would also come **adesp. F 289** 'Out came the Hectors and the Sarpedons' (Snell F incert. 65 with p. 37, Budé F **24; Hygin. *fab.* 273.12 lists Sarpedon as well as Hector amongst competitors at the games).   Eur. **F 867** 'But here close by is the woman devoted to Phoebus' might refer to Cassandra in this play (Hartung; Snell F incert. 64, p. 27; Budé F *31), and a Hellenistic commentary-fragment includes a few damaged lines perhaps from Cassandra's prophetic speech (**adesp. F 721b–c**: cf. Luppe in Hofmann and Harder, *Fragmenta Dramatica* 153–9).   Three fragments with no very distinctive features are assigned doubtfully to Paris at the altar: **F 937** 'Don't kill (me?): it is unlawful to kill a suppliant' and **F 938** 'So now you are going to kill me because of my words?' are a pair of which the second was assigned by Hartung; both are printed with reservations by Snell (F incert. 66–7, pp. 48–9) and Jouan (Budé F **35–6), as is **adesp. F 71b** 'I call Zeus Herkeios to witness' (Snell F incert. 68, p. 49 n. 1; Budé F **38); Timpanaro (47 n. 1) favours including all three.   Against including Eur. **F 1082** (F 45* Snell, F *40 Budé) in a concluding divine speech see p. 41 above. Other suggested placings of this fr. in *Alexandros* are even less plausible (Cassandra prophesying, Stinton 68; Aphrodite in a prologue-speech, Kovacs 70).

Myth. Alexandros (less frequently 'Paris') is important in the *Iliad* for having caused the Trojan war by abducting Helen. He is portrayed as an effective archer but a second-rate warrior, worsted by Menelaus in the duel from which Aphrodite rescues him (Book 3) yet destined to kill Achilles with Apollo's aid (22.358–60; the event was related in the lost *Aithiopis*). He is also characterized as divinely handsome ('Aλέξανδρος θεοειδής, *Il.* 3.16 etc.) and excessively devoted to the sexual gratification which Aphrodite's patronage and his marriage with Helen have brought him. There is a brief allusion to the famous Judgement of Paris in *Il.* 24.27–30, when Hera and Athena are said to have been remorseless in their hatred for Troy 'because of the fatal folly (*âtê*) of Alexandros, who insulted them when they came to his homestead and approved the one who offered him pernicious lust'. The story of the Judgement is always set in the countryside with Paris herding his flocks, but this does not necessarily presuppose a story of his being raised as a herdsman in humble circumstances, since herding was not an unusual activity for epic heroes (such as Anchises when seduced by Aphrodite, *Hom.Hymn* 5.53ff.). In Proclus' summary of the lost epic *Cypria* the Judgement leads directly to Paris's expedition to Sparta to get his prize, Helen, and it looks as if the original poem did not include a narrative of his early life (cf. Robert [1881] 233–9, Snell 58, Stinton 60; Jouan [1966] 135–7 maintained that it might have done). But as Stinton notes, if the early epics did not mention a story of Paris's early life it does not follow that such a story did not already exist (still less that it was only invented by the tragedians as Robert had argued). The story makes him a 'curse-child' (Murray 138), like Oedipus and others, fated to bring ruin on his family and community. His parents are prophetically warned of this but allow him to survive by having him exposed rather than killed outright; he grows up *incognito* but with extraordinary abilities, and eventually returns to fulfil his destiny. This is a subtype of the widespread 'hero exposed at birth' tale pattern, whose presence in Euripidean tragedy is exhaustively studied by Huys (*Tale*). It could have been attached to the figure of Paris early or late, and quite likely early insofar as the Judgement story (itself a folktale)[3] and the ambivalent character of Paris in epic needed some such underpinning. The earliest actual indication of its possible attachment, however, is either in vase-paintings of the 480s or 470s (but the identifications are very doubtful: see *Illustrations*) or in a papyrus-fragment of a paean of Pindar (F 52i(A).14–25). This fragment contains a speech in which

---

[3] The tale pattern is most recently discussed by Malcolm Davies, *CQ* 53 (2003), 32–43.

Cassandra recalls the pregnant Hecuba's dream of bearing a torch-wielding Hundred-hander and warns that the portent is now being fulfilled; the occasion might be Paris's departure for Sparta as in the *Cypria*, or possibly his homecoming as in our play, but at any rate it suggests that the essentials of the story of Hecuba's dream and Paris's exposure, survival, and return to Troy were current in Greek poetry in the first half of the 5th century at the latest. Details, of course, were open to variation and continued to be so, including the content of the dream, who interpreted it, who was required to kill the baby, who saved his life, who reared him, and how he came to return and be recognized. The chorus of *Andromache* recalls Cassandra begging for the baby to be killed, presumably because of the dream (*Andr.* 293–300). The failed exposure is recalled by Andromache in *Tro.* 597–8, by Helen in *Tro.* 919–24 (referring to the dream), and by Iphigenia in *IA* 1283–99. The Judgement and its destructive consequences are recalled in these and other contexts (*Andr.* 274–92, *Hec.* 629–56, *Hel.* 357–60, *IA* 573–85, 1299–1318).

It may have been the tragedians who elaborated the story of Paris's return by inventing the memorial games and his successes, his brothers' plot against him, and his escape in the nick of time through recognition. Sophocles' *Alexandros* is known only from four one-line and seven one-word fragments including a comment on a herdsman defeating townsmen (F 93) and references to town and country people (F 92, 94), midwifery and suckling (F 95, 98, 99). Probably, then, he told a similar story, and Euripides differentiated his version from Sophocles' (assuming Sophocles composed first, though the date is unknown). Snell (63–5) argued that Hyginus' summary was close to Euripides, but since Hyginus makes no mention of a plot, while the Hypothesis ignores the bull-motif and makes Hecuba attack Paris (as Snell 41–2, 46–7, 64 thought she must even though Hyginus ignores her), it now seems that Hyginus' summary is at best partially Euripidean or may even derive from Sophocles.[4] Be that as it may, Euripides' chief inventions were probably the conflict between Paris and the herdsmen leading to the highly Euripidean debate scene, the central role and characterization of Hecuba as grieving mother and murderess, and a young Paris who displayed nobility, talent, and a high-mindedness verging on arrogance. These features were set, of course, against an awareness of his future as the

---

[4] Scheidweiler (330) noted the eclectic nature of Hyginus' summary; see now M. Huys *APF* 43 (1997), 20–1. Robert (in Preller-Robert 982 n. 2) supposed that the bull-motif was Hellenistic, but Stinton (55) suggested that Sophocles invented the funeral games and the bull-motif together. This is likely since the invention of the games requires a mechanism whereby Paris can enter them (a mechanism which Euripides seems to have supplied more artificially).

destroyer of Troy, but that was a reality only for Cassandra amongst the play's characters, and even the Judgement of Paris was set in the future.[5]

Illustrations. In Greek art only two Attic red-figured cups of the early 5th C. have been identified, by Hampe and others, with Paris's homecoming (*LIMC* nos. 16–17; doubted by e.g. Stinton 53–5, Jouan 1966, 137 n. 3, and for no. 17 Davreux 117–8); they are non-dramatic and have no features suggestive of Euripides' plot (beyond, perhaps, Cassandra delivering a warning). The identification of Polykleitos' bronze statue known as the Diadoumenos ('Man Tying a Headband') as Paris, and as inspired by Euripides' character (cf. Hampe on *LIMC* no. 18), is also conjectural. All other relevant material is Italian (*LIMC* nos. 19–43), principally some seventy Etruscan mirror-backs and ash-urns which show Paris taking refuge at an altar, with one knee placed on it and usually a victor's palm-branch in one hand and sword in the other. The mirror-backs, from the late 4th through 3rd C., all show him attacked by an armed man, presumably Deiphobus, and an axe-wielding woman who has been identified as either Hecuba or Cassandra. The urns (2nd–1st C. B.C.) show these figures (in some cases omitting one or other attacker) and up to five others which may include a goddess protecting Paris (Aphrodite?), a male figure restraining Deiphobus (Hector?), and an older male figure restraining the woman (Priam?). The three-figure scene could be a nucleus from which the larger scenes were developed with loose reference to a mythical vulgate, or possibly all the scenes derive from a many-figured 4th C. Greek wall-painting or a vase-painting tradition. Euripides' play could be more or less accurately represented, but the scenes cannot be used with any confidence in reconstructing its dramatic action, except perhaps for the three-figure scene. The more complex scenes would give at best (like many South Italian vase-paintings of other plays) an assemblage of the main characters focused on the play's crucial scene, and the presence of Aphrodite is not evidence that she actually appeared in the play. It seems likely, however, that the axe-wielding woman did appear in the altar-scene. The Hypothesis now strongly supports identifying her as Hecuba, as Snell (46 with n. 3) maintained. Cassandra was preferred by Davreux, who suggested that her prophecies were interpreted iconographically as an actual attack on Paris, or that she might even have attacked him in Euripides' play (cf. Coles 26, Krauskopf in *LIMC*). But the claim that the woman is too young to be Hecuba is not strong;

This follows from Cic. *De Diu.* 1.114, where Cassandra's description of the Judgement (= Enn. F 17.47–9) is cited as a prediction of a *future* event: cf. Stinton 69 n. 17, and in general on this fr. Timpanaro 40–1. These and others rightly reject Snell's contention (53–4) that Eur.'s *Alex.* ignored the Judgement.

Hecuba can be thought of as in her late thirties in this play, and depictions of the figure as very young are late and probably confused.

On the terracotta dramatic masks from Lipara perhaps associated with *Alexandros* see below, *Staging*.

Themes and characters. The plot of *Alexandros* followed a pattern in which a mother became reunited with her long-lost and illegitimate (or forbidden) son or sons. The pattern was used by Sophocles in *Tyro B*, and by Euripides in *Ion, Captive Melanippe, Antiope* and *Hypsipyle* (cf. our Vol. I, 246 and in detail Huys, *Tale*). *Alexandros* particularly resembles *Ion* in which Ion's mother Creusa, like Hecuba, has retained her royal status rather than been persecuted or enslaved, and is hostile to the 'intruder' to the point of planning to kill him through a plot which leads paradoxically to the recognition. It differs from all the others, however, insofar as Paris is a 'curse-child' (*Myth* above). The contrast between the long-lost son's heroic reclamation of his birthright and the destiny furthered by his return makes for a tragedy of multiple ironies and heavy emphases on the limits of human knowledge, understanding and happiness.

These ironies are implicit in the characters of the play's leading figures. Paris himself is a youth of boundless potential – strong and handsome, intelligent and eloquent – but also ambitious and immoderate in his dealings with his fellow-slaves and in his athletic victories (F 62d.27–8). The way lies open for his development into Homer's vain and selfish hedonist, talented but underperforming, seduced by Troy's luxury and Aphrodite's gifts. Priam's 'Time will show what you are' (F 60) is all too true; Paris's choice of sexual success in the Judgement would be a voluntary one. The fatal consequences of his survival are vividly foreshadowed in recollections of the dream (especially in the prologue and following scenes), and in Cassandra's warnings as he returns to his family. But if Paris is the play's subject, its focal character is Hecuba, just as the mothers in other 'long-lost son' plays are. At the outset she is torn between remorse over the killing of her son and consciousness that her dream required his death. Her remorse turns to rage against the intrusive slave (like Creusa's in *Ion*),[6] which paradoxically brings her close to doing the 'right' thing by killing him, only for maternal feelings to prevail when she realizes he is her own child. Her ambivalence is reflected in the conflicting attitudes of the other characters (cf. Snell 65). Priam's and Hector's sympathy for Paris, reflecting their Homeric personalities, is attractive in its immediate context but will prove naively optim-

---

[6] The younger Hecuba's behaviour in this play probably shared to some extent the ferocity (motivated by maternal emotion) which she showed in punishing Polymestor in *Hecuba*, and which was traditionally associated with her character (cf. F *62h Comm.).

istic in the longer term by contrast with the seemingly perverse yet justified hostility of Cassandra and Deiphobus. Cassandra's foreboding may have been set against Hecuba's remorse in the first episode (above, p. 38), and her climactic vision of the future probably sketched all the essentials, including her own death as well as Hecuba's (F *62h), Hector's (Enn. F 25), and those of the other main characters. Euripides will have drawn on the pathos of Cassandra in Aeschylus' *Agamemnon* for this play as well as for *Trojan Women*, while also giving her the sharper awareness of her own paradoxical role and predicament that she has in the later play.[7]

Several references to time and its effects (cf. F 42 Comm.) underline the play's ironic setting of present joy against future ruin. But the fragments give no insight into how, if at all, it might have treated the reasons for the destruction of Troy. It is certainly relevant that in the third play of the 'Trojan Trilogy', the extant *Trojan Women*, Paris's survival is blamed as having led to the Judgement, the seduction of Helen, and the resulting punishment of Troy (cf. *Tro.* 498–9, 597–8, 919). But it also appears that the gods have abandoned Troy and their obligations to it for deeper reasons which the human characters cannot grasp (*Tro.* 469–71, 821–58, 1060–80, 1240–5, 1280–1) but which may have to do with the spite of Hera and Athena (presumably due to the Judgement as in the *Iliad*; cf. *Tro.* 23–4) or a general desire of the gods to bring down the mighty (*Tro.* 612–3). On the whole, as Scodel (130–7) shows, *Trojan Women* points to no rational ordering of the world which can explain or justify the fall of Troy; the gods are portrayed as at best uncaring, at worst irresponsible. It is unlikely, then, that, as Kovacs (66–70) suggests, *Alexandros* portrayed Paris in Aeschylean fashion as an instrument of divine justice, destined to bring about the punishment of Troy for its excessive prosperity and consequent tendency to hybris.[8]

What is evident from the fragments is the play's emphasis on divergences between appearance and reality, and the fallibility of human insight and decisions, emotions and good intentions. It is through humane instincts that the child who should have been killed survives, the games which will bring him

---

[7] On the tragic Cassandra see Davreux 25–47; P. G. Mason, *JHS* 79 [1959], 80–93; Scodel 69–71. But the Euripidean Cassandra's 'bacchic' terminology need not be specifically Dionysiac, as Mason and Scodel suggest.

[8] Kovacs' argument is not strongly supported by Enn. F 17.49 (Cassandra's description of Helen as a 'fury') and *Tro.* 597 (Andromache's assertion that Paris survived through the ill-will of the gods). Eur. F 1082 is probably irrelevant (p. 41 above). In *Colby Quarterly* 33 (1997), 162–76 Kovacs argues that the Trojan trilogy portrayed divine malevolence (though not necessarily divine justice) as the cause of Troy's destruction.

back to Troy are established, and Priam allows the slave a chance to show his virtue. Hecuba and Deiphobus hate the slave only so long as they do not know his true identity, and they fail to understand the true reasons for wishing him dead. Cassandra's real knowledge is ineffectual, and the happy outcome is the beginning of Troy's destruction. These classically tragic motifs are sharpened by the ironic use of anti-traditional, 'rational' arguments concerning nobility and virtue in the debates about Paris's participation and successes in the games.[9] The case for virtue in slaves is made, and its proof provided, by a man who thinks he is a slave but who in fact owes his virtues to heredity. Priam's open-mindedness rightly overcomes the conservative prejudices of Paris's opponents, yet is itself misplaced. The Chorus in endorsing Priam's decision (F 61b–c) complacently rejects the use of social distinctions as measures of virtue, but seems to underestimate the difficulty of getting that god-given intelligence and understanding on which they assert true virtue depends. As Scodel (89–90) notes, the debate has left undetected both the identity of Paris and his ultimate value.

In *Alexandros* human optimism and miscalculation allow Paris to embark on his fatal career as the destroyer of Troy. In *Trojan Women* the process is complete, and the survivors can only contemplate its outcome, still without comprehension. The meaning of Troy's fall is sought in vain, and Hecuba's demands to see some kind of order and justice in the world's events remain unanswered. The linkage that is generally seen between the first and last plays of the Trojan trilogy is real but not simple, for while the events of *Alexandros* sow the seeds of Troy's destruction in a limited sense, they do nothing to explain or justify the city's fate; they are simply part of it, and have no decisive prominence in the later play. Rather than presenting a comprehensible historical process, the two plays express, each in its own way, the tragic futility of human hopes, aspirations and reliance on 'reason' which an event such as the fall of Troy represents. Between them in Euripides' production of 415, in conjunction and contrast, stood a very different play, *Palamedes*, which portrayed man's capacity for using his own greatest gifts to malevolent and self-destructive ends, and focused significantly on the Greeks at Troy rather than the doomed Trojans.[10]

---

[9] See especially Scodel 83–90 on the *agôn* in *Alex.* and its ambiguities.

[10] On *Palamedes* (and the fourth play *Sisyphus*, of which almost nothing is known) see below, pp. 92–104. For discussions of the Trojan trilogy or tetralogy see especially Snell 66–8, Murray, Pertusi, Conacher, Koniaris, Scodel, Kovacs (n. 7 above). Koniaris argued that the three plays were essentially unconnected and wholly understandable in isolation from each other. Scodel makes the boldest and most extensive case for a unity of conception, tracing linkages speculatively but often persuasively, and seeing a thematic emphasis on the uncertainty of life in a disordered world and the limited consolations of

Staging. The play was set before the royal palace, with the temple of Apollo probably close by. On the Chorus (probably Trojan women) and secondary chorus of herdsmen see above, p. 38. Snell (42–3) and Scodel (40–1) distribute the roles between three actors as follows: (1) Hecuba, Priam; (2) Paris, Hector; (3) Cassandra, Deiphobus, Herdsman (the Messenger can be either (2) or (3). This however is based on the assumption that Deiphobus was Paris's opponent in the debate-scene. If the opponent was Hecuba (above, p. 39), or indeed someone else, we could have (1) Hecuba (and the debate-speaker if different), (2) Paris, Hector, (3) Priam, Cassandra, etc. The one important scenic item was the altar (probably the theatre's central altar) at which Paris took refuge. There is no evident need for machinery or special effects, but much striking dramatization: Hecuba's grief (probably conveyed in a monody), Paris dragged in by the secondary chorus of complaining herdsmen, the debate scene, a colourful messenger-speech, the plotting scene and following suspense, Cassandra's unheeded prophecies, the crisis at the altar, and the recognition.

A set of small 4th C. terracotta dramatic masks from a tomb on the island of Lipara (north of Sicily) may give an impression of how some of its characters were visualized: see Webster in L. Bernabò-Brea and M. Cavalier, *Meligunis-Lipara* II.321–2 and Pls., and, after earlier publications listed in their Bibl., Bernabò-Brea and Cavalier, *Maschere e personaggi del teatro greco nelle terrecotte liparesi* (Rome, 2001), 29–30, 40–1 with Pls. 12–15 (Eng. tr. on pp. 279–80, 283). The identifications of these masks with *Alexandros* are however uncertain (see e.g. L. Battezzato, *JHS* 123 [2003], 247–50).

Date. Aelian, *Var. Hist.* 2.8: 'In the ninety-first Olympiad [415 B.C.]...Xenocles and Euripides competed with each other. First was Xenocles, whoever he was, with *Oedipus, Lycaon, Bacchae,* and satyric *Athamas.* Second to him was Euripides with *Alexandros, Palamedes, Trojan Women* and satyric *Sisyphus.*'

Other dramatizations; influence. Sophocles' *Alexandros* and Ennius' Latin *Alexander* are considered above under *Myth* and *Reconstruction* respectively; the fragments of Ennius' play are printed below, pp. 88–91. A third *Alexandros*, by Nicomachus of Alexandria Troas (*TrGF* 127: 3rd C. B.C.?), is known only by its title and a single verse. There are no other extensive treatments of the story in ancient literature, although Hecuba's dream, Paris's exposure and the recognition are mentioned in works of larger scope, e.g. Lycophr. *Alex.* 224–8, Ov. *Her.* 16.43–52, 89–92, 359–62 (his athletic victories), 17.237–40, Dict. Cret 3.26, Dracont. 8.78–212. From more recent times Hecuba's dream is treated episodically in George Peele's *Tale of Troy* (1579–81) and Hilda Doolittle's *Helen in Egypt* (1952–6), and a few Renaissance paintings depict this and the exposure etc. (cf. *OGCMA* II.818–20).

---

human virtue and recollection. Other discussions argue for particular unifying ideas such as the illusoriness of human values (Murray), or human (rather than divine) responsibility for human suffering (Pertusi).

ΑΛΕΞΑΝΔΡΟΣ

T iii (– N) Hypothesis P. Oxy. 3650 col. i

'Αλέξαν]δρ[ος οὗ ἀρχή·
   c. 9 letters] καὶ τὸ κλεινὸν ['Ί]λιον,
   ἡ δὲ ὑ]πόθεσις·
   c. 9 letters] Ἑκάβης καθ' ὕπνον ὄψεις
7–8 *letters* ἔ]δωκεν ἐκθεῖναι βρέφος   5
   c. 9 letters]ν ἐξέθρεψεν υἱὸν 'Αλέ-
ξανδρ[ον Π]άριν προσαγορεύσας. Ἑκάβη δὲ τὴ[ν ἡ]μέραν ἐκείνην πενθοῦ-
σα ἅμα κ[αὶ] τιμῆς ἀξιοῦσα κατωδύ-
ρατο μὲν [τὸ]ν ἐκτεθέντα, Πρίαμον [δ' ἔ-   10
πε[ι]σε πο[λυτ]ελεῖς ἀγῶνας ἐπ' α[ὐ]τῶι κα-
ταστήσ[ασ]θα[ι]· διελθόντ[ων δὲ ἐτῶ]ν εἴ-
κοσι ὁ μὲν παῖς ἔδοξε [*c. 7* τ]ὴν
φύσιν εἶναι βουκολ [*c. 9*]ντος,
οἱ δ' ἄλλοι νομεῖς διὰ [τ]ὴν ὑπερήφανον   15
συμβίωσιν [δ]ήσαντες ἐπ[ὶ] Πρίαμον ἀνήγα-
γον αὐτόν·_____ηθεὶς [δ]ὲ ἐπὶ τοῦ δυνά-
στου .... ω[ ]......[.(.)]ρειτο καὶ τοὺς δι-
αβάλλοντας ε ... [.]υς ἔλαβε καὶ τῶν
ἐπ' αὐτῶι τελ[ο]υμέν[ων] ἀγώνων εἰάθη   20
μετασχεῖν. δρόμον δὲ καὶ πένταθλον,
ἔτι δαπα ...(.) την στεφ .... ἀπεθηρίωσε
τοὺς περὶ Δηΐφοβον, οἵτινες ἡττῆσθαι δια-
λαβ[ό]ντες ὑπὸ δούλου κατηξίωσαν τὴν
Ἑκάβην ὅπως ἂν αὐτὸν ἀποκτείνηι· πα-   25
ραγενηθέντα δὲ τὸν 'Αλέξανδρον
Κασ[σάν]δρ[α μ]ὲν ἐμμανὴς ἐπέγνω
καὶ π[ερὶ τῶ]ν μελλόντων ἐθέσπισεν,
Ἑκάβη [δὲ ἀπο]κτεῖναι θέλουσα διεκω-
λύθη. π[α]ρα[γενό]μενος δ' ὁ θρέψας αὐτὸν   30
διὰ τὸν κίνδυνον ἠναγκάσθη λέγειν τὴν
ἀλήθειαν. Ἑκάβη μὲν οὖν υἱὸν ἀνεῦρε...

ALEXANDROS

T iii Hypothesis

Alexandros, <which begins>, '. . . . . . and glorious *Ilium',*
and the plot (is as follows):
. . . Hecuba . . . visions in her sleep . . . gave his infant son
. . . to expose[5] . . . reared *him* as his son, calling Alexandros
Paris. But Hecuba, grieving over that *day and* also thinking it
worthy of honour, lamented *the* exposed child, *and persuaded*
Priam[10] *to establish lavish* games for *him. When* twenty *years*
had passed, the boy seemed to be . . . in his nature . . .
herdsman . . . and the other shepherds, because of his
arrogant[15] behaviour towards them, *bound* him and brought him
before Priam. *When he* . . . before the ruler, he . . . . . and
caught out those slandering him . . . and was allowed to take
part in the games *which were being celebrated* in his honour.[20]
And . . . *crown(ed?)* in running and the pentathlon, *and* also
. . . *he infuriated* Deiphobus and his companions who, realising
that they had been worsted by a slave, demanded that Hecuba
should kill him.[25] When Alexandros arrived, *Cassandra* became
inspired and recognized him, and prophesied *about* what would
happen; *<but>* Hecuba, who was ready to kill him, was
prevented. The man who had raised him *arrived,*[30] and because
of the danger was compelled to tell the truth. Thus Hecuba
rediscovered her son . . .

T iii Hypothesis   P. Oxy. 3650 (early 2ⁿᵈ C. A.D.), col. i, ed. Coles 1974, 1984; see also van
Rossum-Steenbeek 186–7, Diggle *TrGFS* 80–1, Kannicht *TrGF*   2 = F 41a   4–5 perhaps
Πρίαμος μὲν] and ἰδούσης ἔ-] Coles (ἐσιδούσης Bremer)   7 Π]άριν deleted by Luppe
11 -σε πο[λυτ]ελεῖς or -σεν δ[ιατ]ελεῖς Coles   13 -σι⟨ν⟩ Diggle   ἔδοξε[ν ἀμείνων Coles
ἔδοξε [κρείττων or [καλλίων Luppe   14 βουκόλο[υ τοῦ θρέψα]ντος (or τρέφο]ντος) Coles,
noting that βουκόλω[is equally possible: then βουκόλω(ι) [γεννηθέ]ντος Luppe
17 ἐπερωτηθεὶς Coles (ἀν- Bremer)   ἀπολογηθεὶς Luppe   18 ῥα(ι)δίω[ς] συνη[γο]ρεῖτο
declined by Coles, favoured by Kannicht   19 ἑκάστ[ο]υς Coles   22 ετιδαπαξητην read by
Coles, who conjectured ἔτι δὲ πὺξ at the start, whence ἔτι δὲ πυγμὴν Huys   στεφθεὶς Bremer

EURIPIDES

41a (– N)   x – ᵛ – x] καὶ τὸ κλεινὸν ['Ί]λιον

42   x – ᵛ – x] καὶ χρόνου προύβαινε πούς.

42a–c N-Sn   = 62f–h

42d (~ 64 N)   Paraphrase:
γενόμενος δὲ νεανίσκος καὶ πολλῶν διαφέρων
κάλλει τε καὶ ῥώμηι αὖθις 'Αλέξανδρος προσ-
ωνομάσθη, λῃστὰς ἀμυνόμενος καὶ τοῖς
ποιμνίοις ἀλεξήσας.

43 (46 N)   ΧΟΡΟΣ πάντων τὸ θανεῖν· τὸ δὲ κοινὸν ἄχος
μετρίως ἀλγεῖν σοφία μελετᾶι.

44 (45 N)   (Χο.) ὥστ' οὔτις ἀνδρῶν εἰς ἅπαντ' εὐδαιμονεῖ.

45 (44 N)   (Χο.) οἶδ'· ἀλλὰ κάμπτειν τῶι χρόνωι λύπας χρεών.
(ΕΚΑΒΗ) χρή· τοῦτο δ' εἰπεῖν ῥᾶιον ἢ φέρειν κακά.

46   Χο. ἔστιν τέκνων σοι πλ[
'Εκαβ. ἐ[γὼ δὲ θ]ρηνῶ γ' ὅτι βρ[έφ-
Χο. τλήμων γε Πρίαμος κ[αὶ
'Εκαβ. ὡς ἴσμεν οἱ παθόντες ο[
(43 N)   Χο. παλαιὰ και̣νοῖ̣ς δακρύοις οὐ χρὴ στένειν.   5

41a (– Budé) = Hypoth. 2   Τροία μὲν ἤδε] (e.g.) Scodel ὦ κλειτὺς 'Ίδης] (e.g.) Diggle
42 (2 Sn, 1 Budé) Schol. Ar. *Frogs* 100, attrib. Eur. *Alex.*; similarly Suidas 'παρα-
κεκινδυνευμένον' (π 356 Adler). Other derivative sources and Schol. *Frogs* 311 (repeating
Frogs 100) attribute Ar.'s phrase to Eur.   προύβαινε Elmsley (and a corrector in Suid. ms.
M) πρόβ- Schol. Ar., Suid.   42d (~ 17 Sn) Apollod. 3.12.5, unattrib.; cf. Varro *Ling. Lat.*
7.82 citing Enn. *Alex.* F 20 (below) with ref. to Eur.   43 (3 Sn, 2 Budé) Stob. 4.44.47,
attrib. Eur. *Alex.* (*'Cho(rus)'* Stob. ms. S)   44 (4 Sn, 3 Budé) Stob. 4.41.33, attrib. Eur. *Alex.*
45 (5 Sn, 4 Budé) Stob. 4.49.8, attrib. Eur. *Alex.* Assigned to Chorus-leader and Hecuba by
Hartung, to Priam and Hecuba by Welcker (but cf. F 46.3)   1 κάμπτειν Trincavelli κνάμπτ-
Stob.   2 χρή Stob. ms. S χρῆν Stob. mss. MA   46, 46a, 61d, 62a–e, 62k P. Strasb. inv.
gr. 2342–4, ed. Crönert, 1922 (see Bibl. p. 35 for this and other editions); dated c. 250 B.C. by
E. Turner in P. Cockshaw et al., *Miscellanea Codicologica F. Masai dicata* (Gent, 1979), 1–5;

52

ALEXANDROS

F 41a–42d: prologue-speech (41a the play's first line;
speaker uncertain).

41a . . . and famous Ilium

42 . . . and time's foot moved on.

42a–c N-Sn = *62f–h*

42d *When he (Paris) became a young man and excelled*
many in beauty and strength, he was given a
second name, Alexandros, because he drove off
brigands and protected the flocks.

F 43–46: parodos and first episode: the Chorus tries to
console Hecuba's grief for her lost son.

43 CHORUS All of us must die; but wisdom practises feeling the
pain of this common woe in moderation.

44 *(Cho.)* And so no man is fortunate in everything.

45 *(Cho.)* I know, but one should bring grief to an end in time.
(HECUBA) One should, but saying this is easier than bearing troubles.

46 *(Cho.)* You have . . . . . . of children . . .
Hecub. And yet I grieve because . . . . . . *my/our child.*
Cho. Unhappy Priam, and . . .
Hecub. As we well know, who suffered . . .
Cho. One should not lament old troubles with fresh tears.[5]

---

perhaps 35–40 lines per column, Coles 57 n. 1, Turner 2 **46** (1 Cr, 6 Sn, pp. 40–1 Coles,
1 D, 5 Budé) P. Strasb. 2344.1 5 Stob. 4.56.20, attrib. Eur. *Alex.* 1 πλ[ῆρες ἀρσένων
στέγος Crönert, πλ[ῆθος ἀρσένων ἔτι Diggle perhaps πλ[οῦτος Kannicht 2–5 paragraphi
mark speaker-changes 2 ἐ[γὼ δὲ Lefke θρ]ηνῶ Reitzenstein (in Crönert) βρ[έφος
(Crönert) κατέκταμεν (e.g.) Snell (διώλεσα Diggle, κτανεῖν ἔτλην Lee) 3 perhaps κ[αὶ ἡ
(= χὴ) τεκοῦσα (Crönert) δύσμορος Snell 4 ο[ἱ τλάντες θ' ἅμα Collard ο[ὐ λελησμένοι
Cropp

53

(Ἑκαβ.)]ε.. ων τις ἡ τεκοῦσ[α

(Χο.?) .. (.)]. (.)μεν, ὥς φασ', ὤλετ[

(Ἑκαβ.) .. μα]κάριον τἄρ' οὐκ[

    ]εστι τοῖ' ἐμο[

    ]πνας πρὸς κακ[10

(Χο.?) δέ]δορκα παῖδα κ[

    ]ν ἀδύτων ω[

traces of two more lines

46a (– N) *col. i* *last twenty-one lines of a column:*

    remains of three lines

    ]μν[..(.)]ος[..]λλοις ἔριν

    ].τ[..]ω.[.]δηις λάτρις   5

    ]νδε πω[λι]κοῖς ὄχοις

    ]ντατη[...]ους θανεῖν

    ] ὃν τετίμη[κ]ας τέκνων

    ].ελ.[...]υ[..]αι γένος

    ]ρ οἵπερ ἵσταν[τ]αι πον[10

    ] τήνδ' ἀφαγνίζεις χθόνα

    κα]ὶ ἐπικηδείους πόνους

    ]ων ἤδη πόλιν

    ]ονωι σπουδὴ λάβηι

    ]υδενωνεμων πόλιν   15

    ]τασιν τε γῆς

    π]ορσ[ύν]οις κακῶν

    τ]ῶι τεθ[ν]ηκότι

    ] καλὸν τόδε

    ]ναι γονάς   20

    end of one more line

  col. ii *upper half of col. lost, then beginnings (1–6 letters each) of its last seventeen lines; paragraphi give lines 30–40 to one speaker (Priam?) and 41ff. probably to the Chorus.*

6 ξ]είνων τις, ἡ τεκοῦσ[α δ' οὐ λέγει τάδε Schadewaldt (in Snell)   7]η or]ις (then doubtfully ὁ πα]ῖς μέν) Crönert end [ἐν μυχοῖς ὀρέων (e.g.) Münscher 8 μα]κάριον Crönert 9 ἐμο[ὶ Snell 10 τερ]πνὰς Crönert]μνας also possible, Kannicht; then perhaps μερί]μνας

ALEXANDROS

(Hecub.) Some . . . . . . , his mother . . . . . .

    (Cho.) . . . perished, so they say . . .

(Hecub.) . . . not, then, blessed . . .

      . . . . . . such . . . *are there for me(?)* . . .

      . . . . . . because of (*or* added to) *troubles(?)*. . .[10]

    (Cho.) . . . . *I see* your(?) child . . .

      . . . . . (from?) the shrine . . .

F 46a: probably Priam discussing preparations (with whom?) for the festival for his dead son.

46a

  . . . . strife

  . . . . servant[5]

  . . . . *horse-drawn* carriage

  . . . . to die

  . . . . the child you have honoured(?)

  . . . . family

  . . . . which are being put on . . .[10]

  . . . . you are cleansing this land

  . . . . *and* funereal labours

  . . . . already . . . the city

  . . . . eagerness grips (you?)

  . . . . city[15]

  . . . . of the land

  . . . . . *you could provide* . . . of/from evils

  . . . . *for the* dead . . .

  . . . . this (is/is not?) fine

  . . . . offspring[20]

The dialogue continued for some 30 lines in the next column, ending with a short speech (of Priam?) followed by (probably) lines for the Chorus.

Cropp   11–12 (Xo.) καὶ μὴν δέ]δορκα παῖδα Κ[ασσάνδραν σέθεν Ι ἤκουσα]ν ἀδύτων ὦ[δε Φοιβείων πάρος (e.g.) Wilamowitz (in Crönert: στείχουσα]ν Diggle; end ἄπο Webster) **46a** (3 Cr, 16 Sn, pp. 41–2 Coles, 6 Budé) P. Strasb. 2342.1 10 πόν]οι Crönert   12 κα]ὶ (i.e. κἀπικηδείους) Crönert   15 ὦ νέμων πόλιν Crönert   ἐμῶν also possible: Snell; then ο]ὐδὲν ὢν ἐμῶν (or ἐμὴν)? Kannicht   16 ἀνάσ]τασίν Crönert   17 beg. ἀποστροφὴν δ᾿ ἂν τῶνδε (e.g.) Snell   18 παιδὶ τ]ῶι Crönert

55

47 N   *See 61a below*

48   σοφὸς μὲν οὖν εἶ, Πρίαμ', ὅμως δέ σοι λέγω·
δούλου φρονοῦντος μεῖζον ἢ φρονεῖν χρεὼν
οὐκ ἔστιν ἄχθος μεῖζον οὐδὲ δώμασι
κτῆσις κακίων οὐδ' ἀνωφελεστέρα.

49   ἤλεγχον· οὕτω γὰρ κακὸν δοῦλον γένος·
γαστὴρ ἅπαντα, τοὐπίσω δ' οὐδὲν σκοπεῖ.

50   δούλων ὅσοι φιλοῦσι δεσποτῶν γένος
πρὸς τῶν ὁμοίων πόλεμον αἴρονται μέγαν.

51   δούλους γὰρ οὐ
καλὸν πεπᾶσθαι κρείσσονας τῶν δεσποτῶν.

52, 53 N   *See 61b, c below*

54   *See after 61a below*

56 (ΑΛΕΞΑΝΔΡΟΣ) ἄναξ, διαβολαὶ δεινὸν ἀνθρώποις κακόν·
ἀγλωσσίαι δὲ πολλάκις ληφθεὶς ἀνὴρ
δίκαια λέξας ἧσσον εὐγλώσσου φέρει.

55   ('Αλεξ.?)   ἄδικον ὁ πλοῦτος, πολλὰ δ' οὐκ ὀρθῶς ποιεῖ.

57   ('Αλεξ.?)   ὦ παγκάκιστοι καὶ τὸ δοῦλον οὐ λόγωι
ἔχοντες, ἀλλὰ τῆι τύχηι κεκτημένοι.

58 N   *See 62i below*

---

48 (32 Sn, 18 Budé) Stob. 4.19.14, attrib. Eur. *Alex.*   2–4 partly preserved in an inscription on a herm (of Euripides?) now in Copenhagen (Ny-Carlsberg Glypt. 414b)   2 μεῖζον inscr. (previously Blaydes) μᾶλλον Stob.   **49** (33 Sn, 10 Budé) Stob. 4.19.15, attrib. Eur. *Alex.* **50** (27 Sn, 11 Budé) Stob. 4.19.16, attrib. Eur. *Alex.*   2 αἴρονται Elmsley αἰροῦνται Stob. **51** (28 Sn, 9 Budé) Stob. 4.19.20, attrib. Eur. *Alex.*   **56** (34 Sn, 14 Budé) Stob. 3.42.3, attrib. Eur. *Alex.*   2–3 Clem. Alex. *Strom.* 1.8.41, attrib. to an unnamed tragedy   2 ἀγλωσσίαι

47 N   *See 61a below*

F 48–51, probably criticisms of Paris in the debate:

48   You are certainly wise, Priam, but still I tell you: there is no greater burden than a slave who has bigger ideas than he should, nor a possession more vile or more useless for a household.

49   I've tested it: so vile is the race of slaves, all belly and looking to nothing beyond that.

50   Slaves who become attached to their masters' kind get serious hostility from their own sort.

51   It is no good thing to own slaves who are stronger than their masters.

52, 53 N   *See 61b, c below*

54   *See after 61a below*

F 56, 55, 57: probably Paris defending himself in the debate scene.

56   (ALEXANDROS) My lord, slander is a terrible thing for men. Often a man gripped by ineloquence, though he has spoken justly, gets less credit than an eloquent one.

55   (Alex.?) Wealth is an unjust thing and does much wrongly.

57   (Alex.?) O vilest creatures – slaves not in name but in reality.

58 N   *See 62i below*

Clem. εὐγλ- Stob. 3 φέρει Stob. -ειν Clem.   **55** (37 Sn, 17 Budé) Stob. 4.31.71, attrib. Eur. *Alex.*   **57** (38 Sn, 8 Budé) Stob. 4.19.18, attrib. Eur. *Alex.*   2 φύσει Jacobs (then 1 οὐ τύχηι, 2 ἐν τῆι φύσει Cobet)

59   ἐκ τῶν ὁμοίων οἱ κακοὶ γαμοῦσ' ἀεί.

61   †μισῶ σοφὸν ἐν λόγοισιν, ἐς δ' ὄνησιν οὐ σοφόν.†

60   (ΠΡΙΑΜΟΣ)   χρόνος δὲ δείξει σ'· ὧι τεκμηρίωι μαθὼν
               ἢ χρηστὸν ὄντα γνωσόμεθά σ' ἢ κακόν.

61a   *See after 61d below.*

61b (52 N)   Χο.   περισσόμυθος ὁ λόγος εὐγένειαν εἰ
                  βρότειον εὐλογήσομεν.
                  τὸ γὰρ πάλαι καὶ πρῶτον ὅτ' ἐγενόμεθα, διὰ
                    δ' ἔκρινεν ἁ τεκοῦσα γᾶ
                  βροτούς, ὁμοίαν χθὼν ἅπασιν ἐξεπαί-   5
                  δευσεν ὄψιν· ἴδιον οὐδὲν ἔσχομεν.
                  μία δὲ γονὰ τό τ' εὐγενὲς καὶ δυσγενές,
                  νόμωι δὲ γαῦρον αὐτὸ κραίνει χρόνος.
                  τὸ φρόνιμον εὐγένεια καὶ τὸ συνετόν, ὁ δὲ
                    θεὸς δίδωσιν, οὐχ ὁ πλοῦτος . . .   10

61c (53 N)   Χο.   οὐκ ἔστιν ἐν κακοῖσιν εὐγένεια, παρ' ἀ-
                  γαθοῖσι δ' ἀνδρῶν.

---

59 (29 Sn, 13 Budé) Stob. 4.22.87, attrib. Eur. *Alex.*   **61** (35 Sn, 15 Budé) Orion 1.3,
attrib. *Ale(xa)n(dros)* in a series of Euripidean excerpts   μισῶ σοφὸν Ι ὄντ' ἐν λόγοισιν
(etc.) Meineke μισῶ δ' ἐγὼ Ι σοφὸν λόγοισιν (etc.) Schneidewin μισῶ σοφὸν λόγοισιν, ἐς δ'
ὄνησιν οὗ Cobet   **60** (39 Sn, 19 Budé) Clem. Alex. *Strom.* 6.2.10, attrib. Eur. *Alex.*,
assigned to Priam by Matthiae   1 δείξει σ' Grotius δείξει Clem.   γνωσόμεθά Schneidewin γνώσομαι Stob.   **61b** (40 Sn, 20 Budé) Stob. 4.29.2, attrib. Eur. *Alex.* ('Cho(rus)' ms.
S)   6 ἔσχομεν Stob. ms. S ἔχ- mss. MA   7 καὶ δυσγενές Diggle, Kannicht καὶ τὸ
δυσγ- Stob. ⟨πέφυκε⟩ καὶ τὸ δυσγ- Wilamowitz   8 γαῦρον Stob. ms. S γαύρων ms. M
γαυρῶν ms. A   9 ὁ δὲ Wilamowitz ὁ Stob.   **61c** (41 Sn, 21 Budé) Stob. 4.29.7, attrib.
Eur. *Alex.*

59   The lower sort always marry from their own kind.

Another jibe at Paris?

61   †I loathe a man who is clever in words but not clever at doing good service.†

One speaker in the debate criticizes the other's eloquence.

60   *(Priam)* Time will show what you are; by that evidence I shall learn whether you are good or bad.

Priam permits Paris to compete in the games.

61a   *See after **61d** below*

F 61b, 61c, from a choral stasimon following the debate scene:

61b   *Cho.*   Our talk will be idle if we sing the praises of human good birth. For long ago at the beginning, when we were born and mother earth produced distinct human beings, she bred for all of us a similar[5] appearance; we got no special feature. Well-born and low-born are a single breed, but time through convention has made the well-born proud. It is intelligence and understanding that make nobility, and god that gives it, not wealth . . .[10]

61c   *Cho.*   Nobility is found not in men who are bad but in those who are good.

EURIPIDES

61d (– N)   *remains of three lines*
(Χο.)   τύχηι δ[. . .] ι πα[
ΑΓΓΕΛΟΣ   κρείσσων πεφυκὼς [5
Χο.   ἢ καὶ στέφουσιν αὐτὸ[ν
Ἀγγ.   καί φασιν εἶναί γ' ἄξιον [
Χο.   ὁ δ' ὧδε μορφῆι διαφερ[
Ἀγγ.   ἅπανθ' ὅσ' ἄνδρα χρη[
(Χο.)   *c. 9 letters*]γαν βουκ[ολ-   10
(Ἀγγ.)   *traces of one line*
(Χο.)   ἀγῶνα ποῦ κ[
(Ἀγγ.)   Πρίαμος τίθησιν [
Χο.   εἰς τόνδε νικη [
Ἀγγ.   *remains of one line*   15

61a (47 N) (Ἀγγ.?)   ὅθεν δὲ νικᾶν χρῆν σε, δυστυχεῖς, ἄναξ·
ὅθεν δέ σ' οὐ χρῆν, εὐτυχεῖς. δούλοισι γὰρ
τοῖς σοῖσι νικᾶις, τοῖς δ' ἐλευθέροισιν οὔ.

54 (Ἀγγ.?)   κακόν τι παίδευμ' ἦν ἄρ' εἰς εὐανδρίαν
ὁ πλοῦτος ἀνθρώποισιν αἵ τ' ἄγαν τρυφαί·
πενία δὲ δύστηνον μέν, ἀλλ' ὅμως τρέφει
μοχθεῖν τ' ἀμείνω τέκνα καὶ δραστήρια.

62   *See after 62i below*

62a (– N)   *trace of one line*
(Χο.)   καὶ μὴν ὁρῶ τόν]δ' Ἕκτορ' ἐξ ἀγωνίω[ν
μό]χθων σύγγονόν τε, παῖδε σώ,
] εἰς δ' ἅμιλλαν ἥκουσιν λόγων.

61d (2 Cr, 18 Sn, pp. 42–3 Coles, 2 D, 22 Budé) P. Strasb. 2344.2, context and speakers identified by Schadewaldt in Snell   4 δ[ίδω]μι Crönert, Kannicht   πά[ντα Lefke 5–9 paragraphi mark speaker-changes   5 κρείσσων Crönert -ω P   7 [τυραννίδος (e.g.) Crönert   8 διαφέρ[ων or -[ει Crönert   9 χρὴ Crönert   [τὸν εὐγενῆ τελεῖν (e.g.) Page perhaps χρή[σιμον Coles, χρη[στὸν ὄντα Kannicht   12 κ[ρίνουσι Crönert 14–15 paragraphi mark speaker-changes (not written in 13)   14 νικητ[ήρι(α) Crönert 61a (26 Sn, 23 Budé) Stob. 3.4.31 (om. ms. S), attrib. Eur. *Alex.*   1 χρῆν Valckenaer χρῆ Stob.   2 χρῆν Stob. ms. A χρὴν ms. M   3 τοῖς σοῖσι νικᾶις Musgrave τοῖς σοῖσιν ἥκεις Stob. ms. A (τοῖς σοῦσιν ms. M)   54 (36 Sn, 16 Budé) Stob. 4.33.3, attrib. Eur. *Alex.*

60

F 61d, 61a, 54, messenger's arrival and probable extracts from his speech:

61d   *(Cho.)*   To (*or* through) fortune . . . . . .

    MESSENGER   Being naturally superior . . . . . .⁵

        Cho.   And are they crowning him . . . . . ?

        Mess.   Yes, and declaring him worthy . . . . . .

        Cho.   And he *is/being* so *outstanding* in beauty . . . . ?

        Mess.   Everything that a man *should(?)* . . . . . .

        (Cho.)   . . . . . *herdsman* . . . . . . .¹⁰

        (Mess.)   . . . .

        (Cho.)   Where . . . the contest . . . . . ?

        (Mess.)   Priam is placing/arranging . . . . . .

        Cho.   To this man . . . *victory* . . . . . .

61a *(Mess.?)* Those who should bring you victory bring you failure, my lord, and those who should not, bring you success. You win with your slaves, and not with your free men.

54   *(Mess.?)* Wealth and excessive luxury, it turns out, are a bad training for manliness. Poverty is a misfortune, but all the same it rears children who are better at working hard and get things done.

62   *See after 62i below*

F 62a–d, Hector and Deiphobus return from the games; Deiphobus and Hecuba plot to kill Paris:

62a   *(Cho.)*   <And now I see> Hector <here> . . . from the *toils* of the games, and his brother . . . , your two sons . . . and they have come into conflict in words.

1–2 Clem. Alex. *Strom.* 4.5.24, attrib. Eur. *Alex.*   1 παίδευμ' Musgrave (κακὸν οὖν ἦν τὸ παίδευμα Clem.) βούλευμ' Stob.   4 μοχθεῖν τ' (or μοχθεῖν) Conington μοχθοῦντ' Stob. **62a** (4 Cr, 23 Sn, p. 45 Coles, 3 D, 25 Budé) P. Strasb. 2342.2   2 καὶ μὴν ὁρῶ τόνδ'] Jacob: τόν]δ' Lee, Diggle ἀλλ' εἰσορῶ γάρ] Crönert ἀγωνίω[ν Wilamowitz -ικῶ[ν P 3 ἥκοντα μό]χθων Crönert στείχοντα Jacob, Diggle περῶντα Kannicht   4 Δηίφοβον] (e.g.) Diggle πρὸς οἶκον] (e.g.) Kannicht   δ' proposed by Coles, read by Kannicht, Lee   θ' Crönert

(ΔΗΙΦΟΒΟΣ)   οὐ]δέν' ὅστις ἐστὶ δυσχερής   5
              ] κακοῖσι μαλθάσσει φρένας.
(ΕΚΤΩΡ)   ἐγὼ δέ γ' ὅσ]τις σμίκρ' ἔχων ἐγκλήματα
              μεγάλα νο]μίζει καὶ †συνέστηκεν φόβω[ι†.
(Διιφ.)   καὶ πῶς, κα]σίγνηθ' Ἕκτορ, οὐκ ἀλγεῖς φρένα[ς
              δούλου πρὸς] ἀνδρὸς ἆθλ' ἀπεστερημέν[ος;   10
('Εκτ.)   ] εἰς, Δηΐφοβε· τί γάρ με δεῖ
              ] καιρὸς ὠδίνειν φ[ρέ]νας.
(Διιφ.)   ] ῥαιδίως φέρεις τάδε
              Φρ]υξὶν ἐμφανὴς ἔσηι.
('Εκτ.?)   ]ς νέον φῦσαι με[15
              βο]ύλεται δ' οὐ σωφρ[ον
              ]νεζευχθοι[
              κ]αθέστηκεν[
              ]εγω γὰρ ουχ [
              ] πρόσθεν λ[20
              remains of one more line

62b (– N)   col. i   Minimal line-ends from the lower half of
                      possibly the same column as F 62a.

            col. ii   Lower half of the next column:

                      traces of one line
(Διιφ.?)   ἐλε]ύθεροι μὲν πα [
                      δο]ῦλοι δ' ἂν ἤσκουν [
                      πα]ντοῖ' ἐκείνων ατ[25
                      ...]ν δ' ἀπῆσαν μν[
                      remains of three lines
('Εκτ.)   οὔ[τ' οἶκο]ν αὔξων οὔτ[ε   30
                      πρόθυμ' ἔπρασσε δοῦλος ὢν απ [
                      ψυχῆς [ἐ]μαυτοῦ μὴ κατα[
                      εἰ δ' ἐστὶ κρείσσων, σοῦ κόλαζε τὴν φ[ύσιν,
                      ὑφ' ἧς ἐνίκω· κυριώτερος γὰρ εἶ.

5 beg. ἐπήινεσ' (e.g.) Münscher αἰνῶ μὲν (e.g.) Kannicht   οὐ]δέν' Crönert   6 ἁλοὺς δὲ τοῖ]ς Crönert   ἁλοὺς δὲ δ]ὴ Kannicht   αὖθις δὲ τοῖ]ς Diggle   7 beg. Pohlenz in Crönert   σμίκρ' Diggle   μικρα P   8 μεγάλα Diggle   δεινὸν νο]μ- Crönert   perhaps φθόνω[ι Collard, Cropp   9 καὶ πῶς Diggle   πῶς γὰρ Wilamowitz   10 δούλου πρὸς] Wilamowitz (δούλου παρ') and Diggle   11 λίαν ἀθυ]μεῖς Wilamowitz (μάτην Kannicht) λίαν μ' ἐπαί]ρεις Coll–

(*DEIPHOBUS*) . . . . . . *no one* who is ill-disposed[5] . . . . .
bad . . . softens his attitude.

(*HECTOR*) <*And I of no one*> *who* having minor complaints
considers <*them major*> and †contends with
fear†.

(*Deiph.*) <*And how,*> *brother* Hector, are you not pained in
your spirit, when you have been robbed of prizes
<*by a slave*>?[10]

(*Hect.*) *You . . . . . . , Deiphobus. Why do I need . . . ?*
. . . . . an occasion for tormenting *one's spirit.*

(*Deiph.*) . . . . . you are bearing these things lightly . . .
. . . . . you will be conspicuous to the Trojans.

(*Hect.?*) . . . . to produce a(?) new/young . . .[15]
. . . . and *wants* . . . *intemperate* . . . . . .
. . . . *to be yoked/joined(?)* . . .
. . . . *is established(?)* . . . . .
. . . . *for* . . . .
. . . . *previously* . . . .[20]

62b   *Possibly some 30 lines after the end of F 62a:*

(*Deiph.?*) . . . *free* . . . . . , while *slaves* would practise
. . . their . . . *of all kinds* . . .[25] . . . *would be*
absent . . .
(three fragmentary lines)

(*Hect.*) . . . *neither* building up *his estate nor.* . . . . .[30]
he acted resolutely, though being a slave . . . . . .
not . . . my own spirit . . . . And if he is superior,
punish your own nature which is what defeated
you — you have more authority over that.

ard   12 οὐ] Crönert μισεῖν νιν; οὐ γὰρ] Wilamowitz (οὔ τοι Page) is too long   ὀργὴν ἔχειν;
οὐ] or δυσθυμίας; οὐ] (e.g.) Collard   φ[ρέ]νας so read by Coles   13 σὺ δειλίαι μὲ]ν
ῥαιδίως φέρεις τάδε, | ἥσσων δὲ δούλου Φρ]υξὶν ἐμφανὴς ἔσηι (e.g.) Lefke (Φρ]υξὶν
Reitzenstein in Crönert)   15 perhaps μέ[νος Cropp   16 σωφρ[ονεῖν Crönert σώφρ[ονα
Collard, Cropp   17 συ]νεζεῦχθαι Crönert (ἐζεῦχθαι? Kannicht)   νεόζευκτοι Snell (wrongly
reading]νεοζ-)   18 κ]αθέστηκεν[Crönert (]ατ- P)   **62b** (6b + 6c.15–35 Cr; 43.58–64,
85–105 Sn; detached as 23a by Coles (pp. 46–9); ~ 26 Budé) P. Strasb. 2343.2, lower part
(detached from F 62d)   23–4 beg. Coles (previously supplied wrongly from F 62d.57)
23 παῖ[δες Crönert πάν[τες Snell   25 beg. Kannicht   30 οὔ]τ' οἶκο]ν αὔξων οὔτ[ε πρὸς
κέρδος βλέπων Reitzenstein   32 [ἐ]μαυτοῦ Snell   33 κρείσσων, σοῦ Latte in Snell
κρείσσων σου, Crönert (κρεισσω σου P)   end Reitzenstein

ἐγὼ †δενε[ ]ρω† κεῖνον· εἰ γὰρ [35
κράτιστος [

Χο.?   ἀε[ὶ γὰρ] Ἕκτωρ [ ] ... [
     τα [ ] ι αὐτοῦ καὶ δομ[

Ἑκαβ. οὗτος μὲν ἀεὶ τέκν[ο]ν[
     Δηίφοβε, καὶ τἆλλ' ουθ[40
     ῥέξεις δ' ἃ λυπούμεσθα [
     κτανόντες ἄνδρα δοῦ[λον

62c (– N)   *end of possibly the next column (F 62d col. i intervening?):*

     beginning of one line

(Ἑκαβ.?) πάρεργον [
     νῦν οὖν ἐμοισο[
     καὶ τοὺς λαθραι [
     δούλης γυναικὸς [5
     μή νυν ἔτ' εἰσιν τ[
     ἀλλ['ο]ὺκ, ἰώ μοι, δ[

62d (– N) col. i *Ten minimal line-ends from the top of a column, possibly straight after F 62b, including 4 λάτριν, 5 νέων.*

     col. ii *Top half of the next column:*

(Ἑκαβ.) κεῖνον μὲν ὄνθ' ὅς ἐστι θαυμάζειν Φρύγας,
     Πριάμου δὲ νικ .... γεραίρεσθαι δόμους.
(Δηιφ.) πῶς οὖν [...(.)] .... ὥστ' ἔχειν καλῶς;
(Ἑκαβ.) .... ιδε χειρὶ δεῖ θανεῖν.   25
(Δηιφ.) οὐ μὴν ἄτρωτός γ' εἶσιν εἰς Ἅιδου δόμους.
(Ἑκαβ.) ποῦ νυν [ἂ]ν εἴη καλλίνικ' ἔχων στέφη;
(Δηιφ.) πᾶν ἄστυ πληροῖ Τρωϊκὸν γαυρούμενος.
(Ἑκαβ.) ...... δ]εῦρ', εἰς βόλον γὰρ ἂν πέσοι.
(Δηιφ.) ....]ιδηις γ' ὅτ[ι κρ]ατεῖ τῶν σῶν τέκνων.   30

35 δ' ἐνε[ί]ρω Snell δ' ἐπαινῶ Körte εἰ γὰρ ἐ[στ' ἀνὴρ Reitzenstein 37, 39 paragraphi mark speaker-changes 37 ἀε[ὶ γὰρ] Kannicht (to fit the space) ἀε[ὶ μὲν] Ἕκτωρ Lefke 39 possibly τέκν[α] [Coles **62c** (5 Cr; 43.29–35 Sn; 23b Coles (pp. 49–50); 27 Budé) P. Strasb. 2342.3 4 λέ[γοντας Snell (ας[or λε[read by Kannicht) καὶ τοὺς λάθραι λε[γοντας ὡς ἐλεύθερα ǀ δούλης γυναικὸς [παῖς ἐνίκησεν τέκνα (e.g.) Page 6 εἰσίν or

But I †. . .† him; for if . . .[35] *strongest* . . .

Cho.? Hector *always* . . . his . . . and . . . house . . .

Hecub. This man always . . . *(my) child* Deiphobus, and
(in?) other matters . . .[40] But you will do . . .
which we feel distress at, killing a man who is *a
slave* . . . .

62c   *Some 30 lines after the end of F 62b?*

(Hecub.?) . . . an incidental matter . . . . . . so now for me
(*or* for my) . . . . . . and those secretly . . .
of/from a slave woman[5] . . . . . . Surely they are
not (*or* surely he will not go) . . . . . . ? But . . .
not – woe is me! – . . .

62d   *Col. i: ten minimal line-ends from the top of a
column, perhaps immediately after F 62b, including
4 servant, 5 new/young (men?)*

*Col. ii: some thirty lines later (perhaps immediately
after F 62c):*

(Hecub.) . . . that he, being who he is, should be admired by
the Trojans, and Priam's house . . . be honoured
. . . *victory.*

(Deiph.) How then . . . . so as to turn out well?

(Hecub.) . . . . he must die by . . . hand.[25]

(Deiph.) He will surely not go unwounded to Hades' halls!

(Hecub.) Where might he be then, wearing his victor's garlands?

(Deiph.) He is filling the whole town of Troy with his exultation.

(Hecub.) . . . . . . *here,* for he would fall into the net.

(Deiph.) . . . *you* . . . that he has power over your sons.[30]

εἰσιν 7 ἀλλ[' ο]ὐκ Snell δ[υνατόν ἐστ' ἰδεῖν τόδε Körte **62d** (6a + 6b + 6c.1–21 Cr;
43.1–10, 36–56, 71–91 Snell; 43 Coles (pp. 50–4); ~ 4 D; ~ 28–29 Budé) P. Strasb. 2343.1,
2343.2, upper parts (lower parts now detached as F 62b) 22 beg. Schadewaldt 23 νίκηι
μὴ Page 24–9 paragraphi mark speaker-changes 24 'traces very uncertain' Kannicht
(ὀ[κέλ]λει ταῦτα γ' Snell) 25 τῆιδε Crönert σῆι δὲ Murray 26 εἰσιν Lekfe ἐστιν P
27 νυν Cropp νῦν editors [ἄ]ν Wilamowitz 30 μηπώποτ' ἐπ]ίδηις γ' ὅτ[ι Snell beg. οὐ
μὴ Lee ε]ἰδῆις Page κρ]ατεῖ Crönert

(Ἑκαβ.?)

ἀ]μμάτων ἔσω
]ειν σε βούλομαι
ἐσ]τὶ δοῦλος, ἀλλ' ὅμως
] . λ[.] . δ' ἐμοῖς
] . . . φόνον   35
]ην ἅπαξ
]αύσεται

traces of five more line-ends

col. iii   *Top half of the next column:*

δουλου ρ[
ἡμιχορ. α'?   μεταβολ[ὰ
νικω . . . [45
σιν παραεθ[
οἶκον εξ . [
ἡμιχορ. β'?   δέσποινα[(ἐ-)
πὶ δεσποτ[
φύλλοις ν[50
Ἀλεξ.?   ποῦ μοι π[
Ἑκάβη, φρά[σον μοι
τὴν καλλ[ίνικον
Χο.?   πρέσβυς πε[
Ἑκάβην δὲ β[55
*minimal remains of eight more line-beginnings;
speaker-changes at 56, 63*

62e (– N)   ]ης ἤκουσ' ἔπος
β]ακχεύει φρένα[
remains from two more line-ends

*62f (935 N, 42a N-Sn)
ΚΑΣΣΑΝΔΡΑ ἀλλ' ὦ φίλιπποι Τρῶες

31 ἀ]μμάτων Wilamowitz 33 ἐσ]τὶ Crönert 37 π]αύσεται Crönert perhaps κλ]αύσεται
Cropp 44, 48 paragraphi with coronis mark speaker-changes μεταβολ[ὰ κακῶν Crönert
45 νικώμεσ[θα Snell νικωντο[Crönert 46 παρ' ἀέθ[λοις Snell 48 δέσποινα[Kannicht
δέσποιν', ο[Crönert, Snell, Coles 49 πι (i.e. ἐπὶ) rather than τι read by Coles, Kannicht

ALEXANDROS

(Hecub.?) . . . . inside the net

. . . . I wish you to . . . . . .

. . . . *he is* a slave, but still

. . . . my . . .

. . . . murder[35]

. . . . once

. . . . he will . . .

Col. iii top: some 20 lines later, line-beginnings including:

. . . of/from a slave . . .[43]

Semichor. 1? A change . . .[44] . . . house . . .[47]

Semichor. 2? The(?) mistress . . . . . . *to the master* . . . . . .
with leaves . . .[50]

Alex.? Where, tell me . . . . . . Hecuba, *tell <me>* . . . . .
. . . the *victory-song* . . .[53]

Cho.? The old man . . . . . . , but Hecuba . . . . . .[55]

F 62e–h: from Cassandra's prophetic scene:

62e . . . . heard a/the pronouncement

. . . . she is raving

*62f CASSANDRA Come now, horse-loving Trojans

τ[rather than λ[or δ[read by Kannicht, Lee   51, 54 paragraphi mark speaker-changes
51 μοι or ποι Coles, Kannicht   52, 53 suppl. Crönert   **62e** (8 Cr, 7 Sn, pp. 54–5 Coles, 30
Budé) P. Strasb. 2344.4   2 β]ακχεύει Crönert]αχχ- P   φρένα[ς Snell   ***62f** (9* Sn,
*32 Budé) [Longin.] *De Sublim.* 15.4, attrib. Cassandra in Eur.; assigned to *Alex.* by Toup and
Musgrave

67

EURIPIDES

62g (adesp. 414 N, 42b N-Sn)

Κασ. ἄκραντα γάρ μ' ἔθηκε θεσπίζειν θεός,
καὶ πρὸς παθόντων κἂν κακοῖσι κειμένων
σοφὴ κέκλημαι, πρὶν παθεῖν δὲ μαίνομαι.

*62h (968 N, 42c N-Sn)
(Κασ.) Ἑκάτης ἄγαλμα φωσφόρου κύων ἔσηι.

62i (58 N) (Ἀλεξ.) οἴμοι, θανοῦμαι διὰ τὸ χρήσιμον φρενῶν,
ἢ τοῖσιν ἄλλοις γίγνεται σωτηρία.

62 Ἑκάβη, τὸ θεῖον ὡς ἄελπτον ἔρχεται
θνητοῖσιν, ἕλκει δ' οὔποτ' ἐκ ταὐτοῦ τύχας.

Unplaced Fragments

62k (– N) *Minor fragments, P. Strasb. 2344.5–15*

63 ἄρρητος κόρη

64 N *See 42d above*

**62g (11* Sn, **34 Budé) Plut. *Mor.* 821b, attrib. Cassandra, author and play unnamed; cf. Cic. *Ad Att.* 8.11.3; assigned to Eur. *Alex.* by Toup and Musgrave   *62h (14* Sn, *33 Budé) Plut. *Mor.* 379d, attrib. Eur.; assigned to *Alex.* by Welcker. Imitated by Ar. F 608 καὶ κύων ἀκράχολος, Ἑκάτης ἄγαλμα φωσφόρου, γενήσομαι ('And I shall become an ill-tempered dog, a favourite of light-bearing Hecate'), which is cited by Paus. Att. α 7 ('ἄγαλμα Ἑκάτης'), an entry repeated by Eustath. on Hom. *Od.* 3.274 and abbreviated by lexicographers including Hesych. ε 1267, α 252 Latte, Phot. ε 344, α 114 Theodoridis   ἔσηι Xylander ἐσσίν Plut. mss.   62i (44 Sn, 37 Budé) Stob. 3.38.20, attrib. Eur. *Alex.*   2 ἢ Barnes ὂ Stob.   62 (13 Sn, 39 Budé) Stob. 4.47.10, attrib. Eur. *Alex.*   62k (9–19 Cr, 47–58 Sn, ~ 41 Budé)   63 (60 Sn, 42 Budé) Hesych. α 7439 Latte, attrib. Eur. *Alex.*

68

**62g *Cas.* The god caused me to make vain prophecies; by those who have suffered and are beset by troubles I am called wise, but before they suffer I am mad.

*62h *(Cas.)* You will be a dog, a favourite of light-bearing Hecate.

62i *(Alex.)* Ah! I am going to die because of my virtue, which for others is a source of protection.

Paris threatened by his attackers.

62 Hecuba, how unexpected does divine action prove to be for men, and never draws its outcomes from the same source!

Probably the Chorus commenting on the recognition.

Unplaced Fragments

62k *Minor fragments of the Strasbourg papyrus with a few isolated words not printed here*

63 The maiden who cannot be named.

64 N *See* **42d** *above*

Commentary on *Alexandros*

T iii Hypothesis. P. Oxy. 3650 contains this hypothesis and line-beginnings from a hypothesis of *Andromache* largely identical with the one known from medieval mss. It is from the same roll as P. Oxy. 2457, which has fragmentary hypotheses of *Alcestis* and *Aeolus*. The hypotheses are in a standard format (see General Introd. in Vol. 1, 1–2) giving title, first line and narrative outline beginning with background information from the play's prologue (lines 4–12 here). How much is lost at the end is not clear, but the last surviving words may be the start of a conclusion (see 32 n.).

2. The play's first line was quoted (F 41a).

4–7. Hecuba's dream and the attempted killing and survival of her baby were all no doubt included in the prologue (below, F 41a–42d n.; Introd., p. 37. The summary is very brief, omitting the dream's content and moving from exposure to rearing in a few words. Coles' supplements (or Bremer's adjustment of them) give '<*Priam, because*> **Hecuba** <*had seen*> **visions in her sleep**'. ἔδωκεν ἐκθεῖναι βρέφος '*gave his infant son...to expose*' could be the end of an iambic trimeter from the prologue (cf. esp. *Pho.* 25: Coles 17, Timpanaro 16). **calling** *Alexandros* **Paris:** i.e. giving the name Paris to the boy later known as Alexandros (Scodel 41–2, Timpanaro 16 n. 1). Other accounts have him named Alexandros later by the local community: see on F 42d; Huys, *Tale* 317–8. The wording is condensed and possibly garbled; or the summarizer might have meant (wrongly) 'calling the boy Alexandros-Paris', the double name found in mythographic sources such as Hygin. *Fab.* 91 (title), 92.2, 98.1 etc. Luppe suggests deleting **Paris** so that the herdsman names the infant Alexandros in anticipation of his future strength (*APF* 45 [1999], 19–20). Deleting **Alexandros** would be more appropriate, but the summarizer probably wanted to register both names.

7–12. The Hypothesis has the games founded soon after the exposure and before the twenty-year interval mentioned in 12–13, probably reflecting the play accurately: cf. Huys, *Tale* 253–4. The games are presumably periodic (like the biennial Nemean games commemorating Archemorus: pp. 173, 177 below on *Hyps.*). Hecuba's grief and the founding of the games are reflected in the play's early scenes (F 43–46a).

[11. πο[λυτ]ελεῖς, lavish: the word occurs frequently in the Euripidean scholia (of burials: Schol. *Alc.* 55, *Hec.* 623, *Tro.* 1248), and is a likelier restoration than δ[ιατ]ελεῖς 'perpetual'.]

13–14. Perhaps '**the boy seemed to be** <*better*> **in his nature** *than the herdsman who had raised him*' (Coles), or '...**seemed to be** <*superior* (or *finer*)> **in his nature** *than one born to a* **herdsman**' (Luppe). Luppe's κρείττων 'superior' is attractive since it is applied to Paris elsewhere (F 51.2, 61d.5, 62b.33) and (as Bremer notes) to Neleus and Pelias in similar circumstances, Menand. *Epitr.* 329. **nature:** φύσις includes both physical qualities and character and intelligence, the former displayed in the games, the latter in the debate-scene (and cf. F 62i). The traditional motif of the foundling's extraordinary qualities is discussed by Huys, *Tale* 335–63.

70

15–17. Paris's arrogance and arraignment, reflecting the beginning of the debate-scene. No specifics are given, and the implication may be simply that his natural superiority and the herdsmen's resentment led him to abuse them, like the young Cyrus in Hdt. 1.114: cf. Huys, *Tale* 350. This account seems incompatible with that of Hygin. *Fab.* 91, where the seizure of Paris's favourite bull as a prize leads him to enter the games, and there is no mention of his arrogance or an arraignment (cf. Introd., p. 39).

17–21. The debate scene itself, source of many of the book-fragments (see on F 48–51 etc.). In 17–19 tentative supplements (see App.) suggest: '*When he was questioned* [Coles/Bremer; or '*defended himself*', Luppe] **before the ruler, he** <*easily*> argued his case [Coles/Kannicht] **and caught out** *each of* [Coles] **those slandering him**'. For 'caught out' see LSJ λαμβάνω I.4. Paris may have rebutted a series of accusations attributed to individuals or divided among members of the secondary chorus in the scene's opening lyric exchange, or '*each*' (if correct) could be due to generic summarizing; it need not be inferred (as by Kovacs 49–50) that the argument was reported, not staged.

21–3. Paris's victories and the reaction to them were reported by a messenger (F 61d, 61a?, 54?, Enn. F 19, 24 etc.). In 21–2 perhaps '**And** *being crowned* [Bremer] *in* **running and the pentathlon,** *and* **also** <*boxing*> [Coles/Huys]'. Paris is remembered as a great boxer in Verg. *Aen.* 5.370. **Deiphobus and his companions:** lit. 'those around Deiphobus', a vague phrasing often used in hypotheses (Hypoth. *Andr.* 9, *Rhes.* 6, 13) and scholia (Schol. *Andr.* 414, *Hipp.* 1062, *Tro.* 31, *Pho.* 204, 868). It is likely that companions of Deiphobus were mentioned in the messenger's speech, and they may have appeared with him in the next scene (see next note). [*infuriated*: the first two letters in ἀπεθηρίωσε are not certain (cf. Coles 1984, 16), but the compound form used metaphorically (LSJ I.2) is rather common in Hellenistic and later Greek texts.]

23–5. who... demanded that Hecuba should kill him: this seems to imply that the companions appeared with Deiphobus in the plotting scene, but it may be a careless summary (cf. Huys 1986, 13–14). On this and the planning see Introd., p. 40; Comm. on F 62d col. ii; Huys 1986, 15–16.

25–30. Paris returns from the games, Cassandra recognizes him and prophesies future disasters (cf. F 62e–h, Enn. F 17, 25, 26), and Hecuba is prevented from killing him (cf. F 62i). For possible reconstructions of this sequence see Introd., pp. 40–1. **Hecuba...was prevented** suggests she had to be restrained by a third party and/or by servants: cf. Huys 1986, 31, supported by Luppe (1986, 9–10) who compares similar wording in Hypoth. *Andr.* 11 and Hypoth. *Hcld.* 7.

30–2. The man... was compelled to tell the truth: presumably he revealed that Paris was the exposed child of Priam and Hecuba in order to save his life.

32. Thus Hecuba rediscovered her son...: this may well be the incomplete final sentence of the Hypothesis, stating the outcome for Hecuba on the one hand (μὲν) and Paris or Troy in general on the other. The phrasing tells, if anything, against the possibility that the Hypothesis went on to mention a *deus ex machina* (though Bremer 311 favours this).

41a, 42, 42d. Fragments of the prologue-speech; see also Hypoth. 1–12, Enn. F 18 and 20. On the speech as a whole and its speaker (perhaps a neutral god such as Hermes) see Introd. p. 37. Recent comments in L. Di Giuseppe, *ARF* 3 (2001), 67–73.

41a. The second half of the play's opening line, given in the Hypothesis. For the first half Scodel (22) suggested '<*This is Troy*>', Diggle (finding this tautologous) '<*O slope of Ida*>' (*CR* 31 [1981], 106). Mt. Ida is the site of Paris's exposure and early life.

42. and time's foot moved on: the verse 'aether, Zeus's bedroom, and time's foot' is cited by Dionysus to illustrate Euripides' poetic virtuosity in *Frogs* 100, and repeated by Xanthias at *Frogs* 311. The scholia cite *Mel.S.* F 487 and this fr. as Eur.'s actual words. 'Time's foot' appears again in *Bacc.* 889. The placing of this fr. in the prologue is likely, with ref. to Paris's childhood (cf. Hypoth. 12–13). Time's changes and revelations are stressed, perhaps thematically, in F 44, 45, 60, 61b.8: cf. Huys 1986, 34.

42d (~ 64 N). Apollodorus (see App.) indicates that the exposed child was named Paris by the herdsman who raised him, but gained the name Alexandros as a powerful youth 'protecting' (ἀλεξήσας) the local flocks. Varro (see App.) links this etymology with Euripides, and hence very probably with this play, noting that Ennius' Latin rendition, *defensor hominum*, 'defender of men', misses the verbal connection. The etymology suits the prologue-speech (cf. on *Antiope* F 181–182; Bremer 310 cites van Looy in *Zetesis* [Antwerp-Utrecht, 1973], 344–67), although some have placed it later, e.g. Snell 35–6 (assigning the prologue to Cassandra), Coles 23 (assuming Paris's origin was not yet revealed to the audience). The verse of Ennius which Varro quotes (Enn. F 20 below), 'And so the herdsmen now call Paris Alexander', presumably reflects Eur.'s text. See also on Hypoth. 6–7. In the summary of the exposure story in Schol. *And.* 293 the name Paris is connected with the satchel (πήρα) in which the herdsman is supposed to have carried the baby; this too may have appeared in Eur.'s prologue. **excelled...in beauty and strength:** cf. Hypoth. 13–14, F 61d.8.

43–46. These fragments are generally grouped together and placed in an anapaestic dialogue between Hecuba and the entering Chorus (F 43) followed by spoken dialogue between her and the Chorus-leader (F 44–6): cf. Introd., pp. 37–8, Crönert 12, Snell 5, 24, Scodel 25–6, 41. The Chorus probably consisted of Trojan women friendly to Hecuba. Priam is not the second speaker since he is mentioned in F 46.3. Hypoth. 7–10 emphasizes Hecuba's grief and lamentation over the baby's exposure, probably reflecting this scene. Admetus receives and resists consolation similarly in *Alc.* 1070–86.

43 (46 N). All of us must die, etc.: a common consolation for the loss of loved ones: see on *Hyps.* F 757.920–7, also *Alc.* 416–9, *Cresph.* F 454, *Temenid.* F 733.   **wisdom practises:** i.e., wise people train themselves. **feeling the pain...in moderation:** again common advice, e.g. *Alc.* 1077, S. *El.* 140ff.; many examples in the source of this fragment, Stob. 4.44. METRE: anapaestic.

44 (45 N). no man is fortunate in everything: cf. on *Androm.* F 152–3; *HF* 1314. The thought may include the equally common idea that no human can expect to be wholly fortunate at any time, like *Sthen.* F 661.1–5 (almost identical in its first line), *IA* 15–34, Bacchyl. 5.50–5; cf. on *Androm.* F 143.

45 (44 N). one should bring grief to an end in time: a conventional thought, e.g. F 46.5 below, *Ino* F 418, *Mel.* F 507; first at Hom. *Il.* 24.46–9, 128–9, 522–6, 549–51. The Greek verb is a race-course metaphor, 'turn griefs (around the turning-post and back towards the finishing-line)': *Supp.* 748, LSJ κάμπτω II. **saying...easier than bearing...:** the topic of Stob. 4.49, which also cites *Alc.* 1078.

46.1. *E.g.* 'You have <*a house that is full*> of <*male*> children' (Crönert), or 'You have <*an abundance/wealth*)> of <*male*> children <*still*>' (Diggle, Kannicht).
2. '*And yet I* grieve because <*we killed*> *our child*' Snell (or '< *I have lost*>' Diggle, or '<*I brought myself to kill*>' Lee).
3. E.g. '**Unhappy Priam, and** <*unfortunate the child's mother*>!' (Crönert and Snell).
4. Perhaps '**As we well know, who** <*both*> **suffered** <*and brought ourselves to act*>', i.e., Priam and Hecuba caused their own misery by killing the baby (Collard, cf. Lee in 2 n. above). Or perhaps '**As we well know who suffered**, <*not having forgotten it*>', provoking the next response (Cropp).
5. One should not lament old troubles, etc.: the whole line (= F 43 N) is cited in Stob. 4.56 *(Consolatory Advice).* Cf. on F 45 above.
6–10. Probably Hecuba (6, 8–10) continues to resist the Chorus-leader's advice (5,7). In 6 Schadewaldt offered '**Some** <*stranger can say this, but*> **his mother** <*cannot*>'. In 7 Crönert suggested '<*The*> **child perished, so they say**', and Münscher added (e.g.) '<*in the mountain-hollows*>'. Assignment of 8–10 to Hecuba (Snell) is plausible in view of ἐμο[(= ἐμο[ὶ '*for me*'?) in 9. She may be insisting on her loss of happiness, the extent of her griefs, and (with Crönert's τερ]πνὰς '*pleasant*' in 10) either the paradoxical pleasures of grief or the pleasures she cannot now enjoy; Snell reconstructed tentatively on these lines (see his or Kannicht's app.). The alternative]μνας in 10 might give μερί]μνας '*cares*'. Then **because of troubles** (πρὸς κακ[ῶν) and **added to troubles** (πρὸς κακ[οῖς) seem equally possible.
11–12. E.g. '<*And now*> *I* see your child <*Cassandra arriving here before*> the shrine <*of Apollo*>' (Wilamowitz). Diggle's '*coming*' fits the space better. Webster's '*from* (the shrine)' accommodates the location of the play before the palace, not the temple. On Cassandra's possible entry here see Introd., p. 38.

46a. Content and placing are uncertain. Most scholars accept the view of Crönert (13) that the fr. contains a dialogue between Priam (addressed in 8, 11, 17) and someone else about the games established for his dead son (8, 10, 12, 18). Hypoth. 10–12 suggests that this may have followed the discussion of Hecuba's grief. In general see Snell 34–5, Coles 41–2 (in light of the Hypothesis, and with some textual revisions), Scodel 27–8. An allusion in Ar. *Birds* 508–12 to Priam appearing on the tragic stage with a sceptre surmounted by a bird may refer to his entry here, as Hartung first suggested. If all this happened at the start of the second episode, Priam will have been interrupted on his way to the games by the complaining herdsmen (second chorus) arriving with the captive Paris. The other speaker has been identified as the Chorus-leader, Hecuba, Cassandra, a retainer, or Deiphobus: the last is favoured by e.g. Snell, Scodel, Jouan (1998, 49).

Crönert and Snell offer some speculative supplements in col. i which are not recorded here. Col. ii gives the end of the scene, including the first few letters of lines from a scene-closing speech (30–40) and probably the start of a choral passage (41–3) indicated by the marginal coronis-mark. (Turner 1979, 4 warns that the meaning of the coronis in this early papyrus is uncertain; there are similar signs at F 62d.44, 48).

5. servant: in F 62d.4 the word λάτρις may refer to Paris, but the inference that it does so here (Jouan 1966, 118; Coles 42) is very insecure. It could refer to a servant assisting Priam.

6. *horse-drawn* carriage: élite transport (cf. *El.* 966, 998–9, 1135–6, *IT* 370, *IA* 613, 623), so probably Priam's conveyance to the games (Snell 34–5).

8. the child you have honoured(?): presumably Paris, honoured by the games.

10. Crönert's πόν]οι gives '<*labours*> **which are being put on**', i.e. the games (cf. 12).

11. you are cleansing this land: the verb ἀφαγνίζω and noun ἀφαγνισμός regularly refer to ritual cleansing, e.g. Hippocr. *Sacr. Disease* 1.112 Littré, Dionys. Hal. *Ant.Rom.* 2.68.4; cf. J. Rudhardt, *Notions fondamentales de la pensée religieuse (etc.)* (Geneva, 1958), 172. ('Deconsecration' may be meant in the special case of Alcestis returning from the dead in *Alc.* 1146: Parker, *Miasma* 329 n. 10). What kind of cleansing is meant here is unclear. As Coles (42) and Scodel (28) note, Paris's death by exposure would not have caused pollution or plague. The present-tense verb can hardly refer to a purification prompted by the supposed killing of Paris twenty years previously. Huys (*Tale*, 128–9) suggests a response to continued fear of the prophecies about Alexander's birth. Cf. Di Giuseppe (above, F 41a–42d n.), 71–3.

12. funereal labours: cf. 10 above.

15. Crönert's word-division gives '*O you who govern the* **city**', with solemn vocative participle (cf. *Hyps.* F 757.853). Unlikely as this seems, it is hard to construct sense with the alternatives sketched by Kannicht.

16. Crönert's ἀνάσ]τασίν giving '<*ruination*> **of the land**' is commonly printed and seems apt (cf. 11, 17), but there are plausible alternatives: στάσιν 'discord', κατάστασιν 'condition', μετάστασιν 'alteration', ἐφεστᾶσιν 'they are in charge'.

17. evils: probably those that Priam sought to avert by having the baby killed. Snell's supplement gives '<*and*> **you could provide** <*an escape*> **from** <*these*> **evils**'; but there could be a past reference, e.g. '<*You acted so that*> **you could provide** <*a relief/defence*> **from evils**'.

18. Crönert (App.) suggests '*for the* **dead** <*child*>'.

48–51, 56, 55, 57, 59, 61, 60. These fragments probably belong together in the debate scene in which Paris was brought before Priam by irate fellow-herdsmen (a secondary chorus), justified himself to the king, and won permission to compete in the games: Hypoth. 17–21, Introd., pp. 38–9. The exact order and contexts of the frs. remain unclear. Priam is addressed in F 48 and 56, and he probably addresses Paris in F 60. Five frs.

attacking slaves (F 48–51, 57) are known from a single chapter of Stobaeus; the order of citation (48, 49, 50, 57, 51) might match their order in Eur.'s text (cf. R. Piccione, *RFIC* 122 [1994], 175–217 at 188 n. 3, 202–3, 209–11), but F 57 is perhaps better ascribed to Paris along with the frs. attacking his opponents' abuse of rhetoric and wealth (F 56, 55). F 59 and 61 are harder to pin down, while F 60 is probably Priam bringing the debate to a close by allowing Paris the opportunity to prove himself. F 54, often assigned to this scene, is better placed at the end of the messenger's speech. Eur. F 958, 976, 1068 have been doubtfully placed in this scene (see Introd., *Other proposed ascriptions*).

48. a slave who has bigger ideas than he should: Paris's arrogance is the cause of his fellow-slaves' hostility (Hypoth. 15–16). The fr. bears on the identification of his opponent (cf. Introd., p. 39). Coles (24) proposed Deiphobus (cf. Scodel 29–30), but Kovacs (52, 56) points out that Deiphobus could not address his father as **Priam** (he assigns the fr. to Hecuba trying after the games to persuade Priam to kill Paris). Huys makes this a Chorus-leader's comment on the debate (*AC* 64 [1995], 187–90; cf. Jouan 1998, 50; Kannicht app. on F 48–61c). But the advisory tone is unlikely if the Chorus was female (Introd., p. 38), and the phrasing of **You are certainly wise...** (with 'transitional' μὲν οὖν: Denniston, *GP* 470–3) shows that these lines are part of a larger argument: cf. e.g. *El.* 1035, *Tro.* 400, *IA* 924.   [**has bigger ideas:** the Copenhagen herm's μεῖζον recurs in F 963.2 and is appropriate here (cf. Huys cited above, and *Tale*, 351 n. 932). Stob.'s μᾶλλον giving 'is cleverer' is less apt though often printed.]

49. so vile is the race of slaves: for prejudice against slaves cf. e.g. *Alcmaeon* F 86.6–7, and F 57 n. below for contrary stress on slaves' capacity for good.   **all belly, etc.:** i.e. driven solely by their appetite for food, like the shepherds who are 'mere bellies' in Hes. *Theog.* 26 (see West's Comm. for further examples), Odysseus in Hom. *Od.* 18.53 (cf. Russo on *Od.* 18.44), or the unknown speaker of Eur. F 915; cf. *Antiope* F 201.3–4, Soph. F 564.   **beyond that:** i.e. beyond their next meal (ὀπίσω 'in the future', LSJ II).

50. Slaves who become attached, etc.: probably criticizing Paris's wish to gain Priam's favour and enter the world of free men at the games. The sentiment is an obvious one, but it is also easy to find commendations of slaves' loyalty to masters, e.g. *Meleag.* F 529.   [Elmsley's αἴρονται '**get**' replacing Stob.'s αἱροῦνται 'choose' restores a common metaphor for incurring conflict; cf. LSJ ἀείρω IV.4.]

51. slaves...stronger than their masters: probably Priam is warned against favouring the gifted Paris, but the plotting against Paris after his victories is another possible context: see Snell 39 n. 5, Kovacs 53, 57.   [Wilamowitz (in Crönert 16 n. 2) reordered the words to read οὐ γὰρ καλὸν | δούλους πεπᾶσθαι, and then identified the second line with F 62d.43. The re-ordering avoids an enjambment which is typically 'Sophoclean' but not unknown in Eur., e.g. *Mel.D.* F 492.4–5, F 494.19–20, *Archelaus* F 240.1–2.]

56. slander is a terrible thing, etc.: the opening of a speech of self-defence, presumably addressed by Paris to Priam (**My lord**). Such appeals typically include complaints that the speaker may be worsted by slander (e.g. Antiphon 6.7, *Tetral.* 1.4.1, Andoc. 1.6, Lys. 19.5) or dishonesty (cf. Collard on *Hec.* 1187–94) or his own lack of eloquence (cf. Barrett on *Hipp.* 986–7).   **ineloquence...eloquent:** the abstracts ἀγλωσσία, εὐγλωσσία seem to have been invented in the rhetorical discourse of Eur.'s day. For ἀγλωσσία see Antiphon 87 B 97 DK (on Antiphon B 44(a).i.18 see Pendrick [cited on F 61b], 350–1). In Pind. *Nem.* 8.24 the adj. ἄγλωσσος refers to Ajax, also ineloquent and traduced. For εὐγλωσσία see *Antiope* F 206.4, F 928b.2 (= F 156.2 Austin), Anon. Iamblich. (89 DK) 1.1, Ar. *Knights* 837 (cf. Critias 88 A 17 DK), and for εὔγλωσσος A. *Supp.* 775, Eur. here and F 899.1, Ar. *Clouds* 445. εὐγλωσσία is associated with dishonesty in F 206, F 928b, *Knights* 837, *Clouds* 445.   **gets less credit:** lit. 'wins less', an image from competition (LSJ φέρω A.VI.3).

55. Wealth is an unjust thing, etc.: an old truth (e.g. *Ino* F 419, *Hipp.Cal.* F 438, A. *Ag.* 772–81, Theogn. 153–4 = Solon F 6.3 *IEG*). Probably Paris is protesting against actual or expected mistreatment by the royal family.

57. The speaker is probably the 'slave' Paris himself, and probably in the debate-scene (although Murray 133 and Kovacs 61 place the fr. during the later physical attack on him).   **slaves not in name, etc.:** lit. 'not having the slavish in word but possessing it through circumstance', i.e. probably 'nominally free yet actually slavish' (addressed to free men) rather than 'slavish not just nominally but actually' (addressed to slaves). A free man may have the character of a slave just as a slave may have the character of a free man (cf. on *Mel.* F 511, Kannicht on *Hel.* 726–33). The distinction between title and reality is sophistic. [Jacobs' φύσει would replace **in reality** with 'in your nature'.]

59. The lower sort, etc.: quoted among similar passages by Stob. *On marriage*; cf. on *Antiope* F 214, *Mel.* F 502. Kannicht cites Cleobulus' saying (DK 10 3.α.18), 'Marry from your own kind, for if you marry one of your superiors you will get masters, not kinsmen'. The fr. is usually included in the debate-scene, as a disparagement of Paris's aspirations. The comment probably refers to class rather morals, but there could be an ironic allusion to Paris's future marriage with Helen.

61. I loathe a man who is clever, etc.: either directed at Paris in the same vein as F 48, or by him at his opponent in the same vein as F 56.   [All the conjectures in the App. adjust an unmetrical text without altering the meaning, Cobet's most simply.]

60. Time will show, etc.: usually ascribed to Priam addressing Paris at the end of the debate scene (after the recognition, Kovacs 61–3 disputed by Huys 1986, 34). For time's influence in this play cf. F 42 n. Its revelatory power is an old topic, e.g. Solon F 10, Theogn. 967, Pind. *Ol.* 10.53–5; cf. on *Antiope* F 223.107–8.

61b (52 N). This and the next fragment are cited in Stob. 4.29, *On nobility*. They have generally been assigned to a stasimon following the debate scene because of their relevance to its main issue and in particular Priam's rejection of prejudice against Paris in

F 60. In light of the Hypothesis they might fit almost as well after the messenger-scene when Paris has proved himself in the games, especially if the messenger-speech ended with F 54; a stasimon at that point is possible but not certain, cf. Introd., p. 40. The argument is simple, but hinges on an ambiguity in the word εὐγένεια, 'nobility'. In its literal sense 'good birth', *eugeneia* should not be identified with 'virtue' (F 61b, 1–2), for in origin or 'in nature' (φύσει) all men are similar (3–7); it is only by convention (νόμωι, an artificial human construct) that we have come to distinguish 'good birth' and 'low birth' and to identify 'good birth' as 'nobility' in the sense of 'virtue' (8). Nobility in *that* sense is really a product of moral discernment which is a gift of god (9–10), and so moral virtue is the measure of true nobility (F 61c). For this interpretation see especially Lanza 241–3, and cf. Scodel 31, Jouan 1998, 50–1 (differing from Jouan 1966, 127–8). Lanza showed that these fragments are very unlikely to involve the second chorus, and this is even less likely now that it is known to have been hostile to Paris. Some scholars had attributed both fragments to the second chorus; others including Snell attributed F 61b to the second chorus and F 61c to the main chorus, thus creating a debate between defenders and critics of Paris (see on F 61c below, and for documentation Snell 40 n. 2, Kannicht app.).

The discussion is conventional in pointing out the unreliability of apparent criteria of virtue such as birth, wealth (cf. F 54 n. below), or a 'noble' appearance (cf. *El.* 550–1, *Ion* 237–40), and conversely the lack of a reliable visible indicator (cf. e.g. Theogn. 117–28, *Carm. Conv.* 889 *PMG*, Eur. *Med.* 516–9, *Hipp.* 925–7, *Hipp.Cal.* F 439, *HF* 655–72. *El.* 367–79). But the supporting argument is cast in the rationalistic or 'sophistic' terms of Euripides' day: *(a)* it rests on the distinction between 'nature' (*physis*), which is real and permanent, and human convention (*nomos*), which is artificial and temporary (7–8); *(b)* real human nature is traced by an anthropological enquiry into the origin of the human race (3–6); and *(c)* a conclusion is drawn about the irrationality of current moral and social values (1–2, 9–10). Antiphon's contrast between the natural similarity of all human beings and the artificial differences of their *nomoi* (Antiphon 87 B 44(b)) has rightly been compared, although there is no explicit attack on social distinctions in the extant text of Antiphon. Cf. also Hippias 86 C 1.17–20 DK (= Pl. *Prot.* 337c–d), Hdt. 3.38. In Soph. *Tereus* F 591 (again quoted in Stob. *On nobility*) a chorus reflects that humans are 'a single breed' (ἓν φῦλον) divided only by their differing lots in life. See S. Luria, *Aegyptus* 5 (1924), 326–30, *Hermes* 64 (1929), 491–7; Wilamowitz, *Kl.Schr.* 4.443–5; E. Hall, *Inventing the Barbarian* (Oxford, 1989), 218–21; G. Pendrick, *Antiphon the Sophist: the Fragments* (Cambridge, 2002), 65–6, 351–6.

METRE: lyric iambics. F 61c could be the beginning of an antistrophe since it matches the metre of F 61b.1–2 nearly enough and the word εὐγένεια recurs in the same position. For this and the colometry see Snell 40 n. 2.

1–2. Our talk will be idle: lit. 'Redundant-in-telling (will be) our tale'. Pleonasm in compound adjective and noun ('-telling...tale') is much used by Euripides: see on *Arch.* F 242. **human, βρότειον:** an important word contrasting the false nobility defined by human criteria with the true nobility determined by god (9–10).

3–5. distinct human beings: i.e. 'distinct from other creatures': cf. Luria 1929 (above), 491–2 and esp. Archelaus 60 A 4 DK: 'as the earth first warmed...creatures appeared in great numbers, including humans. All of them had the same diet, getting nourishment from the mud, and were short-lived. Later they developed reproduction from each other, and humans were distinguished (διεκρίθησαν) from the other creatures and established rulers, laws, crafts, communities, etc.' [Meineke placed ὁμοίαν...ὄψιν before διὰ δ' ἔκρινεν...βροτούς, thus altering the argument radically so that mother earth gave the same appearance to all humans and racial differences were generated later, by climate. This misinterpretation was followed by Wilamowitz, *Kl.Schr.* I.205, IV.443–4.]

5–7. she bred: the verb ἐκπαιδεύω, lit. 'educate, train', is here applied to natural endowment. The creatures of earth and air are their παιδεύματα, 'pupils', in *And.* 1101, *Aeolus* F 24b.5. **similar:** not clones, but a **single breed** (7) with the same basic physical features; cf. Antiphon F 44(b).ii–iii. **no special feature:** i.e. no physical feature differentiating 'well-born' from 'low-born', 'noble' from 'low', 'good' from 'bad' (see general note above). [7. καὶ δυσγενές: this correction of Stob.'s unmetrical καὶ τὸ δυσγενές is simpler than Wilamowitz's ⟨πέφυκε⟩ καὶ τὸ δυσγενές (giving '**Well-born and low-born are** <*by nature*> **a single breed**'): cf. Diggle, *Euripidea* 283 n. 42.]

8. has made the well-born proud: lit. 'fulfils it (so as to be) proud'(?). ['it' can easily be 'the well-born' since 'good birth' is the subject of the whole passage, but κραίνω ('fulfil, accomplish, deliver') is not used elsewhere with a predicate and the text may be corrupt or defective: cf. Diggle (above) 282–3, and other conjectures in Kannicht's app. (none convincing). For γαῦρον '**proud**' (questioned by Diggle) cf. especially *Bell.* F 285.11, 'the man with proud (γαῦρον) and noble (γενναῖον) blood'.]

9–10. intelligence and understanding...make nobility: other Euripidean speakers rejecting false criteria of nobility/virtue identify various moral virtues as the proper criteria: decent conduct in general (*El.* 383–5), justness (*Dictys* F 336), courage and justness (*Mel.D.* F 495.40–3). **and god that gives it:** if all men are alike by nature, and true nobility exists but cannot be humanly acquired like wealth or family status, then true nobility must come from another source, i.e. 'god'. [These lines complete rather than contradict the argument of the whole fragment. There is no need to think that they do not belong here, although οὐχ ὁ πλοῦτος '**not wealth**' is a little crudely phrased and could be paraphrase rather than quotation.]

61c (= 53 N). The conclusion of F 61b is reaffirmed. Those imagining a debate between the two choruses took the meaning to be, 'Nobility belongs not to low-born men but to well-born ones'.

61d, 61a, 54. Messenger scene: see Hypoth. 21–3 for some of the content, and notes below for the placing of F 61a and 54. Enn. F 19 is a remark of the Chorus-leader or Hecuba from the beginning of the scene. Enn. F 24 and probably F 22* Sn, 22 and 23 are from the messenger's speech; also perhaps *TrGF* adesp. F 286 and 289 (see Introd., *Other proposed ascriptions*).

61d. Schadewaldt's identification of context and speakers is generally accepted: the messenger announces Paris's victories in a brief dialogue with the Chorus-leader before

Hecuba comes out to receive his report (cf. *IT* 1284ff.). Speculative supplements by Crönert, Schadewaldt and Page are collected in Kannicht's app.

4. Crönert's and Lefke's supplements give '**To fortune** *I ascribe* [lit. *'give'*] *everything*', the Chorus-leader commenting on the unexpectedness of Paris's victory.

5. naturally superior...: Paris's natural superiority explains and justifies his victory. The topic recurs in Hector's argument with Deiphobus, F 62b.33–4; cf. on Hypoth. 13–14.

7. Crönert's '**worthy** <*of the kingdom*>' is favoured by Huys (*Tale*, 352), but such a suggestion is hardly compatible with Hector's nonchalance in the next scene.

8. he <*is/being*> so *outstanding*: probably a comment on Paris's combining athletic success with beauty (cf. F 42d), as the reply suggests.

9. Page's supplement gives '**Everything that a man** *should* <*achieve who is well-born*>'. Coles and Kannicht suggest '**a** <*good*> **man**' (cf. F 60.2).

12. Crönert's κ[ρίνουσι giving '**Where** <*are they deciding*> **the contest**' has been widely adopted but hardly suits the placing of this fragment in the messenger-scene (Crönert had placed it earlier).

13–14. Perhaps referring to Priam awarding the victory-prizes, Crönert's νικητ[ήρι(α).

61a (47 N). Those who should bring you victory, etc.: lit. 'From where you should win, you fail, etc.'; Priam is credited with victories won by Paris rather than his own sons (a dramatic irony, since Paris *is* his own son). The fr. has often been placed at the end of a messenger-speech delivered to Priam (Hartung, Murray 130, Webster 170) or, recognizing that Priam was present at the games himself, as a comment addressed to him by the Chorus-leader on his return from the games (Snell 39). But the Hypothesis makes it unlikely that Priam returned at this point, so others have proposed that the Chorus addresses him in his absence (e.g. Scodel 31, 117, Huys [1986] 35), or that this is a comment on Priam's decision in the debate scene (Kannicht app.). The first of these solutions is far-fetched: these three pointed and argumentative lines have little in common with the passages compared by Huys, which are either brief outbursts of emotion (*Alc.* 144, *Pho.* 1425–6, *Bacc.* 1031 [addressing a god], S. *Ant.* 572), or spurious (*Med.* 1233–5), or not addressed to absentees (*Hcld.* 640, S. *OT* 1236). The second is hard to reconcile with the speaker's insistence on Priam's *success* through a slave's *victory*. The complaint may be quoted by the messenger as one made to Priam during the games as Paris's successes became evident. Direct speech is a regular dramatizing feature of messenger-speeches: cf. *Pha.* 168–71, 176–7, *Mel.D.* F 495.8–9, 15–17, and for Eur.'s extant plays De Jong, *Narrative in Drama* 131–9, 199–200. A report of dissension at the games links well with Deiphobus' angry arrival in the next scene and is probably represented in Enn. F 22.

2–3. You win with your slaves, etc.: suggesting that Priam can claim his slave's victories like a racehorse or chariot-team owner.   [**You win:** νικᾶις, picking up the verb from line 1, is Musgrave's emendation of an obviously confused ms. tradition.]

54. Wealth and excessive luxury, etc.: the disjunction between wealth and virtue is a common topic in archaic and classical Greek poetry (cf. e.g. Cropp on *El.* 368–72), although a connection between poverty and wrongdoing can also be asserted, e.g. *El.*

375–6. This fr. has usually been assigned to Paris in the debate-scene, but Kovacs (53) puts it at the end of the messenger's report (or less probably in Hecuba's reaction to it); cf. Huys, *Tale* 353. This makes good sense of **it turns out** (ἄρα with past-tense verb indicating an old truth newly realized, cf. Denniston, *GP* 36–7). For such sententious conclusions to messenger-speeches see on *Mel.D.* F 495.40–3. There may have been an ironic foreshadowing of Paris's own corruption by luxury after he joined the royal family (cf. Introd., p.000). εὐανδρίαν, **manliness:** cf. *Supp.* 913, F 1052.5, 7 in similar arguments; more generally 'virtue', *El.* 367. [Clement's παίδευμ(α) '**train-ing**' fitting with the child-rearing metaphor in lines 3–4 is preferable to Stob.'s banal βούλευμ(α) 'strategy' (retained by e.g. Snell and Jouan). In line 4 Stob.'s μοχθοῦντ(α) gives awkward sense, 'children who do better hard work'.]

62a–d. These fragments of the Strasbourg papyrus were re-arranged by Coles (1974, 38–58), who saw that F 62b (his fr. 23a) had been wrongly combined with F 62d to make the end of P. Strasb. 2343 (= Crönert's fr. 6, Snell's fr. 43), and that the four separate fragments 62a–d may well come from a sequence of columns containing a single extens-ive scene: Hector and Deiphobus return from the games to meet Hecuba in F 62a, the three converse in F 62b col. ii, and Hecuba and Deiphobus plot to kill Paris in F 62c and 62d. In the most economical reconstruction, five columns containing about 175–200 lines would have contained F 62a (upper half of col. 1), F 62b.i (foot of col. 1), F 62b.ii (lower half of col. 2), F 62d.i (top of col. 3), F 62c (foot of col. 3), F 62d.ii (top half of col. 4), F 62d.iii (top half of col. 5): see the diagram in Coles 1974, 39, reproduced in Huys 1986, 10. The reconstruction of this scene has been discussed, after Coles, by Scodel 31–4 and extensively by Huys 1986 (with summary, p. 33). Either a choral song or a dialogue between Hecuba and the Chorus intervened between the messenger's exit and the entry of Deiphobus and Hector in F 62a, since the actor playing the messenger was needed for one of them (cf. Huys 1986, 11–12).

62a. Deiphobus and Hector enter quarrelling, like Neoptolemus and Odysseus in S. *Phil.* 1222ff., Menelaus and the servant in *IA* 303ff. Hecuba is already on stage (line 3). The text of lines 2–8 is discussed by J. Diggle, *CQ* 47 (1997), 98–100.

2–4. Probably *<And now, I see>* Hector *<here coming home>* **from the *toils* of the games, and his brother, your two sons, and they have come, etc.**', with 3 στείχοντα (Jacob/Diggle) or περῶντα (Kannicht, perhaps better for the space) and 4 πρὸς οἶκον 'home' (Kannicht). [For the wording in 2–3 see Diggle. In 4 Diggle's suggestion gives awkward phrasing, '**and his brother – your two sons – *<Deiphobus>*...**'. The name may have been unneeded if Deiphobus was prominent in the messenger-speech.]

5–6. Probably '*<I approve of>* **no one** who is **ill-disposed**, *<but then in turn>* **softens his attitude,** *towards* **bad** *people*', with supplements by Münscher or Kannicht in 5 and Diggle in 6. [In 6 Crönert and Kannicht suggest '*<but when seized by his troubles>*'.]

7–8. Diggle's '*considers <them major>*' provides a neat antithesis (cf. *Auge* F 275.4), improving on Crönert's '*considers <it terrible>*'. †**contends with fear†:** for the sense of the verb cf. LSJ συνίστημι B.II.2; but what fear would Deiphobus be contending with? Huys (1986, 16–17) suggests fear of Paris's rivalry, but this has little to do with turning minor complaints into major ones, and is not reflected in Deiphobus' response. [No good alternative for the verb has been found. Huys takes it to mean 'conspires through fear' (cf. LSJ B.III.1), as if Deiphobus were already plotting, but the bare singular verb can hardly mean this. φθόνωι seems an attractive alternative to φόβωι, but 'contends with envy' is still unconvincing.]

9. *<And how>:* καὶ conveys indignation, as e.g. *Hcld.* 254, *El.* 225; Denniston, *GP* 309–11.   **pained in your spirit:** here and in 12 'the almost physical pain of humiliation' is expressed (Huys 1986, 16 n. 22).

11–12. Perhaps (with Collard) *'You <incite me excessively>*, **Deiphobus; what need do I have** *<to feel anger* (or *for ill feeling)? This is not>* **an occasion, etc.'.**   [For Collard's ἐπαί]ρεις cf. *Supp.* 581, LSJ ἐπαίρω II.1. Wilamowitz's *'You <are too dispirited>'* and Kannicht's *'You <are needlessly dispirited>'* give inappropriate sense. In 12 Wilamowitz's *'<to hate him? For this is not>'* is far too long. One expects about ten letters (which favours Collard's δυσθυμίας *'for ill feeling'*.]

13–14. Lefke's supplements give *'<Through faint-heartedeness>* **you are bearing these things lightly,** *<and>* **you will be conspicuous to the Trojans** *<as inferior to a slave>.*

15. Cropp's μέν[ος might give 'to generate youthful passion' (cf. LSJ φύω A I.4).

16. Hector may now be talking *about* Deiphobus. In 16 *'wants <to be> intemperate'* (Crönert) or *'wants intemperate <things>'*, i.e. 'has intemperate desires' (Collard, Cropp), are plausible.

17–21. The distribution of lines between speakers becomes impossible to guess.

17. *to be yoked/joined(?):* presumably metaphorical as in e.g. *Hel.* 1654 'joined in marriage', *Alc.* 482 'yoked to wandering' (both compared by Kannicht).   [The correction of –χθοι to –χθαι seems needed. Snell's misreading of the papyrus (see App.) and his conjecture νεόζευκτοι 'newly wed' led to the idea that Deiphobus was blaming Hector's complacency on his recent marriage to Andromache.]

62b. Context and placing: see above on 62a–d. The papyrus shows speaker-changes at 37 and 39, and might have done so anywhere before 30 where the left margins are missing. Lines 23–6 could be Deiphobus describing the possible consequences of Paris's successes. Lines 30–6 must be Hector rebuking Deiphobus, and he probably exits after this speech. The brief comment in 37–8 is probably from the Chorus-leader. Lines 39ff. addressed to Deiphobus are reasonably assigned to Hecuba, already the third party in this scene. See further the notes below, and generally Snell 41–5, Coles 48–9, Huys 1986, 18–20.

22–8. What were thought to be the beginnings of these lines before Coles detached them from Snell's fr. 43.85–91 are now F 62d.57–63.

23. Either *'free sons'* (Crönert) or *'all free (men?)'* (Snell).

30. *neither* **building up** *his* **estate:** as a slave Paris must have acted for honour rather than gain?

33. if he is superior, etc.: Paris's natural superiority is again advertised (cf. on Hypoth. 13–14). Hector suggests that D.'s loss was due to his own physical limitations (**nature**); there would be no point in punishing himself for these, and there is no point in blaming Paris for his physical superiority. Scodel (106) compares Helen's rhetorical ploy in *Tro.* 948: 'Punish Aphrodite (rather than me, since she made me fall in love with Paris)'. Crönert (15) took it that Deiphobus should discipline and train himself better, but this is less conciliatory and misses the point of the appeal to *physis*. There is perhaps a reminiscence of Paris's riposte to Hector in Hom. *Il.* 13.785-7: 'I declare that I do not lack prowess insofar as my power goes; but one cannot fight beyond one's strength, however hard one tries'. [Latte's σοῦ '**your own**' (cf. Snell 45 n. 3) provides a clearer caesura and a more emphatic contrast than Crönert's σου ('if he is superior to you...'), although Eur. often uses phrases like τὴν φύσιν to mean 'my/your/one's nature', e.g. *Ion* 643, *IA* 1411, *Auge* F 265a.1, *Chrysippus* F 840.2, F 904.2. The sense 'punish Nature', recommended by Luria (cited on F 61b; cf. Scodel 106), leaves κυριώτερος γὰρ εἶ unexplained.]

34. **which is what defeated you**: lit. 'by which you were defeated'.   **you have more authority over that**: D. is more entitled to punish himself than to punish Paris, who is Priam's slave and was permitted by him to compete.   [For κυριώτερος used in this way cf. Thuc. 4.18.1. The more obvious sense 'you have more authority than Paris has' (cf. e.g. *And.* 580, *Hel.* 1634, *Bacc.* 505) seems less apposite here. Hardly '*tu es trop grand seigneur*', '*tu es trop imbu de tes droits*' (Jouan 1966, 129; 1998, 70 and 71).]

35. **But I...**: the papyrus may have had ἐνείρω ('I weave in, insert'), but Snell's (43-4) interpretation of this as 'I (am prepared to) crown him' is implausible. Körte's ἐπαινῶ makes good sense, 'I commend him', but the corruption would be hard to explain. At the end, Reitzenstein suggests 'for if <*he is the*> strongest <*man*> . . . .'

37. [**Hector**: Lefke's Ἕκτωρ, questioned by Coles (48), is confirmed by Kannicht (although ων written as in e.g. F 62d.27 ἔχων, 31 ἀμμάτων, seems possible). A reference to Hector seems presupposed by **his** (38) and **This man** (39).]

39–42. Hecuba comments on Hector's attitude, then on Deiphobus' wish to kill Paris. It is unclear whether she *approves* it by saying it will be painful but in the long run valuable (Snell 45, with supplements quoted in Kannicht's app.), or that D. will eliminate what is causing them grief (Murray 133), or *disapproves* it (for now) because of the pain that the killing of a slave will cause (Huys 1986, 19–20).   **(my) child Deiphobus**: reading and interpretation are defended by Huys (1986, 18–19), noting similar phrasing in *Pho.* 528–9.   **you will do**: the Greek verb (ῥέζω) suggests drastic or damaging action (cf. *Alc.* 263, *Med.* 1292, *Andr.* 838, *El.* 1226).

62c. Placing and context: see above on F 62a–d, with Coles 38–9, 44–5, 49–50. If this fr. immediately precedes F 62d col. ii, the sentence begun in line 7 here continues with lines 22–3 there (see on 6–7 below). The speaker, preoccupied as it seems with Paris's usurpation of the rightful position of the royal princes, is probably Hecuba (so e.g. Snell, Page, Huys, Kannicht rather than Deiphobus (e.g. Crönert, Lefke). Possibly she suspects that Paris is a secret bastard son of Priam (Introd., p. 40).

2. an incidental matter: incidental to the plot, or subordinate to the intruder Paris? For the latter Crönert (10) compares *El.* 63; cf. Huys 1986, 22 n. 42.

4–5 Page developing on Snell (see App.) suggested '**and those secretly** <*saying that the son*> **of a slave-woman** <*has defeated free-born offspring*>'. Huys (above) expects '**those secretly** <*born from*> **a slave-woman**...'. [Kannicht's alternative reading (App.) suggests the adj. λαθραίας['secret').]

6–7. Surely...But...: Hecuba contemplates an undesirable outcome, then vows she will not allow it to happen. For μή + Indic. in an apprehensive question cf. e.g. *Hipp.* 799, *Hec.* 1272, *El.* 568 (Diggle, *Euripidea* 160); and for this followed by a strong contrary assertion (ἀλλά...) cf. A. *Pers.* 344–5. **woe is me:** this seems to be the only instance of ἰώ μοι used in dramatic dialogue, which suggests a female speaker (Hecuba). In 7, Körte's supplement shows how this sentence could continue in F 62d.22: '**But** <*it is*> *not – woe is me! – <possible to behold (= endure) this,*> | **that he, being who he is, should be admired, etc.**'.

62d, col.ii. Placing and context: see above on F 62a–d and F 62c. The plotting continues. Snell's speaker-identifications (Hecuba 22–3 etc., Deiphobus 24 etc.) are fairly secure. Coles (49, cf. 25, 52) argued for the reverse assignment, but it is much more appropriate for the mother to lay down the essentials of the plan (25, 29) while the headstrong son seeks guidance (24), reacts to it with assurances of action (26, 30), and provides information about Paris's latest activities (28): cf. Lanza 236 n. 1, Huys 1986, 22–3.

23. Page's supplement gives '**and Priam's house** <*not*> **be honoured** <*with the*> *victory*', accurately reflecting the μέν/δέ contrast between Paris and the royal family. [Kannicht sees ω rather than η, then possibly ιμη. Wilamowitz's νικῶνθ' ὡς ('**and to be honoured** <*for defeating*> **Priam's house**') was read by Snell but does not fit the traces according to recent editors; nor does it make the required contrast.]

24. Presumably '**How then** <*will you/shall we arrange things*>, etc.' [Snell's reading (App.) gives '**How then** *do these things* <*run ashore*>', but the traces are very uncertain and the metaphor (cf. *Hipp.* 140, A. *PV* 183) too strong for this context. Collard suggests e.g. πῶς οὖν σ[ὺ θῆσ]εις (or middle θῆσ]ει) ταῦτά γ' for the likely sense.]

25. '**he must die by** *this* (= *my*) **hand**' (with Crönert's τῆιδε) is more likely than '*but* **he must die by** *your* **hand**' (with σῆι δέ, Murray 132). The later iconography and especially Hypoth. 25, 29 support an assault by Hecuba herself, though not necessarily an unassisted one (see Introd., p. 45). Huys (1986, 23–4) rightly argues that Hecuba should take the initiative here, but his comparison with Electra taking charge of the planning of Clytemnestra's murder in *El.* 646ff. is not conclusive. Electra in fact plans to lure Clytemnestra into her house so that *Orestes* can kill her there, like Merope luring Polyphontes to be killed *by her son* in *Cresph.*, and the Chorus and Electra respectively luring Aegisthus to be killed by *Orestes* in A. *Cho.* and S. *El.*

26. He will surely not go unwounded: not 'He is not invulnerable' (Snell 42). Lefke compares S. *OC* 906. [μὴν in the combination οὐ μὴν...γε is usually a strong 'but' or 'yet' (cf. Denniston, *GP* 335), but here seems to be emphatic as in S. *Phil.* 811 (Denniston 331 rejects Jebb's adversative interpretation there).]

27–8. Where might he be, etc.: this exchange may be reflected in Enn. F 208 (printed below with the frs. of Enn. *Alex.*). [**then:** unaccented νυν, as Hecuba gets down to business, seems better than νῦν 'now (at this moment)'.]

28. filling the whole town: for the metaphor cf. *Ion* 1107, *IT* 804.

29. fall into the net: metaphor from animal-hunting (cf. 31), like *HF* 729.   [The beginning of the line is difficult since probably six missing letters must provide four syllables. See Kannicht's app.]

30–37. Deiphobus speaks in 30 (**your children**), probably Hecuba in 31 (continuing the metaphor of 29). The words in the next few lines might be Hecuba instructing Deiphobus (**I wish you to...**) and requiring sufficient numbers to overpower Paris ('*he is a slave, but still...*'), rather as Orestes warns Electra that Clytemnestra will be no pushover (S. *El.* 1243–4).

30. Snell's μηπώποτ' ἐπ]ίδηις, '<*Never yet*> *may you behold*', would fit better with a following participle-construction than with '**that he has power, etc.**'. Perhaps better οὐ μή, '<*Never*> *will you...*' (Lee). Page suggested ε]ἰδῆις, '*...may you (not) know...*'.

31. inside the net: lit. 'within the knots', i.e. knotted cords of the hunting-net. Kannicht compares *Cyc.* 196, *Pho.* 263.

37. Perhaps '*he will cease*' (Crönert) or '*he will regret it*' (Cropp).

62d. col.iii. These brief line-beginnings are the top of the next column, some twenty lines after F 62d col. ii broke off. The analysis of Crönert (15) is generally accepted with variations of detail, and is adopted here with some refinements. In 44–7 the Chorus seems to be commenting on the now completed plot (see 44 n.); the lines are marked with a coronis (like F 46a.41), and the incomplete word beginning 46 suggests they were written as prose, not unexpectedly in an early papyrus text. Lines 48–50, also with coronis and probably lyric written as prose (49 again beginning with an incomplete word), either refer to Hecuba (**mistress**, 48) or call for her attention (**mistress** vocative), so they may either continue the comments in 44–7 or announce the character who seems to arrive in the next lines asking for Hecuba (see 51–3 n.; Coles' suggestion [54] that 51–3 are also choral is based on a doubtful reading, and 44–7 are unlikely to belong to Hecuba as suggested by Coles and Kannicht). Lines 54–5 seem to be the Chorus-leader answering the arriving character's enquiry about Priam and **Hecuba** (52), and saying that **The old man** (54) is absent but **Hecuba** (55) is available. The arriving character is hardly Paris's foster-father (Crönert) since Hypoth. 30 suggests he only arrived later to confirm the recognition, nor Hector (Körte, Snell 42–3, Kannicht's app. on 51–3) since there is nothing for Hector to do at this point (this suggestion was made when F 62d was thought to follow F 62b). Hypoth. 25–6 suggests that the next character to arrive after the plotting is Paris himself, and this may well be what we have here. The wording in 51–5 suggests a character not closely connected with the royal household, and the references to **leaves** (50 n.) and a **victory-song** (53 n.) fit. In *El.* 985ff. and *Antiope* F 223.15ff. there is no interval between the ends of the plotting scenes and the entries of the victims (Clytemnestra, Lycus), accompanied in each case by a few choral lines. Coles, Scodel 34 and Huys 1986, 30 expect a full stasimon after the plotting scene, i.e. after this fragment since there is not enough room for one between cols. ii and iii of F 62d; but the examples just mentioned show that a stasimon is not needed. The dialogue in the plotting scene could have indicated that Paris would arrive at the palace shortly. Deiphobus would not then have needed to go in search of him, and could be lying in wait in the palace.

44. A change: the Chorus anticipates Paris's downfall and the triumph of Priam's family, probably in dochmiac rhythm, as *HF* 735ff. (μεταβολὰ κακῶν, 'A change from evils (comes)', *El.* 1147ff. (ἀμοιβαὶ κακῶν· μετάτροποι πνέουσιν αὗραι δόμων, 'Requitals of evils (come); the winds of the house's fortune are changing direction').

45. The papyrus traces (App.) seem to allow *'we are defeated'* (Snell) or *'winning/ defeating'* (Crönert).

46. *'At the games'* (Snell)?

50. with leaves: probably leaves crowning the victor or scattered on him: cf. *Hec.* 573–4 with Schol. His crowning has been advertised (F 61d.6, 62d.27, Enn. F 23, 208).

51–2. Where, tell me, etc.: probably an enquiry from a newly arriving character, like Lycus seeking Antiope and her rescuers (*Antiope* F 223.19–21, Aegisthus asking for the 'messenger' who has reported Orestes' death (S. *El.* 1442–4), Agave for Cadmus (*Bacc.* 1211), Teucer for Ajax's son (S. *Aj.* 984). [The last two of these examples illustrate the phrasing ποῦ μοι **Where, tell me...**, and make the reading μοι more likely than the alternative ποι mentioned in the App.]

53. *victory-song*: part of Paris's celebration (cf. F 62d.27): cf. *HF* 180, 680 with Bond's notes, *El.* 865 etc.

54. The old man: probably Priam, since Hecuba is mentioned in the next line. Paris's foster-father (often identified here) is not immediately relevant, and a self-reference by the Chorus-leader (Kannicht app.) seems unlikely. Priam is similarly identified in *Tro.* 921 (on the debated identification in both these passages see M. Huys, *AC* 54 [1985], 250–1). In *Alex.* Priam is well into middle age, like Laius when Oedipus kills him (ὁ πρέσβυς, S. *OT* 805, 807).

62e–h. Hypoth. 25–7: 'When Alexandros arrived, Cassandra became inspired and recognized him, and prophesied *about* what would happen.' The Euripidean fragments are minimal and unhelpful (see also Introd., *Other proposed ascriptions* on Eur. F 867 and *TrGF* adesp. F 721b–c). Substantial fragments are quoted, chiefly by Cicero, from the equivalent scene of Ennius' play (Enn. F 17, 25, 26), but these still do not reveal how this scene fitted with the attack on Paris and the recognition process: cf. Introd., pp. 40–1. In *Andr.* 293–300 Eur. had made Cassandra prophesy at the birth of Paris, perhaps altering or elaborating the story of Hecuba's dream: Stinton 23–4.

62e. Snell (24–5) on grounds of physical resemblance placed this fr. (his F 7) shortly after F 46 (his F 6) with its possible reference to Cassandra's arrival, and inferred that Cassandra not only appeared but prophesied early in the play: cf. Introd., p. 38. Coles (40) finds the physical resemblance uncompelling.   ἔπος, **pronouncement:** see on *Oed.* F 540a.6.   βακχεύει, **is raving:** probably referring to Cassandra; cf. Enn. F 17.32–3, Eur. *Tro.* 170, 341, 408, 500.

*62f. Come now, etc.: quoted by ps.-Longinus in a discussion of highly evocative poetic descriptions (φαντασίαι) such as Orestes' vision of the Furies (*Or.* 255ff.) and

Phaethon's chariot-ride (*Pha.* 168–77 = F 779). The play is not named, but ps.-
Longinus does allude to a famous and evocative speech of Cassandra; cf. Enn. *Alex.*
F 17.41–2, Snell 28–9, Jocelyn, *Ennius* 208.   **horse-loving Trojans:** the phrase
recalls the Homeric ἱππόδαμοι Τρῶες, 'horse-taming Trojans'. The adj. is applied
elsewhere to Aitnaians (Pind. *Nem.* 9.32) and Thracians (Eur. *Hec.* 9, 428, Soph. F
582) as well as Trojans (Soph. F 859).

62g. The god caused me, etc.: Cassandra's prophecies are disbelieved until they are
fulfilled, a motif canonical in tragedy after A. *Ag.* 1210–2. The assignment of this fr. to
Alex. is almost certain since Cicero (see App.) alludes to a similar declaration while
directly quoting part of Enn. *Alex.* F 17.43: cf. Snell 30 with n. 2. Scholars have argued
variously and inconclusively for placing it in Cassandra's probable early dialogue with
Hecuba or in the climactic prophetic scene, and if the latter, in a dialogue before or
after her mantic fit. The phrasing evokes the proverbial idea of 'learning through
suffering' (πάθει μάθος, A. *Ag.* 177), i.e. through experiencing the consequences of
one's ignorance (παθὼν δέ τε νήπιος ἔγνω, 'the fool learns through suffering', Hes.
Works 218). Cf. S. *El.* 1055–7, Chrysothemis warning Electra.

*62h. You will be a dog, etc.:** the fr. is unlikely to come from any other play (the
scepticism of Koniaris [120–1] is extreme). The speaker must be Cassandra so that her
prediction can be disbelieved by those who hear it, and the fr. probably belongs in her
prophecy rather than a supposed later altercation with Hecuba (see Timpanaro 64–6,
Jouan 1998, 55, 74 n. 68, against Snell 29–30). Cassandra alludes to her prophecy at
Tro. 428–30, insisting that Hecuba will die 'here' rather than going to Ithaca as
Odysseus' slave but refusing to humiliate her mother by spelling out the details to
Talthybius. In *Hec.* (several years before *Alex.* and *Tro.*) Polymestor declares that
Hecuba will become a fiery-eyed dog, leap into the sea, and be commemorated by the
Kynos Sêma ('Dog's Memorial'), a promontory in the approaches to the Hellespont
(*Hec.* 1265, 1270–3): cf. J. Mossman, *Wild Justice* (Oxford, 1995), 194–201. Hecuba's
wish to feast on Achilles' liver (Hom. *Il.* 24.212ff.) may have contributed to the
tradition.   **a favourite of...Hecate:** an ἄγαλμα is something the goddess delights in
(ἀγάλλεται). This is one interpretation offered by ancient grammarians commenting
on the phrase Ἑκάτης ἄγαλμα in Ar. F 608 (see App.); thus Hecuba will be a dog-
attendant of the torch-bearing Hecate (for dogs with Hecate see *LIMC* 'Hekate' nos.
65–8). The other ancient interpretation, 'a likeness of (the dog-formed) Hecate' is less
apt, and identifications of Hecate as fully dog-formed are late and syncretistic.   **light-
bearing:** torches are an attribute of Hecate (cf. *Pha.* 268–9 n., Kannicht on *Hel.*
569–70) as well as Artemis (Cropp on *IT* 20–4).

62i, 62. Hypoth. 30–2: '...and Hecuba, who was ready to kill him, was prevented. The
man who had raised him arrived, and because of the danger was compelled to tell the
truth. Thus Hecuba rediscovered her son...'. These fragments add little to the reconstruction of the climactic scenes, on which see Introd., pp. 40–2 (also Introd., *Other proposed
ascriptions* on F 937–8 and *TrGF* adesp. F 71b).

62i (58 N). Ah! I am going to die: this fr. has sometimes been placed in the debate-scene
(e.g. Nauck by his numbering, Hose 41), but the final crisis is far more likely (cf. Snell
48, Huys 1986, 35–8, *Antiope* F 223.59).   **my virtue:** lit. 'the usefulness/worthiness'
of (my) mind'; cf. Mastronarde on *Pho.* 1740–1 comparing Theognis 406, S. *Aj.* 410.
This need not be an allusion to some particular piece of virtuous conduct (as Snell 51
thought, suggesting Paris knew something about his birth but could not reveal it
because of a promise to his foster-father; similarly e.g. Scheidweiler 333–4, Timpanaro
48). Rather, he refers generally to his intellectual and moral qualities and high self-
esteem (the μεγαλοψυχία attributed to him in Ar. *Rhet.* 1401b20) which were featured
in the debate-scene (Hypoth. 15–21, F 48, 60, 61b–c) and have alienated him from his
fellow-slaves (F 50, 51, 57) and antagonized his well-born opponents. Cf. Introd., p.
38–9, 46; Huys, *Tale* 349–54.   [**which:** Barnes changed Stob.'s Neuter ὅ to Fem. ἥ so
that the relative pronoun is attracted to the case of σωτηρία as in *Tro.* 743 (an
interpolation based on our passage) and *Med.* 14.]

62. Hecuba, how unexpected, etc.: an exclamation provoked by an amazing event; very
likely the Chorus-leader commenting on the recognition (Hartung, cf. Huys 1986,
34–5). As Huys notes, such amazement is common after recognitions, e.g. *El.* 579–80,
Ion 1510–11 (a Chorus-leader's couplet like this), *IT* 836–40. Kannicht's numbering of
this fr. places it between the report of Paris's victory and the plotting scene, but the
victory is not a strong example of the gods' unfathomable ways. After the recognition
the comment is fraught with dramatic irony. Other suggestions are not compelling
(Cassandra in her early dialogue with Hecuba, Snell 31; the consolation of Hecuba
represented by F 43–46, Scodel 41).   **divine action:** lit. 'the divine', a vague way of
describing presumed supernatural influence on human fortune(s) (τύχη, τύχαι), e.g.
IT 911 (see Cropp there), *Ion* 1456.   **draws:** a metaphor from drawing water from a
well or supplies from storage (cf. LSJ ἕλκω II.6, II.10).

63. The maiden who cannot be named: the underworld goddess Persephone. Similarly
Hel. 1307, Carcinus II *TrGF* 70 F 5.1: cf. Kannicht on *Hel.* 1307, A. Henrichs in
Hofmann and Harder, *Fragmenta Dramatica* 178 with n. 36. The context in *Alex.*
cannot usefully be guessed.

APPENDIX ONE: ENNIUS, *ALEXANDER*

Fragment- and line-numbers are those of Jocelyn, Ennius, *but the fragments are given here in their probable dramatic order: 18, 20 prologue; 19, 24, 22 Sn, 22, 23 messenger-scene; 208 plotting-scene; 17, 25, 26 Cassandra-scene; 21 uncertain. The fragment-numbers in Snell's and the Budé editions of Euripides'* Alexandros

18	mater grauida parere se ardentem facem	50
	uisa est in somnis Hecuba. quo facto pater	
	rex ipse Priamus somnio mentis metu	
	perculsus curis sumptus suspirantibus	
	exsacrificabat hostiis balantibus.	
	tum coniecturam postulat pacem petens,	55
	ut se edoceret obsecrans Apollinem	
	quo sese uertant tantae sortes somnium.	
	ibi ex oraclo uoce diuina edidit	
	Apollo puerum primus Priamo qui foret	
	postilla natus temperaret tollere;	60
	eum esse exitium Troiae, pestem Pergamo.	
20	quapropter Parim pastores nunc Alexandrum uocant.	64
19	*(Hecub.?)* iam dudum ab ludis animus atque aures auent	62
	auide exspectantes nuntium.	
24	*(Nunt.)* multi alii aduentant, paupertas quorum obscurat nomen.	68
— (22* Sn)*(Nunt.)* omnis aequalis uincebat quinquertio.	—
22	*(Nunt.?)* hominem appellat. 'quid lasciui\<s\>, stolide?' non intellegit.	66
23	uolans de caelo cum corona et taeniis	67
208	is habet coronam uitulans uictoria.	381

18 (1* Sn, 1 Budé) Cic. *De Diu.* 1.42, unattrib.   **20** (17 Sn, 2 Budé) Varro, *Ling. Lat.* 7.82, attrib. Enn.   **19** (19 Sn, 4 Budé) Varro, *Ling. Lat.* 6.83, attrib. Enn. *Alex.*   **24** (20 Sn, 6 Budé) Macrob. *Sat.* 6.1.61, attrib. Enn. *Alex.*   **22* Sn** (p. 206 J, 7* Budé) Festus, *De Verb. Signif.* p. 306.10 Lindsay, unattrib.   **22** (21 Sn, 8 Budé) Festus, *De Verb. Signif.* p. 418.2–3 Lindsay, attrib. Enn. *Alex.*   *lascivi\<s\>* Scaliger   **23** (59 Sn, 9 Budé) Festus, *De Verb.*

APPENDIX ONE: ENNIUS, *ALEXANDER*

are added in the apparatus. Two fragments of Ennius quoted in Cic. De Diu. *1.115
(15* Sn, *11 Budé* O sancte Apollo *etc.) and 2.127 (180 J, *12 Sn, **3 Budé*
Aliquot somnia uera *etc.) should not be attributed to this play: see now Timpanaro
61–2, 63–4.*

18   His mother Hecuba while pregnant imagined in a
dream that she was bearing a burning torch. There-
upon his father,[51] king Priam himself, struck through
with fear in his mind by the dream, and seized with
sighing anxieties, made sacrifices with bleating
victims. Then, begging the god's favour, he sought
an interpretation,[55] beseeching Apollo to help him
understand what direction the strange fortunes in
these dreams were taking. Then from his oracle with
divine voice Apollo proclaimed that Priam should
forbear to take up the son who first thereafter was
born to him;[60] for he would be destruction for Troy, a
pestilence on Pergamum.

20   And so the herdsmen now call Paris Alexander

19 *(Hecub.?)* For a long time now my mind and ears have been
eagerly awaiting news from the games.

24   *(Mess.)* Many others arrive, whose names poverty obscures.

—(22* Sn)
    (Mess.) He defeated all his age-group in the pentathlon.

22 *(Mess.?)* He accosts him: 'What are you swaggering about,
blockhead?' – but he does not understand.

23   Flying down from the sky with crown and ribbons

208   He is wearing a crown, rejoicing in victory.

Signif. p. 496.4 Lindsay, attrib. Enn. *Alex.*   **208** (42* Sn, 10* Budé) Paulus, *Excerpt. Fest.*
p. 507.12–13 Lindsay, attrib. Enn.

89

17   (*Cho.*) sed quid oculis rabere uisa est derepente ardentibus?   32
                  ubi illa paulo ante sapiens uirginalis modestia?

* * * * *

         Cas. mater, optumatum multo mulier melior mulierum,   34
                 missa sum superstitiosis hariolationibus;
                 †neque† me Apollo fatis fandis dementem inuitam ciet.
                 uirgines uereor aequalis, patris mei meum factum pudet,
                 optumi uiri. mea mater, tui me miseret, mei piget.
                 optumam progeniem Priamo peperisti extra me. hoc dolet:
                 men obesse, illos prodesse, me obstare, illos obsequi.   40

* * * * *

         Cas. adest adest fax obuoluta sanguine atque incendio.   41
                 multos annos latuit. ciues ferte opem et restinguite.

* * * * *

         Cas.   iamque mari magno classis cita   43
                         texitur. exitium examen rapit.
                         adueniet. fera ueliuolantibus
                         nauibus compleuit manus litora.

* * * * *

         Cas. eheu uidete: 47
                 iudicauit inclitum iudicium inter deas tris aliquis,
                 quo iudicio Lacedemonia mulier Furiarum una adueniet.

25   (*Cas.*) o lux Troiae, germane Hector,   69
                  quid ita cum tuo lacerato corpore miser?
                  aut qui te sic respectantibus tractauere nobis?

26   (*Cas.*) nam maximo saltu superauit grauidus armatis equus   72
                  qui suo partu ardua perdat Pergama.

21   ⟨. . .⟩ †amidio† purus putus   65

---

17 (8*, ~ 10* Sn, 12–16 Budé) Cic. *De Diu.* 1.66–7, attrib. Cassandra   37 *patris...pudet* Cic.
Orat. 155, unattrib.   43 *iamque mari magno* Cic. *Ad Att.* 8.11.3, unattrib., and *De Diu.* 2.112,
attrib. Cassandra   44 *texitur...rapit* Cic. *Orat.* 155, unattrib.   47 *eheu uidete* Cic. *De Diu.* 2.112,
attrib. Cassandra   32 *rabere* Lambinus *rapere* Cic.   33 paul<ul>o Timpanaro   **25** (~ 10* Sn,
17 Budé) Macrob. *Sat.* 6.2.18, attrib. Enn. *Alex.*   **26** (~ 10* Sn, 18 Budé) Macrob. *Sat.* 6.2.25,
attrib. Enn. *Alex.*   **21** (61 Sn, 5 Budé) Festus, *De Verb. Signif.* p. 240.14 Lindsay, attrib. <Enn.>
Alex.; Aul. Gell. 7.5.10, attrib. Enn. *Alex.*

17   *(Cho.)* But why does she suddenly seem to be raving with burning eyes?[32] Where is that discreet, virginal modesty she had just now?

* * * * *

Cas. Mother, best woman by far of all noble women, I have been spurred by prophetic premonitions,[35] †nor† does Apollo move me to madness with his declarations against my will. I feel shame before the girls of my age, and shame for my father, a most noble man, because of my behaviour. I feel pity for you, my mother, and loathing for myself. You have borne fine children for Priam except for me. It gives me pain, that I am harmful while they are useful, I an impediment, they obedient.[40]

* * * * *

Cas. It is here, it is here – the torch encircled with blood and fire.[41] Many years it lay hidden. Citizens bring aid and extinguish it!

* * * * *

Cas. And now a swift fleet is being assembled on the broad sea.[43] It brings a host of deaths. It will come here. A savage horde has filled our shores with sail-winged ships.

* * * * *

Cas. Aha, look![47] Someone has made a famous judgement between three goddesses. Through this judgement a Spartan woman, one of the Furies, will come here.

25   *(Cas.)* O light of Troy, Hector my brother, why thus afflicted with your body torn? What men have dragged you about as we looked on?

26   *(Cas.)* With a great leap a horse pregnant with warriors has crossed the battlements, ready to destroy high Troy with its offspring.

21   †......† pure and clean

APPENDIX TWO: EURIPIDES, *PALAMEDES*

Texts, testimonia: *TrGF* F 578–90 with T i–*vi.   F. Jouan, ed. Budé VIII.2 (2000), 487–513; R. Falcetto, *Euripide*. *Palamede* (Alessandria, 2002: not seen).

Myth. *Cypria* F 20 Davies; Aeschylus. *Palamedes, TrGF* III F 181–*182a; Sophocles, *Palamedes, TrGF* IV F 478–81, and *Nauplius*, F 425–38; Gorgias, *Palamedes* (82 B 11a DK); Schol. Eur. *Or.* 432; Schol. Ar. *Thesm.* 770; Apollod. *Epit.* 3.6–8; Hygin. *Fab.* 105; Verg. *Aen.* 2.81–5 with Servius' comm.   Preller-Robert III.2.1127–35; *RE* XVIII.2 (1942), 1500–12 ('Palamedes': E. Wüst); R. Scodel, *The Trojan Trilogy of Euripides* (Göttingen, 1980), 43–54 (sources analysed); Gantz 603–8; S. Woodford in *LIMC* (below) and *JHS* 114 (1994), 164–9; *Neue Pauly* 9 (2000), 167 ('Palamedes': L. Käppel).

Illustrations. *LIMC* VII.1.145–9 nos. 1–24, with Pls. in VII.2.96–7 ('Palamedes': S. Woodford, 1994; cf. *JHS* [above] with Pl. VId).

Main discussions (for citations by name only see under *Alexandros*, p. 35 above): Murray, *Greek Studies* 138–41; Pertusi 258–62; Jouan, *Euripide et les légendes* (1966), 339–63 and ed. Budé; Webster, *Euripides* (1967), 174–6; F. Stoessl, *WS* 79 (1966), 93–101; Koniaris 87–92; M. Szarmach, *Eos* 63 (1975), 249–71 and earlier papers; Scodel (above), 53–63; Aélion, *Euripide* (1983), I. 47–59; D. Sutton, *Two Lost Plays of Euripides* (New York, 1987), 111–55; M. Huys, *APF* 43 (1997), 24; D. Kovacs, *Colby Quarterly* 33 (1997), 168–9.

The fragments are disappointingly few. Huys (1997), 24 reports a fragmentary 'narrative hypothesis' in an unpublished Michigan papyrus which has important bearing on the play's reconstruction (see below).

Palamedes' tragic victimization by Odysseus at Troy is known to us largely from Hellenistic and Roman sources, although its outline was familiar to 5th and 4th century Athenians from the tragedians. Euripides himself had referred to it in his *Philoctetes* (F 789d.8–9). The fragmentary plays of Aeschylus and Sophocles on this subject are undated and their plots uncertain. Aeschylus seems to have had Nauplius coming to Troy to accuse the Greeks of his son Palamedes' murder (F 181). Sophocles dramatized Odysseus' plot against Palamedes and their extended argument (F 479) in his *Palamedes*, and Nauplius' appearance at Troy and retaliation in *Nauplius* (testimonia, F 431, 433, cf. 432). There are a number of loose references to the story 'in tragedy' which might include Euripides' play: Polyaenus, *Strateg.* 1 proem 12, 'Odysseus overcame Palamedes in a court-trial of the Achaeans after putting Trojan gold secretly into his tent; through deceit and stratagem the wisest of the Greeks was convicted of treachery' (T *va); Xenophon, *Mem.* 4.2.33, 'All the poets sing how his wisdom incurred

Odysseus' jealousy, and Odysseus destroyed him' (T *vb); Plato, *Rep.* 522d, 'Palamedes showed up Agamemnon as a wholly laughable commander' (T *vi).

For Euripides specifically, Aristophanes and his scholia afford some evidence. Schol. Ar. *Thesm.* 770 Rutherford (T iiia, see below on F 588a): 'In the *Palamedes* Euripides made Oeax, Palamedes' brother, inscribe his death on oar-blades so that they might be carried (by the sea) and reach Nauplius his father and report his death'. Verbal quotations or parodies occur in Schol. Ar. *Birds* 842 (T iib, see on F 589) and perhaps in Ar. *Frogs* 1451 (T iv, see on F 582 N), then more generally *Thesm.* 847–8: '(Euripides) must be ashamed that his *Palamedes* fell flat' (T iiib). This last may be compared with Aelian, *Var. Hist.* 2.8 (T iia, see on *Alexandros*, p. 49): '...ridiculous that Xenocles should win (the prize at the Great Dionysia of 415 B.C.) and Euripides lose (in second place), and that with such plays. One or other of two things was the case: either those in charge of the voting were mad and ignorant and way beyond correct judgement, or they were split by faction; but both are extraordinary and most unworthy of Athenians'. Both these last two testimonies may be set beside the Hypothesis to Isocrates, *Busiris*, 24–30 (T iic): '...when Euripides wanted to speak of Socrates but was afraid, he invented Palamedes in order to have the opportunity through him to allude darkly to Socrates and the Athenians, "You have killed, you have killed the best of the Greeks" (cf. F 588.1–2); and the whole theatre understood and wept, because he was alluding darkly to Socrates'. With the aid of these few hints, and of mythographers, the play's content can be loosely defined; artistic representations however are unreliable for reconstruction.

The fullest and most succinct account of Palamedes' myth lies in Schol. Eur. *Or.* 432. After noting Palamedes' services in organizing a fair distribution of food for the Greeks immobilized at Aulis, through the use of Phoenician writing (i.e. numerals), and in encouraging the use of dice-games to prevent boredom, the narrative continues:

> He won a great name among the Greeks. The party of Agamemnon, Odysseus and Diomedes became jealous on this account, and devised the following scheme against him. They took a Phrygian captive who was bringing gold to Sarpedon and forced him to write a treasonable letter in Phrygian letters, as if from Priam to Palamedes. They killed this man and bribed a servant of Palamedes to put the written tablet under Palamedes' bed, together with the Trojan money. They came along themselves to accuse the hero of treachery and to order an investigation of his tent. When the tablet and the money were found under Palamedes' bed, he was stoned to death. Nauplius heard of this and came to Troy to avenge his son's murder. When the Greeks scorned him out of favour toward their princes, he sailed back to his country; and after learning that the Greeks had set sail he went to Euboea, waited for a storm, and lit beacons round Euboea's headlands. Think-

ing the area safe for landing, the Greeks came in to moor and were destroyed on the rocks.

Hyginus, *Fab.* 105 has much in common with this Euripidean scholion. In summary:

(1) Odysseus' plot is conceived; he tells Agamemnon a dream which foretold moving the Greek camp for one day. (2) Agamemnon agrees; overnight, Odysseus buries the gold where Palamedes' tent had stood and forges the letter, giving it to a Phrygian captive to take to Priam; then Odysseus' man kills the Phrygian and leaves the letter on his body. (3) The letter is brought to Agamemnon; purporting to come from 'Priam to Palamedes', it promises as reward for betrayal the amount of gold buried under Palamedes' tent. (4) Discovery of the gold leads to Palamedes' execution, although innocent.

The essence of (2) and (3) in Hyginus stands also in Apollod. *Epit.* 3.8, and is abbreviated and rhetoricized in Vergil, *Aeneid* 2.81–5.

In his services to mankind, the inventive, skilful and wise Palamedes (his name means roughly 'handy, skilled Contriver') is a mortal counterpart of beneficent gods like Prometheus; the scholia on *Prometheus Bound* 457 and 458a suggest that Palamedes learned from Prometheus (cf. Aesch. *Pal.* F *182a). He is credited with the introduction of writing, number, and measures, board-games and dice, but also of beacon-signals (this last perhaps a back-projection of his father Nauplius' revenge-plan). For these and other services to the Greeks during the war against Troy, he incurred the great jealousy of Odysseus (e.g. Xen. *Mem.* 4.2.33 and Polyaen. *Strateg.* 1 proem 12 quoted above). Myth told too how he had uncovered Odysseus' feigned madness when he tried to avoid going to the war (e.g. *Cypria* in Proclus' summary, Hygin. 105.1, cf. 95, Apollod. *Epit.* 3.6–7). Odysseus snared Palamedes in a false accusation of betraying Greeks to Trojans, through the planting of false evidence – Trojan gold in his tent and a forged incriminating letter from Priam (Hygin. 105.2–4, Apollod. *Epit.* 3.8; allusively in *Philoctetes* F 789d.8). After being condemned, Palamedes was put to death, perhaps by stoning as a communal enemy (cf. Apollod.); an alternative myth-version had him drowned by Odysseus and Diomedes while fishing (*Cypria* F 20; cf. *Illustrations*).

The myth went further: Palamedes' brother Oeax, a ship-master (his name means 'Tiller, Helm'), tried to secure vengeance upon the Greeks, especially Agamemnon (see *Orestes* at *Or.* 432–3), through a remarkable if improbable plan worthy of Palamedes' own inventiveness: he described the murder by chiselling characters ('Palamedean' ones?) on a number of oar-blades and launching them into the sea, hoping that their father Nauplius (another 'speaking name', roughly 'Seaman' or the like) might eventually find one (Schol. Ar. *Thesm.* 770; see on F 588a); he did, and when the Greeks eventually returned from Troy he lured their ships onto the dangerous headlands of Euboea by siting false beacon-signals to guide their mooring (Schol. Eur.).

That summary of Palamedes' story expands a little upon the Euripidean Scholion, and the majority of scholars think that the Scholion contains rather more than Euripides' plot. Schol. Ar. *Thesm.* 770 = F 588a implies that Oeax launched the oar-blades within the play; and it now seems from the Michigan papyrus (above) that the play ended with Nauplius threatening Agamemnon with revenge. If this is so, Nauplius must in some way have found an oar-blade very soon. His threat to Agamemnon is not in Hyginus 105, but it was in both Aeschylus and Sophocles (see above), and its presence in Euripides looks more likely given its record in the Euripidean scholion and Apollodorus. The papyrus would thus confirm the play-end reconstructed by Stoessl, 98–100. With this ruin threatened for the Greeks by man, *Palamedes* would end only to give way to the gods' own intentions against them with which *Trojan Women* begins (lines 48–97), and for destruction by sea in a storm, supporting Nauplius's own revenge (cf. Schol. Eur).

Reconstruction can suggest only an approximate dramatic sequence on the following lines. The scene is the Greek camp at Troy; prologue-speech by Odysseus; parodos of the Chorus of fellow-Greeks, perhaps recalling a night incident (**F 589**). Episode 1, Odysseus' design against Palamedes with the planted gold and letter, featuring the Phrygian captive. Then perhaps Episode 2, accusation and trial of Palamedes, no doubt in a 'formal debate' or *agon*, with Agamemnon judging between Odysseus and Palamedes: **F 579** may belong to an initial investigation of the alleged treachery, perhaps by Agamemnon; **F 578**, **580**, possibly **581**, and almost certainly **583–5** relate to various stages of the accusation and Palamedes' defence; such a scene mirrored the accusation and self-defence of Paris before Priam in *Alexandros* (F 48–61), and was in turn mirrored in the argument of Helen and Hecuba before Menelaus in *Trojan Women* (895–1059). Episode 2 might end with a sentence of death, and Episode 3 might include both a messenger's report of the execution and Oeax's violent grief (**F 588**) and intended retaliation (**F 588a**). Episode 4 (or Exodos) would then contain Nauplius' unexpected arrival to threaten Agamemnon; he may even have had a clairvoyant role, as some mortal persons do at play-end (e.g. Cassandra at the end of *Alexandros* [pp. 40–2 above] and in *Trojan Women* 353–406, 424–61), Euripides substituting such persons for a god (cf. also *Tro.* 90–91 quoted under *Other proposed ascriptions* below, pp. 102–3). All this makes for a typical Euripidean drama of intrigue and revenge. Yet even of the very few fragments we have, **F 586–7** and **590** cannot be placed.

Such a scheme, at least for the play's start, is followed approximately by almost all recent scholars, inevitably with some variations but with considerable agreement over the location of F 578–81, 583–4, 588, 588a, 589: e.g. Webster (1967), with a terminal 'god'; Szarmach (1975), but with an active prologue-scene of Odysseus with Palamedes, and possibly Achilles speaking F 581 to defend him (Szarmach excludes F 585); Scodel (1980), with Episode 1 between Odysseus and Agamemnon, and a long Episode 2 of confrontation and trial divided by a short astrophic lyric including F 910 (printed with our *Antiope*, pp. 296–7), Exodos with Oeax in dispute or saved by a god from murder by Odysseus); Jouan (2000), with prologue-speech by Oeax (changed from Poseidon in his 1966 discussion) and F 585 also given to Oeax in the Exodos. Only Scodel and Sutton doubtfully retain F 582 N; Sutton declines to locate F 584–5.

The speaking characters are principally Odysseus and Palamedes, secondarily Agamemnon and Oeax, almost certainly a messenger who was possibly Diomedes himself (Odysseus' complicit partner in the design, Schol. Eur.: compare their partnership in the *Philoctetes*, p. 6), and apparently Nauplius. The stage-use of a false letter recalls Phaedra's to Theseus (*Hipp.* 856ff.) and is close in date to Iphigenia's well-meant letter to Orestes (*IT* 584ff.). There are however ironies here: Palamedes is destroyed by one of his own inventions, writing, in the forged letter (cf. Kovacs 169; see esp. F 578.8–9 where Palamedes says 'The troubles which befall men and lead to strife, a written tablet settles, and allows no falsehood to be said'); but he is also to be avenged through writing (Oeax's message on the oar-blades), and so Odysseus' jealousy of his inventiveness recoils upon all the Greeks.

F 580–1 (if 581 belonged to the trial-scene) and 583–5 contain just enough to suggest that the scene contrasted Odysseus' ruthless individual sophistry with Palamedes' selfless intelligence. The issue of true wisdom appears in F 581, 583–5 and, outside the trial, in 588 where Palamedes is credited with its absolute possession. A comparable issue may have been raised in the earlier *Philoctetes*, for at F 789d.(8)–(9) (see p. 19) Philoctetes abuses Odysseus for destroying the public-spirited Palamedes; and later in *Antiope* Euripides developed these issues differently when contrasting the practical Zethus and the thinking artist Amphion (*Ant.* F 182b–202 etc.; cf. Scodel 92). Agamemnon seems to have been an easy victim to Odysseus' manipulation; perhaps in our play Palamedes' intellect exposed Agamemnon's weakness (Pl. *Rep.* 522d locates this only in 'tragedy', but cf. F 581, which could have been spoken by Nauplius), and helped to secure his execution.

Palamedes was the middle play of Euripides' tragic trilogy of 415; its relation with *Alexandros* and *Trojan Women* has been intensively discussed (see bibl. above under *Main discussions*). In his Introduction to *Alexandros* (p. 48 above), Cropp suggests it was very different in tone, portraying 'man's capacity for using his own greatest gifts to malevolent and self-destructive ends'.

The play's failure at its first production provided Aristophanes with a jibe (*Thesm.* 847–8) and surprised later antiquity (Aelian, *Var.Hist.* 2.8); to us also it is astonishing that Euripides failed when his tetralogy included the powerful *Trojan Women*. A commentator on Isocrates' *Busiris* (quoted above, p. 93) interpreted Euripides' portrayal of Palamedes and his undeserved end as disguised sympathy for Socrates; but his statement that 'the whole theatre understood and wept' could only apply to a revival of the play after Socrates' execution in 399, not to the first production of 415. Sutton (esp. 111–13, 133–55) relates this whole testimony to the historical (but undated) trial of the sophist Protagoras, who was not less suspect as an intellectual than Socrates. Sutton thinks the play might in part reflect Eupolis' comedy *Kolakes* ('Flatterers') of 421, in which Protagoras was named as presently in Athens.

Illustrations. For reviews of the sporadic and often uncertainly identified ancient representations see Woodford in *LIMC* and in *JHS* (see bibl. above under *Myth*). There were fifth-century paintings (long-lost), especially Polygnotus' composite picture of Palamedes' activities at Aulis and his murder while fishing (= *LIMC* no. 8), both of which were narrated in the *Cypria*, His murder was depicted also in a Roman copy of a lost mid-5th C. sculpture (= *LIMC* no. 6).

Other dramatizations; influence. A final surprise is the play's lack of successors: Astydamas' fourth-century *Palamedes* (*TrGF* 60 F 5a) is only a title for us. No other Greek or Roman plays are known (a single fr. is doubtfully attributed to a comedy by Philemon, F 60 *PCG*). The myth was used as the basis for rhetorical display-pieces by Gorgias (see bibl. above: late 5th C. B.C.), Alcidamas (B XXII.16. 17–29 in Radermacher, *Artium Scriptores*: 4th C.) and Philostratus (*Heroicus* 33–4: 3rd C. A.D.). Frustratingly, we do not know whether Gorgias' speech was earlier or later than Euripides' play, and so whether there was influence one way or the other with the trial-scene (Scodel 90 n. 26 is confident that Gorgias came first). As for the later effect of the story as told by mythographers and in literature (e.g. Verg. *Aen.* 2.81–5), *OGCMA* 801–2 lists poems, plays and art from the 12th to the 20th century, including Canova's sculpture of Palamedes detecting Odysseus' feigned madness, of about 1755.

ΠΑΛΑΜΗΔΗΣ

579 πάλαι πάλαι δή σ' ἐξερωτῆσαι θέλων,
σχολή μ' ἀπεῖργε.

578 ΠΑΛΑΜΗΔΗΣ
τὰ τῆς γε λήθης φάρμακ' ὀρθώσας μόνος
ἄφωνα φωνήεντα συλλαβὰς τιθεὶς
ἐξηῦρον ἀνθρώποισι γράμματ' εἰδέναι
ὥστ' οὐ παρόντα ποντίας ὑπὲρ πλακὸς
τἀκεῖ κατ' οἴκους πάντ' ἐπίστασθαι καλῶς,   5
παισίν τε τὸν θνήισκοντα χρημάτων μέτρον
γράψαντ' ἐνισπεῖν, τὸν λαβόντα δ' εἰδέναι.
ἃ δ' εἰς ἔριν πίπτουσιν ἀνθρώποις κακὰ
δέλτος διαιρεῖ, κοὐκ ἐᾶι ψευδῆ λέγειν.

580 Ἀγάμεμνον, ἀνθρώποισι †πᾶσιν αἱ τύχαι
μορφὴν ἔχουσι, συντρέχει δ' εἰς ἓν τόδε†·
†τούτου† δὲ πάντες, οἵ τε μουσικῆς φίλοι
ὅσοι τε χωρὶς ζῶσι, χρημάτων ὕπερ
μοχθοῦσιν, ὃς δ' ἂν πλεῖστ' ἔχηι σοφώτατος.   5

---

579 (2 Budé) Schol. Hom. *Il.* 2.353 Erbse, attrib. Eur. *Pal.*; Eustath. on *Il.* 2.353, attrib. Eur.
578 (3 Budé) Stob. 2.4.8, attrib. Eur. *Pal.*; cf. Schol. Vatic. on Dion. Thrax p. 190.27–8 Hilgard
(cf. p. 183.14–15): 'Stesichorus (F 213 *PMGF*) makes Palamedes their inventor (of letters and
writing), with whom Eur. too agrees'.   2 φωνήεντα Nauck καὶ φωνοῦντα Stob.   6 τε τὸν
θνήισκοντα Wecklein   τ' ἀποθνήισκοντα Stob.   χρημάτων Scaliger γραμμάτων Stob.
7 γράψαντ' ἐνισπεῖν Gomperz   γράψαντας εἰπεῖν Stob.   γράψαντα λείπειν Grotius
λαβόντα Stob.   λαχόντα Emper   8 text suspect: beg. οἳ δ' or εἰ δ'...κακήν (Heath) Hense
580 (5 Budé) Stob. 4.31a.14, attrib. Eur. *Pal.*, repeated after 31a.30 by mss. MA   1 πᾶσι(ν)
Stob. πᾶσαν Hense   χρήματα (for αἱ τύχαι) Stob. mss. MA in 14   2 εἰς ἓν τόδε Stob. mss.
MA in 14 εἰς χρήματα ms. S in 14, mss. MA in 30 εἰς ἓν τάδε Hense   lacuna after 2:
Szarmach   3 τούτων Stob. mss. MA in 14 θνητοὶ Hense βροτοὶ Herwerden

98

PALAMEDES

579   Long, long have I wanted to question you thoroughly, but
(lack of) leisure kept me from it.

*Speaker unidentified; any of Agamemnon, Odysseus and Palamedes
might have said these words, and to any of the other two; but
Agamemnon seems most likely.*

578 PALAMEDES. Alone I established remedies for forgetfulness; making
consonants, vowels, syllables, I invented knowledge of writing
for men, so that one absent over the sea's plain might know
well everything back there in his house,[5] and a dying man
might write down and declare the measure of his wealth, and
the heir know. The troubles which befall men and lead to
strife, a written tablet settles, and allows no falsehood to be
said.

*Palamedes defends his past services to mankind and the Greeks,
perhaps in an initial exchange with Agamemnon, perhaps at the
start of the trial-scene.*

The next five fragments almost certainly come from the trial-scene:

580   Agamemnon, †their fortunes have shape for all men, but (it?)
runs together into this one thing (*or* but this runs together into
one)†:[1] †of this† all (men), both close friends of music (i.e.
Palamedes) and all who live without it, labour for money, and
whoever has most is wisest.

Perhaps Odysseus attacking Palamedes.

---

[1] In 1-2 one expects '...every shape' (so Hense), or a plural as in *Ion* 382 'the shapes
of misfortunes differ'; cf. *Antiope* F 211.2. In 2, 'runs together' has no clear Subject
(Hense suggested 'these things', i.e. the variety of fortunes), In 3, 'of this' has no
reference or syntax, so that Szarmach's lacuna is a good suggestion.

581   (Παλ.?)   στρατηλάται τὰν μυρίοι γενοίμεθα,
σοφὸς δ᾿ ἂν εἶς τις ἢ δύ᾿ ἐν μακρῶι χρόνωι.

582 N   *See below, Other proposed ascriptions.*

583   ὅστις λέγει μὲν εὖ, τὰ δ᾿ ἔργ᾿ ἐφ᾿ οἷς λέγει
αἰσχρ᾿ ἐστί, τούτου τὸ σοφὸν οὐκ αἰνῶ ποτέ.

584   (Παλ.?)   εἷς τοι δίκαιος μυρίων οὐκ ἐνδίκων
κρατεῖ τὸ θεῖον τὴν δίκην τε συλλαβών.

585   (Παλ.?)   τοῦ γὰρ δικαίου κἂν βροτοῖσι κἂν θεοῖς
ἀθάνατος ἀεὶ δόξα διατελεῖ μόνου.

586, 587   *See below, Unplaced Fragments.*

588   (ΟΙΑΞ?)   ἐκάνετ᾿ ἐκάνετε τὰν
πάνσοφον, ὦ Δαναοί,
τὰν οὐδέν᾿ ἀλγύνουσαν ἀηδόνα Μουσᾶν.

588a   Οἴαξ   ὦ χεῖρες ἐμαί,
ἐγχειρεῖν χρῆν ἔργωι πορίμωι.
ἄγε δή, πινάκων ξεστῶν δέλτοι,
δέξασθε σμίλης ὁλκοὺς
κήρυκας ἐμῶν μόχθων.   5
<   >
βάσκετ᾿ ἐπείγετε πάσας καθ᾿ ὁδοὺς   6
κεῖναι ταύται· ταχέως χρή.

---

581 (4 Budé) Stob. 4.13.6 attrib. Eur. *Pal.*   **583** (6 Budé) Stob. 2.15.15, attrib. Eur. *Pal.*; Orion 1.6 Haffner; cf. John Damasc. *Flor.* I.7, attrib. *Pal.*   2 ἐστί, τούτου Mekler ἐστίν, αὐτοῦ Or. ἔστιν αὐτοῦ τοῦτον Stob.   ποτέ Stob., John Damasc. τόδε Or.   **584** (7 Budé) Stob. 3.9.12, attrib. Eur. *Pal.*   **585** (8 Budé) Stob. 3.9.20 attrib. Eur. *Pal.*   **588** (10 Budé) Philostr. *Heroic.* 34, attrib. Eur. *Pal.*; there are other sources, e.g. Isocrates' adaptation in the Hypothesis to *Busiris*. METRE: probably dactylo-epitrite.   3 οὐδέν᾿ Valckenaer οὐδὲν sources   **588a** (9 Budé) Ar. *Thesm.* 776–80 (1–5), 783–4 (6–7), which Schol. 770 Rutherford paraphrases in attributing the action to Oeax in Eur. *Pal.*; Ar.'s lines are paratragic and may echo or imitate rather than repeat Euripidean wording (cf. Rau, *Paratragodia* 52–3).   METRE: anapaestic.

581 *(Pal.?)* Commanders without number certainly we might become, but wise ones – just a single man or two in a long time (*or sardonically*: but just one or two wise men in a long time).

> *The words suit Palamedes or Oeax or Nauplius; if Palamedes, probably part of his defence of his exceptional abilities (and perhaps a sneer at Agamemnon: see Pl. Rep. 522d); if either of the other two, they attend hopes or threats of vengeance.*

582 N   *See below, Other proposed ascriptions*

583   Whoever speaks well while the actions upon which he speaks are shameful – this man's cleverness never has my approval.

> *Probably Palamedes implying that villainy underlies Odysseus' over-clever speaking; or Odysseus cynically rebutting Palamedes?*

584 *(Pal.?)* One just man overcomes numberless unjust men, when he has the gods and justice on his side (*less well*: since he comprehends the divine and justice).

585 *(Pal.?)* The reputation of a just man lasts for ever among both men and gods without dying, and his alone.

586, 587   *See below, Unplaced Fragments*

588 *(OEAX?)* You have killed, you have killed, you Danaans, the famous all-wise one, the Muses' nightingale who harmed no man.

> *A lament for Palamedes, the voice of the intellectual powers in the protection of the Muses (cf. F 580.3); probably a grieving and angry Oeax, possibly the Chorus.*

588a Oeax. O my hands, you should be handling productive work! Come now, you tablets of smoothed blades, receive a chisel's furrows, messengers of my woes . . . . . Depart, hasten over all the sea-roads, that way, this way: quickly, it should be!

> *Oeax scratches a message about Palamedes' murder on oar-blades so that Nauplius may find it and avenge his son.*

EURIPIDES

Unplaced fragments

586   Χο.   †τοῦ σὰν† Διονύσου
†κομᾶν† ὃς ἄν' Ἴδαν
τέρπεται σὺν ματρὶ φίλαι
τυμπάνων ἰάκχοις.

587   κώπην χρυσόκολλον

589   Lexical items:

(a) οἱ περίπολοι οἱ τὰς φυλακὰς περισκοποῦντες ἐρχόμενοι ἐπὶ τοὺς φύλακας κώδωνας εἶχον . . . μήποτε δὲ παρα-κωμωιδεῖ τὸν Εὐριπίδου Παλαμήδην οὐ πρὸ πολλοῦ δεδιδαγμένον.

(b) δικωδώνισε· Δημοσθένης . . . . ἡ δὲ μεταφορὰ ἤτοι ἀπὸ τῶν περοπολούντων σὺν κώδωσι νυκτὸς τὰς φυλακάς, ⟨ὡς⟩ Εὐριπίδης ἐν Παλαμήδει, ἢ . . .

590   ἔμβολα

Other proposed ascriptions

- (582 N)   εἰ τῶν πολιτῶν οἷσι νῦν πιστεύομεν,
τούτοις ἀπιστήσαιμεν, οἷς δ' οὐ χρώμεθα,
τούτοισι χρησαίμεσθ', ἴσως σωθεῖμεν ἄν.

adesp. 591c (p. 542 N)

λωπιστός· ὁ Παλαμήδης, ἐκ τῆς τῶν ἱματίων ἐπιρίψεως.

Tro. 90-1   αἱ Καφήρειοί τ' ἄκραι
πολλῶν θανόντων σώμαθ' ἕξουσιν νεκρῶν.

586 (12 Budé) Strabo 10.3.14, attrib. 'the chorus in *Pal.*' (the citation is fully discussed by S. L. Radt, *Noch einmal zu*...[Leiden, 2002], 439–40).   METRE: uncertain, either dactylo-epitrite or aeolo-choriambic.   **587** (13 Budé) Pollux 10.145, attrib. Eur. *Pal.* (the lexicographer is listing the names of hand-weapons)   **589** (1 Budé) (a) Schol. RV etc. Ar. *Birds* 842a Holwerda (cf. Suidas κ 2221 Adler) on the word κωδωνοφορῶν 'carrying a bell' in *Birds* 842   (b) Harpocrat. *Lex.Rhet.* Δ 56 Keaney   **590** (14 Budé) Hesych. ε 2307 Latte, attrib. Eur. *Pal.*; Photius, *Lex.* ε 697 Theodoridis, unattrib. (glossing the word as 'bars, means of safety')   **582 N** (*11 Budé) Ar. *Frogs* 1446–8: cf. 1451 εὖ γ' ὦ Παλάμηδες, ὦ σοφωτάτη φύσις, 'Bravo, Palamedes, you wisest of beings!'. Schol. R etc. 1451a–b Chantry (repeated in Tzetzes 1451 Koster) says this was 'probably addressed to Euripides' and fashioned from *Palamedes*. 'Not a quotation, but from a pastiche of Euripidean style', Rau, *Paratragodia* 123 n. 18.   **adesp. 591c** Hesych. λ 1511 Latte unattrib.

102

Unplaced fragments

586 *Cho.* †...† of Dionysus †...†[2], who up on Ida delights with the dear mother (the Asiatic Cybele) in the revel-cries of tambourines.

> *Dionysiac worship on Mt. Ida near Troy probably provided decorative content for a choral stasimon, or even the parodos (cf. F 589).*

587   hilt inlaid with gold

> *Sometimes assigned to the parodos, as if the play began soon after dawn.*

589 *(a) The patrols who inspected the guard-posts approached them with bells . . . maybe (Aristophanes) is parodying Euripides'* Palamedes, *which had been produced not long before.*

   (b) 'He went round ringing a bell': Demosthenes (speaking of Philip of Macedon) . . . the metaphor is either from those who went round the night-watches with bells, as in Euripides' Palamedes . . .

590   door-bars

Other proposed ascriptions

– (582 N) If we were to distrust those of our citizens we now trust, and use those we do not use, perhaps we might be saved.

adesp. 591c
   Cowled: Palamedes. From throwing one's cloak over (one's head, in shame or grief).

Tro. 90–1 ... and the Capherean promontories will have the corpses of many dead men (when Nauplius' revenge is achieved).

> *These words probably do not conceal a 'fragment' of our play, only perhaps allude to the story: see Koniaris 91–2.*

---

[2] There are numerous conjectures in 1–2, mostly directed to filling out a description of bacchic ecstasy, with hair flowing (like *Bacc.* 150, 241); but 'hair' in 2 may refer to the ivy-clad Dionysiac thyrsus (cf. *Antiope* F 203.2 and n.).

APPENDIX THREE: EURIPIDES, *SISYPHUS*

Texts, testimonia. TrGF F 673–4 with T i.   N. Pechstein, *Euripides Satyrographos* (Stuttgart, 1998), 185–217 and (briefly, with German tr.) in R. Krumeich et al., *Das griechische Satyrspiel* (Darmstadt, 1999), 442–8; H. Van Looy, ed. Budé VIII.3 (2002), 29–38. The disputed attributions to the play of a fragmentary 'narrative hypothesis' in P. Oxy. 2455 fr. 7 and of the 40-line book-fragment Critias 43 F 19 are fully discussed by M. Davies, *BICS* 36 (1989), 16–32 and by Pechstein (1998). Van Looy 35–8 like Pechstein favours attributing P. Oxy. 2455 fr. 5 to *Sisyphus* (with Turner, ed. pr.), and fr. 7 to *Skiron*.

This satyr-play concluding the tetralogy is scarcely visible, and its plot beyond reasonable conjecture; it may have maintained the theme of deception and lying which varies in prominence in the three tragedies. There are only two book-fragments: F 673 indicates that Heracles was a play-character; F 674 is a reference to devious talk, perhaps by Sisyphus, whom the play may have presented as Odysseus' father (as often in drama, and most appropriately in this tetralogy).

Fragments

673   χαίρω σέ γ', ὦ βέλτιστον 'Αλκμήνης τέκος,
        <σωθέντα,> τὸν δὲ μιαρὸν ἐξολωλότα . . .

        I rejoice at your <safety>, most excellent son of Alcmena
        (i.e. Heracles), and the destruction of that foul (man?)...

674   ἐλίσσων

                        twisting

673 (1 Budé) Suidas χ 174 Adler and two other lexica, attrib. Eur. Sisyphus   2 <σωθέντα> Cobet   674 (2 Bude) Hesych. ε 2115 Latte, attrib. Eur. *Sisyphus*, with gloss οὐκ ἐπὶ εὐθείας λέγων 'not speaking straightforwardly': hence <λόγους> ἐλίσσων ('twisting <words>') Matthiae

OEDIPUS

Texts, testimonia. P. Oxy. 2455 fr. 4 (= *TrGF* T iii) and 2459; *TrGF* F 539a–557, T i–iii; Austin, *NFE* frs. 82–101; H. Van Looy, ed. Budé VIII.2 (2000), 429–58; John Malalas, *Chron.* II.17 Thurn (= 2.42 Jeffreys) (= T ii). See also on F 554b, 556. (P. Vindob. G 29779, once tentatively identified by R. Kannicht as from a commentary on *Oed.*, has been shown by W. Luppe, *Act.Ant.* 33 (1990–2), 39–44 to relate to Sophocles.)

Myth. Hom. *Od.* 11.271–6 (and Schol.); Eur. *Pho.* 44–5 and (in Schol. there) Antimachus Coloph. F 70 Wyss; Schol. *Pho.* 26, 61, and 1760 (= Pisander *FGH* 16 F 10); Hygin. *Fab.* 66.2, 67.7 (see M. Huys, *APF* 43 [1997], 17–18); Apollod. 3.5.8–9; Nicol. Damasc. *FGH* 90 F 8.   Preller-Robert II.3.877–908 (1921); *RE* XXXIV (1937), 2013–2117 and Suppl. VII (1940), 769–86 (both 'Oidipous': L. W. Daly); F. Wehrli, *MH* 14 (1957), 108–17; J.-M. Moret, *Oedipe, la Sphinx et les Thébains* (Rome, 1984); Gantz 490–506, esp. 499–500; *LIMC* VII.1.1–15 with VII.2.6–15 ('Oidipous': I. Krauskopf, 1994); *Neue Pauly* VIII.1129–32 ('Oidipous': A. Henrichs, 2000).

Illustrations. Robert (below), Figs. 48, 49; Séchan, *Études* 434–41 with Fig. 124; Webster, *Euripides* (1967), 307; Moret (above); T. H. Carpenter, *Art and Myth in Ancient Greece* (London, 1991), Pls. 261, 264; *LIMC* (above).

Main discussions. N. Wecklein, *SBAW* 1901, 661–92 (esp. 689–92); C. Robert, *Oidipus* (Berlin, 1915), I.305–31, II.107–18; L. Deubner, *Oedipusprobleme* (Berlin, 1942) = *Kl. Schr.* 735–77; J. Vaio, *GRBS* 5 (1964), 43–55; Webster, *Euripides* (1967), 242–6; J. Dingel, *MH* 27 (1970), 90–6; L. di Gregorio, *CCC* 1 (1980), 49–94 (based in part on P. Vindob.: see *Texts*); Aélion, *Mythes* (1986), 42–61; M. Hose, *ZPE* 81 (1990), 9–15; Huys, *Tale* 357–8; C. Collard discusses the contribution of P. Oxy. 2459 in F. McHardy et al. (eds.), *Lost Dramas of Classical Athens. Greek Tragic Fragments* (forthcoming).

Euripides' treatment of the Oedipus-story was characteristically individual.

Recovery and study of the fragments. Until the 1960's only one fragment certainly attributed in the ancient source (F 541, the forcible blinding of Oedipus) and one attributed with probability by scholars (F *545a, Jocasta's resolve to share her husband's suffering) hinted at Euripides' innovative dramatization. Fourteen anthological fragments from Stobaeus and two lexicographical fragments had long been known, but only two or three had a content permitting plausible location. A text recovered just before 1940 confirmed F 554a for the play. Papyrus-finds in the 1960s *(a)* expanded F 556, assured F 539a for the play but made F *555 even more uncertain, and *(b)* brought new short stretches of a narrative (F 540, 540a–b: the Sphinx and her riddle) and one further intriguing

book-fragment (F 554b, an apparent invocation of Athens); it was disappointing
that P. Oxy. 2455 preserved nothing substantial of a narrative hypothesis.

   The new finds have not wholly invalidated earlier reconstructions, although
they have provoked some very differing ones; since their first assessment by
Turner (1962, ed. pr. of P. Oxy. 2459), Vaio (1964) and Webster (1967), they
have been studied most helpfully by Aélion (1986) and Hose (1990). These last
two scholars were able to discount P. Vindob. (see on *Texts*), which di Gregorio
(1980) had understandably used.

Myth. Few myths have been shaped so firmly for modern readers by a single
ancient poet as that of Oedipus in Sophocles' extant play *Oedipus Tyrannus*,
with other episodes in *Oedipus at Colonus* and *Antigone*; the first and third of
these predated Euripides' *Oedipus*, the second was a little later. The essence of
the myth was to hand for all three tragedians in Homer, *Odyssey* 11.271–6, the
earliest surviving account: parricide, incest and suffering (undefined, and it may
be unsafe to infer that blinding is meant; this first appears in Aeschylus); all
three are attributed to the 'deathly design of heaven' (276). In Homer Oedipus
goes on ruling at Thebes after his mother's suicide, and it may be that Euripides
alone, in both *Oedipus* and *Phoenissae,* had Jocasta survive her son's revelation
and blinding. Without doubt early Epic (now lost) held many further details, but
there survives one fragment telling of Oedipus' subsequent curse upon his sons,
Thebais F 2 *EGF*. Aeschylus' dramatization of the whole history, from Oedipus'
father Laius and his defiance of the god Apollo in begetting his son (cf. our F
539a) to the fulfilment of his curse, was in a tetralogy of 467 B.C.; its final
tragedy, the extant *Seven against Thebes*, apparently recapitulates the events of
the preceding but lost plays *Laius* (esp. *Sept.* 741–57) and *Oedipus* (esp. *Sept.*
772–90). The two plays went as far as the curse's pronouncement, which *Seven*
enacts (see 70, 655, 695, 720–6, 832–3 etc.). Aeschylus emphasizes the
punishment inevitable for Laius' ancient sin (742–4, 766–7, 790–1, 842); at
e.g. 689, 719, 947–8 he reflects Homer's attribution of it to divine will, like his
contemporary Pindar at *Ol.* 2.38–40 (476 B.C.), who has it that Oedipus'
parricide fulfilled his fated destiny, as in Apollo's oracles to Laius (S. *OT* 711ff.)
and to Oedipus (787ff.). Neither Homer nor Pindar says how the gods arranged
Oedipus' revelation, or how slowly. Nor do we know Aeschylus' mechanism,
but just possibly he anticipated in some way the uncanny interaction of god,
man and chance which so baffles interpreters of Sophocles' play; the ironic
(mis)calculation of Eteocles which brings Oedipus' two sons to fulfil his curse
in *Seven* may repeat similar multiple causation in the earlier plays *Laius* and
Oedipus. Aeschylus' version of the myth must have been influential upon both
Sophocles and Euripides; but with the forcible blinding of Oedipus Euripides

clearly intended effects different from the self-blinding, in which he followed his predecessors in *Phoenissae* (close in date to *Oedipus*).

The entire myth is recounted in later learned sources, for example Schol. Hom. *Od.* 11.271 Dindorf, Hyginus and Apollodorus.

Reconstruction. The primary evidence yields only two hard facts. The play contained a description of the Sphinx and her riddle (F 540, 540a–b) – and therefore almost certainly also of her defeat by Oedipus; and Oedipus was forcibly blinded by servants of the murdered king Laius while known to them as the son of Polybus king of Corinth (F 541) – and therefore not yet revealed as the son of Laius himself.[1]

The attribution of F *545a is however being gradually accepted; in this fragment, as in *Phoenissae*, Euripides differs from Sophocles in having Jocasta live on after Oedipus' catastrophe (at *Pho.* 1549–50 she has tended him in his blindness). The fragment coheres in temper and in trochaic metre with F 545; together they imply quite a major role for Jocasta, something also implicit in Malalas' terse statement that the play 'was about Oedipus and Jocasta and the Sphinx'. The new F 540, 540a–b seem also to bear out Malalas for the Sphinx. It is possible that Oedipus' eventual refuge in Athens, as in Sophocles' *Oedipus at Colonus*, was anticipated (F 554b, if the text is sound: see Comm.). A few of the nearly twenty other book-fragments can perhaps be associated in a scene with F 545 and *545a (542–4, 546–51); 552–554a can be given a possible location; but 555–7 cannot be placed.

Secondary and other material is nevertheless most suggestive; it ranges from art of the 2nd C. B.C. to Malalas of the 6th C. A.D. Two sentences in Hyginus (2nd C. A.D.?) state respectively (*Fab.* 66.2) that the infant Oedipus was rescued from exposure by Periboea the wife of Polybus and (*Fab.* 67.7) that when Oedipus, now king of Thebes, was distressed by news of Polybus' death, it was Periboea who revealed to him his rescue from exposure and adoption, while Menoetes the old servant of Laius who exposed the infant, recognised him by the scars on his feet. These two statements may stem from a myth-version differing from that of Sophocles in *OT*, but their origin, let alone their combination, specifically in Euripides' play itself, is far from certain; in particular, Hygin.

---

[1] Deubner (1942), 19ff. = *Kl. Schr.* 653ff. nevertheless rejected F 541 because of the inconsistency between the forcible blinding and the self-blinding recorded both in Schol. *Pho.* 1760 (Pisander), which he thought reflected Euripides' play quite faithfully, and Hygin. *Fab.* 67.8. The Pisander-text has been finally invalidated for reconstruction by E. L. de Kock, *AC* 5 (1962), 15–37; cf. H. Lloyd-Jones, *CQ* 52 (2002), 4 with bibl.

67.8 goes on to Oedipus' self-blinding, conflicting with F 541.[2] Periboea appears however on a 2nd C. B.C. cup which shows her rescuing the infant Oedipus and handing him to Polybus (see *Illustrations*).[3]

We have the play's first line, **F 539a** (= T iii): it gave the cardinal fact of Oedipus' existence, that he was fathered by Laius although Apollo forbade him when he consulted the god upon his childlessness. We cannot know whether this detail was merely a convenient starting-point for the play's expository prologue, or whether it set a tone and heralded a truth borne out in the action, that human life is subject to extraordinary chances, god-willed or not (see *Myth* above; F 549, 550, 554; compare *Or.* 1–3). The prologue-speaker was either the god Hermes (most scholars cite his prologue in *Ion*, disclosing Apollo's will for Ion, cf. the 'Homeric' cup in *Illustrations*) or a person ignorant of Oedipus' true identity (again cf. F 541), for example a surviving servant of Laius (Vaio 50); earlier scholars had favoured Creon, Robert in particular, giving his jealousy of Oedipus a large part in the action (see Comm. on F 551); but after the discovery of P. Oxy. 2459 also Webster and lately Van Looy.

The expository prologue-speech certainly did not include **F 540, 540a–b**, for the elaborate style of these fragments suits only an in-play narrative by a participant. Some have thought therefore that Oedipus' victory over the Sphinx happened at the play's very start and was immediately reported (cf. the speedy start of *IT*, with the capture of Orestes and Pylades reported at 260–339). Dingel (1970), 93–4 has gone furthest here; he limits the plot to Oedipus' victory, his accession to the kingship, marriage to Jocasta, revelation as Laius' killer and then blinding, and finally Jocasta's support for him – with no disclosure of his true parentage to reveal also his parricide and incest. This gives the play no final catastrophe (most unlikely: Aélion [1986], 47, cf. Hose [1990], 14), unless Euripides wanted an unrealised but inevitable calamity, as for the Trojans in *Alexandros* and the Greeks in *Troades*.

F 541 is also from a report-speech, but by a conventional messenger, a servant of Laius who describes the blinding in which he shared. Two such speeches in one play would not be unusual for late Euripides (cf. e.g. *IT, Pho.* and *Bacc.*). Nor is it necessary to suppose that F 541 must follow F 540 in dramatic order: indeed it is on this point that Hose (1990) has made an attractive

[2] Opinion has moved increasingly against crediting Hyginus with access to 'narrative hypotheses' of Euripides: see Huys cited under *Myth* in the Bibl. above, and e.g. on *Antiope*, p. 261 below.

[3] Reconciliation of diverse secondary matter with primary evidence is more than usually difficult in the case of *Oedipus* (cf. Collard, 2004). There is a very balanced evaluation of everything potentially significant, of progress made by previous reconstructions, and a qualified endorsement of Aélion's, by Van Looy 430–44.

reconciliation of our gappy indications how the plot developed. Hose thinks that the narrative of the Sphinx was Oedipus' own, telling Periboea in detail how he became king; she has come from Corinth to Thebes to bring her 'son' comfort over the death of his 'father' Polybus (Hygin. 67.7 above; cf. Robert 1.317–8).

Hose's suggestion accommodates Oedipus' gradual revelation, first to himself as outcast foundling and therefore not the natural son of Polybus; second, to the Thebans, as Laius' killer – this second, Hose suggests, because Periboea would have come to Thebes in the chariot which belonged to Laius and was in the murder-incident, and which Oedipus had sent to Polybus as thanks for his upbringing, *Pho.* 44–5. The scholiast there records the gift, but of horses, in Euripides' near contemporary Antimachus of Colophon; so too in Hyginus; in Nicol. Damasc. it is Laius' mules which Oedipus himself takes to Polybus. Laius' men would have recognised the chariot when it came with Periboea and inferred that Oedipus was the killer, so blinding him, perhaps under the leadership of Creon; the use of the chariot as a 'recognition-token' goes back to Hartung (1844) and especially Wecklein (1901, 689ff.). Third, the now blind Oedipus, deposed from the kingship, has a scene with Jocasta, perhaps in Periboea's company (Hose 13), in which his true parentage comes out. Laius' old servant Menoetes, who exposed the baby Oedipus, may have contributed to the identification from Oedipus' scarred feet (Hygin. 67.7); Robert thought this corroboration unnecessary, while Webster (246) suggested it may have given Creon another chance to force the revelation through, and located F *555 here. Such a development in the plot would be wholly tragic: Periboea, a family-member rather than an outsider, initiates from concern what becomes a catastrophe for her 'son' (compare Deianeira's attempt to win back her husband in S. *Trach.,* and the reward-seeking Corinthian servant who brings disaster in *OT*). For this typically Euripidean reversal of the happy reunion normal in 'lost-and-found' plays see also on *Alexandros*, p. 46. The 'recognition' and disastrous 'reunion' of Oedipus with his birth-mother Jocasta is verified by at least one physical token, the chariot (compare the cradle at *Ion* 1337ff., the letter at *IT* 791ff.), and perhaps also by bodily wounds (compare the scar at *El.* 573ff.).

Thus the major part of the play would acquire shape and sequence; its second and final catastrophe is Oedipus' complete revelation and exile, its closing scene is Jocasta's support for her blinded husband in **F 545** and ***545a** (compare Theseus' support for his friend Heracles after the killing of the children, *HF* 1215ff., only a little earlier in date). At F *545a.11–12 she states expressly that she will share his moral responsibility, a reference to their incestuous marriage rather than to his parricide; the gnomic fragments apparently bearing upon marriage (**F 542–4, 546–51**) may come from this scene between the two – especially if it was a 'debate' in which Jocasta had to convince Oedipus (again, like Theseus convincing Heracles), even more so if their argument is held in the presence of Creon trying to prevent her support or to punish Oedipus further (**F 554a**); in **F 551** Jocasta may be criticising Creon's long jealousy of Oedipus. Oedipus' unexpected joy (**F 550**) perhaps belongs to this ending, possibly also the two reflections on life's mutability (**F 549, 554**), whether also spoken by him or by the Chorus.

Here too would belong **F 554b**, an invocation of Athens (if the text is sound: see Comm.). Oedipus invokes the place of his ultimate refuge and death, as after Euripides in S. *OC* 84ff. where he senses the end promised him in an oracle, a motif found also at the probably inauthentic *Pho.* 1703ff. Indeed, Aélion (52) suggested that he may be recalling such an oracle here, or responding to a god's instructions to go to Athens, in a further typical Euripidean turn (compare the gods' spoken orders for Orestes' future movements before he finds release at *El.* 1251ff., *Or.* 1643ff.). F 554b cannot have been spoken in Athens itself by an Oedipus already removed from Thebes; such a change of scene at play-end is unthinkable, although suggested by di Gregorio 91.

Webster's reconstruction (inferred from his discussion; he gives no scheme): Prologue by Creon with F 539a, 540, 540a–b. Oedipus discovered as Laius' killer, and blinded, through the jealous energy of Creon, early in the play, F 541, cf. 551. Towards the end, Oedipus has been revealed also as Laius' son through Periboea's intervention, Creon sends him into exile and Jocasta supports him, F 545, *545a (F 543–4, 546, 553–4 belong in this context); F 557 is spoken by Jocasta only 'after the truth comes out'. Webster notes that F 542, 547, 552, 556 and 554a establish a contrast between the characters of Oedipus and Creon, but he marks all of them as impossible to locate confidently.

Aélion's reconstruction (largely shared by Van Looy): F 539a represents the prologue (Creon); Oedipus' victory over the Sphinx begins the action, F 540, 540a–b (after the parodos, Van Looy); Oedipus is offered the throne by Creon, to his joy (F 550; Van Looy has Oedipus and Creon discuss the music for his wedding to Jocasta, F 556; followed by a stasimon). Laius' servants recognise Oedipus as their late master's killer, tell Creon, and Oedipus is blinded, F 541, and deprived of the throne. Periboea arrives and becomes the agent of the further revelation; a 'formal debate' or 'agon' of Oedipus and Creon follows, in F 542, 547, 553, 554a (Van Looy adds 552) and perhaps 549, 554 (Van Looy has 554a as Oedipus' resigned acceptance, 549 and 555 as comments by the Chorus). Jocasta gives Oedipus her support, F 548, *545a, 545, 546, 551, 543 (Van Looy [458 n. 43] adds 544 but regards 543 as impossible to locate and textually intractable). Creon insists that Oedipus should leave Thebes, F 554b (Van Looy dismisses its association with an oracle), and he goes off with Jocasta.

Other proposed ascriptions. For **F 1029.4–5** see Comm. on F 542.3. **F 912**, a short lyric excerpt in praise of a divine 'Mind' as a source of relief from troubles (cf. the notorious *Tro.* 884–8), was ascribed to the beginning of our play by A. Mehat, *REG* 80 (1967), XXVIII. All now discounted are: **Eur. Phil. F 799a** (see p. 24), formerly Soph. F 667 N = 733 Pearson (attrib. Eur. *Oed.* by Unger); **Diog. Sinop. TrGF I 88 F 4**, formerly adesp. F 284 N (attrib. Eur. *Oed.* by Valckenaer); **adesp. F 8** (from an unknown poet's *Oedipus*; suggested for Eur. *Oed.* by Welcker).

Illustrations. There are two pictures of the Corinthian Polybus receiving the infant Oedipus. One is an Attic red-figure amphora of c. 450 B.C., earlier than Sophocles and Euripides (*LIMC* 'Oedipus' no. 3; Moret P 1. 1; Carpenter, *Art and Myth* Pl. 261): a herdsman hands the baby to him, as in *Pho.* 28–9 (at S. *OT* 1142–3 a herdsman of Laius gives it to Polybus' servant; in Schol. Eur. *Pho.* 1760 (Pisander) it is a herdsman of Sicyon who hands it to Polybus' wife Merope). Euripides may have named a herdsman in *Oed.*; if Hose (1990) is right, however (see *Reconstruction*), he had Periboea as Polybus' wife discovering the infant and bringing it to Polybus for adoption – exactly as in the composite scene depicted on a 'Homeric cup' of the 2nd C. B.C. (*LIMC* 'Oedipus' no. 4; Robert I. 326 fig. 49; Séchan fig. 124): a seated Nereid symbolizes the sea-shore where the baby is found (in Schol. E. *Pho.* 26 Laius has the baby exposed in a chest at sea; in Schol. 28 it comes ashore at Corinth); the god Hermes (named) presides over the 'lucky' discovery; Periboea appears in two adjacent scenes (her name is between her two figures), lifting the baby above a chest near a rock and later handing it (now named) to an enthroned Polybus (part-name); and all this is consistent with Hygin. *Fab.* 66.2.

Oedipus' encounter with the Sphinx was pictured with extraordinary frequency. From over eighty works documented by Moret (1984), one in particular is regularly reproduced, which may be earlier even than Aeschylus' Theban plays of 467, let alone those of Sophocles and Euripides, an Attic red-figure cup of c. 470 B.C. (*LIMC* no. 19; Moret Pl. 50.4, and e.g. Carpenter, *Art and Myth* Pl. 264); this and many other paintings show the Sphinx 'perched', often on a column, in a posture like that described in F 540 (see Comm.); it seems certain that an established painters' tradition here influenced Euripides.

Oedipus' forcible blinding (F 541) has so far been found in only one work of art, an Etruscan alabaster urn of the 2nd C. B.C. (*LIMC* 'Oedipus' no. 85 = 'Iokaste' no. 6 with Pl.; Robert I.307 fig. 48). Oedipus is held to the ground as described by Euripides; the artist shows a figure with a sceptre, presumably Creon, and may be ultimately indebted to the play, but has added the figures of Jocasta and Oedipus' children to make a composite scene; the former would hardly be present at a blinding, the latter are not provably present in the play (but see Comm. on F 543.3).

Themes and characters. We cannot know whether Euripides allowed an eventful action to speak for itself or commented explicitly on its surprising turns (see *Reconstruction* on F 539a); or whether he gave particular colour to the main participants Oedipus and Jocasta, as implied by Malalas, and perhaps to Creon, combining action with individual interest especially in Jocasta, as in *Pho.*; many reconstructors have seen Creon's jealousy of Oedipus as a major theme (Comm. on F 551). The play bears Oedipus' name, so that it is frustrating so little survives of his reactions to his disasters (perhaps F 543, 548–50); it would be illuminating to set these against the physical and mental self-laceration of Sophocles' hero, and to compare Euripides' Oedipus with his Heracles (see *Reconstruction*). Huys (*Tale,* 357) suggests, from the references to intelligence in F 548 and *545a, that Euripides depicted Oedipus' qualities solely as intellectual (see also F 540.7–10 n.). Something of a noble acceptance in Oedipus may have prompted Jocasta's own (Webster 246 notes that his quietude and her strength match the couple's roles in *Pho.*). In this respect she is the one character of the play who is at all visible; and the fragments of her long speech in tetrameters (F 545, *545a) suggest that Euripides made a big thing of her, possibly in the style of Electra supporting her sick brother in *Or.* 1–315, or of Antigone true to her father Oedipus in *Pho.* 1679 ('I shall go into exile with my wretched father') and 1690 ('So must I too not share your troubles?': cf. Jocasta in F *545a.12). It may be that Euripides, no less than Sophocles before him in *Antigone* and after him in *OC*, seized upon the unique family-relationships to portray extreme devotions. Perhaps Euripides made room for Periboea herself urging Jocasta to comfort Oedipus.

Staging. The fragments permit only one inference: if Oedipus was blinded (off-stage) during the play, at his reappearance Euripides achieved the same theatrical effect through a change to a bloody mask as had Sophocles at *OT* 1296, and he himself with his blinded Polymestor at *Hec.* 1056. It is not credible to rest upon F 554b a change of scene from Thebes to Athens at play-end: see above on *Reconstruction*, and the Comm.

Date. The use in the play of trochaic tetrameters permits a dating shortly before 415 at the earliest (see the Comm. on F 545); but it would not quite match the general inference from metrical resolutions in the dialogue trimeters (the test-base is too small for sureness). Cropp-Fick 85 nevertheless say 'dates after 415 are clearly the most likely'; on 70 they give the range 419–406, i.e. the last quarter of Euripides' career, and note that the resolution in F 553.2 is of a late type. Hose (1990) has conjectured 410 for the first production, shared with *Auge* and *Temenidae*.

Other dramatizations; influence. The story of the self-destructive royal house of Thebes was popular with tragedians from the start (see *Myth* above). Tragedies entitled *Oedipus* are known from Euripides' contemporaries Achaeus, Philocles and Xenocles, and from a number of 4th C. tragedians, in particular Meletus with his tetralogy '*Oedipodeia*': see *TrGF* II.336, III.288; Van Looy 434–5. Only one Athenian comedy is known: in the 4th C. Eubulus wrote an *Oedipus* which was probably at least allusive to Euripides' play (the scrappy fragments do not help reconstruction); but the Oedipus-Sphinx encounter was burlesqued in a number of South Italian farces of the 4th and 3rd centuries: see Trendall-Webster IV. 32 (bibl.). Epicharmus in the early 5th C. wrote a comic *Sphinx*, and Aeschylus a satyr-play of this name (very fragmentary; it concluded his Theban tetralogy of 467). Among later plays, Seneca's 1st C. A.D. *Oedipus* (its debt to Euripides cannot be known) was staged in an adaptation by Ted Hughes in London in 1969; for modern performances of Sophocles (first in 1585), see R. C. Jebb, *Sophocles. Oedipus Tyrannus*, xxxiii–li and Flashar, *Inszenierung* 27–34, 393, 404–6.

For the literary development of the Oedipus-myth throughout antiquity see Gantz and e.g. F. Wehrli, *MH* 14 (1957), 108–17. For the incalculable later effect of the central Oedipus-story see L. Edmunds, *The Sphinx in the Oedipus Legend* (Königstein, 1981), 1–39, repr. in L. Edmunds, A. Dundes (eds.), *Oedipus: a Folklore Casebook* (New York, 1983), 147–73; L. Edmunds, *Oedipus: the Ancient Legend and its Later Analogues* (Baltimore, London, 1985, repr. 1996); B. Gentili, R. Pretagostini (eds.), *Edipo. Il teatro greco e la cultura europea* (Rome, 1986); *OGCMA* 754–62; Henrichs in *Neue Pauly* (bibl. above, *Myth*). As to Freud, an excellent starting-point is J. Bremmer, 'Oedipus and the Greek Oedipus Complex' in J. Bremmer (ed.), *Interpretations of Greek Mythology* (London, 1987), 41–59 (with rich bibliography); also P. L. Rudnytsky, *Freud and Oedipus* (New York, 1987).

ΟΙΔΙΠΟΥΣ

–/T iii Hypothesis P. Oxy. 2455 fr. 4.40–2

Ο]ἰδίπους, [οὗ ἀρχή·
Φοί]βου ποτ' οὐ̣κ̣ [ἐῶντος ἔσπειρεν] τέκν̣[ο]ν

539a (adesp. 378 N)

Φοί̣βου ποτ' οὐκ ι̣ἐῶντος ἔσπειρενι τέκνιοιν

540   *Ends of nine trimeters, then scrappy centres of six more:*

]. ιδῆ τε βοστρύχ[ων] φόβην·
οὐρὰν δ' ὑπί]λασ' ὑπὸ λεοντόπουν βάσιν
καθέζετ'[– x]δ' ἀποφέρουσ' ὠκύπτερον
]ν ἐπιπα . . ιριζ[.]ν̣ χρόνωι
]υ̣ διήλεσε . . φυλλων φόβην   5
x – ◡ – x] προσβάληι τ' αὐγαῖς πτερόν·
εἰ μὲν πρὸς ἵπ̣ιπους Ἡλίου, χρυσωπὸν ἦ̣ιν
νώτισμα θηριός· εἰ δὲ ιπριὸς νέιφος βάλοι,
κυανωπὸν ὥ̣ις τις ῞Ιριις ἀντηύιγει ισέλας.
only a few letters are legible in 10–15

T iii Hypothesis P. Oxy. 2455 fr. 4.40–2 (2nd C. A.D.), ed. Turner (1962); fr. 18 col. 1.1–6
was identified as from *Oed.* by W. Luppe, *ZPE* 60 (1985), 20; there are a few letters, including 5 ἐ]πὶ γήρως 'in old age'.   **539a** (82 A, 1 Budé) See Hypoth. above; complete verse
in Plut. *Mor.* 205c and *Life of Cicero* 874d, unattrib.; already attrib. *Oed.* by Meineke;
assigned variously to Creon, a servant of the dead Laius, or Hermes   τέκνα Plut.
540, 540a, 540b (83 A, 2 Budé) P. Oxy. 2459 (4th C. A.D.), ed. Turner (1962); re-ed.
H. Lloyd-Jones, *Gnomon* 35 (1963), 446–7, Vaio (1964, 43–7, in part); frs. i and ii are almost
certainly from one column (Dingel [1970] reversed them: see Comm. on F 540); fr. iii cannot
be placed in relation to them; frs. iv and v are exiguous and not reproduced here. Readings,
corrections and supplements are by ed. pr. except where noted. The three frs. are almost
certainly from one speech (assigned to Oedipus by Hose: see *Reconstruction*).

OEDIPUS

T iii Hypothesis

Oedipus, <which begins,> 'Although *<Phoebus forbade him>,* (Laius) once *<got >* a child . . .'

539a   Although Phoebus forbade him, (Laius) once got a child . . .

F 540, 540a, 540b are from a narrative describing the Sphinx preparing to pose the famous riddle:

540   . . . locks of her hair. Curling her tail beneath her lion's legs and feet she sat down . . . putting away her swift-flying . . . in time(?) . . . she(?). . . (of leafy?) foliage(?).[5] . . . *<so as to?>* . . . and hold(?) her wing to the rays. If the creature held her winged back towards the Sun's horses, its hue was golden; and if towards the cloud, like a rainbow it shone back a dark-blue gleam . . .

540 P. Oxy. fr. i.1–3; cf. Apollod. 3.5.8, '(the Sphinx had) a woman's face but a lion's breast and legs and tail and the wings of a bird.' 1]ρ ed. pr.]ω Austin (or ọ) Kannicht πυρσ]ώδη conj. Diggle   2–3 καθέζετο Ael. *NA* 12.7 (on the Sphinx part-maiden, part-lioness), attrib. Eur. 2 Erot. *Gloss.Hippocr.* υ 23 (p. 89.19 Nachmanson), attrib. Eur. *Oed.*; Athen 15.701b, unattrib.   δ' om. Erot.   ὑπίλλασ' Ael. (ὑπήλας Athen.), corr. Valckenaer ὑπείλλει Erot.   καθίζετο Ael.   εἶτα] δ' or ὦμον] δ' (e. g.) Austin   4 ἐπὶ (prepos.) ed. pr.   παραι or παλαι ed. pr.   πασαι Kannicht   5 διήλεσ(ε) P ('perhaps from διαλέω' Lloyd-Jones) διήλασ(ε) conj. ed. pr.   φυλλων read by Kannicht (ἐριφύλλων or ἐπι-φύλλων conj. Lloyd-Jones) ἐπιφράσων conj. ed. pr.   6 beg. ὅταν (ὅπως Vaio) μεθῆι τε] (e.g.) ed. pr.   7–9 Stob. 4.20.68 = Plut. *Mor.* F 136 Sandbach (VII p. 133.16 Bernadakis), both unattrib. (= F adesp. 541 N); first suggested for *Oed.* by Valckenaer   7 ἵπ]πους P αὐγὰς Stob.   8 P has the colon   νέφος P νέφη Stob.

540a *Centres of fourteen verses, but only vestiges of the first line:*

x – ⏑ –]μον ἐλίπομεν [x – ⏑ –   2
x – ⏑]πων ἵσταντ' ἀ[– x – ⏑ –
x – ⏑ σ]υρίξασ' ἱ . . . . [
x – ⏑] αἴνιγμ' ἡ μιαι[φόνος κόρη   5
x – ⏑]πειποῦσ' ἐξά[μ]ετ[ρ(α) x – ⏑ –
– ⏑ ⏑ – ⏑ ⏑]εν· ξύνεσιν δ' ἔχο[ν – ⏑ ⏑ – –
τέτραπον ἠδὲ δί]πουν τι τρίπο[υν ⏑ ⏑ – ⏑ ⏑ – –
– ⏑ ⏑ – ⏑ ⏑]νῇ τρισὶ δ' [– ⏑ ⏑ – ⏑ ⏑ – –
– ⏑ ⏑ – ⏑ ⏑]ίν δ' ἄρσεν κα[ὶ (⏑) – ⏑ ⏑ – –   10
x – ⏑] εύεις ἢ πάλιν β[x – ⏑ –
x –]ὸν ὕμνον οπ[
x – ⏑] ὑμεῖς λέξ[ατ(ε) – x – ⏑ –
only two letters legible in line 14

540b *Right-centres of six lines (almost certainly trimeters), but only vestiges of lines 1 and 6 and a few letters in 2, 4 and 5:*

ἀν]ταγωνιστῇ[ι   3

541 ΛΑΙΟΥ ΘΕΡΑΠΩΝ
ἡμεῖς δὲ Πολύβου παῖδ' ἐρείσαντες πέδωι
ἐξομματοῦμεν καὶ διόλλυμεν κόρας.

542 οὗτοι νόμισμα λευκὸς ἄργυρος μόνον
καὶ χρυσός ἐστιν, ἀλλὰ κἀρετὴ βροτοῖς
νόμισμα κεῖται πᾶσιν, ἧι χρῆσθαι χρεών.

540a P. Oxy. fr. ii   3]πων Kannicht   4 ἵνα[Turner   5 end Snell in ed. pr.   6 beg. τοιόνδ' ἐ]πειποῦσ' ed. pr.   τοσόνδ' ὑ]πειποῦσ' 'not unsuitable' Kannicht   end ἐξά[μ]ετ[ρ' ἀφῆκ' ἔπη Barrett   7–10 a version of the Sphinx's riddle in five dactylic hexameters is found in Athen. 10.456b (transl. in Comm.), who acknowledges as source Asclep. Trag. (FGH 12 F 7), as does Schol. Pho. 50; also in Hypoth. Pho. 5, S. OT Hypoth. III, Schol. (Tzetzes) Lycophr. Alex. 7, Anth.Pal. 14.64 (cf. Apollod. 3.5.8 in App. to 540.1–3 above)   7 beg. ἔστι τι φωνῇεν (ex. gr.) Lloyd-Jones, after ἔν τι τὸ φωνῇεν Snell (but both seem too short): line 1 of the five-line version ends with οὗ μία φωνή   double-colon (:) after]εν P   end δέχο P, with no elision   δ' ἔχο[ν ed. pr. ('χ most uncertain' Kannicht)

116

540a   . . . we left . . . they were placing themselves . . . . .
(the Sphinx) hissing . . . riddle . . . the murderous
<*maiden*>⁵ . . . pronouncing . . . hexameter(s) . . .
intelligence . . . <*on four feet and on two*> feet (?) a
thing on three feet . . . three . . . male (and?) . . .¹⁰
. . . again . . . song . . . you are to say . . .

540b   . . . (to an, the) antagonist . . .

541   *SERVANT OF LAIUS*
Pressing Polybus' son firmly to the ground we blind
him and destroy the pupils of his eyes.

The forcible blinding of Oedipus is narrated.

*Most of frs. 542–554a are assigned by editors, with
varying confidence, to an episode involving Oedipus and
Jocasta and perhaps Creon or even also Periboea:*

542   I tell you, pale silver and gold are not the only
currency, but virtue too is an established
currency for all mankind, which they should use.

---

10 end κα[ὶ θῆλυ Snell   11] ευς (ed. pr.) or].ους Kannicht   ἤ ed. pr. ἦ P
540b P. Oxy. fr. iii   **541** (84 A, 5 Bude) Schol. Eur. *Pho.* 61 attrib. (Eur.) *Oed.* ('...the
servants of Laius blinded him ...')   **542** (85 A, 11 Budé) Stob. 3.1.3 attrib. Eur. *Oed.*;
Orion, *App.Eur.* 21 Haffner, attrib. Eur.   1–2 Philodemus, *Rhet.* I p. 262.5 Sudhaus, attrib.
Eur.; paraphrased by Clem. Alex. *Strom.* 4.5.24.6, attrib. Sophocles   1–2 οὔκουν μόνον
τοῦτο νόμισμα λευκὸς ἄργυρος ἢ χρυσός Clem. οὔτοι βροτοῖσι κέρδος ἄργυρος
μόνος...κἀρετὴ μέγα Orion   3 ἦν κτᾶσθαι Nauck, doubting the verse's authenticity.
For this verse Gomperz substituted, after a lacuna, F 1029.4–5 ἀρετὴ δ' ὅσωιπερ μᾶλλον
ἂν χρῆσθαι θέλης, | τόσωι δὲ μᾶλλον αὔχεται τελουμένη

543 (ΟΙΔΙΠΟΥΣ?) μεγάλη τυραννὶς ἀνδρὶ τέκνα καὶ γυνή
<   >
ἴσην γὰρ ἀνδρὶ συμφορὰν εἶναι λέγω
τέκνων θ' ἁμαρτεῖν καὶ πάτρας καὶ χρημάτων
ἀλόχου τε κεδνῆς, ὡς μόνων τῶν χρημάτων
<   >
ἢ κρεῖσσόν ἐστιν ἀνδρί, σώφρον' ἢν λάβηι ...   5

544   ἄλλως δὲ πάντων δυσμαχώτατον γυνή.

545 (ΙΟΚΑΣΤΗ)
πᾶσα γὰρ δούλη πέφυκεν ἀνδρὸς ἡ σώφρων γυνή·
ἡ δὲ μὴ σώφρων ἀνοίαι τὸν ξυνόνθ' ὑπερφρονεῖ.

*545a (909 N)
('Ιοκ.) οὐδεμίαν ὤνησε κάλλος εἰς πόσιν ξυνάορον,
ἀρετὴ δ' ὤνησε πολλάς· πᾶσα γὰρ κεδνὴ γυνὴ
ἥτις ἀνδρὶ συντέτηκε σωφρονεῖν ἐπίσταται.
πρῶτα μὲν γὰρ τοῦθ' ὑπάρχει· κἂν ἄμορφος ἦι πόσις,
χρὴ δοκεῖν εὔμορφον εἶναι τῆι γε νοῦν κεκτημένηι,   5
οὐ γὰρ ὀφθαλμὸς τὸ κρῖνον < – ‿ > ἐστιν ἀλλὰ νοῦς.
εὖ λέγειν δ', ὅταν τι λέξηι, χρὴ δοκεῖν, κἂν μὴ λέγηι,
κἀκπονεῖν ἂν τῶι ξυνόντι πρὸς χάριν μέλληι πονεῖν.
ἡδὺ δ', ἢν κακὸν πάθηι τι, συσκυθρωπάζειν πόσει
ἄλοχον ἐν κοινῶι τε λύπης ἡδονῆς τ' ἔχειν μέρος.   10
σοὶ δ' ἔγωγε καὶ νοσοῦντι συννοσοῦσ' ἀνέξομαι
καὶ κακῶν τῶν σῶν ξυνοίσω, κοὐδὲν ἔσται μοι πικρόν.

543 (86 A, 21 Budé) Stob. 4.22a.1, attrib. Eur. *Oed.* Assigned to Oedipus by Robert. 1 Men. *Mon.* 506 Jaekel separated from 2–5 by Weil 3 χρημάτων Stob. κτημάτων Hermann 4–5 lacuna after 4 Welcker, Meineke μόνον τῶν χρημάτων | γυνή 'στι κρεῖσσον ἀνδρί Robert (μόνον Musgrave, γυνή 'στι κρεῖσσον Dobree) 5 ἢ Stob. ms. Trinc. ἣ ms. A (and Kassel, after the lacuna) ἡ ms. M τί Madvig 544 (87 A, 20 Budé) Stob. 4.22.140, attrib. Eur. *Oed.* Spoken perhaps by Creon or Chorus: Van Looy. ἄλλως Stob. mss. SA ἄλλων ms. M δὲ Stob. τε Meineke 545 (88 A, 7 Budé) Stob. 4.22.85, attrib. Eur. *Oed.*; Clem. Alex. *Strom.* 4.8.63.3, attrib. Eur. (with debased text), after citation of F 546 1 also Stob. 4.22.2, attrib. Eur. Assignment to Jocasta is consistent with F *545a; F 545 was inserted after F *545a.10 by Robert (see App. there) 2 ἡ δὲ Stob. ms. S, Clem. εἰ δὲ Stob. mss. MA, whence in 1 εἰ σώφρων γυνή Blaydes ὑπερφρονεῖ

543 *(OEDIPUS?)* Children and wife are a great kingdom for a man
< . . . > For it is an equal disaster for a man, I say,
to lose children, fatherland and money, as (to lose) a good
wife, since his money alone < . . . > Truly it is better for a
man, if he gets a virtuous (wife) . . .

544 And besides, a woman is the hardest of all things to fight.

Context and speaker uncertain

545 *(JOCASTA)* Every sensible wife is her husband's slave; any who
is not sensible looks down upon her partner out of folly.

*545a *(Joc.)* Beauty benefits no wedded woman with her husband,
but virtue benefits many. Every good wife who has melted
in union with her husband knows how to be sensible. Her
first principle is this: even if her husband is unhandsome,
to a wife with a mind at all he ought to appear handsome;[5]
what judges is not the eye (*a word missing*) but the mind.
She should think that he has eloquence whenever he says
anything, even if he has not; and she should work to
achieve whatever she intends to work at to gratify her
partner. It is pleasing too, if her husband has some setback,
for a wife to put on a sad face with him and to join in
sharing his pains and pleasures.[10] You and I – now you are
guilty of sin, I will endure sharing your guilt and help to
bear your troubles; and nothing will be (too) harsh for me.

Stob. ὑπερφέρει Clem.   ***545a** (– A, 8 Budé) Clem. Alex. *Strom.* 4.20.125.1–126.4,
quoting 7–8, 9–10, 11–12, 1–3, 4–6 separately in sequence: see Comm. Musgrave proposed
the order 1–6, 7–12 (adopted by Nauck, Van Looy; 'probable', Kannicht in *TrGF*).
Assigned to Jocasta in *Oed.*, by C. F. Hermann, noting the common ground between 5–6 and
F 543–8.   2 κεδνή Nauck ἀγαθή Clem. καλή and 3 σωφρονεῖν <τ'> Musgrave (<τ'>
Heath)   4 γὰρ Grotius γε Clem. τοῦθ' Clem. ταῦθ' Musgrave (cf. on 6)   6 τὸ κρῖνον
Sylburg τὸ κρίνειν Clem. (then <δυνατόν> Nauck, <ἱκανόν> Heimsoeth) τὸ <ταῦτα>
κρῖνον Musgrave   end: νοῦς <μόνος> Duentzer νοῦς <ὁρᾶι> Wilamowitz (then
ὀφθαλμοῦ τὸ κρίνειν Nauck)   7 εὖ λέγειν Sylburg εὐλογεῖν Clem.   μὴ λέγηι Clem.
μὴ δοκῆι Nauck   8 ἄν Valckenaer ἄν Clem.   πονεῖν Collard λέγειν Clem. τελεῖν
Wecklein (then δοκεῖν· κἄν μὴ λέγηι | ἐκπονεῖν... Weil)   9 πάθηι τι Blaydes πράξηι
τι Clem. τι πράξηι Grotius   10 τε λύπης Sylburg λύπης τε Clem.   lacuna after 10
Nauck; F 545 inserted here by Robert   12 ἔσται Musgrave ἐστι Clem.

546 (ΧΟΡΟΣ?) πᾶσα γὰρ ἀνδρὸς κακίων ἄλοχος,
κἂν ὁ κάκιστος
γήμηι τὴν εὐδοκιμοῦσαν.

547 ἑνὸς <δ'> ἔρωτος ὄντος οὐ μί' ἡδονή·
οἱ μὲν κακῶν ἐρῶσιν, οἱ δὲ τῶν καλῶν.

548 ('Ιοκ.?) νοῦν χρὴ θεᾶσθαι, νοῦν· τί τῆς εὐμορφίας
ὄφελος, ὅταν τις μὴ φρένας καλὰς ἔχηι;

549 (Οἰδ.?) ἀλλ' ἦμαρ <ἕν> τοι μεταβολὰς πολλὰς ἔχει.

550 (Οἰδ.?) ἐκ τῶν ἀέλπτων ἡ χάρις μείζων βροτοῖς
[φανεῖσα μᾶλλον ἢ τὸ προσδοκώμενον].

551 ('Ιοκ.) φθόνος δ' ὁ πολλῶν φρένα διαφθείρων βροτῶν
ἀπώλεσ' αὐτὸν κἀμὲ συνδιώλεσεν.

552 πότερα γενέσθαι δῆτα χρησιμώτερον
συνετὸν ἄτολμον ἢ θρασύν τε κἀμαθῆ;
τὸ μὲν γὰρ αὐτῶν σκαιὸν ἀλλ' ἀμύνεται,
τὸ δ' ἡσυχαῖον ἀργόν· ἐν δ' ἀμφοῖν νόσος.

553 (Οἰδ.?) ἐκμαρτυρεῖν γὰρ ἄνδρα τὰς αὐτοῦ τύχας
εἰς πάντας ἀμαθές, τὸ δ' ἐπικρύπτεσθαι σοφόν.

546 (89 A, 10 Budé) Clem. Alex. *Strom.* 4.8.63.2, attrib. Eur. (cf. on 545) 1 κακίων... εὐ-
δικιμοῦσαν Stob. 4.22.187, attrib. Eur. *Oed.* Assigned to Chorus by Robert. 1 κακίων
Clem., Stob. χείρων anon., Heimsoeth 2 κάκιστος Stob. κράτιστος Clem. 547 (90
A, 12 Budé) Stob. 1.9.2a, attrib. Eur. *Oed.* 1 <δ'> Grotius 2 κακῶν Grotius τῶν
κακῶν Stob. 548 (91 A, 9 Budé) Stob. 4.21.19, attrib. Eur. *Oed.* Assigned to Jocasta by
Aélion. 1 θεᾶσθαι, νοῦν· τί Elmsley θεάσασθαι οὐδέν τι Stob. mss. SMA (but
θεᾶσθαι ms. Paris. 1985) 2 μὴ φρένας Gesner μὴ τὰς φρένας Stob. 549 (92 A,
17 Budé) Stob. 4.41.45, attrib. Eur. *Oed.* Tentatively assigned to Oed. by Robert. <ἕν>
Nauck 550 (93 A, 3 Budé) Stob. 4.47.4, attrib. Eur. *Oed.* Oedipus suggested as speaker by
Robert. 1 χάρις Stob. χαρὰ Nauck 2 del. Herwerden, def. Gomperz and others

546 *(Cho. ?)* Every wife is inferior to her husband, even if the most inferior of men marries a woman of high standing.

Context uncertain.

547 Although love is a single thing, its pleasure is not single: some love what is bad, some love what is good.

Context and speaker not known

548 *(Joc.?)* The mind is what to watch, the mind! What use is handsomeness when one does not have good sense?

549 *(Oed.?)* But one day truly holds many changes.

550 *(Oed.?)* Delight resulting from unexpected events is greater for men [when it appears rather than what is expected].

551 *(Joc.)* Envy which ruins the wits of many men destroyed him, and destroyed me with him.

552 Is it indeed more useful to be intelligent without courage, than both headstrong and crass? The one of these is foolish but defends itself, the other, which is peaceable, is lazy; and there is weakness in both.

Context and speaker uncertain.

553 *(Oed.?)* It is stupid for a man to testify to his misfortunes in front of everybody; concealing them is wise.

551 (94 A, 6 Budé) Stob. 3.38.9, attrib. Eur. *Oed.* Assigned to Jocasta by C. F. Hermann.
552 (95 A, 13 Budé) Stob. 3.7.9, attrib. Eur. *Oed.* Jocasta suggested as speaker by Aélion.
2 κἀμαθῆ Grotius κ' ἐμμανῆ Stob. ms. M and after correction ms. A (perhaps κεὑμενῆ ms. A itself) **553** (96 A, 14 Budé) Stob. 4.45.6, attrib. Eur. *Oed.* Assigned to Oedipus by Robert; possibly Chorus, Collard.

EURIPIDES

554   πολλάς γ' ὁ δαίμων τοῦ βίου μεταστάσεις
         ἔδωκεν ἡμῖν μεταβολάς τε τῆς τύχης.

554a (1049 N)

(ΚΡΕΩΝ?) ἐγὼ γὰρ ὅστις μὴ δίκαιος ὢν ἀνὴρ
         βωμὸν προσίζει, τὸν νόμον χαίρειν ἐῶν
         πρὸς τὴν δίκην ἄγοιμ' ἂν οὐ τρέσας θεούς·
         κακὸν γὰρ ἄνδρα χρὴ κακῶς πάσχειν ἀεί.

554b   (Οἰδ.?) < x – ᴗ > ὦ πόλισμα Κεκροπίας χθονός,
         ὦ ταναὸς αἰθήρ, ὦ < ᴗ – x – ᴗ – >

Unplaced fragments

*555   ἀλλ' ἡ Δίκη γὰρ καὶ κατὰ σκότον βλέπει.

556   τόν θ' ὑμνοποιὸν δόνα[χ' ὃν ἐκτρέφει Μέ]λας
         ποταμός, ἀηδόν' εὐπνόων αὐλῶν σοφήν

557   ἄναρθρος

554 (97 A, 16 Budé) Stob. 4.41.44, attrib. Eur. *Oed.* (followed there by F 549). Assigned to Oedipus by Robert, to Chorus by Van Looy.   **554a** (98 A, 15 Budé) Stob. 4.5.11, attrib. Eur.; assigned to Creon by Aélion   3   *Mantiss.Prov.* 1.83 *CPG* II.757.3, unattrib. 4 Theosoph.Tubing. §86 Erbse (1955[1] p. 201.6, 1995[2] p. 55), attrib. Eur. *Oed.*   πάσχειν Stob., *Mantiss.* πράσσειν Theosoph.   **554b** (– A, 19 Budé) = Men. *Samia* 325–6 (with self-interruption by the speaker after the second ὦ), attrib. Eur. *Oed.* by a marginal scholion in P. Bodm. 25 of Men. Tentatively assigned to Oedipus by Kannicht, comparing F 550 1 Καδμείας (or Θηβαίας) Cropp (Καδμείας also Van Looy)   ***555** (*99a A, 18 Budé) Stob. 1.3.6 has after the lemma 'Eur. *Oed.*' a part-dactylic line now known to be Callim. *Aetia* F 239.5 *Suppl.Hell.* (= P. Ant. 113 fr. 1.b.5), followed directly by this iambic verse. Its attribution to the play is therefore wholly uncertain.   σκότον Kannicht σκότους Stob. **556** (100 A, 4 Budé) P. Oxy. 2536 col.i.28–30 (2nd C. A.D.), from Theon's commentary on Pind. *Pyth.* 12.25–6, attrib. Eur. *Oed.*; Hesych. α 1500 Latte (ἀηδόνα· γλωττίδα μεταφορικῶς), attrib. Eur. *Oed.* = *Anecd.Gr.* I p. 349.3 Bekker = Photius α 441 Theodoridis, attrib. 'the tragedian(s)'   ἐκτρέφει Gentili ἐκφύει Turner (ed. pr.)   **557** (101 A, 22 Budé) Hesych. α 4544 Latte, attrib. Eur. *Oed.*

122

554   The god gives us many transformations of our life and changes to our fortune.

554a *(CREON?)* Any man who unrighteously sits in sanctuary at an altar – I would myself dismiss the law and take that man to justice without fear of the gods; for a bad man should always be treated badly.

554b *(Oed.?)* O citadel of the land of Cecrops, O outspread heaven, O . . . !

Unplaced fragments

*555   The truth is, Justice sees even in darkness.

556   . . . and the reed, maker of song, <*which*> the Black River <*grows to fullness*>, the skilful nightingale of pipes sweetly-blown

557   limp (of limbs)

Commentary on *Oedipus*

Hypothesis. For P. Oxy. 2455 and its preservation of many Euripidean fragmentary 'hypotheses' see our Vol. 1 pp. 26 (*Telephus*), 86 (*Stheneboea*), 204 (*Phaethon*), and this vol. pp. 14 (*Philoctetes*), 184 (*Hypsipyle*).

539a. The abrupt narrative start to a prologue-speech is typical: cf. Comm. on *Phil.* F 789a, and *Mel.S.* in our Vol. 1 p. 248; also the openings of several Euripidean plays travestied at Ar. *Frogs* 1177ff. For possible speakers see App. and Introd., *Reconstruction.* **Although Phoebus forbade him:** when Laius consulted Apollo's Delphic oracle about his childlessness, he was told not to father a child in defiance of the gods, for any son would kill him and destroy his house (A. *Sept.* 742–52, *Pho.* 13–20 where 18 has 'don't seed the furrow for children in despite of the gods'; cf. S. *OT* 711–3). **got:** lit. 'sowed, seeded'. [**child:** 'children' in Plut., who recounts Cicero's unkind adaptation of the verse upon meeting Voconius accompanied by his three ugly daughters.]

540, 540a, 540b. For Hose's assignment of these three frs. to Oedipus see Introd., *Reconstruction.*

540. The Sphinx: she has the face of a girl (see Apollod. in App. to 1, cf. 540a.5 n.), a body at least in part glistening (scaly: 7–9 and n.) and with wings (3, 6), lion's legs (2, cf. Apollod.) and possibly hair like a lion's mane (1 and textual n.); she is apparently settling to rest (2–3; 4?); then she reflects rainbow-colours to the sun as she turns about (5?, 6–9). She is a hybrid creature: cf. *Cret.* F 472.bc.29–31 (the Minotaur), S. *Inachus* F 269a.35–45 (Io transforming into a cow), Ezekiel, *Exagoge* (*TrGF* I no. 128), 254–63 (the Phoenix). [This description of the Sphinx (P. Oxy. fr. i) more logically precedes F 540a (fr. ii), its utterance of the famous riddle; but some eds. entertain Dingel's reversal of the order (a 'technical possibility' consistent with the papyrus-fibres; for such a reversal cf. *Cret.* F 472bc in our Vol. 1, p. 61 – though Cozzoli (see Addenda, p. 364 below) now prefers the first editor's order there).]
1. **locks:** φόβην, tumbling hair, a metaphor from thick and hanging foliage; used of a horse's mane at *Alc.* 429; here it suggests a lion's mane [whence Diggle's supplement '<*fiery*> locks', the colour of a lion's head and mane at *HF* 361].
2. **Curling:** ὑπίλασα, a rare compound of the chameleon-like verb εἰλέω (Chantraine, *Dict.Etym.* 319), 'bend, fold etc.' In the countless ancient depictions of the Sphinx (see Moret, 1984), her tail is usually raised into an 's' behind her as she crouches or sits. **lion's legs and feet:** the adj. λεοντόπους, lit. 'lion-footed', resembles ταυρόπους 'bull-footed' (*IA* 275); -πους '-foot(ed)' duplicates βάσιν **legs** (lit. 'going, motion'). Cf. *IA* 421 θηλύπουν βάσιν 'women's (i.e. delicate) legs and feet', and for other such phrases *Arch.* F 242 n.

124

3. swift-flying: the adj. presumably qualified a noun for 'wing' lost in this line or the next; it is used of a hawk at Hom. *Il.* 13.62. The noun ὠκύπτερον is attested only in the Plural, 'wing-feathers', Ar. *Birds* 803 etc. [**3.** 'she sat down *<and then>* ' or 'putting away her swift flying *<shoulder>*' Austin. **4.** Turner (ed. pr.) identified the preposition ἐπὶ ('on, for?'), but his πάλαι ('long ago') is judged less likely than the letters πασαι by Kannicht.]

5. Even the approximate meaning of this line is unsafe to guess. [P. Oxy.'s Aorist διήλεσε is unattested, and no translation is given here; if it is from διαλέω (suggested by Lloyd-Jones), the sense 'she ground down' seems most unlikely in context; if Turner was right to alter it to διήλασε, the doubtful intransitive meaning 'she drove through' conflicts with the Sphinx's seated posture in 3, and the transl. 'spread, distributed' with φόβην 'locks' as object is scarcely possible. The letters before φόβην seem to point to 'leaves', Gen. Pl. φύλλων (half-read by Kannicht), or 'leafy', Gen. of e.g. the adj. ἐριφύλλων (Lloyd-Jones) – in which case φόβην must have its commoner meaning in Eur., 'foliage' (see on 1).]

6. [*<so as to?>*: the Subjunctive is better explained as Final (with Vaio's ὅπως) than as Indefinite (with ὅταν 'whenever', ed. pr.); thus e.g. ὅπως μεθῆι τε] προσβάληι τ(ε), '*<so as to relax> and hold...*'. An Indefinite construction is difficult after the Aorist in 5, and appears in the Optative of 7–9: see Vaio 51–2.]

7–9. The verses show Eur.'s interest in contrasting light- and dark-colour-effects, mocked at Ar. *Frogs* 1331: cf. e.g. *Tro.* 549 'the black gleam of fire' in the night, with Barlow's note; Barlow, *Imagery* 8–14; at *IT* 1245–6 a snake is pictured amid foliage (5 here?). Kannicht in *TrGF* cites an observation by Carolin Hahnemann that our lines may have inspired Virgil's portent-snake at *Aen.* 5.87–9, its back dotted with dark-blue marks, its scales lit by a golden gleam, like a rainbow striking the clouds with a thousand different colours opposite the sun. **creature:** θήρ of the Sphinx as at A. *Sept.* 558; but she is a 'maiden' at F 540a.5 (n.).

Eur.'s expression is compressed here, with 'If (she held it) towards the Sun's horses, the creature's back was golden; and if she held (it) towards the cloud, like a rainbow etc.' **winged back:** νώτισμα means something with which a νῶτον 'back' is provided, i.e. wings; cf. the verb νωτίζω *Pho.* 654, of ivy lying on the back of the infant Dionysus and providing shade. **the Sun's horses:** his chariot and four, daily crossing the sky with his light, e.g. *Pha.* 2–5 Diggle (= F 771.2–5). **golden:** lit. 'gold-faced', χρυσωπόν, of the sunlight *El.* 740; a colour-adj. formed like 9 κυανωπόν (**dark-blue**). **like a rainbow:** lit. 'like some Iris', the rainbow goddess depersonalized as in Hom. *Il.* 11.27 etc. **shone back:** the verb ἀνταυγεῖν is almost always transitive, e.g. *Or.* 1519; probably intransitive in a similar light-study Chaeremon *TrGF* 71 F 14.7.

10–15. [Nothing can be done confidently with the few scrappy letters; if ed. pr. was right with 12 ἀφρόν[ων, this may describe foolish (and unsuccessful) past challengers of the Sphinx.]

540a.2. we left: it is frustrating that P. Oxy. does not preserve the verb's object: a place, a thing or even a person.

3. they were placing themselves: presumably bystanders when the Sphinx spoke the riddle, 5–6; 13?

4. hissing: this translation of the verb συρίζω suits the dangerous Sphinx better than 'piping, whistling, singing', despite 'song' in 12; used of a murderous monster at *PV* 355, of horses dangerously snorting A. *Sept.* 463.

5. <maiden>: her girl's face (see Apollod. in 540.1 App.) dictates this part-for-whole description; κόρη similarly of the Sphinx at S. *OT* 508, παρθένος at *Pho.* 1042; she is **murderous** at *Pho.* [1760].

6. A fairly constant version of the **riddle** occurs throughout antiquity (see App.), with five not four hexameters as follows (approximate line-divisions): 'It is two-footed and four-footed on the ground, with one voice ('one form' in a few versions),[1] / and three-footed, and alone changes its nature ('voice' in a few versions) of all things born[2] / and moving on the earth and up in the sky and down in the sea.[3] / Whenever it goes supported on the greatest number of feet,[4] / then the quickness of its limbs is feeblest'. The 4th C. tragedian Theodectas had a different dactylic riddle from the Sphinx in his *Oedipus* at *TrGF* 72 F 4, as also in an unknown play at F 18: see Kannicht on *Hel.* 353–6. **pronouncing:** the compound ἐπειποῦσα (ed. pr.) suits a portentous or ritual utterance (LSJ ἐπιλέγω I.4) better than ὑπειποῦσα 'intimating, suggesting <this much>' (offered by Kannicht; cf. *HF* 962). **hexameter(s):** this dactylic metre was regular in oracles (Hdt. 7.220 with ἔπη 'verses' [whence Barrett's supplement '<uttered verses> in hexameters', cf. ἔπη at *IT* 723, *Med.* 675, the Sing. at *Alex.* F 62e]. Eur. here strikingly inserts dactylic hexameters into iambic trimeters, as Aristophanes does with the bogus oracles at *Birds* 967ff., *Peace* 1063ff.; in the lyric S. *Phil.* 839–42 hexameters indicate oracular authority.

7–10. intelligence: added by Eur. to the riddle-subject's attributes (but as ed. pr. observes, it almost destroys the riddle), like the subject's apparently indifferent gender (10 **'male (and?)** <female?>). Since the word is embedded in the hexameter riddle, it is difficult to interpret it (with Lloyd-Jones) as the intelligence of those challenged to solve it; the longer version contains no such wording; cf. *Pho.* 1505ff. where the 'intelligent' Oedipus had understood the Sphinx's unintelligible song. Huys (*Tale,* 358) observes that whether 'intelligence' has to do with solver or subject, it 'finally refers to Oedipus, since the man from the riddle is the image of the man who solves it'; cf. Introd., *Themes etc.* [7. '<It is a thing with a voice>' Lloyd-Jones, following Snell's '<There is one thing which has a voice...>'. At the end P. Oxy. is uncertainly read, but its lack of an elision (contrast e.g. 3, 9) seems to rule out ed. pr.'s 'and possessing (intelligence)'; and the *chi* is very unclear.]

11–13. Back to the narrator's trimeters, it appears; but **again** (or 'back') is unclear in reference, **song** seems to describe the intoned or hissed riddle (*Pho.* 1506), and **you are to say!** (Imperative) looks like the Sphinx's challenge to the bystanders (3) to solve the riddle.

540b.3. antagonist: any would-be solver, or Oedipus himself – or is the Sphinx herself meant, if Oedipus is the narrator?

541. For the importance of this fr. see Introd., p. 107. **blind:** a unique sense of the verb ἐξομματόω which elsewhere is '(re)endow with sight', Soph. F 710 etc. **destroy the pupils:** so too *Hec.* 1117 (Polymestor blinded) and *Cyc.* 611 (the Cyclops). For blinding as a punishment in both myth and history see the material in Collard on *Hec.* 1035–55 (fuller lit., Kannicht in *TrGF*). Eur.'s version of Oedipus' blinding may underlie a 2nd C. B.C. bronze urn-relief (see Introd., *Illustrations*) and Suet. *Nero* 21.3, where Nero sings of Oedipus 'blinded'.

542. Axiomatic lines impossible to locate. **pale silver:** also *Phil.* F **790a (n.). **gold:** just gold, not 'pale' or 'white' gold, a term for the gold-silver alloy *electrum* (e.g. Hdt. 1.50.2). For virtue 'shining' from regular use like a bright metal see Pearson on Soph. F 864. Cf. also *Mel.S.* F 486 'Justice's golden countenance', Soph. F 12. Gold itself as a metaphor for things of high value: *Tro.* 432, LSJ χρυσός 3.
[3. The repetition of νόμισμα from 1, and 3's absence from Philod. and Clem., caused Nauck's doubt of the verse; but his conjecture 'which they should possess' is needless. He and Wilamowitz were attracted by Gomperz's suggestion that F 1029.4–5, two verses which fit badly after 1–3 there, belong after our 1–2 and a lacuna: '...**not the only currency, but virtue too** <*is preferable for mortals and more lasting, since mortals are worn away and consumed by use;*> (1029.4–5:) *but the more you are willing to practise virtue, the more it grows from being tendered*' (τελουμένη, like money, suiting 'currency' in 1–3: cf. perhaps *Alc.* 132; LSJ τελέω II.1.b, esp. 2, 3).]

543. Possibly Oedipus praising the virtues of such a wife as Jocasta (rather than her own praise of her sex: F 545, *545a). [If Oedipus is speaking, τυραννίς in line 1 means **kingdom** (he values Jocasta as highly as the literal kingdom of Thebes which he has now lost: Robert II.110 n. 11), and a brief lacuna after 1 (Weil) seems necessary. If τυραννίς is 'tyranny' (so e.g. Webster 244), this is hardly Oedipus talking of Jocasta; and the lacuna must be large, or 2–4 must be supposed to come from a different context or even play, and to be conflated with 1 through loss of the intervening lemma in Stob. (see on **Truly** in line 5, and on F *555 below).]
3. to lose children: life's greatest disaster, e.g. *Supp.* 782–5, 792–3. Oedipus is not necessarily foreseeing the loss of his own children (it is unknown whether Eur.'s play ended with his separation from them, as in Sophocles, or with his curse upon them, or even if they appeared in the play at all).
4–5. as (to lose) a good wife: that τε (as) introduces the single term **wife** in contrast with the preceding three terms is shown by the immediate but now incomplete explanation **since his money alone....** The repetition of **money** between 3 and 4 seems unstylish, but cf. e.g. F 542.1 and 3. Kannicht indeed suggests that the repetition may have been important in the now incomplete

clause. [So Hermann's 'possessions' in 3 is not needed. It is easier to mark a
lacuna after 4 (Welcker) than to emend 4 and 5 into coherence with 3, as many
scholars have done, e.g. Robert in App.: 'since only a wife is better than money
for a husband'. In 5 **Truly** either confirms a statement about the superiority of a
wife which is missing in the lacuna, or it may be yet another originally separate
(but incomplete) quotation conflated by the loss of its lemma (see on 1); similarly
Madvig's 'What is better...?' Kassel follows Stob. ms. A, '...or it is better...', an
alternative to the lost statement, as in *Mel.D.* F 494.23–5, a repudiation of men's
blame for women already questioned in 1–3 of that fr.]

544.   Probably a remark about Jocasta when she determinedly supports Oedipus;
Creon or Chorus-leader are suggested speakers. The fr. belongs in the same overall
context as F 545–548.   **woman...hardest...to   fight:** an age-old prejudice,
Hes. *Works* 702–3, Semonides F 6 *IEG*, Eur. *Hipp.Cal.* F 429, *Phoenix* F 808 etc.
[Stob's ἄλλων gives 'And of all other things woman is....']

545.   Jocasta's commendation of a wife's prudent support for a husband (cf.
F *545a.2–10) anticipates her intention of joining Oedipus in his punishment
(11–12 there). The dialogue-metre has changed to trochaic tetrameters, adopted by
Eur. in his latest plays for stirring or emotional scenes and reviving their use from
the earliest Greek tragedy. They reappear first in *HF* 855ff. and *Tro.* 444ff., around
415 B.C. (see Webster, *Euripides* (1967), 285–6 and Mastronarde on *Pho.* 588–
637); they are used for not more than eighty lines at a time, and it is not improbable that in *Oed.* they were confined to a single speech by Jocasta (or part-speech:
cf. Cassandra in *Tro.* 425–61).   **sensible...folly:** contrasted in a woman also at
Hipp. 398.   **partner:** ξυνόντα, a participle, lit. 'being with'; this neutral word
of a husband also at F *545a.8, *Hel.* 297; a wife *And.* 206.

*****545a.** Hermann's attribution (see App.) was followed by Deubner, *Oedipusprobleme*
24–7 = *Kl. Schr.* 658–61; but he placed the fr. before Oedipus was uncovered (and for
his reconstruction he was following Schol. *Pho.* 1760: see Introd., *Reconstruction*).
Clem. (App.) has 'Euripides gives a dignified sketch of a wife who loves her
husband'. [Musgrave's reversal of Clem.'s line-order, generally accepted, creates in
11–12 a powerful climax for Jocasta's devotion to the now polluted Oedipus.]
1–2. Cf. *And.* 207–8 'It is not beauty, woman, but virtues which delight husbands'.
2–3. Compare *El.* 1052 'A wife should agree with her husband in everything'; *And.*
213–4 'A wife must learn to love her husband, even if she is married to a bad one,
with no rivalry of spirit'.   **melted in union with:** (συντήκειν, lit. 'fuse, melt,
dissolve') with a wife *Supp.* 1029, a lover Pl. *Symp.* 192e. [**good** (wife): Nauck's
κεδνή is certain: cf. F 543.4. Clem.'s ἀγαθή is either an adaptation for prose or a
slip (cf. Musgrave's καλή); it gives an unparalleled metrical resolution (full word-
break within resolved sixth longum of the tetrameter, or fourth of the trimeter: cf.
Cropp-Fick 53–4 [esp. type 8.2c], 67; M. L. West, *Greek Metre* (Oxford, 1982),
91). Heath's <τ'> makes 'good' the predicate, 'every wife is good who, etc.']

4–6. (Her first) **principle** is this: ὑπάρχει with demonstr. pronoun at e.g. *Hcld.* 181, 351, cf. *Aeolus* F 15.3. **even if her husband is unhandsome:** cf. *Ino* F 405.1, of a bride. **at all:** γε emphatic with a noun: Denniston, *GP* 116–7. **what judges:** lit. 'the judging (part, element etc.)', Neuter Participle and Definite Article like *Supp.* 709 τὸ κάμνον οἰκείου στρατοῦ 'the faltering (part) of his own army' and *Antiope* F 219.2 τὸ ἐκλαλοῦν 'this blathering'; KG I.267f. [This is Sylburg's conjecture, and is best supplemented with Musgrave's '**what judges** <*these things*>', less well with Duentzer's '**but the mind** <*alone*>'. Clem.'s Infin. τὸ κρίνειν 'judgement' can be either (1) Acc. of Respect in 'it is not the eye but the mind which is <*able*> in judgement' (Nauck: or '<*adequate*>', Heimsoeth), or (2) Nom. of the Subject with Nauck's Gen. ὀφθαλμοῦ, 'judgement is not the eye's'; this latter is supplemented by Wilamowitz, '**but the mind** <*sees*>'.] **not the eye but the mind:** cf. F 548, and the similarly worded *Antiope* F 212 (see n. there); *Med.* 219 has 'Justice does not inhere in the eyes of men' (they are too quick to detest a man on sight). The idea that the mind 'sees' goes back to Epicharmus 23 B 12 DK, appearing also at e.g. *Hel.* 122, cf. A. *Eum.* 103–4.

7–8. eloquence: εὖ λέγειν, lit. 'to speak well', a phrase commoner in Eur.'s contrast of it with glib or false eloquence (e.g. *Antiope* F 206.1–2 and n., *Arch.* F 253 and n., *Palamedes* F 583, *Hel.* 1190 etc.) than in its praise (e.g. *Supp.* 299, *Or.* 239, *Pho.* 526). **work to achieve:** this is the full meaning of the compound verb ἐκπονεῖν, a favourite word of Eur. (over twenty times): for his love of compounds in ἐκ- see Lee on *Ion* 375. [**to work at:** πονεῖν (Collard) replaces Clem.'s λέγειν, a visual slip from 7; the conjecture creates a structure within line 8 matching εὖ λέγειν...λέγηι in 7. Wecklein's τελεῖν gives either 'to accomplish' or perhaps 'to render, to tender', as in F 1029.5 quoted on F 543 above.]

9–10. It is pleasing, etc.: for the thought cf. *Phrixus* F 823, 'a wife must always bear sharing fortune with the husband of her bed'. **put on a sad face with:** cf. A. *Cho.* 738. **join in sharing:** ἐν κοινῶι, lit. 'in common', almost tautologous with ἔχειν μέρος 'have a share', like *Supp.* 1078, *IT* 1299 etc.; cf. 11 below νοσοῦντι συννοσοῦσα. [Nauck supposed a lacuna after line 10 because Clem. interposed his own transitional paraphrase of lines 11–12 before citing them; but 9–12 cohere well enough. Robert's insertion of F 545 in fact destroys the coherence.

11–12. guilty of sin...sharing your guilt: cf. *IA* 407 'I want to join you in good sense, not moral wrong'. **help to bear your troubles:** κακῶν is partitive Gen. with ξυνοίσω, like *Med.* 946 συλλήψομαι...σοι...πόνων, *IA* 160 μόχθων; KG I.343f.

546. These anapaestic lines are probably by the Chorus – but their scorn for a wife almost certainly locates them earlier in the play than Jocasta's support for Oedipus. Robert I.316 left it open whether they can belong to the same context as F 545 and *545a. For wives' subordination to husbands see F *545a.2–3 (n.). **most inferior:** Huys, *Tale* 358 translates **κάκιστος** as 'most miserable', asking whether the word points to the blind Oedipus or his position as a presumed bastard; at S. *OT* 1063, 1397 it is used of low birth, cf. LSJ I.2.   [**1. κακίων, inferior:** a short iota in the Comparative is very rare, uncertainly attested in Tragedy; *TrGF* accepts it here (as did Austin in *NFE* and initially Collard on *Supp.* 1101 ἥδιον), despite Diggle, *Studies* 29–30, and notes a few instances in Comedy. A reason for retaining κακίων is that 2 κάκιστος takes it up expressly, and more effectively than would Heimsoeth's conjecture χείρων ('worse').]

547. Usually placed among the sequence F 541–8, as part of a general discussion of the moralities of marriage; possibly related to F *545a.8–9. **1.** For loves categorized as good and bad cf. *Sthen.* F 661.22–5 (n.), *Androm.* F 138. **2.** For the article attached only to the second of two entities Kannicht (*TrGF*) compares *Alcmena* F 96 πλοῦτος ἤ τ' ἀπειρία, *Aeolus* F 21.5; cf. Mastronarde on *Pho.* 496, 1258.

548. Probably further defence of Oedipus by Jocasta, and of her esteem for his intelligence (demonstrated over the Sphinx): with **mind** cf. her F *545a.5–6. For the sentiment in general cf. *Chrys.* F 842 (a man) 'I wish I might have cleverness of thought and bravery in acting, and be ill-looking, rather than handsome but weak', *Antiope* F 212 (a woman), cf. on *Antiope* F 199. For the emphatic doubling of **mind** cf. *Bell.* F 285.7 and n.; Kannicht cites S. *Phil.* 462, F adesp. 382. **watch:** keep in view, keep one's eyes and attention on, θεᾶσθαι as at *Or.* [911] (eyes on a leader), Pl. *Phaedo* 84b (on the truth), cf. *IA* 674 τό γ' εὐσεβὲς σκοπεῖν, 'keep reverence in view'.   [Meineke gives 'when one's wits are poor'; compare the word-orders in identical ideas at *Antiope* F 212.2, *Hel.* 732.]

549. changes: i.e. reversals for the worse, for this is presumably Oedipus reflecting on his revelation not only as regicide but also as parricide: cf. F 554. 'One day destroys everything' and the like: *Hec.* 285, *Pho.* 1689 etc. [whence Nauck's supplement here of 'one', restoring the metre].

550. Almost certainly Oedipus' delight either at Jocasta's support (F *545a.11–12) or the prospect of refuge in Athens (F 554b?), rather than at a future return to Corinth as king (after Periboea's news of Polybus' death: Robert I.323, comparing Phineus for a blind man becoming king).   **unexpected:** reversals of bad fortune are a commonplace: *Bell.* F 301 and n. (for reversals of good fortune, F 549 and n.). [**1. χάρις, delight:** Nauck's χαρά 'joy' is rejected by e.g. Robert I.323 n. 43 and Kannicht in *TrGF*, who cites χάρις LSJ IV, *Supp.* 79, *Tro.* 1108 etc.   Line 2 is a clumsy expansion of line 1; Kannicht thinks it an actors' interpolation.]

551. Jocasta attributes her joint destruction with Oedipus to Creon's jealousy of Oedipus' kingship (see Introd., *Reconstruction*); all editors compare Oedipus' suspicion of Creon at S. *OT* 382–6, 624.   **envy:** destructive of honourable men *Bell.* F 295, cf. F 294, Pind. *Pyth.* 7.19.

552. Who speaks, and when? If an observer, perhaps a witness of Laius' murder (Robert I.330, hesitantly); or Jocasta may be reflecting on Oedipus' destruction (Van Looy, following Aélion [1986], 52; cf. F 551): the contrast of stupidity and intelligence appears in F 553.2.

2. intelligent...foolish: note the effective chiasmus, two antithetical words embracing two others, like *Bell.* F 290 (a similar context), *Chrys.* F 842 cited on F 548 above, *And.* 639, *Danae* F 326.6–7: in all these, one side of the comparison has two words merely juxtaposed (asyndeton). [Grotius corrected mere copying errors in Stob., 'mad' (ms. M) and 'well-intentioned' (perhaps ms. A).]

3. peaceable...lazy: for the correlation see on *Antiope* F 183.2, 187.4.

4. weakness: lit 'disease', a metaphor of weak political character at e.g. *Antiope* F 226; moral wrong at F *545a.11 above.

553. Perhaps Oedipus is explaining his silence after an initial realisation that he was Laius' killer; conversely (e.g. Robert I.313, Van Looy), he may be commenting on his disastrous openness about himself: the **misfortunes** he refers to may have been the wounds made in his feet at exposure, or his murderous encounter with Laius, but probably not his identification as parricide – and to whom might he be speaking? Alternatives: a comment by the Chorus, expressed as often in a distich (Collard), or someone objecting to Oedipus' exhibiting himself after the blinding, now that he is polluted: cf. Creon's horror at S. *OT* 1424–7.   **testify to:** quasi-legal terminology; the same nuance in the compound verb at e.g. A. *Ag.* 1196, *Eum.* 461, the simple verb at *Hipp.* 1075.   **concealing:** shameful acts are best hidden, not made public: *Cret.W.* F 460.1–3, *Scyr.* F 683, cf. on *Cret.* F 472bc.31–3; also *Ino* F 416 'many men seek through boldness to obscure their disasters and to hide their woes', *And.* 1054, *Hipp.* 915 etc.

554. Possibly Oedipus reflecting on his own fate (**our:** cf. F 549; Robert I.313 links it with F 553 as the start of a long narrative by Oedipus: cf. F 540); possibly the Chorus (Van Looy) offering a general observation (in a distich: see on F 553; the language is appropriately tautologous). For **the god** as source of changing fortunes cf. e.g. *And.* 1007, *Supp.* 331, *HF* 885; Hdt. 1.32.1 and 9.

554a. The inclusion of these lines in Stob.'s chapter *On rule and the necessary character of a ruler* suggests that Creon as successor to the Theban kingship is asserting his right to remove Oedipus for punishment should he seek sanctuary at an altar – or if he has already sought it. Both history and myth exposed the impossible alternatives, whether to drag a criminal from sanctuary or to let him die there from starvation, for both offended divine and human law: see the exemplary case of Pausanias (Lycurg. *Leocr.* 128, cf. Parker, *Miasma* 182–3) and the theatrical moments at *And.* 246–60, *Ion* 1312–15, *Hcld.* 259–60.   **take to justice:** an Athenian legal formula, LSJ ἄγω I.4.   **bad man...be treated badly:** *Hec.* 903–4, 1085–6 etc. [For 'be treated' Theosoph. has 'fare': for this common ms. alternative see App. on F *545a.9.]

554b. For the importance of this fr. see Introd., *Reconstruction*. Oedipus is the most likely speaker, his tone consistent with his unexpected joy at F 550 (n.). In Menander's play the speaker is appealing passionately in mock-Tragic style to Athens as the paramount guarantor of justice, and to the heavens as the ultimate court of appeal in witness. [So Cropp thinks Menander has substituted 'of Cecrops' for 'of Cadmus' or 'of Thebes'; then Oedipus is appealing generally to his home earth and sky for understanding of his predicament. Van Looy also proposed 'of Cadmus', independently.]   **citadel...of Cecrops:** the acropolis of Athens (*Med.* 771), named for the mythical king at e.g. *Ion* 936 'the Cecropian rock', *Mel.S.* F 481.10.   **outspread heaven:** perhaps that of Athens, when seen from the acropolis, but the description is common, e.g. *Or.* 322, Hom. *Il.* 15.36, 192.

*555. If the verse belongs to the play, it was perhaps a black comment on justice for the blinded Oedipus. Justice's vision is comprehensive, *El.* 771 etc.; herself un-seen, she sees the criminal clearly, *Arch.* F 255; she appears to use the dark itself as a punishment at A. *Cho.* 61–4 (cf. our n. on *Mel.* F 506); further material in Pearson on S. *Ajax Locr.* F 12.   [Authenticity: it is possible that the original line(s) cited from the play by Stob., together with the lemma for the Callimachus fr., have been lost: similar likelihood at e.g. *Antiope* F 215. Kannicht's σκότον restores the 2nd Decl. Masc. noun regular in Eur.; for the Accus. with κατά cf. *Tro.* 1072 κατ' ὄρφνην 'in darkness', *IA* 109.]

556. The **Black River** flowed into Lake Copais near Orchomenus in Boeotia; for its famous reeds see Pind. F 70, Theophr. *Hist.Plant.* 4.11.8–9. Passages collected by Kannicht on *Hel.* 1107–12 show the regular poetic connotation of melodic dirge through the image of the **nightingale** (after the myth of Procne's transformation into the bird, to mourn her murdered son: first at A. *Ag.* 1139–45, cf. S. *Tereus* F 581–595b). So the context of our fr. may be a description of the funeral music long ago for the murdered Laius, early in the play (but Van Looy thinks of music for the marriage of Oedipus and Jocasta).

    Hesychius defines **nightingale** here with 'tongue-piece, metaphorically', i.e. that part of the pipe where the tongue modulates the notes (M. L. West, *Ancient Greek Music* [Oxford, 1994], 83ff.); and he follows our fr. with Eur. F 931 λωτίνας ἀηδόνας 'nightingales of the lotus(-pipe)': it seems best to keep the full translat-ion **nightingale**, although the word etymologically is 'singer'; the bird's unique vocal range registers exceptional human ability at *Palam.* F 588.3, *Hec.* 337. **skilful:** for σοφός of music cf. *IT* 1238, *Hom.Hymn.* 4.483, 511, Pind. *Paean* 18.3.   [For Gentili's supplement ἐκτρέφει cf. Hdt. 1.193.1 and perhaps Soph. F *730c.16; it fits the space better than Turner's ἐκφύει (same sense).]

557. limp: Hesychius glosses this word at its occurrence in *Oed.* with 'slack, with-out strength'; cf. *Or.* 228 'my limbs are limp and without strength' (the sick and bed-ridden Orestes), also S. *Trach.* 1103 (the crippled Heracles). In Hesych.'s preceding entry (α 4543 Latte, unattrib.) the same word is glossed with 'unformed'.

ANDROMEDA

Texts, testimonia. P. Oxy. 2628 fr. 1 (see App. for F 119–120); PSI 1476 (see App. for F 140); Ar. *Thesm.* 1009–1135 with scholia (cf. F 114–5, 117–8, 120–5, 127–8); *TrGF* F 114–156; F. Bubel, *Euripides, Andromeda* (Stuttgart, 1991); R. Klimek-Winter, *Andromedatragödien* (Stuttgart, 1993); Van Looy in ed. Budé I (1998), 147–90.

Myth. [Hes.] F 135.5–7; Pherecydes *FGH* 3 F 10–12; Hdt. 7.61.3; Soph. F 126–136; Ov. *Met.* 4.668–5.238; Manil. 5.538–618; Apollod. 2.4.2–4; Hygin. *Fab.* 64; Conon *Narr.* (*FGH* 26 F 1) 40; Luc. *Dial. Mar.* 14; astronomical texts (cf. *TrGF* T iii): [Eratosth.] *Catast.* 15, 17; Hygin. *Astr.* 2.9–11; Schol. AP German. *Arat.* p. 77–8. Preller-Robert II.1.237–43; M. L. West, *The Hesiodic Catalogue of Women* (Oxford, 1985), 82–5, 144–54; Bubel (above), 24–44; Gantz 211–2, 307–11; Klimek-Winter (above), 1–21.

Illustrations. Séchan, *Études* 256–73; K. Schauenburg, *Perseus in der Kunst des Altertums* (Bonn, 1960) and *A&A* 13 (1967), 1–7; Webster, *Monuments*[2] (1967), 154–5 and *Euripides* (1967), 304–5; K. Phillips, *AJA* 72 (1968), 1–23 with Pls. 1–20; Trendall-Webster 78–82 (III.3.10–13: Eur.), 63–5 (III.2.1–3: Soph.); V. Saladino, *Prometheus* 5 (1979), 104–16; *LIMC* I.1.775–90 with I.2.622–42 ('Andromeda': K. Schauenburg, 1981); J. R. Green, *GRBS* 32 (1991), 42–4 and *Theatre* 20–3. Ancient texts describing lost works of art (cf. *TrGF* T v): Luc. *De Domo* 22; Ach. Tat. 3.7; Philostr. *Imag.* 1.29.

Main discussions. N. Wecklein, *SBAW* 1888, 87–98; E. Müller, *Philologus* 66 (1907), 48–68; Séchan (above); Schmid 517–9; Webster, *BICS* 12 (1965), 29–33 and *Euripides* (1967), 255–7; Rau, *Paratragodia* 65–89 and in H.-J. Newiger, ed., *Aristophanes und die alte Komödie* (Darmstadt, 1975), 339–56; Aélion, *Mythes* (1986), 151–83; R. Moorton, *AJP* 108 (1987), 434–6; Bubel (above), 45–63, with review by A. Bierl, *BMCR* 3.6.1 (1992); Klimek-Winter (above), 55–315, with reviews by M. Hose, *Drama* 5 (1997), 193–8 and D. Bain, *JHS* 115 (1995), 191–2; A. M. Bowie, *Aristophanes: Myth, Ritual and Comedy* (Cambridge, 1993), 205–27; F. I. Zeitlin, *Playing the Other* (Chicago, 1996), 375–416 (orig. 1981); Van Looy (above), 147–67; E. J. Beverley, *The Dramatic Function of Actors' Monody in Late Euripides* (diss. Oxford, 1997), 112–26; J. Gibert, *ICS* 24/25 (1999/2000), 75–91.

Reconstruction. An innovative and influential play, with an unusual plot in which eligible young lovers overcome all obstacles to live happily ever after. Reconstruction depends on two main sources: Aristophanes' extended parody of the opening sequence in his *Thesmophoriazusae* (1009–1135), produced the year after *Andromeda* (see below, *Date*), and, regarding the *exodos*, a set of brief notices derived from the Alexandrian scholar Eratosthenes' book about constellations (*Catasterisms*). What happened in the middle of the play is quite uncertain; proposed reconstructions depend on the outlines of the myth known from other sources and analogy with surviving plays which *Andromeda* may have resembled.

In Aristophanes, 'Euripides' persuades his Kinsman to infiltrate the festival of the Thesmophoria being celebrated by Athenian women when he hears that the women are plotting revenge for his alleged misogyny. The Kinsman ineptly defends the poet but is discovered, arrested, and threatened with dire punishment. He tries to escape by enacting scenes from Euripides' plays: *Telephus* (cf. Vol. 1, 18–19), *Palamedes* (see *Pal.* F 588a, this volume, pp. 100–1), *Helen*, and finally *Andromeda*. Assuming the title role, the Kinsman sings portions of Andromeda's lyric exchange with the Chorus and her monody. In between, Echo arrives; when the Kinsman, instructed by her to 'wail piteously', sings what the scholia identify as the play's first words (F 114 n.), Echo echoes. The Scythian archer responsible for guarding the Kinsman returns and scuffles with Echo, who amusingly repeats the Scythian's broken Greek. Soon 'Euripides' arrives in the role of Perseus. His ludicrous attempt to re-play the hero's rescue of the damsel in distress is punctured by exchanges with the Scythian, who is uncomprehending but refuses to let 'the girl' go, and 'Euripides' must exit without achieving his goal. The *exodos*, in which he finally succeeds in duping the Scythian, may allude to yet another of Euripides' plays, *IT*: see p. 62 of Cropp's edition.

The parody covers only the opening of Eur. *Androm.*, and that not in the original sequence (see below). In a few places it draws on other tragedies. The problem of identifying frs. of *Androm.* and drawing inferences from *Thesm.* is handled with exemplary caution by Klimek-Winter, followed in the main by Kannicht. Rau (1967) and (1975) remain good general treatments of the parody; see also Zeitlin, Bowie, Gibert, and the introduction to Austin and Olson's commentary on *Thesm.* (Oxford, forthcoming).

The main action of Euripides' play was the rescue of Andromeda from a sea-monster by the hero Perseus who, arriving unexpectedly, found the damsel in distress and fell in love with her. Despite the opposition of Andromeda's father, the Ethiopian king Cepheus, the two escaped to Greece together. The play opened with Andromeda on stage alone, bound to a rock in front of a cave by the sea. In a unique substitute for the usual expository prologue in iambic trimeters (unless the beginning of *IA* is authentic as transmitted), she describes her situation in plaintive anapaests, perhaps recitative at first, rising to fully lyric delivery (**F 114–6 n.**). Her plight is highly pathetic: the sea-monster to whom Cepheus has exposed her is expected at any moment. Unlike other Euripidean monodists, she cannot engage with props (Ion's broom, Electra's jug, Hypsipyle's castanets; cf. Beverley, 120–1), but Euripides enhances the scene's interest by a bold stroke. At some point while Andromeda sings, she hears the echo of her own voice – almost certainly not as early as in Aristophanes, where the first repeated phrase comes after a mere 5 lines. In Euripides, Echo was only heard from off-stage ('in the caves'), but she is personified in Andromeda's request that she allow her to fulfil her desire for lamentation (**F 118**). The scene must have been moving and effective, but it was risky and offered Aristophanes temptation he could not resist. His Echo is a hag (*Thesm.* 1075) who quickly makes a nuisance of herself by echoing Andromeda and then the Scythian at ever shorter intervals. Moreover, her appearance is a surprise (a characteristic 'concretization' of poetic conceit) and carries the plot backward: because Kinsman-as-Andromeda has already parodied portions of the Parodos (**F 117, 119–120, 122**), Echo arrives at a point when the audience is expecting Euripides-as-Perseus (so Sommerstein on *Thesm.* 1056–97). In Euripides, Echo is probably silenced with a minimum of fuss, as the Chorus of Ethiopian maidens enters and begins a sympathetic lyric exchange with the heroine (**F 117–22** n.). In places where we depend on Aristophanes alone, it is imposs- ible to be sure where Euripides ends and Aristophanes begins (cf. esp. F 122).

In the first Episode, Andromeda may have given a calmer exposition of her situation, before or after Perseus' arrival. In fact we cannot be sure he arrived directly after the Parodos, though this is usually assumed on the basis of Aristophanes. An exception is Schmid 518, who suggests that 'lyric effusions' occupied the better part of the first half of the play. More plausibly, some imagine a scene involving Andromeda's parents or fiancé, if he had a part (see below). In any case, **F 124** announces the arrival of Perseus (on the theatrical crane: see *Staging*). When the dashing young hero expresses sympathy and seeks information from the vulnerable heroine, she may at first be reluctant to speak (**F 126** n.), but Diogenes Laertius preserves an exchange which must belong later in this scene and shows Andromeda boldly promising herself to Perseus if he should save her (**F 129, 129a**). Perseus probably tells a little of his background and adventures (**F 130, 133–4, 134a**). On the development of the love interest, see below on *Themes and characters*.

We now lose sight of the exact course of the plot. As noted, some imagine an appearance of Cepheus before Perseus' arrival. Others have him enter during the first Episode, while Perseus and Andromeda are conversing, and still others hold him off until the second Episode. A related question crucial for evaluation of his character is whether or not Cepheus gives an oath to Perseus. Some interpret **F 151** as Perseus reminding Cepheus of an earlier commitment, but this is far from certain. Likewise, it cannot be known what part Andromeda's mother Cassiepeia played, if any. If Perseus acted entirely on the strength of his under- standing with Andromeda, her dramatic importance and initiative at this stage are magnified. These qualities could even have been underscored by having Perseus free her before his ordeal and take her with him; it seems more likely, however, that he returned to free her later, if indeed this task fell to him, as it does in Apollodorus and Ovid. Nearly all agree that Perseus spoke **F 136**, a famous invocation of Eros, before leaving to fight the monster. His departure was presumably followed by a Choral ode and, in the next Episode, a Messenger speech relating his conquest (**F 145–6**).

In Ovid, Perseus next claims Andromeda as his prize and proceeds with her

to a banquet in Cepheus' palace; it is on this scene that the previous fiancé
Phineus intrudes. Passing mentions of a feast (**F 147**) and a libation (**F 148**) do
not prove that Ovid was following Euripides, and whether Phineus had a part in
the Greek play remains a matter of keen controversy. We have hints (esp.
F 141; also perhaps **F 142–3, 137** on the value of wealth and of a noble spouse) of a
scene in which someone opposes the marriage of Perseus and Andromeda, but
Cepheus, Cassiepeia, and Phineus are all candidates. One of the astronomical
texts that mentions Euripides (Hygin. *Astr.* 2.11 = *TrGF* T iiia(b)) says 'neither
her father Cepheus nor her mother Cassiepeia could persuade [Andromeda] not
to leave her parents and country and follow Perseus'. This suggests a two-part
agôn like *Hel.* 894–995 or *IA* 1146–1252. Less helpfully, the other sources say
that Andromeda 'was unwilling to remain with her parents' or the like. Klimek-
Winter concludes that the opposition thus attested for the parents (strongly by
Hyginus, weakly by the other notices) makes involvement of a previous fiancé
unlikely. It seems entirely possible, however, that there was opposition of two
kinds, and at two different stages. On learning the course events were taking,
Phineus might urge Cepheus to reject Perseus, employing the kind of argument
we hear in **F 141**, with its reference to bastards. Perhaps Cepheus vacillated and
Phineus resorted to violence leading to his petrification (related in a second
Messenger speech). Now one or both of Andromeda's parents could make a plea
full of pathos: their kinsman (along with partisans?) turned to stone by the
dangerous foreigner, they face a miserable old age without their only daughter,
and so on. All of which elicits from Andromeda the high-minded loyalty to her
saviour for which she is praised in the astronomical texts (esp. ps.-Eratosth.
Catast. 17: 'by her own choice she left for Argos with Perseus, a noble
decision', εὐγενές τι φρονήσασα). The parents remain distraught and perhaps
actively opposed, until Athena arrives *ex machina* and announces that Perseus,
Andromeda, Cepheus, Cassiepeia, and Cetus (Greek for sea-monster: see F 115a
n.) will all become constellations, the family thus reunited in death.

In the reconstruction without Phineus, Cepheus and Cassiepeia might have
taken on more differentiated roles (one can imagine either playing the less
sympathetic part). Analogy with *Hel.* and *IT* shows that opposition of this kind,
without the complication of a fiancé, could provide ample incident for a long-
drawn-out intrigue, as Perseus and Andromeda plot their escape from her
unwilling parents. The intervention of Athena to avert violence might have been
more necessary and exciting in this version than in one in which Cepheus and
Cassiepeia are relatively sympathetic. With or without Phineus, Euripides must
either avoid drawing attention to the fact that Perseus and Andromeda could
escape at any moment with the help of his winged sandals and irresistible
weapon, or contrive a reason why they don't do this. For judicious consideration

of the Phineus question and a résumé of earlier arguments, see Bubel 17–23. For analysis of the complex astronomical tradition and what may be deduced from it, Klimek-Winter 96–9.

Other proposed ascriptions. Further passages of Ar. *Thesm.* have sometimes been claimed for *Andromeda*; in an Appendix to his edition (311–13; cf. 89), Klimek-Winter gives reasons (including esp. the silence of the scholia) for rejecting them. After identifying *Thesm.* 1098–1100 as spoken by Perseus in *Androm.*, the scholion on 1098 adds καὶ λοιπὸν ἐπέζευξεν τὰ ἑξῆς ('then he attached what follows'), which *could* mean 'then Aristophanes (or his character Euripides) attached (in *Thesm.*) what follows (in *Androm.*)'. It is open to debate whether this justifies ascribing *Thesm.* 1101–2 (= **F 124.5–6**) to Euripides, but clearly it provides no support for Euripidean authorship of other tragic-sounding verses nearby (cf. F 127 n.). The 'Berlin Photius' (α 2153 Theodoridis = F 955h Nauck-Snell = *fr. dub.* 7 Budé) quotes a trimeter and a half of an oracle given by Ammon; Zielinski's assignment to *Androm.* would be very attractive if we knew that Euripides used the oracle mentioned by Ov. *Met.* 4.670–1 and Apollod. 2.4.3 to motivate the exposure of Andromeda (see on *Myth*). There is little in favour of other proposed ascriptions, which include **F 977, 985, 1008, 1062, 1064,** *adesp.* **F 537,** and *lyr. adesp.* **F 926(e)** *PMG* (= Eur. No. 170 M); see Klimek-Winter 90–3, 313–15.

Myth. The available evidence and general considerations suggest that Perseus' acquisition of a bride through the killing of a monster, which belongs to an old and widespread tale-type, was known from early times, but we know little about details supplied by the tragedians' predecessors. Perseus, son of Zeus and Danae, is already 'renowned among all men' in the *Iliad* (14.320), and Hesiod tells of the birth of Chrysaor and Pegasus from the body of the Gorgon Medusa after Perseus beheaded her (*Theog.* 280–1). The visual record reveals that knowledge of Perseus' other adventures is also old and widely diffused, but we encounter Andromeda daughter of Cepheus first in a late Corinthian (mid-6th C. B.C.) amphora (*LIMC* 'Andromeda' no. 1) on which the names Perseus, Andromeda, and Cetus are inscribed, and in a fragment of the Hesiodic *Catalogue of Women* (F 135). The amphora is intriguing for its depiction of the heroine in a more active role than she will play in later versions of the myth: while Perseus hurls stones at the monster, Andromeda, who is not bound, stands close by and helps him with a supply of further stones (cf. Schauenburg [1960], 56; Phillips 71 and Pl. 1). Perseus has his usual attributes (winged sandals, Hades-cap, pouch for the Gorgon's head), but the fact that he does battle with stones rather than *harpê* ('scimitar') is unusual, as is the wolf-like appearance of Cetus (whose head only is represented). The Hesiodic fragment, from the portion of the *Catalogue* dealing with the descendants of Inachus, merely mentions Andromeda as the mother of Alcaeus, Sthenelus, and Electryon (the first and third names restored by conjecture). A valuable detail is her epithet 'daughter of Cepheus', but we get no hint of Andromeda's home (see further below).

An influential literary version earlier in the 5th century will have been by Pherecydes of Athens, but the portions cited by the Scholia to Apollonius of Rhodes (*FGH* 3 F 10–12) unfortunately do not include the exposure and rescue of Andromeda or her marriage to Perseus. (F 12 mentions in passing that Andromeda was with Perseus when he returned to Argos.) Details are also lacking from Herodotus' mention of Perseus' and Andromeda's son Perses, who is said to have been left behind with his grandfather Belus and later to have given his name to the Persians (7.61.3).

Among later versions, those of Apollodorus, Hyginus, and Ovid are most informative. According to Apollod. 2.4.3, after killing Medusa Perseus arrived in Ethiopia, where he found king Cepheus' daughter Andromeda bound by the sea. The cause was queen Cassiepeia's boastful claim to be more beautiful than the Nereids. An angry Poseidon sent a flood and a monster to ravage the land, and no remedy was found until the Libyan oracle of Ammon demanded Andromeda's exposure. Apollodorus says Cepheus had to be forced to take this measure by the Ethiopians. Perseus saw the girl and fell in love; he promised Cepheus he would kill the monster in exchange for her hand, and the deal was sealed with oaths. Perseus killed the monster and released Andromeda, but her previous fiancé, Cepheus' brother Phineus, tried to prevent the marriage. In the end, Perseus could only stop the plot against him by using the Gorgon's head to turn Phineus and his supporters to stone. The shorter version of Hyginus (*Fab.* 64) offers two significant differences of detail: Cassiepeia's offence was to boast not that she but that Andromeda excelled the Nereids in beauty, and the fiancé (here called Agenor) secures Cepheus' aid in the plot against Perseus. The long treatment of the myth in Ovid (*Met.* 4.668–5.238) shows clear traces of Euripidean influence but, as usual in such cases, cannot be assumed to draw only on him. Similarities include the setting (Andromeda bound to a rock by the sea in Ethiopia, 4.669–772), Perseus' mistaken impression that Andromeda is a statue (673–5 ~ Eur. F 125), and the motif of love at first sight (672–7). The modest silence of Ovid's heroine (681–3) may derive from Euripides (cf. F 126 n.), as may details of Perseus' encounter with the sea-monster (711–34), not found in the Euripidean fragments but represented in what look like remnants of a messenger speech in Ennius (F 113, 115–8 Jocelyn = 3, 5–7 Klimek-Winter). Ovid uses Cassiepeia's boast and the oracle of Ammon to motivate Andromeda's exposure (670–1), and he also has the opposition of the earlier fiancé Phineus who, against Cepheus' will, does battle and is finally petrified along with other enemies of the happy pair, who depart for Argos (5.1–237).

The question of Phineus is discussed above (*Reconstruction*). Whether Euripides had the boast and the oracle is unclear. The former is clearly attested for Sophocles, whose *Andromeda* is undated but probably preceded Euripides' (see below on *Illustrations* and *Other dramatizations*). Noting its recurrence in Ovid, the mythographers, and especially Ennius (F 119 Jocelyn = 8 Klimek-Winter), who is thought to have followed Euripides closely, Kannicht accepts the boast for Euripides, but Klimek-Winter 99 suspends judgment. As for the oracle, there is no trace of it in Sophocles; Zielinski introduced it to Euripides by attributing F 955h to *Andromeda*, but this fragment could be located elsewhere (Wilamowitz [*Kl.Schr.* 4.541] thought of *Busiris* or *Phaethon*).

The 'exotic' setting of Euripides' play in Ethiopia is discussed below (*Themes and characters*). West argues that Cepheus was originally Arcadian, and that the relocation of myths originally set in the Peloponnese to distant lands belongs to a trend of the early archaic period; as the Greeks increased their contacts around the Mediterranean, they adapted and extended heroic genealogies to provide eponyms and dynastic links everywhere (West [1985], 144–54).

Illustrations. The adventures of Perseus are a popular subject in the visual arts of all periods. The earliest appearance of Andromeda, on a Corinthian amphora, has been discussed above (*Myth*). A Caeretan hydria from a little later in the 6th C. shows a hero (Perseus, Heracles, or perhaps another) and a sea-monster, but no heroine (Gantz 308). Next comes a series of five vase-paintings from roughly the decade 450–440, often linked to Soph. *Andromeda* and thus thought to provide it with a mid-century date. On them, Andromeda appears bound to a stake or stakes, or being escorted to be bound, by attendants who are sometimes depicted as 'Africans' with curly hair and flat noses (see further on *Staging*). If the vases derive from Sophocles, it seems to follow that the binding of Andromeda (in a manner different from that in Eur.) took place in the course of his play and thus that we cannot know how many of the antecedents to this action were enacted, how many narrated as background. It has been argued that objects represented in the background on the vases (chests, cloth, perfume vessels, mirrors) suggest marriage or an erotic theme for Sophocles' play (Green [1994], 20–3). See further Schauenburg (1967); Green (1991); Klimek-Winter 32–4.

Later, Andromeda is usually shown bound to a rock and/or before a cave (for the 'arch-rock', see on *Staging*). Only one vase, a red-figure crater of c. 400 B.C. (*LIMC* no. 8; Trendall-Webster III.3.10; O. Taplin, *Greek Tragedy in Action* [London, 1978], fig. 7; A. Pickard-Cambridge, *Dramatic Festivals of Athens* [Oxford, 1990³], fig. 60), has a strong claim to stand in a direct relation to Euripides. The labeled figures include Andromeda, in eastern dress, bound and with arms outstretched (as described in the astronomical texts); Perseus with all his standard attributes; Cepheus, his eyes fixed on Perseus; and a pair of flanking deities: Aphrodite placing a floral wreath on Perseus' head, and Hermes standing above Cepheus. Framing the entire composition are a smoking altar and an unlabelled young woman in eastern dress and perhaps with 'African' features who may represent the Chorus. The eyes of Perseus and Andromeda meet. Aphrodite, who does not appear in the fragments, is easily understood as an embodiment of the play's erotic theme, and Hermes may have been chosen as Perseus' traditional helper (so Klimek-Winter). If the vase is connected to the play despite these differences, clearly the absences of Cassiepeia and any previous fiancé may not be used as evidence for Euripides.

For surveys of the numerous other representations of the myth in visual art later than Euripides, see Phillips, *LIMC* 'Andromeda', Klimek-Winter 108–12. Literary descriptions of lost art-works are collected by Kannicht as T v; on these, see Klimek-Winter 112–8.

Themes and characters. It is unfortunate that uncertainties of reconstruction drastically limit what can be said about the characters of *Andromeda*, for this popular play was likely among those that most influenced the later dramatic tradition. Plays of the same period, especially *Hel.* and *IT*, treat non-Greek kings, queens, and princesses in ways that doubtless recurred with variations in *Andromeda*. Thus either Cepheus or Phineus, if he appeared, will have played the part of a savage villain. Cassiepeia will have been vainglorious, full of maternal love, or both. One of these characters may well have shown some noble tendencies.

What we know of Andromeda's character is intriguing but tantalizingly incomplete. She is first set up as a passive victim, moving the audience and Perseus to sympathy and outrage against her cruel father. Her offer of herself to Perseus 'as servant, wife, or slave' (F 129a) may have delivered a decisive impulse to a Perseus not yet sure what to do, and she perhaps continued, like other Euripidean heroines (including Helen in the companion play *Hel.*), to take a leading role. Unfortunately, we lose sight of her until her refusal to stay with her parents, which earned her praise and will have been the occasion of at least one impressive *rhesis*. We would very much like to know whether Andromeda reciprocated Perseus' love, but the fragments are silent, and she may not have stated any motive for her defiance beyond loyalty to her saviour. An important point here is that the union is destined to be lasting and fruitful, and the audience will have been inclined to view what Andromeda and Perseus felt for each other in a positive light. This is not necessarily true of some roughly comparable situations known from other plays. Thus tragic treatment of the passions of Pelops and Hippodamia, Jason and Medea, and Theseus and Ariadne may have been coloured by the well-known disasters belonging to these legends, though in all these cases there is an oppressive father from whom the audience will have been glad to see the princess escape. Initiative shown by these heroines – for example, by Hippodamia in suggesting to Myrtilus the means of Oenomaus' undoing (Pherecydes *FGH* 3 F 37a), or Medea in aiding Jason's escape from Aeetes or revenge on Pelias – will not have won unmixed approval. Tragic heroines in such 'helper' roles are often represented as dangerous, and there are few signs that audiences of classical Athenian drama, including New Comedy, ever developed a predisposition favouring children who defy their parents in the cause of true love.[1]

Perseus seems to have had all the trappings of the gallant saviour. Strong, sympathetic, just, and moderate, he also had the support of the gods. The representation of such a hero falling in love before the audience's eyes may have been a new event on the tragic stage. Certainly there are other tragic characters who are *in* love, but it is also rare that anything good comes of it: yet that is the expectation the audience of *Andromeda* must have had. How much complexity and depth accompanied Perseus' erotic passion is hard to say. The tale-type itself of successful romantic intrigue was surely known in popular forms and may have been a staple of satyr-play. The ethically serious treatment of characters and situations that is the usual hallmark of the tragic genre would tend to legitimate the pattern in a way rarely seen in public Athenian sources. For more on this subject and its relation to Aristophanes' extended parody of *Andromeda*, see Gibert (1999/2000).

It is often observed that the eligible young lovers of *Andromeda* have a counterpart in the middle-aged couple reunited in the companion play *Hel.*, where marital fidelity is celebrated (but eroticism muted). Some (e.g. Klimek-Winter 132–4) infer from Andromeda's opening invocation of Night that the performance order of the plays followed the chronological order of the relationships. Beyond the love element, the tone of *Andromeda* is in general likely to have resembled that of other 'romantic tragedies'. Like some of them (*Hel.*, *IT*), it is set in a distant land where Greek and 'barbarian' values collide. Like Theonoe in *Hel.*, Andromeda chooses to do the right thing; she is brought to Greece and becomes the ancestor of the quintessentially Greek hero Heracles.

Staging. The opening sequence was daring in the extreme. Whereas Sophocles included the binding of Andromeda in the action of his play (cf. [A.] *PV*), Euripides begins with the heroine, probably dressed as a bride (cf. F 120, 122), already bound to her rock by the sea. Use of the *ekkyklêma* is supposed by

---

[1] An interesting comparison can now be made between Andromeda and Ariadne. A papyrus hypothesis of Eur. *Theseus* (produced before 422), to be published in vol. 68 of *Oxyrhynchus Papyri*, shows that the Cretan princess had a more active role than was previously known. There is a hint that she was motivated by desire for Theseus, and the affair may have been essentially 'happy', but the mere fact that the pair were not destined to remain together suggests that the tone was rather different from that of *Andromeda*.

many, including recently van Looy 153 n. 15 and Beverley 119–20. This offers one way of accounting for Perseus' description of the setting below him as a 'hill' (ὄχθος, F 125.1, but Klimek-Winter 200–1 defends use of the term for a cliff seen from a distance) and making it unnecessary for the audience to witness the binding of Andromeda before the start of the play. The *ekkyklêma*, however, seems not to be used for outdoor scenes, and the binding may just as well have been part of a 'cancelled first entry' (O. Taplin, *The Stagecraft of Aeschylus* [Oxford, 1977], 136). Andromeda may have been bound to the prop known as the 'arch-rock' found on vases (see Taplin, *Comic Angels* [Oxford, 1993], 25–6); at any rate, there is no sign of stakes, assumed for Sophocles on the basis of vase-painting. (The σανίς 'board' to which Kinsman-as-Andromeda is bound in Aristophanes is not good evidence for the Euripidean staging.) Behind her (through the central door of the *skênê*?) lies the cave from which the voice of Echo is heard (F 118 n.). The off-stage voice was bold, as was the entrance of Perseus, for which most scholars assume use of the *mêchanê* (references in Klimek-Winter 194). The flying hero's standard equipment includes winged sandals, Hades-cap, *harpê* ('scimitar'), and *kibisis* ('pouch' for the Gorgon's head); only the sandals are mentioned in the fragments, but the rest should be assumed (cf. Sommerstein on *Thesm.* 1098).

In other plays, Euripides describes various people, including Ethiopians, as 'dark-skinned'. On the 5th C. vases thought to be inspired by Soph. *Andromeda*, attendants are represented with flat noses, curly hair, and dark skin; on one of them, this is true also of Cepheus, as apparently of the figure who may represent the Chorus on the Berlin crater probably inspired by Euripides (see on *Illustrations*). On the 5th C. vases, Andromeda herself is always 'white' (Hall [1989], 141–2), as probably in Eur. (cf. Diggle on *Pha.* 4), but later artists and authors make her dark-skinned and treat the 'race' theme variously (Müller 56–8).

Other (reconstructed) events of the play pose no special problems of staging. There is no positive reason to assume a change of scene from the seashore to Cepheus' palace with Webster (*Euripides*, 196–7). The battle with the sea-monster took place off-stage and was related by a Messenger, as were the struggle with the previous fiancé and his petrification, if they occurred. Appearance of Athena *ex machina* is safely deduced from the astronomical sources (see on *Reconstruction*).

Date. Schol. Ar. *Frogs* 53 says *Androm.* 'preceded [*Frogs*] in the eighth year'. Since the hypothesis to *Frogs* dates it by archon-name to 405, this gives, by inclusive reckoning, 412 for *Androm.* This date is consistent with the most likely interpretation of information we have on the date of Ar. *Thesm.*, in which Echo speaks of herself as one 'who assisted Euripides myself in last year's competition in this same place' (1059–61, with schol. on 1060: '*Androm.* was produced in the previous year'): a scholion on 841 dates *Thesm.* to the 'fourth year' after the death of the Athenian general Lamachus, and another on 190 puts it in the 'sixth year' before Eur.'s death. The last two notices, however, can be made to yield an alternative date of 410 for *Thesm.* and thus, if one believes the scholion on 1060, 411 for *Androm.* These dates are preferred by a minority of scholars, whose arguments are summarized and extended by Vickers (*Alcibiades on Stage* [forthcoming], nn. 1–5 to ch. 5), but they involve rejection of the apparently unimpeachable Schol. *Frogs* 53 (unless, desperately, one takes the re-performance of *Frogs* in 404 as the scholion's point of reference). For the majority view placing *Androm.* in 412 and *Thesm.* in 411, see Andrewes in *HCT* V.184–93, and the Introd. to Austin and Olson's edition of *Thesm.*

Schol. *Thesm.* 1012 attests that *Androm.* and *Hel.* were produced together, and *Hel.* too is fixed in relation to *Thesm.*, in this case by Schol. *Thesm.* 850, which explains the phrase 'the new Helen' with the comment 'produced last year'. The metrical evidence supports a date in the 410's but not a choice between 412 and 411 (Cropp-Fick 73–4).

Other dramatizations, influence. Something has been said already (on *Illustrations*) of Sophocles' *Andromeda*, dated c. 450 B.C. on the strength of vase-paintings thought to have been inspired by it. Apart from the role played by Cassiepeia's boast (see on *Myth*), not much is certain. In particular, whether love played any part is unknown (but see Green, cited above on *Illustrations*). Casaubon concluded from Schol. Theocr. 4.62/63d,e (= Soph. F 136) that Sophocles' play was satyric; although this remains a minority view (cf. Klimek-Winter 53), it may receive slight additional support from P. Oxy. 2453 (overlapping F 133 and containing scraps of satyr-plays: cf. Klimek-Winter 46–8). For the purpose of gauging the originality of Euripides' treatment of *erôs*, it would of course be essential to know whether Sophocles' play included this theme, and whether it was tragic or satyric. The fragments of Sophocles' play are edited with commentary in Klimek-Winter 23–54. According to Schol. Ar. *Clouds* 555/6, an unspecified play by the 5th-century comic poet Phrynichus (F 77 *PCG*) featured an old woman who was threatened by a hungry sea-monster 'in imitation of Andromeda [or *Andromeda*]'.

Aristophanes' lengthy parody is the first of many ancient texts attesting the popularity and lasting influence of Euripides' play. Some others, beginning with Ar. *Frogs* 52–4 (where, in a passage full of implications for reception history, the theatre god Dionysus describes the experience of *reading* the play), are surveyed in Gibert 76–8. See also the collections of testimonia in Kannicht and Klimek-Winter (with commentary).

A single word of an *Andromeda* is attributed to the 4th C. comic poet Antiphanes (F 33 *PCG*; the poet's name is an emendation of ms. 'Aristophanes'), and there were Hellenistic tragedies by Lycophron (*TrGF* 100 T 3) and Phrynichus II (*TrGF* 212 T 1), of which we know only that they existed. In Latin, Livius Andronicus, Ennius, and Accius wrote plays called *Andromeda*, the remains of which are edited with commentary by Klimek-Winter 317–75. Of these, the fragments of Ennius reveal Euripidean influence (esp. F I *TRF* ~ Eur. F 114) but allow few if any safe inferences back to Eur. One would particularly like to know whether F 2, which looks like the Athenian betrothal formula familiar from Menander (see e.g. Gomme-Sandbach on *Dysc.* 842), goes back to Eur. (Cepheus acceding to Athena's wishes by betrothing his daughter, or Athena rounding out the bastardy theme [F 141] by predicting the birth of 'legitimate' children?).

Ovid's treatment ensured that the legend remained popular in modern times, when it has been the subject of paintings by, among many others, Titian, Rubens, Rembrandt, Delacroix, and Burne-Jones; plays by Corneille and Calderón; and operas by Monteverdi (lost), Lully, Haydn, and Ibert. See details in *OGCMA* under 'Perseus and Andromeda'.

ΑΝΔΡΟΜΕΔΑ

114 ΑΝΔΡΟΜΕΔΑ   Ὦ νὺξ ἱερά,
                     ὡς μακρὸν ἵππευμα διώκεις
                     ἀστεροειδέα νῶτα διφρεύουσ᾽
                     αἰθέρος ἱερᾶς
                     τοῦ σεμνοτάτου δι᾽ Ὀλύμπου   5

115   Ἀνδρ.   τί ποτ᾽ Ἀνδρομέδα
                     περίαλλα κακῶν μέρος ἐξέλαχον,
                     θανάτου τλήμων μέλλουσα τυχεῖν;

115a (121 N)
       (Ἀνδρ.)   ἐκθεῖναι κήτει φορβάν

116   (Ἀνδρ.?)   ποῖαι λιβάδες ποία σειρήν

117   (Ἀνδρ.)   φίλαι παρθένοι, φίλαι μοι

118   Ἀνδρ.   κλύεις ὤ;
                     προσαυδῶ σε τὰν ἐν ἄντροις,
                     ἀπόπαυσον, ἔασον, Ἀχοῖ, με σὺν
                     φίλαις γόου πόθον λαβεῖν

119–120   (Ἀνδρ.)   συνάλγησον, ὡς ὁ κάμjνων
                     δακρύων μεταδοὺς ἔjχει
                     κουφοτῆτα μόχθjων.

114 (1 Budé) Ar. *Thesm.* 1065–9, attrib. *Androm.* and assigned to Andromeda in the Prologue by Schol. 1065   1–3 Schol. *Theocr.* 2.165/166b, attrib. Eur.   1–2 Schol. Oribasius, *Coll. Med.* lib. inc. 42.1 (*CMG* 6.2.2), attrib. 'the tragedian' (i.e. Eur.)   1 Schol. Hom. *Il.* 24.12–13, naming Andromeda   **115** (2 Budé) Ar. *Thesm.* 1070–2 with Schol. 1072 λείπει 'μέλλουσα τυχεῖν' ('the words "I am on the verge" are missing'), assigned to the Prologue by Schol. 1070   **115a** (*3 Budé) Schol. Ar. *Birds* 348, attrib. Eur. *Androm.*   **116** (4 Budé) Schol. Ar. *Lys.* 963, attrib. *Androm.*   ποῖαι λιβάδες Dobree   ποῖαι αι (i.e. αἱ) λιβάδες Schol. Ar. ms. R   ποία λιβάς Schol. Ar. ms. Γ   **117** (5 Budé) Schol. Ar. *Thesm.* 1016, attrib. Eur. *Androm.*   **118** (6 Budé) 1 Ar. *Thesm.* 1018, attrib. *Androm.* by Schol. 1018   2–4 Schol. Ar. *Thesm.* 1018–9, assigned to Andromeda speaking to Echo   2 προσαυδῶ σε τὰν Bothe

144

ANDROMEDA

114   *Alone and bound to a rock, Andromeda begins the play with semi-lyric exposition and complaint:*

ANDROMEDA Holy night, how long the course you drive in your chariot across the starry back of the holy sky, through most august Olympus.[5]

115   *(Andr., continuing)* Why ever did I, Andromeda, receive a share of troubles beyond all others? I am miserable and on the verge of death.

115a   *(Andr.)* (to) expose (me) as fodder for the sea-monster

Probably Andromeda, continuing in a slightly higher stylistic register.

116   *(Andr.?)* what tear-drops, what Siren . . .?

Context uncertain (Andromeda, still alone?)

117   *(Andr.)* Friendly maidens, dear to me

Andromeda to the entering Chorus.

118   *(Andr.)* Do you hear? Oh! I call on you who are in the cave: stop, Echo, let me attain the object of my desire, lamentation with my friends.

Andromeda, the first line perhaps to the Chorus, then to Echo.

119–120 *(Andr.)* Grieve with me, for when one who is in trouble shares his tears, he has relief from his toils.

προσαιδοῦσσαι τὰς Schol. Ar.   3 ἀπόπαυσον Seidler ἀπόπασον Schol. Ar.   4 πόθον Seidler πόθου Schol. Ar. χάριν Kannicht κόρον Herwerden   λαβεῖν Schol. Ar. λακεῖν Collard   **119–120** (8 Budé) P. Oxy. 2628 fr. 1 (= P: 1st-2nd C. A.D.) ed. E. Lobel, *Oxyrhynchus Papyri* 32 (1967) 123, Pl. 5; assigned to Eur. *Androm.* by Th. Brunner, *ZPE* 88 (1991), 165–6   1–3 (= **119 N**) Stob. 4.48.17, attrib. Eur. *Androm.*, assigned to Chorus in ms. S   4–6 (= **120 N**) Schol. Ar. *Thesm.* 1022, attrib. *Androm.*, assigned to Chorus   2 ἔχει Stob. mss. SM ἔχει τινὰ Stob. ms. A

145

EURIPIDES

ΧΟΡΟΣ ἄνοικτος ὃς τεκ〕ών σε τὰν
πολυπονωτάτα〕ν βροτῶν   5
μεθῆκεν ῞Αιδα π〕άτρας ὑπεριθανεῖν.

121 N   = 115a *above*

122   (᾽Ανδρ.)   **ὁρᾷς; οὐ χοροῖσιν οὐδ᾽**
ὑφ᾽ ἡλίκων νεανίδων   *1030*
κημὸν ἕστηκ᾽ ἔχουσ᾽,
ἀλλ᾽ ἐν πυκνοῖς δεσμοῖσιν ἐμπεπλεγμένη
κήτει βορὰ Γλαυκέτηι πρόκειμαι.
γαμηλίωι μὲν οὐ ξὺν
παιῶνι, δεσμίωι δὲ   *1034–5*
γοᾶσθε μ᾽ ὦ γυναῖκες,
ὡς μέλεα μὲν πέπονθα μέλε-
ος, ὦ τάλας ἐγὼ τάλας,
ἀπὸ δὲ συγγόνων ἄλλ᾽ ἄνομα πάθεα,
φῶτα **λιτομένα, πολυδάκρυτον ᾽Αί-**
δα γόον φλέγουσα   *1041*

124 (124 + adesp. 157 + 123 N)
ΠΕΡΣΕΥΣ ὦ θεοί, τίν᾽ ἐς γῆν βαρβάρων ἀφίγμεθα
ταχεῖ πεδίλωι; διὰ μέσου γὰρ αἰθέρος
τέμνων κέλευθον πόδα τίθημ᾽ ὑπόπτερον,
ὑπέρ τε πόντου χεῦμ᾽ ὑπέρ τε Πλειάδα
Περσεὺς πρὸς ῎Αργος ναυστολῶν τὸ Γοργόνος   5
κάρα κομίζων.

125   (Περσ.)   ἔα· τίν᾽ ὄχθον τόνδ᾽ ὁρῶ περίρρυτον
ἀφρῶι θαλάσσης; παρθένου δ᾽ εἰκὼ τίνα
ἐξ αὐτομόρφων λαΐνων τυχισμάτων,
σοφῆς ἄγαλμα χειρός;

---

4 τὰν (followed presumably by πολυπονωτάτα]ν) P τὴν -την Schol. Ar.   6 π]άτρας P, previously conj. Düntzer πατρὸς Schol. Ar.   **122** (7 Budé) Ar. *Thesm.* 1029–41; uncertainly
demarcated portions attrib. *Androm.* by Schol. 1029–30, 1034–5, 1040   1039 ἄλλ᾽ Scaliger
ἀλλὰν Ar. αἴν᾽ Reiske   1040 λιτομένα Enger (implied by parts of Schol. Ar. *Thesm.* 1040)
-αν Ar. (reflected in other parts of Schol. Ar.)   1041 φλέγουσα Enger (-σαν Musgrave)
φεύγουσαν Ar.   **124** (9 Budé) 1–3 Ar. *Thesm.* 1098–1100, identified as from *Androm.*
and assigned to Perseus by Schol. 1098   4 (= **adesp. F 157 N**) Euseb. *Praep. Evang.* 15.62.8,

146

CHORUS Pitiless the man who sired you, the most afflicted of
mortals,[5] and gave you over to Hades to die for your
fatherland.

Andromeda and the Chorus in the amoibaion/Parodos.

121 N   = 115a *above*

122   *(Andr.)* Do you see? Not with dances nor accompanied by
girls my age[1030] *do I stand holding a funnel, but tied up by
many bonds I am set out as food for the monster Glaucetes.*
Not with a wedding paean, *but with a binding one*[1035]
wail for me, *women*, for I am wretched, and I've
suffered wretchedly – *poor, poor man that I am* – and at
the hands of my relatives other, outrageous sufferings, as I beseech *the man* and kindle my tearful
Hades-lament.[1041]

Andromeda, during the amoibaion/Parodos.

124   PERSEUS Oh gods! To what foreign land have I come with
my swift sandal? Cutting a path through the middle
of the sky, above the flow of the sea and the Pleiad, I,
Perseus, ply my winged foot, as I sail to Argos
bringing the Gorgon's head.

Perseus arrives on the theatrical crane.

125   *(Pers.)* But lo, what hill is this I see, with sea-foam flowing
round? What image of a maiden perfectly carved in
stone, the beautiful product of an artful hand?

Perseus catches sight of Andromeda.

---

naming Perseus; assigned to Eur. *Androm.* by Meineke and placed here by Snell following
Knaack   5–6 (= **123 N**) Ar. *Thesm.* 1101–2, assigned to Eur. *Androm.* by Fritzsche and
placed here by Wilamowitz on the strength of Schol. Ar. *Thesm.* 1098 (see Comm.)   **125** (10
Budé) 1–2 Schol. Ar. *Thesm.* 1105, attrib. *Androm.*   2–4 (παρθένου...χειρός) Maximus
Confessor, *Scholia on Works of Dionysius the Areopagite* 234 (PG 4.424a), attrib. Eur.
Androm.   2 δ' Battezzato τ' Schol. Ar., Max.   εἰκὼ τίνα Thiersch, according to Blaydes
εἰκὼ τινά (i.e. εἰκώ τινα, printed by many editors) Schol. Ar. εἰκόνα τινὰ Max. εἰκώ τινος
Diggle   3 τυχισμάτων Maas (τυκισμάτων Jacobs) τειχισμάτων Max.

EURIPIDES

126   (Περσ.?) σιγᾷς; σιωπὴ δ᾽ ἄπορος ἑρμηνεὺς λόγων.

F 127–8 are probably not genuine:

127   (Περσ.) ὦ παρθέν᾽, οἰκτίρω σε κρεμαμένην ὁρῶν.

128   (᾽Ανδρ.) ὦ ξένε, κατοίκτιρόν με, τὴν παναθλίαν.
               λῦσόν με δεσμῶν.

129   Περσ.   ὦ παρθέν᾽, εἰ σώσαιμί σ᾽, εἴσηι μοι χάριν;

129a (132 N)
    ᾽Ανδρ. ἄγου δέ μ᾽, ὦ ξεῖν᾽, εἴτε πρόσπολον θέλεις
            εἴτ᾽ ἄλοχον εἴτε δμωΐδ᾽ . . .

130   Περσ. τὰς συμφορὰς γὰρ τῶν κακῶς πεπραγότων
            οὐ πώποθ᾽ ὕβρισ᾽, αὐτὸς ὀρρωδῶν παθεῖν.

131   (᾽Ανδρ.) μή μοι προτείνων ἐλπίδ᾽ ἐξάγου δάκρυ·
            γένοιτό τᾶν πόλλ᾽ ὧν δόκησις οὐκ ἔνι.

132 N   = 129a *above*

133   (Περσ.?) ἀλλ᾽ ἡδύ τοι σωθέντα μεμνῆσθαι πόνων.

134   (Περσ.?) εὔκλειαν ἔλαβον οὐκ ἄνευ πολλῶν πόνων.

134a (149 N)
    (Περσ.?) νεότης μ᾽ ἐπῆρε καὶ θράσος τοῦ νοῦ πλέον.

126 (11 Budé) Stob. 3.34.12 mss. SM, attrib. Eur. *Androm.*   127 (*12 Budé) Ar. *Thesm.*
1110, assigned to Eur. *Androm.* by Barnes   128 (*13 Budé) Ar. *Thesm.* 1107, assigned to
Eur. *Androm.* by Canter   129 (14 Budé) Diog. Laert. 4.29, attrib. Eur. *Androm.*; Schol.
Hom. *Il.* 14.235c, attrib. Eur.; Eubulus F 26, attrib. Eur.   εἴσηι Diog., Schol. Hom. ἕξεις
Eubulus   129a (15 Budé) Ps.-Herodian *On Figures* 45, attrib. Eur. and assigned to
'Andromache ('Andromeda' Villoison) speaking to Perseus'; quoted and said to follow F 129
by Diog. Laert. 4.29   1 δέ μ᾽ Ps.-Herod. με Diog.   130 (17 Budé) Stob. 4.48.2, attrib.
Eur. (mss. MA) *Androm.* (mss. SA: *Andromache* ms. M); Stob. 3.3.39 (ed. Trinc. only), attrib.
Eur.; Ammon. *De Diff.* 80, attrib. Eur. and assigned to Perseus   131 (16 Budé) Stob. 4.47.2
mss. MA, attrib. Eur. *Androm.*   1 ἐξάγου Canter ἐξ ἅδου Stob.   γένοιτό τᾶν Gaisford
(γένοιτό τ᾽ ἂν already Canter) γένοιτο. ταν Stob. ms. M γένοιτο τῶν Stob. ms. A γένοιτο δ᾽
ἂν Schott, Grotius   133 (18 Budé) Stob. 3.29.57, attrib. *Androm.* (two frs. attrib. Eur. pre-

126 *(Pers.?)* You are silent? Silence is an ineffective conveyor of words.

Context uncertain (Perseus to Andromeda?)

F 127–8 are probably not genuine:

127 *(Pers.)* Maiden, seeing you hanging I feel pity.

128 *(Andr.)* Stranger, take pity on me, for I am utterly wretched. Loose me from my bonds.

129 Pers. Maiden, if I should save you, will you show me gratitude?

129a Andr. Take me, stranger, whether for servant, wife, or slave.

Probably the reply to F 129.

F 130–135 may come from the same context as F 129 and 129a, a conversation between Perseus and Andromeda before he departs to fight the sea-monster:

130 Pers. I have never treated the troubles of the unfortunate insultingly, through fear of suffering them myself.

131 *(Andr.)* Don't make me cry by holding out hope: much that is unexpected can happen.

132 N = **129a** *above.*

133 *(Pers.?)* It is pleasant for a survivor to recall his troubles.

134 *(Pers.?)* I got my good reputation not without many toils.

134a *(Pers.?)* Youth and audacity incited me more than good sense.

cede in ms. S).   The line is often quoted unattrib., or attrib. Eur. without play title, or attrib. Men. (= *Monost.* 859).   ἀλλ᾽ Stob., Arist. *Rhet.* 1370b4 ὡς others   τοι σωθέντα some sources τῶι σωθέντι, τῶι συνθέντι, τοῖς σοφοῖσι others   **134** (19 Budé) Stob. 3.29.20, attrib. Eur. *Androm.*   **134a** (24 Budé) Stob. 4.11.4, attrib. Eur. *Androm.*; Lucian, *Menippus or Necromancy* 1, unattrib. amid Euripidean quotations   θράσος Lucian σθένος Stob.

135   ἦ που τὸ μέλλον ἐκφοβεῖ καθ’ ἡμέραν·
ὡς τοῦ γε πάσχειν τοὐπιὸν μεῖζον κακόν.

136   Περσ. σὺ δ’ ὦ θεῶν τύραννε κἀνθρώπων Ἔρως,
ἢ μὴ δίδασκε τὰ καλὰ φαίνεσθαι καλά,
ἢ τοῖς ἐρῶσιν, ὧν σὺ δημιουργὸς εἶ
μοχθοῦσι μόχθους, εὐτυχῶς συνεκπόνει.
καὶ ταῦτα μὲν δρῶν τίμιος †θεοῖς† ἔσηι,   5
μὴ δρῶν δ’ ὑπ’ αὐτοῦ τοῦ διδάσκεσθαι φιλεῖν
ἀφαιρεθήσηι χάριτας, αἷς τιμῶσί σε.

137   *See under Unplaced Fragments below*

145   (’ΑΓΓΕΛΟΣ?) ὁρῶ δὲ πρὸς τῆς παρθένου θοινάματα
κῆτος θοάζον ἐξ ’Ατλαντικῆς ἁλός.

146   (’Αγγ.?)   πᾶς δὲ ποιμένων ἔρρει λεώς,
ὁ μὲν γάλακτος κίσσινον φέρων σκύφος
πόνων ἀναψυκτῆρ’, ὁ δ’ ἀμπέλων γάνος.

138   ὅσοι γὰρ εἰς ἔρωτα πίπτουσιν βροτῶν,
ἐσθλῶν ὅταν τύχωσι τῶν ἐρωμένων,
οὐκ ἔσθ’ ὁποίας λείπεται τόδ’ ἡδονῆς.

138a (1054 N) ἔρωτα δεινὸν ἔχομεν· ἐκ δὲ τῶν λόγων
ἑλοῦ τὰ βέλτισθ’· ὡς ἄπιστόν ἐστ’ ἔρως,
κἂν τῶι κακίστωι τῶν φρενῶν οἰκεῖν φιλεῖ.

---

135 (20 Budé) Stob. 4.35.22, attrib. Eur. *Androm.*   136 (21 Budé) Ath. 13.11, 561b, attrib.
Eur. 1–3 (σὺ δ’…ἐρῶσιν: see further on 3) Stob. 4.20.42, attrib. Eur. 1 Lucian *How To
Write History* 1, attrib. Eur. *Androm.* and assigned to Perseus 1 σὺ δ’ ὦ θεῶν τύραννε
(etc.) Lucian σὺ δ’ ὦ τύραννε θεῶν τε (etc.) Ath. σὺ δ’ ὦ κάκιστε πάντων θεῶν τε (τε om.
ms. S) κἀνθρώπων Stob. 3 ἢ τοῖς ἐρῶσιν εὐμενὴς παρίστασο Stob. 5 †θεοῖς†: βροτοῖς
or θνητοῖς Dobree   145 (22 Budé) 1 Tiberius *On Figures* 47, attrib. Eur. *Androm.*
2 Plut. *Mor.* 22e, attrib. Eur.; κῆτος θοάζων *(sic)* Schol. Eur. *Or.* 335, attrib. (Eur.) *Androm.*
1 assigned to *Androm.* by Heath, 2 joined to it by Fritzsche 1 τῆς Tib. τὰ Nauck
θοινάματα Boissonade θυνάματα Tib. 2 θοάζον Plut. -ων Schol. *Or.*   146 (23 Budé)
Ath. 11.53, 477a, attrib. Eur. *Androm.*; Macrob. *Sat.* 5.21.13, attrib. Eur. *Androm.* 2 σκύφος
Ath. σκύφον Macrob.   138 (32 Budé) Stob. 4.20.22, attrib. Eur. *Androm.* 3 ἔσθ’ ὁποίας

135   No doubt what is yet to come causes terror daily, for impending trouble is greater than suffering.

136   *Pers.* You, Eros, ruler of gods and human beings: either don't teach beautiful things to appear beautiful, or strive along with lovers as they engage in toils of which you are the author, so that they succeed. If you do this, you will be honoured †by the gods†,[5] but if you don't, by the very process of teaching love you will be deprived of the expressions of gratitude with which they honour you.

Perseus invokes Eros, perhaps just before departing to fight the sea-monster.

137   *See under Unplaced Fragments below*

F 145–6 appear to come from a Messenger speech relating Perseus' encounter with the sea-monster and its aftermath:

145   *(MESSENGER?)* I see the sea-monster moving swiftly from the Atlantic brine to feast on the maiden.

146   *(Mess.?)* All the shepherd-folk came streaming, one bringing an ivy bowl of milk, refreshment from his labours, another the sparkling liquid of the grape-vines.

F 138–143 may belong to a formal debate on the proposed marriage of Perseus and Andromeda. Assignments to individual speakers are very uncertain.

138   For mortals who fall in love, when they find that those they love are good, there is no pleasure this falls short of.

138a **(1054 N)** The love we have is terrible. Choose the best from these words, for (*or* that) love is an untrustworthy thing and tends to dwell in the worst part of the mind.

Pflugk ἔστι ποίας Stob.   τόδ' Stob. mss. MA τόθ' Stob. ms. S   **138a** (dub. 3 Budé) Stob. 4.20.44, attrib. Eur. *Androm.*   1 ἔχομεν Trinc. ἔχωμεν Stob. mss. SM ἔχομεν with ω added above o Stob. ms. A   2 ὡς Pierson ὥστ' Stob.

— **(139 N)**   = Ar. *Thesm.* 1128–9: see Comm.

140   ὦ τλῆμον, ὥς σοι τ↓ὰς τ↓ύχας μὲν ἀσ↓θενεῖς
         ἔδωιχ' ὁ δαίμ↓ων, μέγα φρονοῦσι δ' οἱ λόγοι

141   ἐγὼ δὲ παῖδας οὐκ ἐῶ νόθους λαβεῖν·
         τῶν γνησίων γὰρ οὐδὲν ὄντες ἐνδεεῖς
         νόμωι νοσοῦσιν· ὅ σε φυλάξασθαι χρεών.

142   χρυσὸν μάλιστα βούλομαι δόμοις ἔχειν·
         καὶ δοῦλος ὢν γὰρ τίμιος πλουτῶν ἀνήρ,
         ἐλεύθερος δὲ χρεῖος ὢν οὐδὲν σθένει.
         χρυσοῦ νόμιζε σαυτὸν οὕνεκ' εὐτυχεῖν.

143   χρήμασιν γὰρ εὐτυχῶ·
         ταῖς συμφοραῖσι δ', ὡς ὁραῖς, οὐκ εὐτυχῶ.

Unplaced Fragments

137   (Χο.) τῶν γὰρ πλούτων ὅδ' ἄριστος
             γενναῖον λέχος εὑρεῖν.

**144   μὴ τὸν ἐμὸν οἴκει νοῦν· ἐγὼ γὰρ ἀρκέσω.

147, 148   *See after 154 below*

150   οὐκ ἔστιν ὅστις εὐτυχὴς ἔφυ βροτῶν,
         †ὸν μὴ τὸ θεῖον ὡς τὰ πολλὰ συνθέλει†.

151   τήν τοι Δίκην λέγουσι παῖδ' εἶναι Διὸς
         ἐγγύς τε ναίειν τῆς βροτῶν ἁμαρτίας.

140 (30 Budé) Stob. 2.4.7, attrib. Eur. *Androm.*; PSI 1476 (2ⁿᵈ–3ʳᵈ C. A.D.) ed. V. Bartoletti, *Atti del XI Congr. Int. Pap.* (1966) 1–14 (fr. F, col. 2.1–4 = no. 19 Bartoletti)   **141** (27 Budé) Stob. 4.24.45, attrib. Eur. *Androm.*   3 ὅ σε Grotius ὡι (or ὡς) σε Stob. ms. S ὦ σε ms. M ὥς, with ε written above ς, ms. A   **142** (25 Budé) Stob. 4.31.21 and 22, attrib. Eur. *Androm.* 4 νόμιζε σαυτὸν Stob. ms. A   νόμιζε αὐτὸν ms. M   νόμιζ' αὐτὸν ms. S (see Comm.)

— (139 N)   = Ar. *Thesm.* 1128–9: see Comm.

140   Intrepid man, the god has given you weak fortunes, but your words are high-minded.

141   I forbid the getting of bastard children. Though not at all inferior to legitimate ones, they are disadvantaged by custom (*or* law). You must guard against this.

142   Most of all, I want to have gold in my house. A rich man is held in honour even if he is a slave, but a free man in need has no strength. Consider that it is because of gold that you are fortunate.

143   In regard to money I am fortunate; in regard to circumstances, as you see, I am not fortunate.

Unplaced Fragments

137   *(Cho.)* This is the best of riches: to find a noble spouse.

**144   Don't manage my mind: I'll take care of that myself.

147, 148   *See after 154 below*

150   There is no mortal who is fortunate, †whom the divine does not for the most part also wish.†

151   They say that Justice is the child of Zeus and dwells near mortal transgression.

---

143 (26 Budé) Stob. 4.34.30, attrib. Eur. *Androm.*   1–3 and 4 transmitted as one excerpt in Stob., separated by Musgrave, who judges 4 not by Eur.   **137** (33 Budé) Stob. 4.22.11, attrib. Eur. *Androm.*   ****144** (*29 Budé) Schol. Ar. *Frogs* 105, attrib. Eur. *Andromache*; assigned to *Androm.* by Matthiae   **150** (28 Budé) Stob. 4.41.32 mss. MA, attrib. Eur. *Androm.*   2 ὃν μὴ...συστελεῖ Hense ἂν μὴ...συνθέληι Klimek-Winter, after Blaydes   **151** (34 Budé) Stob. 1.3.23, attrib. Eur. '*Andromachus*'; Orion *Floril. Eur.* 16, attrib. Eur.; assigned to *Androm.* by Musgrave   1 τοι omitted by Orion   Διὸς Stob. χρόνου Orion (cf. *Antiope* F 222.1)   2 ἁμαρτίας Orion τιμωρίας Stob.

EURIPIDES

152   (Χο.)   τὸ δαιμόνιον οὐχ ὁρᾶις
               †ὅπηι μοῖρα διεξέρχεται;†
               στρέφει δ᾽ ἄλλους ἄλλως εἰς ἀμέραν.

153   Χο.   ὁ μὲν ὄλβιος ἦν· τὸν δ᾽ ἀπέκρυψεν
              θεὸς ἐκ κείνων τῶν ποτε λαμπρῶν·
              νεύει βίοτος, νεύει δὲ τύχη
              κατὰ πνεῦμ᾽ ἀνέμων.

154   τὸ ζῆν ἀφέντες τὸ κατὰ γῆς τιμῶσί †σου†.
          κενόν γ᾽· ὅταν γὰρ ζῆι τις, εὐτυχεῖν χρεών.

Lexical items:

147   *ἄγορος· καὶ ἄγοροι· Εὐριπίδης Ἀνδρομέδαι· †οἱ κατ᾽*
         οἶκον ἀμφὶ δαῖτα καὶ τράπεζαν Αἰθίοπες σημαίνει†.

148   *ἔλεγον δὲ αὐτὸν (sc. τὸν τρίτον κρατῆρα) καὶ **τέλειον,***
         ὡς Εὐριπίδης Ἀνδρομέδαι καὶ Ἀριστοφάνης
         Ταγηνισταῖς (F 540)

155   *ἀγρεύματα· σκῦλα. Εὐριπίδης Ἀνδρομέδαι*

155a   *ἀμβλωπὸς ὄψις*

156   *ἀμείβεται· παραιτεῖται. Εὐριπίδης Ἀνδρομέδαι*

---

152 (35 Budé) Stob. 1.5.2, attrib. (out of place but unambiguously) Eur. *Androm.*   2 μοῖρα Stob. ms. P μοίρα Stob. ms. F   3 στρέφει Barnes, Heeren στρέφεις Stob.   **153** (36 Budé) Stob. 4.41.17, attrib. Eur. *Androm.*, assigned to Chorus by ms. S   1 τὸν δ᾽ Valckenaer τὸ δ᾽ Stob.   2 ἐκ κείνων Grotius ἐκείνων Stob. ἐκκλίνων Conington, Wilamowitz   3 τύχη Stob. mss. MA -α Stob. ms. S   **154** (42 Budé) Stob. 4.55.4, attrib. Eur. *Androm.*   1, 2 assigned to different speakers by Musgrave   1 γῆς Boissonade γῆν Stob.   2 εὐτυχεῖν χρεών

152 *(Cho.)* Don't you see the divine †in what way fate goes through?† Day by day it turns different men different ways.

153 *Cho.* The one prospered, but the god obliterated the other from those who once were successful. The condition of life sways, fortune sways with the winds' gust.

154 Neglecting to live, they honour what is beneath the earth †of you† – inanely, for it's when one is alive that one should enjoy good fortune.

147 *'gathered' (sing.) and 'gathered' (pl.): Euripides in 'Andromeda': †those in the house around feast and table Ethiopians he* (or *it*) *signifies†.*

148 *And they also called it (sc. the third mixing-bowl)* ***final**, as Euripides in Andromeda and Aristophanes in Tagenistae (F 540).*

155 *catches: spoils. Euripides in* Andromeda.

155a dim vision

156 *exchanges: begs off. Euripides in* Andromeda.

Musgrave εὐτυχεῖ κρέων Stob. mss. SA εὐτυχεῖ κρεῶν Stob. ms. M **147** (37 Budé) *Anecd. Gr.* 1.339.5 Bekker, attrib. Eur. *Androm.* ἀμφὶ δαῖτα Bekker ἀμφιδέτα ms. **148** (38 Budé) Schol. Pl. *Phlb.* 66d = Schol. Pl. *Rep.* 9, 583b, attrib. Eur. *Androm.* **155** (39 Budé) Hesych. α 768 Latte **155a** (40 Budé) Phot. α 1164 Theodoridis (ἀμβλωπός), attrib. Eur. *Androm.* **156** (41 Budé) Hesych. α 3539 Latte; cf. Phot. α 1177 Theodoridis, *Et. Magn.* α 1053 Lasserre-Livadaras

Commentary on *Andromeda*

114–116. Four fragments of Andromeda's monody. Most scholars now accept the Aristophanic scholion's identification of F 114 as the εἰσβολή or 'beginning' of the Prologue of *Androm.* (Passages adduced by Klimek-Winter and Kannicht show beyond doubt that this term can only refer to the play's very first words.) The mode of delivery at first may have been recitative, not song (Attic vocalization in τλήμων, F 115.3), though the placing of catalectic dimeters close together (F 114.2, 5) is one of the hallmarks of lyric anapaests, and F 115a, if correctly placed, indicates modulation to a higher register (see note). In any case, the delivery is more emotional than the trimeter exposition with which all other Euripidean prologues except *IA* and *Rhes.* (both of doubtful authenticity) begin. It is night, and Eur. sets his character's psychic turmoil against vast, elemental stillness. However, unlike e.g. Agamemnon at the beginning of Books 2 and 10 of the *Iliad* (models, perhaps, for the opening of *IA*), Andromeda cannot take an important decision; she can only wait, and the night wears long.

114. Holy night: like **sky** a few lines on, night is holy because it fills Andromeda with what we call 'religious awe' or dreadful anticipation (cf. *Ion* 85); similar addresses to night are collected by Cropp on *El.* 54 (cf. Beverley 124). Eur. may have remembered that 'day' and 'darkness' are ἱερόν in Homer, or he may recall the exact phrase ἱερὰ νύξ in Stes. F 185.3 *PMG* or Aesch. F 69. The degree to which night is personified is, as often in such cases, elusive: lesser in the conception of it as 'holy', greater when she drives a chariot. For the latter, cf. *Ion* 1150–1, where Lee cites the collection of examples from the visual arts in *LIMC* II.906–7 ('Astra'). **holy sky**: repetition of the epithet so soon after 'holy night' offends some tastes, but cf. *Ion* 117–20. Eur.'s increasing fondness for the word αἰθήρ (documented in Bubel's note) caught the attention of Aristophanes (*Thesm.* 14–18, 272 [~ *Mel.S.* F 487], *Frogs* 100 = 311, 892), but there is nothing new-fangled about having it traversed by night, and it is also traditional as the home of Zeus (Hom. *Il.* 2.412, Hes. *Works* 18, etc.) or the gods in general (cf. *Mel.S.* F 487 n.). **Olympus**: more or less identical to οὐρανός 'sky', as occasionally from Homer on (e.g. *Il.* 8.18–27, *Od.* 6.42–7 with Hainsworth's note). In Aristophanes, the character Echo repeats the last two Greek words, δι' Ὀλύμπου, which mark a metrical pause (period-end) in Andromeda's delivery. In Eur., a voice from off-stage probably did the same thing, though perhaps not so near the beginning of Andromeda's monody (see Introd., *Reconstruction*). After this first instance, the Aristophanic Echo no longer waits for a pause and soon makes a nuisance of herself; see further F 118 n.

115. Why ever did I, etc.: these lines (with interruptions by Echo) follow directly on F 114 in Aristophanes and may have done the same in Eur. (but see Bubel 45). Appropriately for a Prologue, they contribute both pathos and information. Euripidean characters regularly introduce themselves by using their names in first-person state-

156

ments at the beginning of a play (e.g. *And.* 1–5) or when appearing on the theatrical crane (e.g. F 124.5, *Ion* 1555–6), apparently a matter of technique as much as tone. Tragic intensity is conveyed by the plaintive **why ever** and **miserable**, the poetic adverb περίαλλα **beyond all others**, and the fulsome **share of troubles** and ἐξέλαχον 'I received (as my lot)', identical in meaning to the uncompounded ἔλαχον. The opening with the heroine already on the verge of death is an innovation of Eur. vis-à-vis Sophocles (see Introd., *Illustrations*).

115a (121 N). (to) expose (me) as fodder, etc.: Webster 194 sees in the catalectic dimeter (consisting of seven long syllables and showing Doric vocalization in φορβάν, both characteristic of fully lyric delivery) a continuation or development of what Kannicht calls the 'semi-lyric' anapaests of F 114–5, still before the entrance of the Chorus (after which no anapaests are attributable to Andromeda, hence the renumbering of the fr. and placement of it here). As Kannicht notes, the movement from lower to higher stylistic register within a monody is paralleled at *Tro.* 98–121/122–52 (where the two types of anapaest are contiguous) and *Ion* 82–111/144–83 (where a pair of aeolic stanzas intervenes), both followed immediately by *parodoi* which include further lyrics from the monodist.   **sea-monster**: an epic word of unknown etymology not found in tragedy outside *Androm.* (again F 145.2; cf. Ar. *Clouds* 556), κῆτος becomes the regular term for the monster to which the heroine was exposed, and as such comes to be used for the constellation still known as Cetus (Klimek-Winter 170–1). The place of *kētē* in the real and imaginary lives of ancient Greeks is well discussed by J. K. Papadopoulos and D. Ruscillo in *AJA* 106 (2002), 187–228.

116. what tear-drops, what Siren: in the passage of Ar. *Lys.* said by a scholion to parody this anapaestic dimeter, the Chorus expresses mock-tragic sympathy for the sexually frustrated Cinesias, and some infer that our fr. likewise belongs to the Chorus. Andromeda is the speaker according to others, including Kannicht, who compares *Hec.* 159–60 and *Hel.* 164–6. Ar. would then have given to his Chorus words recited or sung by an actor in Eur., the reverse of what he does (apparently) in F 120. If the fr. belongs to the Chorus, they approach ('marching anapaests') and exclaim about the figure who is streaming tears and singing as beautifully as a Siren. (F 117 shows that Andromeda is already known to them, so the questions do not actually seek information.) If it belongs to Andromeda, she perhaps asks what tears of pity will be shed for her plight, what Siren will sing a comforting lament for her death. Sirens first become visible in this role around the time of Eur.'s play (Kannicht on *Hel.* 167–78, J. Neils in B. Cohen, ed., *The Distaff Side: Representing the Female in Homer's Odyssey* [Oxford, 1995], 180–1), so if Sirens are connected with laments here, the coincidence of form and content with *Hel.* 164–78 is all the more striking. Hypsipyle invokes 'lyre's music…with Calliope's aid' (*Hyps.* F 752h.6–9 nn.).

117–122. Four fragments of the lyric exchange ('amoibaion') between Andromeda and the Chorus that served as the play's Parodos. While such an exchange is regular when the prologist remains to greet the entering Chorus (Kannicht, cited by Klimek-Winter 160), no two examples are identical, and detailed reconstruction (as e.g. by Webster, *Euripides*, 194–5) should be resisted. F 118 gives vital information on the handling of Echo; F 122 is valuable for its suggestion of themes sounded in this part of the play, though the possibility of distortion by Aristophanes must not be forgotten.

117. maidens, dear to me reveals the Chorus to be age-mates and friends of Andromeda, who welcomes them. Their affectionate relationship rules out the suggestion, based on analogy with [A.] *PV*, that the Chorus are Nereids (Schmid) or Oceanids (Mette).

118. Do you hear, etc.: however 2 is restored, it locates Echo 'in the cave', and this indicates that in Eur., unlike Aristophanes, she was represented only by an off-stage voice (see Introd., *Reconstruction* and *Staging*). Whereas Echo no doubt effectively heightened the sense of Andromeda's initial isolation, the proposed **lamentation with my friends** suggests communal ritual, theatrically realized as the amoibaion/Parodos. For pleasure in lamentation, see F 119–120 n.   [The text of *Thesm.* 1018–19 and the scholion give 2 in the same corrupt form; Bothe's restoration gives straightforward sense. Some try to restore προσάιδουσα ('singing in response', referring to Echo); the sense is appealing but requires further changes, and none of the solutions yet proposed is convincing. Seidler's simple correction of 3 produces an aor. act. imp. ἀπόπαυσον 'stop' used intransitively. No exact parallel has been found, but pres. παῦε is so used at S. *Phil.* 1275 and often in Ar., and Kannicht notes that the Kinsman's κατάνευσον in the same position in Ar.'s parody provides some support; see further Klimek-Winter 155–7. In 4 the transmitted gen. πόθου 'desire' cannot be right. Seidler's simple correction to the acc. produces an unparalleled collocation 'take desire' which must be understood as 'attain the object of desire', with γόου 'lamentation' apparently still understood as the objective gen. after πόθον 'desire of lamentation'. This is difficult, and a phrase like γόου χάριν λαβεῖν 'to obtain the pleasure of lamentation' would certainly meet our expectations (Kannicht), though it leaves the corruption unexplained. Likewise Herwerden's κόρον, which yields the attractive sense 'to take my fill of lamentation' (*pace* Klimek-Winter, κόρον λαβεῖν is well supported by *Alc.* 185). Accepting πόθον, Collard suggests λακεῖν 'cry out' for λαβεῖν 'attain'.]

119–120. Grieve with me, etc.: the discovery by Brunner (see App.) that P. Oxy. 2628 preserves remnants of F 119 and F 120 presented as a continuous text confirms that editors were right to reject the assignment of F 119 to the Chorus by Stob. ms. S, for if F 119 belongs with F 120, which because of its content and place in Aristophanes' parody cannot be located outside the amoibaion/parodos, then the command to **grieve with me** can only be given by Andromeda to the Chorus. (The suggestion of P. Carrara in *ZPE* 95 [1993], 29 that F 119 is addressed by one part of a divided Chorus to the other is not convincing.) F 120, on the other hand, is correctly assigned to the Chorus by the Aristophanic scholion that quotes it.   **his...he...his**: though Andromeda is the **one who is in trouble**, her generalizing pronouncement includes two masc. sing. participles; cf. S. *El.* 770–1, Eur. *Med.* 1018. The thought that there is comfort in tears is common in Greek poetry from Hom. *Il.* (23.10, 98; 24. 513) and *Od.* (e.g. 19.213) on;

see *El.* 126 with Cropp's n., *Tro.* 608–9, *Oenomaus* F 573, *Arch.* F 263 n. That shared grief brings relief points to the communal nature of lamentation (e.g. *Supp.* 71 ff.). A further note of pathos is struck by **gave you over to Hades**, which evokes the familiar Bride of Hades motif (F 122 n.) which, to judge from vases, played a part in S. *Androm.* as well (see Introd., *Illustrations*).

122. Do you see, etc.: there is no sure way to separate the Euripidean from the Aristophanic in this portion of the Kinsman's song, where the otherwise helpful scholia become vague. General probability is in favour of assigning the bits and pieces printed in bold type to one of Andromeda's lyric contributions to the amoibaion/Parodos, in which she goes on bitterly lamenting her fate, perhaps because it puts a stop to her participation in the carefree life of girls (of which festive dances are the emblem: cf. [Cropp on] *El.* 175–80, *Pho.* 1264–5), perhaps because it will prevent her age-mates from singing and dancing at her wedding. Aristophanes, bent on mocking Eur.'s tragic adaptations of the 'New Music', embeds the quotations in a wildly heterogeneous metrical context, but the original may not have been so outlandish.   **girls my age**: as the sea-monster's victim, Andromeda is destined to lose forever the company of her age-mates, a regular feature of the life of girls as depicted in poetry, often with reference to ritual song and dance (C. Calame, *Choruses of Young Women in Ancient Greece* [Eng. tr. Lanham, 1997], 26–30 and *passim*). Of course, she is also destined to lose it when she becomes Perseus' bride, in a transition such as often forms the background of ritual and poetry involving girls. For paeans and weddings, see Sappho F 44.31–3, Aesch. F 350, Ar. *Birds* 1763–5; I. Rutherford, *Pindar's Paeans* (Oxford, 2001), 56–7. After **not with a wedding paean**, the text of Aristophanes continues, 'but with a binding one' (δεσμίωι δέ): these words are more likely the comic poet's joke than part of Andromeda's song; a magic-ritual 'binding song' such as the δέσμιος ὕμνος of A. *Eum.* (321–96) may be faintly evoked.   **wretched...wretchedly**: the Greek has two forms of the adjective μέλεος, in a variety of 'polyptoton' characteristic of high tragic style.   **Hades-lament**: similarly A. *Sept.* 868–70 Ἀίδα...παιᾶν' 'Hades-paean', Eur. *El.* 143–4 μέλος Ἀίδα 'Hades-chant'. While the primary meaning is that Andromeda laments her death, Eur. also sounds the 'Bride of Hades' theme again (F 119–120 n.).   [Enger changed the forms of **beseech** and **kindle** (participles in the Greek) to agree with the subject of **I've suffered**. As transmitted, they agree with 'me' of **wail for me**, but this construction seems less likely. Musgrave detected a form of φλέγειν 'to set ablaze, kindle' beneath φεύγουσαν in the transmitted text of Ar. With the object 'song', the metaphor is 'synaesthetic', that is, it describes an aural phenomenon visually. Bubel cites Bacchyl. *Pae.* 4.80 for the verb so used, and Diggle collects many similar expressions (*Euripidea* 12). The same error occurs in the mss of *Rhes.* 110 (Kannicht).]

124. Oh gods, etc.: the context in Aristophanes strongly suggests that these were Perseus' first words as he made his spectacular entrance by means of the theatrical crane.   **swift sandal, winged foot**: Perseus' winged sandals are a fixture in art as early as the 7th C. B.C., in literature from the Hesiodic *Shield* 220 on (K. Schauen-

burg, *Perseus in der Kunst des Altertums* [Bonn, 1960]). On the Euripidean phrase
cutting a path, see Mastronarde on *Pho.* [1], Dunbar on Ar. *Birds* 1398–1400.
Pleiad: collective sing. for Pleiades. For this constellation as representative of stars in
general, see West on Hes. *Works* 383–4, Diggle on *Pha.* 66. The Gorgons live 'beyond
renowned Ocean' already in Hesiod (*Theog.* 274), but a journey of Perseus 'over the
stars' seems a little, well, over the top – unless Eur. alludes to the position of the
Pleiades 'near the left knee' of the constellation Perseus (Arat. *Phaen.* 254).
[Knaack's discovery of a passage in the 96th letter of Procopius (p. 569 Hercher)
which contains echoes of both 1–3 and a line quoted by Eusebius (4 = adesp. 157 N) in
what looks like paraphrase of a single poetic text confirmed Meineke's attribution of
the latter to *Androm.* The status of 5–6 is more controversial. They follow directly on
1–3 in Ar., and the scholion on *Thesm.* 1098 *can* be read as supporting attribution to
Androm. (see Introd., *Other proposed ascriptions*). Appropriate expository information
is provided in tragic style, but too economically, according to Klimek-Winter, who
thinks that Aristophanes composed the lines with a view to getting on quickly with his
parody. The self-introduction of Perseus is in Eur.'s manner (F 115 n.), and
ναυστολῶν 'as I sail' is one of his favourite words. If he really used it here, it is hard
not to credit him with a sense of fun, for Aristophanes surely meant his audience to
smile when his Peisetaerus, two years earlier in *Birds*, asked Iris τὼ πτέρυγε ποῖ
ναυστολεῖς; 'whither pliest thou thy pair of wings?' (1229), and it was nothing if not
daring of Euripides to allow the winged Perseus to re-cycle the metaphor at the start of
his already sufficiently daring turn on the theatrical crane. Of course, some will see
this as an additional reason to deny Euripidean authorship of 5–6.]

125. Perseus now notices his surroundings, but still from a distance, so that he can
mistake Andromeda for a statue. There is a pleasing irony in the fact that Perseus, who
can turn people to stone, at first takes his flesh-and-blood future wife for a stone
effigy, but the tone is hardly comic (*contra* Klimek-Winter 199). Rather, the image is
tinged with eroticism; cf. *Alc.* 348–54 (Admetus describes the statue of Alcestis he will
commission and then take to bed), *Hec.* 557–65 (Talthybius describes Polyxena's
exposure of her body, 'beautiful as a statue'), and A. *Ag.* 414–19 (the Chorus describes
how Menelaus took no more pleasure in 'the grace of shapely statues' once Helen had
gone).   **But lo**: ἔα marks Perseus' surprise (Page on *Med.* 1004) as he makes visual
contact with his surroundings (Mastronarde, *Contact* 24).   **hill**: Andromeda is to be
imagined bound to a rock rising abruptly out of the sea; it is not clear what effort was
made to represent any part of this conception realistically in the theatre (Introd.,
Staging).   **perfectly carved in stone**: praise for accuracy and realism is a constant
feature of ancient art criticism. For αὐτόμορφος in this sense, see Battezzato (cited
below), 158–60. Others think the word indicates that the craftsman found the rock's
natural endowment suited to his creation.   [The transmitted text of 1–2 gives 'What
hill is this I see and some image of a maiden?' While some defend this, Diggle, *Studies*
42 n. 2 proposes at the end of 2 τινος agreeing with παρθένου and yielding 'What...
image of some maiden?' L. Battezzato argues for the reading adopted here (apparently
due to Thiersch), a second interrogative τίνα, with a question mark after θαλάσσης

(*MD* 44 [2000] 141–73, at 141–61; for the further change of τ' to δ', see 158). For τειχισμάτων 'fortifications', Jacobs brilliantly conjectured τυκισμάτων 'chiselings' here and at *Her.* 1096 (cf. 945); P. Maas (*Kleine Schriften* [Munich, 1973], 219–20) showed that the spelling τυχ- is preferable.]

126. You are silent, etc.: the line is usually given to Perseus, who is supposed to be trying to get an ashamed or reluctant Andromeda to answer his questions about her plight (cf. Ov. *Met.* 4.681, after undoubted imitation of F 125 at 672–7). The speaker's reference to **words** is paradoxical no matter what silent character is addressed and does not count against the usual assignment. It is likely enough that Andromeda had to be prodded to speak to the flying stranger.

127. Maiden, seeing you, etc.: this line, spoken by Euripides-as-Perseus in *Thesm.*, should not be claimed for Eur., as the scholia are silent. (The scholion on 1098, for which see Introd., *Other proposed ascriptions*, should not be invoked here.) It is likewise arbitrary to identify a distant line in *Thesm.* (1058) as the direct reply to it (Barnes, followed by Nauck). The address ὦ παρθένε 'Maiden' is typically Euripidean (around a dozen times in his works, once in Soph., not in Aesch.), and the sentence as a whole resembles *Ion* 618–19, *IA* 1336–7; such is Aristophanes' skill in representing Eur.'s style. While most literary sources for the legend have Perseus fall immediately in love with Andromeda, pity (in advance of love) is mentioned by Conon *Narr.* (*FGH* 26 F 1) 40, Lucian *Dial. Mar.* 14.3.

128. Stranger, take pity, etc.: like the previous fr., these lines, spoken by Kinsman-as-Andromeda, should not be claimed for Eur.

129, 129a. Maiden, if I should save you, etc.: the connective particle δέ prevents us from taking F 129a as the *immediate* reply to F 129, and some scholars, thinking it too forward of Andromeda to 'throw herself' at Perseus in this way, keep the frs. apart. Wilamowitz even advocated moving F 129a to the end of the play, where the sources derived from Eratosthenes' *Catasterisms* indicate a scene in which Andromeda chooses to disobey her parents and go with Perseus to Argos. But Diogenes calls F 129a 'what follows' (τὰ ἐχόμενα) F 129, and it is better to suppose that as little as one prefatory line of Andromeda's came between Perseus' question and her answer. Perseus' word for **gratitude**, χάρις, can suggest 'sexual favours', and the anecdote in which Diogenes embeds his quotation of the lines trades on this nuance. If, however, Perseus speaks vaguely of 'favour' and Andromeda answers with **servant, wife, or slave**, she must still be credited with a decisive initiative, the suggestion that he might seek her hand in marriage (see Introd., *Themes etc.*). Her formulation recalls Hom. *Il.* 3.406–9, where an embittered Helen asks Aphrodite why she doesn't go and dote on her favourite Paris, until he makes her his wife or slave. [If editors have correctly restored his quotation of Eur. from the corrupt Schol. Eur. *Med.* 476, Eubulus has ἕξεις for εἴσηι, which gives the same meaning and is actually better attested for Eur. in the idiom χάριν ἔχειν/εἰδέναι 'to feel or show gratitude'. Nonetheless, the version of the other sources is to be preferred, as Eubulus, who is mocking the alleged profusion of s-sounds in Eur. ('sigmatism'), has a motive (he gets another s) for misquoting the line.]

130. I have never treated the troubles, etc.: the injunction not to abuse the unfortunate because one's own fate could turn out to be no better belongs to traditional wisdom: Thgn. 155–8, Democr. DK 68 B 293 (cf. Hes. *Works* 717–18, Chilon the Spartan DK 10.3.3.11), [Men.] *Monost.* 470; in tragedy, Eur. *And.* 462–3 and esp. S. *Aj.* 121–6.

131. Don't make me cry, etc.: assignment of the lines to Andromeda depends on the likelihood that the person **holding out hope** is Perseus; Andromeda fears disappointment. The following maxim about the unexpected recalls the anapaestic lines found at the end of several Euripidean tragedies (for which see Kannicht on *Hel.* 1688–92 or Mastronarde on *Med.* 1415–9) and sounds a theme that is found throughout his work (cf. *Antiope* F 223.104 n.). [Some assign the first line to Andromeda and the second to Perseus. The connective particle, whether τοι or δέ, is not against this.]

133. It is pleasant for a survivor, etc.: one of the best known maxims of antiquity, a version of which is found already at Hom. *Od.* 15.400–1 (cf. 12.211–12), which Aristotle quotes along with our fr.; for variations, see (Pearson on) Soph. F 374 and 636, (Kannicht on) Eur. *Hel.* 665. Cicero (*De Fin.* 2.32.105) indicates that our line, which he translates into Latin, was very well known, as its use by Aristotle without the name of author or play suggests. Related thoughts occur in prominent positions in Lucretius (beginning of *DRN* 2) and Virgil (*Aen.* 1.203, Aeneas' first speech), and Klimek-Winter collects many more Latin variations. The context in *Androm.* cannot be determined.

134. I got my good reputation, etc.: for the thought, cf. *Arch.* F 237 n. Perseus is usually assumed as the speaker, but the context cannot be determined.

134a. Included by Stob. in his chapter *On youth* among passages equating youth with immaturity or audacity (hence his variant σθένος 'strength' is inferior to θράσος **audacity** preserved by Lucian); this typically Greek way of thinking is discussed by K. J. Dover, *Greek Popular Morality* (Oxford, 1974), 102–6; Euripidean examples are collected by Collard on *Supp.* 160. Nauck's placement of the fr. derived from Wecklein's assignment of it to Andromeda's previous fiancé; if there was no such character in the play (Introd., *Reconstruction*), it is better placed here, where it could be spoken by Perseus and refer to either his slaying of the Gorgon or his present adventure.

135. The compressed 2 means '<fearing> impending trouble is worse than suffering <present trouble>' (Kannicht). [If Wecklein's assignment of this line to a second speaker is correct, ὡς...γε is 'asseverative' ('indeed': cf. Willink on *Or.* 93, improving on Denniston, *GP* 143); however, a 'causal' sense (**for**) and assignment to a single speaker seem more natural (Kannicht).]

136. You, Eros: Perseus invokes the god of love, either while asserting his right to the promised marriage or, more likely, just before departing to fight the sea-monster. A. M. Dale, *Collected Papers* (Cambridge, 1969), 180–4 included this passage among mostly act-ending 'challenging-nouthetetic' addresses to gods at decisive moments in the 'happy-ending' plays of Eur.'s latest period, in particular Menelaus to Zeus at *Hel.* 1441–50, Ion to Apollo at *Ion* 436–51 (this one, as Dale notes, at a decisive moment of character or thematic development more than action), Iphigenia to Artemis at *IT* 1082–8. As similar passages are found just before the entrance of a new character at *Ion* 384–9 (Creusa to Apollo) and *Antiope* F 223.11–16 (Amphion to Zeus), the usual placement of our fr. cannot be regarded as certain. Prayer elements include the initial Voc. **You** and the epithet τύραννε **ruler**, with the 'polar expression' **over gods and human beings** emphasizing Eros' great power, traditional at least since Hes. *Theog.* 120–2 (cf. S. *Phaedra* F 684 = Eur. *Hipp.Cal.* F 431, *Auge* F 269, Pl. *Smp.* 178b-80b). Where a typical prayer might then continue with relative clauses illustrating the god's influence, Perseus presents a disjunctive pair of commands: **either don't teach…or strive along with lovers**. As a description of how Eros instills love, to **teach beautiful things to appear beautiful** recalls *Hipp.* 525–34, especially ὁ κατ᾽ ὀμμάτων στάζων πόθον 'the one who distills longing upon the eyes' (and note 538, Eros as τύραννος ἀνδρῶν 'ruler of men'); Eros is a teacher also in *Hipp.Cal.* F 430 and the famous *Sthen.* F 663 (see Comm. there). The address begins to be 'challenging-nouthetetic' with mention of lovers' toils (cf. *Hel.* 1446) and continues in this vein with the threat that Eros will cease to be thanked and honoured if he does not help. To the extent that **expressions of gratitude** and **honour** suggest cult, they conflict with *Hipp.* 535–42, where the Chorus claim that Greeks foolishly do *not* worship Eros (cf. Pl. *Smp.* 189c), but Barrett shows in his note that this is something of an overstatement. The idea that people might cease to worship an unworthy god is hardly confined to the plays in which everything eventually turns out well: it reaches a desperate climax in *HF* 1341–6 (cf. 1303–8), on which see H. Yunis, *A New Creed* (Göttingen, 1988), 139–71. **so that they succeed**: attached as an adverb to **strive along with**, εὐτυχῶς, lit. 'successfully', is used in anticipation ('prolepsis') of the outcome of the striving (KG 2.115–16). **teaching**: διδάσκεσθαι appears to be the middle used like the active, as at *Hyps.* F 759a.1622; Ar. *Clouds* 783. [There is not much to choose between Lucian's and Athenaeus' versions of 1. In 5, the transmitted reading τίμιος θεοῖς 'honoured by the gods' would give acceptable sense if gods alone were imagined as under the sway of Eros. Perseus, however, has mentioned Eros' power over human beings and is invoking the god's aid in his own behalf; the lovers in 3 and those who bestow gratitude and honour in 7, then, include mortals, whom Dobree accordingly restored here with θνητοῖς or βροτοῖς, 'by mortals'.]

145. to feast on the maiden: θοινάματα pathetically evokes a social occasion gone awry; so also in the only other classical occurrences, at *Ion* 1495 (Ion exposed to wild animals and carrion birds, an image ultimately derived from Hom. *Il.* 1.4–5) and *Or.* 814 (of the 'banquet of Thyestes'), and with related words at A. *Ag.* 1502, E. *Cyc.* 550, *Hec.* 1072, *Phil.* F 792, etc. **Atlantic brine**: Homer mentions two groups of

Ethiopians, one inhabiting the far east and the other the far west (*Od.* 1.23–4). We learn from this fr. that Eur. set his play among the latter, and Perseus thus arrives by a direct route leading from the Gorgons (placed in the far west by Hes. *Theog.* 274–5; cf. *Hel.* 769) to his home in Argos (F 124.5–6).

146. All the shepherd-folk came streaming, etc.: Philostratus undoubtedly has this fr. in mind when he describes cowherds offering Perseus milk and wine as he rests after killing the sea-monster (*Imag.* 1.29). It thus fits easily into a continuation of the Messenger-speech assumed as the context of F 145.   **ivy bowl of milk:** Dale, *Collected Papers* (see 136 n.) 98–102 pointed out the absurdity of supposing that Greeks made large drinking vessels out of 'ivy wood' and suggested that Eur., in whom phrases such as 'ivy bowl' are first found, was rendering the Homeric κισσύβιον (*Od.* 9.346, 16.52), which (1) occurs in rustic contexts, as do the Euripidean examples, (2) remains obscure etymologically (but is not now thought to have anything to do with ivy), and (3) does not easily fit into iambic trimeters. The false association spawned learned Alexandrian controversy, which in turn led to the preservation of our fr. in Athenaeus and Macrobius.   **refreshment from his labours:** There is word-play in the unique ἀναψυκτήρ, lit. 'cooler'. While cooling beverages are very much in context (Philostratus mentions the sweat dripping from Perseus), so is the metaphorical refreshment of being delivered from trouble. The latter is usual in related phrases such as ἀναψυχὴ πόνων (*Ion* 1604) or κακῶν (*Supp.* 615), but the ψυκτήρ of *Tel.* F 726 is apparently literal, whether it refers to a cup or a larger vessel used to cool wine (see Preiser's note). When Hesiod recommends food and drink for a picnic at the hottest time of year, he too mentions milk along with wine (*Works* 590–6).   **sparkling liquid:** in his parody of Euripidean lyrics at *Frogs* 1309–22, Aristophanes recognizes the poet's fondness for the word γάνος in high-style periphrases for wine (cf. *Hyps.* F 757.891). It suggests joy as well as (usually liquid) brightness (Fraenkel on A. *Ag.* 1392, Dodds on Eur. *Bacc.* 261).

138. fall in love: the expression is almost unique in classical Greek (cf. Antiphanes F 232.3, Hypoth. Men. *Her.* 4–5; εἰς ἔρον/ἔρωτα πίπτειν in the sense 'conceive a desire for something' at *IT* 1172, *Bacc.* 813; and related material in P. Flury, *Liebe und Liebessprache bei Menander, Plautus, und Terenz* [Heidelberg, 1968], 19). Klimek-Winter remarks that the casting of 1 as a rel. clause results in an epigrammatic structure in which 1 is the general, 2 the specific 'set-up', and 3 arrives as a kind of punch-line; he adds that such phrasing endeared Eur. to anthologists (cf. Handley on Men. *Dysc.* 766ff.).

138a. The love we have, etc.: the reasons that led Fritzsche to deny this fr. to *Androm.* are insufficient, and it has been reclaimed by most recent editors, including Kannicht. **we:** probably poetic plural for 'I', but possibly Perseus or Andromeda speaks of his/her own *and* the other's love as δεινός (**terrible,** 'strange' or 'awe-inspiring'). Alternatively, someone tries to persuade either or both of them to choose reason over passion – an interpretation that becomes more attractive if Meineke was right to judge the syntax at the beginning of the excerpt incomplete (cf. *Arch.* F 250 n.). He suggested that the previous line ended with δεσπότην: 'We (i.e. humans generally) have a terrible master in Love'). **words**: the λόγοι could be just the statements in 2–3 (ὡς = 'that'); alternatively, the person told to **choose** has heard two sides of a debate, and the untrustworthiness of love is offered as a reason (ὡς = 'for') to choose the better (i.e. sensible) course.

139 N. Although they recognize *Thesm.* 1130 (or 1130–1) as coming from *Med.*, the Aristophanic scholia are silent on 1128–9, which Fritzsche (following Matthiae) attributed to *Androm.* Recent editors reject them; as Rau (1967), 88 notes, Ar. was well able to write tragic-sounding lines of his own. See further Introd., *Other proposed ascriptions.*

140. Without context, the nuances of several words remain indeterminate: τλῆμον **Intrepid man** can be sympathetic or disapproving of what someone endures/dares (cf. e.g. Gregory on *Hec.* 326–7); the addressee's τύχαι ἀσθενεῖς **weak fortunes** could consist in physical, social, or economic disadvantage; the **words** that **are high-minded** (μέγα φρονοῦσι) could be approved as signs of a noble spirit or disapproved as arrogance.

141. I forbid the getting of bastard children: it is likely enough that Cepheus held it against Perseus, who was born (obviously out of wedlock) to Zeus and Danae, that he was a bastard, but the transmitted text cannot mean 'I forbid my children (i.e. Andromeda) to take bastards (as husbands)', for only a man can 'take' a woman in this sense (e.g. Men. *Asp.* 263; *Perikeir.* 1014; LSJ λαμβάνω II.1.c). Probably Andromeda is addressed, and the **bastard children** are those she will bear if she marries Perseus. In some other places where Eur. talks of bastards (e.g. *Hipp.* 1083 and especially *Ion* 592), it is easier to see why he might want to evoke their legal status in contemporary Athens, though even then the gain in interpreting his language technically is hard to measure. As the traditional descendants of Perseus and Andromeda are destined for illustrious mythical careers, the suggestion that Andromeda should accept an approved (Ethiopian?) marriage is heavily ironic from a Greek point of view. For the assertion that bastards are not naturally inferior to legitimate children, see Eur. *And.* 638, *Antig.* F 168, *Eurysth.* F 377; D. Ogden, *Greek Bastardy* (Oxford, 1996), 204.

142. Most of all, I want to have gold, etc.: for praise of money, see Thgn. 523–6, 699–718, etc.; Solon F 13.7, Soph. F 354, (Mastronarde on) Eur. *Pho.* 439–40, *Danae* F 324. Although rich slaves were not unknown at Athens ([Xen.] *Ath. Pol.* 1.11 with Frisch's note; A.R.W. Harrison, *The Law of Athens* I [Oxford, 1968], 177–8), the claim that they are held in honour (τίμιος) is contentious. There is similar exaggeration in 3, though there can be no doubt (or surprise) that the rich had disproportionate 'strength'. [Stob. transmits the four lines as one excerpt, but Musgrave convinced Hense that 4 is a separate fr. by an unknown poet (hence the two Stob. numbers). It is also possible that 4 belongs to *Androm.* but did not immediately follow 1–3 (Klimek-Winter).]

143. Similar thoughts and expression at *IT* 850–1, *Ion* 307.

137. This is the best of riches, etc.: even if their reference to a **noble spouse** is merely general, these lyric lines, which look like Choral reflection, are more likely to follow than precede the scene(s) in which the proposed marriage of Perseus and Andromeda becomes a subject of controversy. If the reference is specifically to Andromeda, and 'noble' means that she has just given evidence of her good character, the fr. could belong near the end of the play (see Introd., *Reconstruction*).   **spouse**: the poetic λέχος, lit. 'bed', may refer by metonymy to 'marriage' or 'spouse' of either sex. The passages quoted with this one in Stobaeus' chapter *That marriage is a very fine thing* (including Thgn. 1225–6, Soph. F 942, Eur. *Oed.* F 543, *Phrixus* F 822, Hippothoon *TrGF* 210 F 3a [= Eur. F 164 N]) mostly concern good *wives*.

**144. Don't manage my mind: underlying the expression τὸν ἐμὸν νοῦν οἰκεῖν 'manage my mind' is τὸν ἐμὸν οἶκον οἰκεῖν 'live in, be master of, manage my own house' (*And.* 581, where see Stevens). Hence Ar.'s witticism at *Frogs* 105 (which gave an ancient commentator the occasion to quote our passage): 'don't manage my mind: you've got a house'. No precise parallel has been found for the notion of inhabiting another's mind; F 138a.3 (where see note) and *And.* 237 are somewhat similar.

150. There is no mortal who is fortunate, etc.: for mortal happiness subject to divine whim, see *Arch.* F 152 n.   [After surveying fifteen attempts to emend line 2, Klimek-Winter endorses Blaydes' ἂν μὴ...συνθέληι 'unless the divine also wishes it for the most part'. The thought, like that produced by most of the conjectures, would then closely resemble *Supp.* 596–7, where see Collard for further examples. As Kannicht points out, however, this commonplace does not suit the anthologist's heading *That human prosperity is unstable because fortune easily changes*; comparing *Tel.* F 716, Hense therefore proposed ὃν μὴ...συστελεῖ 'whom the divine will not bring low for the most part'. Nauck must have intended something similar by ὃν μὴ...προυσελεῖ 'whom the divine does not for the most part maltreat' (sc. 'sooner or later', unless he was thinking of an unattested future form). Certainly the rare verb would be liable to corruption, and the vivid sense of outrage it seems always to convey might have caught an anthologist's eye, but it is not very close to the transmitted text.]

151. Justice...the child of Zeus: traditional ('they say'), as at Hes. *Theog.* 901–2, *Works* 256, A. *Sept.* 662, *Cho.* 949, etc. For divine power 'dwelling nearby' and related expressions of faith that the wicked will be punished, cf. *Arch.* F 255 n. Reference to a specific **transgression** (of Cepheus, who has broken a promise? See Introd., *Reconstruction*) provides only one possible context for the fr.   [Except for the omission of τοι, Orion transmits 1 in a form identical to *Antiope* F 222.1, where Justice is the child not of Zeus but of time. The variant is easily explained as a result of confusing the two passages. In 2, on the other hand, Orion's ἁμαρτίας 'transgression' gives better sense than Stob.'s τιμωρίας 'punishment', for if Dike *brings* or even *is* punishment, what is the point of saying that she *dwells near* it?]

152. Don't you see the divine, etc.: the metre of this brief lyric is syncopated iambic, or perhaps dochmiac, or a blend of the two. The content suggests attribution to the Chorus but is too general for assignment to a specific context. The old commonplace that human happiness depends on the changeable will of the gods (e.g. Hom. *Od.* 18.130–40, Archil. F 130) recurs in F 153 (cf. F 150 n.) and many Euripidean passages, often blended with some notion of fate. Most like our fr. is *And.* 1007–8; for further references, see Collard on *Supp.* 269–70, 331, 412–13.   [Line 2 has not been convincingly explained or emended. In 3, the change of 2nd person στρέφεις to 3rd person στρέφει **it turns** must be right, as the person addressed in οὐχ ὁρᾶις **Don't you see?** can hardly be endowed with this power.]

153. The one prospered, etc.: again the changeability of human fortune according to the gods' whim (F 150, 152 nn.). Such a reflection by the Chorus could come at several points in the play.   **those who...were successful**: like Latin *clarus*, λαμπρός, lit. 'bright', is used of various kinds of success.   **gust**: change of wind is a very common poetic emblem of change of fortune: Pind. *Ol.* 7.95, *Pyth.* 3.104–5, *Isthm.* 3/4.23–4, A. *Pers.* 942–3, Eur. *El.* 1147–8, *Ion* 1506, (Bond on) *HF* 216.   [In the transmitted text of 1, **the one** who prospered (ὁ μέν, masc.) is balanced by 'it' (τὸ δ'), where 'it' = 'his prosperity'. Valckenaer's simple change produces a more satisfactory antithesis between two individuals. In 2, some change is needed for the anapaestic metre; Grotius' ἐ<κ> is very simple; Conington and Wilamowitz independently proposed ἐκκλίνων 'causing to decline', from the same metaphorical sphere as νεύει 'sways' in 3.]

154. Neglecting to live, they honour, etc.: the speaker evidently intends some contrast between good fortune in this life and honour after death, but much remains obscure. One would expect τὸ ζῆν ἀφέντες to mean 'letting go of life', i.e. 'dying', but since 'they' are alive and bestowing honour on the dead, the participle must mean **neglecting** as at S. *OC* 1537 (cited by Kannicht), Eur. *Supp.* 491, for which παρείς would be more usual. Most editors since Musgrave have divided the lines between two speakers, but though exclamatory γε (Denniston, *GP* 126–30) is at home in a stichomythic exchange, it is not found only there, and κενόν **inanely** could express the speaker's reaction to what he or she has just said 'they' do (cf. *Pho.* 551).   [If correct, σου at the end of 1 must be construed with τὸ κατὰ γῆς to give 'the part of you that is beneath the earth'. The word order is troublesome, however, and various emendations have been proposed (see Klimek-Winter). Collard suggests που 'I suppose'. At the end of 2, mss. SA of Stob. give the name Creon; since he has no place in *Androm.*, some assume that the lemma mistakenly gives *Andromeda* for e.g. *Antigone* or *Alcmeon*. Musgrave's easy change gives good sense but cannot be regarded as certain.]

147. After Bekker's correction, the Greek words from οἱ to τράπεζαν (*those in the house around feast and table*) constitute three trochaic metra and may quote Eur. directly. Some form of the lemma ἄγορος/-οι **gathered** must have occurred, although the word occurs elsewhere only in lyric. The end of the note is ungrammatical but appears to identify the participants as Ethiopians. Those who reconstruct *Androm.*

from Ovid imagine the context as a wedding feast for Perseus and Andromeda, into which the rejected suitor Phineus/Agenor will make an angry entrance (cf. *Met.* 4.757ff.). The rather general phrasing allows many other possibilities.

148. *final*: in explaining the Greek proverbial equivalent of 'last but not least' (τὸ τρίτον τῶι σωτῆρι, lit. 'third to [Zeus] the Saviour'), the Platonic scholia cite Eur. and Aristophanes (F 540) for use of the word τέλειος, which means both 'final' and 'perfect', of the third and last libation poured during symposia, to Zeus Sôtêr. The custom is alluded to often in tragedy: A. *Ag.* 1387, (Sommerstein on) *Eum.* 757–61, F 55; Soph. F 425. Zeus received cult as both Sôtêr and Teleios, but separately: although the two aspects of the god were at some point thought to be united in the practice of libation, it is attested for Aristophanes and Eur. only that they called the last κρατήρ ('bowl, libation') τέλειος (Jacoby on Philochorus *FGH* 328 F 87; Burkert, *Greek Religion* 70–1). The context in *Androm.* may be a feast, but it is also possible to think, for example, of Perseus making a thanksgiving offering after his ordeal (cf. Ov. *Met.* 4.753–6).

155. *catches*: if the ἀγρεύματα of the original were associated with warfare, as indicated by the gloss *spoils*, the usage was unusual though perfectly natural. The primary association is with hunting; at *Hyps.* F 754 (where see n.), the sing. is used of a child's gathering of flowers.

155a. dim vision: the Berlin Photius records that Eur. used the form ἀμβλωπός **dim** in *Androm.* and *Theseus* (F 386a), alongside ἀμβλῶπας (from ἀμβλώψ) in *Thyestes* (F 397a). Aeschylus (*Eum.* 955) and Critias (88 B 6.11 DK) also have ἀμβλωπός.

156. *exchanges: begs off*: many scholars disbelieve the lexicographers' gloss. Comparing Hesych. α 3623 Latte, where ἀμείβεσθαι and περαιώσασθαι ('cross over' and 'pass through') are among the words used to gloss ἀμεύσασθαι 'surpass, pass over', Küster emends παραιτεῖται 'begs off' to περαιοῦται here. Of other suggestions, Collard's παραμείβεται is closer to the transmitted text than Kannicht's παραλλάσσει (both meaning 'passes by').

HYPSIPYLE

Texts, testimonia. P. Oxy. 2455 frs. 14 (cols. xiii–xiv, xvi) and 15 with P. Oxy. 3652 (= *TrGF* T iiia, hypothesis: see app. crit. there); *TrGF* F 752–769 including P. Oxy. 852 (ed. B. Grenfell and A. Hunt, *Oxyrhynchus Papyri* VI [1908], 19–106: by far the most extensive source), P. Petrie II.49c (= P. Lit. Lond. 74: see F 757.830–50), P. Hamb. 118b col. ii (= F 752a). Von Arnim 46–67; G. Italie, *Euripidis Hypsipyla* (Berlin, 1923); U. Scatena, *Studio sull' Ipsipile Euripidea* (Rome, 1934); Page, *GLP* 76–109; G. W. Bond, *Euripides: Hypsipyle* (Oxford, 1963); W. Cockle, *Euripides: Hypsipyle* (Rome, 1987); Diggle, *TrGFS* 135–49; H. van Looy, ed. Budé VIII.3 (2002), 155–223. Descriptions and illustrations of P. Oxy. 852: Grenfell-Hunt 19–21, Pl. II–III; B. Donovan, *Euripides Papyri* I (New Haven and Toronto, 1969), 60–4, Pl. VII–XIII; Cockle 19–39, Pl. II–V; E. G. Turner, *Greek Manuscripts of the Ancient World* (Princeton, 1971; ed. 2, London, 1987), Pl. 31.

Myth etc. Hypsipyle at Nemea: Pind. *Nem.* hypoth. 2–4 (hypoth. 2 = *TrGF* T iiib(1)); Schol. Clem. Alex. *Protrept.* 2.34 (= T iiib(2)); Apollod. 3.6.4 (= T iiib(3)); *Anth.Pal.* 3.10 (= T iv); Hygin. *Fab.* 74 and (= T vb) *Fab.* 273.6; Mythogr. Vat. 2.141 Bode = Schol. Stat. *Theb.* 4.740 (= T va). These are collected in Bond 147–9 as well as *TrGF.* Stat. *Theb.* 4.711–5.753 is a creative reworking of the story. Other accounts of the death of Archemorus: Bacchyl. 9.10–17 (cf. Simonides F 553 *PMG*); Aesch. *Nemea, TrGF* 3.261–2; Paus. 2.15.2. C. Robert, *Hermes* 44 (1909), 376–402; J. Mahaffy, *Hermathena* 35 (1909), 347–52; *RE* IX.i.436–44 ('Hypsipyle': O. Jessen, 1916); Simon (below, *Illustrations*); P. Vicaire, *BAGB* (1979), 1–45 (Amphiaraus); Brillante (below, *Illustrations*); *LIMC* I.i.691–713 ('Amphiaraus': I. Krauskopf, 1981), II.i.472–5 ('Archemorus': W. Pülhorn, 1984), III.i.59–62 ('Euneos et Thoas': G. Berger-Doer, 1988), VIII.i.645–50 ('Hypsipyle': C. Boulotis, 1997); B. Deforge, *REG* 100 (1987), 36–8 (A. *Hyps.*); Gantz 345–6, 511–2. *Nemea (site):* Pausanias 2.15.2–3; S. G. Miller, *Nemea: A Guide to the Site and Museum* (Berkeley, 1990), and annual reports in *AR* since 1975. *The Euneidai:* J. Toepffer, *Attische Genealogie* (Berlin, 1889), 181–206 (sources 181–5); F. Pfister, *Der Reliquienkult im Altertum* (Giessen, 1909), 162–4; Bond 20; E. Kearns, *The Heroes of Attica* (London, 1989), 70; W. Burkert in A. Bierl (ed.), *Orchestra: Drama, Mythos, Logos* (Stuttgart, 1994), 44–9; M. Cropp in Csapo and Miller, *Poetry, Theory, Praxis* 129–45.

Illustrations. Séchan 358–66; Scatena (above, *Texts*), 109–14, Pl. 1–6; Webster, *Monuments*[2] 73ff., 158–9; Trendall-Webster 90–1 (III.3.25–6); E. Simon, *AA* (1979), 31–45 (Archemorus); C. Brillante, in *Omaggio a Piero Treves* (Padua, 1983), 43–55 (Archemorus); *LIMC* (above, *Myth*); Cockle 142, 147–8, 166–7, Pl. 1.

Main discussions (since publication of P. Oxy. 852: fuller lists in Bond and Cockle). Grenfell-Hunt (above, *Texts*); Robert (above, *Myth*); N. Wecklein, *Über die Hypsipyle des Euripides* (Munich, *SBAW* Abh. 8, 1909); E. Menozzi, *SIFC* 18 (1910), 1–18; E. Petersen, *RhM* 68 (1913), 584–95 = *Die attische Tragödie (etc.)* (Bonn, 1915),

476–86; Italie (above, *Texts*), V–XII, 58–80; W. Morel, *De Euripidis Hypsipyla* (Leipzig, 1921); Séchan 341–58; A. W. Pickard-Cambridge in Powell, *New Chapters III*, 68–134; Scatena (above, *Texts*), 45–107; W. H. Friedrich, *Hermes* 69 (1934), 300–3; Schmid 563–9; G. Schiassi, *RFIC* 81 (1953), 193–208 and 82 (1954), 1–17; Bond (above, *Texts*), 6–20, and reviews by A. P. Burnett, *CPh* 60 (1965), 129–31, H. van Looy, *AC* 35 (1966), 574–80; T.B.L. Webster, in *The Classical Tradition...Studies...H. Caplan* (Ithaca, 1966), 83–97; Webster, *Euripides* (1967), 211–5; G. Giangrande, *MPhL* 2 (1977), 165–75; Aélion, *Euripide* (1983), 187–95 and *Mythes* (1986), 119–35; F. Zeitlin in T. Carpenter and C. Faraone (eds.), *Masks of Dionysus* (Ithaca, 1993), 147–82; Hose, *Drama und Gesellschaft* 134–7.

Text. *Hypsipyle* is the best preserved of all Euripides' lost plays, although in 1889 Nauck could print only nineteen short book-fragments. It was also one of his longest plays, at well over 1700 lines. The text now available comes largely from P. Oxy. 852, published by Grenfell and Hunt in exemplary fashion in 1908 with contributions from Wilamowitz, Murray and J. B. Bury. This includes extensive extracts from near the play's beginning (F 752d–k), middle (F 757) and end (F 759a). A reconstruction of the papyrus-roll can be determined from physical features and text-layout, the content of the document on whose back the play-text was copied, and the survival of some of the marginal notations marking every hundredth line of the play (see e.g. line 400). A new level of accuracy was achieved in Cockle's intensive study, following those of the first editors and of Bond with J. Barns (cf. Bond 1–3, Cockle 19–39). Minor additions have come from P. Petrie (F 757.830–50), P. Hamburg (F 752a), and the papyrus hypothesis. This edition, like Kannicht's in *TrGF*, follows Cockle's reconstruction of P. Oxy. The line-numbers (exact or approximate) of the reconstructed P. Oxy. are included where possible and used in references to F 757, 758a, 759a (e.g. F 757.800).

Reconstruction. Many older ideas about the plot of *Hyps.* have been invalidated by P. Oxy. and the now accepted reconstruction. Crucial features of this include (1) the rapid succession of fragments giving Hypsipyle's reactions to the death of Opheltes between the end of Stasimon 1 (about line 575) and the entrance of Eurydice (about 690: see Comm. on F 753d–754b); (2) the opening of the 'trial' scene well before line 800 (cf. F 757) rather than some three hundred lines later as was widely supposed before the work of Barns and Bond (cf. Bond 2, and earlier Menozzi 11); and (3) the securing of F 758d (= P. Oxy. frs. 61+82) towards the end of the play rather than in the prologue-speech as Barns and Bond asserted following E. Petersen.

  The basis of the plot is evident in Hypsipyle's exchanges with the Chorus and Amphiaraus as each arrives (F 752f–h) and from the extant part of the reunion-scene near the end of the play (F 759a). Hypsipyle is the daughter of Thoas, son of the god Dionysus and king of the island of Lemnos. When young she bore twin sons to Jason during the Argonauts' visit to Lemnos. Jason and his men stayed on until these sons, Euneos and the younger Thoas, were weaned, whereupon he took them with him to Colchis (F 759a.1614). He later died in circumstances not clear from the fragments (see on F 759a.1616), and the sons were educated by his comrade Orpheus in Thrace, Euneos as a musician and Thoas as a warrior (F 759a.1619–23). Meanwhile Hypsipyle had fled from Lemnos to escape punishment for sparing her father when the rest of the Lemnian women massacred the entire male population of the island in the well-known 'Lemnian troubles', which here seem to have followed rather than preceded the Argonauts' visit (F 759a.1593–9: cf. *Myth* below). While fleeing she was seized by marauders, transported to Nauplion, the port of Argos, and sold as a slave (F 759a.1600–8) to Lycurgus, priest at the rural sanctuary of Zeus at Nemea (F 752h.26–8). She then lived with Lycurgus and his wife Eurydice as nurse to their infant son Opheltes. Her father, having somehow survived with Dionysus' help (F 759a.1627), was reunited with his now adult grandsons and returned with them to Lemnos (F 759a.1624–6).

The play's opening was tripartite: speech, dialogue, monody.[1] Hypsipyle must have started with a lengthy speech telling her genealogy (**F 752, 752a**) and the story of her affair with Jason, separation from him and their sons, and later tribulations (**F 752b**), and emphasizing her servitude and isolation, despair of seeing her loved ones again, and compensating love for the infant boy now in her charge. She then re-entered the house to attend to the child, and Euneos and Thoas arrived (like Orestes and Pylades after Iphigenia's prologue-speech in *IT*), travelling in search of their mother.[2] After an expository conversation while viewing the temple (**F 752c**), they seek hospitality at the priest's house and are met by Hypsipyle (**F 752d**). Learning that Lycurgus himself is absent, they hesitate to press their request but with Hypsipyle's encouragement (**F 752d–e**) seem to have gone inside (**Hypoth.** 22–3, 25–6).[3] The fragments reveal no more of their involvement until the reunion-scene (but see below, pp. 175–6).

---

[1] Grenfell-Hunt 23: cf. Wecklein 16–20, Morel 1–10, Italie 58–63, Bond 7–12 (but with frs. 61+82 misplaced).

[2] Cf. Hypoth. (= T iiia) 21–2, hypoth. Pind. *Nem.* 2 (= T iiib(1)) 4, Mythogr. Vat. (= T va), Stat. *Theb.* 5.715. They were perhaps sent by their grandfather Thoas after being reunited with him (Webster [1966] 85, [1967] 212; cf. F 759a.1624–6).

[3] So e.g. Morel 9–10, Bond 12, Burnett 129. The Hypothesis introduces them after Opheltes' death, but the inference that they accepted hospitality only at this point (cf. Webster [1966], 86, 89, 90–1 and *Euripides* [1967], 212) is not compelling.

Hypsipyle remained on stage, and is singing a song to calm the baby when the Chorus of friendly local women enters with news that the Seven and the Argive army are passing on their march to Thebes (**F 752f**). The parodos is a lyric exchange, Hypsipyle dwelling on her lost past and present misery, the Chorus trying vainly to console her (**F 752g, 752h.**1–9). Then Episode 1 begins with the entrance of the seer Amphiaraus, one of the Seven, who has foreseen his own death at Thebes; he requests Hypsipyle's help in finding spring-water to assist a sacrifice (**F 752h–k**, cf. **Hypoth.** 19). Their conversation continued beyond line 400 (near the end of F 752k) and ended with her agreeing to help, probably over the objections of the Chorus (**F 753, 753a**, placing not certain; the danger from the serpent may or may not have been mentioned).[4] The conclusion of Episode 1 is lost, but Hypsipyle must have left for the spring with Amphiaraus and the baby. Stasimon 1 (roughly lines 500–75) was largely or wholly concerned with the expedition of the Seven and its epic background (cf. *IT* 392ff. commenting on the newly arrived Greeks); its extant part describes the arrival of Polynices and Tydeus at the court of Adrastus (**F 753c**).

The sequence from Stasimon 1 to Eurydice's entrance has been much debated, but Cockle's reconstruction precludes expansive possibilities such as a 'messenger' reporting the baby's death or a cortège bringing the body to the house (see Comm. note on F 753d–754b). After the stasimon Hysipyle has returned in distress and is telling the Chorus of the baby's seizure by a monstrous serpent near the spring where she has incautiously left him on the ground (**F 753d–e, 754**). This lyric exchange leads to a dialogue in which she seems to have narrated these events (**F 754a**), then discussed with the Chorus her predicament and possible ways of escaping it (**F 754b**), only to be fore-stalled by Eurydice's entrance from the house about line 690, apparently looking for Hypsipyle and the baby (**F 754c**). The next hundred lines, including **F 755a**, contained dialogue and speeches – Hypsipyle explaining the boy's death, Eurydice reacting with grief and accusing her of plotting against the family (cf. F 757.866–7), Hypsipyle beginning a speech in her own defence. **F 757** (giving lines 800–949 almost continuously, with half of the lines complete) starts with the ending of her speech, an appeal to Eurydice's good judgement which the Chorus supports. Eurydice's intransigent reply provokes from Hypsipyle a final desperate appeal for protection which is answered by the return of Amphiaraus from the spring. In a scene which became emblematic of the play (see below, *Illustrations*) he explains the circumstances of the child's death, persuades

---

[4] Wilamowitz placed F 754a (P. Oxy. fr. 18), a description of the terrifying serpent, in this episode; cf. Webster (1966), 88–9. For its placing in Episode 2, after the disaster, see Grenfell-Hunt 25, Bond 98, Cockle 155–6.

Eurydice to relent and accept the misfortune, interprets the event as prefiguring the deaths of the Argive leaders at Thebes, renames the child Archemorus ('First in Death'), and proposes his commemoration in funeral games which will live on as the Nemean Games. Eurydice readily accepts his advice.

The structure and content of the second half of the play have to be inferred from much sparser fragments, the testimonia, and our knowledge of Euripides' dramatic style. The testimonia demand caution: most are summaries of the myths of the Seven or the founding of the Nemean Games; only the play-hypothesis is based explicitly on Euripides' plot. *Anth.Pal.* 3.10 and its introduction seem largely Euripidean, but the epigram may have adjusted the story to its own purpose of praising the filial piety of the brother-kings Attalus and Eumenes of Pergamum. Statius' extensive account, much used for reconstructing the play before P. Oxy. was discovered, must be understood as a work of Statius' own design, even if it includes much that is Euripidean.[5] As for the fragments themselves, a gap of 140 lines precedes **F 758a–b** which give the end of an episode and the beginning and a later part of a stasimon, all very damaged. This is probably the end of Episode 2 followed by Stasimon 2, in which case Episode 2 continued until 1088; a long and complex episode is not untypical of the central dramatic developments of Euripides' later plays (e.g. *IT* 467–1088, *Hel.* 386–1106), and Amphiaraus, Eurydice and Hypsipyle may have continued to discuss the funeral of Opheltes and the games, perhaps with some preparation for the participation of Euneos and Thoas and the eventual reunion (cf. below, pp. 175–6). It is possible, though, that lines 960–1088 comprised a brief Stasimon 2 and a brief Episode 3 (cf. e.g. *IT* 1089–1233).[6] At any rate, the stasimon celebrates the power of Dionysus, his gifts to mankind, the joys of worshipping him, and the story of his birth (**F 758a–b**), and seems to cast him in 'Orphic' terms as a god of cosmic significance (see on F 758a.1103–8). This praise may have reflected a sense that Dionysus was bringing about the liberation of his grandchild Hypsipyle and the reunion of his son's family. After this nearly 300 lines are lost (c. 1155–1450), then a further pair of damaged dialogue-fragments (**F 758c–d**) seems to be concerned with Hypsipyle's liberation (perhaps now accomplished) and her need to find her sons (perhaps continuing). A hundred lines later still, at 1579ff., the second column of **F 759a** has 55 almost complete lines in which Amphiaraus makes his farewell and Hypsipyle and her sons

---

[5] On Statius' use of Euripides see Grenfell-Hunt 22–3; A. Reussner, *De Statio et Euripide* (Diss. Halle, 1921), 37–44; G. Aricò, *Dioniso* 35 (1961), 56–67; D. Vessey, *BICS* 17 (1970), 48–51.

[6] Van Looy (ed. Budé, 167) places a second stasimon soon after 949 but gives no reasons and overlooks the stasimon at F 758a–b as well as the later dialogue-fragments F 758c–d.

celebrate their reunion and relate to each other their earlier experiences.

This framework must have supported some kind of continuing dramatic movement, and some scholars have supposed that Hypsipyle remained under threat of punishment despite Eurydice's apparent readiness to forgive her. Hygin. *Fab.* 74 mentions that the Seven had to pacify 'Lycus' on Hypsipyle's behalf, and in Statius' *Thebaid* (5.638ff.) Lycurgus, returning from a sacrifice on nearby Mt. Apesas, has to be restrained by the Seven from attacking her, which leads to a general mêlée between Argives and Nemeans. Welcker's and Hartung's attribution of this motif to Euripides is now generally rejected, as is Robert's attempt to sandwich a return of Lycurgus between the reunion-scene and Dionysus' intervention;[7] the motif is best seen as an expression of Statius' own theme of uncontrollable internecine strife. Also improbable is the idea that Euneos and Thoas became involved in the condemnation of Hypsipyle (Hartung) or her arrest and punishment (Wecklein).[8] The likeliest source of a continued threat is Eurydice herself, but the grounds are still not strong. The play-hypothesis (T iiia) says that the sons 'having lodged with Lycurgus' wife...were keen to compete in the funeral games for the boy' and that Eurydice 'approved them, but planned to kill their mother as having killed the child on purpose...', but this probably distorts the order of events and refers to Eurydice's initial condemnation rather than any later threat. Pind. *Nem.* hypoth. 2 (T iiib(1)) likewise introduces Euneos and Thoas after the child's death and relates that Eurydice imprisoned Hypsipyle in a secret place with a view to killing her, but Amphiaraus through his seercraft revealed her whereabouts to her sons, and she on being released challenged the heroes to compete with them: but in *Hyps.* the games must have preceded the recognition (see below), and an imprisonment is unlikely since it would have removed Hypsipyle from the scene.[9] Lastly, *Anth.Pal.* 3.10 (T iv) has Hypsipyle rescued from death *by her*

---

[7] So also Schiassi (1953) 206–8. Cockle (40, 49, 141) places an intervention of Lycurgus before the recognition, but wrongly assumes support for this in the archaic iconography (cf. below, n. 15).

[8] Cf. e.g. Grenfell-Hunt 28–9, Morel 23–8, Italie 69–70, Séchan 352–5. Wecklein's idea that the sons arrested Hyps. before the trial scene is incompatible with an early placing of F 757. In Stat. *Theb.* 5.710–22 the sons side with Lycurgus and Eurydice until they realise who Hyps. is; but they have not appeared earlier, nor met Hyps., as they did in Eur.'s play.

[9] Menozzi's attribution of an imprisonment to Euripides is followed by (e.g.) Scatena, Bond, Burnett; he had wrongly assumed that the games occurred after the end of the play (Menozzi 9). Bond's suggestion that Eurydice meant to have Lycurgus decide about Hypsipyle's punishment on his return is unlikely if (as Bond himself maintains) Lycurgus did not return during the play; and it relies on a false placing and unsound interpretation

sons (rather than by Amphiaraus as in the extant trial scene), but this is probably due to the politically motivated adjustment mentioned above.

Probably, then, the second half was concerned not with further dangers for Hypsipyle but with the recognition itself, her redemption from slavery, and her reunion with her family (so e.g. Italie 65, Solmsen, Friedrich, Webster 1966, 92–3). Solmsen (416–7) showed eloquently how Hypsipyle's continuing predicament and emotional reactions to events could have been the focus of the drama, like Creusa's in *Ion*. If this is right, she will have remained on stage, or close by, throughout. As for events, a celebration of the games with Euneos and Thoas participating is mentioned by some testimonia (Pind. *Nem.* hypoth. 2, Mythogr. Vat., Hygin. *Fab.* 273.6, cf. Stat. *Theb.* 6.340ff.) and is confirmed by the papyrus hypothesis. This must have occurred before the recognition since at the end of the play Amphiaraus and the Seven are already leaving for Thebes. A narrative report of the funeral and games is thus very likely, with Euneos' and Thoas's participation leading somehow to the recognition (Petersen 591 = 482–3, Italie 70-1, Friedrich, Schiassi [1953] 198–202, Bond 18). As Webster says (1966, 94), a messenger-scene and following stasimon could have occupied most if not all of the 300-line interval between the second stasimon (F 758 a–b) and the scene in progress in F 758c–d. The speech was surely delivered to Hypsipyle, not Eurydice as Schiassi and Webster supposed; it seems unlikely that Eurydice reappeared after the conclusion of the trial-scene.

The Vatican Mythographer (T va) supplies a likely mechanism for the recognition (Friedrich, Schiassi 199–202, Bond 18–19): Euneos and Thoas 'won at running, and when the herald announced that they were the sons of Jason and Hypsipyle, their mother recognized them'. The alternatives offered by ancient sources seem remote from the play: Amphiaraus discovers the imprisoned Hypsipyle by divination (see above), or Hypsipyle calls out the names of Thoas and Lemnos during a fray provoked by Lycurgus (Stat. *Theb.* 5.718–22). If Hypsipyle did not attend the games, the summary is slightly distorted: either she recognized the names from an announcement reported in the messenger-speech, or Amphiaraus recognized them and brought them to Hypsipyle for confirmation (this would account for his presence at the reunion and his claim to have brought it about, F 759a.1686). The description in *Anth.Pal.* 3.10 (T iv) of the sons 'being recognized by their mother and showing her the golden vine' suggests the vine served as a proof after the initial recognition (cf. *IT* 808–26, *Ion* 1412–36).

Euneos and Thoas, having entered the house around line 180 (between F 752e and 752f) must then have left it between the trial-scene and the

---

of P. Oxy. fr. 63 (see Comm. on F 758c–d and 758c.2). Others (e.g. Burnett) prefer to see Eurydice simply postponing the execution until after the funeral and games.

messenger-scene to compete in the games. The hypothesis perhaps refers to this: '...having lodged with Lycurgus' wife they were keen to compete in the funeral games for the boy. And she having accepted the aforesaid youths as guests approved them....' Allowing for some confusion in the order of events, this suggests that Euneos and Thoas remained in the guest-quarters (like Heracles in *Alcestis*) until they heard of Opheltes' death, then obtained Eurydice's permission to join in the games, and departed in order to do so.[10] A scene involving them may have come right after the trial-scene, or after a lost intervening stasimon (see above), or even after the stasimon represented by F 758a–b (though its Dionysiac theme fits better *after* a major step towards the recognition and Hypsipyle's liberation has been taken). It remains unclear whether the twins conversed with Eurydice (as perhaps implied by the hypothesis, but this would have made role-allocation more difficult and could have occurred inside the house), or with Hysipyle (offering further dramatic ironies), or with Amphiaraus (who then took them with him to the funeral), or with two of these.

The papyrus shows that Dionysus appeared in the play's final scene at F 759a.1673. He is prominently featured elsewhere (F 752, 752a, 752g.35–7, 758a–b, 759a.1627–32, and the grapevine-token). Nothing survives, but he presumably ordained the future of his Lemnian family and commanded Euneos and Thoas to take Hypsipyle back to Lemnos (cf. *Anth.Pal.* 3.10 = T iv, Mythogr. Vat. = T va). Wilamowitz suggested that he also told Euneos to go on to Attica and there establish the family of the Euneidai, official musicians and dancers in the Attic cult of Dionysus Melpomenos, thus creating a perpetual connection between Athens and Lemnos (cf. Grenfell-Hunt 28 and Bibl. above). This suggestion has been generally accepted, and its implications are discussed under *Myth* below.

Other proposed ascriptions. None is convincing. **P. Petr. 2.49(d) DX**, from an argument about the death of a child, ascribed to *Hyps.* by Milne, is now *TrGF* **adesp. F 634** (see Kannicht-Snell there; Bond 52, 140).   Ar. *Frogs* 1309–12 (**F 856**), where scholia ascribe 1310 wrongly to *IA*, was assigned to *Hyps.* by Bakhuyzen (cf. Bond 140; E. Borthwick, *Phoenix* 48 [1994], 29) since it follows an allusion to Hypsipyle's castanets and precedes *Hyps.* F 765, 765a, 765b; but it is probably pastiche (as schol. 1310 itself observes) based on *IT* 1089–90.   The declaration about gods and chance quoted after F 765c by John Lydus, *On Months* and ascribed to *Hyps.* by Wilamowitz, Grenfell-Hunt and others is now known to be from *Phrixus B* (**F 820b**).   For *TrGF* **adesp. F 37a**, 'Aietes' golden fleece', identified by Cockle with F 752f.22–3, see Comm. on that passage.

---

[10] Hypoth. 2 and 4 Pind. *Nem.* contain inklings of a resistance by the Seven to the admission of Hypsipyle's sons to the games (Cropp [2003], 141 n. 75); cf. the resistance of Hecuba's sons to Alexandros' admission to the games in *Alex.*

Myth.[11] There is no firm evidence before Euripides for Hypsipyle's migration to Nemea. Robert's inference that Euripides invented it is widely though not universally accepted.[12] The *Iliad* mentions Hypsipyle simply as the mother by Jason of Euneos, who ruled Lemnos during the Trojan War (*Il.* 7.468–9, 21.41, 23.740–9). The Argonauts' visit to Lemnos and participation in an athletic contest there were mentioned by Simonides (F 547 *PMG*) and Pindar (*Pyth.* 4.252–8, *Ol.* 4.19–27); Pindar places it on their return journey from Colchis and mentions unions between the Argonauts and the 'husband-slaying' Lemnian women, which presumably served to repopulate the island after the 'Lemnian troubles' as in later accounts (though in these the visit occurs on the outward voyage). A tetralogy by Aeschylus and plays by Sophocles and Aristophanes seem to have used the same components,[13] and there are allusions to the massacre in A. *Cho.* 631–8, Hdt. 6.138, and E. *Hec.* 887. As for Nemea, there was probably a local tradition about the founding of the games at least from the time of their development as a panhellenic event in 573 B.C.: Opheltes/ Archemorus was killed by the serpent as the Seven and their army passed through Nemea on their way to Thebes, Amphiaraus interpreted the portent, and the games were founded to commemorate the child's death (cf. Bacchyl. 9.10–17, Simon. F 547 *PMG*, Pind. *Nem.* 8.51, 10.28). Such an episode may have occurred already in the cyclic *Thebais*, but its sparse fragments include nothing relevant.[14] Attempts to trace Statius' account of a vengeful assault on Hypsipyle by Lycurgus (*Theb.* 5.660ff.) back to the archaic *Thebais* and related iconography are not compelling.[15] Hermann's argument that Hypsipyle had a

---

[11] For full discussion and documentation of this topic see Cropp (2003).

[12] E.g. Italie (differing on other points), Bond 128–9, Giangrande, Gantz 511–2. The suggestion that Hypsipyle might have been the name of a Nemean deity (cf. Jessen 436, Burkert 1994, 49) is speculative, though it fits well with the likelihood that the Nemean cult was originally focused on child-raising (excavations suggest it went back to late Mycenean times: Miller, *AR* 47 [2001], 25; for possible Mycenean elements of both the cult and the Thebaid narrative see E. Vermeule, *PCPhS* 213 (1997), 122–52, esp. 137, 141 on Opheltes and the Games). An early connection of the Euneid family with Nemea has been suggested (Pfister 162–4). That Euneos was a competitor in archaic accounts of the first Games seems unlikely since Bacchyl. 9.11 calls the first competitors Argives.

[13] Aeschylus: *TrGF* 3.118 and Deforge. Sophocles' *Lemniai*: *TrGF* 4.336–8 (F 384–9). Aristophanes' *Lemniai*: *PCG* 3.2.207–14 (F 372–91).

[14] Nor do the fragments of Antimachus' *Thebais*, unless frs. 32–36 Wyss refer to the chariot-race in the first Nemean Games as Wyss thought.

[15] Cf. Simon and Brillante, reviving and extending Welcker's arguments; also Cockle 40, 141. In question are a scene on the lost Amyclaean throne (Paus. 3.18.12) and an engraved shield-strap from Olympia showing a conflict between Amphiaraus and

role in Aeschylus' *Nemea* (*TrGF* 3.261–2, F 149a) has been favoured by some scholars (cf. Séchan 342, Aélion [1983] 1.188) but rests on the unneeded supposition that *Nemea* was part of a Lemnian tetralogy.[16]

Euripides' myth used the common motifs of a mother's exile and enslavement, the sons' orphanhood and wanderings, and a fortuitous reunion. The separation of Hypsipyle from her sons in their infancy seems to be contrived, and events at Lemnos ordered so that the Argonauts' visit and Jason's liaison with Hypsipyle occurred in normal circumstances and Jason stayed there until he could take his sons with him to Colchis.[17] Thus the sons know little of the massacre and Hypsipyle's flight until she tells her story during the reunion (F 759a.1593–1603), and Hypsipyle remains conveniently unimplicated in the massacre or in covering it up (contrast Ap. Rhod. 1.653ff., Stat. *Theb.* 5.322ff.). The novelty, or at least abstruseness, of all this for Euripides' audience is suggested by the care with which Euneos explains his and Thoas's history to his mother (F 759a.1616–23). Thoas himself may have been invented to allow Euneos' migration to Attica, which would require an alternative ruler for Lemnos; there is no trace of a twin brother in the older tradition, and the re-use of the grandfather's name is a symptom of this kind of *ad hoc* invention.

The myth in this form seems to have had political overtones, dignifying the Athenian family of the Euneidae as direct descendants of Dionysus, and giving Athens a claim to religious and temporal authority in Lemnos. This probably reflects Athens' strong interest in the control of Lemnos, which with Scyros and Imbros straddled the sea-route from Euboea to the Hellespont and had been a dependency of Athens since the beginning of the fifth century. The descendants of Athenian settlers on Lemnos maintained a special relationship with Athens, used Athenian-style political institutions, and blended Attic with pre-Greek elements in their religious cults. Just as Miltiades' acquisition of the island gave rise to justificatory myth-making (Hdt. 6.137–40), so Athens' need to proclaim kinship with its allied states probably influenced Euripides' choice and treatment of the Hypsipyle myth for his play when Athenian dominance in the Aegean was at risk, and the democracy disrupted, in the years following the Sicilian

---

Lycurgus; but no female figure is involved, and Lycurgus is probably featured as one of the Seven (cf. Stesich. F 194 *PMGF*). See Cropp 2003, 134–5.

[16] The only relevant data are that Aeschylus wrote a *Nemea* and that he mentioned Nemea, no doubt the local nymph, as mother of Archemorus. This suggests that the play was about the baby's death but made his mother herself responsible for it: cf. Gantz 511.

[17] Robert 380–7, 398, not invalidated for the most part by Italie 72–80, who followed Grenfell-Hunt 105 and Mahaffy in supposing that Euripides made Jason revisit Lemnos on his return journey, after Hypsipyle's disappearance. See Comm. on F 759a.1614–19.

disaster.[18] At the same time the story asserted Athenian connections with Nemea, a panhellenic cult-centre promoted by Sparta's Peloponnesian rival Argos and lying close to a strategic route between the Peloponnese and central Greece,[19] and with Oropos, the sanctuary of the heroized Amphiaraus, which lay in contested territory on the borders of Attica and Boeotia.[20]

Illustrations. Nothing is extant before the mid-fourth century, unless one accepts the disputed interpretation of an archaic shield-strap from Olympia as involving Hypsipyle (see n. 15 above). Thereafter the death of Archemorus is often represented. Various items including Hellenistic cups (*LIMC* 'Hypsipyle' nos. 13a–c), a wall-painting from Herculaneum ('Hypsipyle' no. 9, 'Archemoros' no. 3, 'Septem contra Thebas' no. 16), monumental relief-sculptures and Argive coins of the 2nd C. A.D. ('Hypsipyle' nos. 4–8, 11–12, 'Archemorus' nos. 4–7, 'Septem' nos. 17–20) show the snake coiled around the infant Archemorus while a woman looks on or flees in distress and one or two men attack it. E. Simon postulates a 4th C. wall-painting inspired by Euripides' play as the source of this series, and includes in it a Paestan pottery-fragment (*LIMC* 'Hypsipyle' no. 2, 'Archemorus' no. 2) showing the snake starting to devour the infant in front of a distressed woman. Boulotis in *LIMC* adds a recently-discovered Hellenistic relief-cup fragment ('Hypsipyle' no. 10) showing the head and raised left arm of Hypsipyle, here named. These images have few if any 'dramatic' features (though the woman's dress in the Paestan fragment may reflect tragic costume), and they do not assist reliably in reconstructing Euripides' narrative. The same can be said of the well-known Apulian crater now in St. Petersburg (*LIMC* 'Hypsipyle' no. 3, 'Archemorus' no. 8, 'Septem' no. 13, 'Nemea' no. 14; Séchan fig. 105, Scatena pl. 3, Trendall-Webster III.3.25) showing two young warriors attacking the snake coiled around a sacred tree while two others watch, and in the foreground the dead

---

[18] Cf. Cropp (2003), 139. This kind of motivation would explain a radical development of the story of Hypsipyle and her family. By contrast, Burkert (1994) suggests that Euripides only added the figure of Orpheus to a pre-existing story of Hypsipyle at Nemea, and that the motivation for this lay in internal Athenian political rivalries.

[19] For Nemea's strategic importance cf. Thuc. 5.58–60, 6.95. The archaic temple seems to have been destroyed amid military action around 410, close to *Hypsipyle*'s production. It was probably this destruction which led to the removal of the Games from Nemea to Argos until the sanctuary was redeveloped in the 330s (Miller, *AR* 27 [1981], 12, and *Nemea* 43, 58–63, 130).

[20] The sanctuary of Amphiaraus at Oropos was either founded or substantially developed under Athenian control in the 420s, but in 411 was seized by a Boeotian force and the nearby port used as a base for a Peloponnesian fleet: see Thuc. 8.60, 8.95.

Archemorus discovered by his nurse and a second woman bringing funeral offerings. A few minor items show the immediate aftermath of the child's death in abbreviated form (*LIMC* 'Hypsipyle' nos. 11–13).

By contrast, a mid-4ᵗʰ C. Apulian crater now in Naples (*LIMC* 'Hypsipyle' no. 15, 'Archemorus' no. 10, 'Septem' no 14, 'Nemea' no. 15, 'Euneos and Thoas' no. 1; Séchan fig. 103, Scatena Pl. 1, Trendall-Webster III.3.26) focuses on another crucial moment in the play and shows, with names, all of its known characters and several ancillary figures. Before a central architectural façade Hypsipyle pleads with Eurydice, and Amphiaraus intervenes with an admonitory gesture. To the left are Thoas, Euneos and (above) Dionysus; to the right Parthenopaeus and Capaneus representing the Seven, with Zeus and Nemea (local god and local nymph) above. Below, the corpse of Archemorus (here a boy rather than an infant) is laid out for burial, attended by two women and his lamenting tutor, while two servants bring funeral offerings.

Another Apulian crater now in the Louvre (*LIMC* 'Archemorus' no. 9, 'Septem' no 15, 'Euneos and Thoas' no. 3, Séchan fig. 102, Scatena Pl. 2A–B) seems to evoke several of the play's key features, though none of the figures is named. Amphiaraus (identifiable by a pose similar to that on the Naples vase) addresses the mourning Eurydice who is seated holding her son's body. Four spear-holding youths look on, one of them from above (where also Hermes leads a chariot driven by a winged goddess, perhaps suggesting the boy's transition to heroic status). The youths can be identified as Euneos (wearing a diadem and holding a bag which probably denotes recognition-tokens), Thoas (wearing a traveller's hat and holding two headbands, perhaps signifying athletic victory), and (again) two of the Seven. Hypsipyle is not present: the scene emphasizes Archemorus' death and the founding of the Games rather than her story.

Doubtful identifications: (1) An Apulian amphora also in Naples (*LIMC* 'Euneos et Thoas' no. 2, Séchan fig. 104, Scatena Pl. 4) shows three pairs of conversing figures who have been interpreted (e.g. Séchan 364) as Hypsipyle and Eurydice, Lycurgus and Amphiaraus (or Adrastus), and Euneos and Thoas, but the identification of the second pair seems arbitrary and puts the whole interpretation in doubt. (2) A wall-painting from Pompeii shows in tragic costume a woman holding a baby and addressing a man who carries a jug and wears a sword under his himation – perhaps Hypsipyle responding to Amphiaraus' request for help: cf. Webster (1966), 88, *Euripides* (1967), 306, *Monuments*² NP 9; Cockle 147–8.   The recognition-scene is known in art only indirectly through *Anth.Pal.* 3.10 (see p. 175 above).

Themes and characters. The play is akin to some other highly inventive late plays of Euripides (*Iphigenia in Tauris, Ion*) whose principals move fortuitously from suffering to *eudaimonia* and in doing so become associated with Attic cult and genealogy. The framework is the recognition-plot, in which long-separated relatives find each other unknowingly and must go through further crises which lead to recognition and restoration. The knowing audience both shares and observes their vicissitudes, feels for their fallibility, and appreciates how their humane instincts combine with luck and divine providence to bring about a happy outcome. The major scenes of *Hypsipyle* were highly emotive: the sons' first encounter with their enslaved mother, Hypsipyle's decision to help Amphiaraus, her panic at the baby's death, Eurydice's grief and punitive reaction restrained by Amphiaraus' wisdom, a vivid report of the funeral and athletic contests, the final bringing together of mother and sons, and an epiphany of Dionysus. At the same time these confrontations were carefully calibrated in moral terms, showing good decisions contributing to good outcomes. Hypsipyle presses hospitality on the young strangers (F 752e) so that they remain to join in the funeral games and to be recognized there. Hypsipyle's deference (*aidôs*) in helping Amphiaraus with his sacrifice (F 753, cf. F 757.846–63) is rewarded by his defence of her (F 757.868ff.) and his good offices in the reunion (F 759a. 1584–6). Her terrible mistake in causing the baby's death is balanced by her devotion to him (F 752f.1–14) and grief at his loss (F 753d–e, F 757.840–3), and by her pious service to the Seven, as well as by the fact that the boy's heroization is pre-ordained (F 757.930–43). Eurydice avoids committing her own terrible mistake (F 757.879–80). Amphiaraus is idealized as a figure of wisdom and authority, piously fulfilling his religious duties as he goes towards his fate (F 752h.29–32, F 752k.20–1), conscious of the *charis* he owes to Hypsipyle (F 757.859, 871–3, F 759a.1584–6), reconciling Eurydice to her loss, and seeing the significance of her son's death. His virtue was traditional (cf. Hes. F 25.37–38, A. *Sept.* 382, 568–614, and in general Vicaire), but the play seems to have enhanced it, especially in the understanding of death expressed in his famous consolation of Eurydice (see Comm. on F 757.921–7). The female characters by contrast are more vulnerable to their emotions, Hypsipyle's being conditioned by her long experience of loss and slavery (the lost prologue-speech; F 752f–h); but both she and (as far as we can tell) Eurydice exhibit a saving moral rectitude. Euneos the musician and Thoas the warrior recall Amphion the musician and Zethos the man of action in *Antiope* (cf. below, pp. 266–8), but the fragments give no sign that the contrast here had any dramatic significance; it may have suggested simply that the twins together possessed an ideal combination of practical and intellectual accomplishments.

   The plot of *Hypsipyle* interweaves legends with an expansiveness notable in other late plays of Euripides (*Phoenissae, Orestes, IA*: cf. A. Michelini, *ICS* 24/25 [1999/2000], 41–57). The mythical world of epic is evoked through reminiscence and offstage action, especially in the songs of Hypsipyle and the Chorus and (presumably) the messenger-speech. This expansiveness would be compounded if *Hypsipyle* were part of a coherent trilogy. Possible trilogies have been proposed on various grounds, the most widely canvassed being *Hypsipyle–Phoenissae–Antiope* which are mentioned together by a scholiast on Ar. *Frogs* 53; but the inference that they are mentioned as a trilogy is unsafe (see below, *Date*). Suggestions about the larger themes of possible trilogies remain tentative, but it is notable that the play shares with *Antiope* a concern with Dionysus as forebear, liberator and object of cultic devotion (F 752, F 758a–b, F 759a.1627–32, and his epiphany), and with the integrating power of music which in this play is associated with Hypsipyle (F 752f.1–14), Amphion (F 752f.32–3), Orpheus (F 752g.8–14, F 759a.1619–23), Euneos (F 759a.1622), and the cultural legacy represented by the Euneidai. On the possible significance of these themes see Burkert (1994), Zeitlin 171–82, and P. Wilson, *ICS* 24/25 (1999/2000), 440–9.

Staging. The scene is the sanctuary at Nemea, whose remoteness and isolation (F 752h.15–21) stand in contrast with its later fame, though it already has regional importance (F 752h.26–8) and a substantial temple with architectural features (F 752c). In reality Nemea was a cult-site in late Mycenean times but achieved prominence only with the early sixth-century development of the Panhellenic festival, expansion of the hero-tumulus, and building of the archaic temple (see Miller in the bibl. above, and Comm. on F 752c.2, F 752h.31). The stage-building is the priest's house where Hypsipyle lives with Lycurgus and his family. The temple is adjacent and visible (F 752c). Surrounding the sanctuary is the marshy plain of Nemea, including the Argive army's encampment and the meadow and spring inhabited by the fatal serpent. This important offstage space is evoked in the parodos (F 752f.29ff.), Amphiaraus' arrival (F 752h.15ff.), Hypsipyle's account of the baby's death (F 752, 752a), and no doubt the lost report of the funeral and games. Movement to and from it is dramatically important: Hypsipyle sets off for the spring with Amphiaraus and the baby but returns alone and distraught; Amphiaraus returns just in time to save her life; Euneos and Thoas leave unrecognized to join the games and return in triumph to greet their mother; Amphiaraus leaves at the end to join the army and march to his death. Dionysus probably appeared on the roof of the stage-building to deliver his instructions at the end (an arrival on the *mêchanê* seems unneeded).

The Chorus consists of local women friendly to Hypsipyle. Her arduous role must have been played by the first actor: she is the focus of all the major scenes, sings extensively in several scenes, and was on stage for at least three-quarters of the play. Other roles can easily be distributed between the second actor (Thoas speaking in the prologue only, Amphiaraus, Dionysus) and third actor (Euneos and Eurydice, unless they appeared together: above, p. 176).

Either of these could have played the Messenger. Extras are needed for Thoas in the reunion scene (cf. Comm. on F 759a.1590–2) and the household servants who seize Hypsipyle (F 757.851, 860–1). The baby Opheltes was probably represented by a dummy, but his presence is strongly established in the opening scenes where Hypsipyle calms the fretting child and lulls him to sleep with her music. As in *Ion*, the mundane sentimentality of these scenes balances and alleviates the play's tragic and melodramatic elements.

Date. Schol. Ar. *Frogs* 53 (*TrGF* T ii) says that *Hypsipyle, Phoenissae* and *Antiope* were 'fine' plays produced 'shortly before' *Frogs* and after *Andromeda* (of 412). This suits the character and length of *Hyps.* and the metrical style of its dialogue passages (cf. Cropp-Fick 80–1). The scholiast's contrast between the dates of *Andromeda* and of *Hyps.*, *Pho.* and *Antiope* tells against 411, and the biographical tradition suggests that Eur. did not produce plays in 407 because he had left Athens (see however S. Scullion, *CQ* 53 [2003], 389–400). If the three plays were produced together this cannot have been in 408, the recorded date of *Orestes*, but the scholiast may have chosen them not as a trilogy (a matter irrelevant to his point) but simply as three outstanding late plays. (On the date of *Antiope* see further p. 269, and for *Pho.* the cautious summation of Mastronarde, *Phoenissae*, 11–14; on the political circumstances see above, pp. 178–9.)

Other dramatizations; influence. That *Hyps.* was a notable play is indicated by Schol. *Frogs* (above), by the targeting of it in *Frogs* (cf. F 752, 752f.8, 9–11; 763; 765, 765a; 765b, and Comm. on F 753c.4, 758b.1), and by the later iconographic tradition. There are traces of later performance (the Pompeii wall-painting, and some kind of production before Juba II of Mauretania in the time of Augustus, Ath. 8.343e) and of recycling (the 'Odes of Epagathus', see Cockle 42; pantomimes of 'Hypsipyle and Archemorus', Lucian, *On Dance* 44.1). Its originality and fame perhaps discouraged imitations, although the *Hypsipyle* with which Cleaenetus won third prize at the Lenaea in 363 B.C. (*TrGF* 84 T 4) may have been one. By contrast, Aeschylus' *Nemea* may have been the source for a comedy by Theopompus (fl. 410–370 B.C.: F 33 *PCG*) and for Ennius' Latin tragedy *Nemea* (F 124–5 Jocelyn), but nothing definite is known about the content of these.

In poetry likewise, while the story of Hypsipyle's rescue of her father and her affair with Jason was much used (especially Ap. Rhod. 1.601–909, Ov. *Her.* 6, Val. Flacc. 2.72–427, Stat. *Theb.* 5.17–485), her involvement with Nemea and the death of Archemorus is recalled only through an Ovidian allusion (*Ibis* 481) and in Statius' major re-creation of the story (Stat. *Theb.* 4.680–5.16, 5.486–6.237). It was the Lemnian events again that inspired the medieval poets' virtuous Hypsipyle (Dante, *L'Ovide moralisé*, Boccaccio, Chaucer) and many treatments of this theme in renaissance and classical opera and tragedy (see *OGCMA* I.617–8: twenty-five operas about Jason and Hypsipyle are recorded for the period 1732–1818, nearly all using Metastasio's 1732 libretto). Since the early nineteenth century, it seems, her story has hardly been touched.

ΥΨΙΠΥΛΗ

T iiia (– N) Hypothesis P. Oxy. 2455 (with P. Oxy. 3652)

fr. 14 (col. xiii)

Ὑ[ψι]πύλη ἧς ἀρχή,
ιΔιμόνυσιος ὃς θιύρσοισιιν καὶ νειβριῶν
    δοραῖς, [   ] ἡ δ' ὑπ[όθεσις·

*a dozen lines largely lost: P. Oxy. 3652 col. i supplies line-
ends of a few letters each, P. Oxy. 2455 fr. 15 (if it belongs
here) two successive line-beginnings:*

Ἀμ]φιαρα[...   π]αραγε[ν...

fr. 14 (col. xiv)   *traces of one line*

γ[....]θεισατο [
κρήνην ἔδ⟨ε⟩ιξ[ε   δρά-
κ[ο]ντος διεσπ[......]αδε [20
τ[ό]πους οἱ γεγονότες [....]... παῖδες παρ[ῆσ]αν
ἐπὶ τὴν τῆς μητρὸς ζήτησιν καὶ κατα-
λύσαντες παρὰ τῆ⟨ι⟩ τοῦ Λυκούργου γυναικὶ
τὸν ἐπιτάφιον τοῦ παιδὸς ἠθέλησαν ἀ-
γωνίσασθαι· ἡ δ[ὲ] τοὺς π[ρ]οειρημέν[ο]υ[ς   25
ξενοδοχήσασα τούτους μὲν ἐπη⟨ί⟩νεσ[ε]ν,
τὴν μητέρα δ' αὐτῶν ἀποκτείνειν [ἤμελ-
λεν [ὡ]ς ἑκουσίω[ς ἀπ]ολωλεκυ[ί]ας α[ὐ-
τῆ[ς τὸ] τέκνον· Ἀ[μφια]ράου δὲ ......[
σαμ[....] τουτω[...] χ[ά]ριν ἔδω[κε   30
traces of two more lines

*P. Oxy. 3652 col. ii has 15 more lines including near the end
of this hypothesis:*

Ἀρ]χεμορ[– ...   ...τὸ]ν παῖδ[α...

P. Oxy. 2455 fr. 14 (col. xvi) has in the last line of the hypothesis:

ἐθ]έσπισ[εν

T iiia Hypothesis (p. 21 Bond, p. 135 Diggle)   P. Oxy. 2455 (2nd C. A.D., ed. E.G. Turner, 1962), fr. 14 cols. xiii–xiv (lines 185–203: photo, ed. pr. Plate IV), fr. 15 (position uncertain), fr. 14 col. xvi (lines 218–220 assigned to *Hyps.* hypoth. by Luppe); remains of a similar text in

184

HYPSIPYLE

T iiia Hypothesis

Hypsipyle, which begins, 'Dionysus, who with thyrsuses and fawnskins', and the *plot* (is as follows):

(a dozen lines largely lost)

. . . *Amphiaraus* . . . . . . *arriving* . . .

. . . *putting the?* . . . . . . *showed* the spring . . . of/by a serpent[20] . . . . . . the sons who had been born (*or* had come) . . . *had arrived <in the>* vicinity in search of their mother, and having lodged with Lycurgus' wife they were keen to compete in the funeral games for the boy. And she having accepted the aforesaid youths[25] as guests approved them, but *planned* to kill their mother *as having killed <the> child on purpose*. But when Amphiaraus . . . . . . *<she?> thanked him*[30] . . .

isolated phrases from the end of the hypothesis:

. . . *Archemorus* . . .   . . . *the child* . . .

. . . *prophesied* . . .

P. Oxy. 3652 (early 3rd C. A.D., ed. H. M. Cockle, 1984: photo, Pl. I). See also W. Luppe, *ZPE* 52 (1983) 43–44, 72 (1988) 27–33; van Rossum-Steenbeek 204–5, 219–21, Diggle *TrGFS* 135, Kannicht *TrGF*.   18 γ[ῆν τι]θεῖσα τὸ τ[έκνον Turner (better τον[Kannicht)   19–21 ἐν τούτωι δὲ ὑπὸ δρά]κ[ο]ντος διεσπ[άσθη· ἔπειτ]α δὲ π[ρὸς τοὺς] τ[ό]πους οἱ γεγονότες ʽ Υ[ψιπύ]λης Turner   21 τ[ό]πους above line   perhaps ἐ[ν ἡλικ]ίαι van Rossum-Steenbeek ἐ[ξ αὐ]τῆς Cropp   28 [ὡ]ς ἐκ- read by Kannicht (ἀλλ᾽ ἀκ- Turner)   29–30 δὲ παραιτη|σαμ[ένου Turner

752 (ΥΨΙΠΥΛΗ) Διόνυσος, ὃς θύρσοισι καὶ νεβρῶν δοραῖς
καθαπτὸς ἐν πεύκαισι Παρνασσὸν κάτα
πηδᾶι χορεύων παρθένοις σὺν Δελφίσιν
very few lines missing, then:

752a P. Hamb. 118 b
('Υψ.) Σταφ[υλ-
Πεπαρ.....[
τούτων.....[
ὥραις γε ... ονγ[
Ἥρας εδοιδ [5
Διονυσο νολ[
τρίτος Διονυ[σ
Χίου παρα[
οι ντατ[
Λῆμνον [10
ἐγὼ δε [
beginnings of four more lines

752b P. Oxy. 852   *(col. 2)*

frs. 96 + 70   *Ends of twelve iambic trimeters from the lower half
of col. 2 (~ lines 90–120), including:*

('Υψ.) 1 ἀπ]όπτολιν   6] . φάος
2]ι τύχαις   7]αζω ζυγῶι
5 Συμ]πληγάδων

Later in the lower half of col. 2, or top of col. 3:

752c (764 N)
(ΘΟΑΣ) ἰδού, πρὸς αἰθέρ' ἐξαμίλλησαι κόρας,
γραπτούς <τ' ἐν αἰετ>οῖσι πρόσβλεψον τύπους.

752 (p. 23 Bond; 1–3 Diggle) Ar. *Frogs* 1211–13, attrib. (Eur.) *Hyps.* by Schol. (which supply
the correct ending παρθένοις σὺν Δελφίσιν); Schol. Ar. *Clouds* 603, attrib. Eur. 1–3 (to
χορεύων) Macrob. *Sat.* 1.18.4, attrib. Eur. 1 P. Oxy. 2455 (see above) 2 Philoxenos F 413
Theodoridis, attrib. Eur. (= *Etym. Sym.* 2.18–19, cf. *Etym. Magn.* 1.37) 2 κάθαπτος (*sic*)
Hesych. κ 85 Latte, unattrib. 1 ὃς θύρσοισι P. Oxy., Ar. *Frogs* most mss. θύρσοισι Ar.
Frogs ms. R, Macrob. ὃς πεύκαισι Schol.ᴱ *Clouds* ἐν πεύκαις Schol.ⱽ *Clouds* 2 πεύκ-
αισ(ι) or πεύκη(ι)σι variously attested 3 σὺν παρθένοις (om. Δελφίσιν) Schol.ᴱ *Clouds*

752 *Hypsipyle entering from the house begins her prologue-speech:*

(*HYPSIPYLE*) Dionysus, who girt with thyrsuses and fawnskins leaps in the torch-lit dance across Parnassus with the Delphic maidens . . . .

752a *A few lines later (line-beginnings):*

(*Hyps.*) . . . *Staphylos* . . . . . . *Peparethos* . . . . . . of these . . .
. . . in/at? seasons . . . . . . of/from? Hera . . . . . .
Dionysus . . . . . . ⁵ a third . . . Dionysus . . . . . .
of/from(?) Chios . . . . Lemnos . . . . . . ¹⁰
and I . . . .

752b *Towards the end of the prologue-speech (line-ends):*

(*Hyps.*)	1	. . . abroad/exiled	6	. . . light/salvation
	2	. . . (mis?)fortunes	7	. . . yoke
	5	. . . *Symplêgades*		

752c *Hypsipyle has withdrawn into the house. Euneos and Thoas have arrived by a side-entrance and are conversing:*

(*THOAS*) Look – run your eyes up towards the sky, and take a look at the painted reliefs on the pediment.

752a (p. 157 Bond) P. Hamb. 118b col. ii, ed. E. Siegmann (Hamburg, 1954), corr. and suppl. H. Lloyd-Jones, with advice from B. Snell and C. Voigt, in Bond 157–60   2 Πεπαρηθον read doubtfully by Snell   7 Διονύ[σου Lloyd-Jones   **752b, d–k, 753a–c, 754a–c, 755a, 756a, 757, 758a–d, 759a** P. Oxy. 852 (here = P), ed. B. P. Grenfell and A. S. Hunt in *Oxyrhynchus Papyri* VI (1908); for subsequent editions see above, p. 169.   **752b** (p. 24 Bond) P. Oxy. 852, frs. 96+70   7 αἰ]άζω Bond   **752c** (764 N; p. 24 Bond; 4–5 Diggle) Galen XVIII, I.519 Kühn, attrib. Eur. *Hyps.*   1 κόρας Hermann –αι Galen –αις Musgrave   2 ⟨τ' ἐν αἰετ)οῖσι πρόσβλεψον Nauck ((ἐν αἰετ)οῖσι προσβλέπειν Valckenaer, –βλέπων Musgrave) οἶσι πρόσβλεπον Galen

752d   P. Oxy. 852   *(col. 3)*

fr. 1.i   ('Yψ.)   *remains of one line*

ἤξε[ι . . . . .]σπ . [. . . . . ἀ]θύρμα[τ]α
ἃ σὰς [ὀ]δυρμῶν ἐγαλη[νιεῖ φ]ρένας.
ὑμεῖς ἐκρούσατ᾽, ὦ νεανία[ι, πύλα]ς;
ὦ μακαρία σφῷν ἡ τεκο[ῦσ᾽, ἥ]τις ποτ᾽ ἦν·   5
τί τῷ[ν]δε μελάθρων δε[όμε]νοι προσήλθετον;

Θο.   στέγ[η]ς κεχρήμεθ᾽ [ἐ]ν[τὸς ἀ]χθῆναι, γύναι,
εἰ δυ[να]τὸν ἡ[μῖ]ν νύκτ᾽ ἐ[ναυλίσ]αι μίαν.
ἔχο[με]ν δ᾽ ὅ[σ]ων δεῖ κ[α]ὶ ο[ὐχὶ] λυ[π]ηροὶ δό[μοις
ἐσό[μ]εθα τοῖσδε, τὸ δὲ σὸν ὡς ἔχει μ[εν]εῖ.   10

('Yψ.)   ἀδέσ]ποτος μ[ὲν ο]ἶκ[ο]ς ἀρσένων κυ[ρε]ῖ   ~141
        about 20 letters   ] δώμ[α]τα

at least six lines lost, then from lower half of col. 3 (~ 150–180):

752e fr. 2   ('Yψ.)   *traces of one line*

Λυκοῦρ[γ-
γυνὴ δ[

Θο.   οὐκ ἐν ξε[νῶσι
πρὸς δ᾽ α[5

('Yψ.)   ἥκιστ[α
ξένο[
ἀεὶ δε[
ἀλλ᾽ εἰς ν[
remains of one more line   10

rest of col. 3 and about 12 lines from top of col. 4 lost, then:

752f fr. 1.ii   ('Yψ.)   *remains of one line-end*   *(col. 4)*

. . . .]ος ἰδέσθαι
. . . .] . . χον ὡς ἐνόπτρου
. . . . . .]οφαῆ τιν᾽ αὐγὰν   ~190
. . . . . .] αὔξημα τὸ σὸν   5
. . .] νησωμαι, τέκνον, εὐ-
ωποῖς ἢ θεραπείαις.

752d (p. 25 Bond; 6–17 Diggle) P. Oxy. fr. 1.i   2 πατὴρ οὐ] σπά[νι᾽ ἔχων Wecklein
πατὴρ σὸ]ς πό[λλ᾽ ἔχων K.F.W. Schmidt   3 σὰς Wilamowitz in ed. pr. σῶν P   9 κ[α]ὶ

752d   *Hypsipyle, answering the young men's knock at the house-door, calms the baby:*

(*Hyps.*) . . . *will come* . . . *toys* which *will calm* your mind
from crying.

Was it you, young gentlemen, who knocked at the
door? *(Noticing their looks)* O blessed she who *bore*
you, whoever she was![5] Why have the two of you
come to this house and what do you want from it?

Tho. We need to be given shelter inside, woman, if *we*
may bed down here for just one night. *We* have *all* we
need *and will not be a nuisance to your household*;
for your part you'*ll stay* completely undisturbed.[10]

(*Hyps.*) *The household has no* men *in charge at present* . . .
. . . *the house* . . .

752e   *A little later, more of the same conversation:*

(*Hyps.*) . . . Lycurgus . . . . . . his wife . . . .

Tho. . . . not . . . in the *guest-quarters*. . . but to . . .[5]

(*Hyps.*) By no means . . . . . . *guest(s?)* . . . . . . *and/*
but(?) always . . . . . . But . . . into . . .

752f   *Thoas and Euneos have entered the house. As Hyps. sings to*
the baby, a group of local women (the play's Chorus) arrives
by a side-entrance with news that the Argive army is nearby:

(*Hyps.*) . . . . . . to look at . . . . . . like a mirror's . . .
. . . -lighted gleam . . . . . your growth[5] I may . . .
. . . , child, or with cheerful tending.

---

o[ὐχὶ] (= κοὐχὶ) Diggle τ[ί] πο[τε] ed. pr.   10 ἔχει ed. pr. ἔχεις P (read correctly by Cockle)
11 paragraphus marks speaker-change   **752e** (p. 25 Bond) P. Oxy. fr. 2   3 δ[ὲ ed. pr.
5 πρὸς δ' ἄ[λλο δή τι δῶμ' (e.g.) ed. pr.   6 paragraphus marks speaker-change
752f (p. 25–7 Bond; 18–57 Diggle) P. Oxy. fr. 1.ii   13 the word νεαρός is listed as
equivalent to νέος 'young' and attrib. Eur. *Hyps.* in Bekker, *Anecd. Gr.* I.109.15 (= **770 N**)
32–3 Hesych. α 4076 records without attrib. the adj. Ἀμφιονίη applied to a κιθάρα
4 λευκ]οφαῆ (e.g.) ed. pr. (and see Comm.)   6] μνήσωμαι ed. pr.

ἰδού, κτύπος ὅδε κορτάλων
(one(?) line omitted in papyrus main text)
οὐ τάδε πήνας, οὐ τάδε κερκίδος
ἱστοτόνου παραμύθια Λήμνια   10
Μοῦσα θέλει με κρέκειν, ὅτι δ' εἰς ὕπνον
ἢ χάριν ἢ θεραπεύματα πρόσφορα

[B]   π]αιδὶ πρέπει νεαρῶι   ~200
τάδε μελωιδὸς αὐδῶ.

(ΧΟΡΟΣ)   τί σὺ παρὰ προθύροις, φίλα;   στρ.
πότερα δώματος εἰσόδους   16
σαίρει[ς], ἢ δρόσον ἐπὶ πέδωι
βάλλεις οἷά τε δούλα;
ἦ τὰν Ἀργὼ τὰν διὰ σοῦ
στόματος αἰεὶ κληιζομέναν   20
πεντηκόντερον ἄ[ι]δεις,
ἢ τὸ χρυσεόμαλλον
ἱερὸν δέρος ὃ περὶ δρυὸς   ~210
ὄζοις ὄμμα δράκοντος
φρουρεῖ, μναμοσύνα δέ σοι   25
τᾶς ἀγχιάλοιο Λήμνου,
τὰν Αἰγαῖος ἑλί[σ]σων
κυμοκτύπος ἀχεῖ;
δεῦρο †ταν† λειμῶνα Νέμει[ον·
ἀσ[τ]ράπτει χαλκέο[ι]σιν ὅπλο[ις   30
Ἀργεῖον π[ε]δίον πᾶ[ν·
ἐπὶ τὸ τᾶ[ς] κιθάρας ἔρυμα
τᾶς Ἀμφιονίας ἔργον[~220
ὠ[κυ]πόδας Ἄ[δρ]ασ[το]ς [
ὅ[ς] ἐκάλεσε μένο[ς   35
ποικίλα σάματα [
τόξα τε χρύσεα [
κα[ὶ] μονοβάμονε[ς
ἀειρόμενοι χθ[ον
remains of one more line, then about 22 lines lost, then:

8 κορτάλων Maas κροτ– P   8a marginal note ἄν(ω) 'above' indicates an omitted line added
in the now lost upper margin   11 θέλει Morel μέλει P   13 [B]: notation for line 200 lost but

Look, here is the sound of castanets . . . *(a line missing)* . . . These are not Lemnian songs for relieving the labour of weft-thread and web-stretching shuttle[10] that the Muse wants me to voice, but what serves for a tender young boy, to lull him or charm him or tend to his needs —this do I tunefully sing.

(CHORUS) What are you doing at the doorway, dear friend?[15] Are you sweeping the entrance to the house, or casting water on the ground, as a slave-woman does? Are you singing now of Argo, whom your voice is always celebrating,[20] that famous penteconter, or the sacred gold-fleeced hide on which around the tree's boughs the serpent's eye keeps watch; and does your memory dwell[25] on sea-bound Lemnos which the Aegean encircles and beats with echoing waves?

Come now †to the† Nemean meadow. *All of* the Argive plain *is flashing* with armaments of bronze.[31] Against the bastion(?) built by Amphion's lyre swift-footed Adrastus . . . . . . who has summoned the might . . . . . . [35] intricate devices . . . . . . and golden bows . . . . . . and single-treading . . . . . . lifting . . . *(from?) the ground* . . .

A few more choral lines and the first half of Hypsipyle's response are lost, then:

indicated by a related mark at line 9   15 paragraphus marks speaker-change   19 ἦ Page ἡ P
26 Λήμνου corr. from νήσου P   28 κυμοκτύπος ed. pr. κυμοτύπος P   29 δ' ἂν (suggested in ed. pr.) Dodds (δ' ἀνὰ Collard)   30 ἀσ[τ]ράπτει read by von Arnim ἀπάγει ed. pr. χαλκέο[ι]σιν ed. pr. χαλκειο[ι]ς P   31 'Αργεῖον P –ων von Arnim πᾶ[ν von Arnim 33 [χερός ed. pr.   34 [ἄγει στρατόν K. F. W. Schmidt   35 ὅ[ς] von Arnim ὁ [δ'] ed. pr. ἐκάλεσε P κάλεσε⟨ν⟩ Diggle   36 σαεματα corr. from συεματα (or σαματα from e.g. συιματα) P σάγματα Wilamowitz in ed. pr.   39 χθ[ονός von Arnim

752g   (col. 5)

fr. 1.iii   ('Υψ.)   *traces of one line*   ~250

.... Θ]ρηικίαν
.....]σ[ ]μενης ὀρούσας
ἐπ᾽ οἶδμα γαλανείας
πρυμνήσι᾽ ἀνάψαι,   5
τὸν ἁ τοῦ ποταμοῦ παρ-
θένος Αἴγιν᾽ ἐτέκνωσεν
Πηλέα, μέσωι δὲ παρ᾽ ἱστῶι
᾽Ασιάδ᾽ ἔλεγον ἰήιον
Θρῆισσ᾽ ἐβόα κίθαρις   10
μακροπόλων πιτύλων
ἐρέταισι κελεύσματα μελπομένα,   ~260
τότε μὲν ταχύπλουν,
τότε δ᾽ εἰλατίνας ἀνάπαυμα πλάτα[ς.
τ[ά]δε μοι τάδε θυμὸς ἰδεῖν ἵεται,   15
Δαναῶν δὲ πόνους
ἕτερος ἀναβοάτω.

Χο.   παρὰ σοφῶν ἔκλυον λόγο[υ]ς   ἀντ.
προτερον ὡς ἐπὶ κυμάτων
πόλιν καὶ πατρίους δόμου[ς   20
Φοίνικος Τυρία παῖς   ~270
Εὐρώπα λιποῦσ᾽ ἐπέβα
Διοτρόφον Κρῆταν ἱερὰν
Κουρήτων τροφὸν ἀνδρῶν,
ἃ τέκνων ἀρότοισ[ι]ν   25
τρισσοῖς ἔλιπεν κρά[τος
χώρας τ᾽ ὄλβιον ἀρχάν.
᾽Αργείαν θ᾽ ἑτέραν κλύω
λέκ]τρωι βασίλειαν ᾽Ιὼ
...]φας ἀμφὶς ἀμεῖψαι   30
κερ]ασφόρον ἄταν.   ~280
ταῦ]τ᾽ ἦν θεὸς εἰς φροντίδα θῆι σοι
...᾽].[.]ς δή, φίλα, τὸ μέσον

752g (~p. 27–8 Bond; 58–103 Diggle) P. Oxy. fr. 1.iii+67   9 ᾽Ασιάδ᾽ ἔλεγον Beazley
(ἔλεγον Wilamowitz in ed. pr.) ᾽Ασιὰς ἔλεγεν P   10 κίθαρις A. Mette κίθαρις ᾽Ορφέως P

752g *(Hyps.)* . . . . . . Thracian . . . . . leaping forth over the calmly lapping water to fasten the stern-cables,[5] he whom the river's daughter Aegina brought forth, Peleus; and by the mast amidships the Thracian lyre cried out a mournful Asian plaint[10] singing commands to the rowers for their long-sweeping strokes, now to speed forward, now to take rest from the pinewood oar. These things, yes these, does my spirit yearn to see;[15] but as for the Danaans' labours, let someone else acclaim them.

Cho. From learned tellers I have heard the story, how in the past, leaving her city and her ancestral home,[20] Phoenix's daughter from Tyre Europa went upon the waves to Crete where Zeus was raised, the sacred nurse of the Kourêtes, and to her threefold harvest of children[25] left *power* and prosperous government of the land. And another princess, I hear, the Argive Io, by *her mating* altered <*her form's?*>[30] *horn*-bearing affliction. If god puts <*these things*> into your thoughts, surely, dear friend . . . moderation . . .

12 μελπομένα ed. pr. -αν P   21 Φοίνικος West Φοινίκας P   29 λέκ]τρωι Bond
30]φας read by Cockle πάτ]ρας ed. pr. perhaps μορ]φᾶς Diggle   32   . . .]ταν P
33 στέρξει]ς Radermacher

> ....] ἀπολείψει
> .... π]ατέρος πατέρα   35
> ....]τεχει σέθεν
> ....] ὠκύπορο[ς] μετανίσεται
> *remains of nine more lines*
>
> *12–15 lines lost, then:*

752h   fr. 1.iv   (Ὑψ.)   *trace of one line*   (*col. 6*) ~310

νεμον ἄγαγέ ποτε [
κυναγόν τε Π⟨ρ⟩όκριν τὰν πόσις ἔκτα
κατεθρήνησεν ἀοιδαῖς [
θάνατος ἔλαχε· τὰ δ' ἐμὰ πάθε[α   5
τίς ἂν ἢ γόος ἢ μέλος ἢ κιθάρας
ἐπὶ δάκρυσι μοῦσ' ἀνοδυρομένα
μετὰ Καλλιόπας
ἐπὶ πόνους ἂν ἔλθοι;

(Χο.) ὦ Ζεῦ Νεμέας τῆσδ' ἄλσος ἔχων   10
τίνος ἐμπορίαι τούσδ' ἐγγὺς ὁρῶ   ~320
πελάτας ξείνους Δωρίδι πέπλων
ἐσθῆτι σαφεῖς πρὸς τούσδε δόμους
στείχοντας ἐρῆμον ἀν' ἄλσος;

ΑΜΦΙΑΡΑΟΣ ὡς ἐχθρὸν ἀνθρώποισιν αἵ τ' ἐκδημίαι   15
ὅταν τε χρείαν εἰσπεσὼν ὁδοιπόρος
ἀγροὺς ἐρήμους καὶ μονοικήτους ἴδηι
ἄπολις ἀνερμήνευτος ἀπορίαν ἔχων
ὅπηι τράπηται· κάμὲ γὰρ τὸ δ[υ]σχερὲς
τοῦτ' εἰσβέβηκεν· ἄσμενος δ' εἶδον δόμ[ους   20
τούσδ' ἐν Διὸς λειμῶνι Νεμεάδος χθον[ός.   ~330
καί σ', εἴτε δούλη τοῖσδ' ἐφέστηκας δόμ[οις
εἴτ' οὐχὶ δοῦλον σῶμ' ἔχουσ', ἐρήσομαι·
τίνος τάδ' ἀνδρῶν μηλοβοσκὰ δώματ[α
Φλειουντίας γῆς, ὦ ξένη, νομίζεται;   25

Ὑψ. ὄλβια Λυκούργου μέλαθρα κλήιζεται τά[δε
ὃ]ς ἐξ ἁπάσης αἱρεθεὶς Ἀσωπίας
κληιδοῦχός ἐστι τοὐπιχωρίου Διός.

752h (~p. 28–30 Bond; 104–46 Diggle) P. Oxy. frs. 1.iv+92+3   3 κυναγόν ed. pr. κυμαγον
(corr. from κυματον) P   10 paragraphus marks speaker- change   11 ἐμπορίαι Wecklein

. . . will *(not?)* desert you . . . . . . your father's
father[35] . . . . . . of/for you . . . . . . will come
swift-voyaging after you . . .

*remaining choral lines and first part of Hypsipyle's response
lost, then:*

752h   *(Hyps.)*   . . . . . . once brought . . . . . . and the huntress
Procris, whom her husband killed . . . . . . lament-
ed with songs . . . . . . death claimed <*her*>; but
my sufferings – [5] what grieving cry or song or lyre's
music, bemoaning them with Calliope's aid amidst
my tears, will come to mourn my troubles?

(Amphiaraus approaches by a side-entrance)

(Cho.) O Zeus, possessor of this Nemean grove,[10] what
business brings these newcomers I see close by,
distinctively dressed in Dorian clothing, and coming
towards this house through the lonely grove?

AMPHIARAUS How hateful to men are absences from home,[15] and
times when a traveller, falling into need, sees
deserted country with solitary dwellings – homeless,
unguided, not knowing which way to turn. This very
hardship has befallen me, and I was glad to see this
house[20] in Zeus's meadow here in the land of Nemea.
So to you who stand there at the doorway, whether a
slave, or whether you are no slave, I'll put this
question: what man is reckoned as owner of this
pastoral dwelling in Phlius' country?[25]

Hyps. People call these Lycurgus' wealthy halls. Chosen
from out of all Asopia, he is temple-keeper of our
local Zeus.

–ας P   15 ἐκδημίαι Wilamowitz in ed. pr. (cf. ἐκδημία attrib. Eur. *Hyps.* in Bekker, *Anecd.
Gr.* I.93.26 = **768 N**) ἐρημίαι P   18 ἄπολις Murray in ed. pr. ἄπορον (corr. from ἀπόιν') P
ἀνερμήνευτος ed. pr. –ον P   27 αἱρεθεὶς Ἀσωπίας ed. pr. εὐρ– –ία(ι) P

'Αμφ. ῥ]υτὸν λαβεῖν [χ]ρῄι[ζοι]μ' ἂν ἐν κρωσσοῖς ὕδωρ
χ]έρνιβα θεοῖσιν ὅ[σιον] ὡς χεαίμεθα.   30
στατῶν γὰρ ὑδάτων [ν]άματ' οὐ διειπετῆ,   ~340
στρατοῦ δὲ πλήθει πάντα συνταράσσεται.

'Υψ. τίν]ες μολόντες καὶ χ[θ]ονὸς ποίας ἄπο;

('Αμφ.) ἐκ τῶν Μυκηνῶν [ἐσ]μὲν 'Αργεῖοι γέν[ος,
ὅ]ρια δ' ὑπερβαίνοντες εἰς ἄλλην χθόνα   35
στρ]ατοῦ πρ[ο]θῦσαι βουλόμεσθα Δαν[α]ϊδῶ[ν.

frs. 1.iv + 92   ('Υψ.) ὑ]μεῖς [πορ]εύεσθ'[ἆ]ρα πρὸς Κάδμου πύλας;

('Αμφ.) ....] ρομ[.... ε]ὐτυχῶς, γύναι.

('Υψ.) ....]λε[....] σου θέμι[ς μ]αθεῖν;

('Αμφ.) .....] κατάγομ[εν φυγ]άδα Π[ολυνεί]κη πάτρας.

('Υψ.) ...]ω[........]ὰς θηρᾶ [~350

frs. 1.iv + 3   ('Αμφ.) παῖ[ς] Οἰκ[λέους ....] 'Αμφιάρ[εως   42

('Υψ.) ὦ μεγάλ[α ....]ια και[

('Αμφ.) πῶς δ' οιλ[.........]σα [

last 2–4 lines of col. 6 lost, then within the first c. 13 lines of col. 7:

752i   fr. 4   remains of five line-beginnings including: (col. 7)

2   ('Αμφ.) ὄνομα [
3   ('Υψ.) ἡ Λημ[ν   ~370?

then starting about line 14 of col. 7:

752k   fr 1.v   'Αμφ. γυ[
'Υψ. ὁσία φ[
'Αμφ. ἐδεξ[α-
'Υψ. πόθεν μ[
'Αμφ. ἔγημ' ὁ κλε[ινὸς   5
'Υψ. εἰς ἦν τις ω[
'Αμφ. ταύτηι δίδωσ[ι
'Υψ. θεοὶ θεῶν γα[ρ
'Αμφ. Πολύδωρος οὖ[ν   380

30 ὅ[σιον] Stengel ὅ[διον] ed. pr. (Murray) χεαίμεθα ed. pr. (Wilamowitz) χρησαίμεθα P
31 στατῶν ed. pr. στρατ– P   37–40 so read by Cockle (ἆ]ρα Turner) after joining
fr. 92 with fr. 1.iv   38 ειδη[added in right margin (see Comm.)   39 λέ[γ',
εἴ τί] Diggle   40 ἡμεῖς] Cockle Θήβας] Diggle   Π[ολυνεί]κη Herwerden Π[ολυνί]κην P

Amph. *I'd like to ask* if I may get some *running* water in pitchers, so that we can pour a *pure* libation to the gods.[30] The runnels of stagnant water are not clear, and all are being churned up by our massive army.

Hyps. Who are you, and what country have you come from?

(Amph.) We come from Mycenae and are Argives by race. As we are crossing the *border* into another country[35] we want to sacrifice for our Danaid *army*.

(Hyps.) So you are *making your way* to Cadmus' gates?

(Amph.) . . . . successfully, lady.

(Hyps.) . . . . (if) one may learn it from you?

(Amph.) . . . *we are restoring Polynices, who is exiled* from his homeland.[40]

(Hyps.) . . . . . . *(you?) seek* . . . . . .

(Amph.) *The son of Oiclês* . . . . . . Amphiaraus . . .

(Hyps.) O . . . great . . . . . .

(Amph.) And how . . . . . .

The conversation continues after a short break:

752i (Amph.) . . . . . . name . . . . . .

(Hyps.) *Lemnos/The Lemnian* . . . . . .

and within a few more lines:

752k Amph. . . . woman/wife . . . . . .

Hyps. . . . pure . . . . . .

Amph. . . . *received* . . . . . .

Hyps. Whence/Why . . . . . .

Amph. The *famous*. . . . . . . married . . . . . .[5]

Hyps. He (*or* there) was one . . . . . .

Amph. To her . . . gave . . . . . .

Hyps. The gods . . . . . . the gods' . . . . . .

Amph. So Polydorus . . . . . .

---

42 paragraphus marks marks speaker-change   **752** (p. 30 Bond) P. Oxy. fr. 4   3–5 paragraphi mark speaker-changes   **752k** (~p. 30–2 Bond) P. Oxy. frs. 1.v+5+65+75+85. Paragraphi mark speaker-changes in 2–11, 13–16, 27–36 (others lost).

Ὑψ. εἴ που θεᾶς φὺ[ς   10
Ἀμφ. τούτου δὲ παι[

frs 1.v etc.   (Ὑψ.)]ει [ἡ]δύ τοί[
Ἀμφ. ὃν καὶ σ[υ]νείπο[
Ὑψ. εἰς χρησμὸν οὖν σοι θα[
Ἀμφ. χρὴ γὰρ στρατεύειν μ' ει[15
Ὑψ. ἐ]δέξατ' οὖν ἑκοῦσα δυ[
(Ἀμφ.) ἐδέ]ξαθ', ἥκω δ' [οὔ]ποτ' ἐκ[
(Ὑψ.) ...]αι σαφῶς [ ]θανατ[
(Ἀμφ.) ... ἔ]στιν αι[ ] [ ] [390
(Ὑψ.) τί δῆιτα θύειν ιδιεῖ σε κιατθανούμενον;   20
(Ἀμφ.) ἄμεινοιν· οὐδιειὶς κάμαιτος εὐσεβεῖν θεούς.

stichomythia continues through fourteen largely or wholly   393–406
lost lines, the eighth marked Δ̲ (= 400)

F 753 and 753a probably belong within the next thirty lines:

753   (Ὑψ.) δείξω μὲν Ἀργείοισιν Ἀχελώιου ῥόον.

753a   (col. 8?)
frs. 23 + 37   — τί φ[ήι]ς; ἐκε[
               — ἐκεῖ λο α [
               — ὦ παντάλα[ινα
               remains of three more lines of stichomythia

fr. 24   beginings of six further lines of stichomythia

753b   Minimal fragments from col. 9 and top of col. 10

753c fr. 7 (Χο.)   remains of one line   (col. 10)
               ....] πολυκα[
               ...... αι σταχύω[ν
               .... δρ]οσιζομεν[
               .....] δώτορες ει .[5
               remains of one line (and perhaps a further line lost) ~550

13 ὃν corr. from ὃς P   σ[υ]νείπο[(= σ[υ]νείπο[) corr. from σ[υ]νηγ[P: i.e. perhaps συνεῖπον or συνειπόμεσθα Kannicht   15 εἴ[περ ἀξιοῖ γυνή (e.g.) Roberts in Page   16 δύ[σ-

Hyps. If *born* from a goddess . . . . . .[10]

Amph. And his *son/descendants* . . . . . .

(Hyps.) . . . *pleasant* . . . . . .

Amph. One whom also . . . . . .

Hyps. So to the/an oracle . . . . . . for you . . . . . .

Amph. Yes, for I must join the campaign *if(?)* . . . . . .[15]

Hyps. She accepted willingly, then . . . . . .

(Amph.) *She accepted it* – and *never* shall I come *from* . . . . . .

(Hyps.) . . . . . . plainly . . . *death* . . . . . .

(Amph.) . . . . . . *is* . . . . . .

(Hyps.) Then why do you need to sacrifice if you're going to
 your death?[20]

(Amph.) It's better so; it's no labour to worship the gods.

*Remainder of this dialogue largely lost. The next two frag-
ments probably belong to the continuation of the scene:*

753 *(Hyps.)* I'll show the Argives Achelous' stream.

753a — What *are you saying?* . . . . . . *there(?)* . . .

 — There . . . . . .

 — *You foolhardy* (or *much afflicted?*) *woman* . . . . . .

753c *Hypsipyle, carrying the baby, has left with Amphiaraus
 for the spring. Part of the Chorus's first stasimon:*

(Cho.) . . . . . . *<fruit?>ful* . . . . . . (*of?*) corn-ears/harvest . . .
 . . . *moistening* . . . . . . *givers* . . . . . .[5]

(one or two more lines largely lost)

ποτμον τέλος (e.g.) Cropp   18]αι or]ει   19 Above αι[P has νο[(correction or insertion?)
20–1 (= **F adesp. 350** N; 147–8 Diggle) Plut. *Mor.* 20d, unattrib., located here by Italie
20 θύειν P (as Cobet conjectured) οὖσι(ν) Plut.   **753** (p. 32 Bond; 149 Diggle) Didymus,
Lex. Trag. F 2, p. 85 Schmidt (from Macrob. *Sat.* 5.18.12), attrib. Eur. *Hyps.*   **753a** (~p.
38 Bond) P. Oxy. frs. 23+37, 24   1 ἐκε[ῖ (as in 2) Kannicht   2–5 paragraphi mark speaker-
changes (also in fr. 24)   2 εκειλο corr. from εκειγαρ P   perhaps λοχαγ[οί (e.g.) Cockle
3 παντάλα[ινα Cockle   **753c** (~p. 32–3 Bond) P. Oxy. frs. 7, 8+9+M+E+42, K.
Paragraphi and/or speaker identifications visible at 4, 5 7, 9, 11, 16   2 πολυκά[ρπων ed. pr.

frs. 8 + 9 etc.   *remains of one line*

Πλευρ[ων

ἀλατευ[

πατρα[. . .]οισι . [. . .] . [10

φυγὰς [. . .] . ῎Αργος [

νυ[*c. 10 letters*] . [.] ἐν κοίταισι παρ' αὐλα[

ἐριδ[. . . . . ἀ]μειβόμενοι

σιδ[. . . . . .]εσια

σφαγα[. . . .]λον   15

κλισίας π[ερ]ὶ νυκτέρου   ~561

γενναίων π[α]τέρων

φ[υ]γάδες δορὶ θυμόν.

Φοίβου δ' ἐν[ο]πὰ[ς] βα[σ]ιλεὺς ἐνύχευ-

ε[ν] ῎Αδραστος ἔχων   20

τέκνα θηρσὶν [ζ]εῦ[ξ]αι

. . . .]ομο[

     c. 13 letters] ἀμπετάσας

     trace of one more line

     about eight lines lost, then:

753d   frs. 12 etc.   *traces of one line*

φευ[

μέ[γε]θος αδ[ ]αβ[ ]δ[~580

οὐ γὰρ ἐμμεν[

῾Υψ.   ὤ μοι . [4

     five very damaged lines; 5, 7 and 9 seem to be   5–9

     assigned to the Chorus

(῾Υψ.?)   ποῦ μάλα;   10

Χο.   ἤδη [τόδ'] ἐγγύς, οὐχὶ μα[κράν

       λε]ύσσειν ἀλλὰ σο[~590

      . [γυνα]ῖκες οἵας ειθευ . . [

(῾Υψ.)   οἴ] ἐγώ·

(Χο.)   τί θροεῖς;   15

(῾Υψ.)   ὠλόμαν·

     remains of one more line

---

12 αὐλᾶ(ι) or αὐλα[ῖς ed. pr.   15 perhaps]χον ed. pr.   22 δ]ομο[ν ed. pr. (Bury)
753d (~p. 33–4 Bond) P. Oxy. frs. 12+56, 14, 13, 10+17. Paragraphi marking speaker-changes

. . . *Pleuron(ian?* . . . . . . wander<*ing?*> . . . . .
homeland(?) . . . . . . [10] a fugitive . . . . . Argos
. . . . . . <*by night?*> . . . amongst the beddings by
the courtyard, exchanging *quarrel(s?)* . . .
iron/sword . . . . . . *slaughter* . . . . . . [15] *over* a
couch for the night, the fugitives . . . . . . their
noble fathers' temper in conflict. And King Adrastus
lay pondering in the night the proclamation of
Phoebus that he had,[20] to yoke his daughters with
wild beasts . . . . throwing open . . .

753d   *A few lines later, Hypsipyle has returned alone from the*
spring. Part of her anguished sung dialogue with the Chorus:

Alas(?) . . . . . .
magnitude . . . . . .
For . . . not *(to?) remain* . . . . . .

Hyps.   Oh woe . . . . . . [4]

remains of five lines probably divided between
Hypsipyle and the Chorus, then:

(Hyps.?)   Just where?[10]
Cho.   Already <*this*> is close by, not *far away,*
to see, but . . . . . .
. . . . . . *women*, what . . . . . .
(Hyps.)   Woe is me!
(Cho.)   What cry is this?[15]
(Hyps.)   I am lost!

visible at 4, 5, 9, 11, 16; speaker-identifications visible at 4, 7, 9, 11.   4 ω read by Haslam,
Cockle ιω ed. pr.   11 [τόδ]' Turner   13 γυνα]ῖκες Haslam (in Cockle)   o inserted above ε
of θευ P   14 οἴ] ἐγώ Kannicht

753e Minimal fragments from the upper part of col. 11,   (col. 11)
including the notation Ζ (= 600) and, a little later,   **600**
screams of Hyps. (ἐὲ ἐέ)

754   (Ὑψ.)   ἕτερον ἐφ' ἑτέρωι †αἰρόμενος†
ἄγρευμ' ἀνθέων ἡδομέναι ψυχᾶι,
τὸ νήπιον ἄπληστον ἔχων.

754a   κρήνη [σ]κιαζ[(col. 12)
δράκων πάροικ[ος
γοργωπὰ λεύσσω[ν
πήληκα σείων, οὗ φοβ[
ποιμένες ἐπεισιγ' εν[ ] [5
παν[ ]μα δρᾶσαι καὶ ρυ [
— φ[εῦ· γυ]ναικὶ πάντα γίγνε[ται
.....]ς ἥκει· φύλακα δ' οὐ π[
remains of four lines, and about three lines lost, then:

754b frs. 20 etc. (Ὑψ.)   ω [ ] αι [
ἕστηκα μ π [
ἀνά[ξι'] ἕξειν· οἱ φόβοι δ[ ]τικτο [~670
Χο. εὐελπ[']υτι[ ]' ἔχεις ἐν[ ] [4
Ὑψ. δέδο[ι]κα θ[α]νάτωι παιδὸς οἷα πείσομ[αι.   7
Χο. οὔκουν ἄπειρός γ', ὦ τάλαινα, σ[υμφορῶν.   8
(Ὑψ.) ἔγνωκα κἀγὼ τοῦτο καὶ φυλάξ[ομαι.   9
Χο. τί δῆτά γ' ἐξεύρηκας εἰς ἀλκ[ὴν κακῶν;   6
Ὑψ. φεύγειν στ [ ]ων των[ ]δρ[5
(Χο.) ποῖ δῆτα τρέψηι; τίς σε δ[έ]ξεται πό[λ]ις;   10
Ὑψ. πόδες κριν[ο]ῦσι τοῦτο κα[ὶ π]ροθυμία.
Χο. φυλάσ[σ]εται[ι] γῆ φρου[ρίο]ισιν ἐν κύκλωι.

753e (~p. 34 Bond) P. Oxy. frs. 25 col. ii, 11, 52   **754** (p. 34-5 Bond) Plut. Mor. 93d and 661e-f, both attrib. 'Hyps.' (i.e. Eur. Hyps., Valckenaer)   1 ἐφ' ἑτέρωι Mor. 93d some mss. ἐφ' ἕτερον or –ων others ἐφετέρας Mor. 661e   αἰρόμενος Mor. 93d most mss. αἰρούμενος others ἱέμενος Mor. 661f   2 ἄγρευμ' ἀνθέων ἡδομέναι Mor. 93d ἄγρευμα ἂν συνηδομέναι Mor. 661f   3 ἄπληστον ἔχων Amyot ἄχρηστον ἔχων Mor. 93d ἄπληστος ἐών Mor. 661f   **754a** (p. 36-7 Bond) P. Oxy. frs. 18, 19   1 σ[κ]ιάζεται (von Arnim) or σ[κ]ιάζει Kannicht   4 φόβ[ωι ed. pr.   5 ἐπεὶ σῖγ' or ἔπεισί γ' ed. pr. (Wilamowitz)

753e   *Hypsipyle responds to the Chorus with screams.*

754   *Probably more of the same sung dialogue:*

    (Hyps.) . . . . . . picking(?) one quarry of flowers after another
    with joyful spirit, his child's mind unsatisfied.

754a   *Hypsipyle describes the serpent in a spoken dialogue:*

       . . . a spring . . . is *shadowed* (or *shadows*) . . . . .
       a serpent living by it . . . . . . fiercely staring . . .
       . . . shaking its helm, *in fear?* of which . . . . . .
       shepherds . . . . . . when silently?[5] . . . to do . . .
       . . . and . . .

    Cho.? *Alas, for a woman* everything *becomes/is* . . . . . .
       (and?) comes . . . but . . . not . . . guardian . . .

754b   *A few lines later, Hypsipyle discusses her plight with the Chorus:*

    (Hyps.) O . . . . . . I stand . . . . to get undeserved
       (sufferings). My fears . . . . . .
       Cho.   . . . *optimistic* . . . . . . you have . . . . . . [4]
       Hyps. I fear what I shall suffer for the child's death.[7]
       Cho. Well, you are not inexperienced in misfortunes, poor
       woman.[8]
    (Hyps.) I am aware of that myself, and shall guard against it.[9]
       Cho. What then have you discovered for a *protection*
       <from harm>?[6]
       Hyps. To flee . . . . . . [5]
    (Cho.) Where then will you turn? What community will
       accept you?[10]
       Hyps. My feet and my eagerness will determine this.
       Cho. The land is guarded by watch-towers that surround it.

---

7 paragraphus marks speaker-change   perhaps ὤ[μοι corr. from ἐ[μοὶ Cockle
754b (~p. 35–6 Bond; 150–66 Diggle) P. Oxy. frs. 20+21+44   1 ὦ φί[λτα]ται γυ[να]ῖ[κες
ed. pr. (Bury)   end ὡς ἐπὶ ξυροῦ (e.g.) ed. pr.   3 end: see Comm.   4–16 paragraphi mark
speaker-changes (lost in 9, 10)   7, 8, 9, 6, 5 so ordered by Wecklein   4 accent above lacuna:
P   6 δῆτά γ' corr. from δή ποτ' P   [κακῶν Wilamowitz in ed. pr.   5 στε[γ]ῶν τῶν[δ'
ἔ]δρ[αν(α) Bury in ed. pr.

Ὑψ. [ν]ικᾶι[ς]· ἐῶ δὴ τοῦτ[ό] ⟨γ'⟩· ἀλλ' [ἀ]πέρχομαι.   *~680*

Χο. σκόπει, φίλας [γ]ὰρ τά[σδε] συμβούλους ἔχεις.

Ὑψ. τί δε ....[ ]ιμ[τ]ις ἐξάξε[ι] με γῆς;   15

Χο.   *c. 12 letters*   ] .. [......] δούλους ἄγειν.

remains of one more line

about three lines lost, then:

754c frs. 34 etc.   *trace of one line*

(Ὑψ.?)   ]τη[.... δέσ]ποινα[

(ΕΥΡΥΔΙΚΗ?) ......] . ι κλῆιθρ['] ὦσ[......] ουσε[

      ......]ωμαι δωμάτων [....] τιδα

      ......]τ' ἔξω δμωῒς ἡ τροφ[ὸς τέ]κνου   5

      ......]δίδωσιν οὐδ' ἔσω βαίν[ει δό]μων.

remains of lines 7–10; speaker-changes at 9 and
perhaps 10; line 9 marked **Ḥ** *(= 700)*   **700**

(Εὐρ.?) π]έλας θυρῶν ἇ[ρ'] ὕπνον ἐκτελεῖ γλυκ[ύν,   11

      ἢ π]α[ι]δὸς εἴργε[ι] δάκρυ' ἔχουσ' ἐν ἀγκάλ[αις;

(Ὑψ.?)]π[ ]τ' ἀπ' οἴ[κ]ων· οἴχε[τα]ι φίλας τέκν[ον

  ..]σασ[........] η [.....]ηλημματο[ς

  ..] σηδ[*c. 15 letters*   ] ει λόγων   15

  ..]αιθοα[*c. 11–12 letters* ἐ]π' ἀγκάλαισί[μου

  ..] . οχη[*c. 12 letters*   ]ς ἀπωλόμ[ην

  ....]κετ[*c. 12–13 letters* ἐ]κ χερῶν ν[

755 N   *See* **765b** *(at end)*

755a   *Minor fragments from col. 13. Line-beginnings from the*
upper part of the column include:

frs. 30 + 40   2   πῶς δ' ἂν . [*(col. 13)*

            3   θανόντα τονδ[

            4   — οἴει στα[

Line-ends towards the middle of the column include:

frs. 36 etc.   3   ] κτανεῖν

            4   ] . ζων λαβεῖν

            6   ]δειξ[.] χέρνιβα

            7   ] ἀπώ[λ]εσεν[.]α . [.]ν

Hyps. You win; I'll give up that plan – yet I am leaving.

Cho. Consider, though; you have friends *here* to advise you.

Hyps. But what . . . who will take me out of the country?[15]

Cho. . . . . to take slaves.

754c   *A few lines later, Eurydice enters from the house, perhaps
with servants, looking for Hypsipyle and the child:*

(*Cho.?*) . . . . *mistress* . . .

(*EURYDICE?*) . . . . . . the door-bolts so that . . . . . . *I may* . . .

. . . (from?) the palace . . . . . . The slave-woman

who is *my child's nurse* . . . outside[5] . . . is giving

. . . and is not going about inside the house.

(*remains of four lines*)

(*Eur.?*) Is he finishing a pleasant sleep by the doorway,[11] or
is she holding the boy in her arms to stop his tears?

(*Hyps.?*) . . . from *the house*; the child *is gone* . . . dear . . .

. . . . *of/from mischief* (or *magic*) . . . . . . of/from

words[15] . . . . . . *upon my* arms . . . . . . I am

ruined . . . . . . *out of* (my?) hands . . .

755   *See 765b (at end)*

755a   *A little later in the same scene Hypsipyle is accused by
Eurydice: beginnings of five lines including 2–4:*

frs. 30 + 40 (*Hyps.?*) But how could . . . . . . who has died . . .

Euryd.? Do you suppose . . .

a little later again, ends or near-ends of twelve lines including:

frs 36 etc.   3 . . . to kill   6 . . . a libation

4 . . . to take   7 . . . destroyed . . .

---

15 τί δ' εἴ τιν' εὑρ[ο]ιμ' [ὅστ]ις ed. pr. (Murray), but reading of traces 'very doubtful'
Cockle (δ' εἰ ed. pr., Kannicht, δερ Cockle, Diggle)   754c (~pp. 35–7 Bond) P. Oxy. frs.
34+35, 26, 33, 32+48+50+53   2 δέσ]ποινα ed. pr.   3 χαλᾶτέ μ]οι Bury in ed. pr.   ὡς
[ἂν ἐξελ]θοῦσ' ἐ[γώ Dale (ὡς [ἂν εἰσελ]θοῦσ' ἔ[σω Bury in ed. pr.)   3–6 assigned to Euryd.
by Bury in ed. pr.   4 perhaps φρο]ντίδα ed. pr.   5 ἡ ed. pr. ἤ Herwerden   9 (and perhaps
10) paragraphus marks speaker-change   11–12 assigned to Euryd. by Cockle   11 ἂ[ρ']
Cockle ἔ[θ'] Turner   12 ἢ π]α[ι]δὸς εἴργε[ι] Cockle (π]α[ι]δὸς Bond)   13–18 assigned to
Hyps. by Cockle   13]π[or]τ[, then]τ' or]γ' Cockle   14 δ]ηλήματο[ς Bond   15 σηδ[
(not ησδ[) P   755a (~pp. 32, 37–9 Bond) P. Oxy. frs. 30+40, 43, 36+6+28+55, 38   frs.
30+40.3 τόνδ[ε Cockle τὸν δ[ύστηνον Handley   4 paragraphus marks speaker-change

756 N   *See 765a (at end)*

756a   *Unplaced minor fragments within cols. 8–14*

757   P. Oxy. with P. Petrie   *(col. 14)*

frs. 27 etc. **Θ** (Ύψ.)   *traces of one line*   **800**

καὶ χ[έρ]νιβ[
ἑῷ δε[̣ ̣] λα[
 ̣] ητ' ἀπε‌νν[επ-   'Ἰος
ἀρετὴν ξενο[   ]μα   5
δοκῶ δὲ ταυ[τ   ]άβηι   805
ἢν μὴ σὺ πεισθ[ῆις   ]υ

remains of thirteen lines   *8–20*

κεῖται [̣ ̣] [*21* 820
καλαῖσι τὸν ο[
Φ[οί]βου τὰ λε[
καὶ μὴ δι'ὀρ[γῆς
χρόνωι δὲ βού[λ-   *25*
τὸ τῶν γυναι[κῶν   825
καὶ πα[ῖ]δα τ[
κἂν διαριθμ[
ἢν δ' ἐξαμα[ρτ

Χο. γενν[αῖ' ἔ]λε[ξας   *30*

P. Petr. begins   ἐν σώφροσιν [γ]ὰρ κἄμ' ἀριθμεῖσθα[ι θέλω.   830

(Εὐρ.) τί ταῦτ[α] κομψῶς ἀντιλάζυσαι λό[γων

fr. 60.i   ………] ̣εχουσα μηκύνεις μ[ακράν,   *(col. 15)*
κτανοῦσ' 'Οφέ]λτην, τῶν ἐμῶν ὄσσω[ν χαράν;
………] ̣ ̣ μηδ' ἀναμν[ησ- – ᴗ –   *35*
 ̣ν ̣π[̣ ̣ ̣] ̣ ̣ [̣]μοι παιδί θ' ὃν διώ[λεσας.   835

(Ύψ.) οὕτω δοκ[εῖ μ', ὦ [π]ότνι', ἀποκτείνε[ιν ᴗ –
ὀργῆι πρὶν ὀρθῶς πρᾶγμ[α] διαμαθε[ῖν τόδε;
σιγᾶις, ἀμείβηι δ' οὐδέν; ὦ τάλαιν' ἐγ[ώ·
ὡς τοῦ θανεῖν μὲν οὕνεκ' οὐ μέγα στ[έν]ω,   *40*

756a P. Oxy. frs. 16, 31 (p. 37 Bond), 39, 41, 45–7, 49, 64 (p. 46 Bond)   757 (~p. 39–44
Bond; ~167–243 Diggle) P. Oxy. col. 14 (frs. 27, 68, 116, 29+A+51+22), col. 15 (fr. 60.i+87),

756 N   *See 765a (at end)*

756a   *Numerous minor fragments unplaced within cols. 8-14*

757   *Some sixty lines later, the same scene continues with line-beginnings from Hypsipyle's speech in self-defence including 801–6:*

(*Hyps.*) and *the libation* . . . . . . I leave aside . . . . . .
. . . *forbid* . . . . . . virtue . . . *strange(rs?)* . . .
and I consider *these things* . . . . . .⁸⁰⁵ if you *are*
not *persuaded* . . .

   and 820–8:

he(?) lies . . . . . . with(?) fine . . . . . . *Phoebus'*
. . . . . . and do not *in anger* . . . . . . but *deliber-at(ing?)* in time . . . . . . women's . . . . . .⁸²⁵
and the/a child . . . . . . and if *<you?> discriminate*
. . . . . . but if *<you?> make an error* . . .

Cho. *You have spoken nobly* . . . . . . For I too want to
be counted amongst those with good sense.⁸³⁰

(*Eur.*) Why do you seize upon this specious *talk* (and) . . .
. . . carry on *at length <when you have killed>*
Opheltes, <the joy> of my *eyes?* . . . . . . and do
not *remind* . . . . . . for me and my son whom *you
have killed.*⁸³⁵

(*Hyps.*) *Are you determined*, mistress, to kill me thus . . . in
anger before properly *learning* the truth of *<this>*
affair? You are silent? You give me no reply? O
wretched am I!   I do not greatly *grieve* if I must die,

col. 16 (fr. 60.ii)   803 ητ' ἀπενν[επ– Cockle δῆτα τηνι[ed. pr.   accent above lacuna: P
805 λ]άβηι ed. pr.   827–8 διαριθμ[ήσηι . . . ἐξαμά[ρτηις Cropp   830–50 = P. Petr.
II.49c (= P. Lit. Lond. 74), 3ʳᵈ–2ⁿᵈ C. B.C., identified with *Hyps.* by F. Petersen, *Hermes* 49
(1914), 156–8, 623–6; re-ed. Cockle 135–6. Negligible variants not reported here.   830 θέλω
Wilamowitz 831 ἀντιλάζυσαι λό[γων Robert ανλαζεσαι λ [P. Petr. (P. Oxy. lacking)
832 μ[ακράν Roberts 833 suppl. Morel 834 μηδ' ἀναμν[ήσης τέκνου Petersen οὐ (μὴ)
. .] . μήδ' ἀναμνή[σεις κακῶν Diggle 1995 835 μοι read by Milne (cf. Diggle 1995)
διώ[λεσας Petersen 836 end: ἄρα Diggle 1995 837 ὀρθῶς πρᾶγμ[P. Oxy.]ἐχρῆν παῖδα
P. Petr. τόδε Wilamowitz 839 μέγα Wilamowitz μεταστ[P. Petr. (P. Oxy. lacking)

εἰ δὲ κτανεῖν τὸ τέκνον οὐκ ὀρθῶς δοκῶ,   840
τοὐμὸν τιθήνημ', ὃν ἐπ' ἐμαῖσιν ἀγκάλαις
πλὴν οὐ τεκοῦσα τἄλλα γ' ὡς ἐμὸν τέκνον
στέργουσ' ἔφερβον, ὠφέλημ' ἐμοὶ μέγα.
ὦ πρῷρα †καὶ† λευκαῖνον ἐξ ἅλμης ὕδωρ   *45*
'Αργοῦς, ἰὼ παῖδ', ὡς ἀπόλλυμαι κακῶς.   845
ὦ μάντι πατρὸς Οἰκλέους, θανούμεθα.
ἄρηξον, ἐλθέ, μή μ' ἴδῃς ὑπ' αἰτίας
αἰσχρᾶς θανοῦσαν, διὰ σὲ γὰρ διόλλυμαι.
ἔλθ', οἶσθα γὰρ δὴ τἀμά, καὶ σὲ μάρτυρα   *50*

P. Petr. ends

σαφέστατον δέξαιτ' ἂν ἥδ' ἐμῶν κακῶν.   850
ἄγετε, φίλων γὰρ οὐδέν' εἰσορῶ πέλας
ὅστις με σώσει· κενὰ δ' [ἐ]πῃδέσθην ἄρα.

'Αμφ. ἐπίσχες, ὦ πέμπουσα τ[ή]νδ' ἐπὶ σφαγά[ς,
δόμων ἄνασσα· τῶι γὰρ εὐπρεπεῖ σ' ἰδὼν   *55*
τοὐλεύθερόν σοι προστίθημι τῆι φύσει.   855

Ὑψ. ὦ πρός σε γονάτων ἱκέτις, 'Αμφιάρεω, πίτνω,
κ]αὶ πρὸς [γ]ενείο[υ τ]ῆς τ' 'Απόλλωνος τέχνης,
κ]αιρὸν γὰρ ἥκεις τοῖς ἐμοῖσιν ἐν κακοῖς,
ῥ]ῦσαί με· διὰ γὰρ σὴν ἀπόλλυμαι χάριν.   *60*
μέλλω τε θνήισκειν, δεσμίαν τέ μ' εἰσορᾶις   860
πρὸς σοῖσι γόνασιν, ἢ τόθ' εἱπόμην ξένοις·
ὅσια δὲ πράξεις ὅσιος ὤν· πρ[ο]δοὺς δέ με
ὄνειδος 'Αργείοισιν "Ελλησιν τ' ἔσηι.
ἀλλ' ὦ δι' ἁ[γνῶ]ν ἐμπύρων λεύσσων τύχας   *65*
Δαναοῖσιν, [εἰπ]ὲ τῆιδε συμφορὰν τέκνου·   865
παρὼν γὰ[ρ οἶσ]θα· φησὶ δ' ἥδ' ἑκουσίως
κτανεῖν μ[ε π]αῖδα κἀπιβουλεῦσαι δόμοις.

'Αμφ. εἰδὼς ἀφῖγμαι τὴν τύχην θ' ὑπειδόμην
τὴν σὴν ἃ πείσηι τ' ἐκπεπνευκότος τέκνου.   *70*
ἥκ[ω] δ' ἀρήξων συμφοραῖσι ταῖσι σαῖς,   870
τὸ μ[ὲ]ν βίαιον οὐκ ἔχων, τὸ δ' εὐσεβές.
αἰ[σ]χρὸν γὰρ εὖ μὲν ἐξεπίστασθαι παθεῖν,
δρᾶσαι δὲ μηδὲν εὖ παθόντα πρὸς σέθεν.

---

841 deleted in P. Petr.   842 γ' ed. pr.   δ' P. Oxy. (P. Petr. lacking)   843 ὠφέλημ' ἐμοὶ
P. Oxy. ωλενμεμο[P. Petr.   845 παῖδ' P. Petr. παῖδες (perhaps corr. to παῖδε) P. Oxy.

but if I am wrongly thought to have killed the child,[840] my nursling, whom I fed and cherished in my own arms in every way except that I did not bear him, a great boon to me. O prow of Argo †and† stirring the water white from the brine, O my twin sons, how shamefully I am dying![845] O seer, son of Oiclês, I am facing death. Defend me, come now, don't see me killed because of a shameful accusation; for you are the cause of my destruction! Come now, you know my side of it, and she would accept you as a most reliable witness of my misfortune.[850] *(To Eurydice's servants)* Take me, then – I see no friend nearby to save me; my deference, it seems, was wasted.

(Amphiaraus re-enters from the direction of the spring)

Amph. Hold there, you who are despatching this woman for slaughter, mistress of this house – for by your bearing I can tell on sight that you are of free birth.[855]

Hyps. (falling on her knees before Amphiaraus) O, by your knees I fall in supplication, Amphiaraus, and by your chin and your Apolline art, for you have come here just in time amidst my troubles: save me, for I am dying because of my service to you. I am facing death, you see me bound and at your knees[860] – me, who lately went along with you strangers. You who are blameless will be acting blamelessly; but if you forsake me, you will be a disgrace to Argos and all Hellas. Come, you who see fortunes for the Danaans in *pure* burnt offerings, *tell* her what happened to her son.[865] You were there, *you know*, though she claims I killed the child on purpose and plotted against her family.

Amph. I have come with full knowledge and had guessed your plight and what you would suffer because of the child's death. I am here now to defend you in your misfortune,[870] relying not on force but on my piety. It would be shameful to know all about accepting services, and yet do no service in return for yours.

850 σαφέστατον ed. pr. –αν P. Oxy.]τατον P. Petr.   854 εὐπρεπεῖ σ' ed. pr. εὐτρεπὲς corr. to εὐτρεπεῖ σ' P   857 τ]ῆς τ' ed. pr. τ]ῆς P   860 τέ ed. pr. δέ P   865 τῆιδε ed. pr. τήνδε P

πρῶτον μὲν οὖν σὸν δεῖξον, ὦ ξένη, κάρα·   *75*
σῶφρον γὰρ ὄμμα τοὐμὸν ('Ελλήνων λόγος   **875**
πολὺς διήκει) καὶ πέφυχ' οὕτω, γύναι,
κοσμεῖν τ' ἐμαυτὸν καὶ τὰ διαφέρονθ' ὁρᾶν.
ἔπειτ' ἄκουσον, τοῦ τάχους δὲ τοῦδ' ἄνες·
εἰς μὲν γὰρ ἄλλο πᾶν ἁμαρτάνειν χρεών,   *80*
ψυχὴν δ' ἐς ἀνδρὸς ἢ γυναικὸς οὐ καλόν.   **880**

Εὐρ. ὦ ξένε πρὸς "Αργει πλησία[ν] ναίων χθόνα,
πάντων ἀκούουσ' οἶδα σ' ὄ[ν]τα σώφρονα·
οὐ γάρ ποτ' εἰς τόδ' ὄμμ' ἂν ἔβλ[ε]ψας παρών.
νῦν δ', εἴ τι βούληι, καὶ κλύε[ι]ν σέθεν θέλω   *85*
καὶ σ' ἐκδιδάσκειν· οὐκ ἀνάξιος γὰρ εἶ.   **885**

'Αμφ. γύναι, τὸ τῆσδε τῆς ταλαιπώρου κ[α]κὸν
ἀγρίως φέρουσάν σ' ἤπιον θ[έσθαι θέλ]ω,
οὐ τήνδε μᾶλ[λ]ον ἢ τὸ τῆς δ[ί]κης ὁ[ρ]ῶν.
αἰσχύνομα[ι] δὲ Φοῖβον οὗ δι' ἐμπύρ[ω]ν   *90*
τέχνην ἐπασκῶ, ψεῦδος ε[ἴ τ]ι λέξομεν.   **890**
ταύτην ἐγὼ 'ξέπεισα κρηναῖον [γά]νος

frs. 60.i + 87   δεῖξαι δι' ἁγνῶν ῥευμάτων [. .] υχ [
στρατιᾶς πρόθυμ', 'Αργεῖον ὡς δ[.] νην πυρ[

fr. 60.ii   *three lines wholly and one largely lost, then:*   *(col. 16)*

. . . .] παῖς με[
    ]ασαμεν[*100*
[Γ]   ἡμ]εῖς δὲ[.] '[**900**
. . . .]αι θέλ[οντες
δρ]άκων ασ[
ἠκόντισ' ἀ[
καί νιν δρομ[*105*
εἵλιξεν ἀμφ[**905**
ἡμεῖς δ' ἰδό[ντες
ἐγὼ δ' ἐτόξευσ['
ἀρχὴ γὰρ ἡμῖν [
'Αρχέμορος ε [*110*
σύ τ' οὐχὶ σαυτὴ[ν   **910**
ὄρνιθα δ' 'Αργείο[ισι
καὶ μὴ . . . . [

(To Eurydice) So to begin with, lady, unveil your head. My eye is discreet[875] (that is well known in Hellas) and I have been bred to govern myself and see what matters. And next, listen to me and let go this haste. To err over anything else is allowable, but over a man's or a woman's life it is not well.[880]

Eur. *(unveiling herself)* O stranger, dweller in the land near Argos, from all reports I know you are a discreet man, or you would never have stood there and looked on my face. As it is, if you wish it, I am ready to listen and explain things to you. You are not unworthy of that.[885]

Amph. Lady, you are reacting cruelly to this unfortunate woman's offence, and I *would like to make you* lenient. I am looking not so much to her as to the interests of justice. And I shall be shamed before Phoebus, whose art I practise with burnt-offerings, if I say anything false.[890] I myself persuaded this woman to show me the *bright* spring-water . . . through its pure streams . . . a sacrifice for the army, so that(?) . . . Argive . . .[893]
. . . . . *(four lines missing)* . . . . . the child . . .[898]
. . . *(one line missing)* . . . . . . And *we* . . . . .[900]
wanting . . . . . . *the serpent* . . . . . . shot forth . . .
. . . and . . . him . . . *rapid* . . . . . . coiled *around*
. . . . . .[905] And we *on seeing* . . . . . and I shot . . .
. . . For . . . the beginning . . . for us . . . Archemorus . . . and you . . . not . . . yourself . . . . . .[910]
but an omen *for the Argives* . . . . . . and not . . . . .

875–6 parenthesis indicated by Collard   875 Ἑλλήνων P -ας Lloyd-Jones   882 πάντων ed. pr. πάντων δ' P   883 ὄμμ' ἂν ed. pr. ὄμμα P   890 ἐπασκῶ ed. pr. –ῶν P   893 πρόθυμα ἀργεῖον ὡς P, corrected from προθυμασωστιν[ ]αν   νην corr. from νον (i.e. δεινὴν from δεινὸν?)   901 σῶσ]αι von Arnim θῦσ]αι Wecklein   912 στολ[('all very doubtful') ed. pr.

ἀλλουχ[
πολλοὶ δ[*115*
Κάδμου [*915*
νόστου κυρησ[
Ἄδραστος ἵξετ᾽ αρ[
ἑπτὰ στρατηγ[
τὰ μὲν γενόμεν[α   *120*

(757 N)   ἃ δ᾽ αὖ παραινῶ, ταυτά μοι δέξαι, γύναι.   *920*
ἔφυ μὲν οὐδεὶς ὅστις οὐ πονεῖ βροτῶν·
θάπτει τε τέκινα χἄτερα κτᾶται νέα,
αὐτός τε θνήισκει· καὶ τάδ᾽ ἄχθονται βροτοὶ
εἰς γῆν φέροντες ιγῆν. ἀναγκαίως δ᾽ ἔχει   *125*
βίον θερίζειν ὥστε κάρπιμον στάχυν,   *925*
καὶ τὸν μὲν εἶναι, τὸν δὲ μή· τί ταῦτα δεῖ
στένειν ἅπερ δεῖ κατὰ φύσιν διεκπερᾶν;
ἃ δ᾽ εἰκὸς Ἀργο[
θάψαι δὸς ἡμ[ῖν   *130*
οὐ γὰρ καθ᾽ ἡμ[*930*
ἀλλ᾽ εἰς τὸν αἰε[ὶ
τοῖ[ς σο]ῖς βρότε[
κλεινὸς γὰρ ἔσ[ται
ἀγῶνά τ᾽ αὐτῶ[ι   *135*
στεφάνους διδ[*935*
ζηλωτὸς ἔστ[αι
ἐν τῶιδε με [
μνησθήσετα[ι
ἐπωνομάσθη[*140*
Νεμέας κατ᾽ ἄλσ[ος   *940*
ἀναιτία γάρ· τοῖσ[
σὺν γὰρ καλῶι σο[
θήσει σε καὶ παιδ᾽ [

Εὐρ. ὦ παῖ, τὸ μέν σοι τ[*145*
    ] ἧσσον ἢ μην[*945*

---

917 ιξεταρ[P ἥξει τ᾽ Ἄρ[γος Page   919 τὰ μὲν γενόμεν[α δὴ σαφῶς ἐπίστασαι (e.g.) ed.
pr.   920–7 = **757.1–8 N** cited by Clem. Alex *Strom.* 4.7.53 (920–3, 926–7 ταῦτα...διεκπερᾶν,
attrib. Eur.), [Plut.] *Mor.* 110f–111a (921–7, attrib. 'Amphiaraus consoling Archemorus'
mother'), Stob. 4.44.12 (921–7, attrib. Eur. *Hyps.*), M. Ant. 7.40 (925–6 βίον...μή, unattrib.)

but not(?) . . . . . . many . . . . . Cadmus' . . . .⁹¹⁵
achieve their homecoming . . . . . Adrastus will reach
. . . . . the seven commanders . . .
    What has happened . . . . . But now, lady, please
accept this counsel that I offer.⁹²⁰ No mortal was ever
born who does not suffer. We bury children and get other
new ones, and die ourselves; and mortals grieve at these
things as they bring earth to earth. But so it must be: we
must harvest life like a fruitful crop,⁹²⁵ and one of us live,
one not. Why should we lament these things, which by
our very nature we must endure?
    But what it is proper . . . . . . *Argos* . . . . . .
Give . . . *to us* to bury . . . . . . For not in . . .
. . .⁹³⁰ but for eternal (time) . . . . . . mortal . . .
with(?) your . . . . . . For *he will be* famous . . .
. . . and . . . a contest to/for him . . . . . . giv<*ing?*>
crowns . . . . . .⁹³⁵ *he will be* envied . . . . . . in this
. . . . . . will be remembered . . . . . . was given the
name . . . . . in the *grove* of Nemea . . . . . .⁹⁴⁰ For
she is blameless . . . . . . For with good . . . . . . will
make you and your son . . . . . .
    Eur. My son, the . . . to you . . . . . . less than . . . . .⁹⁴⁵

---

and 11.6 (925, unattrib.); transl. Cic. *Tusc.* 3.59 (~921–7, attrib. Eur.; cf. Epictet. 2.6.11–14 (allusion to 925–6, unattrib.). Clem. Alex. and [Plut.] cite a further line, also cited alone by Stob. 3.29.56 ms. S (attrib. Eur. *Tel.*), [Plut.] *Mor.* 117d (line 927a = **F 1043a**): δεινὸν γὰρ οὐδὲν τῶν ἀναγκαίων βροτοῖς, 'Men need fear nothing that is inevitable' (so [Plut.] 111a), or similar. 920 ἃ δ' αὖ P ἅ γ' οὖν Clem. μοι Valckenaer μου Clem. 921 οὐ πονεῖ βροτῶν Clem., [Plut.] (*mortalis nemo est...* Cic.) οὐκ ἀεὶ πονεῖ Stob. 922 θάπτει τε Clem. θάπτειν τε P, Stob. θάπτει δὲ (or καὶ θάπτει or θάπτει) [Plut.] χἄτερα Clem., Stob. χἄτερος (or χἄτερος αὖ) [Plut.] κτᾶται νέα [Plut.] σπείρει νέα Clem. κτᾶσθαι πάλιν Stob. 923 αὐτός τε θνῄσκει Clem., [Plut.] αὐτοὺς δὲ θνῄσκειν Stob. (αὐτοί τε θνησκε[P) καὶ τάδ' Clem., [Plut.] κατὰ δ' (κᾆτα δ', Grotius) Stob. 924 ...γῆν. ἀναγκαίως δ' ἔχει Grotius (cf. Cic. *Reddenda terrae est terra. Tum vita omnibus metenda ut fruges: sic iubet necessitas*) τὴν ἀναγκαίως ἔχει Stob. τὴν δὲ ἀναγκαίως ἔχειν (or ἔχει) [Plut.] 926–7 τί ταῦτα δεῖ | στένειν...διεκπερᾶν [Plut.], Stob. (στενειναπε[P) ταῦτα δεῖ στέγειν (στέργειν, Postgate)... δεῖ δ' ἐκπερᾶν Clem. 930 καθ' ἡμέραν...μίαν Page (καθ' ἡμέρας...μιᾶς φάος von Arnim) καθ' ἡμ[ᾶς Bond 940 end: τήνδε δ' οὖν λῦσαί σε χρή (e.g.) ed. pr.

(759 N)

πρὸς τὰς φύσεις ιχρὴ καὶ τὰ πράγματα σκοπεῖν
καὶ τὰς διαίτας τῶιν κακῶν τε κἀγαθῶν,
πιειθὼ δὲ τοῖς μὲιν σώφροσιν πολλὴν ἔχειν,
τοῖς μὴ δικιαίοις ιδ ᾿ οὐδὲ συμβάλλειν χρεών.   150

135 lines lost (all of cols. 17, 18, first third of 19), then:

758a   *(col. 19)*

fr. 57   *Near-beginnings of iambic trimeters, then Choral stasimon:*

5–6 *?*] ἔοικε δε[
5–6 *?*] Διόνυσός τ[ε   1085
4–5 *?*]αντος εισε [
4–5 *?*]φέστηκ᾿ ουδ[
4–5 *?*] ιδ᾿ ουτ[

(Χο.)   τίς ποτ᾿ [στρ.?
         θαλαμο[1090
         βάλλει ὑπ[
         ἀνά τ᾿ αἰθ[έρ-
         τί τὸ σῆμα [10
         βότρυς α [
         ἀναδίδω[σι   1095
         ῥεῖ δὲ γά[
         στάζει[
         νέκταρ[15
         λιβάνου[
Λ̄   τάχ᾿ ἂν ε[**1100**
         χάριν α[
         ἀντάπο[

         ὦ πότνια θεῶ[ν   ἀντ.?
         ]άος ἄσκοπον [21
         ]έρι πρωτόγονο[1105
frs. 81 + 57   ]θελ᾿ Ἔρως ὅτε νυ[
         ]ν τ᾿ ἐτράφη τότε [
         ] α θεῶν γένο[ς   25
         traces of one more line

946–9 = **759 N** cited by Orion 7.5 (946–9, attrib. *Hyps.*), *Flor. Monac.* 104 (= *Flor. Leiden* 100: 946, unattrib.)   946 φύσεις P, *Flor. Mon.* χρήσεις Orion   949 οὐδὲ Schneidewin

HYPSIPYLE

We should look at the natures of the good and the bad, and at their actions and their ways of life, and put much trust in those who are temperate, but not consort at all with immoral people.[949]

135 lines lost, then:

758a   *Near-beginnings of lines 1084–8, ending the same(?) episode, then beginning of the Chorus's second(?) stasimon:*

1084   . . . and it seems . . .
1085   . . . and Dionysus . . .
1087   . . . stand(s) apart (*or* stand(s) upon/by) . . .

Cho.   Who/what ever . . . . . . chamber(s?) . . . . . .[1090]
casts (*or* strikes) . . . . . . up to *the sky* (*or* through *the heaven*) . . . . . . What (is?) the sign . . . . . .
grape-bunch . . . . . . gives forth . . . . . .[1095] . . .
. . . and flows . . . . . . drips . . . . . . nectar . . .
. . . of frankincense . . . . . . perhaps . . . . . .[1100]
. . . . . . joy/grace . . . . . . *reward?* . . .

O mistress . . . of the gods . . . . . . inscrutable *light* (or *Chaos*) . . . . . . *in(?)* heaven/mist first-born . . . . . .[1105] Erôs *willed*, when *Night(?)* . . .
. . . and was nurtured at that time . . . . . . race *(or* offspring*)* of gods . . .

οὐδὲν Orion   **758a** (pp. 44–5, 46 Bond) P. Oxy. frs. 57+81   1087 ἀ]φέστηκε/-κα or ἐ]φέστηκε/-κα   1088 ουτ[: ὡς[ ] ιδ[inserted above line by second hand   1096 γά[λακτι ed. pr.   1102 paragraphus marks last line of strophe   ἀντάπο[(error for ἀντίπο[ινα?) suggested by Bond, read by Kannicht   ἀντάγω[ed. pr.   1104 φ]άος ed. pr. χ]άος resisted by Morel   1105 ἀ]έρι ed. pr. αἰ|θ]έρι Morel   1106 perhaps ἤ]θελ' (]θεα also possible) Cockle   νὺ[ξ ed. pr. (or νυ[κτ-)   1107 τ' ἐτράφη Turner e.g. ἐ]ν τ' ἐτράφη (τε τραφῆι also possible) Cockle   1108]δα or]φα

215

some 20 lines lost (rest of col. 19, first few lines of col. 20), then continuation of stasimon:

758b   frs. 58 etc.

]αὖραι θέλομεν[*(col. 20)*
] σμύρνας καπν[
θα]λάμοις Βρόμιο[ ]ει[
]ἀπ᾽ οἴνας
] τε φίλαι   5
νάρ]θηκα φέρουσα τριπέ[τηλον
]ας παρὰ χειρὸς ἐδε[ξ-
]ς ἐς οἴκους
]ερον· ὡς δ᾽ ἐπ᾽ ἐπώμ[ιον
κυ]παρισσόροφον χερὶ ν[10
ἔ]σωθεν
remains of one line
]ας ἁμᾶς [
]ο κτῆμα [᾽]τασ[
]ς οὐχὶ θιγ[15
]ν οἴκοις
] ἐξάγεται[ι ......] α
]ον γενο [
]εἶπε τ᾽ ἄ[...]εμις
]μεν σα [...]χρη πέρας   20
]η χάριν [...]ασθαι
remains of one more line

over 300 lines lost (lower half of col. 20, all of cols.
21–24, about three-quarters of col. 25), then:

758c   fr. 63   *Middles and ends of iambic trimeters:*   *(col. 25)*

trace of one line

('Υψ.?)   ] ἄνδρα κατέφυγεν[
]θειν ἐστὶν εἰς τα[ ]δε [–
]ους ἀνέθεσαν· τὰς συν[◡ –
] οὐκ ἔχουσι συμμάχους   5
]ς Ἀμφιάρεως· σωσαι[◡ –
]θις ὥσπερεὶ νεὼς [◡ –
λ]α[μ]βάνω[

216

*some 20 lines lost, then middles and ends of more
lines from the same stasimon:*

758b   . . . on the breeze we want . . . . . . myrrh-smoke
. . . . . . *(in the?) chamber*. . . Bromios . . . from
the vine . . . . . . dear . . . ,⁵ bearing *the trefoil wand*
. . . *received* from . . . hand . . . into the/my home
. . . and as onto *the shoulder*- . . . cypress-roofed in
the/my hand . . .¹⁰ . . . *within* . . . *(one illegible
line)* . . . our/my . . . . . . possession . . . . . .
not *touch* . . .¹⁵ . . . home(s) . . . brings (*or* is
brought) forth . . . *(one line with a few letters)* . . .
and said . . . . . . limit²⁰ . . . . . . joy/grace . . .

758c   *Some 300 lines later, near-line-ends probably from a
speech of Hypsipyle including (2–8):*

(Hyps.?) . . . . . . took refuge . . . man . . . . . . is . . .
to . . . into . . . . . (they) dedicated/attributed . . .
. . . (they) do not have (*or* not having) allies⁵ . . .
Amphiaraus; . . . save . . . . . . like a ship's . . .
. . . I(?) take (or find) . . .

758b (~p. 45–6 Bond) P. Oxy. frs. 58+99, 59, 77   1]αυραι (αὖραι or αὗραι) or]λυραι ed. pr.   6 νάρ]θηκα...τριπέ[τηλον von Arnim   14 accent above lacuna: P   **758c** (p. 44 Bond) P. Oxy. fr. 63   6 σῶσαι ed. pr.   7–8 e.g. αὖ]θις ὡσπερεὶ νεὼς σ[άλῳ ǀ πλαγκτῆς κυβερνήτην σε] λα[μ]βάνω [σοφόν Wilamowitz and ed. pr.

several lines lost, then near top of col, 26:

758d frs. 61 + 82   *remains of four line-ends*   *(col. 26)*

fr. 61

]λ᾽ ο[ὔ]ρι᾽ ἀζήλωι κα[κῶι   5
ἦ]λθε καρδίας ἔσ[ω
]σδ᾽ [ἔ]χοις νεανι[–
]λθ᾽ ὁμοῦ παρόνθ᾽ ὁ [–
ζῶ]σιν ἢ τεθνᾶσι δ[ή
]λλα δυστυχοῦν[⏑ –   10
] δουλείαν πικρ[άν
]ς ἀνηνύτους λό[γους
]αύσομαι σε δω[⏑ –
]καταστήσειας ἄ[ν
πρό]σθ᾽ ἐλευθέραν [⏑ –   15
]ρος εἰ σύ μοι, τέκ[νον
]οφῶι δοίης χά[ριν

remains of two more lines

about 95 lines lost (remainder of col. 26 and nearly all of col. 27, for which see below)

759a fr. 64.i *Scattered line-ends of a few letters each. At 1571–2*   *(col. 27)*
marginal notes refer to words in the text, Ἠδωνίσι
and Πάγγαιον.

fr. 64.ii ('Υψ.)   τέκνα τ᾽ ἀνὰ μίαν ὁδὸν   *(col. 28)*
ἀνάπ[α]λιν ἐτρόχασεν   1580
ἐπὶ φόβον ἐπὶ χάριν   60
ἑλίξας, χρόνωι
δ᾽ ἐξέλαμψεν εὐάμερος.

Ἀμφ.   τὴν μὲν παρ᾽ ἡ[μ]ῶν, ὦ γύναι, φέρηι χάριν·
ἐπεὶ δ᾽ ἐμοὶ πρόθυμος ἦσθ᾽ ὅτ᾽ ἠντόμην,   1585
ἀπέδωκα κἀγὼ σοὶ πρόθυμ᾽ ἐς παῖδε σώ.   65
σώιζου δὲ δὴ σύ, σφὼ δὲ τήνδε μητέρα,

758d (p. 23–4 Bond) P. Oxy. frs. 61+82, suppl. ed. pr. (fr. 61) except where noted.
7 [ἔ]χοις: or possibly [ὅ]χοις ed. pr. τού]σδ᾽ [ἔ]χοις νεανί[ας von Arnim   8 ἦ]λθ᾽ (ed. pr.)
or ἔ]λθ᾽ Kannicht   ὁμοῦ corr. from ὅλου   end ὅμ[ως ed. pr.   10 πο]λλὰ (von Arnim) or

758d   *Several lines later, further line-ends (dialogue?) including:*

. . . . . . *favourable* . . . . . . (to/for/by?) unenviable
trouble[5] . . . . . *has occurred in* my heart . . . . .
you might have/be able . . . *young men* . . . . . . *came/*
come . . . present together . . . . . . *they are* (or *are*
they) *alive* or dead . . . . . . suffering . . . misfortunes
. . .[10] . . . bitter servitude . . . . . unavailing *words* . . .
. . . I shall *cease* (or *weep*) . . . you . . . . . . you
would establish/render . . . . . . *formerly* free . . .[15] . . .
you are . . . to me, *my child* . . . . . . you might give
thanks . . .

759a   *Some 95 lines are almost completely lost between F 758d*
and F 759a col. ii. Marginal notes in F 759a col. i show
that lines 1571–2 referred to Edonian women *and* Mount
Pangaeus *in a lyric passage (see Comm.). When the text*
resumes in col. ii, Hypsipyle is rejoicing with Amphiaraus
and her now-recognized sons:

(*Hyps.*)   . . . has driven <*me*> and my sons along a single
path, this way and that,[1580] swerving us first towards
fear, then towards gladness, but with time's passing
has shone out bright and fair.

Amph.   Lady, you have received the service that I owed you.
You were generous to me when I requested your
help,[1585] and I have repaid you generously with regard
to your sons. Take care of yourself, now; and you two
take care of your mother. And now farewell to you all;

ἀ]λλὰ Kannicht   13 π]αύσομαι E. Petersen, κλ]αύσομαι von Arnim   σὲ δ' ὡ[ς πρέπει
von Arnim   σὲ δ', ὦ [τέκνον E. Petersen   16 τέκ[νον von Arnim, E. Petersen τερ[read by
ed. pr.   17 σ]οφῶι ed. pr. τρ]οφῶι von Arnim   **759a** (~pp. 46–8 Bond; ~243–296
Diggle) P. Oxy. col. 27 (frs. 64.1+113+90), col. 28 (frs. 64.ii+91+115), col. 29 (fr. 64.iii)
1581 ἐπί χάριν ed. pr. ἐπί τε χάριν P   1585 ἠντόμην ed. pr. ἦν τότε P   1587 σώιζου
(corr. from σώιζε) δὲ δὴ σὺ τέκνα, σφὼ (corr. from σὼ) δὲ μήτερα P first hand τήνδε (above
line) P second hand

καὶ χαίρεθ'· ἡμε[ῖ]ς δ', ὥσπερ ὡρμήμεσθα δή,
στράτευμ' ἄγοντες ἥξομεν Θήβας ἔπι.

Ὑψ. εὐδαιμονοίης, ἄξιος γάρ, ὦ ξένε.   1590

ΕΥΝΗΟΣ εὐδαιμονοίης δῆτα· τῶν δὲ σῶν κακῶν,   70
     τάλαινα μῆτερ, θεῶν τις ὡς ἄπληστος ἦν.

Ὑψ. αἰαῖ, φυγὰς ἐμέθεν ἃς ἔφυγον,
     ὦ τέκνον, εἰ μάθοις, Λήμνου ποντίας,
     πολιὸν ὅτι πατέρος οὐκ ἔτεμον κάρα.   1595

Εὐν. ἦ γάρ σ' ἔταξαν πατέρα σὸν κατακτανεῖν;   75

Ὑψ. φόβος ἔχει με τῶν τότε κακῶν· ἰὼ
     τέκνον, οἷά τε Γοργάδες ἐν λέκτροις
     ἔκανον εὐνέτας.

Π   Εὐν. σὺ δ' ἐξέκλεψας πῶς πόδ' ὥστε μὴ θανεῖν;   **1600**

Ὑψ. ἀκτὰς βαρυβρόμους ἱκόμαν   80
     ἐπί τ' οἶδμα θαλάσσιον, ὀρνίθων
     ἔρημον κοίταν.

Εὐν. κἀκεῖθεν ἦλθες δεῦρο πῶς, τίνι στόλωι;

Ὑψ. ναῦται κώπαις   1605
     Ναύπλιον εἰς λιμένα   85
     ξενικὸν πόρον ἄγαγόν με
     δουλοσύ[ν]ας τ' ἐπέβασαν, ὦ τέκνον,
     ἐνθάδε νάϊον, μέλεον ἐμπολάν.

Εὐν. οἴμοι κακῶν σῶν.

Ὑψ.   μὴ στέν' ἐπ' εὐτυχίαισιν.   1610
     ἀλλὰ σὺ πῶς ἐτράφης ὅδε τ', ἐν τίνι   90
     χειρί, τέκνον; ὦ τέκνον,
     ἔνεπ' ἔνεπε ματρὶ σᾶι.

1590–2 speaker distribution by A. M. Dale (1590 Tho., 1591–2 Eun.: ed. pr.) οἱ Ὑψιπ. υἱοί ('Hypsipyle's sons') P   1593 φυγὰς ed. pr. φυγάς τ' P   1595 πολιὸν ὅτι πατέρος...κάρα ed. pr. (Wilamowitz) ὅτι πατέρος...πολιὸν κάρα P   1596–1634 paragraphi mark speaker-changes   1598 τέκνον ed. pr. (Wilamowitz) τέκνα P   1602 ὀρνίθων ed. pr. (Wilamowitz) ὀρνεεων P   1608 δουλοσύ[ν]ας Wecklein –α(ι) P   ὦ P ἰὼ Wilamowitz   1609 ἐνθάδε νάϊον von Arnim ἔνθα δὴ νάίων P   1611 ὅδε τ' ed. pr. ὁδε δ' (corr. from ὅτε δ') P

and we, as we set out to do, will lead our army on
and come to Thebes.

(Amphiaraus departs)

Hyps. Good fortune to you, for you deserve it, stranger.[1590]

EUNEOS Good fortune to you indeed. But you, poor mother—
how insatiably some god wished misfortunes on you!

Hyps. Alas, the flight I had to flee, my son, if you
only knew it, from sea-girt Lemnos, because I
did not sever my father's grey head![1595]

Eun. They really ordered you to kill your own father?

Hyps. I feel the terror of that time's evils—O, my
son, like Gorgons they were, slaying their
partners in their beds!

Eun. And you, how did you steal away and escape death?[1600]

Hyps. I made my way to the deep-resounding shore
and the swelling sea, the lonely resting-place
of birds.

Eun. And from there how did you come here, how
conveyed?

Hyps. Seafarers with their oars[1605] brought me on a
foreign voyage into Nauplion harbour and set
me into slavery, O, my son, in this land, ship-
borne, a pitiful piece of merchandise.

Eun. Ah me, your hardships —

Hyps. Don't grieve at what turned out well![1610] But
you, how were you raised, and your brother
her – who took you in hand, my son? O my
son, tell, tell this to your mother!

221

Εὐν. Ἀργώ με καὶ τόνδ' ἤγαγ' εἰς Κόλχων πόλιν.

Ὑψ. ἀπομαστίδιόν γ' ἐμῶν στέρνων.   1615

Εὐν. ἐπεὶ δ' Ἰάσων ἔθαν' ἐμός, μῆτερ, πατήρ —   95

Ὑψ. οἴμοι κακὰ λέγεις δάκρυά τ' ὄμμασιν,
     τέκνον, ἐμοῖς δίδως.

Εὐν. Ὀρφεύς με καὶ τόνδ' ἤγαγ' εἰς Θρήικης τόπον.

Ὑψ. τίνα πατέρι ποτὲ χάριν ἀθλίωι   1620
     τιθέμενος; ἔνεπέ μοι, τέκνον.   100

Εὐν. μοῦσάν με κιθάρας Ἀσιάδος διδάσκεται,
     τοῦτ[ο]ν δ' ἐς Ἄρεως ὅπλ' ἐκόσμησεν μάχης.

Ὑψ. δι' Αἰγαίου δὲ τίνα πόρον ἐμ[ό]λετ'
     ἀκτὰν Λημνίαν;   1625

Εὐν. Θόας [κ]ομίζει σὸς πατὴρ †δυοῖν τέκνω†.   105

Ὑψ. ἦ γὰ[ρ] σέσ[ω]τ[α]ι;

Εὐν.   Βα[κ]χ[ίου] γε μηχαναῖς.

fr. 64.ii + 91   Ὑψ.   [   ]βό[‥]ι πόνων
                        [   ] ι προσδοκία βιοτᾶς
                        [ἐ]πόρευσε ματρί παῖδα σῆι   1630
                        .[   ]ιε μοι   110

fr. 64.ii + 115   Εὐν. κει[   ] Θόαντος οἰνωπὸν βότρυν.

fr. 64.iii   *scattered traces of line-beginnings from the next
                  column, with speaker-notation* διονυϲ   *(col. 29)*
                  (Dionysos) at line 41 (~1673)

                  Lines ~1687–end lost   *(col. 30)*

1617 κακὰ ed. pr. (Murray) κακῶν P   1619 Θρήικης Björck Θράκ– P   1620 τίνα πατέρι χάριν ⟨τίνα⟩ ποτ' ἀθλίωι Willink (…ποτὲ ⟨τίνα⟩ χάριν… Murray)   1622 κιθάρας ed. pr. κίθαρις P   1624 δι' ⟨ἁλὸς⟩ Αἰγαίου Willink   1626 δυοῖν τέκνω P τέκνω δύο ed. pr. δισσὼ (or παιδὸς) τέκνω Wecklein τὼ σὼ τέκνω Collard   1630 παῖδασῆ (so accented) P, interpreted as παῖδας ἦ by ed. pr.

222

Eun. Argo took me and him to the Colchians' city.

Hyps. Yes, you were just lately weaned from my breast![1615]

Eun. And when, mother, my father Jason died —

Hyps. Ah me, you tell of evil events, and tears, my son, you bring to my eyes.

Eun. Orpheus took me and him to the region of Thrace.

Hyps. Doing what service for your unfortunate father?[1620] Tell me about it, my son!

Eun. He taught me the music of the Asian lyre, and trained my brother to Ares' martial arms.

Hyps. And what passage did you make across the Aegean to Lemnos' shore?[1625]

Eun. Thoas your father conveyed †the children of two†.

Hyps. Is he really *safe* then?

Eun. Yes, through *Bacchus'* contriving.

Hyps. . . . . (of/from?) hardships
. . . . expectation of life
. . . . brought (his?) son for your mother[1630]
. . . . (to/for?) me.

Eun. . . . . Thoas'(?) wine-dark grape-bunch.

The remaining text is almost entirely lost, except for the speaker-notation DIONYSUS forty-one lines later.

223

Unplaced Fragments

759b (– N)	*Numerous small fragments of P. Oxy.*
760	ἔξω γὰρ ὀργῆς πᾶς ἀνὴρ σοφώτερος.
760a (758 N)	κακοῖς τὸ κέρδος τῆς δίκης ὑπέρτερον.
761	ἄελπτον οὐδέν, πάντα δ᾽ ἐλπίζειν χρεών.
762	εὔφημα καὶ σᾶ καὶ κατεσφραγισμένα
763	ἆρ᾽ ἐκδιδάσκω τὸ σαφές;
765	οἰνάνθα τρέφει τὸν ἱερὸν βότρυν
765a (756 N)	περίβαλλ᾽, ὦ τέκνον, ὠλένας.
765b (755 N)	ἀνὰ τὸ δωδεκαμήχανον ἄστρον
765c (942 N)	*(Paraphrase)* οὐδὲν γὰρ ἀσφαλές ἐστι τῆς τύχης, ὡς Εὐριπίδης ἐν Ὑψιπύληι.
766	*(Lexicon-entry)* ἀναδρομαί· αὐξήσεις, βλαστήσεις· Εὐριπίδης Ἱκέτισιν, Ὑψιπύληι.
767	*(Lexicon-entry)* . . . ὅτι δὲ αἱ ἀρκτευόμεναι παρθένοι ἄρκτοι καλοῦνται, Εὐριπίδης Ὑψιπύληι, Ἀριστοφάνης Λημνίαις καὶ Λυσιστράτηι.
769	τῆς κροταλισάσης
(768 N, 770 N	*See app. crit. on 752h.15 and 752f.13 above)*

---

760 (p. 38 Bond) Stob. 3.20.31, attrib. Eur. *Hyps.*; mistakenly attrib. Eur. *Archelaus* in Stob. 3.20.12 through combination with F 259 and F adesp. 523; *Flor: Monac.* 150, unattrib. **760a** (758 N; p. 38 Bond) Stob. 3.10.26, attrib. Eur. *Hyps.* **761** (p. 51 Bond) Stob. 4.46.16, attrib. Eur. *Hyps.* **762** (p. 51 Bond) Ael. Dionys. 'σᾶ' (σ 1 Erbse), attrib. Eur. *Hyps.* (similarly Eustath. on Hom. *Il.* 13.773) εὔφημα: εὔσημα Valckenaer **763** (p. 51 Bond) Ar. *Frogs* 64 with Schol., attrib. Eur. *Hyps.* (see Comm.) **765** (p. 51 Bond) Schol. and Tzetz.

Unplaced Fragments

759b   *Numerous small fragments of P. Oxy.*

760   Every man is wiser when free from anger.

760a   Bad people think profit superior to fairness.

761   Nothing is beyond expectation; one should expect everything.

762   auspicious, safely kept and stamped with a seal

763   Am I informing you with clarity?

765   the vine-shoot nourishes its sacred cluster.

765a   Throw your arms around me, my child!

765b   up to(?) the star with twelve devices

765c   *Nothing in the realm of fortune is secure, as Euripides (says) in 'Hypsipyle'.*

766   *'Up-runnings': 'increasings', 'burgeonings': Euripides in 'Suppliant Women' and 'Hypsipyle'*

767   *... that girls playing the bear are called bears (is said by) Euripides in 'Hypsipyle' and Aristophanes in 'Women of Lemnos' and 'Lysistrata'.*

769   of her who sounded the castanets

on Ar. *Frogs* 1320, attrib. Eur. *Hyps.* οἰνάνθα Schol. –ας Tzetz. τρέφει Schol.ᴿ, Tzetz. –ειν Schol.ⱽ φέρει other Schol. **765a** (756 N; p. 51 Bond) Ar. *Frogs* 1322, attrib. by Schol. ᴱⱽᵇ³ to Eur. *Hyps.* περίβαλλ' Ar. some mss. περίβαλ' Ar. other mss., Tzetzes *ad loc.* **765b** (755 N; p. 51 Bond) Ar. *Frogs* 1327 (ἀνὰ ...δωδεκαμήχανον) with Schol. (ἀνὰ...ἄστρον), attrib. Eur. *Hyps.* (similarly Tzetzes on *Frogs* 1328, Suidas 'δωδεκαμήχ-ανον', δ 1442 Adler) ἄντρον variant or conjecture in Schol.ᶿ δωδεκάμηνον Mette **765c** (942 N; ~p. 48 Bond) John Lydus, *On Months* 4.7 (and similarly 4.100, without play-title) **766** (p. 51 Bond) Hesych. 'ἀναδρομαί' (α 4281 Latte). The attribution to Eur. *Suppl.* is false: see F 855. **767** (p. 51 Bond) Harpocrat. 'ἀρκτεῦσαι' (repeated more briefly in several other lexica) **769** (p. 52 Bond) Phot. 'κροταλίζειν' (κ 1111 Theodoridis), attrib. 'Euripides the comic poet(?) speaking about Hypsipyle'.

Commentary on *Hypsipyle*

T iiia Hypothesis. The text in P. Oxy. 2455 is supplemented by a similar but still more fragmentary text in P. Oxy. 3652. Luppe 1983 suggested that Turner's fr. 14 col. xvi belongs before his fr. 14 col. xv, so that its first three lines are the end of the *Hyps.* (not *Phaethon*) hypothesis, and *Hyps.* is followed by *Phrixus A* in both papyri. The texts do not coincide at any point but are probably interlaced (Luppe 1988). P. Oxy. 2455 fr. 15 was tentatively placed before fr. 14 col. xiv by Turner.

18. With Turner's supplement, '*putting the child <on the> ground*'. (Kannicht's reading would allow the same meaning with e.g. τὸν [παῖδα.)

19–21. With Turner's supplements, '*<In the meantime> he was mauled <by> a serpent. <Then>* **the sons who had been born** *<to Hypsipyle>...*'. The last phrase does not fit the trace before the lacuna according to van Rossum-Steenbeek, who suggests 'who were *<in adulthood>*'. Cropp's '**who had been born** *<to her>*' gives common genealogical phrasing as e.g. in Schol. *And.* 32, *Or.* 15, *Pho.* 53.   παρ[ῆσ]αν, **had arrived:** lit. 'were present'; for the sense cf. LSJ πάρειμι I.5, Dodds on *Bacc.* 5. It need not mean or imply 'came onto the stage' (Turner).

26. approved them: i.e., as contestants. This sense for ἐπη⟨ί⟩νεσ[ε]ν seems more appropriate than Turner's 'congratulated (on winning the contest)': see Introd., p. 176.

28–29. *as having killed <the> child on purpose*: cf. F 757.866–7, 'she claims I killed the child on purpose and plotted against her family'. *Andromache* and *Mel.D.* involve situations in which a wife sees an enslaved woman as a threat to her status or family.

29–30. With Turner's παραιτη]σαμ[ένου, '**But when Amphiaraus** had interceded....'
End. *prophesied*: probably referring to Dionysus' speech at the end of the play.

752, 752a, 752b. Prologue-speech of Hyps.: see Introd., p. 171.   F 758d (= P. Oxy. 852 frs. 61+82) was wrongly placed here by Barns and Bond: see Comm. note on F 758c–d.

752. The main source is one of the parodies of Eur.'s narrative play-openings in Ar. *Frogs* 1198ff., each capped by the phrase ληκύθιον ἀπώλεσεν ('lost his little oil-jar'). *Hyps.* seems to have opened with the heroine's genealogy (like *IT, Mel.S.*), starting from Hyps.'s grandfather Dionysus (see on F 752a below) and leading to her personal history.

The picture of Dionysus dancing with his bacchants on Mt. Parnassus is generic, e.g. *Ion* 714–7, *Bacc.* 306–8 (see Bond here, Cropp on *IT* 1243; in *Pal.* F 586 he dances on Mt. Ida). It is appropriate both to the context (introducing Dionysus' union with Ariadne) and thematically (Dionysus will influence the rescue of his granddaughter and will appear at the end of the play to organize a prosperous future for his descendants). The play's opening thus strikes a note of impending release from oppression and misfortune.

1–2. with thyrsuses and fawnskins: a zeugma since thyrsuses are handled, not worn; but the two items belong together as essentials of bacchic equipment, e.g. *Bacc.* 24–5 (cf. Dodds on *Bacc.* 113 (thyrsus); Burkert, *Greek Religion* 166).

752a. The lines missing between F 752 and F 752a, perhaps only one or two, will have mentioned Dionysus' union with Ariadne. P. Hamburg 118 comprises two frs. from what seems to have been a collection of Euripidean prologues. Fr. a has part of the prologue of *Archelaus* (F 228a n.). The sparse line-ends in fr. b col. i were identified with *Hec.* 28–44 by Barrett, the line-beginnings in col. ii with *Hyps.* by Lloyd-Jones in Bond 157–60. We appear to have a listing of four sons borne to Dionysus by Ariadne as in Apollod. *Epit.* 1.9 (number and names vary in other sources: see Lloyd-Jones; Gantz 116, 269). Hyps.'s father Thoas was presumably named last along with his island of Lemnos (line 10).

1–2. *Staphylos...Peparethos...*: Staphylos is a personification of the grape-bunch (σταφ-ύλη). The island Peparethos (modern Skopelos, next to Skiathos) was well known for its vines and wines (e.g. S. *Phil.* 547). Probably the two were named here as sons of Dionysus, though this identification of Peparethos is otherwise known only from Apollod. *Epit.* 1.9 (Staphylos is widely attested). Diod. 5.79 has Ariadne's uncle Rhadamanthys giving the island Peparethos to the man Staphylos (cf. Ps.-Scymnus 580–3), as well as Chios to Oenopion, Lemnos to Thoas, and several other such allocations.

3–6. The content of these lines and the reference to Hera remain unexplained.

7–8. Probably **a third** son of **Dionysus**, Oinopion ('son of wine-face'), to whom the god gave **Chios**: see *LIMC* VIII.i.920–2; A. Henrichs in *Papers on the Amasis Painter and his World* (Malibu, 1987), 108 with n. 88. Oinopion was credited with introducing viticulture and wine-making (*oinopoiia*): Theopompus *FGH* 115 F 276 (= Ath. 1.47, 26b), Diod. 5.79.1. Ion of Chios made Theseus his father (Ion F 29 *IEG*, cited by Plut. *Thes.* 20.2).

752b. Fragment-joins and placing in the lower half of col. 2 of the papyrus: Cockle 144. The wording suggests that the speaker is Hyps. rather than Euneos or Thoas (as Webster [1966, 85] preferred), and that we are near the end of her prologue-speech. It will have been lengthy; no extant Euripidean prologue-speech has over 90 lines, though the near-contemporary *Ion* and *Pho.* have just over 80. But Hyps. has a lot to relate.

1–2. [ἀπ]όπτολιν, *abroad/exiled*: this supplement is much more likely than e.g. φιλ]όπτολιν 'patriotic', νε]όπτολιν 'newly founded', ὁμ]όπτολιν 'of the same city'.]

5–7. Possibly Hyps. longs for Jason to return through the **Symplêgades** (the 'Clashing Rocks' at the entrance to the Black Sea through which he passed safely on his voyage to Colchis), bringing her **salvation** (or the **light** of freedom) and relief from the **yoke** of slavery. [In 7 Bond's αἰ]άζω would give something like '<*this*> **yoke** <*of slavery at which*> I wail'.]

752c. The fr. is cited by Galen to illustrate the use of ἀετός 'eagle' to mean **pediment** (with broad 'wingspan'). The attribution to Thoas (speaker of the next two frs.) addressing Euneos as they arrive at the temple is widely accepted, though von Arnim and Morel (8–9) suggested Hyps. trying to amuse the baby (in what would be a rather sophisticated manner). Cf. Orestes and Pylades viewing the temple of Artemis (*IT* 67ff.), the Chorus noticing the decoration of the Delphic temple (*Ion* 184ff.), Teucer noticing the architecture of Proteus' palace (*Hel.* 68ff.).

1. run your eyes up: the prefix in ἐξαμίλλησαι (Aor. Mid. Imper.) probably suggests 'move urgently (to this new sight)', rather than 'move away (from what you have been looking at)'; cf. Willink on *Or.* 38. At *Ion* 205 the Chorus 'impels' its eye (βλέφαρον διώκω) towards the temple-sculptures.   [These comparisons favour Hermann's Acc. κόρας over Musgrave's Dat. κόραις ('race *with* your eyes'). Galen's Nom. κόραι does not make sense.]

2. painted reliefs: τύπος should be a shape made by striking or stamping (τύπτω), but it came to denote bas-reliefs because of their similarity: see G. Roux, *REA* 63 (1961), 5–14, suggesting that the actual decoration of the archaic temple of Zeus at Nemea is evoked here. Recently found stonework from that temple includes 'many fragments... with a layer of plaster on which were painted designs suggest[ing] that the pediment was decorated with a painted scene': Miller, *AR* 47 (2001), 24.   [Valckenaer restored Galen's defective text with <ἐν αἰετ>οῖσι προσβλέπειν ('to take a look at...**on the pediment**') – a difficult use of the infinitive improved by Musgrave's participle προσβλέπων ('taking a look at...'). Nauck's <τ'>...πρόσβλεψον, '**and take a look at...**', convincingly supplies a third imperative in the sentence.]

752d–k. F 752d, f, g, h, k are all contained in P. Oxy. 852 fr. 1, which partially preserves columns 3–7 of the papyrus, including the end of the prologue, Hyps.'s monody, the choral parodos, and the beginning of Episode 1. F 752e and 752i are separate frs. of P. Oxy. placed by the first editors.

752d. Hyps. answers the door to the two young men, not recognizing them as her sons. (Menelaus is similarly met by a servant in *Hel.* 437ff., and so probably is Cresphontes in *Cresph.* F 448a. The exemplar for such scenes is the encounter between Clytemnestra and the disguised Orestes in A. *Cho.* 668–718.) Hypsipyle has brought the baby with her, calms him as she makes her entrance, and then addresses the young men. She must have been speaking for at least three lines before our text begins; no speaker-changes are indicated in the blank papyrus-margin above.

2. The supplements in the App. would give '<*Father*> **will come** <*with not a few*> *toys*' (Wecklein) or '<*Your father*> will come <*with many*> *toys*' (Schmidt). Both seem a little long for the first space and the idea is quaint, but mention of Lycurgus here and in 11 would emphasize his absence from Nemea which leads to Hyps.'s dealings with Amphiaraus and makes Eurydice central in the reaction to the baby's death.

5. O blessed she...: an obvious but effective dramatic irony as Hyps. unknowingly refers to herself, like Creusa meeting Ion (*Ion* 308, 324), Iphigenia meeting Orestes (*IT* 472–5). Remarking on a person's good fortune (*makarismos*) was a conventional form of congratulation and could be used as a tactful and ingratiating compliment, e.g. by Odysseus in his embarrassing meeting with Nausicaa, Hom. *Od.* 6.154–5. Hyps.'s remark is not quite like this but rather (like Creusa's and Iphigenia's) an unguarded reaction to her first sight of her grown-up sons, highlighting the pathos of the situation. **whoever she was:** such phrases are 'almost a formula in pre-recognition scenes' (Bond: cf. *Alc.* 1062, *IT* 340–1, 483, 628, *Ion* 238, 324, 564, Menand. *Epitr.* 310; also in paraphrase, *Phil.* F 789d(6)).

7. **We need...woman:** Thoas replies politely but curtly, thinking he is addressing an underling (like Orestes at S. *El.* 1106–7).

8. **bed down:** αὐλίζειν/–εσθαι and its compounds suggest rough and temporary accommodation (see Bond).

9. **[and will not be a nuisance:** Diggle's supplement gives better sense and fit than the first editors' 'how could we be a nuisance'?]

10. **you'll stay completely undisturbed:** lit. 'your (situation) will stay as it is'. [Cockle saw that P has ἔχεις 'you hold/you are' rather than ἔχει 'it is'. Diggle and Kannicht also print it, but it is easier to take τὸ σὸν as subject of both ἔχει and μενεῖ.]

11. **has no men in charge:** lit. 'is masterless of males'. Bond compares *Bacc.* 1305 ἄτεκνος ἀρσένων παίδων 'childless of male children, *El.* 1130 ἀγείτων...φίλων 'neighbourless of friends', etc. See also KG 1.401–2.

752e. Placing: Cockle 144. Little remains, but the content is fairly clear. The first editors and von Arnim proposed hypothetical supplements for 4–5, Page for all of 2–7.

2–3. Lycurgus...his wife...: the papyrus does not indicate a speaker-change before line 2, so Hyps. spoke at least three lines here, presumably explaining Lycurgus' absence and Eurydice's presence in the house.

4–5. not...in the guest-quarters (etc.): Thoas tactfully suggests that he and his brother should lodge elsewhere, like Heracles on learning of Alcestis' death, *Alc.* 538. The first editors' suggestion for line 5 (App.) is '**but to <***some other house***>...**'.

6–9. Probably Hyps. presses the twins to accept hospitality, as Clytemnestra presses the seemingly reluctant Orestes in A. *Cho.* 707–15 and the Paedagogus in S. *El.* 799–803; cf. Admetus with Heracles, *Alc.* 539–50. But Hyps. is a slave and presumably encourages them to enter and seek hospitality from Eurydice rather than offering it herself. Hypoth. 22–3, 25–6 indicates that they agreed. The remains of the dialogue seem to reflect this (cf. Bond 11–12, 61): Thoas and Euneos should **by no means** leave (cf. *Alc.* 538–9, 545, S. *El.* 798–9); they are welcome **guests** and the house is **always** hospitable (cf. *Alc.* 566–7, *Cho.* 707–8, S. *El.* 800–1); they should go **into** the house without further ado (cf. *Alc.* 541, 546, *Cho.* 712, S. *El.* 802). Presumably they were lodged in the house's guest-quarters like Heracles in *Alc.* and Cresphontes in *Cresph.* (F 456 n.), and were thus available to intervene later. Hyps. herself presumably stayed outside with the baby, to be joined by the Chorus shortly. The gap of fewer than thirty lines between the end of F 752e and the start of F 752f will have contained this conclusion and the beginning of Hyps.'s song.

Monody and Parodos (752f, 752g, 752h.1–9). Hyps.'s song probably began within a few lines of the end of F 752e and contained about 35–40 lines of which we have the last fourteen. It is followed by her sung exchange with the arriving Chorus, of close to 120 lines. This general pattern is shared with the monody/parodos sequences of Soph. and Eur. *Electra, Androm.* (F 114–22), *Helen* and *Ion,* though shapes and proportions vary; in *IT* Iphigenia responds to the Chorus's lyric anapaests without a preceding monody. The effect of the whole is to bring the heroine's history, predicament and emotional state into perspective. The main tropes in *Hyps.* recur elsewhere: slave's or peasant's work cheerfully or sorely borne (*Ion*, E. *El.*); obsession with the past (E. *El.*, S. *El.*), social activity offered and rejected (E. *El.*); mythical or gnomic consolations offered and rejected (E. *El.*, S. *El.*); insistence on the uniqueness of the heroine's plight and her isolation (E. *El.*, S. *El.*, *Hel.*, *Androm.* F 115-6). The style is that of the 'New Music' of which Eur. was a leading practitioner, characterized by freedom and variety of form and emotional expression, especially through female voices, and mimetic musical performance such as Hyps.'s castanet-song: cf. E. Csapo, *ICS* 24/25 (1999/2000), 399-426.

The Chorus of friendly local women has come inviting Hyps. to join their excursion to view the Argive army, like the chorus of *El.* inviting Electra to the festival of Hera, or of *IA* visiting the shore to view the Achaean army and fleet. Their first question (F 752f.15-18) hardly proves, as Bond suggests, that Hyps. is not holding the baby during this sequence, but neither the Chorus nor Amphiaraus seems to notice him and it is unlikely that she would have held him right through the parodos and first episode. Probably she has put him down to rest during the earlier part of her monody after bringing him out when she answered the door to Thoas and Euneos. If so, there was a visible foreshadowing of her fatally leaving him near the spring later on.

F 752f.15ff. are surely the Chorus's first words, as is generally assumed. The thirty or so lines lost between F 752e and 752f give little room for a choral utterance as well as the lost end of the prologue-scene and beginning of Hyps.'s song; and in F 752f.1-14 Hyps. is still addressing the baby, not the Chorus. In favour of a previous choral utterance J. Diggle, *Eikasmos* 6 (1995), 40 cites Willink's observation that the extant opening lines contain 'not a hint of self-address'. Self-address or collective conversation amongst an arriving chorus is in fact far from universal (it occurs in e.g. *Alc.*, *Hcld.*, *Hipp.*, *HF*, *Or.*, *Ion*, *Cresph.*). The absence of self-*reference*, i.e. 1st-person statements explaining the chorus's identity and arrival or the like, is however notable: cf. S. *El.* 121ff., where a sympathetic chorus addresses Electra almost exclusively. There may have been something identifying the Chorus in the lost beginning of Hyps.'s response, like *Hel.* 191-2, S. *Aj.* 210-2, *Trach.* 140-1, *El.* 129-30.

The lyric sequence comprises Hyps.'s song to the baby, then a pair of exchanges in which she responds to the Chorus. The two choral sections are clearly in strophic responsion. Grenfell and Hunt (84-5) followed Wilamowitz in identifying responsion between Hyps.'s monody and her first response to the Chorus (the metre of the last few lines of each can be closely matched: F 752f.9-14 ~ 752g.11-17). Most editors have agreed, but this muddles the monody with the parodos and requires a series of awkward word-breaks between lines in the 'antistrophe'. Moreover, responsion is much less evident in the preceding lines (cf. e.g. Bond 62). The last four lines of the 'antistrophe' are in fact more similar to the last four of Hyps.'s third sequence (F 752h.6-9), yet there is no responsion to be seen in the preceding lines there. As Diggle argues (above, 39-40), we should infer that Hyps.'s monody and her two responses to the Chorus were loosely but not exactly matched (cf. *IT* 123-235). It is also possible, though perhaps not likely, that the monody itself was strophic with internal responsion like *El.* 112-66, *Ion* 112-43.

METRE. End of monody (F 752f.1-14): aeolic cola, then iambic dimeter (8) leading to a dactylic sequence with ithyphallic clausula (9-14). Choral strophe and antistrophe (F 752f.15-39, F 752g.18-37): again aeolic (15-33 ~ 18-36), then dactylic. Hypsipyle's first response (F 752g.1–17): largely aeolic in 2–9, then dactylic (10–11) and dactylo-anapaestic with ithyphallic clausula (12–17). Hypsipyle's second response (F 752h.1–9) seems to have ionic (2–4), trochaic (5), and again dactylo-anapaestic with ithyphallic clausula (6–9).

752f.3–4. like a mirror's...gleam: probably referring to the child himself (catching attention like a glinting mirror?) or some feature of him (Bond suggested his bright eyes). In *Hec.* 925 the sense of the 'golden mirror's infinite gleamings' (χρυσέων ἐνόπτρων...ἀτέρμονας...αὐγάς) is itself uncertain (see Collard there). [λευκ]οφαῆ (App.) would give 'bright-lighted gleam' (the adj. is used of glistening sand in *IA* 1054), but the supplement is not certain. Eur. invented compounds with –φαής freely: see Kannicht's app. and Diggle, *Euripidea* 350 = *SIFC* 7 (1989), 204. Collard with ref. to *Hec.* 925 suggests χρυσ]οφαῆ 'gold-bright', an adj. which Eur. applies to the gods Helios (*Hec.* 636) and Eros (*Hipp.* 1275).]

5–7. [The syntax and incomplete subjunctive verb in 6 are difficult. The first editors' μνήσωμαι is usually printed and should mean 'I may solicit, seek', but it is hard to supply the two syllables that should precede it: see Bond (comm.) and Kannicht's app.]

8. the sound of castanets: Hyps. uses castanets or clappers to amuse the baby and improvise an accompaniment to her song. The scholia to Ar. *Frogs* identify an allusion to this when Ar.'s Aeschylus summons a music-girl playing *ostraka* (clappers made from pot-sherds) to accompany a parody of Euripidean song: *Frogs* 1305–07, 'Where's that female who bangs away with the *ostraka*? Come on, Euripidean Muse – you're the right accompaniment for these songs of his!' See also below on F 769.

9–11. These are not Lemnian songs (etc.): Hys. must now sing lullabies for the baby she cares for, not the weaving-songs she once sang in her home in Lemnos. Weaving is emblematic of women's lives: at *Tro.* 199–200 weaving in captivity sums up the enslavement of the women of Troy. **songs for relieving the labour:** παραμύθια are 'consolations, alleviations'. In *Ion* 196–7 the Chorus-women are used to telling each other mythical tales as they weave. **weft-thread and web-stretching shuttle:** the terms sum up the activity of weaving; cf. *Bacc.* 118 'away from our looms (ἱστῶν) and shuttles (κερκίδων)'. On a vertical loom the shuttle carries the spooled weft-thread back and forth through the warp-thread, stretching it as it passes through. In Ar. *Frogs* 1315–16 (part of a parodied 'Euripidean' song combining distorted reminiscences of *IT* 1089ff., *El.* 435ff., and several bits of *Hyps.*: cf. F 765–765b; E. Borthwick, *Phoenix* 48 [1994], 29–37), ἱστότονα πηνίσματα, κερκίδος ἀοιδοῦ μελέτας seem to be 'web-stretching threadings, work of the singing shuttle': *kerkis* 'sings' as it makes contact with the warp-thread (cf. Dover on *Frogs* 1315–16). The *kerkis* has also been identified as a 'pin-beater', used for beating the weft into place with a twanging noise (cf. G. Crowfoot, *ABSA* 37 [1936/7], 36–47 at 44–5; E. Barber, *Prehistoric Textiles* [Princeton, 1991], 269–74); but the shuttle is an apter emblem of the weaver's activity. **to voice:** the verb κρέκειν is apt here since it could denote both weaving and the making of musical noises including singing. It may have meant primarily something like 'strum', with ref. to the vibrations caused by the *kerkis* (see above and esp. Barber 273–4; on the semantic development, Dunbar on Ar. *Birds* 682–3). [θέλει, **wants:**

P's μέλει 'is concerned (for me to sing)' is awkward, the personal use of μέλω (active) being rare and not otherwise known with Acc. + Inf. following.]

15–18. What are you doing…as a slave-woman does: the question draws attention to Hyps.'s humble situation in contrast with her romantic royal past.

21. penteconter: the fifty-oared naval vessel of the Archaic period typically ascribed to heroic adventurers (cf. Cropp on *IT* 1124).

22. sacred: Phrixus, after being carried from Thessaly to Colchis by the gold-fleeced ram, sacrificed the ram to Zeus Phyxios ('Protector of Fugitives') and gave the fleece to King Aietes, who hung it in a grove sacred to Ares (Apollod. 1.83.5, Schol. Pind. *Pyth.* 4.431).   **gold-fleeced hide:** Cockle argues that *TrGF* adesp. F 37a τὸ χρυσόμαλλον Αἰήτου δέρος, 'Aietes' gold-fleeced hide', recalls this phrase, but χρυσόμαλλον δέρος is quite commonly used of the Golden Fleece.

24. keeps watch: the present tense φρουρεῖ does not imply that the serpent is still doing this; rather, it makes the description vividly pictorial.

26. [Lemnos: P's original reading was 'island', perhaps correctly since identifications by name do sometimes intrude into texts (Diggle, *Euripidea* 459 n. 79).]

27–8. which the Aegean encircles (etc.): lit. 'encircling which (the) Aegean, wave-beating, resounds.' For ἐλίσσω 'encircle' cf. *Or.* 358, 444, *Pho.* 711 (Bond). On Eur.'s liking for the verb (mocked by Aristophanes) see Borthwick (above, 9–11 n.), 30.

29. [δεῦρο †ταν†, Come now †to the†…: the meaningless ταν could be replaced by δ' ἂν (Dodds) or in full δ' ἀνὰ (Collard): 'But (rather than dwelling on the past) come now to…'. The choice would depend on the scansion of θεὸς in the corresponding line of the antistrophe, F 752g.32: see note there.]

30–1. *All of* the Argive plain *is flashing* (etc.): epic phrasing very like Hom. *Il.* 20.156 (the armies before Troy), E. *Pho.* 110–1 (the Seven before Thebes); cf. *Arch.* F 229 (n.).   [The statement is a little unrealistic, as if the women could survey the Argive plain from Nemea. Von Arnim's 'Αργείων would give 'All of the plain (hereabouts) is flashing with the Argives' armaments', and would be closer to the parallels cited above. But in S. *El.* 1–9 Orestes and his tutor can view the Argive agora and the Heraion from Mycenae.]

32–3. Against the bastion(?) built by (lit. 'work of') **Amphion's lyre:** Amphion was said to have used his lyre-music to collect the rocks which formed the citadel of Thebes (cf. *Antiope* F 223.88–95 (n.)). The reference signals that the Theban citadel will resist the Argive attack. The power of music is thematic in *Hyps.* also (Introd., p. 182).   [The text is problematic as ἔρυμα 'defence/bastion' (cf. *Antiope* F 223.89) sits awkwardly within the phrase 'work of the Amphionian lyre'. The first editors and some others add χερός at the end of 33 to give 'Against the lyre-built bastion, work of Amphion's hand', but this would make line 33 longer than the corresponding line in the antistrophe (F 752g.36) which certainly ends with σέθεν and must have contained eight syllables, not ten. 'Work of the Amphionian lyre' is a convincing phrase and is probably reflected by Hesychius (see App.). Cf. *Pho.* 824, the fortress of Thebes built 'by the Amphionian lyre' (τᾶς 'Αμφιονίας…λύρας ὕπο).]

34. swift-footed Adrastus…: Schmidt's supplement (App.) gives 'leads his army'.

35. [ὅ[ς] (or ὁ [δ']) ἐκάλεσε μένο[ς (**who has summoned the might**...) gives inscrutable
metre with six or seven successive short syllables. Diggle's ὃς κάλεσεν (with unaug-
mented aorist in epic style) plausibly offers dactylic rhythm as in the following lines.]
36. intricate devices: presumably the famous shield-devices (σήματα) of the Seven,
memorably described in A. *Sept.* 387–90, 432–4, etc.   [Wilamowitz's σάγματα would
be 'carrying-cases' for shields etc. (cf. Ar. *Ach.* 574) – perhaps attractive (cf. *And.*
617), but hardly eye-catching or significant enough for this context.]
38. single-treading: the word μονοβάμων occurs only once elsewhere, for a 'one-footed'
metrical measure (*Anth. Pal.* 15.27.5). Eur. has δίβαμος 'two-legged' (*Cret.* F 472bc
32; cf. *Rhes.* 216), τετραβάμων 'four-legged' (*El.* 476, *Tro.* 516, *Hel.* 376, *Pho.* 808)
and perhaps 'four-horsed' (*Pho.* 792, corrupt). Here one-horsed chariots (Morel 38) or
individual riding-horses (like μονάμπυκας in *Alc.* 428 or μονίππους in Xen. *Cyr.*
6.4.1: Bond) would fit well with the next line.
39. lifting... (*from?*) *the ground...*: this is the sense with von Arnim's Gen. χθ[ονός:
perhaps horses raising dust (Morel compared S. *Ant.* 417) or lifting their hooves high.
[The Ionic-Epic forms ἀείρω etc. are confined to lyrics in tragedy: cf. *Alc.* 450, *El.*
873, *Tro.* 546, *Pha.* 81, 111. Attic αἰρόμενοι seems needed at the start of a dactylic
line, unless there was a line-break ἀλειρόμενοι.]

752g. Hyps. will not be distracted from the past by talk of the Argive army, and dwells on
her recollections of the Argo's first arrival at Lemnos. The Chorus then tries another kind
of consolation, reminding her of the princesses Europa and Io who also suffered the pains
of exile but were cared for by gods who loved them and had happy destinies and
distinguished children. They predict Hyps.'s rescue by her grandfather Dionysus and
indirectly foreshadow her reunion with her sons and their bright future.
    METRE. See general note on Monody and Parodos above.
2–14. Part of a word-picture of the Argo as Hyps. first saw her arriving at Lemnos. The
chorus of *IT* similarly sketches Orestes' ship sailing to and from the land of the
Taurians, *IT* 407–38, 1123–37.
2. Thracian: probably the Thracian Sea which Argo crossed from Thessaly to Lemnos.
3–5. Peleus leaps, or prepares to leap, from ship to shore in order to **fasten** the Argo's
stern-cables (cf. Hom. *Od.* 9.137, E. *Med.* 770, *HF* 478).
4. the calmly lapping water: lit. 'the calm's swell', rising and falling at the shore-line.
6–8. The nymph **Aegina**, daughter of the Boeotian river Asopus and identified with the
island of Aegina, was Peleus' grandmother, his father Aeacus being one of her sons by
Zeus (Gantz 220, 814, and on Peleus 222–32). The ἐτέκνωσε (**brought forth**) may
then suggest 'engendered' rather than 'bore' (cf. Morel 39, LSJ τεκνόω II).   [Πηλέα,
though subject of the sentence, is 'inversely attracted' into the Acc. case of the rel.
pron. τὸν: cf. e.g. *Bacc.* 1330–2, S. *Trach.* 283–5, *El.* 160; KG II.413–4.]
8–14. and by the mast (etc.): Orpheus gives rhythmic **commands to the rowers** with
his lyre-music. In real life these were given on the more strident *aulos* (e.g. *IT* 1125–7;
Kannicht on *Hel.* 1575–6). Orpheus is already associated with the Argonauts in a
metope from the Sicyonian treasury at Delphi, c. 570 B.C. (*LIMC* 'Orpheus' no. 6 =
'Argonautai' no. 2); in 5th C. literature cf. Pind. *Pyth.* 4.176–7 (but Pindar's contemp-

orary Pherecydes could deny the association, *FGH* 3 F 26) and later e.g. Ap. Rhod. 1.536–41, Stat. *Theb.* 5.340–5 (a similar description by Hyps. of this scene): see further Gantz 343–5. Orpheus will be important in the play as guardian of Euneos and Thoas after Jason's death and as Euneos' music-teacher (F 759a.1616–23): see Introd., pp. 171, 182; Burkert 1994.

9–10. Asian plaint: i.e. exotic and elaborate (cf. Cropp on *IT* 179–80 and *Erec.* F 369d): thus Orpheus teaches Euneos 'the music of the Asian lyre', F 759a.1622. In *Cyc.* 443–4 'music of the Asian lyre' is Dionysiac music. **['Ασιάδ' ἔλεγον ἰήιον, a mournful Asian plaint:** text and sense are a little uncertain, though the change from P's ἔλεγεν 'told' to ἔλεγον **plaint** (Wilamowitz) and the deletion of the metrically awkward 'Ορφέως as a gloss (A. Mette) are unproblematic. P's 'Ασιὰς (Nom.) gives 'Thracian Asian kithara', i.e. the Thracian Orpheus' Asian-style kithara (cf. F 759a.1622). For Beazley's **'Ασιάδ'** giving **Asian plaint** see Bond here. For P's phrasing Kannicht compares e.g. the 'Phoenician Sidonian ship' of *Hel.* 1451–2 (but the word-order in our passage is harder), and he understands ἔλεγον ἰήιον as the Argonauts' paean-song (ἰὴ παιάν) of thanks for their landfall (but the purpose of the music is to set the rowers' rhythm, 11–12).]

16. Danaans': i.e. Argives', cf. F 752h.36, *Arch.* F 228.6–8 with Comm.   **labours:** heroic undertakings (πόνοι as e.g. *HF* 22, 357, 575, Thuc. 1.123.1).

18. From learned tellers I have heard: the Chorus appeals to myth for precedents, as in *Alc.* 962–4, *Med.* 1282–3 and other such formulae discussed by Bond (but they are not necessarily self-conscious or apologetic as Bond suggests).

19–23. leaving her city (etc.): Europa was abducted from the seashore at Tyre by Zeus, who in the form of a bull carried her across the sea to Crete. Tradition made her the daughter either of **Phoenix** (cf. Hom. *Il.* 14.321, Hes. F 140, 141.7, Bacchyl. 17.31, perhaps Eur. *Cret.* F 472.1) or of Agenor, and either sister or half-sister of Cadmus who also migrated from Tyre to become the founder of Thebes: cf. Collard on *Cret.* F 472.1, Gantz 208–10.   **[21. Φοίνικος, Phoenix's:** West's correction (*BICS* 30 [1983], 77) of P's Φοινίκας, Gen. Sing. with πόλιν etc.,' her city…in Phoenicia' (kept by Kannicht).]

23. Crete where Zeus was raised: in Hesiod's account the baby Zeus was hidden by his mother Rhea in a cave near Lyktos in Crete (more commonly a cave on Mt. Ida) to save him from the jealousy of his father Cronus, who had already consumed all his siblings; he thus grew up to overthrow his father: cf. Hes. *Theog.* 459–84. See West on *Theog.* 477 (topography), Gantz 41–2 (other sources).

24. Kourêtes: young male initiates (*kouroi*) in the Cretan cult of Zeus (cf. *Cret.* F 472.14 (n.)), whose mythical counterparts were supposed to have protected the boy (*kouros*) Zeus with the martial noise of their clashing cymbals etc. See Frazer on Apollod. 1.1.7; Burkert, *Greek Religion* 127, 173, 261–2, 280; Gantz 42.

25–6. her threefold harvest of children: Europa's sons Minos, Rhadamanthys, Sarpedon: so e.g. Hes. F 141.11–14 (as usually restored), Aesch. F 99.7–16, Bacchyl. F 10 (but Homer counts only the first two, *Il.* 14.322, and makes Sarpedon a Lycian). Childbearing is often imaged as agricultural production, e.g. Aesch. F 99.7–11, S. *Ant.*

569, E. *Med.* 1280. Bond notes that Eur. may have been evoking the standard Athenian marriage formula, 'for the sowing/harvesting of legitimate children'.

28–31. And another princess (etc.): Io, daughter of Inachus of Argos, was turned into a cow either by Hera to conceal her from her lover Zeus, or by Zeus to conceal her from Hera. She wandered the earth suffering various afflictions until in Egypt Zeus restored her human form and impregnated her with a son Epaphus. His descendants included Danaus who with his daughters settled at Argos. The story was told in the lost Hesiodic *Catalogue of Women* and *Aegimius* (see Hes. F 124–6, 294, 296) and S. *Inachus* (F 269a–295). The main extant sources (with variances) are A. *Supp.* 40–7, 291–324, 531–89, *PV* 561–886, Bacchyl. 19, cf. Apollod. 2.1.3–4; Gantz 199–203. Since Io's story is paired with Europa's as a source of consolation for Hypsipyle, it must be her release and happy destiny as mother of Epaphus that are mentioned.

29. by *her mating*: Bond's λέκ]τρωι gives an apt ref. to Io's mating with Zeus, although in Aeschylus at least she was impregnated simply by the touch of his hand.

30–1. altered <*her form's?*> *horn*-bearing affliction: i.e. reverted from cow-form to human form. The damage in line 30 and ambiguity of the word ἀμφὶς make text and sense doubtful. For **altered** cf. LSJ ἀμείβω A.4. [The damaged letter in 30 looks much more like φ than ρ. The translation makes Diggle's tentative μορ]φᾶς depend on κερ]ασφόρον ἄταν, and ἀμφὶς adverbial with ἀμεῖψαι ('changed it around'). But ἀμφὶς might belong with a preceding Gen. (thus ed. pr.'s πατ]ρᾶς ἀμφὶς, 'apart/far from her homeland').]

31. κερ]ασφόρον *horn*-bearing: cf. *Pho.* 248 (also Io).

32. [θεὸς is probably one syllable ('synizesis') rather than two: see L. Battezzato, *BICS* 44 (2000), 53 n. 55. Cf. on F 752f.29 above.]

33. στέρξει]ς (Radermacher) fits well at the beginning: '<*you will*> surely <*be content*>, **dear friend, <*with*> moderation**' (i.e., you will not be too discouraged).

34–7. Perhaps roughly: '<*and hope*> **will** <*not*> **desert you** <*that*> **your father's father** (i.e. Dionysus) <*will yet rescue you*>. He has <*concern*> **for you**, <*and soon enough*> **will come swift-voyaging after you**'. See ed. pr. for a bold reconstruction of the Greek on these lines, largely by Wilamowitz.

752h. METRE. 1–9: see general note on the Monody and Parodos above. 10–14: recitative anapaests as often for choral introductions of a new episode.

1–2. ...once brought...: this must be the end of a mythological example of a heroine who, like Procris (3–5), received appropriate lamentation after disaster or death.

3–5. Procris: a daughter of Erectheus of Athens, accidentally killed by her husband Cephalus as she secretly watched him hunting or (as here, cf. Apollod. 3.15.1) hunted with him. Details of their story vary considerably (cf. Gantz 245–6). The incompleteness of the text makes the syntax of 3–5 and the subject of **lamented** uncertain.

6–8. what grieving cry or song (etc.): three kinds of lamentation are identified in an emotive 'ascending tricolon'. Perplexed staccato questioning is characteristic of overwrought laments, e.g. *Pho.* 1509–11 (similar tricolon), 1498–1501 and 1515–18 (cries for assistance in expressing grief), *HF* 1025–7 and *Hel.* 165–6 (choosing between ways of expressing grief). The third and weightiest item, **lyre's music...amidst my tears**, is an elaborate song sung to the lyre. **Calliope** ('Lovely-voice') is the muse of song, and κιθάρας μοῦσα is lit. 'lyre's muse', so the inspired artistic character of this third item is emphasized in contrast with the first two. There is an irony in Hyps.'s conviction that she will get no consolation from music: Orpheus the musician (above, F 752g.8–14) has in fact prepared her sons to rescue her. Calliope is recorded as Orpheus' mother (e.g. Timoth. F 791.221–4, Ap. Rhod. 1.24–6, Asclepiad. Trag. *FGH* 12 F 8). [**6.** P's marginal κιθάρι[, i.e. κιθάρι[σμα 'lyre-playing' (Wilamowitz), is not a variant but a gloss explaining κιθάρας μοῦσα.]

9. will come to mourn my troubles: in the Greek simply 'would come to (my) troubles'. The different kinds of lamentation are thought of as joining Hyps. in expressing her grief (cf. previous n.). As Bond says, this interpretation seems preferable to 'What grieving cry or song (etc.) could come up to the level of (i.e. adequately express) my troubles?' But Hyps.'s point is not, I think, that she feels bereft of musical support (Bond) but that she finds it hard to choose the appropriate kind.

11. what business…: lit. 'In commerce of what do I see these newcoming strangers….'

12–13. distinctively dressed in Dorian clothing: lit. 'distinct in Dorian clothing-attire'. Distinctions of national or regional clothing are sometimes significant in tragedy (cf. *Hcld.* 130, *Hec.* 734–5, *IT* 246–7, A. *Supp.* 234–7). The sleeveless knee-length chiton worn by Amph. was fashionable in democratic Athens and regarded as simple and egalitarian by contrast with traditional Ionian dress. On the stage it will have made a contrast with the elaborate 'Asiatic' costuming of most leading tragic characters, and it is reflected in the vase-paintings (cf. Introd., p. 180). On the nuances of 'Dorian dress' in Athenian life and tragedy see L. Battezzato, *ICS* 24/25 (1999/2000), 343–62, esp. 351–3 on *Hyps.* (Amph.'s dress 'the visual counterpart of his moral qualities').

15–19. How hateful…are absences (etc.): Amph. behaves with courteous reserve, first addressing Hyps. indirectly and using generalities to gain her sympathy and lead up to his direct request for information. [**15. absences from home:** P's 'untended areas' goes badly with 'untended fields' (17). Wilamowitz (in ed. pr.) replaced it on the basis of a lexicographic attribution of the word ἐκδημία to this play (see App.).]

18–19. homeless, unguided, not knowing (lit. 'having uncertainty')…: another emotive 'ascending tricolon', the phrasing compounded by successive negative prefixes (ἄ–, ἀν–, ἀ– : see Bond for many examples). [In P the Nom. ἄπολις ἀνερμήνευτος 'homeless, unguided' were miscopied as Acc. forms agreeing with ἀπορίαν 'uncertainty'; then the acc. form ἄπολιν was miscopied as ἄποιν(α), which in turn was miscorrected to ἄπορον 'perplexed'.]

22–3. whether a slave, or whether you are no slave (lit. 'have a non-slave body'): like Thoas at F 752d.7, Amph. first takes Hyps. to be an attendant at the palace door, but her appearance and bearing make him think again (cf. Stat. *Theb.* 4.748–52).

25. Phlius' country: the town of Phlius lay 7 km. NW of Nemea in the Asopus valley. Both Phlius and Cleonae (7 km. E. of Nemea in the next valley) had an interest in the governance of the sanctuary.

27. Chosen: Greek priests were often appointed by their communities by election or lot, with due regard to their acceptability to the gods, cf. e.g. *Ion* 1323; Burkert, *Greek Religion* 96. **all Asopia:** the river Asopus flows from Lake Stymphalus *via* Phlius and Sicyon into the Corinthian Gulf.   [P's meaningless εὑρεθεὶς 'Ασωπία(ι) is a simple miscopying.]

28. temple-keeper: lit. 'key-holder', the priest being responsible for the security of the temple and its possessions. Cf. *IT* 130–1 with Cropp's note.

29. *running* **water** is suitably pure for ritual use: cf. e.g. *El.* 793–4, S. *OC* 469, 1598; Burkert, *Greek Religion* 77–8.

30. libation: the word χέρ-νιψ ('hand-wash') properly denotes lustral water but is sometimes used loosely for libations: see Garvie on A. *Cho.* 129. So also presumably below, F 755a frs. 36+.6, F 757.801.   [*pure*: both ὅ[σιον] (Stengel, Kannicht) and ὅ[διον] 'for our journey' (Murray in ed. pr. and e.g. Bond, Cockle, Diggle) fit the context, but it is emphasis on the water's purity that leads to the explanation in the next two lines. Amph. will explain the purpose of the libations in 35–6.]

31. runnels of stagnant water: the water seeps from underground springs through the marshy plain, and has been made muddier by the Argive army. Recent excavations show that there is no natural river-channel through the Nemea valley; in the classical period the plain was marshy and a dependable natural supply of drinking-water lacking (S. Miller, *AR* 45 [1999], 25–6; 47 [2001], 24; 48 [2002], 21–2); hence the importance of the isolated spring to which Hyps. will guide the Argives.   [νάματα, **runnels:** for the sense see Bond's note and (cited there) Wilamowitz on *HF* 625.   διειπετῆ, **clear:** the sense 'rain-fed', supposedly derived from the word's etymological sense 'sky-fallen', is not appropriate here: on the word's meanings see Chantraine, *Dict. Etym.* 'διιπετής'.]

35. As we are crossing the *border*: such transitional sacrifices, which might abort the expedition if they produced bad omens, were called *diabatêria*: cf. Thuc. 5.54.2, 5.55.3, 5.116.1, Xen *Hell.* 3.4.3, 3.5.7 etc.

36. to sacrifice for our Danaid *army*: προθῦσαι, with προ- governing the Gen. στρατοῦ, must mean 'sacrifice on behalf of' (so e.g. *Ion* 805, *Erec.* F 370.66; cf. below, F 757.893), but the basic sense 'sacrifice before (the campaign)' can be felt as well: cf. Ar. *Thesm.* 38. On the development of the verb's meaning see J. Casabona, *Recherches sur le vocabulaire des sacrifices en grec* (Aix-en-Provence, 1966), 103–8; cf. J. Mikalson, *AJP* 93 (1972), 77–83.   **Danaid:** i.e. Argive, cf. F 752g.16 n. Eur. seems to have invented the term Δαναΐδαι ('Danaids') and used it frequently: cf. Collard on *Supp.* 130.

37. Cadmus' gates: the city of Thebes, founded by Cadmus, with its seven-gated citadel. On the legendary topography of Thebes see Mastronarde, *Phoenissae* 647–50.

38. E.g., '*<Yes, if the gods are willing to bring us there>* **successfully…**'   [P's marginal note seems to mean εἰ δή 'If indeed', clarifying the syntax of the lost line-beginning.]

39. E.g., '*<And what is the purpose of your campaign, if>* **one may…**'. The reservation is almost formulaic, 'conceding a person's right not to answer' (Mastronarde, *Contact* 102 comparing *Med.* 676, *IT* 938, etc.).   [Diggle's λέ[γ', εἴ τί] gives '*<Tell…if one>* may learn etc.']

40. Either simply '*we are restoring Polynices*' (with Cockle's ἡμεῖς) or '*we are restoring Polynices <to Thebes>*' (with Diggle's Θήβας).

41. Hyps. asks Amph. to identify himself (as his reply shows).

42. *Oiclês*: himself a seer, and grandson of the seer Melampus (Gantz 188, 313).

752i. Amphiaraus in turn, it seems, asks Hypsipyle to identify herself.

752k. The same dialogue continues. Amph. tells how Cadmus married Harmonia (5), who received as a wedding gift a divinely made necklace (7), which passed through their descendants (9, 11) to Polynices. Amph.'s wife Eriphyle (sister of Adrastos) was seduced by Polynices and received the necklace from him (16–17) in return for compelling Amph. to join the expedition against Thebes. Amph. knew this would be fatal but was bound by a promise to let Eriphyle resolve any dispute between himself and Adrastus (13–15, 18–19). For this story in outline see Apollod. 3.4.2, 3.6.1–2; cf. Gantz 471–2, 506–10 (earlier sources and variants).   Extensive speculative reconstructions of the text in this fr. were printed by von Arnim and Page, and of lines 5–11 by the first editors.
1. Probably Amph. begins to tell how his *wife* Eriphyle betrayed him.
3. Probably Eriphyle *received* the necklace of Harmonia from Polynices.
5. Presumably 'The *famous* <*Cadmus*> married <*Harmonia*>.'
7. Presumably 'To her <*Aphrodite?*> gave <*a necklace as a wedding-gift*>.' The donor was variously said to have been Aphrodite, Hephaestus, Athena, or Cadmus himself after receiving the necklace from one of these gods: Gantz 471–2.
9. Polydorus: traditionally the only son of Cadmus and Harmonia along with their daughters Semele, Agave, Ino, Autonoe (cf. Hes. *Theog.* 975–8), and father of Labdacus; otherwise a rather shadowy figure (see Gantz 483–4).
11. his *son/descendants*: i.e. Labdacus himself or Labdacus and his successors Laius, Oedipus, and the brothers Eteocles and Polynices.
13. [P's corrected reading (see App.) seems to suggest the 1st sing. or 3rd pl. Indic. (or an Opt.?) form of συνεῖπον 'agreed, confirmed'. Kannicht thinks also of συνειπόμεσθα (< συνέπομαι) 'we accompanied' (which would need a dative object).]
14. the/an oracle: presumably foretelling the failure of the expedition against Thebes.
15. Roberts's suggestion (App.) gives '*if* <*my wife requires it*>'.
16. Cropp's suggestion (App.) gives '**She accepted...**<*the ill-fated outcome.*>'
17. shall I come: present-tense ἥκω is probably used 'prophetically': cf. e.g. A. *Ag.* 126. Italie suggested ἐκ [μάχης πάλιν: '...<*back*> from <*the battle.*>'
20–1. Amph. shows characteristic courage, piety and moderation (cf. esp. A. *Sept.* 587–91) in facing his situation. The couplet is quoted by Plutarch, with *Arch.* F 254 (see Comm. there) and F 1069, as an example of a bad precept cited so as to be corrected by a good one.   **It's better so:** in such expressons ἄμεινον usually connotes 'better policy' and avoidance of harm, often in view of religious considerations: e.g. Hom. *Il.* 217–8, Hes. *Works* 750, E. *Or.* 788–9, and the common oracular formula λῶιον καὶ ἄμεινον, 'more acceptable and better'.   **no labour:** i.e. easy to bear, however hard it may be, because it is holy work: cf. *Ion* 134–5, *Bacc.* 66–7, 893–6, 1053.

753. Hyps. announces her agreement, either to Amph. himself or to the Chorus. (**I'll show the Argives** need not rule out Amph. as Bond suggests, and he can hardly have left.) The fr. is cited by Macrobius (5th C. A.D.) as an example mentioned by Didymus

(1st C. B.C.) of the word **Achelous** denoting river-water in general. The basic idea seems to have been that the Achelous in NW Greece, as Greece's major river, was the source or 'parent' of its minor rivers. Cf. e.g. *Bacc.* 519 and 625 with the notes of Dodds and Roux.

753a. With Cockle's placing of the fr. (Cockle 151) this may be the Chorus-leader remonstrating with Hyps. (**What** *are you saying...You foolhardy* (**or** *much afflicted?*) *woman...*) and trying to persuade her not to go to the spring (or not to take the baby with her, or not to mix with the Argive army). [Earlier editors had guessed from the content that the lines came later in Hyps.'s confrontation with Eurydice.]

753c. Clearly part of the play's first stasimon. Lines 1–6, apparently involving successful harvests and the beneficence of the gods, are presumably the end of one section. Then lines 7–23 turn to the mythical background of the play's action, as often in the early stasima of Eur.'s plays. The Chorus recalls the famous episode at Argos when Polynices and Tydeus, both arriving as exiles at Adrastus' palace, quarrelled over their lodging and fought until Adrastus separated them. Adrastus recognized them from their savagery (or in later sources from some visible signs such as their shield-emblems) as the 'boar' and the 'lion' who according to an oracle of Apollo were to marry his daughters. Thus Adrastus became implicated in Polynices' disastrous campaign against Thebes. A parallelism (and contrast) between the quarrel of Tydeus and Polynices leading to Adrastus' intervention and its negative outcomes, and the quarrel of Eurydice and Hyps. leading to Amph.'s intervention and its positive outcomes, is perhaps implied. The episode was no doubt told in the epic *Thebais* and by Stesichorus in his *Eriphyle* and/or '*Thebais*', but none of it survives from these. For extant accounts see esp. *Supp.* 131–50, *Pho.* 408–23, Apollod. 3.6.1, Hygin. *Fab.* 69, Stat. *Theb.* 1.390–512 (a creative re-working). Bond 87–8 lists other sources; cf. also Mastronarde on *Pho.* 411 and Gantz 508–9 who include the vase-paintings *LIMC* 'Adrastos' no. 1 (a Chalcidian calyx-crater from c. 530 B.C. showing Tydeus interrrupting Adrastus' banquet) and no. 2 (a Sicilian crater from c. 350 B.C. showing Adrastus separating the combatants).

METRE. Apparently a mixture of aeolic, dactylo-epitrite and dactylo-anapaestic, as in some other choral reminiscences of the past, e.g. *IT* 392–421, 1234–83, *Hel.* 1107–36.

2–3. [*<fruit?>ful...*corn-ears/harvest: πολυκά[ρπων (ed. pr.) would agree with σταχύ-ων and make a phrase like F 757.925 (below) κάρπιμον σταχύν 'fruitful harvest'; cf. *Supp.* 31, *Bacc.* 750, F 516.]

4. *moistening*: probably with ref. to nurturing rain. [The verb δροσίζομαι occurs in Ar. *Frogs* 1312 in a passage noted in the scholia as Euripidean. The noun δρόσος and adj. δροσερός were favourite words of Eur. (e.g. *And.* 227 of rain, *Hipp.* 78 river-water, *IA* 152 spring-water).]

5. *givers*: reminiscent of epic phrases referring to gods as 'giver(s) of good things' (examples in LSJ δωτήρ, δώτωρ). Also possible is βιο]δώτορες 'givers of life/ sustenance', as Cockle notes: cf. the 'life-giving' (βιοδώροις) river-nymphs of Argos, Aesch. F 168.17; 'life-giving earth' (βιόδωρος αἶα), S. *Phil.* 1161.

8. *Pleuron(ian)*: Pleuron and Calydon were the main cities of Aetolia. Tydeus son of Oineus, a member of the ruling family, came to Argos as an exile after killing an uncle or cousins in a political feud: cf. Hom. *Il.* 2.638–44, 14.109–25, Hes. F 10a.49–64.

9–11. Description of the exiled Tydeus reaching Argos.   **wander<*ing?*>:** ἀλητεύω and cognates regularly denote wanderings of fugitives, e.g. *Hipp.* 1048, *El.* 131, 139, 202.

12–18. Description of the fight between Tydeus and Polynices. Perhaps roughly '<*by night*>...amongst the beddings by the court-yard, exchanging *quarrels <thick and fast, with wieldings of>* iron/sword *<and with>* slaughter, over a couch for the night the fugitives *<displayed>* their noble fathers' temper (etc.)'. Ed. pr. reconstructs on these lines (mainly due to Murray, and favoured by Bond).

12. amongst the beddings: at *Pho.* 416 Polynices arrives at Argos (ahead of Tydeus) seeking a bed' (κοίτας ματεύων).

19–21. Adrastus recognizes 'the lion and the boar' (*Supp.* 140, *Pho.* 411).   **proclamation of Phoebus:** both the word ἐνοπή and its plural form suggest the striking public effect of the Pythia's delivery of the oracle: cf. *El.* 1302 with Denniston's note.   **to yoke his daughters:** the verb ζεύγνυμι, lit. 'yoke', often denotes marriage or sexual union.

22. [Bury's δ]όμο[ν 'house' is likely in view of *Alc.* 597 (see next note).]

23. throwing open: Adrastus opens his doors, or house, to the strangers: phrasing as e.g. *Alc.* 597 δόμον ἀμπετάσας 'throwing open his house', *Pho.* 297 ἀμπέτασον πύλας 'throw open the doors'.

753d–754b. About 120 lines fall between the end of the stasimon (shortly after the end of F 753c) and the entrance of Eurydice in **F 754c.** In **F 753d** Hyps. has re-entered in distress to tell the Chorus of the baby's death. A sung exchange (*amoibaion*) between her and the Chorus begins here and continues with her cries of grief in **F 753e**; **F 754** describing Opheltes picking flowers can be assigned to Hyps. in the same exchange. Then comes **F 754a** in trimeters with (presumably) Hypsipyle describing the serpent and the Chorus-leader responding. **F 754b** has the beginning of a stichomythic dialogue between Hyps. and the Chorus, Hyps. knowing that the baby is dead and looking for ways to escape punishment. It is not surprising that Opheltes' death, crucial for both Hyps.'s peril and the founding of the Nemean Games, should have been reported by Hyps. herself in this extended and overwrought scene.   [Until Cockle placed **F 754a** near the top of col. 12, some scholars had supposed that it belonged to a messenger's report (see the reconstruction and survey of opinions in Bond 13–15, 98). There now seems to be no room such a speech (nor for a cortège bringing Opheltes' body back to the house: so Robert 395, Morel 12–13, Bond 14); there is no need to infer it from F 753d.11–12 or F 757.944; the return of the body would be a major event, conflicting with Hyps.'s confrontation with Eurydice.]

753d. Combination and placing of frs.: Cockle 153–4. Reconstruction of text at the left margin and of speaker-indications (see App.) is difficult since the papyrus is defective and some lines were indented, others not. Blank papyrus to the right shows that lines 3–5 were quite short, and lines 9, probably 14, and 15–16 are complete. Editors have distributed the whole passage between Hyps. and the Chorus, but lines 1–10 might possibly be a dialogue within the Chorus hearing offstage cries from Hyps. who then comes into view (11–12) and addresses them (14–16).   METRE. Probably a mixture of dochmiacs (2?), iambics (11–12?) and cretics (10, 14–16), as often in such agitated dialogues.

3. not *(to?)* **remain:** the incomplete word must be some form of the verb ἐμμένω, 'remain', 'stand firm', whether literal or figurative.

11–12. close by, not *far away,* **to see:** if Hyps. only now enters (see above), the Chorus can now see the commotion which to this point it has only heard.   [Similar phrasings in *Pho.* 596, 906, S. *Trach.* 962 justify the supplement *far away.*]

14–16. Woe is me (etc.): οἲ ἐγώ is always a cry of distraught females: cf. *Hel.* 685–6 οἲ 'γώ· – τί φῄς – οὐκ ἔστι μάτηρ, 'Woe is me!' – 'What are you saying?' – 'My mother is dead!'

754. The fr. is quoted by Plutarch both in his essay *On making many friends* (illustrating people's tendency to seek too many new friendships while neglecting established ones, *Mor.* 93d), and in *Sympotic Questions* (discussing our susceptibility to over-elaborate foods, *Mor.* 661e–f). The child's delight in the flowers likewise leads him unthinkingly into danger. Editors have often included in the fr. the unmetrical words which precede it in *Mor.* 93d, εἰς τὸν λειμῶνα καθίσας ἔδρεπεν…, 'settling in the meadow (he) plucked…'. These are surely Plutarch's words (so e.g. Kannicht), though they no doubt reflect something in Eur.'s text. Opheltes in the meadow is featured in Stat. *Theb.* 4.787–97. METRE: dochmiac.

1–2. The baby's flower-picking is imaged as a kind of hunting – forebodingly, since in his innocence he will become the serpent's prey.   [†αἰρόμενος†, **picking(?)** is suspect since the hiatus between ἑτέρωι and αἰρ- is very unlikely (cf. Bond). Its sense might be either **picking** (cf. LSJ ἀείρω I.2) or 'starting (one flower-hunt after another)' (LSJ IV.4).]

3. child's mind: hinting at Opheltes' ignorance of the danger that threatens him. [Metre: τὸ νήπιον ἄπλη- gives a resolved dochmiac. The three remaining syllables are unmetrical and probably do not give Eur.'s text exactly.]

754a. The placing of this fr. near the top of col. 12 (not quite certain: Cockle 155–6) invalidates von Arnim's supplements for lines 1–8, while Page's for lines 1–5 are highly speculative.

1–4. a spring (etc.): description of the spring and the serpent guarding it. For similar Euripidean descriptions cf. *IT* 1245–7 (the serpent slain by Apollo at Delphi), *HF* 398–9 (the serpent guarding the tree of the Hesperides), *Ion* 1263 ('a serpent with murderous fire in its eyes', δράκοντ' ἀναβλέποντα φοινίαν φλόγα), *Pho.* 657–61 (the serpent slain by Cadmus at Thebes); also *Oed.* F 540 with our Comm. (the Sphinx). Stat. *Theb.* 5.505–33 has an elaborate description of the Nemean serpent, and it is prominent in depictions of the death of Archemorus (Introd., *Illustrations*).   **shaking its helm:** a πήληξ is normally a crested helmet, so here the snake's crested head reared for the attack is probably meant (though the first editors and LSJ give simply 'crest' as a unique meaning here): cf. Hom. *Il.* 13. 805 'around his temples the gleaming helmet shook (φαεινὴ σείετο πήληξ)' as Hector advanced into battle. Monstrous mythical serpents are conventionally crested, e.g. Stat. *Theb.* 5.510, 572 (this one), Verg. *Aen.* 2.206–7 (the Laocoon episode), Ov. *Met.* 3.32 (the serpent killed by Cadmus), 4.599 (Cadmus transformed); cf. *LIMC* 'Archemorus' nos. 1, 8.

4–6. in fear(?) of which (etc.): the supplement φόβ[ωι gives this sense, probably describing the local people's fear of the serpent.   [**5.** Either ἐπεὶ σῖγ' or ἔπεισί γ' (Wilamowitz in ed. pr.), giving either *'when silently <the serpent moves?>'* or *'<it?> approaches'*.]

7–8. Alas, for a woman (etc.): probably the Chorus reacts to the description of the serpent and asks a further question. The **guardian** could be the serpent itself (guardian of the spring, cf. *Pho.* 658 cited above) or the protector that Hyps. should have been for Opheltes.   [**7. φ[εῦ, Alas:** the interjection is outside the metre. Cockle, however, thinks the papyrus may have had [μοι corrected from ἐ[μοὶ, which gives roughly the same sense but within the metre, leaving two syllables to be supplied at the line-end rather than four.]

754b. Combination and placing of frs.: Cockle 156. (Dr. Cockle confirms that the absolute line-numbering should be c. 668–684 rather than c. 672–688 as in his edition.) Hyps. now discusses her predicament with the Chorus in a spoken dialogue. The dialogue has some of the mannerisms of the lengthy stichomythiai in which desperate escapes, murders etc. are planned in other late plays of Eur. (*IT* 1020ff., *Hel.* 1035ff. etc.: cf. Bond 95–6 with further refs.). Bond inferred that here too a plan to save Hyps. was devised but was soon aborted by Eurydice's intervention. Cockle's more precise placing of F 754c, with Eurydice's entrance almost immediately after F 754b, leaves no room for the devising of a plan. Whether Hyps. decided to throw herself on Eurydice's mercy is quite uncertain. Her later despairing exclamation, 'my deference (*aidôs*), it seems, was wasted', can hardly refer to such a decision (see below on F 757.852).   [The papyrus's text of the best-preserved lines 7–14 was completed convincingly by the first editors. They also printed less convincing supplements in lines 1, 3–6, 15–16, which were adopted by Page (with Wecklein's reordering of lines 5–9). Von Arnim's alternative supplements for lines 2–6 are inferior.]

1–2. Possibly the beginning the iambic dialogue. Bury's 'O *<dearest women>*' (App.) is apt but the traces after '*O*' are minimal (see Cockle's App. and photograph). Then the first editors' suggested '*<how perilously on the razor's edge>* I stand....' Collard notes *Supp.* 1013, ὁρῶ δὴ τελευτὰν ἵν' ἔστακα, 'I see the end at which I stand'.

3. to get undeserved (sufferings): cf. παθεῖν ἀνάξια 'to suffer undeserved things', *Ion* 1515, and the like (*Tro.* 1289, *IA* 852).   [The first editors' οἱ φόβοι δ' [ἴσχουσί (or ἔχουσί) με, 'my fears *<grip (or restrain) me>*' is impossible if Cockle's joining of fr. 44 with fr. 20 is correct. The join gives a text which is very hard to complete.]

4. optimistic: presumably encouraging Hyps. to hope for the best.

5–9. Wecklein's reordering of these lines provides a logical dialogue-sequence. Cockle is inclined to retain the papyrus order, but it gives a very difficult sequence from line 6 (**What...then have you discovered...**) to line 7 (**I fear what I shall suffer...**).

8. Well, you are not inexperienced (etc.): her previous experience should have taught her to respond patiently to misfortune. This provokes her declaration in the next line

(9) that she will defend herself, which the Chorus receives encouragingly (6). [Bond's comment that 'The chorus is sympathetic, being *non ignara mali*', is misleading. The nom. ἄπειρος, **inexperienced** refers to the subject of the previous sentence, i.e. Hypsipyle. For οὔκουν...γε **Well,** ... see Denniston, *GP* 422–3.]

5. Bury's '**To flee** <*this dwelling-place*>', is plausible. The word ἕδρανον, especially in the Plural, suggests a normally secure place, e.g. *Tro.* 539, *Or.* 1441, A. *Pers.* 4.

10–13. Where then will you turn (etc.): planning-scenes often open with an idea (or ideas) quickly abandoned as impractical or undesirable, e.g. *El.* 614–7, *Ion* 973–7, *IT* 1017–28, etc. (cf. Bond cited in the introductory note above).

11. My feet and my eagerness: poetic phrasing (hendiadys) for 'my eager haste'. Hyps. will go wherever her feet carry her. Editors compare 'eagerness of feet' (προθυμία ποδῶν) in *Ion* 1109–10. Kannicht notes *Hel.* 151 'the voyage itself will show you the way' (πλοῦς...αὐτὸς σημανεῖ).

12. The land is guarded (etc.): for this 'realistic touch' (Bond on *HF* 83) in situations of tragic perplexity cf. *HF* 82–3, *Or.* 443–4, 758–60. In *IT* 883–9 Iphigenia fears flight 'through barbarous tribes and impassable paths'.

14. Consider, though: rather than leave the palace alone (13), Hyps. should stay and listen to the Chorus's advice.

15. Perhaps '**But what** <*refuge can I find...?*>'; then in 16 the Chorus agrees that no one is likely to help a slave to escape. [The first editors printed Murray's '**What** *if I were to find someone who* **will take me**...', but this is very doubtful (see App.). More probably Hyps. herself points out the futility of expecting help from others.]

754c. Almost immediately Eurydice comes out of the house looking for Hyps. and Opheltes, and Hyps. must tell her the dreadful truth. Eurydice either brings with her or later summons the servants who will bind Hyps. (F 757.860–1). The papyrus marks a speaker-change at line 9, and possibly another at 10. At least two changes are needed if Eurydice speaks 3–6 and Hyps. 13ff.

2. *mistress*: either Hyps. or more probably the Chorus observes Eurydice's appearance.

3. Bury's supplement gave '<*Release*> **the door-bolts** <*for me*> so that <*I may go inside and...*>'. Dale rightly preferred '*go outside*' (*JHS* 84 [1964], 166–7). It is clear from the following lines that Eurydice comes out of the house because she cannot find Hyps. and the baby inside (cf. Cockle 158). Phrases like 'Release the door-bolts' are usually used by someone outside shouting to servants inside (*Hipp.* 808, *IT* 1304, etc.). Dale supposed that in this case Eurydice speaks as the doors open and she emerges. Or she might be saying that she has opened the doors herself (cf. S. *Ant.* 1186–7).

4. At the end the first editors' φρο]ντίδα 'concern' (over the baby) fits the context well.

13. More likely the start of Hyps.'s emotional declaration that the child is dead (*is gone*) than a further question from Eurydice as Cockle suggests.

14. Bond's δ]ηλήματο[ς, 'of/from (some) harmful thing', is likely. δήλημα refers to harmful serpents at *Hom. Hymn* 3.364 (Typhaon) and Aesch. F 123.1.

16. *upon my* **arms:** referring to Hyps. holding the baby as 12 above and F 757.841 (and she has let the baby *out of* (**my?**) **hands** in 18 below?)

755a. Kannicht collects here several frs. (not all printed here) assigned by Cockle to P. Oxy. col. 13. The few recognizable words are readily identified with the confrontation between Hyps. and Eurydice.

frs. 30 etc., 3. Cockle's supplement gives *'this (child)* **who has died'.** Handley's alternative is *'the <ill-fated one>* **who has died'.**

frs. 36 etc., 6. *a libation:* see above on F 752h.30.

757. The confrontation between Eurydice and Hyps. probably led to an accusatory speech by Eurydice (roughly lines 740–80 of the whole play) to which Hyps. replied with an emotional defence-speech. In F 757 several frs. of P. Oxy. give, from the lower half of col. 14, the last 29 lines of this speech (800–828, some minimally preserved), then the Chorus-leader's comment, and then the first line of Eurydice's response. Next P. Oxy. fr. 60 gives the 62 lines of col. 15 (832–93) complete or almost complete but for its first few lines, and the beginnings of all but the first three of the 56 lines in col. 16 (894–949). P. Petrie supplies the middles of lines 830–50. The text of Amphiaraus' moral advice in 920–7 and 946–9 can be completed from ancient quotations. We thus have a sequence of 150 lines, half of them virtually complete, from one of the play's climactic scenes. Part of the line-number ϙ (800) is visible in the left margin of the papyrus.

800–28. Probably more than half of Hyps.'s defence-speech. In 801–6 she seems to be arguing that she was right to help the ***stranger(s?)*** (804) with his/their ***libation*** (801: see above on F 752h.30).

822. ***Phoebus':*** Apollo was the divine patron of seers such as Amph. (cf. 889).

823–8. Perhaps, in rough paraphrase, 'and do not judge me in anger, but deliberate carefully and reach your decision in due time. Women's natures are emotional and they will grieve at losing a child; but you should be self-controlled, and if you discriminate well you will be merciful, but if you make an error you will do me a great injustice.' Hyps. renews the plea at 836–7, and Amph. repeats the warning at 880–2. The thought that anger leads to unwisdom and injustice is commonplace: cf. F 760 below, *Pho.* 452–3, Theognis 1223–4, S. *Tereus* F 589, Menand. F 742 *PCG,* and many others collected in Stob. 3.20 (*On Anger*); also Mastronarde on *Med.* 1080.

827–8. **if** *<you?>* **discriminate... but if** *<you?>* **make an error:** thus with Cropp's supplements (in App.). For διαριθμέομαι 'count for yourself, classify' used of assessing moral conduct cf. e.g. Pl. *Laws* 633a8, 728a6.

829–30. The Chorus supports Hyps. Line 830 alludes to Hyps.'s request in 827, with a verbal echo in **I too want to be counted** (ἀριθμεῖσθαι).

831–5. Eurydice abruptly dismisses Hyps.'s defence and insists on her guilt.

831. Why do you seize (etc.): lit., 'why in this way do you speciously seize upon words'. [For κομψός 'elegant' used contemptuously of specious argument see Collard on *Supp.* 426, *Antiope* F 188.5. For τί ταῦτα 'why in this way' cf. *Hipp.* 971, *And.* 851.]

832. [carry on *at length:* this assumes that μηκύνεις is used here without an object (cf. LSJ μηκύνω 3), and μ[ακράν adverbial (cf. *Med.* 1351, *Hel.* 1017, *Or.* 850). The incomplete line-beginning makes this uncertain.]

833. *<the joy>* **of my** *eyes:* χαράν (Morel) a source of joy as in Sappho F 5.6 L-P.

834. and do not…: Petersen's supplement gives '**and do not** *remind* <*me of my child*>'. Diggle (1995, 42–3) plausibly suggests '<*Do not…*> **and do not** *remind* <*me of my/your troubles*>'. Eurydice might also wish not to be reminded of Hyps.'s merits, or about justice, by the woman who has killed her son. [Diggle supposes an idiomatic structure with Fut. Indic. rather than Aor. Subj. verbs, as e.g. *Hipp.* 606 οὐ μὴ προσοίσεις χεῖρα μηδ' ἄψηι πέπλων; ('Won't you not-bring your hand towards me, and not-touch my clothing?')]

836–52. Hyps. moves from reasoned defence to a desperate (yet rhetorical) reassertion of her innocence and love for the child (839–43), and appeals to her 'absent' sons (843–4) and Amph. (844–50) before resigning herself to death (851–2).

836. [Diggle's ἄρα at line-end gives '*Are you determined* <*then*> (etc.)'.]

837. in anger: see above on 823–8.

841–3. my nursling (etc.): this recalls Orestes' nurse lamenting his death in A. *Cho.* 749ff.; also S. *El.* 1143–8 (Electra lamenting Orestes), E. *El.* 506–7 (Orestes' tutor).

842. in every way except (etc.): lit. 'except for not having borne (him), in (all) other things certainly'. [P. Oxy.'s δ(έ) does not quite make sense ('but in all other things'). For the idiomatic τἄλλα γε cf. *Hcld.* 499, *Hel.* 1105, *Or.* 1212, S. *Trach.* 1211.]

843. a great boon: probably the child himself (cf. *Tro.* 703, A. *PV* 613) rather than the process of nursing him.

844–5. O prow of Argo (etc.): recollection of her love for Opheltes (841–3) prompts Hyps. to think of the arrival of the Argonauts (cf. F 752g.1–15) and her own sons by Jason, contrasting earlier happiness and security with her present misery and peril. [Most editors have printed P's wording, though with reservations (see e.g. Italie, Bond). But 'O prow, and water flying white from the brine, of Argo' is very awkward, and λευκαῖνον should probably be transitive (although it does not agree with πρώιρα): cf. Hom. *Od.* 12.172 'they whitened the water (λεύκαινον ὕδωρ) with smoothed oars', E. *Cyc.* 16–17 'whitening the grey brine with surging strokes (γλαυκὴν ἅλα ῥοθίοισι λευκαίνοντες), *IT* 1387 'stir up a whitening surf' (ῥόθιά τ' ἐκλευκαίνετε).]

847. Defend me, come now…: 'ascending tricolon', the first two phrases identical with Megara's desperate appeal to Heracles, *HF* 494 (where Bond gives other examples).

851. Take me, then: a plural Imperative addressed to Eurydice's servants (F 754c n.).

852. my deference, it seems, was wasted: lit. 'In vain did I show *aidôs*, then'. Since this culminates her appeal to Amph., it must mean her respectful behaviour in welcoming and helping him and the Argives, not a decision to submit to Eurydice rather than try to escape as e.g. Grenfell-Hunt 25 (after Murray) and Page 80 supposed.

853–5. you who are despatching: lit. 'O (you) despatching', a solemn use of the Voc. participle (cf. Collard on *Hec.* 1000). Amph. enters abruptly, then softens his intrusion by deferring to Eurydice, just as he was tactful about Hyps.'s status in view of her appearance when he intruded on her (F 752h.22–3). **by your bearing I can tell (etc.):** lit. 'by your seemliness, on seeing you, I attribute freeness to you in your nature.' σοι and τῆι φύσει ('you…your nature') are in 'apposition of whole and part' (*schema Ionicum*): cf. Wilamowitz or Bond on *HF* 162; KG 1.289. For the polite mention of well-born bearing cf. *Ion* 237, Hom. *Hymn* 2.213, S. *El.* 663–4 (ironically nuanced).

856–67. Hyps. formally appeals to Amph. (856–9), then invokes his obligation to return the service (*charis*) she has done him and the Argives (859–63), and his special standing which will help allay Eurydice's suspicions (864–7).

856–7. O, by your knees…and by your chin (etc.): Hyps. throws herself at Amph.'s knees, a conventional demonstration of submission which also compelled attention to the suppliant's plea (**save me (etc.),** 859): cf. J. Gould, *JHS* 93 (1973), 75–6. Like Andromache at *And*. 572–4 she cannot complete the gesture by grasping his knees and chin because she is bound (860: cf. M. Kaimio, *Physical Contact in Greek Tragedy* [Helsinki, 1988], 54); her helplessness is thus emphasized. She appeals to Amph.'s priestly status (**your Apolline art**) as a further compulsion. [Euripidean suppliants sometimes use the formulaic phrase ὦ πρός σε γονάτων without a verb governing σε, e.g. *Med.* 324, *Hipp.* 607, *Hel.* 1237, *Pho.* 923: cf. Mastronarde, *Contact* 60–1. Kannicht punctuates **I fall in supplication, Amphiaraus** as a parenthesis (cf. Bond's note), but line 856 is better taken as one forceful, if slightly incoherent, phrase.]

858. just in time: καιρὸν adverbial Acc., equivalent to ἐς καιρόν; cf. *Mel.D.* F 495.9 n.

862–3. You who are blameless (etc.): rescuing her will maintain his ritual and moral standing. Betraying her would disgrace not just Amph. but **Argos and all Hellas** because her service benefited the whole army. Hecuba reminds Agamemnon of his moral position similarly, *Hec.* 1233–5.

864. you who see fortunes (etc.): besides having witnessed the child's death (865–6), Amph. has the prophetic authority to explain it (as he will do in his long speech). **in *pure* burnt offerings:** i.e., by examining parts of sacrificial animals before and during their burning on the altar, like Teiresias in S. *Ant.* 1005–13; cf. A. *PV* 493–9, E. *El.* 826–9; M. Jameson in M. Cropp et al., *Greek Tragedy and its Legacy* (Calgary, 1986), 59–65; F. van Straten, *Hiera Kala* (Leiden, 1995), 118–44, 156–7.

866–7. she claims I killed the child on purpose (etc.): cf. Hypoth. 11–12 (n.)

868–80. Amph. responds first to what Hyps. has just said about his own knowledge of what happened and Eurydice's false suspicions (868–9: cf. 864–7), then to her call for protection and appeal to his obligation to her (870–3: cf. 859–63). He then approaches Eurydice very tactfully, assuring her that he will not trespass on her modesty (874–7), before calling for her attention with a moral appeal (878–80).

874. unveil your head: Eurydice has veiled herself by covering her face with her robe, thus showing *aidôs* on being approached by a stranger as she explains in 883: cf. D. Cairns, *CQ* 46 (1996), 80 and *JHS* 116 (1996), 153–6, both with further refs.

875–6. that is well known in Hellas: lit. 'the Hellenes' talk (of it) has gone abroad abundant(ly)'. [For διήκει = 'has gone abroad' cf. LSJ διέρχομαι I.3. Thus Lloyd-Jones' Ἕλληνας providing an object ('talk of it has gone throughout the Hellenes') is not necessary, though attractive. The whole phrase is better understood as a parenthesis (Collard) than as linked with the preceding words (Bond: 'the report of the Hellenes (that) my eye (is) discreet is well known…').]

879–80. To err…it is not well: Amph. tactfully understates the case so as not to alienate Eurydice. Human life is uniquely precious because it is irretrievable: Bond cites examples of this argument from Homer (*Il.* 9.406–9), Aeschylus and Eur. Used as a defence against a death-sentence: A. *Eum.* 647–50, Gorgias 82 B 11a.34 DK (*Pala-*

medes), Antiphon 5.91. For χρεών (or χρή) 'is allowable' cf. *HF* 141–2 with Bond's n., *El.* 300.

881–5. Eurydice responds courteously, impressed by Amph.'s address and his reputation.

886–943. Amph.'s great speech, coming at the play's mid-point, was dramatically and morally central to it. It emblematizes the play in two 4th C. vase-paintings (cf. Introd., p. 180). The seer's defence of Hyps. successfully proclaims a humane and rational view of justice and a temperate acceptance of mortality. His instructions for the commemoration of Opheltes provided the basis for the remainder of the play. (On these points see also Introd., pp. 172–3, 181.) The speech falls into six parts: introduction (886–90), narrative of Opheltes' death (891–907), explanation of the event and its implications (908–18), moral advice (*parainesis*) on the acceptance of mortality (919–27), instructions for Opheltes' funeral (928–40), and advice to spare Hyps. (940–3).

Lines 920–7 and 946–9 are quoted in full by ancient authors. Speculative supplements for some of the incomplete papyrus-lines were printed by the first editors (908, 917–9, 929–36, 940, 942–3: see also their notes for 902–3, 938, 944), and for most of them by von Arnim and Page. These vary considerably and are not reliable. The general sense of the whole is discussed in the notes below.

886–90. Introduction: Amph. appeals to Eurydice's better nature, tactfully extenuating Hyps.'s guilt (886–7) and invoking justice (888) and his own reliability as Apollo's prophet (889–90).

889–90. I shall be shamed before Phoebus (etc.): Apollo as patron of seers was thought of as committed to true prophecy, e.g. *Hom. Hymn* 3. 132, Pind. *Pyth.* 3.29, 9.42, A. *Cho.* 559, *Eum.* 615, E. *Or.* 1666–7. **whose art I practise (etc.):** cf. 864 n.

891. *bright* **spring-water:** lit. 'spring-sheen': cf. Broadhead on A. *Pers.* 483 (same phrase) and our comm. on *Androm.* F 146.3.

892–3. through its pure streams (etc.): the syntax becomes unclear as the text fails. The general sense is obvious in light of F 752h.29–36. [Fr. 87, joined by Cockle, supplies the fragmentary ends of each line, invalidating earlier conjectures and making reconstruction difficult. Scribal corrections in 893 (App.) add to the difficulty.]

900–1. These lines might describe either the Argives' ritual activity (hence Wecklein's θῦσ]αι giving '*wanting <to sacrifice>*' in 901), or their first reaction on realising the child was in danger (hence von Arnim's σῶσ]αι giving '*wanting <to save him>*'). The latter is preferable since the Argives' ritual intentions and the child have already been mentioned in 893ff. and 898, and a description of the attack follows immediately.

902–7. Description of the serpent's attack on the child (902–5: cf. F 754a), the Argives' intervention (906), and the shooting of the serpent by Amph. **903. shot forth** may describe the serpent shooting out its tongue or lunging at the child rather than someone throwing a javelin at the serpent (Eur. uses the verb ἀκοντίζω, with or without object, for a variety of rapid motions: cf. Cropp on *IT* 362). **904.** *rapid* may refer to the motion of the snake or its eyes rather than to literal running (cf. *Alc.* 245, *Or.* 837, and the parody at Ar. *Peace* 160 for comparable uses of δρομ- words). **907. and I shot:** Amph. has killed the serpent with an arrow rather than a spear as one might expect from an Argive warrior. The fourth hypothesis to Pindar's *Nemeans* may reflect this passage: 'A serpent...enveloped the child, tightened its coils about him and suffocated him. And they came back and shot (τοξεῦσαι) the serpent...'.

908–18. Amph. interprets the death of Opheltes: it foreshadows the deaths of the Seven, so Opheltes should be known now as **Archemorus**, 'Beginning of Death' (908–9); Eurydice's loss serves as an **omen** *for the Argives* (910–1); their expedition will fail and will lead to the deaths of many on both sides (912–5, details uncertain); few will **achieve their homecoming**, and out of **the seven commanders** only **Adrastus will reach** his homeland (916–8).   [**917.** ἵξετ': elision of ἵξετ(αι) is very unlikely in tragedy, so Page's ἥξει τ' Ἀρ[γος, '**will reach** *Argos*' may well be right.]

919. The first editors' supplement (App.) gives '<*You now understand clearly*> **what has happened**'.

920–7. Amph. consoles Eurydice: death is a burden but a *natural* and *inevitable* part of human lives: they have a season like the harvests, and their ending should be borne without complaint. This consolation was famous in antiquity, as is shown by Cicero's translation of it (with a ref. to its promotion by the Stoic Chrysippus) and the quotations by Marcus Aurelius, Clement, the author of the *Consolation to Apollonius* and others (see App.). These quotations and their gnomological sources are compared and discussed by G. Barabino, *Sileno* 8 (1982), 17–25.

920. [After the μέν-clause in 919 (**What has happened...**) P's δ' αὖ **But now** is clearly the right reading.   Valckenaer's idiomatic Dat. μοι (**please accept**) is much more appropriate than Clement's Gen. μου ('accept from me').]

921. No mortal was ever born who does not suffer: the general consolatory argument 'Not to you alone' (*non tibi hoc soli*: cf. Cic. *Tusc.* 3.79) is so well known that it hardly needs illustration, but cf. esp. Hom. *Il.* 24.524–6, also addressed to a parent (Priam) grieving for a dead son (Hector): 'Nothing can be gained from chill lamentation, for the gods have so spun the lives of luckless mortals that they must live in grief...'; similarly E. *And.* 1270–2 (Thetis to Peleus on the death of their grandson Neoptolemus): cf. R. Kassel, *Untersuchungen zur griechischen und römischen Konsolationsliteratur* (Munich, 1958), 54–5, 70–2.   [Stob. has 'No one was ever born who does not continually bear troubles'.]

922. We bury children: the argument moves from general to present sufferings, so Kannicht's stop at the end of 921 is appropriate ('explanatory asyndeton': so also Cic. *Tusc.* 3.59, *Mortalis nemo est quem non adtingat dolor | morbusque; multis sunt humandi liberi...*,'There is no mortal who is not touched by grief and affliction; many must bury children...'). [Several variants in 922–3 (App.) result from misunderstandings of the syntax. Some of the ps.-Plut. mss. supply an unneeded connective, while P and Stob. create a dependent infinitive-clause ('...who does not suffer in burying...').] **and get other new ones:** inevitable death is balanced by new life. The idea that new children may replace lost ones is itself a consolation ('You should endure also in the hope of other sons, those of you who are still of an age to beget them', Thuc. 2.44.3).

924. earth to earth: the body returns to the earth from whence it came, the source of all mortal life: cf. A. *Cho.* 127–8 (with Garvie's comm.), E. *Supp.* 531–6 (with Collard's comm.), *Antiope* F 195 (n.), *Chrysippus* F 839.1–9, and others cited by Bond.

924–6. we must harvest life (etc.): burying the dead when their time has come is like reaping and storing a ripened harvest. Cf. esp. *Ino* F 415.3–5, 'The same cycle exists for the earth's fruitful plants and the race of mortals: for some life increases, for others it declines and is again harvested (θερίζεται)'. Death's naturalness serves as a consolation even though Eurydice's son has died unnaturally and prematurely.

926–7. [Why should we lament these things (etc.): Clement's slightly confused text gives 'We should conceal (or 'put up with': Postgate) these things which are necessary by our very nature, and we should get through them'.]

928–40. Amph. gives instructions for the burial of Opheltes and establishment of the Nemean Games. Let the Argives perform the burial (929); the tomb will be significant not just for the present but for ever (930–1). Opheltes *will be* **famous** (933), and the Hellenes will perform **a contest** for him (934), giving **crowns** (of wild celery) to the victors (935); thus he *will be* **envied** in his fate (or each victor will be envied in his victory?) (936). **In this** way (or place, or event) your son **will be remembered**, and how the contest celebrated **in the *grove* of Nemea** was named for him (937–40).

930. The supplements in the App. give 'Not for just one day' (Page, adjusting von Arnim's 'Not for just one day's light'), or 'Not just in our time' (Bond).

931–3. but for eternal (time)…: editors have compared Stat. *Theb.* 5.536–7 (*an ut inde sacer per saecula Grais | gentibus et tanto dignus morerere sepulcro*, 'Was it that thus you might in years to come | Be sacred to the Greeks, your death deserve | So fine a sepulchre?') and 5.741 (*mansuris donandus honoribus infans*, 'This babe must be given | Enduring honour': tr. A. D. Melville).   **[931. for eternal (time):** for εἰς τὸν αἰε[ὶ (…) χρόνον cf. *Pho.* 1521, *Or.* 206, Pl. *Phd.* 103E.]

940–3. Eurydice should release Hyps., for she is blameless; what has happened was for the good and will bring blessings to Eurydice and her son. To complete 940 and lead into 941 the first editors suggested '*<And so you should release this woman…>*'.

944. My son: this need not suggest that Opheltes' body is present (cf. above on F 753d–754a). In *Hec.* 585 (compared by Bond following Schadewaldt) Hecuba addresses Polyxena while her body lies elsewhere.

946–9. We should look at the natures (etc.): the complete text is preserved in Orion's 5th C. collection of maxims. Compare *Phoenix* F 812: '(When choosing between men's conflicting judgments) I and any wise man reckon the truth by looking at a person's nature and the way he conducts his daily life. I've never yet asked for an opinion from someone who keeps bad company, for I know he's like those whose company he enjoys'.)

758a–b. Combination and placing of the papyrus-frs.: Cockle 170, 172. Frs. 78+100 (included in F 759b under *Unplaced Fragments* below), including possibly the name of the goddess Dione, might be from the ends of lines 1102–9 (Cockle 179–80). The unplaced book-fr. F 765 might belong in this song (see pp. 224, 257).

F 758a begins with scene-ending iambic trimeters (1084–8), including a mention of Dionysus, perhaps as Hypsipyle's protector, which seems to anticipate the stasimon that follows (compare *IT* 1230ff., a plea to Artemis followed by hymnic praise of her brother Apollo, and *Bacc.* 848ff., invocation followed by celebration of Dionysus). The first 14 lines of the stasimon (1089–1102) are indented in the papyrus and followed by a para-graphus, the remainder are unindented (1103–8): possibly a strophe and opening of an antistrophe (the apparent absence of metrical responsion between 1093 and 1107 could be due to inconsistent line-divisions). The content seems to be Dionysiac throughout. In **758a** the 'strophe' begins with a rhetorical question perhaps expressing longing for contact with the god (1089–92: cf. *Bacc.* 862ff.); then a second question introduces a catalogue of his gifts (1093–9), leading to an expression of hope for experience of his joy or grace (1100–2). The 'antistrophe' turns to a theogonic/cosmogonic narrative, probably giving Dionysus a central significance (see on 1103–8 below). In **758b** attention has turned to the joy (21) of Dionysiac ritual: burning incense (1–2), the cult-building? (3, 10), carrying the thyrsus (6–8), wearing the animal-skin? (9).

The METRE of the stasimon is either largely anapaestic (as indicated by the first editors) or a mixture of anapaestic and dactylic.

1090. chamber(s?): Eur. often uses the Plural of θάλαμος (as below, F 758b. 3). The word connotes privacy or seclusion – here either the women's rooms which they leave in order to worship Dionysus, or a dwelling where the god is worshipped (e.g. *Antiope* F 203), or a cult-building (e.g. *Erec.* F 369.5). A natural cult-chamber or grotto is normally Fem. θαλάμη (cf. Dodds on *Bacc.* 120). **up to *the sky*** (or **through *the heaven*):** this might refer to the open air which is the Bacchants' realm (cf. *Bacc.* 150, 865, 1099), or to the heavenly realm of the gods.

1093–9. What (is?) the sign (etc.): probably 'What is the sign of the presence of Bacchus?', with answers in the following lines (Bond). **grape-bunch:** an emblem of Dionysus and his gifts, common in pictorial representations of the god: cf. e.g. *Bacc.* 11–12, 279, *Pho.* 231, and below, F 759a.1632, F 765. **gives forth:** probably referring to the earth's production of the vine: cf. *Mel.S.* F 484.4, Pl. *Pol.* 272a5. **flows...drips...nectar...frankincense:** probably like *Bacc.* 141ff., 'the ground flows with milk, it flows with wine, it flows with bees' nectar, and the Bacchic One (i.e. Dionysus), holding high the pine-torch's blazing flame, sweet as smoke from Syrian frankincense...'. In *Bacc.* 704–11 the bacchants get water from rocks, wine and milk from the ground, and honey from their thyrsuses. [In 1096 the first editors' γά[λακτι <*with milk*> gives a phrase found in *Bacc.* 142.]

1100–2. τάχ' ἂν, perhaps: probably introducing a hopeful expectation as in e.g. *Alcmene* F 100.1, S. *Aj.* 778. **joy/grace:** probably of Dionysiac ritual, cf. *Bacc.* 139, 535. ***reward(?):*** a tentative translation of ἀντίποινα, usually 'retribution' but here perhaps with a positive sense (cf. Aesch. F 202(?), LSJ ἄποινα II.2). [This assumes that P has ἀντάπο[(Bond, Kannicht) and had intended ἀντίποινα. No supplement is compatible with the first editors' reading ἀντάγω[, unless the accent is incorrectly written in P.]

1103–8. An invocation, probably of the mother of the gods, introduces a narrative of the beginnings of the universe and the gods. The text seems to refer to a primeval darkness or chaos (1104), a **first-born** god emerging within the *heaven* or *mist* (1105), the generative force **Erôs** and the protective goddess *Night* (1106), and a **race of gods** springing from these beginnings (1108). These are common features of early Greek theogonies, but in the context of a Dionysiac hymn they suggest that the narrative may have been of the kind attributed to the prophet Orpheus, and have culminated with the birth and supremacy of Zeus's son Dionysus, god of mystic salvation. This passage and Ar. *Birds* 690–702 (a parody) are widely accepted as evidence that such theogonies were current in the late 5th C. (they are frs. 2 and 1 respectively in O. Kern's *Orphicorum Fragmenta*, Berlin, 1922). The (late 5th C.?) text in the 4th C. B.C. Derveni papyrus, discovered in Thessaly in 1962, quotes a hexameter poem with similar features (see esp. M. L. West, *The Orphic Poems* [Oxford, 1983], 68–115; provisional text and English translation in R. Janko, *ZPE* 141 [2002], 1–62, cf. *CP* 96 [2001], 1–32; A. Laks and G. Most (eds.), *Studies on the Derveni Payrus* (Oxford, 1997); on early Orphism, R. Parker in A. Powell [ed.], *The Greek World* [London, 1995], 483–510). If the narrative is Orphic, πρωτόγονο[**first-born** in line 1105 may be the name or title of the primeval god (also known as Phanes) who was generated by Aithêr and Chaos and joined with Night to generate the race of gods that Uranus and his successors dominated; Zeus on taking power swallowed this god, re-generated the older gods, and sired Persephone by Demeter, then Dionysus by Persephone (cf. West's reconstruction of the 'Protogonos Theogony', summarized on his pp. 100–1).

1103. O mistress: probably a mother of the gods and all living things. Gê/Earth is called πότνια 'revered' *Hec.* 70, A. *Cho.* 722, 'revered mother' S. *Phil.* 391–5. In Eur.'s time earth-goddesses such as Gê, Rhea, Demeter, and the Anatolian Mêtêr/'Mother' (Cybele) were increasingly assimilated with one another and associated with Dionysus: cf. esp. P. Derveni, XXII.7ff. identifying Gê, Mêtêr, Rhea, Hera and Demeter as one; *Bacc.* 275–6, *Pho.* 685–6 (Gê = Demeter); *Hel.* 1301–68 with Kannicht on 1301–2 (Cybele ~ Demeter); *Bacc.* 72–87 with Dodds on 78–9 (Dionysus associated with Cybele); *Bacc.* 120–34 with Dodds on 120–34, 126–9 (Dionysus with Rhea); *Cretans* F 472.9–15 with our Comm. (bacchic rites for Rhea); Burkert, *Greek Religion* 177–9.

1104. inscrutable *light*: probably an oxymoron for darkness: Collard compares S. *Phil.* 297 ἄφαντον φῶς 'concealed light' (of fire in flint), *OC* 1549 φῶς ἄφεγγες 'lightless light' (of the blind Oedipus). Alternatively the dazzling brightness of heaven or *aithêr* (cf. *Pho.* 809 αἰθέρος...ἄβατον φῶς 'heaven's inaccessible light'), or of Protogonos/ Phanes who first illuminated the *aithêr* with an 'unimagined brightness' (φέγγος ἄελπτον, *Orph. fr.* 86 Kern). The reading χ]άος giving '**inscrutable Chaos**' is possible, but the epithet is then less striking; in cosmogonies Chaos is the void or chasm within which all entities developed, e.g. Hes. *Theog.* 116, Acusilaus F 6a–d Fowler, Ar. *Birds* 693, *Orph. fr.* 79 Kern. [See Bond p. 121 for further discussion of text and possible meanings.]

1105. heaven/mist: either αἰ[θ]έρι (the word overlapping from the previous line: Morel), or ἀ]έρι (ed. pr.). Aithêr (Heaven) is an early cosmogonic entity (Hes. *Theog.* 124, *Titanom.* F 1ᴮ Davies, Acusilaus F 6). Aithêr and Gê may be paired as progenitors of all life (see on *Antiope* F 182a). Protogonos/Phanes may be born from Aithêr (*Orph. frs.* 73, 74, 86). Aêr (Mist) was named by the Orphic poet 'Musaeus' as one of the first three cosmogonic entities (with Tartarus and Night); Epimenides named Aêr and Night as the first two: cf. Acusilaus F 6d Fowler with A. Henrichs, *GRBS* 13 (1972), 77–9.

first-born: see above, 1103–8 n. The accent in the papyrus (πρωτόγονο[)indicates the Nom. or Acc. singular form.

1106. Erôs ('Desire'): again a cosmogonic entity, essential to the generation of the gods (Hes. *Theog.* 120–2, Parmenides 28 B 13 DK, Acusilaus F 6b, Ar. *Birds* 696–700). **Night(?):** Nom. νὺ[ξ (ed. pr.) or another case-form (νυ[κτ–) are likely supplements since Night was associated with the births and nurturing of the gods (for nurturing cf. *Orph. frs.* 106, 129, 131 Kern; West, *Orphic Poems* 86–7. According to Aristotle's pupil Eudemus, Orpheus made Night the first of all entities: *Orph. fr.* 28, cf. *fr. 28a*).
1107–8. Probably one sentence, **race of gods...was nurtured**, i.e. subsequent generations of gods were born and raised (or perhaps nurtured by Night: see previous note).

758b.1. on the breeze: editors cite Ar. *Birds* 1716–7 'and the breezes (αὖραι) are gently blowing about the spiral of smoke from the incense' (tr. Dunbar). Cf. also Ar. *Frogs* 313–4, 'a most mystic whiff (αὖρα) of torches has breathed upon me'; Antiphan. F 55.14 (paratragic), 'an air-borne incense-breathing breeze (αὖραν). **we want:** showing eagerness for ritual activity: cf. *Cyc.* 620–1, *HF* 356. [Here the Dat. Sing. αὖραι seems more likely than Nom. Plur. αὖραι ('breezes/whiffs'), or λύραι in either case ('lyres' or 'with lyre').]
3. Bromios: 'the Roaring One' (cf. βρέμω 'roar'), a title of Dionysus: cf. *Bacc.* 66 (with Dodds' note), 115, 151, etc.
5. dear: Fem. Nom. Plur. or Dat. Sing. (the papyrus sometimes gives iota adscript).
6. *the trefoil wand*: i.e. the bacchant's ivy-covered staff (*narthêx*), ivy-leaves being typically three-lobed. [ ]θηκα can hardly be anything but νάρ]θηκα, a verb with this ending being out of place here. τριπέ[τηλον is an adj. for Hermes' staff (ῥάβδος) in *Hom.Hymn* 4.530, which Eur. may be poetically adapting.]
9. shoulder-: perhaps referring to the maenad's animal-skin draped over her shoulder. [The accent in the papyrus, if correct, requires ἐπώμ[ιον rather than ἐπωμ[ίδα 'shoulder'. In its rare occurrences in classical Greek ἐπώμιος is an adj., 'attached to/at the shoulder' or 'carried on the shoulder', but its use as a noun is known in Mycenean ('shoulder-piece' of armour: *LSJ Rev.Supp.*) and patristic Greek ('cape, mantle').]
10. cypress-roofed: probably referring to the *chamber* (3 above) where the god is worshipped. The adj. is known only here and in Mnesimachus F 4.1 (paratragic): 'Come out from the cypress-roofed dwelling (βαῖν' ἐκ θαλάμων κυπαρισσορόφων)'. The temple of Cretan Zeus has a cypress roof in *Cret.* F 472.4–8: see Comm. there.
13. [our/my: Eur. used Homeric and Doric ἁμός (= ἡμέτερος 'our') in both dialogue (see Stevens on *And*.581) and lyric (e.g. *And.* 1174, 1187). It is sometimes confused with ἐμός 'my' in mss.]
15. not *touch*: perhaps indicating a ritual abstention: cf. *Cret.* F 472.16–20 (n.).
20. limit: perhaps of human understanding or experience as in *Hel.* 1140.
21. joy/grace: cf. F 758a.1101 (n.) above.

758c–d. Cockle placed these frs. in the lower part of col. 25 and upper part of col. 26. Wilamowitz and the first editors had placed them loosely between **F 757** and **F 759a**; but Bond (17) and Webster (1966, 92–3) placed **F 758c** at the end of the 'trial' scene, and Bond mistakenly transferred **F 758d** to the prologue-scene. Since some testimonia suggest that Hyps. remained in peril after the 'trial' scene, the first editors suggested that

Hyps. in **F 758d**. was asking one of her sons to help free her and in **F 758c** was asking Amph. for further assistance. But if **758c–d** precede **F 759a** by only a hundred lines, they may well fall between the games and the recognition. Hyps. has usually been identified as the speaker throughout (see esp. lines 9 and 16), but the 2nd person verbs in 7, 13, 14, 16, 17 and the probable question in 9 suggest dialogue. (See also Introd., p. 175 on the reconstruction of this part of the play.)

758c.5. (they) do not have (or not having) allies: the topic may be Hyps.'s defencelessness, the subject 'exiles' or 'slaves' (so e.g. von Arnim, Bond).

7–8. Wilamowitz's reconstruction may be on the right lines: '*<once again>* **I find** *<you>* **like a ship's** *<wise steersman as it wanders in the storm>*'. For the image cf. A. *Sept.* 62, E. *Med.* 523, also S. *OT* 923.

758d.5. *favourable*, οὔρι(α): Neut. Pl. adj., properly of favourable winds, probably referring here to good circumstances relieving Hypsipyle of her **unenviable *trouble*** (cf. *HF* 95, *Ion* 1509, S. *Aj.* 889).

6. *has occurred in* my heart: cf. *Hipp.* 510 ἦλθε δ᾽ ἄρτι μοι γνώμης ἔσω, 'it has just occurred in my mind'.

7. you might have/be able...*young men*: von Arnim's '**you might have** *these young men*' (App.) might be said by Amph. to Hyps. about her recovery of her sons.

8. *came/come*: Indic. ἦ]λθ(ε) or Imper. ἔ]λθ(ε), or compound forms.

9. *they are alive* or dead: probably part of a question put by Hyps. Bond compares Hom. *Od.* 4.833, E. *El.* 229 etc. For δή pointing questions see Denniston, *GP* 210–2.

10. Likely supplements (App.) would give '**suffering *many* misfortunes**' or '**suffering** *other* **misfortunes**' or '*but* **suffering misfortunes**'.

11. bitter servitude: either Hyps.'s or her sons', if she imagines them enslaved.

12. unavailing *words*: perhaps Hyps.'s, unable to bring back her lost sons.

13. The line-end supplements of Petersen and von Arnim (App.) give 'But you, *as <is fitting>*' or 'But you, O *<my son>*' (cf. 16).

15. *formerly* free: a fem. adj. form, so probably Hyps.

16. [*my child*: τέκ̣[νον is very likely here. Hyps. calls on one of her lost sons, or on the dead Archemorus?]

17. At the end, either '*to/with a wise...*' (ed. pr.) or '*to your nurse*' (von Arnim).

759a. The last extensive papyrus-fr. brings us close to the end of the play. Hyps. and her sons have just been reunited in the presence of Amph. The complete surviving column, P. Oxy. fr. 64.ii, begins with the end of what was probably, in view of the style, a celebration-song of Hyps. rather than a choral stasimon (as Menozzi 18, Morel 21–2, Webster [1966] 93 supposed). Amph., having assured Hyps.'s safety and welfare and thus repaid her service to him, makes a brief farewell and departs for Thebes, leaving Hyps. and her sons to continue their celebration. From the preceding col. i only the ends of a few probably lyric lines survive, suggesting that the celebration was already in progress. Marginal notes in the papyrus ('Edonian women: Thracian women', 'Pangaeus: a mountain in Thrace') indicate that lines 1571–2 mentioned the gold- and silver-bearing Mt. Pangaeus (see *OCD*^{3} 'Pangaeus') and the local Edonian women, presumably with reference to Dionysus who was strongly associated with the area. The mountain had a Dionysiac oracle (Hdt. 7.111.2, [E.] *Rhes.* 970–3; cf. *Hec.* 1267), and the region was associated with the killing of Orpheus by Dionysus' maenads, the maddening of the Edonian king Lycurgus, and the blinding of the musician Thamyris by the Muses (see respectively Gantz 722, 113, 55). The education of Euneos and Thoas in this area by Orpheus is clearly relevant, though not mentioned until line 1619.

The celebration follows a basic pattern found in the extant 'recognition-plays' of Eur. (*IT* 827–99, *Helen* 625–97, *Ion* 1437–1509; cf. *El.* 585–95, S. *El.* 1232–87). The heroine expresses her joy in excited and loosely structured ('astrophic') lyrics, while her male partner responds with spoken iambic verses. They first express their joy, amazement and relief at the reunion, then review the vicissitudes and sorrows they have suffered, and finally consider the future they now face (see Cropp on *IT* 827–99 with further refs.; also Kannicht on *Hel.* 625–99). The text here gives the end of the first part in this pattern (1579–83) and much of the second (1591–1633, divided at 1610 between Hyps. and her sons). The question of the future was taken up in the lost speech of Dionysus (1673ff.). Amph.'s exit-speech (1584–9) and the responses to it at the transition from the first to the second part are an unusual feature: he has played a crucial role in Hyps.'s crisis and has presided over the reunion, but his involvement with the family has been temporary and the dramatist now tactfully extricates him.

METRE of Hyps.'s lyrics: mostly dochmiacs (with some cretic or iambic elaborations), occasional dactylic cola (1598, 1602, 1607, 1615 enoplian; 1605–6 dactyls; 1608, 1610b–13 dactylo-epitrite. On the enoplians see A. M. Dale, *The Lyric Metres of Greek Drama* (Cambridge, 1968²), 169 n. 1, 171; K. Itsumi, *BICS* 38 [1991–3], 243–61, esp. 245–6, 248, 251–3 with n. 31.

1579–83. ...has driven <me> and my sons (etc.): the Greek verb images Hyspipyle and her sons as chariot-horses driven remorselessly and veering alternately **towards fear, then towards gladness**; cf. A. *Cho.* 1022–3, E. *El.* 1252–3, *IT* 82–3, 934–5, *Or.* 36–7 (all of Orestes persecuted by the Furies). **this way and that** (ἀνάπαλιν), **swerving us** (ἐλίξας, of winding or zigzag motion): cf. *Ion* 1504–5 (a sailing metaphor), 'We veer this way and that (ἐλισσόμεσθ' ἐκεῖθεν ἐνθάδε) in misfortune, and then again (πάλιν) in good fortune'. The lost subject of this whole sentence should be Masc. like ἐλίξας **swerving**, and should fit both **driven <me>** (etc.) and **has shone out (etc.).** [The first editors suggested δαίμων ('guiding spirit, fortune'), which is plausible even though it mixes the metaphor; cf. *Tro.* 204 ἔρροι νὺξ αὐτὰ καὶ δαίμων, 'may this night and (this) *daimon* be gone (i.e. not befall us)!' A *daimon* can flow favourably (A. *Pers.* 601), change direction like a wind (*Pers.* 942f.), and be both personal and impersonal (Stevens on *And.* 98).]

1582. with time's passing: time's gradual bringing of changes of fortune is a reunion topic (*El.* 585, *Hel.* 645, 652–3).

1584. the service that I owed you: cf. F 757.859, 872–3.

1585 [I requested your help: ἠντόμην, lit. 'I entreated (you)', is the most likely correction of P's ἦν τότε ('I was (generous) then'?)]

1586. with regard to your sons: i.e., in effecting the reunion, corresponding with 'when I requested your help' (with regard to the sacrifice). This seems more appropriate than 'towards your sons' (ed. pr., Page, Bond).

1587. [Take care of yourself: P's text with τέκνα (App.) gives 'Take care of your children', probably because the sense of the middle form σώιζου was misunderstood.]

1590–2. Good fortune to you (etc.): said to Amph. as he departs. [P assigns 1590–2 to 'Hypsipyle's sons', perhaps meaning one farewell from each as the first editors suggested. More probably Hyps. spoke the first farewell and Euneos the second since (1) Amph. has just been chiefly addressing Hyps., and (2) Hyps. proceeds to address one son (1594, 1598 as emended, 1607, 1611–3, 1617–8, 1621), one son responds (1614, 1616, 1619, 1622–3), and this son is clearly identified as Euneos (1622–3). Compare *El.* 1238, assigned to the Dioscuri in ms. L although lines 1240, 1245, 1276 together identify the speaker as Castor and (as here) an unavailable fourth speaking voice would be needed for his brother.]

1592. how insatiably some god (etc.): lit. 'how insatiable with your misfortunes some god was'; cf. *Hel.* 1102 (Helen to Aphrodite), 'Why are you so insatiable with (my) troubles' (τί ποτ' ἄπληστος εἶ κακῶν). No divine hostility towards Hyps. is evident in the frs., but characters in tragedy (as no doubt in ancient Greek life) often highlight their misfortunes by blaming 'the gods' or 'a god' (cf. on 1583).

1593–1608. Hyps. recalls her flight from Lemnos and the Lemnian women's massacre of their men which led to it: cf. Introd., p. 177.

1595. [P's unmetrical word-order has been changed to make two resolved dochmiacs.]

1597. I feel the terror (etc.): the pain of recollecting past sufferings is another reunion topic (*Hel.* 661–4, 673–4, *Ion* 1452, S. *El.* 1245–50).

1598. like Gorgons: i.e. ugly and staring murderously, like the serpent 'fiercely staring' (γοργωπὰ λεύσσων) in F 754a.3 or the mad Heracles with his 'Gorgon's eye' (ὄμμα Γοργόνος) in *HF* 990. [my son: τέκνον (Wilamowitz in ed. pr.) is preferable to P's plural τέκν(α) both because Hyps. is responding to Euneos (cf. 1594, 1612, 1618), and because it suits the the metre (see Dale cited in the metrical note above).]

1600. steal away and escape death: lit. 'steal out your foot so as not to die'.

1605–8. Seafarers…brought me (etc.): cf. the chorus in *IT* 1109–12, 'I went in ships by means of enemies' oars and spears; through gold-rich barter (ἐμπολᾶς: cf. 1609 here) I came (on) a barbarous journey home'. ξενικὸν πόρον is internal Acc. with ἄγαγον: cf. e.g. 1624, *IT* 1112.

1610. Don't grieve at what has turned out well: sorrow giving way to joy is again a reunion topic (*Hel.* 649, *Ion* 1456–61).

1614. to the Colchians' city: cf. Introd., pp. 171, 177–8. In this account Jason took the twins with him to Colchis after staying on Lemnos until they were weaned (1615), and before the Lemnian massacre occurred: cf. Robert, Giangrande. Aélion (1986, 131–3) and van Looy (ed. Budé, 159) put the Argonauts' visit between the massacre and Hyps.'s exposure and flight, but the twins know nothing about the massacre in 1593ff., and these lines suggest that Hyps. fled very soon after it.

1615. just lately weaned from my breast: Giangrande 171–4 shows that ἀπομαστίδιον, occurring uniquely here, means 'off the breast', like ἀπότιτθος ('off the teat') and ἀπογάλακτος ('off the milk', cited by Kannicht), and is opposite to ἐπιμαστίδιος and ὑπομαστίδιος ('on the breast', 'at the breast').

1616. my father Jason died: the surviving frs. of the play give no indication of how or where Jason was supposed to have died in this version of the story. Possibly Eur. left the matter unexplained, although the brevity of Hyps.'s response here (cf. 1620) might suggest she has already heard about it. Bond argues that she has not, noting that she does not know about her father's survival either (1626–7); but there she asks for an explanation whereas here she does not. Perhaps the implication is that she assumes he must have been killed at Colchis. Some iconographic evidence, much debated, suggests there may have been a pre-Euripidean tradition that he was consumed there by the fleece-guarding serpent: see *LIMC* 'Iason', V.i.632 nos. 30–32; Robert 387–9, Giangrande 166–71, H. Meyer, *Medeia und die Peliaden* (Rome, 1980), 81–91.

1619. Orpheus took me (etc.): a further novel feature of Eur.'s story, allowing Euneos to be identified as a musician and founder of the Euneid clan in Attica (Introd., p. 178). For Orpheus with the Argonauts see Comm. on F 752g.8–14.

1620. [The text gives an awkward iambic-dochmiac combination. Repetition of τίνα 'what' (Murray, improved by Willink: cf. Diggle, *Euripidea* 374) would make two more regular resolved dochmiacs]

1622. music of the...lyre: μοῦσαν...κιθάρας is lit. 'lyre's muse' as at F 752h.6–7. For Orpheus' **Asian** lyre-music cf. F 752g.9–10 (n.).

1624. what passage did you make: πόρον is internal Acc. as in 1606.   [Willink's δι' <ἁλὸς> Αἰγαίου, '**across the Aegean** <*sea*>' (a dragged dochmiac) avoids a dubious scansion of δι' Αἰγαίου as an iambic metron with –γαι– shortened by correption.]

1626. †the children of two†: P's δυοῖν τέκνω is obviously wrong but hard to correct. [The first editors and Wecklein offered weak sense with '**the** *two* **children**': the number hardly needs emphasis. Wecklein's alternative '*his daughter's* **children**' is also weak. Collard's '*your two* **children**' is apt but supposes a surprising corruption.]

1627. Is he really *safe* (etc.): the frs. of *Hyps.* give no details of Thoas' survival of the Lemnian massacre beyond the fact that Hyps. spared him (1593–9 above), nor of his reunion with his grandsons. Presumably (as in later poetic and mythographic sources) she or the Lemnian women floated him out to sea in a chest which landed on the island of Sikinos near Paros (Ap. Rhod. 1.620–6) or more commonly Chios, or elsewhere: see *RE* VIA.299, IX.i.440–1.   **through *Bacchus'* contriving:** see Introd., pp. 176, 182 on Dionysus' influence in the story and the play.

1628–31. probably Hyps.'s comments on the revelation of her father's survival, e.g. 'He had little **expectation of life**, yet Dionysus **brought (his) son** safely home **for your mother...**'.   [The articulation παῖδας ἢ (ed. pr.) gives 'brought his sons to (their?) mother, or....']

1632. The line is a complete sentence (followed by a paragraphus in the papyrus). **grapebunch:** a symbol of Dionysus (F 758a.1094 (n.), F 765), perhaps here an ornament which has identified the twins like the 'golden vine' of *Anth.Pal.* 3.10 (T iv.)

760. From Stobaeus' section *On Anger.* The first editors (p. 82) thought of Hyps. defending herself against Eurydice (cf. 823–8 with n.), but **every man** makes a male speaker more likely (Cockle, Kannicht). Perhaps advice to Eurydice from Amphiaraus?

760a. The conflict between κέρδος 'gain' and δίκη 'fairness, justice' is a commonplace, e.g. *Hcld.* 2–3, Hes. *Works* 320–4, Theognis 199–200, 465–6, Pind. *Pyth.* 4.139–41. Grenfell and Hunt (p. 81) thought Eurydice might have accused Hyps. of corruption.

761. A commonplace like e.g. Archil. F 122, S. *Aj.* 648, E. *Ion* 1510–11; others in Stob. 4.46–47. The recognition-scene is the likeliest context (cf. on *Alex.* F 62).

762. The fr. was cited by the Atticist lexicographer Aelius Dionysius to illustrate the use of the form σᾶ for σῶα, 'safe'. εὔφημα **auspicious** is lit. 'well-spoken', avoiding inauspicious speech. Valckenaer's εὔσημα 'well-marked, easy to identify' seems to match the other terms better; the fr. might then have described the well-preserved recognition-tokens which identified Euneos and Thoas, as Zirndorfer (1839) guessed. Wilamowitz (in Grenfell and Hunt, 82) suggested less persuasively that εὔφημα might refer to a secret needing to be concealed by silence; κατεσφραγισμένα **marked with a seal** would then be metaphorical (cf. LSJ σφραγίς II.1).

763. In Ar. *Frogs* 64 Dionysus prepares Heracles for the revelation of his longing for the dead Eur. by reminding him of how one longs for pea-soup, then adds: '**Am I informing you with clarity**, or shall I explain differently?' (ἆρ' ἐκδιδάσκω τὸ σαφές, ἢ ἑτέραι φράσω;). The scholia say 'the half-line is from Eur. *Hyps.*', seeming to mean the second half of the line; but it is the first half which, like some of Dionysus' previous lines (59, 60–1), is tragic in tone. Dionysus thus oscillates comically between vulgar and high-flown explanation of his plight. The Euripidean context is unknown but might have been (e.g.) Amph.'s explanation to Eurydice of her son's death, or the recognition-scene in which one or both parties will have had difficulty in grasping the truth. [For the sense and tragic tone of Ar.'s first half-line see R. Kassel, *RhM* 137 (1994), 36–7; Rau, *Paratragodia* 118–9; Kannicht app.]

765. The 'Euripidean' song in Ar. *Frogs* 1309ff. (cf. on F 752f.9–11) includes at 1320–2: 'sheen of the vine's shoot, toil-terminating cluster's coil – throw your arms around (me?), my child!' (οἰνάνθας γάνος ἀμπέλου, Ι βοτρύος ἕλικα παυσίπονον, Ι περίβαλλ', ὦ τέκνον, ὠλένας). Ancient commentators cited F 765 to illustrate Eur.'s use of the word οἰνάνθη, 'vine-shoot', and also ascribed Ar.'s last four words to Eur. (F 765a). F 765 might be from a choral celebration of Dionysus (cf. F 753c.1–5, F 758a–b), or from the reunion-scene (where the grape-bunch was used as a recognition-token). [*Frogs* 1320–2 as a whole have sometimes been ascribed to *Hyps.*, but the scholia indicate that 1320–1 are not directly quoted; they should be taken as pastiche: cf. Rau, *Paratragodia* 130; Kannicht app.] METRE: dochmiac.

765a. See previous n. for the source. The words must belong to Hyps. in the reunion-scene; such exclamations and accompanying embraces are typical of such scenes, e.g. *IT* 795–9, 827–30, *Hel.* 625–35, *Ion* 1437–44, *Pho.* 304–7, *Or.* 1402–8; cf. Ar. *Thesm.* 912–6 (parody). [Some *Frogs* mss. have Aor. Imper. περίβαλ', giving a normal glyconic rather than a very unusual one with Pres. Imper. περίβαλλ' (cf. K. Itsumi, *CQ* 34 [1984], 74). The metrical anomaly fits with Aeschylus' comment in *Frogs* 1323, 'You see this foot?' — but it could well be Ar.'s own malicious invention. Borthwick (above, F 752f.9–11 n.), 34–6 suggests that Ar. alludes not to metre but to the recognition-scene in Eur. *El.*]

765b. After his first pastiche of Euripidean song, Aeschylus sums up (*Frogs* 1325–8): 'And you dare to fault my songs when you compose songs like *that*, using Cyrene's twelve-trick repertoire (ἀνὰ τὸ δωδεκαμήχανον Κυρήνης)?' The scholia explain that he is comparing Eur.'s meretricious musical technique with the versatile sexual technique of a *hetaira* called Cyrene (also mentioned in Ar. *Thesm.* 98), and that Ar. has adapted the phrase from *Hyps.* On the nuances in Ar. see Borthwick (above), 36–7. The sense and reference of the Euripidean phrase are quite uncertain. The sun passing through the twelve zodiac-signs has been suggested, but μηχανή 'device' is not a proper word for a zodiac-sign, nor for the winding passages of a 'cave' (the variant ἄντρον, giving far-fetched sense). Mette's δωδεκάμηνον would give 'twelve-month star', i.e. again the sun, but the change severs the connection with Aristophanes' text.

765c. A commonplace remark, possibly from the recognition-scene; cf. F 761. (For the lines quoted after this fr. by John Lydus see Introd., *Other proposed ascriptions*.)

766. Context unknown: the choral ode celebrating the gifts of Dionysus (F 758 a–b) is an obvious possibility. For ἀναδρομή = 'growth' see LSJ ἀναδρομή I, ἀνατρέχω II.3.

767. Context unknown. Possibly relevant is the tradition that Pelasgians from Lemnos (Hyps.'s home) once abducted a group of Athenian women from Brauron while they were performing the *arkteia* or bear-ritual for Artemis there (Hdt. 6.138, Philochorus *FGH* 328 F 100–1: on the cult and ritual at Brauron see M. Cropp, *Euripides: Iphigenia in Tauris* (Warminster, 2000), 50–3 with refs.). The Attic cult could also have been mentioned in a choral ode, or by Dionysus at the end of the play.

769. Apparently a reference by another character to Hyps.'s castanet-playing, though some have seen Photius' possibly corrupt wording as no more than a reference to F 752f.8 (against this see Bond).

ANTIOPE

Texts and Testimonia. P. Petrie 1 and 2 (= P. Lit. Lond. 70); P. Oxy. 3317 (ascription disputed: = *TrGF Antigone* F 175); *TrGF* F 179–227 with T i–vii; Pacuvius, *Antiopa* (fragments as in *TrGF* T viib; see Appendix below, pp. 326–9). After P. Petrie (publ. 1891), von Arnim (1913); H. Schaal, *De Euripidis Antiopa* (Berlin, 1914), with comm.; Page, *GLP* 60–71 (only P. Petr., with English tr.); J. Kambitsis, *L'Antiope d'Euripide* (Athens, 1972), with review by J. Diggle, *Gnomon* 47 (1975), 288–91; Diggle, *TrGFS* 85–93 (only F 187, 188, 206, P. Oxy., P. Petr.); H. Van Looy, ed. Budé VIII.1 (1998), 213–74; Huys, *Tale* 104–7, 150–1, 177–81, 313–6, 346–8 (in effect a cumulative commentary).

Myth (principal *testimonia* only). Hom. *Od.* 11.260–5 and Schol. (= *TrGF* T iva); *Anth.Pal.* 3.7; Hygin. *Fab.* 8 (= T iiia), cf. *Fab.* 7; Apollod. 3.5.5 (= T iiib); Schol. Ap. Rhod. 4.1090 (= T iiic) (on the common source of these last three see W. Luppe, *Philologus* 128 [1964], 41–57, M. Huys, *APF* 42 [1996], 171–2); Propertius 3.15.11–42; John Malalas, *Chron.* II.16 Thurn (= 2.29, 35ff. Jeffreys: = T ivc); Horace, *Ep.* 1.18.39–45 and Ovid, *Met.* 6.110–11 (= T ivc); Paus. 2.6.1–2; Dio Chrys. *Or.* 15.9 (= T ivd). Preller-Robert II. 1.114–27; Gantz 484–8.

Illustrations. Haussmann (1958) below; Webster, *Monuments* (1967), 155–6; Trendall-Webster 82–3 (III.3.14–15); *LIMC* I.1 (1981), 718–23 (Amphion: F. Heger), 854–7 (Antiope I: E. Simon), III.1 (1986), 635–44 (Dirke: F. Heger); A.D. Trendall in *Enthousiasmos...Essays...Hemelrijk* (Amsterdam, 1986), 157–66 and *RFV* Pls. 29 (cf. p. 22), 61 (p. 29f.), 211 (pp. 91, 261); Green, *Theatre* 58, and Fig. 3.4a–b; O. Taplin, *AK* 41 (1998), 33–9 with Pls.; L. B. Joyce, *Cl.Ant.* 20 (2001), 221–39 with 2 figs.

Main discussions (after publication of P. Petrie, 1891). N. Wecklein, *Philologus* 79 (1923), 51–69; A. W. Pickard-Cambridge in Powell, *New Chapters* III.105–13; F. Solmsen, *Hermes* 69 (1934), 410–5; Schmid 559–63; U. Haussmann, *MDAI* 75 (1958 [1962]), 50–72, with Pls. 53–7; Webster, *Euripides* (1967), 205–11, 305; E. K. Borthwick, *CQ* 17 (1967), 41–7; Z. K. Vysoky, *LF* 91 (1968), 371–400 (German résumé, 399–400); B. Snell, *Szenen aus griechischen Dramen* (Berlin, 1971), 76–103 (revised from *Scenes from Greek Drama* [Berkeley, 1964], 70–98); P. A. de Nicola, *RAAN* 48 (1973), 195–236; M. Hose, *Studien zum Chor bei Euripides* I (Stuttgart, 1990), 270–4, and *Drama und Gesellschaft* 137–43; Huys, *Tale* (see above, *Texts*); A. J. Podlecki, *Ancient World* 27 (1996), 131–46; P. Wilson, *ICS* 24/25, 1999/2000, 440–9. Main discussions of the two papyri are noted in the apparatus, and those of the 'debate' of Amphion and Zethus in Comm. on F 182b.

The play contained some familiar Euripidean elements such as escape from persecution, reunion of long-lost relatives, and revenge, but also a set-piece debate famous in antiquity once Plato in the *Gorgias* had drawn upon it as an analogue for his own dialogue between Callicles and Socrates (Dodds on *Gorg.* 485e3 observes that since *Antiope* was a late work of Euripides, Socrates and the young Plato may have attended its first performance). While an outline of the action can be established with some confidence and the play's end survives, much detail of its centre is uncertain.

Recovery and nature of the fragments. Writers and anthologists quarried the play for sententious passages both in the debate (perhaps 15 fragments) and elsewhere (16 fragments); there were lexicographers (8 fragments) and various other scholarly citers (7 fragments); many fragments appear in multiple citation. These book-fragments were mostly known and many arranged in plausible dramatic order by Nauck and his predecessors (especially Valckenaer and Welcker) before a long papyrus-fragment from the play's final scene recovered in 1891 (P. Petrie 1–2: F 223) added to confidence that Hyginus, *Fab.* 8 gave a fairly reliable if incomplete outline of the plot. A more recent papyrus-fragment (P. Oxy. 3317 [1980], here located after F 220: = *TrGF Antigone* F 175) also matches a detail in Hyginus well (Dirce while celebrating Dionysus as a bacchant is brought to the Herdsman's dwelling where Antiope has taken refuge); but its ascription to the play is still not widely accepted (see Comm.). One or two long-known book-fragments have since been recovered in part in anthologies on papyrus (F 198, 214, 216; textual differences negligible). Although Cicero, *De Fin.* 1.24 writes of Pacuvius' *Antiopa* as a 'word for word' translation, it was probably no more than a close adaptation, like other Roman copies of Greek models; the fragments however sometimes confirm or illuminate reconstruction.

With so many fragments (about 50, the most for any lost play), there have been continual new arrangements; for those since P. Petrie see *Texts* and *Main discussions* above, and *Reconstruction* below. The editions of Kambitsis (1972) and Van Looy (1998) abandon Nauck's order frequently and head each fragment with a fresh numbering. Kannicht in *TrGF* preserves Nauck's numbering and order entirely, apart from a few additional fragments; but he notes a few probable relocations. This edition follows the *TrGF* numbering and order, except that F 190 and 192 are printed after the new F 182a, 206 after 210, 219 after 188, 220 after 202; and some unplaced fragments are gathered at the end (F 195, 209, 212–18, 226–7); one uncertain fragment, F 910, follows them.

Myth. Euripides' Antiope is daughter of Nycteus (F 223.42), former king in Boeotia, but in earlier versions (first at Hom. *Od.* 11.260) daughter of Asopus, eponym of the Boeotian river (distinguish our Antiope from the Amazon abducted by Theseus of Athens, Gantz 282–5, and from the wife of Laocoon of Troy, Gantz 647–9). Gantz 484–8 traces her entire mythography, together with the destinies of her twin sons Zethus and Amphion, the builders of Thebes' citadel (F 223.86–102 and Comm.). All that is needed to grasp the play's background is found in Hygin. *Fab.* 8 and its probable fellow derivatives from a Hellenistic 'narrative hypothesis' (for such, see our Vol.I p. 2), Apollod. 3.5.5 and Schol. Ap. Rhod. 4.1090 (= *TrGF* T iiia–c: see Luppe and Huys in Bibl., *Myth*); these accounts can be supplemented from other sources offering small details or variations potentially useful in reconstruction. Hyginus 8 indeed purports to summarize both myth and Euripidean play, and its sections 5–9 coincide with the indications given by many play-fragments; but it omits the twins' debate, the mechanisms of their reunion with their mother Antiope and vengeance upon Dirce, and the aetiology of Dirce's Spring: this is stressed by Huys (1996), 171–2, who therefore doubts Hyginus' faithfulness to a 'hypothesis'.

Hyginus 8 reads (with the most significant variations in other accounts noted):

(1) Nycteus king in Boeotia had a daughter Antiope; attracted to her by the excellence of her beauty, Jupiter made her pregnant (Schol. Ap. Rhod. has 'Zeus in the likeness of a satyr raped her', cf. Ovid *Met.* 6.110–11 etc.; Comm. on F 210). (2) When her father wished to punish her for inchastity, Antiope fled from the danger which threatened. By chance Epopeus of Sicyon was staying in the same place to which she came; he took the woman with him and married her at home (on 1–2: Paus. 2.6.1–2 has Epopeus seize Antiope, and both Nycteus and himself die in the consequent war). (3) In his anger at this, Nycteus when dying adjured and enjoined his brother Lycus, to whom he was leaving his kingdom, that Antiope should not go unpunished (cf. *Anth.Pal.* 3.7). (4) After Nycteus' death Lycus came to Sicyon; he killed Epopeus and led away Antiope in bonds. (5) Antiope gave birth to twins on Mt. Cithaeron and abandoned them; a herdsman found and brought them up, naming them Zethus and Amphion (cf. F 181–2; Apollod. has '...at Eleutherae [cf. F 179] a herdsman found and brought the twins up, etc.; in maturity Zethus pastured cattle but Amphion devoted himself to the lyre when Hermes gave it him [F 182a, cf. F 223.90–7]'). (6) Antiope was given to Dirce the wife of Lycus to torture (also *Anth.Pal.* 3.7); she seized an opportunity and took to flight (Apollod. has 'Lycus and Dirce imprisoned Antiope, but when her bonds fell from her of their own accord [cf. Hygin. *Fab.* 7.3], she went unnoticed to the dwelling of her sons, wanting them to take her in'). She reached her sons, of whom Zethus, thinking her a fugitive, did not take her in (cf. Propertius 3.15.29–30). (7) Dirce was brought at once (Kannicht: 'there' Hyginus mss.) to the same place through bacchic possession by Liber (i.e. Dionysus; cf. P. Oxy. 3317 and Comm., and *Illustrations* below); finding Antiope there she began to drag her outside to her death (Schol. Ap. Rhod. has 'the recaptured Antiope was handed over to her own sons'). (8) Assured however by the herdsman who had brought them up that Antiope was their mother, the young men quickly pursued and seized her back; they tied Dirce to a bull by her hair and killed her (F 221; 'tied' as in *Illustrations*; cf. *Anth.Pal.* 3.7.5–6; Apollod. has 'they threw Dirce after her death into the spring called 'Dirce' for her'; Lycus is to throw her in, F 223.112–5).

(9) When they wished to cut down Lycus, Mercury (i.e. Hermes) forbade them (F 223.67) and at the same time ordered Lycus to cede the kingdom to Amphion (78–9: Apollod. has 'they killed Lycus', a deliberate variation; Schol. Ap. Rhod. has 'on the pretence of returning Antiope, they summoned Lycus and were about to kill him...').

Reconstruction. (*Note.* Kambitsis pp. IX–XXX and Van Looy 226–37 include many details of earlier attempts; see also Webster, *Euripides* (1967), 205–11, Podlecki 131–5.)

Prologue by the Herdsman, narrating how he sheltered and brought up Amphion and Zethus after Antiope abandoned them near his dwelling on the slopes of Mt. Cithaeron, near Eleutherae at the border between Thebes and Attica (Hygin. 8.4–6 etc.; fragmentary remains in **F 179, 181–2**); the action is set here. Probably he told of her ancestry (**F 180**) and how she was then taken into repressive slavery by Lycus and Dirce, the rulers of Thebes (Hygin. 8.6). The time may be early morning, if Pacuv. *Ant.* F *1 is from that play's prologue. (Kambitsis IX–XII convincingly rebuts older suggestions that a god was the speaker.)

Parodos: either Amphion enters with his lyre, singing a hymn to the splendours of creation (**F 182a**), and is joined by the Chorus of Attic farmers, or they enter singing themselves, perhaps in honour of Dionysus, and he joins them before singing himself (cf. Pacuv. *Ant.* F 2 from which their identity is inferred; 'Thebans' corruptly for 'Athenians' in Schol. *Hipp.* 58 = *TrGF* T v, for Thebans would know, not guess, Lycus' identity at F 223.17–18).

Episode 1 probably began with Amphion answering the Chorus' questions about the history of the lyre (**F 190, 192**). Zethus' arrival interrupts them; possibly he wanted Amphion to go hunting, and his refusal (Hor. *Ep.* 1.18. 39–40) precipitated the debate (**F 182b**, cf. Pacuv. F 3–*5). Zethus reproves his brother's devotion to music rather than his duty of hard farm-work (**F 183–8, 219?**, cf. Pacuv. F *5); Amphion defends his quieter virtues (**F 193–4, 196–202, 220?**). The outcome appears to have been Amphion's partial concession to Zethus (Hor. *Ep.* 1.18.43–4), but with the paradoxical consequence that he goes on to dominate the later action (see *Themes etc.* below). It is likely that the twins went off at the episode's end, rather than entered the dwelling.

Stasimon 1: a blank, unless **F 910** (p. 296), praise of quiet metaphysical contemplation, is located here as an 'endorsement' of Amphion's stance in the debate.

Episodes 2 and 3 (or 2–4): it is impossible to delimit scenes and identify participants with any confidence. Antiope has now escaped somehow from captivity and comes for refuge in the Herdsman's dwelling where long ago she bore the twins (Hygin. 8.6; Kambitsis p. XV and Van Looy 232 accept the version in Apollod. that her bonds fell from her of their own accord, through the power of Dionysus, like those of the bacchants at *Bacc.* 447). Encountering first the Chorus (F 204), she narrates her miserable history (**F 205, 207**, perhaps in a long speech; cf. Pacuv. F 6–9, 11) to the Chorus alone (e.g. Kambitsis p. XV), perhaps joined by the Herdsman (but see below), or possibly to the twins in mutual ignorance of true identity (Van Looy 233). If the twins have re-entered, Propertius 3.15.29–30 and Hygin. 8.6 may be right with the version that Zethus, not Amphion, refuses Antiope's appeal for sanctuary – but Zethus is more likely to have become a mute figure for the rest of the play after Amphion, as the more eloquent, was the effective winner of their debate (Schaal 25). Antiope seems to have told of her seduction by Zeus in this first encounter (**F 207, 208**? [location not certain]); when Amphion rejects her story (**F 210**), she may then assert her veracity (**F 206**, see Comm.; possibly also in **F 208**); for after she is reunited with her sons, he would hardly reject her story (cf. F 223.2–3).

All those unsure suggestions rest upon some evidence at least; from now on there are merely possible sequences of action, of which this is one: the twins (if still present) go off to their work, leaving Antiope alone (most eds.), perhaps to lament – in a monologue, or a monody, or a (part-)lyric exchange with the Chorus?[1] Did Episode 2 end here? If so, Episode 3 began with Dirce arriving to celebrate Dionysus on Mt. Cithaeron, or having done so (Hygin. 8.7); her fellow bacchants form a secondary chorus (see below, *Staging*), and they may enter singing to honour the god (cf. Pacuv. F 12). Dirce finds the escaped Antiope, and they seem to have had an angry argument (many editors locate **F 216–8** about slavery here, a topic recurring at P. Oxy. 3317.10). This may be the time when the Herdsman learns of Antiope's presence and identity; perhaps he arrived or came out of his dwelling to drive the bacchants away (cf. Pacuv. F 13). Dirce and her women seize Antiope to take her off to death (Hygin. 8.7) – but Schol. Ap. Rhod. has Dirce giving Antiope 'to her own sons', presumably to kill (support for this is sought in Schol. *Pho.* 102, but it is difficult to reconcile with Hyginus; cf. Kambitsis p. XIX). Whatever happened, and however, the Herdsman must go to tell the twins of their mother, so that she may be saved (Hygin. 8.8).

A major issue in reconstruction now arises. Did Episode 3 end here, with Episode 4 holding the Messenger's report not only that Dirce had been killed by the bull (**F 221**), but also that Antiope had been rescued? Or was her rescue done either during a lyric interlude towards the end of Episode 3, so that the twins return with her and Dirce, now herself the captured victim, before the Episode ends, or in a brief Episode 4? Either of these two latter solutions suits and encourages the insertion before F 221 of **P. Oxy. 3317** (Luppe; see

---

[1] 'Antiope's lament' became proverbial, Apostolius II.281.1 *CPG*, cf. Suidas α 2689; Creusa's bitter lyric lament for her abandonment long ago by Apollo, *Ion* 859–922, would be directly comparable.

Comm.): in the fragmentary text Dirce has attempted to gain sanctuary (line 1 – perhaps at the column sacred to Dionysus described in **F 203**); but when faced with violent removal (2–8), she surrenders voluntarily to her death (9–15). When she is taken away by the twins, Antiope remains with the Chorus.

Stasimon 3 (or 4): a blank; located before the Messenger's report by almost all editors.

Episode 4 (or 5), probably running directly into the *Exodos*: Messenger's report (**F 221**) to Antiope and the Chorus (and perhaps the Herdsman); someone may voice moral satisfaction here (**F 222**). After probably a brief lyric interlude, the twins return, shortly before P. Petrie begins (**F 223**); it holds the end of the play. Amphion is already acknowledging that either he and Zethus must pay penalty for Dirce's death or, with their father Zeus' help, complete their triumph by killing Lycus (1–16). With Antiope they now enter the dwelling, before Lycus arrives intending to recapture Antiope (17–27; in these lines he does not mention Dirce). Then there is a gap of 29 lines in P. Petrie after which Lycus is lured into the dwelling unguarded; this is achieved probably by the Herdsman rather than by the unknown Amphion (28–55: see Comm. and below, *Staging*). Lycus is brought out by Amphion for execution, and tormented with news of Dirce's death (56–66); Antiope perhaps comes out too, now played by a mute, so that Euripides may create surprises: the audience are led to expect a killing, which a woman would not normally witness, let alone one on open stage, but the god Hermes suddenly intervenes (67ff., confirming Hygin. 8.9; cf. *Illustrations* below). All the important characters are thus present to hear the god announce Zeus' responsibility for Antiope's suffering, which he has now ended (68–77); he gives Zeus' order for Lycus to cede the Theban throne to the twins (78–9) and to 'bury' Dirce's ashes in Ares' Spring which is to bear her name for ever (80–5). Next, the twins are to build a Theban citadel, with the magical aid of Amphion's lyre moving rocks and trees (86–97); they are to have fine marriages and special honours (98–103). A chastened Lycus accepts Zeus' orders, repeating their details (104–116) – at which point P. Petrie breaks off. Comparison with other Euripidean endings suggests that little further was said, perhaps only formal gratitude from Amphion to Zeus and closing lines from the Chorus; Hermes may leave at 103 as abruptly as he entered, for at 112 he is already 'Third Person'.

Other proposed ascriptions. The strongest candidate is **F 911**, four lyric verses probably beginning an ode and recorded by Satyrus, *Life of Euripides* fr. 39, (col. xvii.19ff. Arrighetti) as Euripides' farewell to Athens when he left it for Archelaus' court in Macedon (for this disputed departure see on *Arch.*, p. 337): 'I have wings of gold upon my back and the winged sandals of the Sirens are fitted to my feet. I shall rise into the great heaven and go to join Zeus' – as if Eur. expected Archelaus to welcome him to a poet's paradise: considered for *Ant.* by Wilamowitz, *Kl. Schr.* I.450 n. 1 and *Der Glaube der Hellenen* (Darmstadt, 1959³), I.263, cf. Webster, *Euripides* (1967), 207; for *Arch.* by Kuiper, *Mnem.* 41 (1913), 242 (scepticism in Harder, *Eur. Kresphontes and Archelaos* [see p. 330, *Texts*], 285); uncertainty in Kambitsis 134 and Van Looy, *Appendix* p. 270; rejected by *TrGF.* **F 224 N** = Eubulus F 9.1–2, 4–5 *PCG*, F 10 Hunter. **F 853**, three trimeters advising honour for gods, parents and the common laws of Greece, is attributed to *Hcld.* by Stob. 3.1.80 mss. MA but to *Ant.* by Trinc.: retained for *Hcld.* by Wilamowitz, *Kl. Schr.* I. 90 and J. Wilkins, *Euripides: Heraclidae* (Oxford, 1993), xxx, 194; asserted for *Antiope*, in the same context as F 206, by Zuntz, *CQ* 41 (1947), 47 and entertained by Diggle, *OCT* I.98; uncertain Van Looy, *Appendix* p. 270; om. Kambitsis; rejected by *TrGF.* **F 941**, two trimeters saying 'consider the boundless heaven embracing the earth as Zeus, as god', much quoted in antiquity; assigned to *Antiope* by Schneidewin, cf. Webster (above) 209; generally rejected. **F 1058** (= *Antigone* F 162a *TrGF*), two trimeters forecasting a good and lasting marriage for the speaker, unattrib. at Stob. 4.22.12, mistakenly attributed to *Antiope* in the fragmentary Euripidean anthology P. Oxy. 3214.3–5 (see Comm. on the correctly attributed F 214 which follows it there). **Adesp. F 88a**: see Comm. on F *187a. Even less probably ascribed are **F 918** and **F 1028**. Some fragments of *Antigone* are confused with *Antiope* in sources: see especially *TrGF* on **F 144, F 177**; for **F 175** see Comm. on P. Oxy. 3317.

Illustrations. No earlier representations are known than three vase-paintings from the 4ᵗʰ C.; these command attention (*TrGF* T vi; studied by Taplin [1998, with Pls.], cf. *LIMC* 'Dirce'). The earliest (1), a Lucanian pelike of c. 400 (Taplin Pl. 8.1; Trendall-Webster III.3.14; A. D. Trendall, *Red Figure Vases of South Italy and Sicily* [London 1989], Pl. 29), has Dirce apparently still tied under the bull, with the twins goading it. It may have been prompted at least by hearsay of Euripides' play (this seems to have been the first telling of the full story: Taplin 38), but evinces no certain association with a performance.

The other two vases do seem to reflect the play. The earlier (2), a Sicilian pelike of c. 370 by the eponymous Dirce Painter (*LIMC* 'Antiope I' no. 6; Taplin, Pl. 8.2; Trendall-Webster III.3.15; Trendall, *Red Figure Vases* [above], Pl. 61; Csapo–Slater 60–2 with Pl. 3A; Joyce Fig.1), combines separate dramatic moments in one picture (a typical vase-painters' device: see our Vol. I p. 3). Dirce lies dead, the bull apparently still trampling her but making off (cf. the Messenger at F 221; in front of a rocky arch (the Herdsman's cave?) the twins manhandle a kneeling Lycus (in tragic costume); one is about to strike him with a sword; a woman turns away in horror (Antiope?); 'above' the arch is a truncated but undamaged figure, clearly Hermes suddenly intervening from the sky (F 223.67). The third vase (3) is an Apulian calyx-crater of c. 320 by the 'Underworld Painter', first published by Trendall, *Enthousiasmos* (*LIMC* 'Dirke' no. 6; Taplin Pl. 9; Trendall, *RFV* Pl. 211; Green, *Theatre* Pl. 3.4a–b). The upper register has amid other figures the twins about to kill Lycus (who is in tragic costume), but Hermes now intervenes physically on the ground to hold them apart. The lower register shows Dirce dead beneath the bull, and still tied to it; a Fury-figure marks her death as blood-vengeance for tormenting Antiope (Taplin 36); an old man, gesturing, may be the Herdsman; a horrified woman, Antiope. Dionysiac emblems lie near Dirce, signifying her bacchic possession (Hygin. *Fab.* 8.7, P. Oxy. 3317 and Comm.).

For other vases and works of art which have been argued to derive ultimately from Euripides' play rather than from myth generally, especially numerous Hellenistic and Roman depictions of Dirce's death, see Webster, *LIMC* and Joyce; cf. below, *Other dramatizations.*

Themes and characters; the debate. There is insufficient detail in near- ly all the fragments – even the long F 223 – and in the testimonia from which to fill out the characters. The Herdsman and Messenger are barely visible, but the former may have had a more active role than the Farmer in *Electra* and have resembled rather the Old Tutor in that play or in *Ion*; his role as both rescuer and foster-father to the twins, continued when he helps with the luring-scene, is well discussed by Huys, *Tale* 313–5. Antiope survives in the text only as a typical Euripidean mother eventually released from long agonies (cf. *Similarities* below). Dirce is a female Lycus, himself a typical persecutor like his son in *HF*; possibly their negative characterization reflects Athenian hostility to Thebes (see e.g. F. Zeitlin in J. Winkler and F. Zeitlin, *Nothing to do with Dionysus?* (Princeton, 1990), 130–67). Dirce may be in the style of the Queen in *Mel.D.* (Vol. 1, p. 243) or the childless Hermione in *And.*, relentlessly jealous and tormenting.

A little more can be said about the twins. As children avenging a parent they are in the long tragic tradition beginning with Orestes and Electra (their 'natural nobility' is brought out in F 185.2, 186 and the unplaced 215); in their preliminary reunion with their mother they are in the particularly Euripidean style (again cf. *Similarities*). They are most visible in the debate, also a familiar Euripidean scene (below). Zethus is shown as direct in argument (especially F 187 and Comm., 185.3–8, 188, 219?); his character and values have a strongly aristocratic cast (cf. Carter [Comm. on F 182b], 171, Wilson 444–5. Amphion's softer and more philosophic nature is hinted first in his devotion to singing (F 182a, 192) before we hear him in the debate calmly deprecating over- exertion (F 193.1, 201); then he defends his own contented quietude (F 193.2, 196) and his reserves of discreet but potentially helpful political *savoir faire* (F 194, 200.2–3, 202, 220?). What surprises about Amphion is his apparent emergence from the debate to dominate Zethus. This change may be anticipated in the fragments if his good sense (F 200.2, 202, cf. perhaps 194) foreshadows his pragmatic analysis of predicament and challenge, and frank appeal for divine aid, once Dirce is dead but Lycus remains to be killed (F 223.1–16); and he later coldly torments the doomed man about his wife's death (60–6). In this determined action he becomes, paradoxically, partly Zethian himself: he is to 'arm himself' with his lyre in building Thebes (F 223.91), as Zethus is to undertake its armed defence (89); their futures are linked, as the singer and 'quiet' man cooperates with the active one (86–8, 98–111).

The debate itself has attracted most discussion (see Comm. on F 182b). It had probably a typical Euripidean form: at its heart, the opposed positions were presented in two long and perhaps combative speeches. Zethus spoke first as 'plaintiff' (the term in M. Lloyd, *The Agon in Euripides* [Oxford, 1992], 17); F 183 shows his principal accusation. Amphion as the more 'sympathetic figure' (Lloyd 16) and 'winner' spoke second. Almost all the fragments can be imagined within the two long speeches; there are no 'one-liners', except perhaps F 191 and 197, which could be attributed to the intense stichomythic exchange characteristically preceding or following Euripides' long debate-speeches (for all these constant features of Euripidean debates see e.g. Collard on *Supp.* 87–262(C) and Lloyd, *Agon* 144–5 with n. 3).[2]

Zethus first attacks socially unproductive idleness as irresponsible in comparison with hard work, but even within his own long speech he shifts towards the merits of clear, constructive thought and brave conduct (F 185.2, 4–8, 188.3–5). Amphion has then to answer on his brother's ground (Carter 171); and he ends by claiming political wisdom for himself (F 199.2–3, 200, 202, cf. 194). This shift in direction was remarked in antiquity (Cicero and Anon. *Ad Herennium* in F 182b.ii).

Scholars argue whether the contrasting philosophies of the debate reflect an urgent political issue of *Antiope*'s own time (see below, *Date*), or a question constantly alive from the earliest poetry into later antiquity. Some like Snell (*Szenen* 87) declare the debate to be of both immediate and general relevance, and evaluate it accordingly against the widest background; others see Amphion's

---

[2] There is broad agreement, which fragments belong to the debate, and which to Zethus and Amphion, but considerable disagreement about their order. For nearly complete summaries of earlier views see Séchan 298 n. 3 (to 1926); Podlecki (1996), 136–7 gives those of Webster (1967), Snell (1971) and Kambitsis (1972) and then his own; for further views see Vysoky 1964, Carter 1986, Slings 1995, Van Looy 1998. A. W. Nightingale (see Comm. on F 182b) regards Amphion as losing to Zethus 'despite powerful arguments', but vindicated by Hermes at the end of the play (F 223.90–7); but a reversal only there is false to the facts of the other fragments (F 210; F 223.1–16, 60–6; and perhaps P. Oxy. 3317.1–8).

emergent superiority as Euripides' endorsement of a political attitude expressed in political disengagement or inactivity, *apragmosunê*; the counter-term was *polupragmosunê*, over-activity or interference, with which Athenians were increasingly charged (or charged one another) throughout the disastrous Peloponnesian War (see Comm. on F 193). Most recently Carter thinks that Euripides has Amphion advocate moderately democratic rather than populist values, in opposition to Zethus' seemingly aristocratic position; Slings sees in Amphion's quiet art and wisdom paradoxically the best accompaniment to the political life; Podlecki counters Carter in arguing that both the debate and the entire play commend a middle, politically practical road between quiet values and the forthright activity represented in Zethus; Wilson emphasizes the significance of Amphion's music, which turns out to have 'foundational value as a "religious" *mousike*' for the future city (p. 447: cf. F 223.90–5).

Similarities with other plays. *Antiope* shares a number of dramatic motifs with other plays after about 425 and particularly 415 (cf. *Date* below). These are: reunion of relatives followed by vengeance upon persecutors (e.g. *Cresph.* in our Vol. 1, pp. 123, 146, and *Mel.*, pp. 245–6); luring of a victim (*Hec.* 951ff., *HF* 701ff., the Orestes-plays *El.* 1008ff. (successful revenge), *Or.* 1366ff. (revenge stopped by a god), and *Cresph.* again; cf. our Vol. I, pp. 6–7). Comparison with *Ion*, very close in date (413?), shows Euripides' reuse of other elements too in subtle variation, so that not just these two plays but others become mutually illuminating (for this phenomenon throughout Euripides see our Vol. I, pp. 6–8). Note especially that both Creusa and Antiope are violated by gods, abandon their babies and suffer long misery before reunion (for which the gods take both responsibility and credit, *Ion* 1556ff. and *Antiope* F 223. 72ff.); Creusa narrowly escapes being killed by her son Ion, Antiope narrowly escapes being killed by Dirce; Ion's conflict with his putative father Xuthus over life-styles (569ff.) has an analogy in the debate in *Antiope* (above, *Themes etc.*).

As to *Hyps.*, apparently from the same original production as *Antiope* (see *Date* below), Wilson (440) follows Zeitlin in Carpenter and Faraone, *Masks of Dionysus* 174 in reasserting corroborative importance for similarities dismissed as 'superficial' by Webster (1967, 214, cf. 211), namely that *Pho., Hyps.* and *Ant.* all portray contrasting brothers, interacting intensely with their mothers; but Hypsipyle's twins Euneos and Thoas have no role comparable with Zethus and Amphion (cf. on *Hyps.*, p. 181 above).

Staging. The entire action plays in front of a cave (F 223.35, 39 etc.), apparently the well-known cult-site of Dionysus at Eleutherae (Paus. 1.38.9; F 179, cf. 203); it seems to be simultaneously the dwelling of the Herdsman and the twins (F 223.42, cf. 29, 47 etc.); it was represented by the central door of the *skênê* (cf. *Phil.*, *Andromeda*, *Cyc.*, *S. Phil.*). There is little in the play that is noteworthy theatrically. There is a brief appearance by a secondary chorus, of Dirce's fellow-bacchants (attested in Schol. *Hipp.* 58 = *TrGF* T v; cf. our Vol. 1, p. 203 on *Phaethon* 227ff.). The central door focuses the excitement, as so often: the Herdsman's dwelling is where Antiope abandoned her twins and returns to seek them, and it is the fateful entrance for both Dirce and Lycus (compare the entrapments at e.g. *Hec.* 1019ff., *El.* 1139ff., *HF* 720ff., 872ff., *Cresph.* F 456 and n.). It is unnecessary to suppose the use of the *ekkyklêma* for Amphion and Zethus bringing out Lycus (F 223.56ff.: Hourmouziades 167, followed by Webster, *Euripides* (1967), 210 and Kambitsis; 'presumably', Taplin, *AK* 42 (1998), 34); nor of the *mêchanê* for Hermes as 'god from the machine' (F 223.67: e.g. D. J. Mastronarde, *ClAnt* 9 [1990], 284; Csapo–Slater 61), for it suffices for him to appear on top of the *skênê* (Wiles 1997, 181). With the dramatic sequence of the play so uncertain, it is impossible to make useful conjectures about the distribution of the parts among the three actors; it seems likely that Zethus at least and probably Antiope were at times played by mutes (see above, *Reconstruction*); after the Herdsman has completed his part in the luring-scene and gone inside his dwelling (F 223.47), he would reappear only if played by a mute, for his actor has to take the part of Hermes from line 67.

Date. Disputed. Schol. Ar. *Frogs* 53 (*TrGF Antiope* T ii = *Androm.* T iic = *Hyps.* T ii) records the performance of *Hypsipyle*, *Phoenissae* and *Antiope* a little before the *Frogs* of 405 B.C., and of *Andromeda* as eight years before it, i.e. 412: many scholars infer that the three plays were produced within a tetralogy in 410 or 408 (e.g. Kambitsis pp. XXXI–V, Hose [1995], 17, 197, Kannicht on *Antiope*). The metrical criteria for dating Euripides' plays (see our Vol. I, pp. 58, 83 etc.) nevertheless point to c. 425–15 for *Ant.*: see Cropp-Fick 75, who point out that features of *Ant.* often taken to confirm a late date, such as a monody (F 182a) or a revenge-scheme against a persecutor (F 223.1–66) are in fact found in earlier plays too, for example monodies at *Hec.* 197ff., *Supp.* 990ff., revenge-entrapments e.g. *Hec.* 870ff. and *Cresph.* (our Vol. 1 p. 125); but other features of *Ant.* strongly resembling those in later plays (see *Similarities etc.* above) seem nevertheless to favour a date of 409/8. Cropp-Fick 76 suggest either that the metrical statistics may be fortuitously 'skewed' by the particular nature of the fragments, or that in Schol. *Frogs* 53 '*Antiope*' is corrupt for '*Antigone*' (approved by W. Luppe, *Mnem.* 45 (1992), 97–8, who argues the reverse corruption in the names for F 175 = vv.14–15 of P. Oxy. 3317; cf. e.g. on F 1058 in *Other proposed ascriptions*). For possible reflection of contemporary relations between Athens and Thebes see Comm. on F 223, at start. Van Looy 221 leaves the problems unresolved.

Other dramatizations; influence. Surprisingly, no other tragedies of the same name are known from the Greek period; nor do Antiope, Amphion and Zethus appear in other Theban plays — but the equally tyrannical son of our Lycus appears in

HF. Yet the play created sufficient resonance in the early 4th C. – presumably through renewed performance – for Plato to exploit it in the *Gorgias* and for it to be burlesqued in Eubulus' fragmentary comedy *Antiope* (see on F 224); J. L. López Cruces (*Prometheus* 29 [2003], 17–36) posits influence of the twins' debate upon a putative 'Cynic' tragedy by the 4th C. philosopher Diogenes of Sinope, *TrGF* 88 F 7; for vase-paintings see *Illustrations* above. This resonance, rather than chance selection, perhaps found its last echo in Pacuvius' translation for the Roman stage in the early 2nd C. B.C.; Pacuvius' editor G. D'Anna thought that he was largely independent of Euripides, a view countered by G. A. Tourlides (*Platon* 46 [1994], 65–70). Much of the story is retold in Augustan poets (T iii, end; for an apparent recreation in Ovid, *Met.* 8 of the twin's debate, voiced there between a sober-sided Daedalus and a voluble

ΑΝΤΙΟΠΗ

179 (ΒΟΥΚΟΛΟΣ)   ...ἔχεις,
εὖ μοι διδοίης δεσπότηι θ' ὃς Οἰνόης
σύγχορτα ναίει πεδία ταῖσδ' Ἐλευθεραῖς.

180   Ὑσίαι or Ὑσιαί

181–182   τὸν μὲν κικλήσκω Ζῆθον· ἐζήτησε γὰρ
τόκοισιν εὐμάρειαν ἡ τεκοῦσά νιν·
τὸν δὲ... Ἀμφίονα...

182a (1023 with 225 N)
ΑΜΦΙΩΝ Αἰθέρα καὶ Γαῖαν πάντων γενέτειραν ἀείδω.

179 (1 Kamb., 1 Budé) Strabo 8.6.16, unattrib.   3 Schol. Hom. *Il.* 11.774a, attrib. Eur. *Ant.*; Apollonius, *Lex.Homer.* p. 48.3 Bekker, attrib. Eur.; *Etym.Gud.* p. 568.43 Sturz, attrib. Eur. *Ant.* (?: play-name corrupt). The passage is alluded to by Dio Chrys. *Or.* 15.9 (= *TrGF* T ivd).   Assigned to the Prologue by Matthiae and to the Herdsman by Wecklein (cf. Pacuv. *Ant.* *1).   1–2 ἔχεις a later hand in Strabo ms. P (formerly V) ἔχειν first hand (whence <ἅ...εὐχόμεσθ'> ἔχειν, | σύ (Aly) μοι Snell   2 Οἰνόης Strabo ms. P Οἰνώνηι other mss.   3 ναίει ms. P ναίειν other mss. ναίω Schol. Hom., Apollon., *Et.Gud.* (for Strabo's text see S. L. Radt, *Noch einmal zu...*[Leiden, 2002], 429–32)   **180** (28 Kamb., 28 Budé) Harpocration, *Lexeis* Y 15 Keaney 'Hysiae...Eur. in *Ant.*'; Steph.Byz. p. 651.15 Meineke, attrib. Eur.; Strabo 9.2.12, unattrib. but naming Antiope (cf. Steph. p. 653.7) Ὑσίαι Harpocrat., Strabo Ὑσιαί Steph.Byz.   **181** = lines 1–2, **182** = 3 (2, 3 Kamb., 2, 3 Budé) 1–2 *Etym.Magn.* 'Ζῆθος', p. 411.12 Gaisford, attrib. Eur. and paraphrasing the etymology   1–2 ζητῆσαι (not ἐζήτησε)...νιν *Etym.Gud.* 'Ζῆθος', p. 230.57 Sturz, attrib. Eur. *Ant.* ('Eur. clearly etymologizes')   3 based on *Etym.Gen.* α 746 Lasserre-Livadaras (*Etym.*

Icarus, see Z. Ritook in the edited volume *Griechenland und Rom* [Erlangen, 1996], 204–21; for possible influence of the debate upon Plutarch's *De Genio* see A. Georgiadou in the edited volume *Teoria e prassi politica nelle opere di Plutarco* [Naples, 1995]). There are late echoes in Dio Chrysostom and John Malalas (T ivc, ivd); many quotations from the play-text were perpetuated in other writers, especially anthologists (above, *Recovery etc.*). For modern times from the 15ᵗʰ C. see Schmid 560 n. 5 (resonance of the debate); *OGCMA* 110–11 'Antiope' (painting, sculpture, opera), 111–12 'Antiope and Dirce' (sculpture, most famously the restoration of the late Roman 'Farnese Bull' in the 1540s and after [bibl. in Taplin 1998, 33 n. 1] and Canova's 'Dirce' of 1819; also poems, operas, ballets, plays) and 94–5 'Amphion' (early 'romances', operas up to Honegger's of 1931, ballets, and even a violin concerto by Hamilton in 1971).

ANTIOPE

F 179–182, prologue-speech:

179 HERDSMAN . . . <you who> hold < . . .>, may you grant good things for me and my master who inhabits the plains of Oenoe with pastures adjoining Eleutherae here!

The Herdsman begins with a prayer for a god's (Dionysus') blessing.

180   *Hysiae*

181–182 One I name Zethus, for his mother 'searched' for comfort for his birthing, <the other. . . . . . . Amphion >.

F 182a, 190, 192, Amphion's entry, singing to his lyre (182a), perhaps in company with the Chorus of Athenian farmers from the neighbourhood:

182a AMPHION Heaven and Earth the begetter of all things are my song.

Magn. ''Αμφίων', p. 92.24 Gaisford), attrib. Eur., printed by *TrGF* in prose-paraphrase as τὸν δὲ 'Αμφίονα, ὅτι ἀμφ' ὁδὸν αὐτὸν ἔτεκεν)   Fragments combined and assigned to the Prologue-speech by Matthiae.   1 κικλήσκω Bothe κίκλησκε *Etym.Magn.*, *Gud.* κικλήσκει Valckenaer **182a** (6 Kamb., 4 Budé) Sext. Empir. *Adv.Math.* 10.314, attrib. Eur.; transl., paraphr. and attrib. Eur. *Ant.* by Probus on Verg. *Ecl.* 6.31 (Servius III.2 p. 343.24 Thilo-Hagen) (= **225 N**). Sext. Empir. is partly reflected and paraphrased in Philostr. *Imag.* 1.10.3 ('Amphion sings') and Hippolytus, *Refut.* 10.7.2 Marcovich, unattribr. Sources correlated by Weil, Wagner, Wilamowitz.

EURIPIDES

190   (’Αμφ.) λύρα βοῶν <γὰρ> ῥύσι’ ἐξερρύσατο.

191   *See after 189 below*

192   ’Αμφ. χρόνος θεῶν <τε> πνεῦμ’ ἔρως θ’ ὑμνωιδίας

182b   *TrGF under this number lists principal* testimonia *for the* DEBATE OF ZETHUS AND AMPHION: *see Commentary.*

183 (184 N with adesp. 395 N)
ΖΗΘΟΣ κακῶν κατάρχεις τήνδε μοῦσαν εἰσάγων
ἀργόν, φίλοινον, χρημάτων ἀτημελῆ.

184   Ζηθ.   ἐν τούτωι <γέ τοι>
λαμπρός θ’ ἕκαστος κἀπὶ τοῦτ’ ἐπείγεται,
νέμων τὸ πλεῖστον ἡμέρας τούτωι μέρος,
ἵν’ αὐτὸς αὑτοῦ τυγχάνει βέλτιστος ὤν.

185   (Ζηθ.) ἀμελεῖς ὧν δεῖ σε ἐπιμελεῖσθαι
ψυχῆς φύσιν <γὰρ> ὧδε γενναίαν <λαχὼν>
γυναικομίμωι διαπρέπεις μορφώματι·
κοὔτ’ ἂν δίκης βουλαῖσι προσθεῖ’ ἂν λόγον

190 (4 Kamb., 5 Budé) *Anecd. Gr.* 4.459 Boissonade (Anon. *On Lyric Poets* 18) = *Lex.Vindob.* Appendix p. 322.18 Nauck, attrib. Eur. *Ant.* ('now it was called a λύρα because (it was) the λύτρον ['penalty in quittance'] given by Hermes for his theft of Apollo's cattle') λύρα with colon Kannicht λύραι Boissonade <γὰρ> Schneidewin ῥύσι’ Boissonade ῥύσα or ῥύσει mss. ἐξερρύσατο mss. ἐξελύσατο Schneidewin **192** (5 Kamb., 6 Budé) Julian, *Ep.* 1.30, unattrib. but cited for the three factors in Amphion's invention of 'ancient music'; repeated in Suidas ''Αμφίων'' (α 1751 Adler); paraphrased by Philostr. *Vit. Apollon.* 7.34, unattrib. πνεῦμα θεῶν Jul. καὶ θεῶν πνεῦμα Philostr. θεοῦ πνεῦμα Suid. <τε> Kuster **183** (7 Kamb., 8 Budé) Dio Chrys. *Or.* 73.10 paraphrases much of this fragment (and cites line 6 of F 188), unattrib. but as words of Zethus censuring his brother. 1 Plut. *Mor.* 634e, unattrib., in parodic form (τήνδ’ ἐμοῦσαν 'this vomiting woman'), repeated at Athen. 14.616c, unattrib. (= adesp. 395 N). 2 Sext. Empir. *Adv.Math.* 6.27, unattrib. 1 κατάρχεις Athen. γὰρ ἄρχεις Plut. after 1 <ἄτοπον, ἀσύμφορόν τιν’ - x ◡ - > inserted from Dio and Sext. by Hartung, in part following Porson (cf. Mette No. 238) 2 ἀργόν Dio ἀργήν Sext. **184** (23 Kamb., 7 Budé) Pl. *Gorg.* 484d–e, with 1–2 slightly adapted and 3–4 quoted and attrib. Eur.; Schol. *Gorg.* p. 149 Greene attributes 'these iambics' to Zethus' speech to his brother Amphion in Eur. *Ant.* 2–4 κἀπὶ τοῦτ’...ὤν Ar. *Rhet.* 1371b31, both paraphrased and quoted, attrib. 'the poet'

272

190 *(Amph.)* <For> the lyre paid by exchange the penalty sought for the cattle.
Amphion explains the lyre's history to the Chorus.

191 *See after 189 below*

192 Amph. Time and the gods' inspiration and the love of singing hymns...
Amphion describes the basis of his art.

F 183–8, 219, 189, 191, 193–4, 196–202, 220 are assigned to Episode 1, including the debate between Amphion and his brother Zethus, who now enters. He attacks Amphion's intellectual and artistic self-absorption as irresponsible and failing in his duties to benefit all.

183 ZETHUS You are the start of mischief, introducing this music which is idle, fond of wine, neglectful of affairs.

184 *Zeth.* ...it is in this, <anyhow>, that each man shines, and for this that he strives, giving this the greatest part of the day – the thing in which he actually is at his personal best.

185 *(Zeth.) You neglect what should be your concerns, <for> when you <have been endowed> with so noble a natural character, you are conspicuous with an effeminate appearance. And you could neither add a word to deliberations about justice nor voice anything prob-*

(Eur. in margin of some mss.); [Ar.] *Probl.Phys.* 917a13, unattrib.   Parts of 2–4 are paraphrased in [Pl.] *Alcib.*II. 146a13, unattrib., and four places in Plut. *Mor.*, attrib. Eur. in one. 1–2 restored by Valckenaer, with <γέ τοι> or <γε πᾶς>   3 νέμων ἑκάστης ἡμέρας πλεῖστον μέρος Ar. *Rhet.*   τούτωι: αὐτῷ [Ar.] *Probl.Phys.*   4 sources divided between τυγχάνει, –ηι and (once only) –οι   βέλτιστος Pl. *Gorg.*, Ar. *Rhet.*   κράτιστος others
185 (9 Kamb., 9 Budé) partly cited, partly paraphrased (1 entirely paraphrase) Pl. *Gorg.* 485e–6a, referring to Zethus and Amphion in Eur., with Schol. p. 150 Greene attrib. Eur. *Ant.* 3 Philostr. *Vit.Apollon.* 4.21, attrib. Eur.; only γυναικομίμωι μορφώματι in Michael Acomin. 1.42.21 Lampros, unattrib., cf. Phot. *Bibl.* 333b2 attrib. Eur.; only γυναικομίμωι in Olympiod. *In Gorg.* p. 26.21 Westerink, attrib. Eur., continuing with parts of 5–6 2–8 progressively restored on the basis of Plato and Olymp. by scholars since Grotius 2 thus Nauck   <λαχὼν> Weil <ἔχων> Ruhnken   3 lacuna after this line: von Arnim 4–5 Dodds κοὔτ' ἂν δίκης βουλαῖσι πιθανὸν ἂν λάκοις (one verse, then 6 οὔτ' ἐν...κύτει) Merkelbach   λάκοις Bonitz λάβοις Plato

οὔτ' εἰκὸς ἂν καὶ πιθανὸν <οὐδὲν> ἂν λάκοις   5
< x – ◡ – x > κοὔτ' ἂν ἀσπίδος κύτει
<καλῶς> ὁμιλήσει<α>ς οὔτ' ἄλλων ὕπερ
νεανικὸν βούλευμα βουλεύσαιό <τι>.

186   (Ζηθ.) καὶ πῶς σοφὸν τοῦτ' ἐστίν, ἥτις εὐφυᾶ
λαβοῦσα τέχνη φῶτ' ἔθηκε χείρονα;

187   (Ζηθ.) ἀνὴρ γὰρ ὅστις εὖ βίον κεκτημένος
τὰ μὲν κατ' οἴκους ἀμελίαι παρεὶς ἐᾶι,
μολπαῖσι δ' ἡσθεὶς τοῦτ' ἀεὶ θηρεύεται,
ἀργὸς μὲν οἴκοι κἀν πόλει γενήσεται,
φίλοισι δ' οὐδείς· ἡ φύσις γὰρ οἴχεται,   5
ὅταν γλυκείας ἡδονῆς ἥσσων τις ἦι.

*187a   *Zethus' words apparently paraphrased in later prose writers:*

(Ζηθ.) *(i) ῥῖψον τὴν λύραν, κέχρησο δὲ ὅπλοις.*

(ii) μάτην κιθαρίζεις μηδὲν ὠφελῶν, ἀλλὰ ἔξελθε·
στρατιωτικὸν βίον ζῆσον καὶ <εὐ>πόρησον
καὶ τυράννησον.

188   Ζηθ.   ἀλλ' ἐμοὶ πιθοῦ·
παῦσαι ματάιζων καὶ πόνων εὐμουσίαν
ἄσκει· τοιαῦτ' ἄειδε καὶ δόξεις φρονεῖν,
σκάπτων, ἀρῶν γῆν, ποιμνίοις ἐπιστατῶν,

---

7 <καλῶς> or <ὀρθῶς> Nauck 'perhaps <ἐχθροῖς>' Kannicht   ὁμιλήσει<α>ς Nauck
7–8 οὔτ' ἄλλων...<τι> Grotius and Gataker   7 end οὔθ' ὑπὲρ φίλων Mette   **186** (22
Kamb., 10 Budé)   adapted by Plato, *Gorg.* 486b (unattrib.), first recognized by D. Canter;
paraphrase in Philod. *Rhet.* 2.176.13 Sudhaus. Valckenaer tried to recover a further, perhaps
separated verse, roughly μήτ' αὐτὸν αὐτῷ δυνάμενον γ' ἐπαρκέσαι (προσαρκέσαι
Matthiae βοηθεῖν Plato).   1 καὶ πῶς Grotius (καίτοι πῶς Plato) πῶς <γὰρ> Nauck
εὐφυᾶ Valckenaer –ῇ Plato   ἥτις Plato mss. BF εἴ τις mss. TW   εἰ ε]ὐγ[ε]νῇ τις read
in Philod. by Sudhaus   **187** (8 Kamb., 11 Budé) Stob. 3.30.1 (ms. S only), attrib. Eur. *Ant.*
1 Diphilus F 74.7 *PCG* among Euripidean borrowings   3–6 Sext. Empir. *Adv.Math.* 6.35,
unattrib. Assigned to Zethus by Gataker, Valckenaer.   2 ἀμελίαι παρεὶς ἐᾶι Grotius,
Valckenaer ἀμέλεια παρειάσει Stob.   4 οἴκοι κἀν Walker, Diggle οἴκοις καὶ Stob.
and Sext.   5 οὐδείς: οὐδέν Wecklein   ἡ φύσις γὰρ Stob.   ἀλλ' ἄφαντος Sext.

able or persuasive,[5] nor <*bravely*> keep yourself close behind a hollow shield, nor give energetic advice on others' behalf.

186 (*Zeth.*) And how is this wise, when art takes over a naturally able man and makes him inferior?

187 (*Zeth.*) Any man possessed of a good living who leaves his house's affairs to neglect and lets them go but delights in songs and pursues this constantly, will be useless at home and in the city, and a nobody for his friends; for anyone's nature is ruined[5] when he is overcome by sweet pleasure.

*187a(*Zeth.*) (*i*) *Throw away your lyre, and use weapons.*

(*ii*) *Your playing of the lyre is idle, you are useless. Go outdoors! Live a soldier's life and provide well for yourself and be a ruler!*

188 (*Zeth.*) But do what I say: cease from useless activities and practise the fine music of hard work. Make such things your song and you will seem to have good sense, digging, ploughing land, minding flocks,

---

6 ἥσσων Sext. ἧσσον Stob.　***187a** ((i) 9 Kamb. in app. [cf. his p. 41 n. 1], part of 9 Budé; (ii) rejected by Kamb. p. 56 on his fr. XVII; om. Budé)　(i) Schol. Pl. *Gorg.* 485e p. 150 Greene ('Zethus says to the musical Amphion ῥῖψον...ὅπλοις'); repeated in Olympiod. *In Gorg.* p. 26.30 Westerink; associated by Valckenaer with F 188.2 (where πολέμων 'war' was once read: see App.); attrib. to ancient commentators on F 185.5f. by Nauck　(ii) Olympiod. *In Gorg.* p. 34.4 Westerink ('Callicles took iambic lines from *Ant.* and said that just as the soldierly Zethus told his brother Amphion the citharode 'μάτην...τυράννησον', so why do you, Socrates, engage in philosophy?')　Borthwick (1967) assigned both (i) and (ii) to Zethus' rebuke of his brother.　**188** (10 Kamb., 12 Budé) reconstructed chiefly by Valckenaer from Pl. *Gorg.* 486c, with the aid of Olympiod. *In Gorg.* p. 26.24–5 Westerink (see on F 185) and of 3–5 τοιαῦτ'...σοφίσματα Stob. 4.145.13, attrib. Eur. *Ant.*　6 Dio Chrys. 73.10, following quotation of F 183 (see App. there). Assigned to Zethus by Wilamowitz.　1 πιθοῦ Canter πείθου Plato　2 ματάιζων Routh ματαιάζων Pl. some mss. δ' ἐλέγχων Pl. most mss.　καὶ πόνων Borthwick (τῶν πόνων δ' Schmidt) πραγμάτων δ' Plato πολέμων δ' Olympiod.　3 τοιαῦτ' ἄειδε Stob. (not in Pl.)　4 Stob. (not in Pl., Olympiod.) ποιμνίοις Valckenaer ποιμνίων Stob.

ἄλλοις τὰ κομψὰ ταῦτ' ἀφεὶς σοφίσματα,   5
ἐξ ὧν κενοῖσιν ἐγκατοικήσεις δόμοις.

219   (Ζηθ.?) κόσμος δὲ σιγή, στέφανος ἀνδρὸς οὐ κακοῦ·
τὸ δ' ἐκλαλοῦν τοῦθ' ἡδονῆς μὲν ἅπτεται,
κακὸν δ' ὁμίλημ', ἀσθενὲς δὲ καὶ πόλει.

189   (Χο.?) ἐκ παντὸς ἄν τις πράγματος δισσῶν λόγων
ἀγῶνα θεῖτ' ἄν, εἰ λέγειν εἴη σοφός.

190, 192   *See after 182a above*

191   ('Αμφ.)   κρεῖσσον ὄλβου κτῆμα

193   ('Αμφ.) ὅστις δὲ πράσσει πολλὰ μὴ πράσσειν παρόν,
μῶρος, παρὸν ζῆν ἡδέως ἀπράγμονα.

194   ('Αμφ.) ὁ δ' ἥσυχος φίλοισί τ' ἀσφαλὴς φίλος
πόλει τ' ἄριστος· μὴ τὰ κινδυνεύματα
αἰνεῖτ'· ἐγὼ γὰρ οὔτε ναυτίλον φιλῶ
τολμῶντα λίαν οὔτε προστάτην χθονός.

195   *See Unplaced Fragments*

196   ('Αμφ.?) τοιόσδε θνητῶν τῶν ταλαιπώρων βίος·
οὔτ' εὐτυχεῖ τὸ πάμπαν οὔτε δυστυχεῖ.
[εὐδαιμονεῖ τε καὖθις οὐκ εὐδαιμονεῖ.]
τί δῆτ' ἐν ὄλβωι μὴ σαφεῖ βεβηκότες
οὐ ζῶμεν ὡς ἥδιστα μὴ λυπούμενοι;   5

---

219 (24 Kamb., 26 Budé) Stob. 3.36.10, attrib. Eur. *Ant.* Assigned to Zethus in the debate by Wilamowitz.   1 σιγή and comma Ellis σιγῆς στέφανος Stob.   2 τοῦθ' Porson οὖθ' Stob.   **189** (21 Kamb., 13 Budé) Stob. 2.2.9, attrib. Eur. *Ant.*; Athen. 15.677b, attrib. Eur. (whence Eustath. on Hom. *Il.* 20.4 p. 355.14 van der Valk). Assigned to Cho. by Valckenaer and located between the long speeches of Zethus and Amphion; to Amphion by Matthiae and located after F 202 by Wecklein.   **191** (11 Kamb., 14 Budé) Philostr. *Vit.Soph.* 2.27.4, 'the practice of declamation called κρεῖσσον ὄλβου κτῆμα, from the hymns of Eur. and Amphion'   **193** (15 Kamb., 19 Budé) Stob. 4.16.2, attrib. Eur. *Ant.*   1 παρόν Stob. χρεών Nauck πόλλ' ἃ (Hense)...χρεών Ribbeck δέον Blaydes   2 this second παρὸν doubted by Slings   **194** (17 Kamb., 20 Budé) Stob. 4.7.10, attrib. Eur. *Ant.*   1 φίλοισί τ' abandoning to others these pretty trifles here[5] from which you will be living in a house of emptiness.

219 *(Zeth.?)* Silence is an ornament, a crown for a man with no evil in him; while this blathering grasps at pleasure but is bad company, and a weakness for a city too.

189 *(Cho.?)* One could make an argument between two positions, upon every matter, if one were clever at speaking.

190, 192 *See after 182a above*

F 191, 193–4, 196–202, 220, Amphion's response to Zethus, defending his art and quietude:

191 *(Amph.)* a possession greater than prosperity

193 *(Amph.)* Whoever is very active when he may be inactive, is foolish, when he may have a pleasant life of inactivity.

194 *(Amph.)* The quiet man is both a sure friend to friends and very good for his city; do not approve adventuring (you people)! I myself do not like too much boldness in either a sailor or a man at the head of his country.

195 *See Unplaced Fragments*

196 *(Amph.?)* Such is the life of wretched mankind: a man is neither completely fortunate nor unfortunate [he both prospers and then again does not prosper]. Why then, when we have entered upon a prosperity which may be insecure, do we not live as pleasurably as possible, without distress?[5]

Stob. ms. S φίλοισιν mss. MA   **196** (14 Kamb., 17 Budé) Stob. 4.41.11, attrib. Eur. *Ant.* 2 *Comp. Men. et Phil.* 1.29 Jaekel, unattrib. and adapted   4–5 Clem. Alex. *Strom.* 6.2.13.4, attrib. Eur. and slightly corrupt.   Assigned to Amphion by Valckenaer.   2 οὔτ᾽ *Comp.* οὐδ᾽ Stob.   οὔτ᾽ εὐτυχεῖ...οὔτε δυστυχεῖ Stob.   οὔτ᾽ εὐτυχεῖν...οὔτε δυστυχεῖν (and 3 εὐδαιμονεῖν twice) Cobet   οὔτ᾽ εὐτυχεῖν δεῖ...οὔτε δυστυχεῖν *Comp.*   οὔτ᾽ εὐτυχὴς...οὔτε δυστυχής Nauck, deleting line 3

197   (Ἀμφ.?) βροτοῖσιν εὐκρὰς οὐ γένοιτ' ἂν ἡδέως.

198   (Ἀμφ.) εἰ δ' εὐτυχῶν⟩ τις καὶ βίον κεκτημένοις
       μηδὲν δόμο⟩ισι τῶν καλῶν θηράσεται
       ἐγὼ μὲν αὐ⟩τὸν οὔποτ' ὄλβιον καλῶ,
       φύλακα δὲ μᾶλλον χρημάτων εὐδαί⟩μονα

199   (Ἀμφ.) τὸ δ' ἀσθενές μου καὶ τὸ θῆλυ σώματος
       κακῶς ἐμέμφθης· εἰ γὰρ εὖ φρονεῖν ἔχω,
       κρεῖσσον τόδ' ἐστὶ καρτεροῦ βραχίονος.

200   (Ἀμφ.) γνώμαις γὰρ ἀνδρὸς εὖ μὲν οἰκοῦνται πόλεις,
       εὖ δ' οἶκος, εἴς τ' αὖ πόλεμον ἰσχύει μέγα·
       σοφὸν γὰρ ἓν βούλευμα τὰς πολλὰς χέρας
       νικᾶι, σὺν ὄχλωι δ' ἀμαθία πλεῖστον κακόν.

201   (Ἀμφ.) καὶ μὴν ὅσοι μὲν σαρκὸς εἰς εὐεξίαν
       ἀσκοῦσι βίοτον, ἢν σφαλῶσι χρημάτων,
       κακοὶ πολῖται· δεῖ γὰρ ἄνδρ' εἰθισμένον
       ἀκόλαστον ἦθος γαστρὸς ἐν ταὐτῶι μένειν.

202   (Ἀμφ.) ἐγὼ μὲν οὖν ἄιδοιμι καὶ λέγοιμί τι
       σοφόν, ταράσσων μηδὲν ὧν πόλις νοσεῖ.

220   (Ἀμφ.?) πολλοὶ δὲ θνητῶν τοῦτο πάσχουσιν κακόν·
       γνώμηι φρονοῦντες οὐ θέλουσ' ὑπηρετεῖν
       ψυχῆι τὰ πολλὰ πρὸς φίλων νικώμενοι.

197 (13 Kamb., 18 Budé) Phot. *Lex.* ε 2231 Theodoridis (εὔκρας), attrib. Eur. *Ant.*; Theod. lists other ancient lexica citing the word, with partial or no attribution; also Schol. Pl. *Critias* 112d p. 292 Greene on the word εὐκράς attrib. Eur. *Ant.* (line not quoted). Herodian 2.635.9 Lentz approves the accentuation εὐκράς, though noting εὔκρας in Eur.   Associated with F 196 by Matthiae, assigned to Amphion by Wagner.   ἡδέως Phot. ἡδονή Lobeck **198** (16 Kamb., 16 Budé) Stob. 3.16.4, attrib. Eur. *Ant.*; P. Petr. I.3(1) (3ʳᵈ C. B.C.: = P. Lit. Lond. 57, 71], 6–9, attrib. Eur., from an anthology 'probably of genuine and "fictitious" Eur. fragments', S. Slings, *ZPE* 33 (1979), 41–5. Assigned to Amphion by Valckenaer.   2 μηδ' ἐν δόμοισι West in *TrGF* ('attested in some mss. of Stob.': Matthiae)   θηρασετ[P. Petr. θηράσεται Kock πειράσεται Stob.   3 αὐτὸν οὔποτ' Stob. ms. A οὔποτ' αὐτὸν mss. STrinc.   4 εὐδαίμονα possibly corrupt, del. Hense δυσδαίμονα Nauck   **199** (18 Kamb., 21 Budé) Stob. 3.3.2, attrib. Eur. *Ant.*   2 φρονεῖν Stob. φρενῶν Valckenaer **200** (19 Kamb., 22 Budé) Stob. 4.13.3, attrib. Eur. *Ant.*; [Plut.] *Vit.Hom.* 156.2 Kindstrand and Orion 18a + 18b Haffner, attrib. Eur.   1–2 cited, in part adapted, by Diogenes F 280 Mullach (from Diog. Laert. 6.104) and Clem. Alex. *Strom.* 2.19.102.7, both unattrib.

197 *(Amph.?)* It (life?) would not be pleasurably well-mixed for mankind.

198 *(Amph.)* If a fortunate man with a good livelihood is going to pursue no beautiful things in his house, I shall never myself call him blest with prosperity, but rather a fortunate guardian of his wealth.

199 *(Amph.)* You were wrong to censure a weak and effeminate body in me; for if I can think soundly, this is stronger than a sturdy arm.

200 *(Amph.)* A man's judgement brings good management to cities, and the same good to a house; moreover, he has great strength in war – for one wise counsel prevails over the hands of the many, while crassness in party with a mob is most destructive.

201 *(Amph.)* Look! All those whose regimen of life is directed to a fine physique are bad citizens if their wealth fails. A man accustomed to a habit of undisciplined eating necessarily remains in the same condition.

202 *(Amph.)* On the contrary, for my own part I wish I might sing and say something wise, without stirring up any of the city's troubles.

220 *(Amph.?)* Much of mankind experiences this trouble: though they have sense they are unwilling to follow their resolve, being generally overcome at heart by their friends.

Probably Amphion too, asserting his strength of mind.

3–4 Schol. Hom. *Il.* 2.372b and Philo, *De Spec. Leg.* 4.47, both attrib. Eur.   There are very many other partial *testimonia* (collected by Mette No. 250, cf. also Haffner and *TrGF*). 1 γνώμαις most *test.* γνώμηι Stob. βουλαῖς Clem.   ἀνδρὸς Stob., [Plut.] ἀνδρῶν others 2 εἴς τ' Stob., Orion εἰς δ' [Plut.]   4 σὺν ὄχλωι: σὺν ὅπλοις Galen, *Protrept.* p. 20.16 Kaibel σύνοπλος van Groningen   πλεῖστον [Plut.], Orion etc. πλέον Stob. μεῖζον Philo   **201** (20 Kamb., 23 Budé) Stob. 3.6.1, attrib. Eur. *Ant.* Located here by Valcke-naer.   3–4 are deemed partly corrupt by eds., but defended by Kannicht in *TrGF*.   3 καὶ γὰρ and 4 †γαστρòς† Nauck (εἰκὸς Schmidt)   4 lacuna after ἦθος Gomperz   **202** (26 Kamb., 24 Budé) Stob. 3.1.63, attrib. Eur. *Ant.*   **220** (25 Kamb., 25 Budé) Stob. 3.30.9, attrib. Eur. *Ant.*   Assigned to the debate by von Arnim, to Amphion by Wecklein. 2–3 ὑπηρετεῖν | ψυχῆι followed by comma Hense

203   ἔνδον δὲ θαλάμοις βουκόλου < x – ◡ – >
             κομῶντα κισσῶι στῦλον εὐίου θεοῦ . . .

204 (ΑΝΤΙΟΠΗ?) πόλλ' ἔστιν ἀνθρώποισιν, ὦ ξένοι, κακά.

205   ('Αντ.) φρονῶ δ' ἃ πάσχω, καὶ τόδ' οὐ σμικρὸν κακόν·
             τὸ μὴ εἰδέναι γὰρ ἡδονὴν ἔχει τινὰ
             νοσοῦντα, κέρδος δ' ἐν κακοῖς ἀγνωσία.

206   *See after 210 below*

207   ('Αντ.)   ἡνίκ' ἡγόμην πάλιν
             κύουσα τίκτω

208   ('Αντ.) εἰ δ' ἠμελήθην ἐκ θεῶν καὶ παῖδ' ἐμώ,
             ἔχει λόγον καὶ τοῦτο· τῶν πολλῶν βροτῶν
             δεῖ τοὺς μὲν εἶναι δυστυχεῖς, τοὺς δ' εὐτυχεῖς.

209   *See Unplaced Fragments below*

210   'Αμφ.   οὐδὲ γὰρ λάθραι δοκῶ
             θηρὸς κακούργου σχήματ' ἐκμιμούμενον
             σοὶ Ζῆν' ἐς εὐνὴν ὥσπερ ἄνθρωπον μολεῖν.

206   ('Αντ.?) ὦ παῖ, γένοιντ' ἂν εὖ λελεγμένοι λόγοι
             ψευδεῖς, ἐπῶν δὲ κάλλεσιν νικῶιεν ἂν
             τἀληθές· ἀλλ' οὐ τοῦτο τἀκριβέστατον,

203 (37 Kamb., 39 Budé) Clem. Alex. *Strom.* 1.24.163.5, attrib. Eur. *Ant.*   1 βουκόλου Toup –ου Clem.   εἶδον (Bothe)...βουκόλων Wilamowitz   <βλέπειν δοκῶ> Mayer <παρῆν ὁρᾶν> Kannicht <– ◡ – ◡> before βουκ. is also possible   1–2 βουκόλον (Clem.)...κοσμοῦντα alternatively Toup   **204** (27 Kamb., 27 Budé) Stob. 4.34.35, attrib. Eur. *Ant.*   **205** (34 Kamb., 30 Budé) Stob. 4.35.24, attrib. Eur. *Ant.*   1 Erotian, *Voc.Hippocr.* κ 22 (p. 50.6 Nachmanson), attrib. Eur. *Ant.* Assigned to Antiope by Valckenaer.   1 ἃ Stob. ὃ Erotian   3 νοσοῦντα Stob. -τι Conti Bizzaro   **207** (29 Kamb., 29 Budé) Ammonius, *De Diff.* 288 p. 74.17 Nickau κύουσα τίκτω(...) ἡνίκ' ἡγόμην πάλιν, with damaged attrib. to Eur. *Ant.*   2 κύουσα τίκτον Eustath. on Hom. *Od.* 15.190, attrib. *Ant.* The printed order of words is due to Wilamowitz; this order with κυοῦσ' ἔτικτον Schaal (cf. Eustath.); Ammon.'s order, with κυοῦσ' ἔτικτον (or κύουσα, τίκτω <θ'>) ἡνίκ' ἡγόμην πάλιν as one verse Valckenaer, who assigned the words to Antiope.   **208** (33 Kamb., 37 Budé) 1–2 τοῦτο M. Aurel. Anton. 7.41, unattrib., and 11.6 'from tragedy'   2–3 Stob. 4.34.37, attrib. Eur. *Ant.*   3 Men. *Monost.* 187 Jaekel, unattrib.   **210** (31 Kamb., 34 Budé) Clem. Alex. *Strom.* 5.14.111.2, 'Amphion is speaking to Antiope',

F 203–11 and P. Oxy. 3317 are from a new episode, in which Antiope arrives in flight, and then Dirce and her fellow bacchants:

203   Inside in the herdsman's dwelling < . . . > a column festooned with ivy for the god of celebration . . .
Someone describes a column dedicated to the god Dionysus.

F 204, 205, 207 are probably all addressed by Antiope to the Chorus, lamenting her misfortunes:

204 *(ANTIOPE?)* Mankind has many troubles, strangers.

205 *(Ant.)* I realise what I suffer, and this is no small misery. Not to be aware when one is in trouble has a certain pleasure; and ignorance amid misery is an advantage.

206   *See after 210 below*

207 *(Ant.)* When I was being brought back again, I was pregnant and gave birth.

208 *(Ant.)* If I and my twin boys were neglected by the gods, even this can be explained: of mankind's great numbers, some must be unfortunate, some fortunate.
Antiope explains her misfortunes, even as the mother of Zeus' sons (location uncertain; possibly after 210).

209   *See Unplaced Fragments below*

210 *Amph.* Nor actually do I think that Zeus imitated the form of an evil beast and came secretly into your bed like a man.
Amphion doubts Antiope's account.

206 *(Ant.?)* My son, words well spoken may be false but overcome the truth through the beauties of their language. That however is not the surest test, it is human

reproduced at Euseb. *Praep.Ev.* 13.13.38 Mras   2 θηρὸς F. W. Schmidt φωτὸς Clem. φηρὸς Wecklein   3 Ζῆν' Valckenaer τήνδ' Clem., Euseb. τόνδ' Bothe   **206** (32 Kamb., 36 Budé) Clem. Alex. *Strom.* 1.8.41.5, attrib. 'the tragedy'   4–6 ὅς δ'...ποτε Stob. 2.15.12, attrib. Eur. *Ant.* Assigned variously by editors.   1 εὖ λελεγμένοι Markland εὖ λεγόμενοι οἱ Clem.   2 κάλλεσιν Clem. καλλονῆι Nauck

ἀλλ' ἡ φύσις καὶ τοὐρθόν· ὃς δ' εὐγλωσσίαι
νικᾶι, σοφὸς μέν, ἀλλ' ἐγὼ τὰ πράγματα   5
κρείσσω νομίζω τῶν λόγων ἀεί ποτε.

211   (Χο.) φεῦ φεῦ, βροτείων πημάτων ὅσαι τύχαι
ὅσαι τε μορφαί· τέρμα δ' οὐκ εἴποι τις ἄν.

212–218   *See Unplaced Fragments below*

219, 220   *See above after 188 and 202 respectively*

P. Oxy. 3317

(Ἀμφ.?) οὔκουν] ἑκοῦσα τήνδ' ἐρημώσ[εις ἕδραν,
μὴ χειρία]ν ἕλκωσί σ' οἵδε πρόσπ[ολοι
ξανθῆς ἐ]θείρας; οὐ γὰρ ἐν τρυφαῖ[ς ἔτι
μέλαθρα] ναίεις Ἡράκλει' οὐδεστ[
  7–8 letters]δ' ἥκεις ἢ δι' οἰωνῶν πλ[άκας   5
  7–8 letters]πεδία δι[ε]φοροῦ χωρὶς μ[
  6–7 letters ν]εβρίδος ἐξανημμένη[
  7–8 letters]ν· ἱερὰ γὰρ τάδ' οὐ σαυτῆς ἔ[χεις.

<ΔΙΡΚΗ> *7–8 letters*]μελλον συνθανεῖν πρε[
μηδεὶς θί]γηι μου δοῦλος ὢν ἐλε[υθέρας   10

4–5 εὐγλωσσίαι | νικᾶι Stob. εὐγλωσσίαν | εἰ καὶ Clem.   5 ἀλλ' ἐγὼ Sylburg ἀλλά
γε Clem. ἀλλὰ γὰρ Stob. 6 κρείσσον Stob.   **211** (30 Kamb., 33 Budé) Stob. 4.34.33,
attrib. Eur. *Ant.*; Clem. Alex. *Strom.* 3.3.23.2, unattrib.   Assigned to Chorus by Wagner.
1 βροτείων Clem. –αι Stob. 2 ὅσαι τε Stob. ὅσαι δὲ Clem.   **P. Oxy. 3317**
(= *Antigone* F 175 *TrGF*, *Antigone* F 22 Budé), 2nd. C. A.D., ed. Hughes (1980), re-ed.
W. Luppe, *ZPE* 41 (1981), 27–30; R. Kannicht, ΚΟΤΙΝΟΣ...*Festschrift... E. Simon* (Mainz,
1992), 252–5; J. Diggle, *APF* 42 (1996), 164–7. Ascribed to *Antiope* by Luppe, first in ed.
pr., cf. esp. *ZPE* 42 (1981), 27–30, *ZPE* 77 (1989), 13–17, *Prometheus* 16 (1990), 201 and
ZPE 102 (1994), 42 n. 10, followed by Diggle (above) and in *TrGFS*, cf. Taplin (1998, cited
in Bibl. above, *Illustrations*). Ascribed to *Antigone* by ed. pr., R. Scodel, *ZPE* 46 (1982),
37–42, Kannicht (1992 above) and in *TrGF*, hesitantly by Van Looy, ed. Budé pp. 197–9
(= his F *22). Rejected for Eur. by G. Xanthakis-Karamanos, *BICS* 33 (1987), 107–11. On
the disputed ascription see also below on vv. 14–15 and Comm. and Introd., *Recovery etc.*
above. The text printed here is largely that of Diggle (1996); supplements by ed. pr. unless
stated.   1–8 assigned to Amphion rather than Herdsman, possibly to Antiope herself, by
Luppe (1989), 15 οὔκουν] Diggle 2 beg. Diggle προσπ[ολοι ed. pr. πρὸς π[έτρας

nature and rectitude. A man who overcomes by eloquence is clever, but I myself[5] have always considered
actions stronger than words.

Almost certainly Antiope, but location uncertain.

211 *(Cho.)* Oh, the pity of it! How many accidents there are and
how many forms of mortal men's sufferings! One
could not speak of an end to them.

The Chorus comment upon Antiope's sufferings.

212–218   *See Unplaced Fragments below*

219, 220   *See above after 188 and 202 respectively*

*From a scene where Dirce is in sanctuary at the column of
Dionysus in the Herdsman's cave and threatened with forcible
removal; the papyrus may begin a speech (following stichomythia?). The first speaker is not certainly identifiable, but
Amphion seems more likely than Antiope and certainly than
the Herdsman:*

P. Oxy. 3317

(Amph.?) <So> abandon your <position> here willingly, so
these . . . do not <lay hands> on you and drag you
by your <auburn> hair: for you no <longer> live in
luxury in Heracles' <palace> nor have you come
< . . . >,[5] you who ranged(?) through the <open
territories> of birds < . . . > plains without . . .
draped <in . . . > of a fawnskin . . . these sacred
emblems do not belong to you.

(Dirce) < . . . the?> future . . . to die with . . . . Let
<no one> who is a slave touch me: I am <free>![10]

(e.g.) is possible   4–5 οὐδὲ στ[έγος | φίλον τό]δ' ἥκεις Diggle   οὐδ' ἐστ[ιᾶι. | ἐς
τέρμα] δ' ἥκεις ed. pr.   5 ἢ Mette η P   πλ[άκας Luppe   6 γαίας τε] Luppe ('a little
short', Diggle)   δυ[σ]φόρου also conj. ed. pr.   μ[ονῆς Diggle μ[όγου ed. pr.   7 beg.
θύουσα ('i.e. θυίουσα') Diggle   end [στολήν with stop ed. pr.   8 οὐ δεινό]ν; hesitantly
Diggle perhaps οὐχ ὅσιο]ν· Collard (P has the raised stop)   9ff. assigned to Dirce by
Luppe (1984)   9 σαφὲς τὸ] μέλλον· συνθανεῖν πρέ[πει φίλοις Luppe σύνες τὸ]
μέλλον· συνθανεῖν πρέ[πει γ' ἐμοί | ἢν τις θί]γηι Kannicht (P has no mid-line punct.
in 9)   10 beg. Diggle   end Handley in ed. pr.

7–8 letters] χρῶτ'· ἀλλ' ἑκοῦσα πε[ίσομαι.
ἐν τοῖς κα̣κοῖς γὰρ ηὐγένει' ὅτωι παρῆι
τραχεῖα κ̣ὠ̣ξύθυμος ἀμαθίαν ἔχιει·
ὅστις δὲ π̣ι̣ρὸς τὸ πῖπτον εὐόργως ι̣φέρει
τὸν δαίμο̣ι̣ν', οὗτος ῥᾶι̣ο̣ν ἀ̣θλιωτ[15

221 (ΑΓΓΕΛΟΣ)   εἰ δέ που τύχοι
πέριξ ἑλίξας < – ⏑ > εἶλχ' ὁμοῦ λαβὼν
γυναῖκα πέτραν δρῦν μεταλλάσσων ἀεί.

222   τήν τοι Δίκην λέγουσι παῖδ' εἶναι Χρόνου,
δείκνυσι δ' ἡμῶν ὅστις ἐστὶ μὴ κακός.

223 P. Petrie 1–2
fr. A col. i   ('Αμφ.)   *7 letters* το]ύσδε μηδ' ὅπως φευξούμεθα.
7 letters ἡ]μᾶς Ζεὺς ἐγέννησεν πατήρ,
σώσ]ει μεθ' ἡμῶν τ' ἐχθρὸν ἄνδρα τείσεται.
ἵ]κται δὲ πάντως εἰς τοσόνδε συμφορᾶς
ὥσ]τ' οὐδ' ἂν ἐκφύγοιμεν εἰ βουλοίμεθα   5
Δί]ρκης νεῶρες αἷμα μὴ δοῦναι δίκην.
μένου]σι δ' ἡμῖν εἰς τόδ' ἔρχεται τύχη
ὥστ' ἢ] θανεῖν δεῖ τῶιδ' ἐν ἡμέρας φάει
ἢ καὶ] τροπαῖα πολεμίων στῆσαι χερί.
πᾶσιν μ]ὲν οὕτω, μῆτερ, ἐξαυδῶ τάδε·   10

11 μηδ' αἰκίσ]ηι Diggle   12–13 (= **adesp. 524 N**) Stob. 3.20.39, unattrib., but in a
sequence of Eur. quotations   12 ὅταν Stob.   14–15 Stob. 4.44.14, attrib. Eur. *Antigone*
(mss. MA; only Eur., ms. S), emended in Stob. to *Antiope* by Luppe (above), comparing the
reverse error at F 216.   14 εὐλόγως Stob.   15 beg.]να P. Oxy.   δαίμονα δ' Stob.
ἀθλιώ[τατος hesitantly ed. pr.   ἀθλιωτάτους | πόνους διαντλεῖ (e.g.) Kannicht   οὗτος
ἧσσόν ἐστιν ὄλβιος Stob.   **221** (39 Kamb., 40 Budé) [Longin.] *De Subl.* 40.4 'on Dirce
dragged by the bull (Eur. says…)'.   Assigned to the play by Valckenaer, to Messenger by
Bothe.   2 <ταῦρος> εἶλχ' Valckenaer   <εἷλκεν> εἷλχ' Adam   **222** (40 Kamb., 41
Budé) Stob. 1.3.33, attrib. Eur. *Ant.*   **223** (48 Kamb., 42 Budé) P. Petr. 1 (frs. A, B) and 2
(fr. C) = P. Lit. Lond. 70, Br. Mus. inv. 485 (3rd C. B.C.). Ed. pr. J. Mahaffy, *Hermathena* 17
(1891), 38–51 and again in *The Flinders Petrie Papyri* (London, 1891), Part I nos. I and II,
with vol. of autotypes; M. was aided by many scholars, esp. Bury in *Hermathena* and Blass
and Wilamowitz in the truer ed. pr. Most recent studies or editions: Pickard-Cambridge (see
bibl., *Main Discussions*; C. H. Roberts, *CQ* 29 (1935), 164–6; Page, *GLP*, 60–71; Kambitsis
(1972); J. Diggle, *PCPhS* 42 (1996), 106–26 and *TrGFS* 88–93; Van Looy in ed. Budé; Kann-

<. . .> my body; <*I shall consent*> willingly. For in one nobly born any harsh and quick temper amid disaster is crass folly; but the man who bears his fate with equanimity in response to what occurs, more easily . . . most wretched . . .[15]

From a new episode; a messenger reports the death of Dirce:

221 (MESSENGER) If (the bull) happened to circle round anywhere, it < . . . > dragged woman, rock, oak along with it as it ranged about continually.

222 They say, Justice is the child of Time, and it reveals which of us is not evil.

Location and speaker uncertain.

From the final scene: Amphion is present with Zethus (mute) and Antiope; the beginning of his speech is missing:

223 (*Amph.*) . . . these men nor how we shall escape (them?) . . . <*If*> Zeus was our father and sired us, <*he will save*> us and together with us punish the man who is our enemy. Things have certainly come to so great a pass <*that*> even if we wanted,[5] we would not escape paying penalty for Dirce's newly shed blood. <*If we stay*> our fortunes come to this: <*either*> we are to die during this day's light <*or*> our hands are <*indeed*> to set up a trophy over our enemies. I speak out here in this way, mother, <*to all of us*>;[10]

icht in *TrGF* (Diggle [1996] and Kannicht give full listings). For attribution to *Antiope* see on lines 57–58b. The edited text printed here is largely that of Diggle in *TrGFS*, which differs hardly at all from Kannicht's in *TrGF*. Diggle uses the commonly accepted line-numbering 1–116; Kannicht numbers 1–145, allowing for the 29 lines calculated as lost after 27. Supplements are Mahaffy's in ed. pr. unless stated. The apparatus is as concise as possible. 1 ('Αμφ.) Bury, cf. 68   2 ἀλλ' εἴπερ ἡ]μᾶς Pickard-Cambridge (ἀλλ' von Arnim, εἴπερ (γὰρ) Weil, ἡμᾶς Bury)   ζευς read in P by Bury   3 σώσ]ει Weil, Wilamowitz ἤξ]ει Bury   4 ἵ]κται Bury (perhaps ει]κται P: Blass)   πάντως Weil, others παντων P   συμφορὰ Blass   5 ὥσ]τ' Bury   6 Δί]ρκης Bury   7 μένου]σι Campbell, others   8 ὥστ' ἢ] Ellis, Blass ἢ γὰρ] Bury   9 ἢ καὶ] Wilamowitz   10 πᾶσιν μ]ὲν Diggle καὶ σοὶ μ]ὲν Blass, others ἡμῖν μ]ὲν Cropp

σοὶ δ᾽ ὃς τ]ὸ λαμπρὸν αἰθέρος ναίεις πέδον,
λέγω τ]οσοῦτον, μὴ γαμεῖν μὲν ἡδέως,
γήμαν]τα δ᾽ εἶναι σοῖς τέκνοις ἀνωφελῆ·
οὐ γὰρ κ]αλὸν τόδ᾽, ἀλλὰ συμμαχεῖν φίλοις.
πιθοῦ] πρὸς ἄγραν τ᾽ εὐτυχῶς εἴη μολεῖν,   15
ὅπως ἕ]λωμεν ἄνδρα δυσσεβέστατον.

(Χο.) ὅδ᾽] αὐ[τ]ός, εἰ χρὴ δοξάσαι τυραννικῶι
σκήπτρωι, Λύκος πάρεστι· σιγῶμεν, φίλοι.

(ΛΥΚΟΣ) ποῦ σ[traces of 22–23 letters   ]αι πέτραν
δρασμοῖς ε[traces of 22–23 letters   ] ;   20
τίνες δὲ καὶ . .   δρῶντες; ἐκ ποίας χθο[νός;
σημήνατ᾽, εἴπατε[traces of at least 16–17 letters
δεινὸν νομίζων αὐτὸς οὐκ ἀτιμάσας
24–7 badly damaged and illegible except for
24 beg. ἦλθο[ν], 26 near end ἀνδρασιν πειρωμεν[

about 9–10 lines missing from foot of fr. A col. i (col. ii is lost)

fr. B col. i   about 20–21 lines missing from top of fr. B col. i

(Βου.)   about 13 letters]σας ἥδομαι κακὸν . . α . [28 = 57 TrGF
(Λυκ.) οὐκ ἀσφαλὲς τόδ᾽ εἶπας, ἄνθρωπε, στέγ[ος.
(Βου.) δρᾶν δεῖ τι· κείνους δ᾽ οἶδ᾽ ἐγὼ τεθνηκό[τας.   30
(Λυκ.) καλῶς ἄρ᾽, εἴπερ οἶσθα, ταξόμεσθα νῦν.   60
(Βου.) τάξιν] τίν᾽ ἄλλην ἢ δόμων στείχει[ν] ἔσω;
about 14 letters] καὶ πρὶν οἰκοῦμεν[
about 14 letters] τοὺς ξένους ἐῶν μ . [.] . [
about 14 letters] δορυφόρους ἔξω πέτ[ρας   35
remains of one line   65
about 11–12 letters ἡμ]εῖς καὶ σὺ θήσομεν καλῶς.

11–12 σοὶ δ᾽ ὅς...| λέγω Blass   σὲ δ᾽ ὅς τ]ὸ...| αἰτῶ Weil   13 γήμαν]τα Campbell
σπείραν]τα Bury ('too long?' Kannicht)   14 οὐ γὰρ κ]αλὸν Bury   15 beg. Schaal end
so read in P by Diggle ([μολ]εῖν conj. Ellis)   16 ὅπως Bury   17 <Χο.> Blass   ὅδ᾽] Weil
21 after και neither πως nor συν– suits the traces (Diggle, Kannicht)   χθ[ονός Blass
24 beg. ἦλθο[ν] Blass   28–45 speakers identified by ed. pr.; in 29–32 P has paragraphi
29 στέγ[ος Sakorraphos   30 τί; West in TrGF   εκεινους P   31 ταξόμεσθα Diggle (–ω–
P)   32 stichomythia may continue wholly or in part through 32 to 37; 32–3 as a distich Page
33 ὠικοῦμεν Blaydes   35 end Diggle   37 beg. τἀνθένδε δ᾽ ἡμ]εῖς Diggle

<and to you who> dwell in the heaven's bright plain
<I say> this much: do not join in union with a
woman for pleasure, and then <when you have
joined> fail to be of help to your children: <for>
that is <not> honourable, but being an ally to your
kin, is. <Do what I say,> and I wish we may go
successfully on our hunt,[15] <so that> we may
<catch> a most impious man.

Amphion enters the cave with Antiope and Zethus.
Lycus is seen approaching; he has armed attendants.

(Cho.) <Here> is Lycus himself, if one is to guess by his
royal sceptre. Let us keep silent, my friends.

(LYCUS) Where . . . (to?) the cave in (her?) running . . . ?[20]
And who (*Plur.*) . . . (and?) . . . doing? From what
country? Tell me, say . . . Thinking it outrageous I
have not disdained <to come> myself . . .[25] . . . (to?)
men(?) trying . . .

about 29–31 lines missing

The Herdsman has come out of the cave, perhaps in
answer to a cry from Lycus:

(Herdsm.) . . . I am happy . . . trouble.[28]

(Lyc.) You speak of this house as unsafe, fellow.

(Herdsm.) Some action must be taken; but I know that those
men are dead.[30]

(Lyc.) Since you know, then they will be good dispositions
that I shall make now.

(Herdsm.) What other <disposition>, except to go inside the
house?
. . . (?) we have been living in before as well.
. . . allowing the strangers . . .
. . . spearmen outside the *cave* . . .[35]
only a few letters legible in 36
. . . you and I will set . . . right.

(Λυκ.) πόσοι δὲ δὴ τὸ πλ]ῆθός εἰσιν οἱ ξένοι;

(Βου.) εἷς ἢ δύ'· ἔγχη] δ' οὐκ ἔχουσιν ἐν χεροῖν.

(Λυκ.) ὅπλοισί νυν φ]ρουρεῖτε περίβολον πέτρας   40

      about 11 letters]ντες, κἄν τι[ς ἐ]κπίπτηι δόμων,   *70*

      λάζυσθ'· ἐγ]ὼ δὲ παῖδα Νυκτέως ἐμῆι

      about 10 letters]σαι χειρὶ καὶ τάχ' εἴσεται

fr. C col. i   *about 14 letters*   ]ντας ὡς μάτην λόγων

                about 12 letters σ]υμμάχους ἀνωφελεῖς.   45

(Βου.)   *about 13 letters*] ος ἦν θεὸς θέληι   *75*

         about 14 letters] τήνδ' ἀνὰ στέγην τάχα.

(Χο.)   *about 14 letters*   ]ριων σθένος

      βρόχοισι κατα[δεῖ *about 10–11 letters*

      βροτῶν δ' αὖ τέχναις [*about 14 letters*]ον.   50a

(Λυκ.) ἰώ μοί μοι.   50b

(Χο.) ἔ]α ἔα·

      καὶ δὴ [πρὸς ἔργω]ι τῶν νεανιῶν χέρες.   *80*

(Λυκ.) ὦ πρόσπ[ολοι   ]ντες οὐκ ἀρήξετε;

(Χο.) ἀλαλάζετα[ι ἀ στ]έγα· βοαῖ   54a

      θανάσιμον μέλος.   54b

(Λυκ.) ὦ] γαῖα Κάδ[μου κ]αὶ πόλισμ' Ἀσωπικόν.   55

(Χο.) κλύεις ὁρᾶι<ς>;   56a

      πα[ρα]καλεῖ πόλιν φοβερὸς αἵματος·   56b *85*

223 N   Δίκα τοι Δίκα χρόνιος ἀλλ' ὅμως

      ἐπιπεσοῦσ' ἔλαθεν ἔλαβεν ὅταν ἴδηι   58a

      τιν' ἀσεβῆ βροτῶν.   58b

(Λυκ.) οἴμοι θανοῦμαι πρὸς δυοῖν ἀσύμμαχος.

(Ἀμφ.) τὴν δ' ἐν νεκροῖσιν οὐ στένεις δάμαρτα σήν;   60

---

38 beg. Diggle following von Arnim (καὶ τὸ) πλ]ῆθος Campbell   39 beg. Diggle
40 beg. Diggle   41 beg. πέριξ κυκλοῦ]ντες Diggle   ἐκτὸς μένο]ντες Campbell
παντῆι βλέπο]ντες von Arnim   end Bury   42 λάζυσθ' Page   ἐγὼ] Campbell
43 θέλω φονεῦ]σαι Bruhn, Schaal   χειρε P   44 λογων read in P by Diggle, λογω[ι by
others   46 <Βου.> von Arnim <Χο.> Blass   ἀλλ' εἴσιθ'· ὄψηι δ' αὐ]τὸς (e.g.) Diggle
ἦν Diggle αν P   47 οὕσπερ σ' ὁρᾶν χρή] e.g. Diggle   48–58b voices identified in ed.
pr.   48 τυραννίδων μακα]ρίων (e.g.) Diggle (μακα]ρίων Wilamowitz)   49, 50a line-
ends after κατα– and τέχναις P   49 κατα[δεῖ Wilamowitz   end θεὸς ῥαιδίως] (e.g.)
Diggle   50b <Λυκ.> Wilamowitz   ιωι P   51 <Χο.> Wilamowitz   ἔ]α Blass   52 Blass

(Lyc.) *<But just how many>* in number are the strangers?

(Herdsm.) *<One or two;>* they do not have *<spears>* in their hands.

(Lyc.) *(to his attendants)* Guard the cave's surroundings *<now, with your weapons>*[40] . . . and *<seize>* anyone who bursts from the house; and *<I>* . . . Nycteus' daughter with my own hand, and she shall soon know . . . how vainly . . . (of?) words . . . useless allies.[45]

Lycus enters the cave alone.

(Herdsm.) . . . if god be willing . . . throughout this house soon!

The Herdsman leaves by the side.

(Cho.) . . . *<ties>* down the strength of . . . with nooses; besides . . . of mortal men with skill . . . .[50]

(Lyc.) *(offstage, in alarm)* Oh! O-oh me!

(Cho.) What? What's that? *<See>*, the young men's hands are *<at their work>*!

(Lyc.) My attendants! Will you not . . . help me?

(Cho.) *<The house>* is loud with triumph! It cries a song of death!

(Lyc.) O land of Cadmus and city of the Asopus![55]

(Cho.) Do you hear? Do you see? He calls the city to his aid in his fear of bloodshed. Justice, I tell you, Justice is slow in coming but still when it sees an impious man it falls on him unseen, it seizes him.

(Lyc.) *(brought out from the cave by Amphion and Zethus)* O-oh! I shall be killed by the two of them, alone without allies!

(Amph.) But your wife who is among the dead – have you no laments for her?[60]

---

53 μολό]ντες Weil κλυό]ντες Snell   54a, 55 paragraphi P   54a Blass, with ἀ inserted by Diggle   54b θανάσιμον (conj. Page, –ωι Wilamowitz) 'suits the traces' Diggle, cf. Kannicht   55 <Λυκ.> Wilamowitz   56a ὁρᾶι<ς> Blaydes   56b beg. von Arnim   57–58b (= **F 223 N**) Stob. 1.3.25, attrib. Eur. *Ant.*   57 δικα[τοι]δικα read in P by Diggle   58a ἐπιπεσοῦσ'Heeren ὑπο– Stob. επεσεν (and line-end) P   ἔλαθεν ἔλαθεν Wecklein ἔλαθεν alone Stob. ελαβεν alone P   ἴδηι Meineke (ι[δ]ηι with no line-end P) ἔχηι Stob.   59–65 speakers identified by ed. pr.; paragraphi P

(Λυκ.) ἦ γὰρ τέθνηκε; καινὸν αὖ λέγεις κακόν.   90

('Αμφ.) ὁλκοῖς γε ταυρείοισι διαφορουμένη.

(Λυκ.) πρὸς τοῦ; πρὸς ὑμῶν; τοῦτο γὰρ θέλω μαθεῖν.

('Αμφ.) ἐκμανθάνοις ἂν ὡς ὅλωλ' ἡμῶν ὕπο.

(Λυκ.) ἀλλ' ἦ τινω[ν] πεφύκαθ' ὧν οὐκ οἶδ' ἐγώ;   65

('Αμφ.) τί τοῦτ' ἐρευν[ᾶ]ις; ἐν νεκροῖς π[ε]ύσηι θανών.   95

fr. B col. ii   (ΕΡΜΗΣ)   7 letters   ] ευω[‚(‚)]ιον ἐξορμωμένους

about 10 letters ἄνα]ξ 'Αμφίον· ἐντολὰς δὲ σοὶ

'Ερμῆς ὁ] Μαίας τ[about 11–12 letters] ενος

. . . . .] Διὸς κήρυγ[μ   c. 8 letters]ν φέρων.   70

καὶ πρῶτα μέν σφ[ῶιν μητ]ρὸ[ς] ἐξερῶ πέρι,   100

ὡς Ζεὺς ἐμείχθη κ[οὐκ ἀ]παρνεῖται τάδε.

τί δητανε[traces of about 18–20 letters]θετο

Ζηνὸς μολοῦσα λέ[κτρ . . . .]τρα . ασας;

ἐπεὶ δ' ὁρίζει καί δι[8 letters]κακά,   75

αὐτή τε δεινῆς [συμφορᾶς ἀπη]λλάγη   105

παῖδάς τε τούσδ' [ἀνηῦρε]ν ὄντας ἐκ Διός.

ὧν χρή σ' ἀκούειν [καὶ χ]θονὸς μοναρχίαν

ἑκόντα δοῦνα[ι τοῖσδε Κ]αδμείας, ἄναξ.

fr. C col. ii   ὅταν δὲ θάπτηις ἄλοχον εἰς πυρὰν τιθείς,   80

σαρκῶν ἀθροίσας τῆς ταλαιπώρου φύσιν   110

ὀστᾶ πυρώσας "Αρεος εἰς κρήνην βαλεῖν,

ὡς ἂν τὸ Δίρκης ὄνομ' ἐπώνυμον λάβηι

κρήνης ἀπόρρους ὃς δίεισιν ἄστεως

πεδία τ[ὰ Θή]βης ὕδασιν ἐξάρδων ἀεί.   85

ὑμεῖς δ', [ἐπ]ειδὰν ὅσιος ἦι Κάδμου πόλις,   115

χωρεῖτε, [παῖδ]ες, ἄστυ δ' 'Ισμηνὸν πάρα

ἑπτάσ[το]μον πύλαισιν ἐξαρτύετε.

σὺ μὲν . [ ] . το . ἔρυμα πολεμίων λαβὼν

one or more lines missing

66 π[ε]ύσηι Diggle −ει P   67 paragraphus P   κε]λεύω [φόν]ιον Weil (]λ fits the traces, but beg. neither ὑμᾶς [Campbell] nor παῦσαι [Schaal]: Diggle, Kannicht)   68 ὁρμὴν ἄνα]ξ (ἄνα]ξ Campbell) Weil ('too short' Diggle)   69 beg. von Arnim ('Ερμῆς] Weil) mid. τ[ά]σδ[ε (i.e. ἐντολάς) Diggle end 'perhaps]μενος' Diggle   70 beg. Λύκωι] Mekler 'ἀφικόμη]ν (Mekler) wholly unsafe' Diggle   φέρων is very un-

(Lyc.) What, is she dead? Further misery, and new, in what you say!

(Amph.) Yes – dragged along by a bull and torn apart.

(Lyc.) At whose hands? By yours? I want to know!

(Amph.) You can know, if you want, that she died at our hands.

(Lyc.) Then you are the sons of parents unknown to me?[65]

(Amph.) Why ask this? When you have been killed, you will find out, among the dead.

The god Hermes appears suddenly above the cave.

(HERMES) . . . in (your?) onslaught . . . *<lord>* Amphion! *<I am Hermes the son>* of Maia . . . orders for you . . . bringing Zeus' . . . proclamation.[70]

First I shall tell the *<two of>* you about your *<mother>*. Zeus lay with her; he does not deny it. Why . . . when she came to Zeus' *<bed>* . . . ? But since he determines and . . . misery,[75] she was herself both released from her dreadful *<fate>* and *<she discovered>* (that?) these (were?) her sons by Zeus.

(to Lycus) You must obey them, my lord, *<and>* cede them willingly sole rule over the land of Cadmus. When you give your wife funeral and place her on a pyre,[80] after gathering the poor woman's mortal substance burn her bones and throw them into Ares' spring so that its outflow be named Dirce for her; it will run through the city, irrigating the plain of Thebe with its waters for ever.[85]

(to Zethus and Amphion) Go, you *<sons>*, and once you are purified and may enter Cadmus' city, by the River Hismenus build a citadel gated at seven mouths. *(To Zethus)* You . . . taking . . . a bulwark against enemies . . . *(one or more lines of Greek text missing)* . . .

---

certain   71 mid. Blass   ]ρο[ς]ε̣ξ read in P by Roberts, Diggle   περι read in P by Blass   72 Blass   73 τί δῆτ' ἂν has been conjectured   74 Blass, Diggle   76 Blass   77 Weil [ἔσωσε]ν West in *TrGF*   78 Blass   79 τοῖσδε Κ]αδμείας Schaal]αδμειοις P   punct. Page   82 ὀστᾶ Sakorraphos οστεα P   87 Ἱσμηνὸν Diggle (Ἱσ– Wilamowitz) –ου P –ῶι Rutherford   89 ἔρυμα read in P by J. U. Powell and ('perhaps') Diggle τ[ο]σοῦτον ἔρυμα conj. Ellis   89–90 defective sense shows one verse (Campbell) or more (Roberts) to be missing

Ζήθωι τάδ' εἶπον· δεύτερον δ' Ἀμφίονα   90
λύραν ἄνωγα διὰ χερῶν ὡπλισμένον   *120*
μέλπειν θεοὺς ὠιδαῖσιν· ἕψονται δέ σοι
πέτραι τ' ἐρυμναὶ μουσικῆι κηλούμεναι
δένδρη τε μητρὸς ἐκλιπόνθ' ἑδώλια,
ὥστ' εὐμ[ά]ρειαν τεκτόνων θήσηι χερί.   95
Ζεὺς τήνδε τιμὴν σὺν δ' ἐγὼ δίδωμί σοι,   *125*
οὗπερ τόδ' εὕρημ' ἔσχες, Ἀμφίων ἄναξ.
λευκὼ δὲ πώλω τὼ Διὸς κεκλημένοι
τιμὰς μεγίστας ἕξετ' ἐν Κάδμου πόλει.
καὶ λέκτρ' ὁ μὲν Θηβαῖα λή[ψ]εται γάμων,   100
ὁ] δ' ἐκ Φρυγῶν κάλλιστον εὐνατήριον,   *130*
τὴν Ταντάλου παῖδ'· ἀλλ' ὅσον τάχιστα χρὴ
σπεύδειν θεοῦ πέμψαντος οἷα βούλεται.

(Λυκ.) ὦ πόλλ' ἄελπτα Ζεῦ τιθεὶς καθ' ἡμέραν
ἔδειξας [5–6 letters] τάσδ' ἀβουλίας ἐμὰς   105
ἐσσφ[7 letters] δοκοῦντας οὐκ εἶναι Διός.   *135*
πάρεστε καὶ ζῆθ'· ηὗρε μηνυτὴς χρόνος
ψευδεῖς μὲν ἡμᾶς, σφῶιν δὲ μητέρ' εὐτυχῆ.
ἴτε νυν, κρατύνετ' ἀντ' ἐμοῦ τῆσδε χθονὸς
λαβόντε Κάδμου σκῆπτρα· τὴν γὰρ ἀξίαν   110
σφῶιν προστίθησι Ζεὺς ἐγώ τε σὺν Διί.   *140*
Ἑρμῆι [9–10 letters] Ἄρεος εἰς κρήνην [β]αλῶ
γυναῖκα θάψας, τῆσδ' ὅπ[ως] ξυνοῦσα γῆς
νασμοῖσι τέγγηι πεδία Θηβαίας χθονός,
Δίρκη πρὸς ἀνδρῶν ὑστέρων κεκλημένη.   115
λύω δὲ νείκη καὶ τὰ πρὶν πεπραγμένα . . .   *145*

The end of the speech and the end of the play are missing.

---

90 δεύτερον read in P by Roberts   Ἀμφίονα Blass, others   –ονι P
91 ἄνωγα (conj. Blass) read in P by Diggle   93 τ' ἐρυμναὶ (conj. Blass) read in P by
Roberts   94 ἐκλιπόνθ' Blass εγλιπουσα P   95 Blass   θήσηι Diggle –ει P –εις Weil
101 εὐνατήριον Housman ευναστηριον P^corr. (ευναυστ–)   104 paragraphus P   Ζεῦ
Blaydes ζευς P   105 εδειξατ read in P by Kannicht, i.e. ἔδειξά τ'   [εἰς φῶς] suppl.
Blass ('–ως matches the traces badly' Diggle) [ἔργωι] Diels   106 beg. only εσσφ legible

That much, I say to Zethus; next, I bid Amphion[90]
equip himself with lyre in hand and sing tunefully of
the gods; bewitched by your music, solid rocks will
follow you and trees leave their seat in mother earth, so
you will make light work for the builders' hands.[95]
Zeus gives you this honour, and I with him, from
whom you had this invention, lord Amphion. You two
shall be called the two white colts of Zeus and have the
greatest honours in Cadmus' city. And your marriages:
Zethus shall have a Theban bride,[100] and Amphion a
very fair partner for his bed from among the Phrygians,
the daughter of Tantalus. But you must hasten with all
speed, now the god has sent to tell you the nature of
his wishes.

(Lyc.) O Zeus, you bring about much that is unexpected, day
by day! You have shown . . . these follies of mine[105]
. . . who seemed not to be Zeus' sons.

    (to Zethus and Amphion) You are here and living:
time the revealer has shown me as deceived but your
mother as happy in her fortune. Go now, rule this land
in my place, both of you taking Cadmus' sceptre; this
is your due[110] which Zeus accords you both, and I
together with Zeus. . . . to Hermes, I shall give my
wife funeral and cast her into Ares' spring, <so that>
united with this land's streams she may water the plains
of Theban territory and be called Dirce by men of later
time.[115] I end my feuding and (. . . ?) what was done
before . . .

The end of the play is missing from the papyrus.

to Diggle εσσφρ read and ἐσσφραγίσας conj. by ed. pr. ἐσσφραγίσας read by Roberts εἰς
φράτερας Wecklein lacuna after this verse Milne (acc. to Roberts) 108 εὐτυχῇ Nauck
ευτυχειν P 112 Ἑρμῆι δ[ὲ π]ίσυνος conj. Page ('not excluded by the traces' Diggle)
Ἄρεος: cf. 82 113 τῆσδ' ὅπ[ως] (conj. Campbell) read in P by Diggle ξυνοῦσα conj.
Weil θανοῦσα Wilamowitz

Unplaced Fragments

195 (Ἀμφ.?) ἅπαντα τίκτει χθὼν πάλιν τε λαμβάνει.

209   οὐ σωφρονίζειν ἔμαθον· αἰδεῖσθαι δὲ χρή,
γύναι, τὸ λίαν καὶ φυλάσσεσθαι φθόνον.

F 212–215 are assigned by some editors, Wecklein first, to Antigone:

212   εἰ νοῦς ἔνεστιν· εἰ δὲ μή, τί δεῖ καλῆς
γυναικός, εἰ μὴ τὰς φρένας χρηστὰς ἔχοι;

213   κόρος δὲ πάντων· καὶ γὰρ ἐκ καλλιόνων
λέκτροις ἐπ' αἰσχροῖς εἶδον ἐκπεπληγμένους,
δαιτὸς δὲ πληρωθείς τις ἄσμενος πάλιν
φαύληι διαίτηι προσβαλὼν ἥσθη στόμα.

214   κῆδος καθ' αὑ̣τὸν τὸν σοφὸν κτᾶσθαι χρεών.

215   πᾶσι δ' ἀγγέλλω βροτοῖς
ἐσθλῶν ἀπ' ἀνδρῶν εὐγενῆ σπείρειν τέκνα
at least one line missing
οὐ γάρ ποτ' ἂν πράξειαν ἐς τέλος κακῶς.

216   οὐ χρή ποτ' ἄνδρα δ̣οῦλον ὄντ' ἐλευθέρας
γνώμας διώκειν̣ οὐδ' ἐς ἰἀρ̣γίαν βἰλέπειν.

217   < – x > τὸ δοῦλον οὐχ ὁρᾶις ὅσον κακόν;

195 (12 Kamb., 15 Budé) Orion II.1 Haffner, attrib. Eur. *Ant.*; cf. Ennius, *Var.* 47
(*Epicharmus* 4) p. 221 Vahlen   **209** (38 Kamb., 35 Budé) Stob. 4.23.18, attrib. Eur. *Ant.*
212 (41 Kamb., 43 Budé) Stob. 4.22.127, attrib. Eur. *Ant.*   1 εἰ νοῦς γ' ἔνεστιν Kannicht
(εἰ νοῦς ἔνεστί γ' Blaydes)   **213** (42 Kamb., 44 Budé) Stob. 4.20.2, attrib. Eur. *Ant.*
4 Athen. 10.421f., attrib. Eur. Assigned to Antiope by Valckenaer (cf. F 210).   2 ἐπ'
Wyttenbach ἐν Stob.   4 ἥσθη Stob. ἥσθην Athen.   **214** (43 Kamb., 38 Budé) Stob.
4.22.93, attrib. Eur. *Ant.* P. Oxy. 3214.5–6 (a Euripidean anthology upon marriage) has the
centre of the line, attrib. *Ant.*   **215** (44 Kamb., 45 Budé) Stob. 4.22.100, attrib. Eur. *Ant.*
2 ἀλόχων Wecklein   3 *And.* 1283 has οὐ γάρ...ἐκ θεῶν κακῶς and follows 1279–82
unsatisfactorily; Stob. 4.22.120 cites 1279–82 without 1283. Lacuna between 2 and 3 Kambitsis, 3 del. Matthiae   **216** (45 Kamb., 46 Budé) Stob. 4.19.4, attrib. Eur. *Ant.* mss. SM

Unplaced Fragments

195 *(Amph.?)* The earth brings everything to birth and takes it
back again.

209 I did not learn to teach moderation; but one must hold
back from excess, lady, and guard oneself against
resentment.

212 . . . if there is sense in her. If not, what's the use
of a beautiful wife, if she were to lack a sound mind?

213 There is surfeit in everything. For example, I have
seen people crazy about an ill-favoured wife after
leaving a more beautiful one, and someone sated with
a banquet glad and pleased to put his lips in turn to
mean fare.

Continuing the topic of F 212.

214 A wise man ought to marry at his own level.

Again, continuing the topics of F 212, 213.

215 I tell all mankind to get well-born children from
noble stock *(at least one line missing)* for they will
never fare badly to the end.

Concluding F 212–4?

216 A man who is a slave ought never to pursue free
thoughts nor look for idleness.

217 *(Amph.)* Do you not see how great an evil slavery is *(or*
slaves are)?

(*Antigone* ms. A) and P. Berl. 21144 (3rd C. A.D.: *BKT* IX [1996], no. 45, anthology on the
theme of masters and slaves), unattrib.   **217** (35 Kamb., 31 Budé) Stob. 4.19.12, attrib.
Eur. *Ant.*   'or τὸ δοῦλον < – x >' Kannicht

218   (Χο.?) φεῦ, φεῦ, τὸ δοῦλον ὡς ἀπανταχῆι γένος
        πρὸς τὴν ἐλάσσω μοῖραν ὥρισεν θεός.

226   νόσον ἔχειν

227   εὐθύδημον

Uncertain Fragment

910   ὄλβιος ὅστις τῆς ἱστορίας
        ἔσχε μάθησιν,
        μήτε πολιτῶν ἐπὶ πημοσύνην
        μήτ᾽ εἰς ἀδίκους πράξεις ὁρμῶν,
        ἀλλ᾽ ἀθανάτου καθορῶν φύσεως   5
        κόσμον ἀγήρων, πῆι τε συνέστη
        χὤθεν χὤπως·
        τοῖς δὲ τοιούτοις οὐδέποτ᾽ αἰσχρῶν
        ἔργων μελέδημα προσίζει.

Fragments in Nauck removed from TrGF

224   See Introd., Other proposed ascriptions

225   See 182a above

---

218 (36 Kamb., 32 Budé) Stob. 4.19.41, attrib. Eur. *Ant.* Assigned to Chorus by Bothe. **226** (46 Kamb., 47 Budé) *Antiatticista* p. 109.17 Bekker, attrib. Eur. *Ant.* and glossed with 'having worthless habits'; repeated at Phot. *Lex.* I p. 449.15 Naber and Suidas ν 494 Adler **227** (47 Kamb., 48 Budé) Hesych. ε 6877 Latte, attrib. Eur. *Ant.* and glossed 'a straightforward citizen'; repeated Phot. *Lex.* ε 2200 Theodoridis, unattrib. εὐθυδήμον Phot. -μονα Hesych. **910** (p. 130 Kamb., p. 271 Budé) Clem. Alex. *Strom.* 4.25.155.1, unattrib.; Themistius, *Or.* 24 p. 109.4 Norman in part (paraphrased), attrib. Eur.; Pollux, *Onom.* 2.14 has only 6 κόσμον ἀγήρω, attrib. Eur. First ascribed to *Ant.* by Wecklein. 3 πημοσύνην Pierson -η Clem. -ας Them. 6 ἀγήρων Nauck -ω Clem., Them., Poll. 7 χὤθεν χὤπως Wilamowitz καὶ ὅπηι καὶ ὅπως Clem. 9 μελέδημα Nauck -τημα Clem.

218 *(Cho.?)* Oh, the pity of it! How the god has in every way marked out the class of slaves for an inferior estate!

226 to have a weakness (of character)

227 a straightforward citizen

Possibly from the debate of Zethus and Amphion.

Uncertain Fragment

910 Blessed the man who has come to possess knowledge through inquiry, setting out neither to harm citizens nor to do unjust acts but contemplating the ageless order of immortal nature,[5] the way in which it came into being, and where from and how. Men such as this are never attended by interest in shameful deeds.

Fragments in Nauck removed from TrGF

224 *See Introd.,* Other proposed ascriptions

225 *See* **182a** *above*

Commentary on *Antiope*

179. Other Euripidean prologues include prayers for a god's blessing against some perceived threat, e.g. *Supp.* 1–3, *Pho.* 84–5, *Cresph.* F 448a.107–8. What may have caused the Herdsman's anxiety here? Possibly news that Antiope has escaped and fear that she may return to the place where she abandoned her baby twins, possibly (Snell [1971], 79) a dream with this implication (Pacuv. *Ant.* *1 may indicate that the play began soon after dawn).

1. **<*You who*> hold:** an invocation-formula which praises and identifies a god through a place occupied or controlled, S. *Trach.* 200, Ar. *Thesm.* 315 etc. The god here is Dionysus (cf. on 2–3 below); Kannicht in *TrGF* notes F *inc.inc.*119 Ribbeck (considered for Pacuv. *Antiopa* by R.), 'Liber (Dionysus), you who inhabit these valleys of Cithaeron'. [In 1–2 Snell tried to rescue Strabo's uncorrected Infin. ἔχειν with '...<*which...we pray*> to have, may you grant...']

2–3. grant good things: a common theme in such invocations, e.g. *And.* 750; for the formula see Fraenkel on A. *Ag.* 121. **my master:** Dio Chrys. 15.9 names 'the tragic poets' for the story in which the twins Amphion and Zethus are found and reared by a herdsman and his wife who were slaves of Oeneus (*TrGF* T ivd); Eur. dramatized his story in his *Oeneus* (F 558–70); the place-name **Oenoe** here alludes to the personal name. Oenoe lay on the border between Theban Boeotia and Attica, close to **Eleutherae** the famous cult-site of Dionysus Eleuthereus, from which the god's wooden image was brought to his Theatre in Athens at the start of each spring's Great Dionysiac Festival: Csapo–Slater 104, 110 (III.9). In this fr. we see the first allusion in the play to Dionysus: cf. F 203, P. Oxy. 3317 and Introd., *Illustrations.* (Strabo cited the fr. to attest the location near Eleutherae of one of the two Attic demes named Oenoe; its source in this play is known through the other ancient sources, who were interested in the word (σύγ)χορτος '(with) **pastures** (adjoining)'.)

180. *Hysiae*: close to Erythrae, on the Boeotian slopes of Mt. Cithaeron (*Bacc.* 751, cf. Paus. 9.2.1) and 'along the river Asopus' (Steph. Byz.). This place-name belongs more probably to the Herdsman's semi-historical prologue than to Antiope's later narrative (F 207, where Kambitsis places it) or to the Messenger's report (F 221). Two of the sources, Steph. Byz. and Strabo, record Hyria as an alternative name, or a different location, for Antiope's birthplace (Steph. yielded Hesiod F 181 M.-W.).

181–182.1. I name: 'historic' Present tense; cf. Hygin. 7.3–4 'the shepherds brought (the twins) up as their own sons and named them Zethus (etc.)' [The attested Imper. κίκλησκε 'Name (one of them Zethus)' is possible only if the Herdsman is narrating a long-ago instruction by a god or Antiope. Bothe's κικλή-σκω **I name** is a better correction than Valckenaer's κικλήσκει 'she names',

298

ANTIOPE 299

which Snell accepts 'because Antiope herself did the searching': see next n.]
Zethus: the name is etymologized as 'He of the Search' (i.e. named from the place sought for his birthing), from the verb *zêt(eo)* 'seek': risible to us, but fitting the Greek perception of names, like Amphion 'He of the Side-Road', reflecting the noun *amph(odos)*. Amphion's etymology may be mocked at Aristophanes F 342 *PCG* ('he ought to have had the name Amphodos'); both etymologies appear at Hygin. *Fab.* 7.3–4. For similar 'etymological' grounding for important persons named in prologues see e.g. *IT* 32–3, *Hel.* 12–13 (see Kannicht), *Tel.* F 696.11–12, *Alex.* F 42d. At *Ion* 661 Ion is so named when he 'comes' (Greek *iôn*, 'coming') into the path of his supposed father Xuthus.

182a. Lyric solos by a principal character preceding or (as perhaps here) accompanying the choral parodos occur at e.g. *Hec.* 59ff., *Ion* 82ff., *Tro.* 98ff; at *And.* 103ff. Andromache sings unique elegiac couplets, just as here Amphion begins with a dactylic hexameter (and may have continued in this rhythm), as if in a formal hymn. Dactylic hexameters are sporadic in tragic lyric, e.g. *Hel.* 164–5, and occur amid dialogue trimeters at *Oed.* F 540a.7–10 (n.). **Heaven and Earth:** often coupled in invocations, e.g. *Pho.* 1290, *Or.* 1496, as the fundamental elements of the world to which to appeal for witness. They are celebrated as such, as 'creators', in hymns, as here and perhaps *Hyps.* F 758a.1103–8 (see Comm.); paired and equated with Zeus at F 941 (see Introd., *Other proposed ascriptions*) and F 877; cf. A. *Heliades* F 70. Eur. may be reflecting cosmogonic theories at *Chrysippus* F 839.1–7: 'Earth the greatest goddess and Zeus' Heaven; the latter is the begetter of men and gods, the former receiving water in soaking raindrops gives birth to mortals, gives birth to vegetation and the tribes of animals, for which not unjustly she is held to be the mother of all'; cf. A. *Danaides* F 44. For such Euripidean reflections see also on F 195 and Uncertain Fragment F 910. Yet the phrase **Earth the begetter of all things** may be quite innocent of such allusions; it is found as early as Hes. *Works* 563; cf. e.g. *Alex.* F 61b.3–5 (n.), *Pho.* 686.

190, 192. The majority of scholars since Wilamowitz have assigned these frs. (and F 191) to the initial exchange between Amphion and Chorus; Kannicht inclines to follow e.g. Nauck, Snell and Webster, in placing 191 and 192 in the debate-scene. Wilson (440–1) suggests that these frs. reflect Eur.'s own attitude in the late 5th C. argument about the 'new music' associated especially with Timotheus; for this generally cf. Csapo, *ICS* 24/25 (1999/2000), 405–26 and, for hymns in Eur., Furley, *ibid.* 183–97.

190. Hermes abducted Apollo's **cattle** (*Hom.Hymn.* 4.14, 18ff., etc.; their recovery is the plot of Sophocles' satyr-play *Ichneutae*, *'Trackers'*). When detected, Hermes paid material compensation by giving Apollo the lyre, which he had invented miraculously as a child by stringing a dead tortoise's shell (*Hom.Hymn.* 4.24 etc., Soph. *Ichn.* F 314.284ff.; see Pacuv. *Ant.* 2); Apollo then became patron of lyreplayers. **paid by exchange the penalty sought:** the Greek noun ῥύσιον and verb ῥυσιάζω express compensation demanded, paid, or seized: life-blood is 'payment' for life-blood, S. *Phil.* 959; cf. Fraenkel on *Ag.* 528.   [Kannicht's punctuation after λύρα puts heavy emphasis on the lyre as postponed Subject of the missing preceding sentence; with Boissonade's Dat. λύραι Hermes is Subject, 'paid the penalty with the lyre by exchange'. Schneidewin's ἐξελύσατο 'redeemed the penalty' accommodates a full but untranslatable etymological play upon the word λύτρον ('quittance') in *Anecd.Gr.*, incorporating λυρα...ἐξελυσατο.]

192. Time: necessary for 'practice', F 191 and n.   **the gods' inspiration:** a fundamental of poetic self-belief, from Homer on; for the particular nature of 'inspiration', literally 'breath', cf. A. *Ag.* 105–6 'persuasion still breathes down on me from the gods', with Fraenkel's note, Hes. *Theog.* 31 (cited by Kannicht in *TrGF*), Democr. 68 B 18 DK.   **singing hymns:** to gods, as in F 182a, 223.91, cf. *Ion* 6.

182b, 183–8 etc. The debate: for the likely content, form and character of this famous exchange see Introd., pp. 262, 266–9.

182b. The testimonia given for this fr. in *TrGF* are: **T ia:** Pl. *Gorg.* 506b4 (cf. 484e, 485e ff.) and Olympiod. *In Gorg.* 34.4 Westerink, where Socrates compares his reply to Callicles with that of Amphion to Zethus (for Plato's technique with the Euripidean material *TrGF* refers esp. to A. W. Nightingale, *Cl.Ant* 11 [1992], 121–41). **T ib:** Aristid. *Or.* 2.394 Lenz-Behr, an obscure and possibly corrupt passage in which *Antiope* is cited to exemplify one man (Eur.?) making both arguments (cf. F 189?), which Aristides wishes to divide between Amphion and Zethus. **T iia:** Cic. *De Diu.* 1.50.94, an orator's technical criticism that Pacuvius' Amphion, like Eur.'s, shifts the debate from music to wisdom. **T iib:** Anon. *Ad Herenn.* 2.27.43, the same criticism at greater length. **T iii:** Hor. *Ep.* 1.18.39–45, Amphion's eventual capitulation to Zethus. From *TrGF*'s bibl. see esp. Snell (1971), 87–96; L. B. Carter, *The Quiet Athenian* (Oxford, 1986), 163–73; S. Slings in *Fragmenta Dramatica* 137–51; Nightingale 121–6; add Podlecki (1996), 135–43; Wilson 440–9; extended bibl. in Budé p. 229 n. 51.

183. The lack of a Greek introductory particle may indicate that these lines develop or explain a preceding charge against Amphion; possibly they begin Zethus' long speech (no initial particle at e.g. *And.* 183, *Hipp.* 935, *Pho.* 469). Their abruptness and the staccato effect in 2 suggest anger, as if Zethus is set upon pursuing an old quarrel.   **the start of mischief:** a formula as old as Homer, *Il.* 3.100, applied to Helen, the archetype of trouble-makers; so too e.g. *Tro.* 919, *Hel.* 426.
1. introducing: the verb εἰσάγω of religious innovation *Bacc.* 260, artistic Ar. *Frogs* 959.   **music:** for μοῦσα without a defining adj. in this sense cf. *Hel.* 165, *Bacc.* 563.
2. idle: i.e. unproductive and therefore politically irresponsible, again at F 187.4 'useless', cf F 188.2, 219, Pacuv. *Ant.* *5 and e.g. Eur. *Mel.* F 512; used of intellectuals also at e.g. *Oed.* F 552.4, Ar. *Clouds.* 316.   **fond of wine:** Zethus identifies love of music with the ways of the symposiast fuddled by wine, like

Nicaenetus 5.1–2 Gow-Page (*Anth.Pal.* 13.29); cf. F 188.5, *Autolycus* F 282.15. **neglectful of affairs:** F 185.1. The line is phrased as a 'negative tricolon with crescendo', the length of each unit increasing; this is a foible of Eur., e.g. *And.* 1216, *Hec.* 714, (Bond on) *Hyps.* I.iv.18 (= F 752h.18); mocked at Ar. *Frogs* 838.

184. In both Pl. *Gorg.* and Ar. *Rhet.* these lines are used to illustrate an individual's natural desire to 'shine' (2) where he thinks himself to be at his best, and the accompanying danger that he will pursue his own excellence to the point of ridicule by others (Pl.) and of selfishness (Ar.), so that he fails to serve the common good (cf. F 219.3, a fr. associated with Zethus here by Wilamowitz and Schaal; and, once again, F 185.4–6, 187.4). Kambitsis entertains attribution to Amphion, thinking that in Plato the speaker may have been applying a general truth taken from *Antiope* rather than one expressed only by Zethus.

1. **\<anyhow\>:** γέ τοι combatively emphasizes the preceding word or proposition, as e.g. *Pho.* 730, *Cyc.* 224.
2. **shines:** the adj. λαμπρός 'brilliant in' with ἐν and Dat., as at e.g. *Aeolus* F 16.1 'in combat', *Autolycus* F 282.10 'in physical prime'.
3. **at his personal best:** lit. 'himself (at the) best of himself'; the emphatic pronoun αὐτός supports the reflexive αὐτοῦ (e.g. *Hcld.* 814); here, the Gen. αὐτοῦ is controlled by the Superlative βέλτιστος, imitating the construction with the Comparative, e.g. Soph. F 871.7 αὐτῆς εὐπρεπεστάτη 'at her fairest' (the moon); KG II.314.6.   In 1–3 the pron. **this** is repeated three times, and thus emphasized as the antecedent to the rel. clause **the thing in which etc.** introduced by Greek ἵνα, a locative 'where' (paraphrased in Pl. by ὅπου) used with the Indic. of circumstances at e.g. *Alc.* 319 of childbirth, cf. *Ion* 1252, *Ino* F 413.2 etc. [some sources attest an indef. Subjunctive 'wherever' without the particle ἄν, like ὅπου at *Cyc.* 526 (cf. KG II.426 n. 1)].

185. 1. *you neglect, etc.*: early scholars tried to construct a verse from Plato's paraphrase, without conviction.
2. **\<endowed\>...character:** for the notion, and the Greek verb λαγχάνω 'be endowed', cf. *Hipp.* 79f. 'naturally endowed with a sense of virtue'.   [A participle controlling φύσιν must be supplied for full contrast of the two ideas in 1–2. The letters of λαχων would resemble –ναιαν in some scripts, leading easily to omission.]   **noble:** γενναῖος, i.e. remaining true to natural nobility of character; so e.g. *Hec.* 597–8, cf. on F 206.4 below.
3. **effeminate appearance:** compare Pentheus mocked by Dionysus when he is made to put on female dress, *Bacc.* 855, 978; similar wording at Soph. F 769. [The abrupt transition to line 4 provoked von Arnim's suspicion that original Euripidean wording may have been omitted by Plato here.]
4–5. **voice:** for the commonplace verb λάσκειν 'talk, cry out' used of formal pronouncements cf. *IT* 976, *Or.* 329 (prophecies).   **anything probable:** εἰκός, an argument dependent upon probability and so potentially successful, *IA* 1134, S. *Phil.* 1373; for this device in contemporary rhetoric see our Vol. 1 on *Cret.*

F 472e.4–41 (lines 11, 19).   **persuasive:** for persuasion in Eur. see esp. *Hec.* 816, where it is 'mankind's sole sovereign', *Antigone* F 170.1, *Hyps.* F 759.3. [Dodds makes the fullest and most likely reconstruction from Plato's paraphrase, in two lines. *TrGF* adopts Merkelbach's single line 'and you would neither voice persuasion in deliberations about justice', which ignores too much of Plato.]

6–7. keep...close behind: an infantry-soldier protects as much of his body (and his neighbour's open side) as possible: Hom. *Il.* 13.408 'all of him crouched under his shield', Callinus F 1.10 'heart and life crouched under his shield'; for Zethus' jibe cf. *HF* 159–60 'who never held a shield in his left hand nor went near a spear'. For the verb ὁμιλεῖν cf. *And.* 791 Κενταύρων ὁμιλῆσαι δορί 'join closely in the war against the Centaurs' [a passage inducing Kannicht to supplement here with 'keep close to <*enemies*> with a hollow shield'; but Nauck's <*bravely*> (καλῶς as e.g. *Hec.* 329, *IA* 1252) (or 'rightly', ὀρθῶς) seems better].   **a hollow shield:** also A. *Sept.* 495; concave and often bossed, the shape giving greater strength and deflection.   [The lost beginning of 6 is beyond conjecture from Plato's text; but the continuation of the syntax in **nor...keep** shows that no more than a few words are lost.]

8. give...advice: alluding to the formulaic proclamation of the Athenian assembly, τίς ἀγορεύειν βούλεται; 'who wishes to address the gathering?', Ar. *Ach.* 45 etc., paraphrased at *Supp.* 438–9 'Who wishes to bring into our midst any excellent counsel he has?' A rhetorical figure here couples verb and Object noun from the same stem βουλ– ('figura etymologica'), a common device of emphasis; this one recurs at *Pho.* 693.   **energetic:** νεανικόν, characteristic of youthful dash and resolution, praised at e.g. *Supp.* 190, 443.

186.   Zethus judges Amphion's natural qualities to have been corrupted (cf. F 185.2ff, 187.5) by the insidious demands of his music and its technique: for τέχνη 'art', pejorative, cf. *Bacc.* 675, *Polyidus* F 635.1–2.   **And how...:** both surprised and sneering; καὶ πῶς appears usually in stichomythia, e.g. *Hec.* 833, *Pho.* 883.   **this...when:** abstract Subject defined by a personal relative clause with ὅστις, 'when (in this instance) the individual etc.': see our Vol. 1 on *Erec.* F 360.1–3, *Pha.* 160–1 (= F 775a).   [The hypothetical third line extracted from Plato by Valckenaer, '(a man) able neither to protect himself' involves substitution of a metrically suitable synonym for Plato's 'help' and would require further reconstruction from Plato's continuation 'nor to save either himself or anyone else from the greatest dangers etc.']

187.1–2. possessed of a good living...neglect: a charge repeated almost word for word in Amphion's riposte, F 198.1–2. Greek βίος **living** as at *Supp.* 450, *Pho.* 400; for the idea cf. *Ion* 581 '(a man) with many possessions in life'.

2. leaves...affairs to neglect and lets them go: pleonastic expression (for strong emphasis) like adesp. F 353 'Zeus leaves the little things and lets them go', *Tro.* 695, F 974.2.

ANTIOPE

3–4. songs...useless: repeating Zethus' accusation of F 183, cf. 187a(ii).
at home and in the city: all good citizens must be actively engaged in both,
e.g. F 200; a life of pleasure or cowardliness (our line 6, F 185.3–7, 188.1; both in
Arch. F 239) or of philosophizing (cf. Pacuv. *Ant.* *5, pp. 326–7 below]; Pl. *Apol.*
23b cited by Kannicht) frustrates such a duty.   [Text: Walker and Diggle independently proposed the locative pairing οἴκοι κἂν πόλει. Stob.'s Datives οἴκοις καὶ
πόλει construe a little awkwardly after 'useless' as '(disadvantageously) to home
and city' (but cf. e.g. F 866.3 τῆι πόλει...ἀμήχανον '(a man) wihout resource for
his city'); less good still is translation as 'in the eyes of home and city'.]
5. a nobody: Greek οὐδείς 'no one' used pejoratively, like *Bell.* F 285.15 'an
absolute nobody' (see n.), *And.* 700 'though they are nobodies they despise the
people'. Wecklein's οὐδέν gives 'nothing, of no significance, useless', like *And.*
50 'useless to his son': for the slim difference between the Masc. and Neut. see
Denniston on *El.* 370.
6. overcome by: ἥσσων (lit. 'less than') with Gen. as e.g. *And.* 631 'overcome by
Aphrodite'; by pleasures Pl. *Prot.* 353c, Xen. *Mem.* 4.5.11.

*187a. Borthwick's (1967) restoration to Zethus of these further two apparent paraphrases in Plato is almost certainly right; but his addition (*CQ* 18 [1968], 199) of
adesp. F 88a οὐκ ἔστι δ' ἐν σοὶ πόλεος ἡγεμὼν ἀνήρ, 'and there is in you no man
to lead a city' (= *Antiope* No.239i Mette), is only a possibility.
(i). throw away your lyre is black humour, for there was an immemorial taunt of
cowards 'who threw away their shields' (see Dover on Ar. *Clouds* 353) – even
though some poets were disingenuously proud to have done it, e.g. Archil. F 5.2
IEG (= 6.2 Campbell).
(ii). lyre...idle: F 183 again, 187.3–4.   **you are useless:** for μηδὲν ὠφελῶν
of damaging 'political' apathy cf. *Supp.* 1112. The phrase is a synonym of the
adjs. ἀνωφελής (*Supp.* 239, with Collard's n.), ἄχρηστος (*Hcld.* 4: see on F 194)
and ἀχρεῖος (*Autolycus* F 282.15); see also on F 183.2 'idle'.   **a soldier's life:**
a predicative adj. in the Greek, cf. *Med.* 249 'we live a life in our homes without
danger'.   For the Imper. **Live** cf. *IT* 699, *Phrixus* F 826.   **provide well for
yourself:** treat war as an opportunity for enrichment, A. *Sept.* 545, *Eum.* 631,
cf. F 188.6 below.   **be a ruler:** absolute rule is applauded and desired for its own
sake, esp. by Eteocles *Pho.* 506, 524–5; its value questioned e.g. *Hipp.* 1012, *Ion*
621, *Tro.* 1169, *Antigone* F 172, S. *OT* 584–9.

188.1. But do what I say: this formula occurs at the end of debate-speeches at
Hcld. 174, *Hel.* 992, and of dialogue exchanges at *Hel.* 323, *IA* 739, 1460 etc.
2. useless activities: cf. on F 183.2, 187.3–4.   **the fine music of hard
work:** recapitulating the attack launched in F 187, cf. 185, with ironic and figurative reversal of 'music'; for music metaphorical of physical training and excellence
cf. *Supp.* 906 (with Collard's n.). [The text of this line has been secured by Borthwick, who gives full illustration of the literary cliché 'work and art are incompatible'. Plato's ἐλέγχων '(stop) fault-finding' is obviously his substitution to suit

his dialogue; in Eur. it is Zethus himself, not Amphion, who is critical. πόνων **hard work** is confirmed by Plato's and Olympiod.'s paraphrase πραγμάτων 'activity'; Olympiod.'s (unmetrical) πολέμων 'warfare' was perhaps a deliberate change to suit Zethus' insistence on the merits of soldiering, F 185.6, 187a. (ii).]

4. Farming affords the Herdsman's 'son' Zethus an appropriate illustration of what is the right 'hard work' (Amphion's F 191 may respond to this); Pacuv. *Ant.* 3 and *4 may reflect our line; cf. e.g. *Or.* 920, *El.* 369ff., Ar. *Peace* 508–11; at *Supp.* 882–7 farming is coupled with military training as ideal service to the community.

5. **pretty trifles**: both Greek words here carry their common pejorative tone: κομψός e.g. *Aeolus* F 16.2 (a similar condemnation to this), *Hyps.* F 757.831, *Supp.* 426 etc., σόφισμα e.g. *Hec.* 258, *Bacc.* 489.

6. **living in a house of emptiness**: the antithesis of F 187a(ii) 'provide well for yourself'. 'Emptiness' perhaps alludes to the empty uselessness of Amphion's neglect of his house and affairs, F 185.1, 187.2, cf. F 198.

219. The ideas match Zethus' criticism of Amphion's politically unproductive music and chatter in social gatherings, F 183.

1. **Silence is an ornament**: the well-born man knows when to be silent and when to speak, *Ino* F 413.1–2, cf. *Or.* 638–9, F 977; Pind. F 180 'do not break out into useless argument with everybody: sometimes the paths of silence are the most reliable'.   [Text: Ellis's correction restores the laconic maxim: see Pearson on Soph. F 64.4. Stob. gives 'the ornament which is silence is a crown' or, less well, 'decorous silence is...']

2. **blathering**: unconstructive prattling (perhaps cf. Zethus at F 188.5), like *Supp.* 462 of an officious herald. For the Greek neuter participle as noun cf. *Oed.* F *545a.5 (n.), *And.* 133 τὸ κρατοῦν 'superior power'. **grasps at**: for ἅπτομαι cf. F 904 'anyone wishing to overcome nature is grasping at extreme folly'.

3. **bad company, and a weakness for a city too**: similarly *Hcld.* 4 'useless to his city and hard to deal with', *Ino* F 425.3 'a bad mixer with associates and the whole city'; cf. F 194 above. For good or bad political 'company' cf. *Aeolus* F 29, *Aegeus* F 7.2. By 'bad company' Zethus may mean 'unmanly inadequacy to fight in close company', cf. F 185.7 and n.

189. The tone of detached observation suits a chorus punctuating a debate (e.g. *Pho.* 526–7 after Eteocles' speech): so Valckenaer. Kannicht however favours Matthiae's attribution to Amphion, at the start of his long debate-speech, comparing the beginning of Eteocles' speech at *Pho.* 499 'if goodness and wisdom were naturally the same for everybody, men would have no disputatious quarrels'. The verses are often cited as a classic statement of ambivalence about contemporary Athenian rhetoric, especially in the mouths of morally equivocal sophists; indeed they probably allude to Protagoras himself, 80 B 6a DK: 'Protagoras was the first to say that there were two antithetical arguments about every matter' (see Kannicht on *Hel.* 138). Ar. *Clouds* 889ff. has 'Right' and 'Wrong' as personified arguments (see Dover's ed., p. lviif.).

1–2. argument between…positions: something of a formula headlining or registering an 'agon', a 'formal debate' or ἀγὼν λόγων: see Collard on *Supp.* 428 or in J. Mossman (ed.), *Oxford Readings in Euripides* (Oxford, 2003), 55. **two positions:** in this context cf. e.g. *Or.* 551, *Tro.* 917; many positions, *Phoenix* F 812.1–3. **upon:** Greek ἐκ 'starting from, on the basis of', e.g. F 188.6.

191. The association of these words in Philostratus with the 'hymns of Euripides and Amphion' suggests their origin in Amphion's entry-scene with the Chorus (where many editors have put them), but persuasive speech is a theme of the debate, F 185.4, 189, 200. The word μελέτη 'practice' in Philostratus is as applicable to music and poetry, e.g. Pind. *Ol.* 14.18, as to rhetoric, for which see LSJ II.1.c. F 192 has time as a musician's need. For the value set upon an abstract **possession** cf. *Meleager* F 518.1–5 (children 'greater than wealth, 'a fine treasure for a house'), *Bacc.* 1150–2 (wisdom and piety), F 1029 (virtue). [The three Greek words fit both dialogue and lyric metrically.]

193. very active: a slightly evasive translation of πολλὰ πράσσει, for lurking behind these words is the familiar accusation, both from within and without Athens, of its policies as interfering, guilty of πολυπραγμοσύνη or busybody-ness: see Introd., p. 268 on the debate, and for the phenomenon in general *Phil.* F 788.2 and commentators on *Supp.* 576–7, Ar. *Birds* 44, Thuc. 1.70.8, 2.40.2 (recently R. Brock in *Modus Operandi. Essays…Rickman*, BICS Suppl. 71 [1998], 227–38). **foolish:** Ion sets the same value on those who are overactive politic-ally, when they need not be, *Ion* 598–601. For the ellipse of Greek 'is' cf. esp. *Tro.* 95, 1203. **inactivity:** Greek adj. ἀπράγμων, equated here with ἀργός 'idle' or ἀνωφελής 'useless' (see on F 181–2, *187a(ii), 194.1 'quiet'); the adverb occurs at *Phil.* F 787.1, where the thought is comparable, and the noun ἀπραξία at *Or.* 426. [The duplication of παρόν between 1 and 2 is not in itself indicative of textual corruption; cf. e.g. repeated χρή at *Hcld.* 491, *HF* 141; but the near-repetition of sense in the two 'when'-clauses has caused suspicion that Eur. wrote more strongly: 1 'when he ought to be inactive', Nauck, 'when he must be…' Blaydes, '(active) with what he ought not to be doing' Hense, Ribbeck.]

194.1. the quiet man: politically laudable to Amphion, cf. *Supp.* 509, 952, *Or.* 698 – but equated with the idle man, *Oed.* F 552.4, *Temenidae* F 736.3, *Supp.* 767, cf. on F 183. **sure friend to friends:** cf. *Or.* 1155, (Collard on) *Supp.* 867–8.
2. very good for his city: like *Hcld.* 4–5 πόλει τ' ἄχρηστος…αὑτῶι δ' ἄριστος 'useless to his city…but very good for himself'.
3. approve: αἰνεῖν as *Palam.* F 583.2, *Or.* 498 etc.; the 2nd Plur. Imper. addresses the world of the spectators, **(you people):** see on *Bell.* F 286.4. **adventuring:** Zethus' challenge to Amphion, F 187a.
4. too much boldness in…a sailor: *Supp.* 508–9 'a bold leader and (a bold) ship's sailor are (both) dangerous'. **a man at the head of his country:** *Pha.* 125 Diggle (= F 774.2) 'a single man at the head is dangerous to his city',

cf. *Pho.* 599. προστάτης, a man recognized as 'standing at the front, a champion, leader', *Hcld.* 964, *Supp.* 243, *IA* 373; it was a title claimed by Athenian demagogues, Ar. *Knights* 1128, Thuc. 3.75.2 etc.

196. Another ethical commonplace, cf. F 193.2: see commentators on *HF* 504, *Supp.* 953–4, *Bacc.* 424–6.
1. a man: the Subject is understood from Plur. θηντῶν **mankind**, as in a very similar context at *And.* 412f., cf. F 200.2 below.
2. The common antithesis **fortunate...unfortunate** occurs at *Bacc.* 1262, *Ion* 699, *Chrys.* F 843.2 etc.; but line 3 is an interpolator's expansion (so Nauck, and Wilamowitz on *HF* 506, who on *HF* 440 gives a classic exposition of the inherent distinction, fading by Eur.'s time, between εὐδαίμων 'blest by heaven' and εὐτυχής 'fortunate by chance'. Cf. below on F 198.3–4).
4. Why then...do we not...: half-colloquial for 'Why, we ought...!': see Barrett on *Hipp.* 1060–1.   **entered upon:** for ἐν and Dat. with the Perf. part. of βαίνω cf. F 1073.2 (sure fortunes).   **prosperity...insecure:** the idea at *Bell.* F 304.1 (also σαφής), *HF* 512, *El.* 941 etc.

197. The fr. more naturally follows the thought ending F 196 than precedes its first line 'Such is the life of wretched mankind', where some editors have placed it. **well-mixed:** i.e. 'with the right internal blend': used of life at *Mel.* F 504, cf. the adj. εὔκρατος of climate at *Pha.* 7 Diggle (= F 772.2). [The fr. was noted by lexicographers to illustrate both the form and the accent of the adj. εὐκράς (correct: Chantraine, *Dict.Etym.*); it is impossible to know whether the fr. is incomplete (see the supply of 'life' in the trans.) or complete (requiring e.g. Lobeck's substitution of ἡδονή: 'pleasure would not be well-mixed for mankind').]

198. Amphion counters F 187 expressly: the first lines of each fr. are similar, and the idea of 'pursuit' occurs in both second verses.
2. beautiful things: activities (Amphion means, his music) or things not necessary or useful but so pleasing as to make a man feel blest (so Snell 1971, 95; cf. Amphion in F 191). For this definition Kannicht cites Ar. *Pol.* 1333a.30, cf. Democr. 68 B 73 DK 'a righteous love of desiring beautiful things without arrogance'.   **in his house:** bare locative Dative, e.g. *El.* 1003 'possess in my house', cf. F 203.1 and n.   [West's conjecture 'will not even (or 'not either'?) pursue beautiful things in his house' is difficult, apparently requiring τῶν καλῶν as Gen. with θηράσεται, a verb with which LSJ attests only the Acc.]
3–4. For the thought cf. Solon's famous 'call no man blest (ὄλβιος) but just 'fortunate' (εὐτυχής) until he dies' Hdt. 1.32.6, cf. *Tro.* 508–9 etc.   **fortunate:** there seems no better translation of εὐδαίμονα here; cf. Solon's εὐτυχής. Amphion devalues the happiness of a rich man indifferent to beauty, from 'blessedness' to mere 'good fortune' (for this looser sense of εὐδαίμων see on F 196.2); or (Kannicht) he is using irony, confining heaven's blessing to temporary guardianship of his

wealth. [Nauck's δυσδαίμονα makes the idea direct: the man is 'unfortunate, unlucky' in this respect]. **guardian of his wealth:** Kambitsis compares Thuc. 6.39.1, 'the rich are the best guardians of money'.

199. Amphion contests Zethus' censure (F 185.2–3, 187.3–4) that 'music' specifically weakens masculine virtues: cf. Pl. *Rep.* 410d, *Gorg.* 491b.
1. censure a weak and effeminate body: for the expression cf. *Tro.* 1035 ψόγον τὸ θῆλύ τε 'blame and the feminine', hendiadys for 'blame for feminine weakness'.
2–3. Amphion gives sound mentality the first place in a city's management, F 200; it is preferred to athletic prowess *Autolycus* F 282.24–8; cf. on F 201.1, S. *Aj.* 1250–2; for intelligence better than brute strength, cf. *Oed.* F 548, Cropp on *El.* 386–90. **if I can think soundly:** i.e. give sound political opinions, with εὖ φρονεῖν as usual specific in its reference – a riposte to F 185.4–6, like Amphion also at F 194.3–4, and perhaps F 220.2. [Valckenaer's conjecture gives 'if my mind is sound', general in application.]

200.1–2. judgement: γνῶμαις Plural, 'instances in which judgement is shown' before concluding a decision, like F 216.2; the Sing. γνώμη (Stob.) is little different in sense, and provides a Subject for Sing. ἰσχύει in 2 (and its sense would continue in 3 'one counsel') – but ἀνήρ 'man' as Subj. is easily supplied from ἀνδρός: cf. F 196.1–2 and n. **cities...house:** paired by Zethus at F 187.4. **strength:** cf. Pearson on Soph. F 939, 'judgements (γνῶμαι) have more power than strong arms'.
3–4. the hands of the many: possibly not just 'strong' hands (1–2 above) but hands raised to vote in the (Athenian) assembly: for this use of the unqualified noun cf. A. *Supp.* 607, Ar. *Eccl.* 264. **crassness:** ἀμαθία as lack of intellectual and moral understanding (*HF* 347, *Med.* 935 etc.: see Denniston on *El.* 294–6, Seaford on *Cyc.* 173); it is characteristic of demagogues (*Or.* 905, Ar. *Knights* 193), leading the **mob** (*Or.* 772, *IA* 526, *Hipp.* 988–9), or of any bad rule (*Pho.* 393); the mob is crudely overbearing (*Supp.* 411, *Hel.* 607). Kambitsis pp. 59–62 gives line 4 a very full discussion. [There are many insignificant textual variants or errors in 3–4. Galen's unique variant σὺν ὅπλοις 'in party with weapons' was likely an adaptation to suit his subject, Themistocles' preference of statecraft to war; van Groningen altered it to the adj. σύνοπλος, 'equipped with weapons', found in Eur. at *HF* 127.]

201. Amphion attacks athletes as over-eaters and therefore 'bad citizens'; in 2 he pursues his antagonism to Zethus' demand for material wealth (F 183.2, 187a(ii), cf. 188.6).
1. Look: καὶ μήν heralding a new argument in a long speech, *Hec.* 1224, *Alc.* 653; Denniston, *GP* 351. **fine physique:** the presence of σαρκὸς with εὐεξία, lit. 'a fine condition of flesh', shows that Eur. refers here to excellent musculature (*HF* 1269, *Cyc.* 380; εὐεξία is used of athletic bodies Pl. *Gorg.* 450a). For the

particular criticism of athletes here cf. Pl. *Rep.* 407b, excessive athleticism making for bad managers and soldiers and for surly indiscipline.
2. if their wealth fails: *Autolycus* F 282.11 comments on athletes' civic uselessness when they age.
3–4. Athletes are said habitually to over-eat at *Autolycus* F 282.5, cf. Xen. *Mem.* 1.2.4 etc. and the gluttonous athletes listed in Athenaeus 10.414–5; moderate eating is commended at *Supp.* 865–6, *Danae* F 328, *Ino* F 413.4. [All the elements of the Greek sentence have been doubted, although reasonable linguistic parallels for each exist. **accustomed to a habit:** ἦθος internal Acc. with (Passive) ἐθίζειν like F 282.8, Pl. *Laws* 706d (both with cognate ἔθη). **undisciplined:** ἀκόλαστον with 'habit' also *Erec.* F 362.22, Critias F 6.12–13 *IEG*. **eating:** lit. 'belly', γαστρός, i.e. 'gluttony'; found in many idioms, e.g. F 915 'my accursed belly', *Ino* F 413.4 'control my belly', cf. e.g. *Alex.* F 49.3 (n.). Schmidt substituted εἰκός, with Nauck's καὶ γὰρ for δεῖ γὰρ, 'and the fact is, a man of undisciplined habit is likely to remain...'. **remains in the same condition:** expression as at *Hel.* 1026, *Tro.* 350, *Ion* 969.]

202. Amphion may be near the end of his speech. **On the contrary:** μὲν οὖν continuative but adversative as *Alc.* 821, 1113 etc.; Denniston, *GP* 475. **I wish I might sing:** Amphion perhaps thinks of a hymn in praise of gods, F 182a. **say something wise:** i.e. politically wise: Amphion at F 199.2, 200.3 (and perhaps Zethus at F 186.1). In this clause the Greek has a strong enjambment in τι | σοφόν, emphasizing the overrun word: for this phenomenon see Collard on *Supp.* 16. **troubles:** translates νοσεῖν, a common metaphor for 'factional strife', *HF* 34 'the city sick with faction', cf. 542.

220. The debate seems the most likely location; if from Amphion, he is arguing that his capacity for clear decision is not hampered by artistic involvement: cf. F 202.
2–3. Text and interpretation much disputed (both Kambitsis 71–5 and Kannicht in *TrGF* give full reviews). The simpler but less popular text (printed) presents a conflict between intellectual decisiveness and subjective blandishments, in which the ruling concepts of **resolve** and **heart** begin the two Greek lines; for ψυχή as 'soul, heart, spirit, feelings, sensibilities or inclinations' cf. e.g. *Alc.* 118 'you touched my heart (ψυχή), you touched my mind (φρένες)', *Hipp.* 255 'the inmost marrow of my soul'. [The more popular sense-division after ψυχῆι (Hense) gives 'though they have sense in their mind they are unwilling to follow their heart, being generally overcome by their friends'; all proponents cite Isocr. 15.180 'to follow what has been decided by the heart'. **by their friends:** πρὸς φίλων as masc. is certainly the more natural interpretation than as neut. 'overcome by what pleases them'. Weil's προσφιλῶν gives 'overcome by friends', νικῶμαι with a bare Gen. as *Med.* 315, S. *Aj.* 1353.]

203. Who describes this scene? Antiope on seeking refuge at the cave (Wilamowitz) is more likely than Dirce arriving with her bacchants (Matthiae; cf. below, P. Oxy.

3317 and Comm.), for the Herdsman or Amphion would not describe their own home, and the Messenger reports Dirce's death away from the cave (F 221). The fr. gives further Dionysiac colour to the play (cf. on F 179 'Eleutherae'); Clement cites it after noting an oracle 'Dionysus, god of many joys, is a pillar for the Thebans' = *Orac.Gr.* F 207 Hendess. Ivy adorns both the emblems and the worshippers of the god (*Bacc.* 25, 81 etc., adesp. F 726); columns bearing masks of the god and hung with ivy are shown in numerous ancient representations: see e.g. *LIMC* III.1.426–7 nos. 29–43 (33–5 illustrated), cf. *Orph.Hymn.* 47.1 Quandt; Burkert, *Greek Religion* 166, 238.

1. inside in: ἔνδον with Dat., cf. *Bacc.* 497, LSJ ἔνδον I.3. A 1st. Pers. verb of seeing may be missing. [Bothe supplied it by altering ἔνδον to εἶδον 'I saw'].

2. festooned with: lit. 'having locks of, hairy with', an easy metaphor for draped ivy; similarly *Bacc.* 1054–5 θύρσον...κισσῶι κομήτην 'a thyrsus hairy with ivy'. **god of celebration:** the adj. εὔιος is almost unique to Dionysus, registering his celebrants' ecstatic cry of εὐοῖ (*Bacc.* 141; but cf. εὐὰν εὐοῖ *Tro.* 325, Cassandra's cry to the marriage-god Hymenaeus).

[1–2. Text: Toup's βουκόλου, with κομῶντα retained, is much preferable to his alternative, retaining Acc. βουκόλον and changing to κοσμοῦντα to give 'inside in the dwelling a herdsman <...> dressing a column with ivy'. Wilamowitz's βουκόλων gives 'inside in the chambers of (Dionysus') worshippers', i.e. a location other than the herdsman's single dwelling (cf. Huys, *Tale* 315); for βουκόλος as a god's 'herdsman' see on *Cret.* F 472.11 βούτης 'herdsman, celebrant'.]

204. Almost certainly Antiope's outburst, when in her flight she first encounters the Chorus, near or outside the Herdsman's cave (see Introd., *Reconstruction*; but Cropp suggests that **strangers** may point to the twins, with ironic 'non-recognition'; cf. Iphigenia at *IT* 479). Her words are a commonplace, e.g. *Ino* F 415.1; more elaborate at F 211 below (perhaps from the Chorus in a subsequent exchange with Antiope). Here, Antiope would go on to appeal for help.

205. The self-analytical style of these lines (and of F 208) led Snell (1971), 85f. to place them in a monologue of Antiope soon after encountering the Chorus (F 204); he compared Phaedra's monologue at *Hipp.* 373ff. Pacuv. *Ant.* 6–9 and 11 perhaps reflect Antiope's account of her torment by Dirce. See Introd., *Reconstruction* on 'Antiope's Lament', and Creusa's loneliness as a long-suffering but bereft mother in *Ion*.

1. I realise: Erotian cited the verse to illustrate the verb φρονεῖν in this sense of νοεῖν: cf. *Bacc.* 1259 φρονήσασαι μὲν οἷ' ἐδράσατε 'when you realise the nature of what you did'; Barrett on *Hipp.* 1401.

2–3. in trouble: lit. 'ill, sick', but the common metaphorical sense is clear from κακοῖς (3), perhaps reflecting κακά F 204.   [νοσοῦντα in Stob. is Acc. of Subject to εἰδέναι, while Conti Bizzaro's Dat. νοσοῦντι depends on ἡδονὴν ἔχει, 'has a certain pleasure for one in trouble']. **ignorance amid misery is an advantage:** S. *Aj.* 552–3, Terence, *Hecyra* 286–7. A related idea, that the man lacking prosperity is ever ignorant of his misfortune, at *Bell.* F 185.15–17.

207. I was being brought back again: by Lycus from Sicyon, after the killing of her husband Epopeus (Hygin. 8.4; she was already pregnant by Zeus, 8.1).

208. For the location see Introd., p. 273. We cannot know whether Antiope offers this near-exculpation of Zeus as part of her narrative, or in response to disbelief of her story by Amphion (so Kannicht; cf. F 210); her reasoning that not all mortals can be fortunate (cf. F 196.2–3 and e.g. *Ion* 381) repeats her F 204; cf. the Chorus F 211.
1. neglected by the gods: i.e. by Zeus himself, whose past conduct but ultimate salvation of Antiope are later explained by Hermes at F 223.71–7; similar complaints against divine fathers for abandoning their children at *HF* 339–47 (Zeus), *Ion* 436–40 (Apollo).
2. can be explained: for the Greek idiom ἔχει λόγον cf. *Hel.* 473.

210. Amphion's disbelief: see on F 208. There was a myth-version that Zeus impregnated Antiope in the guise of a satyr (**beast**: θήρ used of satyrs *Cyc.* 624, Soph. *Ichn.* F 314.221): see Introd., *Myth* on Hygin. 8.1. Incredulity at such divine behaviour, e.g. *El.* 737–8, *HF* 1341–2; for Euripidean scepticism about myth generally see Stinton, *Coll. Papers* 254ff. **imitated:** Zeus as a swan impregnated Leda, *Hel.* 18–19. **evil:** κακοῦργος of sexual misbehaviour also *Hipp.* 642 (a woman), cf. *Tro.* 968, *Bacc.* 232. [In 2 φωτός 'man' (Clem.) is only a miscopying; φηρός 'beast' (Wecklein), though used of both satyrs and centaurs, is the Aeolic form of θηρός, not found in Tragedy.   In 3 τήνδε is another miscopying in Clem.; Bothe's τόνδε 'he' (i.e. Zeus, from a just previous mention) overvalues Clem.'s error, for the explicit name (Valckenaer) is needed, forcefully adjacent to **you** beginnng the verse.]

206. The address to **My son** (the still unidentified Amphion) suggests either Antiope or the Herdsman: if the first, Antiope is pleading to be believed; if the second, the Herdsman may be warning Amphion not against Antiope, whose misery he knows, but against Dirce's pleas. The speech is too long to be a general comment by the Chorus amid such a fraught scene. Zuntz associated F 853 with this fr. because it is attributed to the play in one ms. of Stobaeus and is also a moral homily beginning with 'my son': see Introd., *Other proposed ascriptions*.
1–5. Clever rhetoric can prevail through untruths: *Hec.* 1187–94 are very similar, cf. *Arch.* F 253 (n.), *Med.* 576, *Hipp.* 486–9 etc.
2. beauties: cf. esp. [Longin.] *De Subl.* 5 'the beauties of expression'.
3. surest test: for ἀκριβής in such a context cf. *El.* 367 (how to define manliness).
4. human nature and rectitude: for the association of φύσις and τοὐρθόν in Pre-Socratic thought see Anaxag. 59 A 100 DK, Democritus 68 B 58 DK, then 'rectitude' at e.g. Pl. *Rep.* 540d. Superiority of natural virtue: Zethus at F 185.2 (n.), cf. *Phoenix* F 810. **eloquence:** i.e. glibness, victorious over justice *Alex.* F 56.
5. actions stronger than words: *Hec.* 1187–8 again, *Thyestes* F 394 etc.; men's actions associated with their nature (line 4), *Hyps.* F 759 (946).

211. Oh the pity of it: φεῦ φεῦ begins a choral comment after a long speech at e.g. *Hec.* 1228, *Supp.* 463 and probably F 218; but Snell thinks of the start of Antiope's monologue. [2 τε (Stob.) is sound in a repeated exclamation, *Tro.* 604, Denniston, *GP* 504; but δέ (Clem.) is not rare in repetition, *Alc.* 108 etc., Denniston, *GP* 163.]

P. Oxy. 3317. Ascription to *Antigone* depends upon the apparent equation of lines 14–15 with F 175, attributed to that play by Stobaeus (see App.); it requires imagining circumstances there in which Antigone ranges Cithaeron in celebrating Dionysus (at *Pho.* 1751–7 she says the god gave her no thanks for doing so in the past – but the lines may be inauthentic) and is then arrested (by Creon?). There is an appeal to Dionysus at *Antigone* F 177 (which some scholars have assigned to *Antiope*); perhaps this invokes the god's aid either before Polynices' burial or, after it, for Antigone to evade capture (in S. *Antigone* the Chorus appeals to Dionysus at 153–4, 1115–54); or it comes from an exodos in which Dionysus himself appears (so Van Looy 200).

Hygin. *Fab.* 8.4 and 7.5, however, has a 'bacchic' Dirce, in 7.5 purportedly in the Euripidean *Antiope* (and also – though the text is disputed – in an Ennian adaptation of it); Pacuv. *Ant.* 12 too appears to refer to bacchants, ordered (by Dirce?) to let their hair flow freely. In Hyginus it can be conjectured that Dirce's coming to the Herdsman's cave was engineered by Dionysus himself (8.4 *per bacchationem Liberi*, 'through possession by Liber': cf. on F 203, the Dionysiac column); her coming may have been in response to an appeal for the god's help by the refugee Antiope, the Chorus, or the Herdsman (who began the play with an appeal to the god in F 179). Dirce's fellow-bacchants formed a secondary chorus in *Antiope* (Schol. *Hipp.* 58): see Introd., *Staging*.

The chief difficulties of reconciling the content of P. Oxy. 3317 with these pointers are: (1) the uncertain identities of the participants: P. Oxy. has no speaker-indications. The restoration of 'attendants' in line 2 (popular but not certain: see Comm.) brought Scodel (1982) to object that, if Amphion is the presumed speaker, the twins as a herdsman's sons could not own any, let alone command them to seize Dirce; but the speaker may possibly be Antiope herself, referring to the twins simply as 'these men'. The woman threatened in 1–8 and responding in 9–12 can only be one with freedom, i.e. Dirce (10), for Antiope has lived in 'Heracles' palace' in misery (F 205, cf. Pacuvius 6–9), not the other's luxury (2–3);   (2) the apparent need, in the light of Hygin. 8.4–5, to have Dirce make a second appearance for this scene (Kannicht in *Kotinos*, and in *TrGF*: see App.); for Hyginus states that Dirce discovered Antiope and dragged her off to kill her, and that the twins, told by the Herdsman of their mother's identity, hurried off to rescue her – that is, Dirce and her bacchants left the stage dragging Antiope (cf. Pickard-Cambridge 108) and Dirce was brought back again. This sequence might have occurred within one episode, however: Hyginus states that the twins' rescue of their mother was speedy, or his Imperfect *extrahebat* may mean no more than '(Dirce) began to drag Antiope off (to her death)'; for the speed compare the exit of Polymestor with Hecuba at *Hec.* 1022 and his return after being blinded at 1056, following a brief choral lyric, her re-entry, and his off-

stage shouting;   (3) identifying the person(s) with whom Dirce might foresee her
joint death in line 9 (see note); this is the biggest difficulty.

Accordingly the first speaker in the fr. is more likely to be Amphion than
Antiope, but the latter might well torment Dirce now she is no longer in the safe
luxury of her palace (3–4) and accuse her of wearing improperly the emblems of
Dionysus' worship (8); compare Amphion's taunting of Lycus at F 223.60–6.

1. abandon: Dirce has taken refuge at Dionysus' column (F 203); for commands to
give up sanctuary at a god's shrine cf. e.g. *And.* 135, 262–3, *Ion* 1306, where the
word ἕδρα *<position>* occurs.   [*<So>*: οὔκουν gives a brusque command
expressed with the Fut. Indic. in a negative question, like *Bacc.* 191, *Cyc.* 632.]

2. *<lay hands>* on you: for the predicative adjective χειρίαν cf. *Ion* 1257, *And.*
411. [At the line-end, the supplement of πρόσπ[ολοι 'attendants' remains most
likely but is not necessary to the sense, for bare οἵδε 'these men' would be clear
enough in the stage-moment; πρὸς π[έτρας 'to the rocks' is also possible, if the
twins are already sure of their plan with the bull, for it is among rocks that Dirce is
killed, F 221.]

2–3. Dragging by the hair at *And.* 402, 710 etc., by *<auburn>* hair *IA* 1365–6; the
Gen. is partitive. The speaker makes the normal assumption that this cruel indign-
ity is to be avoided by a woman, as at *Hec.* 207, 225.

4. luxury...*<palace>*: similar wording at *Tro.* 997 'Menelaus' palace was insufficient for your abuse of luxury' (Helen, cf. *Or.* 1113). **Heracles' *<palace>*:** cf.
HF 523. Eur. probably invented the myth-version in which Heracles ruled Thebes
before two tyrants called Lycus (*HF* 27–31), and therefore earlier than Amphion's
building of the Theban citadel (F 223.87–8).

4–5. ['nor have you come *<to a friendly roof here>*' Diggle, with στέγος as in
F 223.29; 'nor *<feast there; but>* you have come *<to the end>*' ed. pr.]

5–6. ranged, lit. 'carried yourself across', but the translation is by no means
secure: (1) Eur. elsewhere uses the verb διαφορέω only in the sense 'tear apart', as
at F 223.62, of Dirce's eventual death (cf. *Bacc.* 739, 746, 1210); (2) LSJ II gives
only one example of the meaning 'carry across' (revenue transferred, Thuc. 6.91),
but at I compares διαφέρω *Supp.* 382 (proclamations circulated); and Eur. has the
noun διαφορά at *Erec.* F 360.9, of board-game 'moves'. [The supplement
διεφορού as 2nd Sing. Imperf. Mid. seems inescapable; Taplin (1998), 38 can hardly be right to read δι[α)φορού as a 'futurative' Imperative, 'you are to die by being
torn to pieces'. Ed. pr. was cautious, apparently preferring δυ[σ]φόρου with
μ[όγου, 'without intolerable effort', rightly doubted by Diggle as not apt from 'an
unsympathetic witness'. No other convincing supplement here or at line-end has
yet been found: Diggle's own μ[ονῆς giving 'without stopping', approximately as
at *Tro.* 1129, is not quite right in tone.] **the *<open territories>* of birds:**
Mt. Cithaeron was wild pasture, and bacchants abandoned their houses in the
communities of Thebes and Boeotia to range the mountain, *Bacc.* 115–9, 135ff.,
677ff. The word πλάξ is used also of the expanses of Cithaeron at *Bacc.* 307, 718.
Perhaps in 'birds' there is an allusion to the bird-like speed of which bacchants are

imagined capable, *Bacc.* 748. **plains:** also *Bacc.* 749, by the river Asopus. [Luppe supplements '*<and the land's>* plains'].

7. fawnskin: the ritual garb of bacchants, cf. *Hyps.* F 752 (n.); so they simulate the animality and speed of one of Dionysus' wild creatures. [The Gen. depends upon a missing Acc., supplied with probability by ed. pr. in στολήν 'draped *<in the costume, livery>* of a fawnskin'; cf. *HF* 549 'draped in the trappings of death'. At the line-start Diggle's θυ(ί)ουσα gives 'possessed, ecstatic', as at A. *Ag.* 1235.]

8. sacred emblems: the adj. ἱερός often describes objects sacred to the god, e.g. *Bacc.* 24, 59, 80, 161 etc. [Diggle's οὐ δεινόν; gives 'Is this not outrageous?', for which he compares F 223.23. Or perhaps οὐχ ὅσιον· 'It is irreligious', Collard (on ὅσιος see on F 223.86); ὅσιον and ἱερὰ would stand together as at *Mel.D.* F 494.20. Diggle shows that neither ἐκδῦσον (ed. pr.) nor ἀποδῦσον (Luppe) provides the appropriate sense 'strip off *your own* raiment'; so Taplin (see on 4–5 above) wonders whether such an Imperative may be abruptly addressed by Amphion to Zethus, with ἐξανημμένη[ν in 7: 'strip her, draped in her...').]

9. Dirce appears to be explaining why she will '*<consent>* **willingly**' (11): she regards her death as inevitable (so Luppe writes '*<the>* **future** *<is clear>*'). Sudden realisation of inevitable death comes not just to virtuous victims in Eur. such as Polyxena at *Hec.* 396 and Menoeceus at *Pho.* 1282 but also to villains like the repentant Eurystheus at *Hcld.* 1016ff. (it may mean little that *Anth.Pal.* 3.7.3–4 has Dirce supplicating in tears for her life). But the end of the line is mystifying; however it is supplemented, it is hard to guess with whom Dirce foresees 'dying together'. [Van Looy in ed. Budé I, 192 n. 17 (on *Antigone* F 175) objects that Luppe's supplement '*<it is fitting that>* I die *<with my kin>*' suits rather Antigone in the name-play, content to die after her brothers Eteocles and Polynices. Kannicht suggests that the whole line within *Antigone* should read '*<Understand>* what will happen: *<it is proper for anyone who>* touches me to die *<with me>*'.]

10–11. Let *<no one>* who is a slave touch me: I am *<free>*: thus Polyxena desires to die 'free', *Hec.* 550–1, 'willingly' 548; cf. the girl at *Hcld.* 551. [Diggle supplies '*<nor outrage>* **my body**': the strong verb αἰκίζω is used of the mutual wounds of the twins Polynices and Eteocles at *Pho.* 1529. Polyxena fears violence to her person at *Hec.* 548–9, cf. 374.]

12–13. quick temper is frightening: in a king e.g. *Bacc.* 671, *Cret.* F 472e.50–1; in the worthless Menelaus *Or.* 1198. For these faults to be coupled in **one nobly born** does extreme harm to accepted standards, as e.g. at *Hipp.* 411, *Alex.* F 53, *Bell.* F 295, 298. **crass folly:** ἀμαθία, cf. F 200 and *Oed.* F 552 'both bold and crassly foolish'.

14–15. The sentiment of these two verses is a commonplace in Eur., e.g. *Hcld.* 302–4 'noble birth better than base at warding off misfortune', cf. 253–4, *And.* 771–2, *Hipp.* 205–6. **his fate:** for impersonal δαίμων cf. *Or.* 504, F 1073.2 etc. discussed by Stevens on *And.* 98. The adverb εὐόργως **with equanimity** is matched in Eur. by the noun εὐοργησία 'equanimity, easy temper' at *Hipp.* 1039, *Bacc.* 641. [Stob.'s inappropriate εὐλόγως 'reasonably' is no more than a scribal error. The damaged end of 15 in P. Oxy. is very different from the inept one in

Stob. ('this man is less blest in prosperity'); Luppe (1990: see App.) supposed a conflation of two frs. in Stob. 4.14.14, with the second lemma and part-text lost after 15 τὸν δαίμονα ('probably right', Diggle [1996]). The ed. pr. doubted the supplement ἀθλιώτ[ατος because Greek usage does not justify the translation 'this man is more easy in extreme suffering' which might be appropriate here, as in e.g. *Hel.* 254 'bear life's inevitabilities most easily', and as in Kannicht's supplement here 'this man <*endures*> the most extreme <*miseries*> more easily'. The paradox is in itself not rare, e.g. *And.* 420 '(the childless person) has less pain, but there is misfortune in the happiness'; *Med.* 1228–30.]

221. 'Longinus' admired the verses for the powerful collaboration of words and phrase structure. The death of Dirce dragged by a bull appealed strongly to both ancient and later artists. **If...:** 'if' + Opt. in the sense 'whenever' is frequent in messenger-speeches, e.g. *Hipp.* 1226, 1230, *Hec.* 1165–6, *IT* 325–6.   (**the bull**): the noun is easy to supply in context, but may well have been written by Eur. (Valckenaer).   [Adam's second 'dragged' matches Eur.'s messenger-style at *Bacc.* 1065, *IT* 1406; numerous other supplements have been suggested.] **woman, rock, oak:** the triple asyndeton (cf. e.g. *HF* 224, *Bacc.* 915) vividly suggests the bull's frantic ranging about as it tried to free itself of Dirce (three 4th C. vase-paintings depicting Dirce's punishment tied to the bull can be related to Hyginus' account (*Fab.* 8.9), and the later two quite confidently to Eur. *Antiope*: see Introd., *Illustrations* and Taplin [1998]). *Anth.Pal.* 3.7.5–6 has the bull dragging Dirce along the bottom of a wooded ravine.

222. Some eds. suppose this to be a comment (from the Messenger, or his hearers – the Chorus?) on Justice coming late to Dirce (as to Lycus, F 223.57–8). Wilamowitz (recorded in *TrGF*) suggested Amphion rebutting those who thought him a slave (F 216–18). Another possibility is that Antiope is rejoicing now she is delivered and reunited with the twins: cf. Pacuv. *Ant.* 15.   **Justice...child of Time:** cf. *Androm.* F 151 (in the version of Orion) and n.; time itself reveals men's weakness, *Bell.* F 303.3–5: so justice is slow (but sure), F 223.57–58b and n. **is not evil:** the seeming paradox is well explained by Kannicht: those not overtaken by Justice, which is slow but sure, are thereby shown to be good.

223. A typical Euripidean play-end: a revenge-plot (1–16) is followed by the arrival of the intended victim who is then lured inside (17–49), with success excitingly imminent (50–66), only to be stopped by the intervention of a god (67), who nevertheless gives directions for a happy future (68–103); then the god's provision is accepted by the victim (104ff., but the final lines of the play are missing). Variations of this final sequence occur in other plays both early and late: see Introd., p. 268.
1. these men: Amphion anticipates retaliation for Dirce's death (6).
2. <*If***>:** a conditional structure for **was our father** seems missing, and εἴπερ 'if indeed' approximating to 'since' is likely, cf. *Hcld.* 563 'if indeed I am my father's daughter' (a girl resolving to show the courage of her father Heracles).

3. *<he will save>*: the supplement suits the theme of 'salvation' in play-ends, e.g. *IT* 1490, *Hel.* 1664.

4. Things have...come (lit. 'it has come'): impersonal use of a verb of motion is not quite unique in Eur.: *Tro.* 401 εἰ δ' ἐς τόδ' ἔλθοι 'if it were to come to this' (also e.g. Thuc. 7.75.6, Herodas 3.7–8, where Headlam gives many examples). Usual is e.g. 7 εἰς τόδ' ἔρχεται τύχη 'our fortunes come to this' [whence Blass's συμφορά 'ill fortune' here].

5–16. Stark alternatives followed by a prayer for a god's aid; cf. *IT* 1065ff., *Hel.* 1090ff. (see also on 11–13 below).

5–6. The sense is clear, lit. 'we would not escape the bloodshed (so as not) to pay penalty (for it)', but the syntax a little unclear, perhaps to convey Amphion's sense of crisis.

7. *<If we stay>*: a very probable supplement. Amphion rejects flight to avoid pursuit, preferring boldness (9–10, 14).

9. The antithesis 'succeed or die' also at *Hel.* 1091–2. *<or...indeed>*: ἢ καί emphasizes the preferred alternative without excluding the first: *Hipp.* 667, Willink on *Or.* 1359. **a trophy over our enemies**: this metaphor of personal vengeance at e.g. *And.* 763; also with redundant and emphatic χερί 'with our own hands' *Hel.* 1380f.

10. mother: this personal address points to translating Diggle's supplement as *<to all of us>*, which comes first in the Greek; the asyndeton and the expressive verb ἐξαυδῶ **I speak out** (e.g. *Pho.* 1249) mark solemnity, as if it is a public announcement (i.e. 'for all to hear': common in Tragedy, e.g. *Alc.* 425, *Cret.* F 472e.33, *Hipp.* 956). [Cropp suggests the explicit supplement ἡμῖν, 'to us'.]

11–13. Both a conventional address to the supreme god (11) and a personal appeal to a father to do his duty by his sons (12–13) – but followed by the speaker's sharper concern (14–15) and then the arrival of his enemy (16–17), not unlike Ion's appeal to Apollo at *Ion* 384–9 before Xuthus' entry at 401 or Iphigenia's to Artemis at *IT* 1082–5 before Thoas' entry (after a choral ode) at 1153. Such challenges and admonitions to deity become common in Eur.'s later plays: *HF* 339–47 (Zeus again), *Hel.* 1090ff.: see on *Androm* F 136. **Zeus inhabits the heaven's bright plain**: *Mel.S.* F 487, *Pho.* 84. The heavenly landscape has plains (also *El.* 1349), just as it has cloud-valleys ('folds': see on *Pha.* 174). **union...for pleasure**: typically of promiscuous gods, Zeus at e.g. *Bacc.* 468 and *HF* 1260, Apollo at *Ion* 437, 936. [The textual supplements in 11–12 are certain: for λέγω *<I say>* cf. esp. *Supp.* 1213 and *Hel.* 1662 (gods to men). γήμαντα *<when you have joined>* is a participle taking up the same ruling verb; for this stylistic trope cf. *Hec.* 25–6 etc., KG II. 80.]

14. ally: continuing the image of 9 'trophy...enemies'. As in 15–16, Amphion both asks and assumes Zeus' support: cf. 3.

15–16. on our hunt: the regular imagery of Pentheus' destruction in *Bacc.*, e.g. 1183. *<catch>*: i.e. 'catch and kill', like hunting-prey: *Bacc.* 1108, *Or.* 1346. [An initial verb is missing from 15, for the connective 'and' is otherwise faulty;

Schaal's convincing *<Do what I say>* gives a common idiom of insistence (*Hel.* 1372–4 with Kannicht's note); differently at F 188.1 above (n.).]

17. if one is to guess by his royal sceptre: identity of a new entrant surmised from costume at e.g. *Supp.* 396–7 (with Collard's n.), *Hyps.* F 752h.12–13.

18. Let us keep silent: untypical of a chorus towards a new entrant, but cf. 22; complicity in a plot leads to a chorus's silence, e.g. *Ion* 758, *IT* 1052ff.

20. running: almost certainly Lycus means Antiope's flight from Dirce rather than Dirce's bacchic ecstasy (of which he may however know; cf. P. Oxy. 3317.5–8).

21. For the style of the (double?) question cf. *Hyps.* F 752h.33 'who (are those) coming and from what country?' [The small gap in the middle is annoyingly hard to fill by conjecture, for in P. Petr. even καὶ is uncertain and συν]δρῶντες, 'acting as accomplices') is ruled out by both Diggle and Kannicht; von Arnim's otherwise attractive καὶ πῶς ('who and how acting?') seems to be excluded too. The line-ending (Blass) occurs at *El.* 780.]

23. thinking it outrageous: that Antiope should escape; for the expression cf. *HF* 281f.

28–45. In the lines missing between 27 and 28, someone has come out from the cave to lure Lycus inside unprotected. Most editors think the Herdsman was commissioned by Amphion for this task, not least because the person is addressed by Lycus as 'fellow' in 29, an underling; then Amphion himself does not have to lure Lycus inside (46) as well as bring him out (59). Amphion is however possible (so Webster in particular): (a) he conducts his own deception, like Hecuba at *Hec.* 1012ff, Electra at *El.* 1139ff etc.; (b) the black irony of some of the dialogue is enhanced (28, 32, 37); (c) 46 'if god be willing' will repeat his 15; (d) the actor playing Antiope (who has gone off at 16) has more time than the one playing the Herdsman to change costume for Hermes at 67. For variations between luring-scenes see Vol. 1 p. 146 on *Cresph.* F 456.

29. house: the theatrical impact of the scene requires repeated mention of the Herdsman's dwelling; cf. 19, 35.   **unsafe:** thus at *Hec.* 981 the evil Polymestor dismisses his bodyguard ony because he thinks he is safe; cf. on 40 below.   **fellow:** see on 28–45; ἄνθρωπε used in contemptuous addresses at S. *Aj.* 791, 1154; a colloquialism.

30. Some action etc.: West's τί makes this a question, 'What action must be taken?'   **those men are dead:** apparently part of the deception, a hint to Lycus that the imagined accomplices in Antiope's flight (21?) are no longer a danger. Yet there are others whom Lycus fears, the 'strangers' of 38. The loss of lines between 27 and 28 makes these two identities impossible to separate confidently; but both may be comprised in 'the men' of 26.

31. then they will etc.: Diggle rightly prefers the Fut. Indic. with inferential ἄρα ('then') to P. Petr.'s Subj. 'let us make good dispositions'.   **dispositions:** to secure Antiope's recapture without danger to Lycus himself, cf. 19–24 and ff.

32–7. The loss of all line-beginnings from 33 to 37 means that we cannot know whether these lines continued the strict stichomythic dialogue, whether 32–3 interrupted them with a doublet (Page: Euripidean examples in Diggle, *Studies*

110f.), whether a line is lost between 32 and 33 (von Arnim), or whether all six lines belonged to the lurer (like the short speech at *Or.* 1336–43). Certainly 33 can belong only to the lurer, for he alone has been 'living in (the cave) before' (here, Blaydes's 'was living' may be right: it adds an extra nuance to the deception, implying 'it was safe enough before').

32. *<disposition>*: making a bridge from the preceding stichomythic line, cf. e.g. *Hyps.* F 752.16–17.

34. the strangers: see on 30.

35. spearmen outside the cave: to prevent a surprise attack.

37. [Diggle's set *<things inside>* right is most attractive (cf. *Bacc.* 49), not least because it gives the Direct Object required with the idiom καλῶς τίθημι/τίθεμαι: see his *Euripidea* 264f.]

38–9. *<One or two;>* is also a convincing restoration (Diggle 1996, 115 gives many examples for this pairing), for the numbers both answer 38 *How many* and square with the Plural **they...have.**]

40. Guard the cave's surroundings: Lycus thus leaves himself unguarded. In other deception-scenes a master's guards lay aside their weapons (*El.* 798–9), or he is induced to come unattended (A. *Cho.* 766ff.).

41. [*<seize>*: the verb λάζυμαι is usual in commanding such on-stage arrests, e.g. *Bacc.* 503, *Ion* 1266, *Cret.* F 472e.46.]

43. Lycus' intended personal action against Antiope may indeed have been 'I *<wish to kill her>*' (Bruhn). **she shall soon know:** such expressions are regular for expected triumph over a despised opponent, e.g. A. *Cho.* 305 (Orestes against Aegisthus), *Hcld.* 65, *Supp.* 580.

44. (of?) words: alluding perhaps to Antiope's false hopes from reports that allies would help her after her escape.

46–7. Confident expectation of the victim's fate 'inside' is usual, e.g. at *HF* 726, *Hec.* 1021–2, *Or.* 1342–3 [so Diggle proposes '*<But go inside; and you shall see for yourself,>* if god be willing, *<those you are fated to see>*...']

48–58b. Excited anticipation of the victim's death by the Chorus, in the common sequence of dochmiacs interrupted by his off-stage cries: cf. *HF* 734ff. etc. cited above. Tentative metrical analysis, interdependent with conjectural supplements, by Diggle (1996) and Kannicht in *TrGF*.

48–50. Apparently a comment on the ease and skill with which gods subdue men (e.g. '*<the god easily>* ties down the strength of *<blissful royalty>* with nooses...' Diggle). For **nooses** metaphorical of the gods' action cf. *Bacc.* 545.

53. hands are *<at their work>*: similar everyday expressions in such dark moments at *El.* 797, S. *Aj.* 116, Thuc. 3.83.3 (all with πρός + Acc.) and *Or.* 1297 (ἐν φόνωι).

54. My attendants: cf. 40–2. [Either 'will you not *<come and>* help me?' (Weil, cf. e.g. *Or.* 1302, S. *El.* 1408) or 'Do you not *<hear and>* will you not help me?' (Snell, cf. *Hec.* 1094) supplies apposite wording.]

54a. *<The house>* **is loud with triumph:** cf. *El.* 691 (the anticipated death of Aegisthus), *Bacc.* 592f. (Dionysus' off-stage destruction of Pentheus' palace).

54b. a song of death: *HF* 751 (the other Lycus' off-stage cries).

55. O land of Cadmus: desperate victims often invoke the help of land and countrymen, even tyrants like Lycus at *HF* 754, cf. Helen at *Or.* 1296 (see West). **city of the Asopus:** community rather than finished city, for Amphion and Zethus are yet to build its citadel (87–8).

56a. Do you see: does Lycus come out here, into the Chorus' sight, and not at 59, or even later? Some think the stichomythia between Lycus and Amphion 59–66 is all off-stage – but this makes a very difficult theatrical moment at 67, with all the human characters, however brought on, appearing simultaneously with the god Hermes. The *ekkyklêma* was not used for Lycus' reappearance: see Introd., *Staging*.

56b–7. in his fear of bloodshed. Justice...: sense and phrasing require this punctuation; for the Objective Gen. with φοβερός eds. cite Pl. *Phdr.* 239b περίφοβον ὄντα τοῦ καταφρονηθῆναι 'very fearful of scorn', KG I.371 n. 19. Page attached 'bloodshed' to 'Justice' (to give 'justice for bloodshed'), marring the impact of the goddess's doubled name (cf. e.g. A. *Eum.* 784), which the particle τοι I tell you emphasizes.

57–58b. The delays of Justice are a commonplace after A. *Ag.* 58, *Cho.* 935, e.g. F 222 above, *Hcld.* 941; cf. also *Arch.* F 255 (n.).   [The textual differences between P. Petr. and Stob. cause problems in restoring a text which satisfies both style and metre. Diggle argues convincingly for Justice 'falling on', ἐπιπεσοῦσα (Heeren), rather than 'falling in a man's path', ὑποπεσοῦσα (Stob.), on the basis of the Furies' crushing descent on their victims at A. *Ag.* 1175, *Eum.* 372ff. Justice is 'unseen' but 'seeing' (ἴδηι Meineke; for the idea cf. e.g. *El.* 771, *Arch.* F 255.3: see n.), but still 'seizes' her victim, as at *Hcld.* 941, *El.* 1169 etc.]

59. alone without allies: the Greek adj. ἀσύμμαχος is unique, but for the idea cf. *Or.* 1301, *Oeneus* F 565 etc.

60. Victims suffering vengeance are taunted for indifference to others' suffering *Hec.* 1085–7, S. *El.* 1411f.

61. What...?: ἦ γάρ asks an intensely emotional question, as at *Hec.* 1124, *Or.* 1595, Denniston, *GP* 284.   **Further...and new:** for αὖ semi-redundant with καινόν cf. *Med.* 705, *Or.* 790 (both concerning new disasters).

62. dragged: the Greek has lit. 'by bull-draggings', adj. and noun like *Hel.* 1555 ταυρεῖος πούς 'a bull-foot', i.e. 'a bull pacing'.   **torn apart:** like animals by the bacchants at *Bacc.* 739, 746 (also διαφορέω; cf. P. Oxy. 3317.6 and n.).

64. You can know, if you want: cruelly mock-deferential; for this contemptuous use of ἄν + Opt., normally a polite colloquialism (e.g. *IT* 673), cf. e.g. S. *Ant.* 444 'you can take yourself off, if you want' (Creon to Ismene).

65. The Greek is tortuous, expressing Lycus' agony of ignorance. ἀλλ' ἦ here asks a question whose answer seems implicit in the phrasing and is realised before its end by the asker; Kambitsis cites Barrett on *Hipp.* 858 'Why, did the poor woman write me a letter about her marriage and the children?' (Theseus sees the dead Phaedra's tablet).

66. you will find out, among the dead: i.e. when you meet Dirce in the underworld.

67. There is no indication in the text- how Hermes enters but almost certainly he appeared on top of the stage-back without the aid of the 'crane': see Introd., *Staging*. F. Jouan in V. Pirenne-Delforge and E. Suárez de la Torre (eds.), *Héros et héroines dans les mythes et les cultes grecques* (Liège, 2000: *Kernos* Suppl. 10), 29–39 makes an extended comparison between the divine intervention here (67–end) and that of Athena in *Erec.* F 370.55–end (our Vol. 1 pp. 171–5 and Comm.); despite the apparent similarities of form and motifs, Jouan stresses Eur.'s originality in composing each scene to meet differing needs of mythical plot, traditional and familiar ritual, and relevance to contemporary events. F. Zeitlin in Carpenter and Faraone, *Masks of Dionysus* 180–2 observes that in Hermes' speech 'all the destructive terms...operating (in the theatre) in Thebes are reversed': Dirce's violent death is to be transfigured in her burial in the ever-flowing spring (81–5); the violent tyrant Lycus is to hand over power voluntarily to the twins who will build Thebes its city-walls; these signal that Thebes will benefit from typical Athenian values, for the play's entire setting and resolution are at Dionysus' Eleutherae, just inside Athenian territory (F 179.3 n.).

67–8. Clearly the god's first words are to stop the intended onslaught upon Lycus at once; cf. Athena halting Poseidon's earthquake at *Erec.* F 370.55, where the goddess appears with similar suddenness to Hermes here (cf. also the gods in *IT, Hel.* and *Or.* (Jouan [67 n.] 31). [Very probably 67 contained '*<I bid>...<bloody>* onslaught' (Weil), but the line's start has so far defied supplements fitting both space and letter-traces. In 68 the supplement ἄνα]ξ 'lord' is made attractive by Hermes' repetition of 'Αμφίων ἄναξ in 97.]

69. [Restoration of Hermes' name is certain but the other traces are too uncertain to permit supplement.]

71. First I shall tell etc.: gods are similarly methodical with such explanations at e.g. *Erec.* F 370.65, *And.* 1233. **the *<two of>* you:** for the 2nd Pers. Dual forms σφῶι, σφῷν (also at 108, *Hyps.* F 752d.5) see LSJ σύ II.

72. he does not deny it: slightly redolent of forensic language, *Hel.* 303, *El.* 796, 1057 etc. Athena apologizes for Apollo who will not face blame in person, *Ion* 1556–9.

73–4. Again, reconstruction is almost hopeless. Is Hermes observing with ironic satisfaction that Zeus would be very unlikely to desert a woman who came to his bed 'voluntarily'?

75. since he determines...misery: so Zeus was able to end Antiope's suffering and reunite her with his own sons by her. For the verb ὁρίζω cf. F 218 'marked out'.

77. Antiope *<discovered>* her children, with the verb ἀνηῦρεν (Weil) as at *Ion* 588 of Ion discovering his 'father' Xuthus. [West's ἔσωσε]ν 'saved' must have Zeus as its Subject, a little awkward with 'by Zeus' in the same sentence – for if Antiope is Subject, she has saved her sons only in the sense that she did not kill them at birth, only abandoned them, an event before her suffering began (76).]

78. obey: for this sense of the verb ἀκούω see *Mel.S.* F 481.5.

80–5. A typical Euripidean aetiology, bedding an ancient but current name or ritual practice causatively in myth, cf. e.g. *Erec.* F 370.73 the Hyacinthids, *Ion* 1577 the tribal names of Athens. For a different play upon the etymology of names see on F 181–182 above.

81. mortal substance: possibly euphemistic, describing Dirce's scattered remains, the pieces of her dismembered body (F 221). In the Greek, φύσις is literally the 'growth, nature' of her flesh, i.e. what flesh she had naturally on her body, with σαρκῶν Plur. 'fleshy parts' as at *Bacc.* 1136 (the dismembered Pentheus) and *Hipp.* 1249 (the mutilated Hippolytus); a similar periphrasis, but with an adj., at *Alc.* 714 χρωτὸς εὐειδῆ φύσιν 'the natural beauty of her body', cf. F 185.2.

82. throw: βαλεῖν is a very rare imperatival Infinitive: cf. *Erec.* F 362.25 and n.

85. outflow: the word only here in Eur., like the compound verbs **run through** and **irrigating**, their rarity perhaps another mark of emphatic solemnity. **Thebe:** the Sing. name is an epic archaism, used to impress; in Eur. also *Hipp.* 555, *Pho.* 823 (both lyric); cf. on 100–2 below.

86. once you are purified and may enter: i.e. the city is open to you (only) when you are purified of Dirce's death, otherwise you will pollute it. This is the full implication of ὅσιος 'holy, pure in the sight of the gods, inoffensive'; as at *IT* 1216, *HF* 923 it is a synonym of βέβηλος, of a place 'which may be (safely) trodden in', but the adj. has a wide application, e.g. *Hyps.* F 757.862 'you who are blameless will be acting blamelessly'; cf. Parker, *Miasma* 330.

87. Hismenus: the second river of Thebes, the other being the Asopus (55). The aspirated form of the name is now regarded as correct: Hutchinson on A. *Sept.* 173.

88. gated at seven mouths: the canonical number, interdependent with the seven attacking heroes: A. *Sept.* throughout, E. *Supp.* 401 etc.; see Mastronarde, *Phoenissae* pp. 642–50. **build:** literally 'fit out': the twins are not to found a new city, but reinforce the existing community with a powerful citadel.

89. Zethus as the working farmer of the debate (F 188.4–6) is to become the physical defender of Thebes, once the artistic Amphion's music has magically aided the construction (90–7); see Introd., *Reconstruction*. Amphion's victory in the debate is now given divine approval (Jouan [above, 67 n.] 36). [Ellis's conjecture τ[ο]σοῦτον ἔρυμα '(so great a) bulwark' seems confirmed by the separate readings of P. Petr. by J. U. Powell (1935) and Diggle (1996), and by the presence in line 93 of the cognate adj. ἐρυμνός (see n. there); the word is used of Amphion's work at Thebes in another papyrus text, *Hyps.* F 752f.32; for 'bulwark against enemies' cf. *Med.* 1322. A finite verb is missing, for which there is no place in 89, so that a lacuna of at least one line must be assumed.]

90. That much, I say...Amphion: the text is uncertain, but consistent with formulaic transitions in gods' speeches, e.g. *Supp.* 1213, *El.* 1276 etc.

91. equip himself with lyre in hand: perhaps, literally, 'arm himself', as if Amphion's weaponry will be that of peace, a mild paradox.

92–5. Kambitsis documents fully the mythic commonplace of music's powerful magic over nature's world, comparable with that of Orpheus, *Bacc.* 562–3, *IA* 1211–

13; Amphion also e.g. Hor. *Ars Poetica* 394–6. **solid:** ἐρυμναί, a rare adj., *Hel.* 68 a mighty palace, *El.* 445 a mountain (conjectural). **mother earth:** just 'mother' in the Greek, as e.g. *Alc.* 757 'black mother (earth)'; for the image cf. *Chrys.* F 839.1–7. **light work etc.:** cf. the god Dionysus miraculously making Pentheus' dismemberment 'light work' for Agave's hands, *Bacc.* 1128. [**you will make:** θήσηι, 2ⁿᵈ Pers. Fut. Mid. (for the ending –ει in P. Petr. cf. 66): Diggle insists that making **light work** for the builders will be Amphion's own achievement, not that of the rocks or trees (the emendation θήσεις gives the same sense); P. Petr.'s θησει may nevertheless be 3ʳᵈ Sing. Fut. Act., with δένδρη as Subject.]

96–7. I with him: σύν 'with' is a bare adverb, used of a fellow-god's partnership also at *Hipp.* 1269, *IA* 268. Hermes claims a part in the gift (as also at 111) because he himself was the inventor of the lyre from a tortoise-shell (see on F 190).

98. the two white colts of Zeus: Amphion and Zethus as at *HF* 29, *Pho.* 606. This title is normally that of Zeus's other twin sons the Dioscuri, Castor and Pollux, who after death rode the sky in horse-form and appear at play-end at *Hel.* 1665, *El.* 1233–5: see Burkert, *Greek Religion* 212. Here they are 'a Theban form of these Indo-European divinities' (Hutchinson on A. *Sept.* 528). Hermes intends the twins to enjoy cult after their death as protective and prophetic heroes (Paus. 9.17.4); and indeed there probably was such cult, given their famous tombs at Thebes: A. *Sept.* 527–8, E. *Supp.* 663, *Pho.* 145.

100–2. Apollod. 3.5.6 (T ivb) 'Zethus married Thebe, from whom comes Thebes the city, Amphion Niobe **the daughter of Tantalus.**' Wilson (48) observes that with Hermes' words Eur. evokes for the audience the horrific loss of their children waiting for Amphion and Niobe (both Aeschylus and Sophocles wrote a *Niobe*).

104. unexpected: a commonplace idea in Euripidean endings, like the tag-lines *Alc.* 1160 and elsewhere, cf. *Alex.* F 62, *Androm.* F 131 (n.) and perhaps *Oed.* F 550.

105. follies: Medea recognizes her own follies, *Med.* 882; cf. *Bacc.* 1121, S. *Ant.* 1261. [Another irritating hole in the text: <εἰς φῶς> (Blass) '*<into the light>*' seems not to suit the traces, and <ἔργωι> (Diels) '*<in reality>*' is a free guess. Kannicht thinks he discerns τ (i.e. –τε) rather than σ after ἔδειξα in P. Petr.: this would appear to give 'and I showed...']

106. [Only εσσφ is now certain in P. Petr. (Diggle and Kannicht). If ἐσσφραγίσας (ed. pr.) is the truth, representing ἐνσφρ-, the sense is 'setting your seal upon, certifying (as real) those who seemed not to be Zeus' sons'; but ed. pr. preferred Wecklein's unlikely εἰς φράτερας, '(shown my follies) *to the clansmen*', i.e. to Amphion and Zethus as members of the royal family of Thebes through their mother Antiope, daughter of the former king Nycteus. Whatever the truth, a certain awkward compression in the Greek suggests that Milne's lacuna may be right.]

107–8. The explanatory asyndeton in **time the revealer (etc.)** suggests that the preceding verbs are Indic. (Kambitsis) not Imper. ('Live with us here!', Van Looy), despite a comparable Imper. 'Live!' at e.g. F 187a(ii). 'Time reveals all' is a cliché since Theogn. 967; cf. *Hipp.* 1051, *Hipp.Cal.* F 441. **deceived:** ψευδής of a person as *IA* 852 'I was deceived and suffered undeservedly'. [**happy:** εὐτυχῆ Nauck, because P. Petr.'s ευτυχειν gives a doubtful Acc. + Infin. construction.]

111. your due...accords: for the translation, see Barrett on *Hipp.* 717.   **and I together with Zeus:** see on 96.

112–13. Page's conjecture πίσυνος gives '<*obedient*> **to Hermes**', like e.g. Hom. *Il.* 9.238 'obedient to Zeus', *Supp.* 121, *Or.* 905; for the idea at play-end cf. *IT* 1476, *Ion* 1606, *S. Phil.* 1447.   [**united with** (ξυνοῦσα Weil) is rightly preferred by Diggle to numerous participles conjectured here, for this verb best suits Dirce's fusion with the existing spring which will give them one name (115); and it clarifies the syntax: ξυνοῦσα controls Dative τῆσδε γῆς νασμοῖσι and τέγγηι governs πεδία Θηβαίας χθονός. Wilamowitz's θανοῦσα 'after her death' leaves the awkward pleonasm 'and with this land's streams water the plains of Theban territory'.]

115. by men of later time: in prophecies at play-end also *HF* 1329–30, cf. *Supp.* 1225.

116. I end my feuding: so Hippolytus at *Hipp.* 1442, cf. *Or.* 1678, *Pho.* 81. Attaching τὰ πρὶν πεπραγμένα **what was done before** to λύω **I end** (but as 'what I did before') involves a slight zeugma, with λύω then understood as 'undo, atone for', as e.g. *Or.* 511 (atone for one killing by another); more likely the missing line(s) provided the verb.

195. This cliché of both popular and scientific thought is quite unplaceable in the play (it was frequently anthologized: see App.). Often related to Amphion at F 182a, it may be part of his response to Zethus at F 184, from an argument that nature's cycle provides for man, without his over-exertion (cf. also F 198). Cf. esp. *Chrys.* F 839.8–9 'what grows from the earth goes back to the earth', *Hyps.* F 757.924 (n.), A. *Cho.* 128, Xenophanes 27 B 27 DK and nn. on F 182a and Uncertain Fragment 910 (below).

209. Interpretation insecure. A rebuke by Amphion of Dirce's vindictiveness towards Antiope (Matthiae, Kambitsis) seems most likely (then the fr. must follow F 220: Kannicht); also the Chorus might suitably offer such a moral comment at that moment (von Arnim).   **to teach moderation:** not 'to show moderation': the verb σωφρονίζειν is regularly transitive (Prose; metaphorical at *HF* 869).   **hold back from excess:** out of moral unease, αἰδεῖσθαι as e.g. *Hcld.* 813 cowardice, cf. *Ion* 179, *HF* 556.   **resentment:** leading to unspecified retaliation, i.e. from both man and especially god, like *El.* 902 (if the dead are violated), *Hec.* 288 (killing women).

212–5. Because these four frs. debate issues of marriage and parentage, Wecklein assigned them to the *Antigone* as more appropriate to that play's content (the marriage of Antigone and Haemon); Kambitsis p. 94 and Webster, *Euripides* (1967), 183 incline to this view. While F 214 appears to be attributed to our play in P. Oxy. 3214, a fragmentary anthology upon marriage, it is very difficult to find a context for it: Antiope may be insulting Dirce (Kambitsis).

212. **...if there is sense in her:** probably a conditional clause run over from a preceding main clause, rather than an elliptical idiom. [An added γε (see App.) could be either '...if there is *sense*...' (Kannicht) or '<Yes,> if there is...' (Blaydes). We cannot know whether the speaker is completing a conditional sentence or answering a proposition.] The thought resembles *Oed.* F 548, cf. *545a.1–2, *And.* 207–8; sense despite femininity *Mel.S.* F 483.1 (n). **What's the use of:** τί δεῖ as e.g. *Hyps.* F 757.926. **if she were to lack:** ἔχοι Opt. of remoter possibility in a primary condition, like *Med.* 630 etc.; KG I. 252.

213. If Antiope is answering Amphion's F 210 (Valckenaer), she gives two examples in which people turn in satiety from superior delights to inferior (as when Zeus abandoned his wife Hera for Antiope's bed). Wilamowitz thought Pacuv. *Ant.* 10, the succession of sun by frost, may have been another comparison made here by Antiope to explain her misery. Editors compare Hom. *Il.* 13.363f. 'There is surfeit in everything: both in sleep and in making love, and in sweet music and fine dancing'.
1–2. For example: καὶ γὰρ adding an explanatory illustration: see Fraenkel on A. *Ag.* 1040 (Denniston, *GP* does not exemplify this usage; KG II.338 gets near it). **crazy:** ἐκπλήσσω as usual of an emotion disrupting balance and self-control, e.g. *Med.* 6, 640, *Hel.* 1397 (all of love's passion), cf. Diggle on *Pha.* F 778 (F 1 D). **wife:** λέκτρα 'marriage-bed' personalized, e.g. *And.* 35, 1281, *Androm.* F 137 (n.). **after leaving:** ἐκ + Gen. marking succession or change, e.g. *HF* 96, 1034 etc. [**about (an ill-favoured wife):** ἐπί (Wyttenbach) 'on the grounds of', with λέκτροις also *Med.* 640. Stob. has ἐν, which gives a different meaning, 'out of their minds in an ill-favoured marriage after a superior one', retained by Kannicht in *TrGF*.]

214. If not part of the continuing discussion of marriage (or of a long speech), possibly part of a comment by the Chorus (Graf). **marry at his own level:** for this concern cf. *Alex.* F 59 (n.), *Mel.* F 502.1–2 (n.), Diggle on *Pha.* 158–9; *PV* 890 τὸ κηδεῦσαι καθ' αὑτὸν ἀριστεύει μακρῷ 'to marry at one's own level is by far the best'.

215. The fr. may continue, and possibly end, the discussion in F 212–4; but the wording suggests a final judgement on the twins' noble birth which is now revealed and wins out to save and avenge their mother. Graf thinks of the Messenger (F 221); for such comments from messengers see de Jong, *Narrative in Drama* 74–6, 191. For the problem of defining nobility as a topic in Eur. see Cropp on *Mel.D.* F 495.40–3 (again ending a messenger-speech).
2. from noble stock: lit. 'from (the daughters of) noble men'. Marriage to and procreation from nobility are male objectives: *And.* 973–5, *Or.* 1675–6, *Meleager* F 520.3 etc. [Wecklein's ἀλόχων 'from noble wives' makes this idea explicit but is unnecessary.]
3. [This line follows neither 1–2 convincingly (del. Matthiae) nor *And.* 1279–82 in the mss. tradition (del. Hartung, where it ends 'do badly at the gods' hands'; it is

omitted from Stob.'s quotation). Editors despair of a solution, suspecting invasion
from either place to the other; but lines quite often resemble those in other plays
innocently (see Mastronarde on *Pho.* 143). Kambitsis well suggests that text has
been lost in our fr. between 2 and 3; or perhaps two separate quotations have
become combined, with loss of the lemma to the second and some text: see App. to
P. Oxy. 3317.14–15, and on *Oed.* F *555.]

216, 217, 218: these three frs. are scattered amid Stobaeus' chapter *On masters
and slaves* (cf. *Alex.* F 48–51 and 57 with Comm.), so that Kannicht in *TrGF* wonders
whether they come from a dialogue on slavery between the twins, or of Amphion with
Antiope; the latter seems more likely. Other editors relate F 216 in particular to an
argument between Antiope and Dirce: see note below and Introd., p. 273. Dio Chrys.
Or. 15.9–10 implies that Amphion and Zethus might have been abused as slaves in
the play before they were revealed as Zeus' sons.

216. Wilamowitz suggested that Dirce is abusing Antiope. Kambitsis thinks of
Dirce rebuking the Herdsman for defending Antiope. 'Slaves must not aspire': *Alex.*
F 48.2–3, *Pho.* 392, *Ion* 675 etc.

217. Amphion may be exclaiming at the evident misery of the refugee Antiope; van
Looy gives the fr. to Antiope herself. The **evil** of **slavery** is a commonplace, e.g.
Hec. 332; cf. on F 218. The alternative translation 'how great an evil slaves are'
would suit a different context, possibly Dirce abusing Antiope (cf. on F 216).
[The line lacks two syllables, either at start or mid-way.]

218. Bothe's attribution to the Chorus, as a typical distich after a long speech, is
attractive; cf. F 211 (n.).   **marked out:** of a god's action also *IT* 979, cf.
F 223.75. **an inferior estate:** *Ion* 973 slavery is all weakness; 'inferior',
ἐλάσσων socially evaluative as at *And.* 190, cf. μείων *Supp.* 437, *Bell.* F. 304.5;
'estate', μοῖρα, a stratum of society as at *Supp.* 244, *Bell.* F 285.3.

226. weakness (of character): for νόσος in this sense cf. *Oed.* F 552.4. The lexicographers indicate that the word was used in the play to describe a person's moral
temper: possibly in the debate-scene, therefore.

227. Also most likely from the debate-scene.

910. The exaltation of metaphysical and cosmological speculation (5–7) by an
intellectual averse to doing political or moral harm (3–4, 8–9) brought most scholars
after Wecklein to associate the fr. with Amphion's stance and then 'victory' in the
debate (with 3–4 and 8–9 compare his F 202). These editors mostly locate the fr. in
the first stasimon, immediately following the debate, like the similarly 'philosophical' stasimon following a debate in *Alex.* F 61b–c (see n. there) ; a few place it in the

third or fourth stasimon, after Amphion's triumphant rescue of his mother and vengeance upon Dirce.

The nine verses make a complete anapaestic system, probably preceding a stasimon; comparable in Eur. are *Chrys.* F 839, the unattributed F 897, and *Med.* 1081–1115, all 'philosophizing'; but in *Med.* the long system substitutes for a whole choral ode (W. Kranz, *Stasimon* [Berlin, 1933], 202f.).

1. Blessed the man who (etc.): a formula of praise for those possessing divine insight into the world's truths (Empedocles 31 B 122 DK) or seeking it through initiation into the mysteries (Pindar F 137, Soph. F 837, cf. *Hom.Hymn* 2.480). Eur.'s application of the formula to the pure inquirer and thinker (1–2 **knowledge...inquiry**, cf. 5 **contemplating**) is striking, and is generally taken (by Valckenaer first) to be praise especially of his contemporary Anaxagoras: see on 4–5 and F 195. The loose combination of terms relating variously to 'philosophy' and 'religion' is like that in *Cret.* F 472 (n.). The verses appear to be echoed in Ar. *Frogs* 1482–7, where the 'blessing' of an exact intellect is coupled with political utility – and attributed to Aeschylus, not Eur. **inquiry:** ἱστορία, the Pre-Socratic concept and term, ascribed to Pythagoras for example in Heraclitus 22 B 129 DK; it is famously the opening word of Herodotus' *History*.

4–5. order (of the universe): a use of the word κόσμος attributed first to Pythagoras (14 no. 21 DK, cf. Parmenides 28 A 44 DK). **ageless...immortal:** e.g. Anaxagoras 59 A 30 DK. On both ideas see DK vol. III, 240–2, Register: 'κόσμος'.

6. came into being: συνέστη, also an early philosophical term: Empedocles 31 B 35.6, cf. Anaxagoras 59 A 67 DK. [**the way in which**, Greek πῆι, is doubted; but for a direct interrogative coupled with a following indirect one see e.g. *IT* 767–8, KG II.439; 'in which way' and 'how' are coupled also at *Alc.* 213, *Hipp.* 673.]

Appendix: Pacuvius, *Antiopa*

For this fragmentary play see above, p. 270. The fragments below are as selected, arranged and numbered by Kannicht in TrGF; *corresponding numbers are added from the standard critical edition by O. Ribbeck,* Tragicorum Romanorum Fragmenta *(1897³ = 'R' below), from E. H. Warmington,* Remains of Old Latin *vol. 2 (Loeb, 1936¹ = 'W' below), and from the standard commentary by G. D'Anna,* M. Pacuvii Fragmenta *(1967 = 'D'A' below).*

*1   (PASTOR?)   . . . orto iubare, noctis decurso itinere . . .

2   AMPHION quadrupes tardigrada agrestis humilis aspera,
        brevi capite, cervice anguina, aspectu truci,
        eviscerata inanima cum animali sono.
        ATTICI non intellegimus, nisi si aperte dixeris.
        Amph. testudo.

3   *(Amph.?)*   loca horrida initas . . .

*4   *(Amph.?)* tu cornifrontes pascere armentas soles.

*5   *(ZETHUS?)* odi ego homines ignava opera et philosopha sententia.

6   *(Ant.)*   . . . inluvie corporis
        et coma prolixa impexa conglomerata atque horrida . . .

7   *(Ant.)*   . . . perdita inluvie atque insomnia . . .

8   *(Ant.)* frendere noctes, miseras quas perpessa sum.

---

*1 (*Inc. Fab. fr.* 1 R, *Unassigned fr.* 55 W, *Ant.* 12 D'A, *1 Budé) Varro, *Ling. Lat.* 6.6 and 7.76, both attrib. Pac.   **2** (*Ant.* 4 R, 4–10 W, 1 D'A, 6 Budé) Cic. *De Div.* 2.133, attrib. 'Pacuvius' Amphion' and 'men of Attica'   **3** (*Ant.* 3 R, 3 W, 5 D'A, 5 Budé) Diomedes, *Gramm.Lat.* I. p. 395 Keil, attrib. Pac. *Ant.*   ***4** (*Inc. Fab. fr.* 3 R, *Ant.* 2 W, 4C D'A, *7 Budé) Nonius p. 280 Lindsay, attrib. Pac.   ***5** (*Inc. Fab. fr.* 2 R, *Ant.* 11 W, 3 D'A, *8 Budé) Aul.Gell. *N.A.* 13.8.4, attrib. Pac.   **6** (*Ant.* 15 R, 13–14 W, 8 D'A, 10 Budé) Schol. Persius, *Sat.* 1.77, attrib. 'Antiopa'   **7** (*Ant.* 5 R, 24 W, 16 D'A, 9 Budé) Charisius, *Art.Gramm.* I p. 129.5 Barwick, attrib. Pac. *Ant.*   **8** (*Ant.* 6 R, 23 W, 17 D'A, 11 Budé) Nonius p. 717 Lindsay, attrib. Pac. *Ant.*

Appendix: Pacuvius, *Antiopa*

*1 *(HERDSMAN?)* . . . at the bright star's rising (i.e. Venus), with night's
journey now having run its course . . .
> *Possibly from the Herdsman's prologue.*

2 *AMPHION* . . . four-footed, slow-walking, from the countryside, low
to the ground, rough-surfaced, small-headed, with a snake-
like neck, grim in its look – disembowelled and lifeless
but alive with sound.
MEN OF ATTICA We cannot understand you, unless you speak plainly.
Amph. A shell-back.
> *Amphion's riddling description of the lyre's invention from a
> tortoise-shell (cf. Eur. F 190 and Comm.)*

> *Frs. 3, *4, *5 are all assigned to the twins' debate:*

3 *(Amph.?)* You often go into places bristling with growth . . .
> *To Zethus? (cf. Eur. F 193)*

*4 *(Amph.?) You* are used to grazing horny-browed cattle.
> *To Zethus?*

*5 *(ZETHUS?)* I myself hate men who are lazy with work and think like
philosophers.
> *To Amphion? (cf. Eur. F 183, 188)*

> *Frs. 6–9, 11 and perhaps 10 are all seemingly from Antiope's
> description of her servitude to Dirce (cf. Eur. F 205.1):*

6 *(Ant.)* . . . with my body all filth, my hair lank, unkempt,
matted and stiff . . .

7 *(Ant.)* . . . lost in filth and sleeplessness . . .

8 *(Ant.)* . . . to grind my teeth at the nights of misery I endured.

PACUVIUS

9 *(Ant.)* fruges frendo sola saxi robore

10 sol si perpetuo siet,
flammeo vapore torrens terrae fetus exusserit:
nocti ni interveniat, fructus per pruinam obriguerint.

11 *(Ant.?)* minitabiliterque increpare dictis saevis incipit

12 *(DIRCE?)* . . . cervicum floros dispendite crines

13 Nonne hinc vos propere a stabulis amolimini?

14 sed cum animum attendi ad quaerendum, quid siet . . .

15 *(Ant.)* Salvete, gemini, mea propages sanguinis!

---

9 (*Ant.* 7 R, 25 W, 18 D'A, 12 Budé) Nonius p. 717 Lindsay (attrib. as no. 8)   **10** (*Ant.* 8 R, 26–8 W, 6 D'A, 14 Budé) Varro, *De Re Rust.* 1.2.5, attrib. Pac.; cf. *Ling. Lat.* 6.6 and Festus p. 482 Lindsay, attrib. Pac. *Ant.*   **11** (*Ant.* 9 R, 12 W, 15 D'A, 15 Budé) Nonius p. 203 Lindsay, attrib. Pac. *Ant.*   **12** (*Ant.* 12 R, 16–17 W, 10 D'A, 19 Budé) Servius Auctus on Verg. *Aen.* 12.605, attrib. Pac. *Ant.*   **13** (*Ant.* 10 R, 15 W, 13 D'A, 16 Budé) Nonius p. 102 Lindsay, attrib. Pac. *Ant.* **14** (*Ant.* 11 R, 21 W, 11 D'A, 18 Budé) Nonius p. 356 Lindsay, attrib. Pac. *Ant.*   **15** (*Ant.* 13 R, 22 W, 14 D'A, 20 Budé) Nonius pp. 90 and 326 Lindsay, both attrib. Pac. *Ant.*

9   *(Ant.)* All alone I grind corn with solid stone.

10   . . . if there were to be sunshine perpetually, with its blazing
          flame it would scorch and burn up the earth's produce; if it did
          not interrupt the night, crops would die stiff from frost.

       Text in part conjectural; context and speaker unknown, but cf.
       Comm. on Eur. F 213.

11   *(Ant.?)* and threateningly (s)he begins to assail (me?) loudly with
          savage words.

       Antiope describes her servitude under Lycus and Dirce
       (cf. Eur. F 205, 207, 223.76).

12   *(DIRCE?)* . . . shake the locks on your necks free, let them bloom!

       Probably Dirce to her bacchants cf. Comm. on Eur. F 203 and on
       P. Oxy. 3317.

13   Take yourselves off from here, away from the cattle-stalls,
          quickly!

       Perhaps the Herdsman or Amphion to the bacchants.

14   . . . but when I have applied my mind to seeking what it is . . .

       Context and speaker unknown.

15   *(Ant.)* Greetings, my twins, progeny of my blood!

       Antiope to her twins, perhaps after Dirce's death (cf. Eur.
       F 222 and Comm.)

ARCHELAUS

Texts, testimonia. P. Hamburg 118a (see App. for F 228a); P. Oxy. 419 (now lost: see App. for F 245); *TrGF* F 228, 228a, 229–264; Austin, *NFE* frs. 1–38; Mette Nos. 279–321; A. Harder, *Euripides' Kresphontes and Archelaos* (Leiden, 1985); H. van Looy, ed. Budé VIII.1 (1998), 275–307; Diggle, *TrGFS* 94–5 (F 228, 228a).

Myth. Generally accepted as Euripidean invention, reflected in Hygin. *Fab.* 219 (= T iiia); Preller-Robert II.2.656–71, esp. 669–70; Harder (above), 131–3. Of some relevance for Macedonian kings as descendants of Argive Temenids are Hdt. 5.22, 8.137–9; Thuc. 2.99.3, 5.80.2. For etymological oracles on the foundation of Aegeae, see Delphic Oracles 225–6 Parke-Wormell (= L 50–1 Fontenrose).   Jacoby in *FGH* II B 401–2; A. Momigliano, *A&R* 12 (1931), 203–10; A. Dascalakis, *The Hellenism of the Ancient Macedonians* (Thessalonike, 1965), 97–146; K. Rosen, *Chiron* 8 (1978), 1–27; N. G. L. Hammond and G. T. Griffith, *A History of Macedonia* II (Oxford, 1979), 3–14; E. Borza, *Hesperia* Supp. 19 (1982), 7–13; Harder (above), 133–7; J. M. Hall in I. Malkin, ed., *Ancient Perceptions of Greek Ethnicity* (Harvard, 2001), 159–86.

Illustrations. None extant.

Main discussions. Schmid 626–7; Siegmann (see App. for F 228a); Webster, *Euripides* (1967), 255–7; D. Lowicka, *Meander* 30 (1975), 263–71 (in Polish); A. Harder, *ZPE* 35 (1979), 7–14; Harder (above), and in *Fragmenta Dramatica*, 117–35; L. di Gregorio, *CCC* 8 (1987), 279–318 and *Aevum* 62 (1988), 16–49; G. Xanthakis-Karamanos, *Parnassos* 35 (1993), 510–33; Van Looy (above), 275–91; C. Sourvinou-Inwood, *Tragedy and Athenian Religion* (Lanham, MD, 2003), 41–5.

Reconstruction. The Archelaus of our play is a descendant of Heracles and the founder of Aegeae (modern Vergina), for a long time the capital city of the Macedonians. His story is found in Hyginus (*Fab.* 219):

> Archelaus, son of Temenus, was cast out [of Argos] by his brothers and came as an exile to king Cisseus in Mygdonia [or Thrace: see F 229 n.]. Under attack from his neighbours, Cisseus promised Archelaus his kingdom and his daughter's hand in marriage if Archelaus (because he traced his ancestry to Hercules – for Temenus was the son of Hercules) would protect him from the enemy. Archelaus routed the enemy in a single battle and sought from the king what he had promised. Now Cisseus, swayed by his friends, broke his word and plotted to kill Archelaus treacherously. He ordered that a pit be dug and filled with burning coals. Light branches were then placed over the pit, so that when Archelaus arrived there he would fall in. A servant of the king revealed the plot to Archelaus. Now aware of what was happening, Archelaus said he wished to speak with the king in private. With witnesses thus out of the way, he picked up the king, threw him into the pit, and so killed him. Following an oracle of Apollo, he then went into exile in

330

Macedonia, a goat leading the way. And so he founded a town and called it Aegeae after the goat [stem *aig–* in Greek]. Alexander the Great is said to be descended from this man.

Hyginus probably reflects the plot of Euripides' play fairly closely (though Huys, *APF* 42 [1996], 168–78 and 43 [1997], 11–30 urges caution in the use of Hyginus to reconstruct tragic plots). In any case, as there are virtually no other sources for the myth, reconstruction depends entirely on the fragments themselves and on Hyginus. While many fragments *can* be fitted into the story he tells, there are no direct points of contact. Reconstruction is thus more than usually tentative.

A papyrus published in 1954 (**F 228a**) gives 25 lines of the Prologue-speech spoken by Archelaus. Internal considerations suggest that this passage came a very short distance (perhaps as few as 3 lines) after **F 228**, which preserves the opening lines of the play and was widely quoted in antiquity for its (probably interpolated) explanation of the annual Nile River flood. Of the remaining 36 fragments, 32 derive from the anthologies of Stobaeus and Orion, and their sententious character severely limits their usefulness for reconstruction. Five topics appear to have had some prominence: good birth and reputation (F 231–2, 242), courage and effort (F 233, 236–40, 243–4), wealth and poverty (F 230, 232, 235, 246–9), anger (F 257–9, to which possibly F 1038 should be added: F 257 n.), and justice and piety (F 252, 255–6); in some fragments these topics are combined. **F 245**, in trochaic tetrameters, was found to be partially included in an Oxyrhynchus papyrus (now lost) first published in 1903. Just before it breaks off, the papyrus changes over to lyric; thus we appear to have the end of the trochaic scene and the beginning of a Choral song. For this reason among others (cf. F 245 n. and Harder 230), Webster's proposed assignment of this exchange to Archelaus and Apollo speaking *ex machina* (*Euripides* [1967], 257, revived by Xanthakis-Karamanos 530) is almost surely incorrect. Finally, **F 264** contains what could be the last words of the play, spoken by the Chorus in anapaests.

The fragments of the prologue present a long genealogy, which some have thought better suited to a Macedonian audience than an Athenian one, which had seen countless dramatizations of Argive myth on the tragic stage. Archelaus just reaches the oracle predicting his own birth when the papyrus breaks off, and we hear nothing of the fraternal discord which Hyginus says led to Archelaus' exile. King Cisseus is addressed in **F 229** (which Musgrave assigned to *Arch.* for just this reason), anapaestic lines that would well suit a choral Parodos. The words 'the plain is shining with fire' could refer to the conditions of siege mentioned by Hyginus. The likewise anapaestic **F 230**, assigned to the Chorus by one ms. of Stobaeus, could come from the same context: the speakers describe an unmanageable crisis which has cast them into poverty. The location of these fragments within the Parodos has a bearing on reconstruction of the early scenes of the play. If the address to Cisseus comes at the beginning, he must have arrived already in a second part of the Prologue. If he found Archelaus still there, some duplication of expository material would have been hard to avoid; so perhaps Archelaus went back off after delivering his opening speech (though he apparently has less reason to do so than the Prologue-speakers in *El.* and *IT*). Alternatively, F 229 announces the arrival of Cisseus to begin the first episode. In either case, the enlisting of Archelaus' aid by promises would seem to be too much too soon in the Prologue, so it probably occurred in the first Episode. Some of the fragments recalling Archelaus' glorious forebears could come from a scene in which he talks himself into accepting Cisseus' offer (cf. *Alc.* 837–60). After he departs for battle and the Chorus sings an Ode, a Messenger arrives to tell how he routed the enemy. If we can trust Hyginus, Archelaus next returns in triumph and demands his due; this could take place in the same scene as the Messenger's speech. A choral Ode would then be followed by a contest scene, either with Cisseus and one of the 'friends' mentioned by Hyginus as antagonists, or with Cisseus as arbiter of a debate in which two of his retainers speak, one for and one against the plan to defraud Archelaus. Some, however, put the scene in which Cisseus is persuaded to break his promises before Archelaus' return, so that the king plays the hypocrite when he welcomes the hero back after battle. The crucial revelation of the plot by the king's Servant surely takes place on stage. The private meeting Archelaus next arranges to have with Cisseus, on the other hand, could be either enacted or reported. If enacted, the witnesses whose removal Hyginus mentions may include the Chorus, whom it is hard to imagine condoning a plot to kill their king. At least the part of the encounter in which Archelaus turns to violent action must, of course, take place off stage. It was reported, then, whether by Archelaus or a second Messenger, and the body of the slain king was probably brought on shortly afterwards. Perhaps his partisans threatened revenge, so that an appearance of Apollo on the machine (generally agreed to be a safe inference from Hyginus' 'following an oracle of Apollo'; that is, a direct command has been altered to an oracle in the mythographer's account) was necessary to put matters in order.

There is no fragment certainly spoken by or to a female character and accordingly no assurance that Cisseus' daughter appeared in the play. On the other hand, no surviving Euripidean play except the satyric *Cyclops* is without at least one female character. F 232 perhaps suggests a difference of opinion about the proposed marriage, and F 234 'Children must obey their father's word' has been taken to imply that the daughter at least initially resisted her father's wishes. We do not know whether, in the end, she was united with Archelaus and went with him into exile. Possibly she was ready to escape a father who proved to be of poor character.

Harder 177 has dispensed with the misguided inference from a passage of Agatharchides (in Phot. *Bibl.* 444b29ff.) that the Theban seer Tiresias played a part in *Arch.* Relying on fragments that warn of the consequences of impiety (F 252, 255, 256), di Gregorio 1988, 41–4 in effect revives the idea, although he thinks of an unknown prophet rather than Tiresias. Hyginus' silence is not a decisive argument against this, but nothing much can be said in its favour.

Other proposed ascriptions. On **F 846**, which Schol. Ar. *Frogs* 1206 says some wrongly identified as the beginning of *Arch.*, see F 228 n. On **F 745**, anapaestic lines attributed to *Temenus* by Stob., see F 230 n. On F 1038, see F 257 n. The claim of **F 969**, which Plutarch says Dicaearchus 'thinks Euripides spoke to Archelaus', depends not on Dicaearchus' (scant) reliability but on Cataudella's argument that *Arch.* would be the natural place to look for lines to offer in support of this piece of biographical gossip. **F 1052** looks like nothing so much as an expanded version of F 237, but whether that makes it likely to belong to *Arch.* is an open question. There is little or nothing in favour of proposed ascriptions to *Arch.* of other book fragments (**F 806, 850, 911, 956, 1045, 1053, adesp. F 108** [cf. T. K. Stephanopoulos in *ZPE* 73 [1988], 216], **193**, Diog. Sinop. *TrGF* **88 F 4**). In an Appendix to her edition (281–90), Harder surveys these and also gives good reasons for rejecting the papyrus fragments **F 953** and **adesp. F 638** and **646**.

Myth. Until recently, it was generally thought that Euripides had invented a mythical Archelaus, whose name conveniently means 'leader of the people', to gratify the Macedonian king Archelaus (ruled c. 413–399 B.C.), his host during the period of exile that is supposed to have occupied the last year and a half or so of his life (but see below on *Date*). The anonymous *Life of Euripides* (2) reports that the play, at any rate, was written as a favour to the king, and many scholars see no reason to doubt this account of its genesis. Certainly a foundation legend drawing attention to descent from legendary Argive rulers and Heracles, and cast as a Heracles-like heroic exploit, would suit the alleged purpose of pleasing Archelaus. If one prefers to put no faith in the *Life*, a stimulus to the play's composition can be found in the generally pro-Macedonian attitude prevailing in Athens from the time of the Sicilian disaster (413), when the newly ascended Archelaus' desire to promote Hellenization coincided with a pressing Athenian need for allies (Hammond and Griffith 137–41). As for Archelaus, Harder (1979, 1985) showed that P. Mich. inv. 1319 (first published in 1968) and P. Oxy. 2455 fr. 9 contain parts of hypotheses to Euripides' *Temenus* and/or *Temenidae*. These plays are undatable but likely earlier than *Arch.*, and both of the papyrus fragments mention Archelaus. *Temenus* and *Temenidae* dramatized episodes in the Heraclid return to the

Peloponnese, with a focus on Argos. (For Euripides' use of these stories, see our Introduction to *Cresph.* [vol. 1, 123–4], which is somewhat loosely related to the Messenian branch of the same complex tradition.) If they are earlier than *Arch.*, it seems likely that Euripides would, if possible, have made *Arch.* continuous with them, in some way redounding to the Macedonian king's glory and endowing his shadowy namesake with an even more serviceable history. One possibility is that in *Temenidae* Temenus awarded Archelaus the Argive throne as the promised recognition of his valour, but his brothers resented his success and drove him into exile. This would maximize his claim to legitimacy as Heraclid ruler of Argos and dovetail nicely with Hyginus' explanation of his exile. The events of *Arch.* would then to some extent be a doublet of what had already happened, with Archelaus' destiny to be a ruler deferred again until his arrival in Macedonia in accordance with Apollo's oracle.

Temenus' promise of the kingship to the son who fought best (in the event, Archelaus) is actually reported in P. Mich.; later dissension between Archelaus and his brothers, however, has to be assumed as a variation or extension of the tale told by the mythographers, involving a sister Hyrnetho in favour of whose (non-Heraclid) husband Temenus passes over his own sons' claims (Nic. Dam. *FGH* 90 F 30, Diod. Sic. 7.13, Apollod. 2.8.5, Paus. 2.19.1, 28.3–6, 4.3.3–5; for discussion, see di Gregorio [1987] and especially Harder [1990]). It is not certain, then, that *Temenidae* followed the outline just described, and moreover, Harder found in F 228a reason to believe that Euripides did not mean his Macedonian audience to assume such a degree of continuity between the earlier play and *Arch.* There Temenus is first mentioned (in line 17) as the son of Hyllus 'who resumed residence at Argos as a descendant of Heracles'. Only then (in lines 19–21) does Archelaus tell the story of Temenus' childlessness and oracular consultation. If the narrative sequence implies that Temenus made his triumphant return before he had any children, it is incompatible with P. Mich. and thus, presumably, *Temenidae*. It may be possible, however, to avoid the inference and maintain the continuity (F 228a.19–22 n.).

For the rest, the claim that the plot of *Arch.* is 'freely invented' needs to be seen in the light of certain traditions regarding the establishment of the Macedonian dynasty to which Archelaus belonged, the Argeadae. (For the much-discussed question of ancient Macedonian 'Greekness', see recently Hall.) Herodotus (8.137–8) tells of three Temenid brothers who, in exile from Argos, came first to the Illyrians and then to Lebaea, in upper Macedonia, where an unnamed king employed them but cheated them of their wages. The youngest brother, Perdiccas, succeeded by a ruse in establishing a claim to the land as payment, and in due course founded a kingdom which prospered and expanded. It is generally agreed that the Argeads would at some point have found this charming folktale insufficiently dignified as an account of the origin of their power and would have welcomed something more heroic. Euripides' *Archelaus* fits the bill, and so do stories involving one Caranus, whose name, like that of Archelaus, suggests 'Ruler' in Greek. Caranus is not mentioned by Herodotus when he gives what clearly purports to be a complete list of Argead rulers up to his own time (8.139), nor is there room for him among the 'eight kings before Archelaus' mentioned by Thucydides (2.100.2). He is a later invention, then, but opinions differ as to whether his story arose before Euripides and was known to him, or later. The constant elements of his story are that he comes to Macedonia from Argos and founds the old Macedonian capital Aegeae in accordance with an oracle which links the name Aegeae with αἶγες ('goats'), as the place to which a goat leads him or where he first sees goats grazing. Some versions show distinct similarities with Herodotus' Perdiccas tale: Caranus first comes to a 'region by Macedonia' ('the Illyrians' in Herodotus); he allies himself with the Orestae ('upper Macedonia' in Herodotus); and expands his power gradually from this base. There is even a connection with goats in Herodotus, who says that Perdiccas was in charge of 'the lesser domestic animals' (τὰ λεπτὰ τῶν προβάτων, 8.137.2), that is, sheep and goats. (In proper folktale fashion, Herodotus' Perdiccas is the youngest of three brothers; the others are in charge of horses and cattle, respectively.) In other respects, the connection with Hygin. *Fab.* 219, that is, *Arch.*, is very close: Caranus aids a king in a war with his neighbours; he is promised half the kingdom as his reward; he founds Aegeae in accordance with an etymological oracle. Pausanias even mentions a battle between Caranus and a Cisseus 'who ruled in the neighbouring country' (9.40.8–9). It seems, then, that Euripides either developed a branch of Heraclid saga and graced Archelaus with a foundation legend containing more typically heroic elements than were to be found in the tale Herodotus had told of Perdiccas; or he learned of a recently promulgated tale of Caranus and oracles leading to the foundation of Aegeae and worked it into his play about the similarly named Archelaus. There are analogues in his work for either procedure, and no convincing grounds for a decision between them. On all this, see Momigliano; Hammond and Griffith 3–14; Harder 133–7.

Themes and characters. Archelaus is young, brave, and strong. The need for him to live up to his Heraclean lineage seems to have been an important theme, but Hyginus and the fragments give no hint that his essential good qualities are ever seriously in doubt. The king's promise of his daughter and (part of) his kingdom is a common folktale motif; Homeric epic alludes to several examples (*Il.* 6.191–3, 9.283–9, 14.119–25, *Od.* 4.5–7), and in Euripides Andromeda is promised (by herself or her father or both) as a reward for Perseus' defeat of a sea-monster. Once he turns to treachery, Cisseus resembles other foreign villains in Euripides' plays (Polymestor, Theoclymenus, Thoas, Cepheus). As far as we can tell from the outline of the plot, it is from this point forward a simple revenge action of a sort that perhaps had been but was no longer popular on the Athenian tragic stage (A. P. Burnett, *Revenge in Attic and Later Tragedy* [Berkeley, 1998]). As such, it has some analogues in satyr play (e.g. Eur. *Syleus*, whose hero was Heracles). Some complexity was perhaps furnished by the king's initial resistance to bad advice and the role of his daughter, if she had one. The decisive action of the Servant is in some measure paralleled by that of the Old Man in *IA* 855ff. (a scene in trochaic tetrameters: cf. F 245?) and the *satelles* of Hygin. *Fab.* 2 (reflecting Eur. *Phrixus B*).

Against the background of Hyginus, it is natural to refer gnomic book fragments about good birth and reputation (εὔκλεια) to Archelaus, the descendant of Heracles. Sourvinou-Inwood 43–5 connects this theme with later archaeological evidence for a cult of Eukleia near the theatre at Aegeae, where she would locate the premiere of *Arch.* (see on *Date*). The theme of courage and hard work (μόχθος and especially πόνος, a quasi-technical term for Heraclean labours) must have helped to assimilate Archelaus to the great hero. As an exile, Archelaus is poor; the exploit narrated by Hyginus offers the chance of wealth and position, including acquisition (again Heracles-like) of a bride, though in the end Archelaus' hopes seem to have been deferred. How to integrate the theme of anger into the play is uncertain; perhaps it reflects someone's judgment on Archelaus' severe punishment of the treacherous king. The fragments on justice and piety may be different reflections on the same action.

Staging. A scene before the palace of king Cisseus is the natural place for Archelaus to arrive and speak the prologue and for the Chorus to enter and report on the progress of the war. The list of *dramatis personae* certainly includes Archelaus, Cisseus, one or more 'friends of Cisseus', a Servant of Cisseus, and very probably a Messenger and Apollo *ex machina*. There is no clear indication of the Chorus' identity, but the suggestion that they were aged local (male) citizens is reasonable (F 229 n.). For the question whether Cisseus' daughter appeared, see above on *Reconstruction*. Harder 172–3 suggests that the audience may have been meant to imagine the pit of burning coals as inside the palace; although this perhaps makes too much of the supposed practical need to choose a place Archelaus was sure to pass on his way back from battle, it can claim some support from Schol. E. *Pho.* 1185 (not cited by Harder), an account, probably derived from a fifth-century tragedy, of Ixion's successful plot to lure his father-in-law Eioneus into his house and throw him into a fiery pit he had constructed there. Otherwise, the pit is simply to be imagined as 'off'. Hyginus' reference to the removal of witnesses presents no problem of staging if the private conversation between Archelaus and Cisseus and what followed were reported by a Messenger; if the encounter began on stage, Euripides may have had the Chorus leave, as in *Alc.* and *Hel.* Such a scene must have continued off-stage, as the conventions of Greek tragedy do not allow us to suppose that Archelaus lifted Cisseus and threw him into the pit in view of the audience.

Date. As mentioned above, the anonymous *Life of Euripides* (2) says that after emigrating to the court of the Macedonian king Archelaus the poet wrote *Arch.* as a favour to his host. According to the usual chronology of Euripides' last years, this puts composition of *Arch.* after the production that included *Orestes* in spring 408, and before the poet's death less than two years later. S. Scullion, however, has recently argued that we should disbelieve the story of exile and death in Macedonia; *Arch.* will have been commissioned by the king for performance in Macedonia, but at a date early enough to allow for re-performance in or near Athens preceding parody of the prologue in Ar. *Frogs* (*CQ* 53 [2003], 389–400; note, however, that many doubt that *Frogs* 1206–8 belong to *Arch.* [F 228.1, 6–8 n.]). Archelaus instituted a dramatic festival called 'Olympia' in honour of Zeus and the Muses at Dion (Diod. Sic. 17.16.3–4, Arrian 1.11.1 with Bosworth's note), and this would have made a suitable setting for the premiere, but Sourvinou-Inwood 41–5 uses later archaeological evidence to argue rather for Aigai (Aegeae). It also seems possible that Euripides conceived the play for an Athenian audience without a direct commission (see above on *Myth*). Metrical evidence confirms a date in the last years of the poet's life but cannot aid in a choice between these alternatives (Cropp-Fick [1985], 76).

Some believe that *Temenus*, *Temenidae*, and *Archelaus* formed a 'Macedonian trilogy'. Of Harder's reasons for opposing this (127–9), the strongest is that one would hardly expect the longest by far of all Euripidean genealogies to come in the third play of a connected trilogy. She might have added that it is odd for *Arch.*, who appeared as an adult in *Temenidae*, to relate the prophecy of his own birth and naming apparently as though the audience had never heard of him (F 228a.23–5). Assumption of a trilogy probably sets too high a value on explaining Euripides' two flattering treatments of the mythical Archelaus economically as the result of a single commission by the historical figure of the same name; however, gaps in our knowledge of the plays themselves and performance conditions in Macedonia make it impossible to rule out the idea definitively.

Other dramatizations, influence. No other playwright of antiquity is known to have treated this story, and there is very little to help us gauge the impact of Euripides' play. If *Frogs* 1206–8 really preserve its opening lines, we have evidence that it was known to Aristophanes, at least, but the ancient commentators who made this claim may have been mistaken (F 228 n.). That the play could be seen as a suitable 'star vehicle' is indicated by the perhaps surprising fact that an unknown third-century B.C. actor won victories with it at the Argive Heraia and the Naia at Dodona (*IG* V 2.118.8–12 = T iib); for some reflections on this, see M. Revermann, *ICS* 24/25 (1999/2000), 462–5.

ΑΡΧΕΛΑΟΣ

228 (ΑΡΧΕΛΑΟΣ) Δαναὸς ὁ πεντήκοντα θυγατέρων πατὴρ
Νείλου λιπὼν κάλλιστον †ἐκ γαίας† ὕδωρ,
[ὃς ἐκ μελαμβρότοιο πληροῦται ῥοὰς
Αἰθιοπίδος γῆς, ἡνίκ' ἂν τακῆι χιὼν
†τεθριππεύοντος† ἡλίου κατ' αἰθέρα,]   5
ἐλθὼν ἐς "Αργος ὤικισ' Ἰνάχου πόλιν ·
Πελασγιώτας δ' ὠνομασμένους τὸ πρὶν
Δαναοὺς καλεῖσθαι νόμον ἔθηκ' ἀν' Ἑλλάδα.

228a P. Hamburg. 118a, Col. II

Three lines almost entirely lost, then:

(Ἀρχ.) . . . . οὐκ ἔψαυσε· Λυγκέως . . . . .
   Ἄ[β]ας ἐγένετο· τοῦ δὲ δίπτυχον γένο[ς·   5
   Προῖτος μανε[ι]σῶν θυγατέρων τρισσῶν πατήρ,
   ὅς τ' ἐγκατῆγεν χαλκέωι νυμφεύματ[ι
   Δανάην . . . θεις . . . . . Ἀκρίσιός ποτε.
   Δανάης δὲ Περσεὺς ἐγένετ' ἐκ χρυσορρύτων
   σταγόνων, ὃς ἐλθὼν Γοργόνος καρατόμος   10
   Αἰθίοπ' ἔγημεν Ἀνδρομέδαν τὴν Κηφέως,
   ἣ τριπτύχους ἐγείνατ' ἐκ Περσέως κόρους·
   Ἀλκαῖον ἠδὲ Σθένελον, ὅς γ' Ἄργους πόλιν
   ἔ[σ]χεν Μυκήνας, πατέρα δ' Ἀλκμήνης τρίτον
   Ἠλεκτρύωνα· Ζ[ε]ὺς δ' ἐς Ἀλκμήνης λέχος   15
   πε[σ]ὼν τὸ κλειν[ὸ]ν Ἡρακλέους σπείρει δέμας.
   Ὕλλος δὲ τοῦδ[ε], Τήμενος δ' Ὕλλου πατρός,
   ὃς Ἄργος ὤικησ' Ἡρακλέους γεγὼς ἄπο.

228 (1 A, 1a Budé) 1–6 Tiberius *On Figures* 48, attrib. Eur. 1–5 Anon., *On the Flooding of the Nile* (= *FGH* 647 F 1) 2, attrib. Eur. *Arch.*; Tzetzes on Hom. *Il.* 1.427, attrib. Eur. 1 + 6–8 Strabo 5.2.4, attrib. Eur. *Arch.* 1 Plut. *Mor.* 497a, unattrib.; [Plut.], *Lives of the Ten Orators* 837e, attrib. to the beginning of a Euripidean play; Anon. *Life of Isocrates* 3.148, attrib. Eur.; Iuba in Rufinus, *Commentary on the metres of Terence* 24, unattrib. 2–4 Diod. Sic. 1.38.4, attrib. Eur. 4 Steph. Byz. *Ethn.* s.v. Αἰθίοψ, attrib. Eur. *Arch.* 7–8 Strabo 8.6.9, attrib. Eur.

ARCHELAUS

228   *Beginning of the Prologue-speech:*

(*ARCHELAUS*) Danaus, the father of fifty daughters, left the most beautiful waters of the Nile †from the earth†, [which fills its streams from the Ethiopian land of dark-skinned people when the snow melts and the sun †drives his chariot† through the sky.] He came to the Argolid and founded the city of the Inachus, and he established the custom throughout Greece that those who had been named Pelasgians before should be called Danaans.

228a   *The Prologue-speech continues:*

(*Arch.*) . . . did not touch: from Lynceus . . . Abas was born. His offspring was twofold[5]: *Proetus, the father* of three daughters who were driven mad, and Acrisius, who once *led* Danae *down into* a bronze bridal chamber . . . . Perseus was born of Danae from the golden-flowing drops. Having severed the Gorgon's head, he went[10] to Ethiopia and married Andromeda, daughter of Cepheus. She bore Perseus three sons: Alcaeus, Sthenelus, who *acquired Mycenae*, city of the Argolid, and *third* Electryon, the father of Alcmene. Zeus entered the bed of Alcmene[15] and begat glorious Heracles. His son was Hyllus, and from Hyllus was born Temenus, who resumed residence at Argos as a descendant of Heracles.

2 ἐκ γαίας Anon., some mss. of Diod., Tzetz. ἐκ γαίης other mss. of Diod. εὐκταίης Tib. ἐν γαίας West   3–5 deleted by Diggle   3 ῥοὰς Tib., Anon. ms. F, Diod. ῥοᾶς Tzetz. θέρει Anon. ms. C ῥοαῖς Valckenaer   5 τεθριππεύοντος Tib., Anon. ms. C τεθρίππου ὄντος Anon. ms. F τέθριππ' ἰόντος Tzetz. τέθριππ' ἄγοντος F. W. Schmidt   κατ' αἰθέρα Tib., Anon. ms. F κατὰ χθόνα Anon. ms. C   6 ἐς Ἄργος ᾤκισ' Scaliger εἰς (κατ' Tib.) Ἄργος ᾤκησεν Strab., Tib.   **228a** (2 A, 1b Budé) P. Hamburg. 118a (= P: 3rd–2nd C. B.C.) ed. E. Siegmann, *Griech. Papyr. der Hamburger Staats- und Universitäts-Bibliothek* (1954), 1–14, Plate 1, with German Comm.; with minor changes Austin, *NFE*; Harder, with English Comm.; Diggle; Kannicht. Photograph of P in Siegmann. Assigned to the Prologue of Eur. *Arch.* by Siegmann.   6 τριῶν read by Harder   7 ἐγκατῆγεν or ἐγκαλύπτει Siegmann   10 σταγόνων Siegmann στανωνων P   13 γ' Lloyd-Jones τ' P   14 ἔ[σ]χεν or ε[ἶ]χεν P

339

EURIPIDES

ἀπαιδίαι δὲ χρώμενος πατὴρ ἐμὸς
Τήμενος ἐς ἁγνῆς ἦλθε Δωδώνης πτύχας   20
τέκνων ἔρωτι· τῆς δ' ὁμωνύμου Διὸς
πρόπολ[ο]ς Διώνης εἶπε Τημένωι τάδε·
῏Ω παῖ πεφυκὼς ἐκ γονῶν Ἡρακλέους,
Ζεύς σ[οι] δίδωσι παῖδ', ἐγὼ μαντεύομαι,
ὃν Ἀρχ[έλ]αον χρὴ καλεῖν …α[ ] [ ] [25

229   (ΧΟΡΟΣ)   βασιλεῦ χώρας τῆς πολυβώλου,
                 Κισσεῦ, πεδίον πυρὶ μαρμαίρει.

230   Χο.   οὐ γὰρ ὑπερθεῖν κύματος ἄκραν
             δυνάμεσθ'· ἔτι γὰρ θάλλει πενία
             κακὸν ἔχθιστον, φεύγει δ' ὄλβος.

231   (Ἀρχ.?)   ἡμῶν τί δῆτα τυγχάνεις χρείαν ἔχων;
      (ΚΙΣΣΕΥΣ?)   πατέρων γὰρ ἐσθλῶν ἐλπίδας δίδως γεγώς.

Unplaced Fragments

232   ἐν τοῖς τέκνοις γὰρ ἀρετὴ τῶν εὐγενῶν
      †ἐν ἔλαβε† κρείσσων τ' ἐστὶ πλουσίου γάμου·
      † πένης γὰρ οὐκ ἐκεῖν' ἀπώλεσεν
      τὸ τοῦ πατρὸς γενναῖον.

233   σοὶ δ' εἶπον, ὦ παῖ, τὰς τύχας ἐκ τῶν πόνων
      θηρᾶν· ὁρᾶις γὰρ σὸν πατέρα τιμώμενον.

234   πατρὸς δ' ἀνάγκη παισὶ πείθεσθαι λόγωι.

20 ἁγνῆς or ἁγνὰς P   229 (*3 A, 2 Budé) Dion. Hal., *On Arrangement of Words* 203, attrib. Eur., assigned to *Arch.* by Musgrave   230 (4 A, 3 Budé) Stob. 4.32b.39, attrib. Eur. *Arch.*, assigned to Chorus in ms. S   231 (5 A, 4 Budé) Stob. 4.29c.42, attrib. Eur. *Arch.*; assigned to Archelaus and Cisseus by Welcker   232 (6 A, 5 Budé) Stob. 4.29c.44, attrib. Eur. *Arch*.   2 ἐν ἔλαβε (ἐν omitted by ms. A) Stob. ἔλαμψε (ἐνέλαμψε already Valckenaer) Nauck λέλαμπε L. Dindorf διέλαμψε Cobet ἔβλαστε G. Wolff κρείσσων Stob. mss. SM κρεῖσσον ms. A   3 πένης γὰρ <ὤν τις> Hartung (<ὢν ὅδ'> Cobet, <ἔμπας> West) <γένος> πένης γὰρ (with κρεῖσσον in 2) Nauck <ἀνὴρ> πένης γὰρ or πένης <ἀνὴρ>

340

Since he was childless, my father[20] Temenus
went to the folds of holy Dodona out of desire for
children, and the priestess of Dione, namesake of
Zeus, said this to Temenus: 'Child born of the
offspring of Heracles, Zeus gives *you* a child,
I prophesy, who must be called Archelaus . . .'[25]

229 *(CHORUS)* King of this fertile land, Cisseus, the plain is
shining with fire.

Probably from the Choral parodos.

230   *Cho.* We cannot run over the top of the wave: for poverty,
the most hateful evil, still flourishes, and prosperity
has fled.

Probably from the Choral parodos.

231 *(Arch.?)* Why then do you need me?
(CISSEUS?) Born of noble ancestors, you give me hope.

*Archelaus and Cisseus discuss how Archelaus can help
with the crisis in Thrace?*

Unplaced Fragments

232   The excellence of the well-born †took one thing† in
their children and is better than marriage with a rich
wife. . . . A poor man does not lose this: the nobility
of his father.

233   I advise you, child, to seek your fortunes from hard
work: for you see that your father is honoured.

Addressed to Archelaus?

234   Children must obey their father's word.

γὰρ Harder <ἐσθλὸς> πένης γὰρ Cropp   **233** (7 A, 8 Budé) Stob. 3.29.13, ms. S only,
attrib. Eur. *Arch.*   **234** (8 A, 29 Budé) Stob. 4.25.19, attrib. Eur. *Arch.* by mss. MA, Eur. by
ms. S

235   πλουτεῖς· ὁ πλοῦτος δ' ἀμαθία δειλόν θ' ἅμα.

236   σὺν μυρίοισι τὰ καλὰ γίγνεται πόνοις.

237   νεανίαν γὰρ ἄνδρα χρὴ τολμᾶν ἀεί·
οὐδεὶς γὰρ ὢν ῥάιθυμος εὐκλεὴς ἀνήρ,
ἀλλ' οἱ πόνοι τίκτουσι τὴν εὐανδρίαν.

238   οὐκ ἔστιν ὅστις ἡδέως ζητῶν βιοῦν
εὔκλειαν εἰσεκτήσατ', ἀλλὰ χρὴ πονεῖν.

239   ὁ δ' ἡδὺς αἰὼν ἡ κακή τ' ἀνανδρία
οὔτ' οἶκον οὔτε πόλιν ἀνορθώσειεν ἄν.

240   ἐμὲ δ' ἄρ' οὐ
μοχθεῖν δίκαιον; τίς δ' ἄμοχθος εὐκλεής;
τίς τῶν μεγίστων δειλὸς ὢν ὠρέξατο;

241   ἐγὼ δὲ τὸν σὸν κρᾶτ' ἀναστέψαι θέλω.

242   φέρει δὲ καὶ τοῦτ' οὐχὶ μικρόν, εὐγενὴς
ἀνὴρ στρατηγῶν εὐκλεᾶ τ' ἔχων φάτιν.

243   ὀλίγον ἄλκιμον δόρυ
κρεῖσσον στρατηγῶι μυρίου στρατεύματος.

244   ὀλίγοι γὰρ ἐσθλοὶ κρείσσονες πολλῶν κακῶν.

---

235 (9 A, 31 Budé) Stob. 4.31c.69, attrib. Eur. *Arch*.   236 (10 A, 9 Budé) Stob. 3.29.44, ms. S only, attrib. Eur. *Arch*. = Men. *Monost*. 252   σὺν Stob. ἐν Men.   237 (11 A, 10 Budé) Stob. 4.10.4, attrib. Eur. *Arch*.; Orion, *Floril. Eur*. 22b, attrib. Eur.   2–3 Stob. 3.29.32, attrib. Eur. *Arch*.; *Corp. Par*. 668 Elter (along with F 1043), unattrib.   3 is nearly identical to Stob. 4.10.26.7 = Eur. F 1052.7.   1 ἄνδρα Stob. ὄντα Orion   ἀεὶ Stob. πονεῖν Orion 3 εὐανδρίαν Stob. 3.29.32, Orion, Stob. 4.10.26.7 εὐδοξίαν Stob. 4.10.4   238 ([12] A, 11 Budé) Stob. 3.29.14, attrib. Eur. *Arch*. in mss. MA, Eur. in ms. S   239 (13 A, 12 Budé) Stob. 3.8.13, attrib. Eur. *Arch*. The lines are made to follow F 364.1 and attrib. Eur. *Erec*. in Stob. 3.29.22 and Orion *Floril*. 7.2   1 ἀνανδρία Stob. 3.8.13 ἀτολμία Stob. 3.29.22, Orion 2 ἀνορθώσειεν ἄν Valckenaer ὀρθώσειεν ἄν Stob. 3.8.13 mss. SMA γαῖαν ὀρθώσειεν ἄν Stob. 3.8.13 ms. Brux., Orion βίοτον (or βίωτον) οὐδέν ὠφελεῖ (or ὠφελεῖν) Stob. 3.29.22

235   You are rich: but wealth is both ignorance and a cowardly thing.

Addressed to Cisseus?

236   Fine things come about through much hard work.

237   A young man should constantly be brave. No man who is slack gains good repute; rather, hard work gives birth to manly courage.

238   There is no one who has acquired good repute while seeking to live pleasurably. It takes hard work.

239   The pleasant life and contemptible unmanliness will raise up neither family nor city.

240   Then is it not right for me to toil? Who earns good repute without toil? What shirker has reached for the greatest achievements?

Archelaus offers help to Cisseus?

241   I want to place a wreath upon your head.

Cisseus wreaths Archelaus as general before the battle, or as victor after it?

242   This too brings no small benefit, when a well-born man with a glorious reputation is general.

243   A small but valiant fighting force is worth more to a general than a vast army.

244   A few brave men are worth more than many cowards.

---

240 (14 A, 13 Budé) Stob. 4.10.8, attrib. Eur. *Arch.* in mss. MA, combined with F 702, 244 and attrib. *Arch.* ms. S   2 ἄμοχθος Grotius ἀμόχθητος Stob.   3 considered a separate fr. by Badham   **241** (15 A, 21 Budé) quoted by Schol. Eur. *Pho.* 1149 because of the masc. gender of κρᾶτ᾽, attrib. Eur. *Arch.*   ἀναστέψαι Schol. ms. A ἀναστρέψαι mss. TB   **242** (16 A, 30 Budé) Stob. 4.13.11 and 4.29c.43, attrib. Eur. *Arch.*   φέρει Stob. 4.29c.43 ἔχει Stob. 4.13.11   **243** (17 A, 6 Budé) Stob. 4.13.10, attrib. Eur. *Arch.*   στρατηγῶι Grotius –οῦ Stob.   **244** (18 A, 7 Budé) Stob. 4.10.11, attrib. Eur. *Arch.* in mss. MA; combined with F 240, 702 and attrib. *Arch.* in ms. S; Orion *Floril.* 7.3, attrib. Eur. *Arch.*

EURIPIDES

245 P. Oxy. 419

```
                    ]ν μεν[
      - ◡ -   ]ρονημα[
      - ◡ -   ]κτείνοντ' ἄχ[
      - ◡ -   ]αρως ἔμελλε π[
      - ◡ -   ]ηθεις παρωτε[                        5
      - ◡  Φοῖ]β' ἄναξ, κάθιζε π[
      - ◡ -   ]τ', ὦ παῖ, προβαλλ[
(245 N)     ἓν δέ σοι μόϳνον προφωνῶ· ἰμὴ 'πὶ δουλείαν ποτὲ
            ζῶν ἑκὼνϳ ἔλθῃς παρόν σοιι κατθανεῖν ἐλευθέρως
            ]των ἔσωθε κα[                          10
      - ◡ -   ]ν· εἰ δ' εὐτυχήσουσ['
      - ◡ -   ]εστω τὸ λοιπὸν [

(Χο.?)      ἄ]νδρα χρὴ διατων[
            ]ν ἁμέραν·
            ]εῖ γὰρ αἱ τύχα[ι                       15
            ]ι τόν θρεκ[
```

246   νεανίας τε καὶ πένης σοφός θ' ἅμα·
       ταῦτ' εἰς ἓν ἐλθόντ' ἄξι' ἐνθυμήσεως.

247   τί δ' οὐκ ἂν εἴη χρηστὸς ὄλβιος γεγώς;

248   οὐκ ἔστι Πενίας ἱερὸν αἰσχίστης θεοῦ.
       μισῶ γὰρ ὄντως οἵτινες φρονοῦσι μέν,
       φρονοῦσι δ' †οὐδενός τε† χρημάτων ὕπερ.

249   μὴ πλούσιον θῇς· ἐνδεέστερος γὰρ ὢν
       ταπεινὸς ἔσται· κεῖνο δ' ἰσχύει μέγα·
       πλοῦτος λαβών ⟨τε⟩ τοῦτον εὐγενὴς ἀνήρ.

245 (19 A, 35 Budé) P. Oxy. 419 (= P: 2nd–3rd C. A.D.) ed. B. P. Grenfell and A. S. Hunt,
The Oxyrhynchus Papyri 3 (1903) 65–6, no plate. After being lost in the First World War, re-
edited on the basis of the ed. pr. by Austin, *NFE*; Harder, with English Comm.; van Looy, with
French Transl.; Kannicht.   8–9 = F 245 N (Stob. 3.7.4 mss. MA, attrib. Eur. *Arch.*), as noted
by Blass in ed. pr.   8 προφωνῶ P, Stob. ms. M προφανῶ Stob. ms. A   μὴ 'πὶ δουλείαν
Macarius, Gesner μὴ πιδοῦ λείαν Stob. ms. M μή που δειλίαν Stob. ms. A   9 ἐλευθέρως

245   *Perhaps a dialogue between Cisseus or his Servant and*
Archelaus:

. . . 3 killing . . . 4 . . . he was about to . . . 6 lord
Phoebus, set . . . 7 child, . . . 8 I urge upon you just one
thing: don't ever enter willingly into slavery while you
are alive, when it is open to you to die as befits a free
man. 10 . . . inside . . . 11 . . . but if they are successful . . . 12 in the future . . .

Lyric (Choral song?) begins here or, less likely, before 14:

13 . . . a man must . . . 14 . . . day . . . 15 . . . for
chance . . .

246   He is young and poor and clever all at the same time:
when these things come together, they deserve
consideration.

247   Since he is rich, why wouldn't he be good?

A rejoinder to F 249?

248   There is no shrine of Poverty, the most shameful
goddess. I truly hate those who, while wise, are wise
†of nothing† for the sake of money.

249   Don't make him rich. If he is poor, he will be
submissive. This is what has great strength: wealth,
and a well-born man who has got it.

A 'friend' urging Cisseus to break his promise?

Stob. ἐλευθέρωι Boissonade, Nauck   **246** (20 A, 15 Budé) Stob. 4.11.9, attrib. Eur.
Arch.   **247** (21 A, 16 Budé) Stob. 4.31a.17 mss. MA, attrib. Eur. *Arch.*   **248** (22 A, 17
Budé) Stob. 4.32b.41, attrib. Eur. *Arch.* in mss. MA, combined with F 230 and attrib. *Arch.* in
ms. S   3 οὐδὲν τῶν γε Duentzer οὐδὲν πλήν γε Hermann   **249** (23 A, 18 Budé) Stob.
4.31a.19, attrib. Eur. *Arch.*   <τε> supplied by Gesner

250   τυραννίδ᾽ ἢ θεῶν δευτέρα νομίζεται·
τὸ μὴ θανεῖν γὰρ οὐκ ἔχει, τὰ δ᾽ ἄλλ᾽ ἔχει.

251   κρείσσω γὰρ οὔτε δοῦλον οὔτ᾽ ἐλεύθερον
τρέφειν ἐν οἴκοις ἀσφαλὲς τοῖς σώφροσιν.

252   ἐκ τῶν δικαίων γὰρ νόμοι ταὐξήματα
μεγάλα φέρουσι, πάντα δ᾽ ἀνθρώποις < ‿ – >.
τάδ᾽ ἐστὶ χρήματ᾽, ἤν τις εὐσεβῆι θεόν.

253   ἁπλοῦς ὁ μῦθος· μὴ λέγ᾽ εὖ. τὸ γὰρ λέγειν
εὖ δεινόν ἐστιν, εἰ φέρει τινὰ βλάβην.

254   <—> πόλλ᾽, ὦ τέκνον, σφάλλουσιν ἀνθρώπους θεοί.
     <—> τὸ ῥᾶιστον εἶπας, αἰτιάσασθαι θεούς.

255   δοκεῖς τὰ τῶν θεῶν ξυνετὰ νικήσειν ποτὲ
καὶ τὴν Δίκην που μάκρ᾽ ἀπωικίσθαι βροτῶν;
ἥδ᾽ ἐγγύς ἐστιν, οὐχ ὁρωμένη δ᾽ ὁρᾶι,
ὃν χρὴ κολάζειν τ᾽ οἶδεν· ἀλλ᾽ οὐκ οἶσθα σύ,
†ὁπόταν† ἄφνω μολοῦσα διολέσηι κακούς.   5

256   μακάριος ὅστις νοῦν ἔχων τιμᾶι θεὸν
καὶ κέρδος αὑτῶι τοῦτο ποιεῖται μέγα.

257   πολλοὺς δ᾽ ὁ θυμὸς ὁ μέγας ὤλεσεν βροτῶν
ἥ τ᾽ ἀξυνεσία, δύο κακὼ τοῖς χρωμένοις.

250 (24 A, 19 Budé) Stob. 4.6.5 mss. MA, attrib. Eur. Arch.   1 ἡ θεῶν δευτέρα Gaisford
ἡ θεῶν (ἠθῶν ms. M) β (= 2) Stob. mss. MA   2 τὰ δ᾽ ἄλλ᾽ ascribed to Scaliger, Grotius
τἄλλα δ᾽ Stob.   251 (25 A, 20 Budé) Stob. 4.19.11, attrib. Eur. Arch.   1 κρείσσω
Pflugk κρείσσον Stob.   252 (26 A, 32 Budé) Orion Floril. 3.1, attrib. Eur. Arch.   1 ἐκ
Meineke ἐ* Orion   2 <ἴσα> Walker   253 (27 A, 22 Budé) Stob. 3.34.2 mss. SM, attrib.
Eur. Arch.; Stob. 3.13.9 ms. L, unattrib.; Corp. Par. 683 Elter, attrib. Eur.   2–3 (τὸ
γὰρ...βλάβην) Gnom. Basil. 392 Kindstrand, unattrib.   1 λέγ᾽ εὖ Stob. 3.13.9 (apparently)
λέγε Stob. 3.34.2, Corp. Par.   254 (28 A, 23 Budé) Plut. Mor. 20d, unattrib. (but with Eur.
in margin Plut. ms. p)   1 Ps.-Justin, Monarch. 5.6, attrib. Eur. Arch.   2 Plut. Mor. 1049e,
attrib. Eur.; repeated without attrib. 1049f.   255 (29 A, 24 Budé) Stob. 1.3.47, unattrib.
1–3 Orion Floril. 5.1, attrib. Eur. Arch.   1 τὰ τῶν θεῶν Orion τὰ θεῶν σὺ Stob. ms. F τὰ
θεῶν Stob. ms. P   2 που μάκρ᾽

250   . . . tyranny, which is considered second to the gods. It does not have immortality, but it has everything else.

251   In the opinion of those who are sensible, it is not safe to maintain in one's house anyone, whether slave or free, who is superior.

Same context as F 249?

252   Through just actions, laws bring great increase, and everything . . . . . . for mortals. If one is pious towards god, that is money.

253   The word is simple: don't speak well. Speaking well is dangerous, if it brings some harm.

254   (—) Child, the gods often trip humans up.
(—) That's the easiest excuse, blaming the gods.

Cisseus excusing his actions to Archelaus?

255   Do you think that you will ever prevail over the intelligence of the gods, and that Justice lives somewhere far from mortals? She is near, and though unseen she sees, and she knows who should be punished. Yet you do not know †when† she will suddenly arrive and destroy the wicked.

Archelaus to Cisseus before throwing him into the pit?

256   Happy is he who sensibly honours god and makes this a great profit for himself.

257   Great rage and stupidity – two evils for those affected by them – have destroyed many mortals.

Grotius που μακρὰν Stob., Orion μακράν γ' (μακρὰν already Schneidewin) Nauck ἀπωκίσθαι Stob. ms. P ἀπωκεῖσθαι Stob. ms. F ἀποκεῖσθαι Orion   3 ἥδ' ἐγγύς ἐστιν Battezzato ἡ δ' ἐγγύς ἐστιν Stob. ἥδ' ἔστιν ἐγγύς Orion   5 †ὁπόταν† Wilamowitz ἕως Wecklein   **256** (30 A, 33 Budé) Orion *Floril.* 3.2, attrib. Eur. *Arch.*   **257** (31 A, 34 Budé) Stob. 3.20.11 mss. SM, attrib. Eur. *Arch.*

258   τῶι γὰρ βιαίωι κἀγρίωι τὸ μαλθακὸν
            εἰς ταὐτὸν ἐλθὸν τοῦ λίαν παρείλετο.

259   ὀργῆι δὲ φαύληι πόλλ' ἔνεστ' ἀσχήμονα.

260   ἔπαυσ' ὁδουροὺς λυμεῶνας

261   ἔσωσα δούλην οὖσαν· οἱ γὰρ ἥσσονες
            τοῖς κρείσσοσιν φιλοῦσι δουλεύειν βροτῶν.

262   πάλαι σκοποῦμαι †τὰς τύχας τῶν βροτῶν†
            ὡς εὖ μεταλλάσσουσιν· ὃς γὰρ ἂν σφαλῆι,
            εἰς ὀρθὸν ἔστη, χὠ πρὶν εὐτυχῶν πίτνει.

263   ἔστι ⟨τι⟩ καὶ παρὰ δάκρυσι κείμενον ἡδὺ βροτοῖς, ὅταν
            ἄνδρα φίλον στενάχηι τις ἐν οἴκωι.

264   (Χο.)   τὰ γὰρ οὐκ ὀρθῶς πρασσόμεν' ὀρθῶς
            τοῖς πράσσουσιν κακὸν ἦλθε.

---

258 (32 A, 37 Budé) Stob. 3.20.25 ms. S only, attrib. Eur. *Arch.*   2 ταὐτὸν Gesner αὐτὸν Stob. παρείλετο Trinc. ‒ατο Stob.   **259** (33 A, 25 Budé) Stob. 3.20.12, combined with F 760 and adesp. 523, attrib. Eur. *Arch.* The frs. were separated by Grotius.   **260** (34 A, 14 Budé) Schol. Pind. *Pyth.* 2.57, attrib. Eur. *Arch.*   **261** (35 A, 36 Budé) Stob. 4.19.13, attrib. Eur. *Arch.*, assigned to Chorus in ms. S   **262** (36 A, 26 Budé) Stob. 4.41.31, attrib. Eur. *Arch.*; Orion *Floril.* 8.2, attrib. Eur. *Arch.*   1 ⟨τὰς⟩ inserted before τῶν βροτῶν in a late ms. of Stob. τὰς ἐφημέρων τύχας Hense τὰς βροτησίας τύχας Busche   2 μεταλλάσσουσιν Stob. ms. M (μεταλλάσουσιν ms. S), Orion μεταβάλλουσιν Stob. ms. A   **263** (37 A, 27 Budé) Stob. 4.54.7, attrib. Eur. *Arch.*   1 ⟨τι⟩ Meineke ⟨δὲ⟩ Herwerden, Wilamowitz   2 οἴκωι mss. MA οἴκτωι ms. S   **264** (38 A, 28 Budé) Stob. 1.3.35, attrib. Eur. *Arch.*

258   When gentleness comes together with violence and savagery, it lessens their excessiveness.

259   There is much unseemliness in petty anger.

260   He (*or* I) put a stop to highwaymen, defilers . . .

261   I saved her when she was a slave. Among mortals, the weaker tend to be slaves to the stronger.

262   I have long reflected how well †the fortunes of mortals† change. The man who stumbles is set aright, and the one who was once fortunate falls.

Chorus-leader or Messenger reflecting on Cisseus' fate?

263   There is <*something*> sweet ordained for mortals even amid tears, when one bewails a dear man at home.

264   *(Cho.)* What was not rightly done rightly turned into trouble for those who did it.

Final words of the play?

Commentary on *Archelaus*

228, 228a. These two fragments preserve nearly half of the Prologue-speech spoken (as is clear from 'my father' at 228a.19 in combination with 228a.25) by Archelaus. For speculation as to how the prologue-scene continued, see Introd., *Reconstruction*. Up to 228a.19, Archelaus outlines his ancestry in a series of brief allusions to very well-known myths. Then, just before the papyrus breaks off, the narrative becomes a little more expansive with the story of Temenus' oracular consultation and the prophecy of Archelaus' birth. Although a genealogical opening is typically Euripidean (F 228 n.), this one covers more than twice as many generations (11) as its nearest competitor (*Or.*, with 5). This fits with a desire to celebrate the heroic and Greek heritage of the Macedonian king Archelaus. Before the Hamburg papyrus came to light, F 228 alone elicited from Wilamowitz the marginal comment (in his copy of the tragic fragments) *tam multa narrat Macedonibus* 'he tells the story at such length for the Macedonians.' Despite this possible motive for thoroughness, it cannot be denied that Eur. runs the risk of tedium. The most noteworthy mythical detail here is that he actually *shortens* the usual succession of Heraclids by two generations (228a.17–18 n.); the allusions to the Argive royal house contain no particularly striking language or mythical variants. Perhaps Eur. designed them to be bland, as the scandalous behaviour of some mythical heroes was potentially embarrassing; here the strongest hint of violence is the allusion to Perseus' severing of the monstrous Gorgon's head (228a.10). Admittedly, we may be missing a reference to the Danaids' murder of their husbands between the two frs., but violence elsewhere attributed to the descendants of Danaus is kept to a minimum in the preserved lines, perhaps deliberately.

228. So many Euripidean prologues launch directly into genealogy (*HF*, *Ion*, *IT*, *Mel.S.*, *Phrixus B* F 819, F 846, and probably *Hyps.* F 752, *IA* 49ff.; cf. *Pho.*, *Or.*) that Aristophanes targeted the allegedly tedious mannerism in *Frogs* (1177–1247). It takes only a little good will, however, to find in those about which we are sufficiently informed meaningful selection of detail and thematic anticipation. If we accept that Eur. wrote *Arch.* to please the historical Archelaus, genealogy itself is the most important point here, and Danaus, the founder of Argos and eponym of the Danaans, makes an ideal point of departure. Eur. may also have wanted to convey a sense of stable, non-violent succession.

1, 6–8. On Danaus' **fifty daughters** see F 228a.3–4 n. According to Apollod. 2.1.4, he left Egypt after quarreling with his brother Aegyptus over the kingship. Besides founding Argos, **the city of the (river) Inachus**, he claimed rule of the Argolid (the meaning of Ἄργος here and at 228a.13, where see Harder) by right of descent from Inachus (the mythical king). Eur. does not say whether he was opposed by its former ruler (contrast Paus. 2.19.3–4, Plut. *Pyrrh.* 32) or how he brought the Pelasgians (for whom see West on *Or.* 692, R. Fowler in Csapo and Miller, *Poetry, Theory, Praxis* 2–18) under his sway and gave his name to them. In 6, νόμον ἔθηκ' **established the custom** could also be rendered 'legislated'; it implies legitimacy as well as power, both

350

flattering to the historical Archelaus. **Danaans** is a general term for Greeks in Homer; while retaining this meaning, Eur. (but not Aesch. or Soph.) sometimes also uses it for 'Argives'.   [1 is identified as the opening of a Euripidean prologue by [Plut.], and other quoting authors name the play as *Arch.* This evidence outweighs Schol. Ar. *Frogs* 1206–8 (= Eur. F 846), where it is recorded that some took those lines to be the beginning of our play. The scholion itself refutes the attribution, noting that no such lines existed in Eur. (that is, in the Alexandrian edition of his works). Aristarchus improvised a solution to this problem by saying that Eur. could have changed the opening himself, and some modern scholars agree, but it is more likely that those who attributed the lines to *Arch.* were simply mistaken, and that they in fact belong to one of the Euripidean plays that did not make it to Alexandria (Harder 179–82); cf. our Vol. 1 on *Mel.S.* Prologue (no. 665a–c M), 1.]

2. [The corruption has not yet been cured convincingly. If 3–5 are spurious, ἐκ γαίας **from the earth** could perhaps be defended as a reference to the alternative theory that the Nile had an underground source, though the bare prepositional phrase displeases. West's ἕν γαίας, in which ἕν 'the single' is used idiomatically with 'most beautiful', is simple and elegant but not finally convincing.]

[3–5]. which fills its streams: Eur. alludes to the theory that the flood of the Nile was caused by melting snow at *Hel.* 1–3 (where see Kannicht); so also A. *Supp.* 559, F 300, Soph. F 882. The question was hotly debated in the fifth century: Herodotus discusses it at length and attributes the melting snow theory, which he is at pains to refute, to Anaxagoras, but as Kannicht notes, A. *Supp.* almost surely predates any promulgation of the theory by Anaxagoras. On the whole topic, see recently R. Thomas, *Herodotus in Context* (Cambridge, 2000), 135–6.   [3–5 were suspected by Harder and deleted by Diggle (cf. Van Looy 292 n. 35). Tiberius' judgment that they are περιττοί 'super-fluous' need not even imply doubt as to their authenticity, but they do present several linguistic difficulties (in μελαμβρότοιο, an epic form of the Gen. not found in tragic trimeters; compression and unparalleled syntax in 3–4; uncured corruption in 5), and it is not hard to imagine that a digression on this popular topic was interpolated at an early date. In 5, F. W. Schmidt's τέθριππ' ἄγοντος 'drives his chariot' may well be right.]

228a. 3–5. According to a widely diffused myth, details of which survive in Archil. F 305 *IEG*, [Hes.] F 129, 135, Aeschylus' *Danaid* trilogy, Pind. *Nem.* 10.6–7, [A.] *PV* 865–6 (cf. Apollod. 2.1.5; Gantz 203–7), Hypermestra was the only one of Danaus' fifty daughters who spared her husband on their wedding night. That husband, **Lynceus**, became the ruler of Argos after Danaus and the father of Abas, next in the succession (adesp. F 454, Apollod. 2.2.1, Paus. 2.16.1–2). According to Apollod. 2.1.5 and Schol. Pind. *Nem.* 10.10, Hypermestra spared Lynceus' life because he spared her virginity; **did not touch**, then, can refer to his restraint (*he* did not touch *her*) or hers (*she* did not touch *him*). A Gen. is expected after ἔψαυσεν in either sense, but the Gen. of Lynceus in 4 is probably to be construed with ἐγένετο in 5 (**from Lynceus...Abas was born**).

6–9. **Proetus** and **Acrisius** are attested as the sons of Abas from the Hesiodic *Catalogue of Women* (F 129, 135) on. The former's daughters **were driven mad** because they offended Dionysus ([Hes.] F 131) or Hera (Bacchyl. 11.40–58); the sources are surveyed by Gantz 312. In a memorable passage of Virgil (*Ecl.* 6.48–51), a symptom of their madness is the belief that they are cows. **bronze bridal chamber**: Eur. here condenses two phrases from the well-known description of Danae's confinement and impregnation by Zeus in the form of a golden rain at S. *Ant.* 944–54 (ἐν χαλκοδέτοις αὐλαῖς 'in a bronze-bound room' and ἐν τυμβήρει θαλάμωι 'in a tomb-like chamber'); in addition, νύμφευμα (here only **bridal chamber**, usually 'marriage' or 'new spouse') may recall νυμφεῖον at *Ant.* 891-2, 1205. Likewise, ἐγένετ' ἐκ χρυσορρύτων | σταγόνων **was born from the golden-flowing drops** (for the pleonasm, cf. F 242 n.) looks to *Ant.* 950 γονὰς χρυσορύτους 'golden-flowing seed'. The story appears to have been told briefly in [Hes.] F 135; cf. Pherecydes F 10, Pind. *Pyth.* 12.17–18; Gantz 300. Sophocles wrote *Acrisius* and *Danae*, Euripides *Danae*. Perseus' later adventures were dramatized in Aesch. *Phorcides*, *Polydectes*, and satyric *Dictyulci*; Soph. *Larisaei*; Eur. *Dictys*, *Andromeda*. [In 7, ἐγκατῆγεν **led...down into** fits the traces but gives questionable sense; perhaps Eur. wrote e.g. ἐγκαθεῖργεν 'confined' (considered but rejected by Siegmann on papyrological grounds).]

10–11. The sources for Perseus' Gorgon adventure are surveyed by Gantz 304–7; his rescue of Andromeda occurred in *Andromeda*.

12–14. Alcaeus, Sthenelus...Electryon: the three sons become the fathers of Amphitryon, Eurystheus, and Alcmene respectively; of these cousins, the first and third are Heracles' 'step-father' and mother, the second his great taskmaster. For later multiplication of Perseus' children, see Harder. [In 13, γ' (Lloyd-Jones) is necessary to make the clause refer to Sthenelus, who according to Apollod. 2.4.6 acquired Mycenae by force after the death of Electryon; Harder's objection that γε distorts the sense is countered by Diggle, *Euripidea* 325–6. Retaining τ', Kannicht refers the clause to Electryon and reads εἶχεν 'inhabited' in 14].

15–16. Alcmene is one of the past lovers Zeus lists to Hera in an amusing passage of the *Iliad* (14.312-28), and Heracles is invariably known as the offspring of this union (Gantz 374–8). **glorious Heracles**: lit. 'the glorious body of Heracles'; for this type of epic periphrasis, which Eur. favours more than the other tragedians, see Harder here, Bond on *HF* 1036, and our Vol. 1 on *Cret.* F 472e.6–7.

17–18. There are usually two generations (represented by Cleodaeus and Aristomachus) between Hyllus and Temenus, less often only one. For other instances in which Eur. varies genealogies, see Harder's note. As **from Hyllus** is lit. 'from Hyllus as father', he seems rather to insist on his departure from tradition. On Temenus' return to the Peloponnese, see Introd., *Myth.* **as a descendant of Heracles**: like the ingressive Aor. ὤικησ' **resumed residence**, this phrase contrasts the Heraclids' legitimacy and Sthenelus' usurpation.

19–22. If the narrative sequence (return to Argos, fertility trouble) reflects the chronological sequence Eur. wants his audience to assume, Archelaus cannot have played the part in the Heraclids' return that he apparently played in *Temenid*. (so Harder). This would mean that for no evident reason Eur. denied to the Archelaus of this play mythical history that would flesh out his claim to military pre-eminence and add to his endurance of Heraclean labour ultimately in the service of founding the Macedonian dynasty. Di Gregorio (1987), 288–92 resists Harder's conclusion, but while it is true that the one sequence only 'implies' the other, a narrative shift back in time such as would make *Arch.* compatible with *Temenid.* is in fact hard to parallel. In Euripidean prologues, *Ion* 57 is closest: after description of Ion's present circumstances, Hermes returns to the time when Xuthus received Creusa in marriage; the connective particle is δέ, as here. But 58ff. render the time-change unambiguous, as in other instances at *El.* 14, *HF* 26, *Bacc.* 43.   **Since he was childless**: the same motive for oracular consultation at *Ion* 64–7 (cf. 1227), where it takes place within the play, and *Med.* 667–9 (cf. 714–15), *Pho.* 13–16.   **holy Dodona**: see notes on *Mel.D.* F 660.15–17 M.   **namesake of Zeus**: unlike many, if not most, etymologies found in Greek texts, this one is correct: the name Dione and the oblique cases of Zeus (Διός, etc.) share the element Δι-, from the Indo-European root meaning '(bright) sky'. See further on *Antiope* F 181–182.

23–5. Child born of the offspring of Heracles: the formal address, filling a whole trimeter, recalls *IT* 17–18 and *Pho.* 17, in both of which, as here, direct discourse lends weight and authority to a prophecy reported in a prologue.   **gives**: oracular present, as at *Hipp.* 47, *Ion* 1585, and often.

229. King of this fertile land, Cisseus: this address very probably belongs to the Chorus's entrance song (*parodos*). It is in recitative (or 'marching') anapaests, which regularly accompany the entrance of the Chorus in early tragedy but are perhaps an archaizing feature in the late *Arch.* The news that **the plain is shining with fire** may reflect the situation described in Hygin. *Fab.* 219: 'when [Cisseus] was being attacked by his neighbors'.   **fertile**: πολύβωλος (lit. 'with many clods') is found only here; it is modelled on epic ἐρίβωλος and ἐριβῶλαξ, the latter used of Thrace at Hom. *Il.* 11.222.   **Cisseus**: assignment of this fr. to *Arch.* depends on this name. The *Iliad* mentions a Thracian Cisses as father of Theano, priestess of Athena at Troy and wife of the noble Antenor (11.223, where some mss. give the name in the same form as in Eur.). At *Hec.* 3, Eur. makes Cisseus the father of the Trojan queen Hecuba; *Hec.* is set on the Thracian Chersonese at the entrance to the Hellespont. The exact setting of *Arch.*, however, is uncertain. Hygin. *Fab.* 219 says that Archelaus came as an exile 'to Macedonia' (*in Macedoniam*). Since Apollo's command that he quit the location of the play, where he has committed murder, for exile 'in Macedonia', where he will found Aegeae, comes just a few lines later in the same text, the first *in Macedoniam* cannot be correct. Relying on Cisseus' Thracian connections, Robert emended to *in Thraciam*, but M. Schmidt's *in Mygdoniam* is better: (1) this region at the head of the Thermaic gulf had a Mt. Cissus, which Eur. may on this occasion (with the help of local Macedonian informants?) have associated with King Cisseus; (2) although Mygdonia was part of Macedonia in Eur.'s time, he would have known that it was correct to treat it as a 'neighbouring country' (as Paus. 9.40.8–9 calls the land ruled by the Cisseus who was defeated by the proto-Macedonian Caranus: see Introd., *Myth*) in the mythical past; (3) the corruption is easily explained by the similarity of *Macedonia* and the less common *Mygdonia*. If correct, location of the play in 'Mygdonia' does not mean giving up Thracian associations: Hammond and Griffith (10 n. 3) write that 'Every-

thing east of the Axius was in Thrace at the time to which the oracle [given to
Archelaus in Hygin.] referred'.   **is shining with fire**: apparently similar passages
(e.g. Hom. *Il.* 20.156–7, 22. 134–5; E. *Pho.* 110–11, *Hyps.* F 752f.30–1) and usage of
the verb μαρμαίρει suggest that the 'fire' here is flashing armour. In the other
passages, however, the subject flashes 'with metal (weapons)' or 'like fire', so perhaps
the Chorus speak of literal fire (e.g. enemy watch-fires, in which case the situation
resembles that at the end of Hom. *Il.* 8).

230. The Chorus speaks of poverty, presumably a result of war with their neighbours.
The anapaestic metre and the subject make it very likely that this fr. belongs in the
Parodos with F 229. Wecklein assigned F 745, attributed by Stobaeus to Eur. *Tem.*, to the
same place because it is also anapaestic and sounds the theme of μόχθος 'toil' prominent
in other frs. of *Arch.* (F 236, 240 nn.).
1. wave: sc. 'of trouble', as in fuller expressions of the common metaphor at *Hipp.* 824,
Ion 927. Notably similar and even more condensed is Thgn. 620: ἄκρην γὰρ πενίην
οὐχ ὑπερεδράμομεν 'we did not run over the top of poverty' (cf. A. *Eum.* 561–2).
2. flourishes: Harder documents Greek poets' fondness for the paradox of a bad thing
'flourishing'. Disparagement of poverty is a traditional theme given similar expression
by e.g. Alc. F 364: ἀργάλεον Πενία κάκον ἄσχετον 'Poverty is a wretched, intolerable evil'. Poverty is naturally associated with war, prosperity with peace; cf. the lyric
invocation *Cresph.* F 453, Εἰρήνα βαθύπλουτε 'Peace, with your depths of wealth'.
In the second quarter of the 4th C. B.C., a famous statue by Cephisodotus represented
Peace and Wealth as mother and child. On ὄλβος 'prosperity', see further F 247 n.

231. If the **noble ancestors** of 2 are those of Archelaus (as is probable but not certain),
two speaker assignments may be considered: either Cisseus addresses both lines to
Archelaus (so Siegmann), or Archelaus asks a question (line 1) which Cisseus then
answers (so most editors). On the first view Cisseus, though he is a king and Archelaus
an exile, expresses surprise that Archelaus needs him (see on **me** below), and adds that
Archelaus is evidently noble (and should therefore be able to take care of himself?).
Without context, this cannot be ruled out conclusively, but it is better to take 2 as
Cisseus explaining to a surprised Archelaus that a king may look at a beggar – if he is
a scion of Heracles – and find hope.   **1. me**: the emphatic position at the head of the
sentence in Greek probably indicates surprise and thus counts against assignment to
Cisseus, who as king would not be surprised to be asked for help. The connective γάρ
(not translated) is not an obstacle to assignment of the two lines to different speakers:
it answers interrogative τί 'why?' as at *Hcld.* 711 and possibly *Hel.* 1230.   **2. noble
ancestors**: the nobility of Archelaus' ancestry is conveyed by the long genealogy in
the prologue and is probably referred to in the many gnomic fragments (232, 233, 242,
249) that sound this theme. Although it is assumed he has inherited his forebears' good
qualities (F 232), this must be tested through 'hard work' (F 236 n.).

232. As with 'nobility' (F 231 n.), mentions of poverty in *Arch.* (except F 230, where see
n.) are naturally referred to Archelaus, as the exile is traditionally impoverished

(cf. esp. *Pho.* 395–405). Mention of marriage suggests Cisseus' promise as reported by Hyginus, but the fr. cannot be placed in a particular scene with any confidence. The assertion in 3–4 may either be general (ἀπώλεσεν gnomic aor. **does not lose**) or refer to Archelaus' actual situation ('did not lose'). The relation between wealth and good character gets a lot of attention in Greek literature; for Eur., see the collection of evidence in Nestle (1901), 319–48; Cropp on *El.* 35–8. We should resist attributing any of the views expressed to Eur.; it is not unusual to find differing opinions within the same play, as here: contrast this fr. and F 235, 247 with F 248, 249. The danger of marrying above one's station is mentioned often in Eur. (*Pha.* 158–9, *Mel.* F 502 nn.) and comedy (Arnott on Alexis F 150).   [The beginning of 2 may have had a form of λάμπειν 'to shine' or one of its compounds (see App.); among the many passages cited by Harder, note esp. Pind. *Isthm.* 1.22, E. *And.* 775–6. G. Wolff's ἔβλαστε 'grew, sprouted' is also plausible. For the next word, the variants κρείσσων ('better', feminine like **excellence**) and κρεῖσσον (neuter, 'a better thing') are both possible. The fact that 3–4 are missing from ms. S has led some scholars to move them or print them as a separate fragment. 3 is two syllables short; on the assumption that this is the result of corruption and not an anthologist's choice of what to quote, scholars have filled out the line in various ways (see App.), among which there is not much to choose.]

233. **I advise you, child:** beyond the observation that it is spoken by an older to a younger person, the fr. cannot be placed in a definite context. Since women were not expected to seek their fortune through hard work, the **child** may be presumed to be male, most likely Archelaus. In that case the **father** is Temenus; why he is said here to be **honoured** we cannot say.   **I advise:** 'I advised' is possible, but εἶπον is probably an instance of the 'tragic' Aor. Indic. conveying the nuance that a pronouncement (or command, or oath) is valid once and for all (KG 1.163–5; cf. Mastronarde, *Medea* pp. 87–8).   **fortunes:** τύχαι are more commonly that which happens (in which case the advice to 'seek' them would be somewhat paradoxical), but the meaning here finds parallels at e.g. *El.* 996–7, F 1077.   **hard work:** see F 236 n.

234. Children must obey (etc.): we cannot locate this quite general sentiment (exactly paralleled in *Alope* F 110) in a precise context; it is hazardous to refer it, as many do, to Cisseus' daughter's duty to marry Archelaus if so commanded by her father, and to deduce from ἀνάγκη ('necessity') that she was reluctant to do so (see Introd., *Reconstruction*).

235. You are rich: the association of riches and stupidity is as old as Thgn. 683; see the collection of examples in Diggle's note on *Pha.* 165. For the connection with cowardice, see esp. Bacchyl. 1.160–2, Ar. *Pl.* 202–3, and (Mastronarde on) *Pho.* 597.

236. hard work: the commonest of commonplaces; to the passages cited on *Tel.* F 701, add [Epich.] F 271, S. *El.* 945, F 397, Eur. *Ixion* F 426, *Hipp.Cal.* F 432, *Cret.W.* F 461, *TrGF* adesp. 526, Philemon F 37, *PCG* adesp. F 892. Most of these are preserved along with our fr. by Stobaeus in his chapter *On love of hard work*.   [There is nothing to choose between the variants σὺν 'with' and ἐν 'in', both of which can be used with instrumental sense.]

237. While the passages cited on F 236 make good things in general depend on hard work, these lines specify its result as **good repute** and (a reputation for) **manly courage** (cf. F 238, 240). Similarly Hes. *Works* 289–90, Simon. F 579 *PMG*, Pind. F 227, Aesch. F 315, Eur. *Androm.* F 134, *Licymnius* F 474, No. 1410 M. The mention of slackness as an alternative to hard work suggests a choice such as the one between Ἀρετή 'Excellence' and Κακία 'Worthlessness, Vice' made by Archelaus' ancestor Heracles in Prodicus' *Horae*, paraphrased by Xenophon at *Mem.* 2.1.21–34. **young**: if the reference is to Archelaus, a connotation of youthful vigour is probably present, as when νεανίας is used of Heracles' body at *HF* 1095; cf. *Andromeda* F 134a (n.), *Antiope* F 185.8 (n.). **gives birth to**: the probably faded metaphor occurs in the context of hard work and good reputation also at Aesch. F 315, where κλέος 'glory' is τέκνωμα τοῦ πόνου 'child of hard work', and Eur. *Tem.* F 745 (quoted F 240 n.). [Orion presents two inferior variants in 1–2: (1) whoever substituted ὄντα 'being' for ἄνδρα 'man' probably did not recognize the poeticism νεανίας ἀνήρ 'young man' (twice in Hom. *Od.*; in Eur. at *And.* 604, *El.* 344, *IA* 933, *Antig.* F 162); (2) πονεῖν 'to labour' for ἀεί 'constantly' looks like the work of someone who took τολμᾶν in the sense 'endure' and thought it required a dependent infinitive. In 2, according to Haffner, Orion too has ῥᾴθυμος 'slack', not ἄθυμος 'spiritless', as believed by earlier editors. That ῥᾴθυμος is right is confirmed by occurrences of the noun ῥαιθυμία 'slackness' at *Med.* 217–18, Theodectas *TrGF* 72 F 11, and Philiscus *TrGF* 89 F 1. For εὐανδρίαν **manly courage** rather than εὐδοξίαν 'good reputation' at the end of 3, see Harder and Kannicht, who give references for the 'pregnant' use of the noun ('courage' conveying 'reputation for courage').]

238. Sentiment very like F 237. The Pres. Infin. βιοῦν **to live** is apparently alien to tragedy though common in later Greek; εἰσεκτήσατο **acquired**, though properly formed, is not elsewhere attested, and the preverb εἰσ– seems to lack point. For these reasons, Wilamowitz denied the fr. to Eur., and later editors have been inclined to agree.

239. The pleasant life (etc.): for the commonplace that a life of pleasure renders a man useless to his family and city, see *Antiope* F 187 n. [At the end of 1, ἀνανδρία **unmanliness** suits the themes of *Arch.* better than ἀτολμία 'lack of endurance or initiative', which is not found in poetry. The end of 2 is transmitted in three versions. It is generally accepted that βίοτον οὐδὲν ὠφελεῖ 'provides no benefit to livelihood' is a banalization of a text that contained (ἀν)ορθώσειεν ἄν **will raise up** and an object, whether γαῖαν 'land' or (better) πόλιν **city**.]

240. Then: except when it follows an interrogative word, the inferential particle ἄρα is extremely rare in questions. Harder aptly cites adesp. F 81: 'Your father was pitiable when he lost his children. Is not then Oeneus pitiable (Οἰνεὺς δ᾽ ἄρ᾽ οὐχί, where note the emphatic position of Οἰνεύς, like ἐμέ 'me' in our fragment), who has lost a glorious child?' The implication is that loss of his glorious child is more serious than the addressee's father's loss of his ordinary children; hence Aristotle's use of the passage (*Rhet.* 1397b18) to illustrate the argument 'from more and less' (that is, *a fortiori*). Our fr. could well belong in such a context. Someone, probably Archelaus, argues that some precedent (the behaviour of his ancestor Heracles in a crisis where the justice of his actions was perhaps not so clear?) makes it imperative for him to toil. Timely **toil** (ὁ ἐν καιρῶι μόχθος) which begets much happiness (πολλὴν εὐδαιμονίαν τίκτει: cf. F 237 n.) is enjoined in the anapaestic F 745, which Stobaeus attributes to *Tem.* but Wecklein joined to F 229, 230 and made a part of the Parodos of *Arch.* [1–2 alone could be written as a trochaic tetrameter (in which case regard 3 as a separate fragment, with Badham), but Wilamowitz' argument that they *must* be so written because of the position of οὐ at the end of 1 is not compelling; cf. *Alex.* F 51 n.]

241. Wreath: while most editors have thought of a wreath of victory promised to Archelaus or (more likely) offered to him upon his return from battle, Harder, who does not think Archelaus and Cisseus met in the immediate aftermath of Archelaus' victory (see Introd., *Reconstruction*), shows that Schmid's interpretation of it as the mark of Archelaus' status as general and consequent location of the fr. in an earlier scene are equally plausible.

242. glorious reputation: the Greek εὐκλεᾶ φάτιν, in which the κλέος element of the adjective is nearly synonymous with φάτις 'reputation', is pleonastic in a way typical of Eur. (e.g. *Arch.* F 228a.9–10 χρυσορρύτων σταγόνων 'golden-flowing drops', *Alex.* F 61b.1 περισσόμυθος ὁ λόγος, *Oed.* F 540.2 λεοντόπουν βάσιν, *Med.* 200–1 εὔδειπνοι δαῖτες, *Hipp.* 605 δεξιᾶς εὐωλένου, *HF* 689 εὔπαιδα γόνον; Breitenbach 188–93). [For φέρει 'brings (benefit)', cf. *Hel.* 1064 (with Kannicht's comm.), *Supp.* 596–7. The object of the at first sight unobjectionable variant ἔχει 'has' in a similar sense (documented by Kannicht on *Hel.* 93) is usually an abstract noun or equivalent (Harder).]

243. fighting force: lit. 'spear'; the use of nouns denoting weapons to refer to a fighting force is common in poetry and, with some nouns (but not δόρυ), in prose as well. For 'the few' (ὀλίγοι) contrasted with 'the many' (πολλοί or equivalent) in a social or political sense (common in prose), cf. *Hipp.* 987, possibly *Erec.* F 356; Ar. *Frogs* 783.

244. brave men...cowards: like F 243, from Stobaeus' chapter on *Commendation of Courage*. In isolation the words might refer simply to 'good' and 'bad' men. On **few** and **many**, see F 243 n.

245. 1–12 are in trochaic tetrameters. On Eur.'s use of this metre see on *Oed.* F 545. The tetrameters are followed directly by lyrics, beginning in 13 or (less likely) 14, as in five of the other instances. On Webster's placement of the fr. at the end of the play, see Introd., *Reconstruction*. **1–7.** Here, as in 10–16, the restorations and supplements are rather uncertain and cannot be checked against the papyrus, now lost. **Lord Phoebus** is agreed to be just about the only possible reading in 6, followed by a form of 'set, establish' or 'sit' (e.g. on the Delphic tripod, as at *Ion* 366). The Voc. **child** in 7 is probably addressed to Archelaus; the speaker could be Cisseus or, perhaps more likely, the Servant. The next word πρόβαλλ[is either 'risk' or 'put forward as an excuse'. **8–9**. For the thought, cf. e.g. *And.* 113–14, *Tro.* 637, and Polyxena's whole speech at *Hec.* 342–78.   **11–12**. Speeches *ex machina* often refer to **the future**, but the conditional clause **if they are successful** seems to look towards events within the play and thus, like the fact that lyric follows, favour an earlier placement.   [**9. as befits a free man:** most editors prefer to change the mss. ἐλευθέρως, lit. 'freely', to the adj. ἐλευθέρωι 'free' (agreeing with 'you': Boissonade, Nauck). The change would be irresistible if ἐλευθέρως had to mean 'of your own free will', since the context demands a contrast between free and slave status, not free and constrained choice; however, ἐλευθέρως means 'as befits a free man' in the very similar *Or.* 1169–70.]

246. Interpretation of this fr. is complicated by the fact that ἐνθύμησις, a prose word with verbal and adjectival relatives in tragedy, can mean either 'worry', in which case the lines would suit someone (e.g. one of the 'friends' mentioned by Hyginus) persuading Cisseus to break his promise; or (neutrally) **consideration**, so that they could come, for example, from an earlier scene and explain why Archelaus might be willing to give his aid to Thrace. Harder notes that on the first interpretation, the speaker sees Archelaus' poverty as cause for concern; yet the speaker of F 249, usually placed in the same scene, believes that poverty keeps a man submissive. See further Harder, and Wilamowitz or Bond on *HF* 722.   **clever:** unfortunately, there is no way of knowing how Archelaus (if he is referred to) earned this description, so fraught in so many plays of Eur.

247. rich…good: the aristocratic assumption stands in stark contrast with F 235. **is** could also be 'was born': perhaps the speaker noted that Archelaus, with his impeccable lineage, had only temporarily run into financial difficulty.   **rich:** ὄλβιος, which can mean generally 'happy, blessed', often (almost always in Eur.) refers specifically to material possessions.

248. Poverty: Πενία (on which see also F 230 n.) is often personified (memorably in Ar. *Pl.*, where she appears on stage, and Pl. *Smp.* 203b–4c, where Socrates tells a story of Πόρος 'Resource' and Πενία as parents of Eros), but unsurprisingly, she hardly if ever receives cult. The speaker of this fr. may be using ἱερόν 'shrine' figuratively, as at *Hel.* 1002–3 (where see Kannicht) and *Antig.* F 170 (shrine and altar of Persuasion in human nature), and mean little more than 'I have no fondness or respect for Poverty'. This is not contradicted by the continuation in which Poverty is a goddess, for many abstractions are so designated by fifth-century Greek writers; in Eur., see e.g. *HF* 557, *Pho.* 506, 531–2, 782, even τὸ γιγνώσκειν φίλους 'recognizing dear ones' at *Hel.* 560, where see Kannicht). On the history of actual worship of deified abstractions, see R. Parker, *Athenian Religion: A History* (Oxford, 1996), 227–37; E. Stafford, *Worsh-*

ipping Virtues: Personification and the Divine in Ancient Greece (London, 2000).
I truly hate: it is something of a Euripidean mannerism to introduce a strong moral
opinion with μισῶ 'I hate' (e.g. *Hipp.* 413–4, *Supp.* 1109, *Alex.* F 61, *Erec.*
F 360.30–1); Aristophanes shaped *Frogs* 1427–8 accordingly (unless he is quoting).
Wilamowitz thought ὄντως 'truly' a creation of the sophistic period; while some
Euripidean instances have a speculative flavour, the present usage in connection with
genuine emotion finds a parallel at Ar. *Clouds* 86.   [3 is unintelligible as transmitted.
For Duentzer's conjecture ('who, though wise, pay no attention to money'), cf. *Pala-
medes* F 580.3–5, Eupolis F 386. If 2–3 are separated from 1 (Boissonade, Musgrave),
Hermann's 'who are wise but think of nothing but money' is also possible.]

249. poor: lit. 'needier'; the comparative degree of adjectives is sometimes used to point
a contrast (here rich vs. poor).   **submissive**: for the thought that poverty is humbling,
see Thgn. 173–8, E. *And.* 164–5, *Alcmaeon* F 81, F 957, Pl. *Rep.* 553c, and other
passages collected by Harder. The power of wealth is also a commonplace, e.g.
Alcaeus F 360, Thgn. 717–18; dramatic passages in Mastronarde on *Pho.* 439–40.

250. tyranny: as the Acc. τυραννίδα is not governed by anything in the fragment, we
have an example (somewhat rare in Stob.) of a syntactically incomplete quotation. For
the idea that royalty confers everything but immortality, see *Hec.* 354–6, (Mastronarde
on) *Pho.* 506. Our fr. says that tyranny **is considered** (νομίζεται) second to the gods,
and Harder rightly points out that nothing enables us to decide whether or not the
speaker approves of the common opinion. Euripidean characters disapprove of tyranny
at e.g. *Hipp.* 1013–20, *Ion* 621–8; see further Collard on *Supp.* 429–32, *Bell.* F 286.5 n.
Whether or not the speaker approves, the evocation of its unfettered power suggests
that tyranny is probably not a neutral synonym of βασιλεία 'kingship' here.

251. maintain in one's house: the speaker may evoke popular tales of domesticated
animals turning against their masters, as memorably in the parable of the lion cub at
A. *Ag.* 717–36; further examples in Harder.   **whether slave or free**: a similar point
about slaves alone at *Alex.* F 48, 51, *Syleus* F 689.

252. Textual problems frustrate clear understanding of this fragment, but as transmitted it
seems to reach a climax in the persuasive redefinition of piety as the equivalent of
money. Possibly the speaker opposes someone who praised the wealth of tyrants, who
were traditionally unconstrained by law or religious scruple (see Harder, and cf. *Supp.*
429–55 with Collard's notes, including Addenda on pp. 440–2). For the sing. **god**,
cf. F 256.1, *Alc.* 514, *El.* 1169, and other passages cited by Harder.   [The two missing
syllables of 2 have been supplied variously; additional arguments for Walker's ἴσα 'is
equitable' were adduced by Ferrari and Harder; it is palaeographically simple and
would suit an argument against tyranny and for the rule of law, especially if the latter
was linked to democracy.]

253. word: if we had a context for this fragment, we could probably specify μῦθος as the speaker's advice or command, as at A. *Cho.* 554. The idea that clever rhetoric is dangerous is very common (e.g. *Tro.* 966–8, *Bacc.* 266–71, *Antiope* F 206); Hecuba's protest at *Hec.* 1187–94 is memorable.

254. The context at Plut. *Mor.* 20d (for which see *Hyps.* F 752k.20–1 n.) and the lines themselves make division between two speakers certain, but not who they are or where in the play the exchange occurred. 'God-blaming' goes all the way back to the *Odyssey*, which begins with Zeus complaining about it (1.32–4). Although Eur. was known for allowing his characters to vent their rage against the gods (see the passages collected by Nestle 126–41), note that the second speaker in our fr. objects to it as facile.   **trip...up:** the figurative meanings of σφάλλειν (found in a similar expression in F 972) range from 'mislead' (*Hipp.* 1414) to 'destroy utterly' (*Med.* 198).

255. Do you think (etc.): the addressee is almost certainly Cisseus. Personification of **Justice** is very common from Hes. *Theog.* 902 on; many tragic instances are collected by Denniston on *El.* 771.   **intelligence:** while the expressions ἡ ξύνεσις, ἡ ἀξυνεσία (F 257.2), τὸ ξυνετόν, and here the unusual plural τὰ...ξυνετά can all describe 'an essentially human quality' (Bond on *HF* 655-6, where the Chorus deny that the gods have 'intelligence and wisdom such as men have') or its lack, they are not restricted to contexts savouring of rationalist criticism, and they occur in other pious warnings not to underestimate the intelligence of the gods at *IA* 394-5, 1189-90, and perhaps F 645.56; *Supp.* 504 and *Tro.* 981-2 are similar.   **She is near** could be very effective if Archelaus said it during the private conversation that ended with his throwing Cisseus into the pit. The thought recurs at Hes. *Works* 248-55, *Androm.* F 151; the different conceit at *Mel. S.* F 506 (where see n.) is that Justice must be discovered among and by humans searching for her.   **though unseen:** another traditional idea, e.g. Hes. *Works* 223 (cf. 255), *TrGF* adesp. 493, E. *Antiope* F 223.57-58b (n.).   **she will suddenly arrive and destroy the wicked:** the idea that the gods or Justice punish the wicked (Hom. *Od.* 14.83-4, Hes. *Theog.* 217-22) is given straightforward expression by the pious Ion at *Ion* 440-1; cf. *Hec.* 799-805. For their delay in doing so, see e.g. Hom. *Il.* 4.160-2, Hes. *Works* 217-18, Solon 4.15-16, A. *Ag.* 58, *Cho.* 935, E. *Hcld.* 941, *Antiope* F 223.57, F 835, 979, Theodectas *TrGF* 72 F 8.   [For punctuation of 1–2 as a question, retention of που μάκρ' in 2, and ἥδ' in 3, see L. Battezzato, *MD* 44 (2000), 164-8. Regarding 5, because the parallels for subjunctive + ἄν in ind. quest. are mostly epic, Wecklein's ἕως 'until' (followed by subj. without ἄν in Soph. but not elsewhere in Eur.) is attractive.]

256. Happy is he: a great many lines beginning this way made their way into the anthologies of Stobaeus and Orion and the collection of 'one-liners' (Μονόστιχοι) attributed to Menander. For sing. **god,** see F 252.3 n.   **makes...for himself:** ποιεῖται can also mean 'considers'.

257. The first of three frs. of *Arch.* appearing in Stobaeus' chapter *On anger* (or possibly four: F 1038 follows F 258 in ms. S alone, where the lemma τοῦ αὐτοῦ might mean 'from the same play', though it more commonly means 'from the same poet'). The translation **great rage** is suggested by the anthologist's context; in itself, ὁ θυμὸς ὁ μέγας could have more neutral or even positive meanings such as great 'passion' or 'spirit'. The destructiveness of θυμός is a theme as old as the *Iliad*; in Eur. one thinks especially of *Med.* 1079–80. ἀξυνεσία can refer to lack of moral feeling as well as intelligence; see Harder's note and cf. (Mastronarde on) *Pho.* 1726–7, the only other occurrence of the word in poetry.

258. gentleness...violence...savagery: the elements described here (lit. 'the soft', 'the violent', and 'the savage', a favourite way of expressing abstractions) **comes together** either in the sense that they are blended in one person's character or in the sense that the union of two people produce an influence of one upon the other. [For παραιρεῖν 'take away from, lessen' + Gen., cf. *Hcld.* 908, possibly *Hipp.* 1103, middle at *IT* 25. A direct object could be supplied by writing τι, με, or μιν after παρεῖλέ: 'takes something' (cf. Hdt. 2.109.2), or 'me', or 'him', 'away from excessiveness'.]

259. There is much unseemliness (etc.): the speaker either (1) belittles the addressee's anger as petty and ineffective (common meanings of φαῦλος) and warns that it will result in degrading failure and retribution, or (2) delivers a more general admonition against anger, which is simply viewed as bad (a less common sense of φαῦλος, but cf. *IT* 390, [Mastronarde on] *Pho.* 94–5).

260. put a stop: the subject ('I' if ἔπαυσ' is for ἔπαυσα, 'he' if for ἔπαυσε) performed a feat of the sort commonly ascribed to Theseus (Apollod. 3.16.1, Paus. 2.1.4; cf. *Hipp.* 976–80, Soph. F 730c.16–21). The subject could even *be* Theseus, though a mythical Archelaus assimilated to Theseus is more likely; the passage perhaps alludes to some stage of his journey towards his fated new home in Macedonia. Some suspect a reference to the historical Archelaus, but this receives no support from the description of his fortifications and other military preparations at Thuc. 2.100.2, and it would mean that when writing for a Macedonian audience (if that is what he did with *Arch.*), Eur. abandoned the usual tragic practice of avoiding direct historical allusions. [A Gen. is expected after **defilers**; comparing Soph. F 730c19 σῦν ἐμπόρων δηλή-μονα ('the sow, destroyer of travelers'), Radt suggests ἐμπόρων 'of travellers'.]

261. I saved her: ms. S of Stobaeus assigns this fr. to the Chorus, but it is hard to contrive a context in which they (or their leader) saved anyone in *Arch.* If the assignment is mistaken, the speaker is probably Archelaus. If he refers to the rescue of Cisseus' land, 'her' in our fr. picks up a fem. noun like χώρα (cf. F 229) or πόλις, previously 'enslaved' because under siege. It may also refer to Cisseus' daughter, but if she was called a slave because her father oppressed her, the explanation in the rest of the fr. (introduced in the Greek by γὰρ 'for') seems unnecessary. The thought that the weak must be slaves to the strong is commonplace (e.g. *Supp.* 492–3, Philemon F 31), but deliberately blunt or amoral expressions of it such as Thuc. 5.89 (in the 'Melian Dialogue') and Pl. *Grg.* 483d (Callicles' declaration of the rights of the naturally superior) were still no doubt shocking.

262. I have long reflected: probably the Chorus-leader or a Messenger (on the fate of Cisseus?), as at e.g. *Hcld.* 863–6 (Messenger), *Supp.* 269–70 (Chorus-leader), but these are not the only possibilities. The instability of human fortunes is a common theme, copiously illustrated by Harder and by Collard on *Supp.* 269b–70. By **how well the fortunes...change** the speaker means 'what a good thing it is that they change' (so Harder, comparing *IT* 532–3). The lines resemble but are spoken more confidently than *Hel.* 711–3 (where see Kannicht). On σφάλλεσθαι 'stumble', cf. F 254 n. When we hear that **the one who was once fortunate falls**, we cannot help but think of the pit of burning coals mentioned by Hygin. *Fab.* 219 (Introd., *Reconstruction* and *Staging*); if this is on target, the irony is a bit obvious for modern taste but not hard to parallel in Greek tragedy.   [None of the conjectures supplying the syllable missing from 1 (see App.) is clearly superior.]

263. Ten metrically continuous dactyls (– ◡ ◡), uncontracted except that the last probably ended the period with catalexis (– –), the cadence familiar from Homeric poetry. Most editors give them to the Chorus to sing, but a few think of Cisseus' daughter. Harder stresses that the thought is not the commonplace 'there is comfort in tears' (*Androm.* F′119–120 n.) but that grief is tinged with sweetness when (ὅταν) it is grief for **a dear man**, or the mourning takes place **at home**.   **ordained:** κεῖσθαι is used as at *IT* 166 (if sound), F 962.1, S. *Phil.* 502–3 (Kannicht).   [Comparing *IT* 144–7 and 656, Kannicht prefers the variant ἐν οἴκτωι 'piteous lamentation' at the end of 2.]

264. What was not rightly done (etc.): these anapaestic verses (with closing cadence) could well be the play's last words, the Chorus' reflection on the appropriateness of Archelaus' punishment of Cisseus.

ADDENDA AND CORRIGENDA TO VOLUME I

ADDENDA

(We regret that we can mention only summarily much excellent and often detailed work which has appeared since 1995.)

General Introduction

p. 1. In I.(i) we ought not to have omitted the still useful appreciation of 'fragmentary' transmission by A. C. Pearson, *The Fragments of Sophocles* (Cambridge, 1917), I.xiii–xciv. C. Collard in F. McHardy (ed.), *Lost Dramas of Classical Athens. Greek Tragic Fragments* (forthcoming) discusses the uneven contribution of papyri to reconstruction, chiefly for *Cretan Women* and *Oedipus.* For Euripidean citations in Stobaeus see R. M. Piccione, *RFIC* 122 (1994), 175–218.

p. 2, n. 1. The two kinds of hypothesis continue to receive attention: see especially M. Huys, *APF* 42 (1996), 168–78 and 43 (1997), 11–30 dissociating Hyginus' *Fabulae* from the 'narrative' kind, and van Rossum-Steenbeek 1–36 endorsing Huys; also W. Luppe, 'Zur 'Lebensdauer' der Euripides-Hypotheseis', *Philologus* 140 (1996), 213–24.

p. 4, n. 1. The full reference is C. Collard, *AC* 64 (1995), 243–51.

p. 5, line 12. On the Budé edition of F. Jouan and H. Van Looy see this vol., p. ix.

p. 5, end of section (i). On *TrGF* V *Euripides* see this vol., p. ix. Kannicht discusses the historical and practical problems of identifying and collecting fragments, and in particular his own task as editor, in ΛΗΝΑΙΚΑ. *Festschrift für C. W. Müller* (Stuttgart, 1996), 21–31, and in G. W. Most (ed.), *Collecting Fragments: Fragmente Sammeln* (Göttingen, 1997), 67–77.

Telephus

p. 17, Texts etc. Add Diggle, *TrGFS* 132–4 (F 696, 727a); van Rossum-Steenbeek 218 (Hypoth.); C. Preiser, *Euripides: Telephos* (Hildesheim, 2000: a very full edition with commentary, to be consulted on all points; for notable features see review by M. Cropp, *Gnomon* 75 [2003], 253–6); F. Jouan, ed. Budé VIII.3 (2002), 91–132.

p. 19, line 11. H. P. Foley's *JHS* article was reprinted in briefer form in R. Scodel (ed.), *Theater and Society in Ancient Greece* (Ann Arbor, 1993), 119–38. On the paratragedy in Ar. *Ach.* see also F. Jouan, *CGITA* 5 (1989), 17–28. The problems of disentangling history from comedy and paratragedy in Ar.'s scene are discussed by C. Pelling, *Literary Texts and the Greek Historian* (London, 2000), 141–63.

pp. 19–20, and Comm. on F 699, F 727. Against the relevance of the sacrifice of Iphigenia in *Tel.* see C. Preiser, *WJA* 24 (2000), 29–35 (as well as in her commentary).

p. 22, Myth. E. Pellizer, *EL* (1998), 43–55 discusses historicizing uses of the Telephus myth. M. Davies, *ZPE* 133 (2000), 7–10 discusses possible folk-tale origins.

pp. 23–4. On the characterization of Achilles in *Tel.* see P. Michelakis, *Achilles in Greek Tragedy* (Oxford, 2002), 182–4.

p. 26, App., Hypothesis. Add van Rossum-Steenbeek, 218.

p. 27, App., F 696. Add Diggle, *TrGFS* 132–3.

p. 43. The text-problem in F 696.14 is discussed at length by Preiser in her commentary and by M. Magnani, *AUFL* n.s. 2 (2001), 35–46.

p. 51. On F 724 and the method of Telephus' healing see C. Preiser, *RhM* 144 (2001), 277–86 (as well as in her commentary).

Cretans

p. 53, Texts etc. Add Diggle, *TrGFS* 115–9 (F 472, 472b, 472e); H. Van Looy, ed. Budé VIII.2 (2000), 303–32; A.-T. Cozzoli, *Euripide: Cretesi* (Pisa and Rome, 2001: full edition with commentary, rev. V. Di Benedetto, *RFIC* 129 [2003], 210–30).

p. 53, Myth. For Malalas see now pp. 33.52ff., 62.58ff., 280.73ff. Thurn, and §§ 2.8, 4.21, 14.12 Jeffreys.

p. 55. Van Looy 316–7 is guarded about a full role for Daedalus and Icarus (with a monologue); he hesitantly includes F 988 *if* there was a debate between Minos and Daedalus, and F 912 as uncertain (p. 315; cf. our *Other proposed ascriptions*).

p. 58. Van Looy accepts Collard's placing of F 472f.

p. 58. F 472.4–15 are extensively reedited, on the basis of P. Oxy. and new editions of Porphyry and Erotian, by Cozzoli and Di Benedetto, who return largely to Porphyry's text and add valuable interpretative matter.

p. 62, F 472bc.31. Diggle conjectures φορεῖ at line-end, accepted by Van Looy.

p. 62, F 472bc.38. Diggle and Van Looy print Luppe's more recent conjecture μ]αστ[ῶι] δὲ [μ]ητρὸς ἢ βοὸς θ[ηλάζεται 'And <is it suckled> by a mother's breast or a cow's (udder)?' Diggle and Luppe read θ[at the end of the line, Di Benedetto reverts to ed. pr.'s σ[, conjecturing σ[φ' οὖθαρ τρέφει 'And *does* a mother's breast or a cow's <*udder nourish it*>?'; but οὖθαρ is not Euripidean, and if the sigma is correct, a possible alternative would be σ[παργῶν τρέφει 'Does a mother's <*swelling*> breast or a cow's (swelling udder) <*nourish it*>?'; for σπαργῶν μαστός of an animal cf. *Bacc.*70.

p. 62, F 472e.1–3. The attribution to Minos and Chorus was first proposed by Koerte, not Collard; it is accepted by Van Looy 313, 329 app.; 1–3 given to Chorus by Diggle (entertained by Cozzoli 104).

p. 63, line 2 of App. for F 472e. Cozzoli 41–3 reports that P. Berlin 13217 has been rediscovered in Warsaw; public access is not yet permitted. She republishes the original photographs of about 1905 (see her p. 43), not clear for confident reading.

p. 64, F 472e.23. ὅνπερ ηὔ]ξατο now Diggle, '<*the exact*> bull <*that*> he vowed.'

p. 64, F 472e.27. For the anaphoric and emphatic pronoun 'you!' Diggle cites KG I.656–7 (some Sophoclean examples, mainly lyric).

p. 66, F 472e.51. Diggle cites Collard's subsequent conjecture θερ]μός 'hot-tempered'.

p. 66, lines 6–7 of Comm. on F 472f. R. Scodel, *Phoenix* 51 (1997), 226 cites S. *Phil.* 461 Ποίαντος τέκνον for a younger person's respectful address of an older.

p. 68, on F 472.3, Crete of the hundred cities: for Homer see Pearson on Soph. F 899.

p. 75, on F 472e.19. For φύτωρ with short first vowel see Jebb on S. *Trach.* 1032 (conjectured by Dindorf).

p. 76, on F 472e.29–30 'hid', *31–33* 'proclaim'. Cf. *Cret.W.* F 460.2–3, *Oed.* F 553.2. Concealing marital infidelity: Men. *Sam.* 507–13 with J. Roy, *Greece & Rome* 44 (1997), 11–22.

p. 78, on F 988 at end. Daedalus' automata: S. Morris, *Daedalus and the Origins of Greek Art* (Princeton, 1992), 215ff.; N. Spivey on 'Bionic Statues' in A. Powell (ed.), *The Greek World* (London, 1995), 446–8.

p. 78, Addenda. A mosaic of the Pasiphae-story was uncovered during the excavation at Zeugma in Syria (BBC 2 TV film, 2000); it is not clear whether it relates to Euripides' play.

Stheneboea.

p. 79, Texts etc. Add van Rossum-Steenbeek 209–11 (Hypotheses, reporting on p. 22 that an unpublished Michigan papyrus has parts of a hypothesis); Diggle, *TrGFS* 128–31 (Hypothesis, F 661, 670); F. Jouan, ed. Budé VIII.3 (2002), 1–27.

p. 80, mid-page. Jouan 8–10 reluctantly abandons Murray's view that Bellerophon at the start of the play is already returning from killing the Chimaera; on 16–18 he has a good review of the two long time-interruptions, showing that Eur. here cleverly and uniquely pushed the limits of one play to an extreme.

p. 81, lines 5ff. Diggle rejects Rabe's παρά του 'by someone' because of the hiatus, and prints Wilamowitz's παρ' αὐτῆς 'by her'.

p. 81, Less certain fragments. Jouan p. 13 n. 28 and p. 27 tentatively admits adesp. F 292 as his fr. *10, placing it before F 670. At p. 13 n. 27 he rejects adesp. F 60.

p. 83, lines 3–7. For 'Potiphar's wife' see also J. Bremmer, *Greek Religion* (Oxford, 1994), 57–8 with n. 20 (bibl.), and S. R. Cavan in *Celebratio. Thirtieth Anniversary Essays at Trent University* (Peterborough, Ontario, 1998), 29–41 (bibl.).

p. 86, F 661.15. Diggle prints von Arnim's Ζηνὸς ἱκεσίου '(reverence for) the laws of Zeus the god of suppliants'.

p. 86, F 661.22–5 and App. Diggle deletes all four lines (22–3 Wilamowitz, 24–5 Holford-Strevens).

pp. 88, 89. Before F 663 add '**662 N** = *F 661.4–5 K*'.

p. 90, on Hypoth. 3. Diggle would have expected the children's names to be given.

p. 97, on F 670.5 ' traps'. Best is Pearson on Soph. F 504.

Bellerophon

p. 98, Texts etc. Add van Rossum-Steenbeek 191–3 (Hypotheses); Diggle, *TrGFS* 98–100 (F 285, 286, 292); F. Jouan, ed. Budé VIII.2 (2000), 1–35.

p. 98, Illustrations. Add *LIMC* VII.1.241–30 with VII.2.142–71 ('Bellerophon': C. Lochin, 1994).

pp. 98–9. On *Bellerophon* and Bellerophon in Comedy see G. Dobrov, *Figures of Play* (Oxford, 2001), 89–104 etc.

pp. 99, 112, 120. F 68 = *Bell.* F 304a *TrGF*. Jouan 14 accepts it for *Bell.* and thinks of a scene with Megapenthes.

p. 100. Jouan 9–10, 14 rejects a single '*agon*-scene'.

p. 101, Characterisation. 'Atheism' is rare in surviving literature; cf. esp. Critias, *TrGF* 43 F 19 (*Sisyphus*) and a few Presocratics cited by H. Yunis, *A New Creed* (Göttingen, 1988), 60 n. 2. For Euripides see M. Fusillo, *Poetica* 24 (1992), 270–99.

p. 103, App. for F 285.13, with Comm. pp. 113–4. Diggle cites F. W. Schmidt's ἣν ἀλγύνεται φέρων '(poverty) which he endures with pain'.

p. 106, F 292.5. Diggle obelizes ἀλλὰ τῶι νόμωι.

p. 106, App. for F 292.6, with Comm. p. 116. Müller reaffirms his lacuna in K. Gärtner, H.-H. Krummacher (eds.), *Zur Ueberlieferung, Kritik und Edition alter und neuerer Texte* (Stuttgart, 2000), 95–7; he reports a suggestion of R. Kannicht that 1–6a may be a digression in Bellerophon's speech, and 6b the resumption of the main theme. W. Luppe in *Dissertationes Criticae. Festschrift G. Hansen* (Würzburg, 1998), 123–6 prefers a lacuna at the end of 5. A long discussion also by Jouan 26 n. 57.

p. 108, F 297.2, with Comm. p. 117. Jouan conjectures μεῖω 'less (pay)', making the contrast plain (with Buecheler).

p. 108, App. for F 304.2, with Comm. p. 118 on 2–3. Jouan conjectures ἁλὸς '(deep) of the ocean'.

p. 117, on F 298. Compare *Antigone* F 176.3–5: 'Who is going to inflict pain on a rocky crag by wounding it with a spear, and who on corpses by outraging them, if they feel nothing of the injuries?'

pp. 119–20. On F 306, 308, 311 see M. Paterlini, *Sileno* 19 (1990), 513–23, and on F 68 (to be assigned to *Bell.*) A. Carlini, *Studi Privitera* (Naples, 2001), 179–84.

p. 120, on F 309a. Cf. perhaps *Hipp.* 1030 (earth and sea refusing welcome), *HF* 1295–6 (earth and sea forbidding human passage).

p. 129, on F 312. J. R. Porter in his *EMC* review rightly objects that ὑφ' ἅρματ' ἐλθὼν does imply yoking, citing the Homeric formula at *Od.* 3.476, 15.47.

Cresphontes

p. 121, Texts etc. Add Diggle, *TrGFS* 111–4 (F 448a, 449, 453); H. van Looy, ed. Budé VIII.2 (2000), 257–88.

pp. 121, 123–4, Myth. Add J. N. Bremmer, *ZPE* 117 (1997), 13–17 (Euripidean invention of plot and main characters; 4th C. political exploitation of the myth); N. Luraghi in H.-J. Gehrke (ed.), *Geschichtsbilder und Gründungsmythen* (Würzburg, 2001), 37-63 (political aspects of the myth of the division of the Peloponnese, especially the elder Cresphontes' role).

p. 125, Date; p. 139, Comm. on F 448a.83–109. E. Medda, *Eikasmos* 13 (2002), 67–84 compares F 448a.83ff. with other monologues addressed to the heart, and suggests Ar. *Ach.* 480-8 is modeled on it, with implications for the dating of *Cresph.*

p. 140, on F 448a.110–128 Metre. Diggle in *TrGFS* app. suggests that the text in P. Mich. is written as prose.

Erectheus

p. 148, Texts etc. Add Diggle, *TrGFS* 101–10 (F 360, 362, 369, 370); F. Jouan, ed. Budé VIII.2 (2000), 95–132.

p. 148, Main Discussions. Add U. Albini, *PP* 40 (1985), 354–60.

p. 154, lines 1–4. J. Breton Connelly's suggestion concerning the Parthenon Frieze was published in *AJA* 100 (1996), 53–80. For E. Harrison's response (to the conference paper) see J. Neils (ed.), *Worshipping Athena: Panathenaia and Parthenon* (Madison, 1996), 202–6; in her view the scene shows the Archon Basileus handing Athena's new peplos to a boy temple-servant.

p. 154, lines 5–10. Weidauer's interpretation of the Lucanian vase is rejected by K. Clinton, *Myth and Cult: the Iconography of the Eleusinian Mysteries* (Stockholm, 1992), 77, who connects it with the contest of Athena and Poseidon.

p. 159, transl. of F 360.6. For λαβεῖν = 'find' see Diggle, *CQ* 47 (1997), 103–4; cf. also *El.* 70 and Ellendt, *Lexicon Sophocleum* 'λαμβάνω' II §5.

p. 167, line 1 of App. Add Diggle, *TrGFS* 106–10; Jouan, ed. Budé VIII.2.126–30.

pp. 168–73, text and App. for F 370, with Comm. pp. 187–91. The conjectures of Diggle mentioned on lines 17, 34, 41, 51 are discussed by him in *CQ* 47 (1997), 103–7; that in 62 is mentioned in his *TrGFS* app. In *CQ* he also suggests in 35 σὺ δ' "Αιδα διῆλθες οἶμον 'but you have completed the path to Hades' (addressed to one of the daughters), and in 42 e.g. θ[άνατον (qualified by the preceding adjectives). His *TrGFS* app. includes a further conjecture: 37–8 φρενομανὴς ἀφῶ δάκρυα '...shall I, distraught in mind, release my tears'.

p. 168, App. for F 370.22. C. Austin notes (by letter) that κοὐ (Diels) was also proposed by W. Headlam, *JPh* 23 (1895), 276–7, comparing Soph. F 837 for the evaluation of life (ζῆν) after death; he thinks the papyrus might have (accordingly)]μαλλον καιου[.

p. 176, on F 350, 'moons'. Cf. E. Kearns, 'Cakes in Greek sacrifice regulations', in R. Hägg (ed.), *Ancient Greek Cult Practice from the Epigraphical Evidence* (Stockholm, 1994), 65–70.

p. 176, on F 352. Cf. Xen. *Cyrop.* 1.5.14, 1.6.44.

p. 177, on F 358, 'Love'. 'Love' (ἔρως) of *polis* also in Pericles' Funeral Speech, Thuc. 2.43.1.

p. 182, on F 362.18–20. For dismissals of discourse aimed 'at gratification (χάρις) and pleasure (ἡδονή)' cf. Critias *TrGF* 43 F 23, Isocr. 8.10, 12.271, Plut. *Mor.* 55e.

pp. 182–3, on F 362.18–20. Pl. *Laws* 694b: the good ruler profits from the intelligence and good counsel of those around him, allows *parrhesia*, and does not show *phthonos*. Xen. *Cyr.* 5.4.36 has *poneroi* in an exactly similar context. *Poneroi* natural associates of tyrants: Xen. *Hiero* 5.1-2 (cited by Collard on *Supp.* 444–6).

p. 184, on F 365. On good and bad *aidôs* see also Bernard Williams, *Shame and Necessity* (Berkeley, 1993), 225–30.

p. 190, on 55–117. Athena's speech is discussed by F. Jouan, cited in the Comm. on *Antiope* F 223.67 in this volume, p. 319.

p. 193, on 90–4. The identification of the Erechtheum is now debated. For a brief introduction to the problem see J. Hurwit, *The Athenian Acropolis* (Cambridge, 1999), with refs. in note 114; cf. N. Robertson in Neils, ed. (cited above), 37–44.

p. 194, on F 370.107–8. On Hyacinthides and Hyades see T. Hadzisteliou-Price, *Kourotrophos* (Leiden, 1978), 127.

Phaethon

p. 195, Texts etc. Add van Rossum-Steenbeek 222–3 (P. Oxy. 2455 Hypothesis); Diggle, *TrGFS* 150–60 (Hypothesis and lines 1–7, 45–126, 158–77, 214–88) with J. Diggle, 'Epilegomena Phaethontea', *AC* 65 (1996), 189–99; H. Van Looy, ed. Budé VIII.3 (2002), 225–68.

p. 195, Illustrations. Add *LIMC* VIII.1.350–4 with VIII.2.311–13 ('Phaethon': F. Baratte, 1997).

p. 196, top. On the study of P see Diggle, 'Epilegomena' (above), 190–1.

p. 200, note 1. Kevin Lee's paper was published in M. Silk (ed.), *Tragedy and the Tragic* (Oxford, 1996), 85–118 (with a response by W. G. Arnott); and our apologies to 'Sidney' (see Eur. *Supp.* 555–7, in part).

p. 202, §4.7. Van Looy 243 is categoric that Oceanus is the god, for he not only 'saves his daughter but restores order': a good point.

p. 203, §5 near end. Delete the sentence 'so it is likely...the end of the Episode.' The mute servant (see Comm. on 245) entered the palace, the entering servant has come from the treasure-house (253–7).

p. 218, line 238. Diggle (and Van Looy) now prints Willink's metrical improvement δόμοις χρυσέ⟨οις θε⟩ῶν 'starry golden palace of the gods'.

p. 218, line 240. Diggle now accepts Hermann's conjectures (printed by us).

p. 222, F 783a = fr. 1 D. Van Looy 265 n. 94 notes Meziriac's supplement (in Plut.) ⟨σε⟩, 'unhinged ⟨you⟩' (i.e., Phaethon speaks ironically to Merops during their discussion of marriage).

p. 226, on 59–60. Diggle, 'Epilegomena' (above) has more on λόγοι here.

p. 226, on 63–101, para.1. For dawn-pictures add Hollis on Callim. *Hecale* 74.23ff.

p. 227, on 67. Diggle, 'Epilegomena' has further notes on nightingales.

p. 231, on 158–9. The construction of Acc. part. with ἔχω occurs 15 times in Herodotus (see J. E. Powell, *Lexicon to Herodotus*), once in Thucydides (1.144.3).

p. 232, on 168. Cf. Nestor's instructions to Antilochus on how to drive, Hom. *Il.* 23.306ff.

p. 233, on 217. Copious illustration of such doubling by Diggle, 'Epilegomena'.

pp. 234–5, on 227–244. J. R. Porter in his *EMC* review observes that if Merops is an *ersatz* bridegroom the difficulty of 241 is resolved.

p. 235 Comm. Diggle, 'Epilegomena' gives many examples of a word or name in corresponding places in strophe and antistrophe, as Aphrodite here in 230 and 239.

Wise Melanippe, Captive Melanippe

p. 240, Texts etc. Add Diggle, *TrGFS* 120–7 (*Mel.S.* Hypoth., F 481; *Mel.D.* F 494 [= No. 660 M], 495, *Mel.* F 506); H. van Looy, ed. Budé VIII.2 (2000), 347–96.

No. 665a–c M is F 481 K; No. 660 M is F 494 K.

pp. 240, 245, Myth. Political aspects of the foundation myths of Metapontium are discussed by D. Giacometti, *Annali della Fac. di Lett. e Filosofia... Perugia* 28 (1990–1), 277–96 and M. Nafissi, *Ostraka* 6 (1997), 337–57.

p. 248, App. for No. 665a M, Hypothesis. Add van Rossum-Steenbeek 199 (P. Leiden), 206–7 (P. Oxy.); Diggle, *TrGFS* 120; ed. Budé VIII.3.356–7.

p. 250, text of No. 665a–c M, with Comm. p. 266. The integrity of the transmitted text is defended further by S. Cives, *RCCM* 40 (1998), 45–53, who notes that a date for *Mel.S.* about 413 would help to explain the omission of Dorus and his descendants from the narrative. Both Diggle and van Looy print a lacuna after line 8, allowing for mention of Dorus. In 12 Diggle obelizes ὄνομά τε τοὐμόν, while Luppe (personal correspondence) suggests the text in 11–12 may have been disrupted (ἀλλ' ἀνοιστέος λόγος Ι ⟨ x – ◡ – x ⟩ κεῖσ' ὅθενπερ ἠρξάμην, Ι ὄνομά τε τοὐμόν ⟨ – ◡ – x – ◡ – ⟩).

p. 255, App. for No. 660 M. Add Diggle, *TrGFS* 123–4; ed. Budé VIII.3.385–7.

p. 256, text of No. 660.25. Diggle in *TrGFS* prints his conjecture ἤν μί' εὑρεθῆι ('if ever' rather than just 'if').

p. 257, App. for F 495. Add Diggle, *TrGFS* 124–6; ed. Budé VIII.3.389–91.

p. 259, App. for F 495 with Comm., pp. 275–6. J. Diggle, *Analecta Papyrologica* 7 (1995), 11–13 proposes in line 18 χερμ[άδων ἔσχον βολάς, 'your brothers put a stop to the rock-throwing', and in 30–1 ἄλλον νεκρὸν [παῖς αὐ]τὸς 'another corpse, by the same youth...' (both printed in *TrGFS*); in 39 he rejects von Arnim, preferring (in *TrGFS* app.) Nauck's τύχην τοιαύτην or μόρον τοιοῦτον ('such is the fortune/death of your brothers that I tell you of'). In *TrGFS* app. he proposes in 23–4 ο]ὐ λῆμ' ἔχο[ντες δοῦλον ἀλλ' ἐλεύθερον Ι ἦιξαν π]ρὸς ἀ[λκήν, 'having a temper not slavish but free, (the twins) leapt to their own defence'.

p. 272, on No. 660 M. J. Butrica, *CQ* 51 (2001), 610–3 sees arguments from this speech reflected in Ar. *Eccl.* 441–54, and suggests a 'Socratic' source for them.

p. 272, on No. 660.12–22. L. Maurizio, *JHS* 105 (1995), 85 discusses this passage in a study of the Pythia's prophetic role at Delphi. On women's religious roles see also M. Lefkowitz in Neils (ed.), *Worshipping Athena* (see on p. 154 above), 78–91.

p. 279, line 5. At end of sentence add M. L. West, *The East Face of Helicon* (Oxford, 1997), 561–2.

CORRIGENDA

(Not including minor typographical and other errors easily corrected.)

General Introduction

> *p. 5, line 10.* Change 'note 1 above' to 'note 1 on p. vii above'.
>
> *p. 10, line 5.* Change 'F 472e.10' to 'F 472e.9'.

Bibliography and Abbreviations

> *p. 13, under I. J. F. de Jong.* Change '*Narrative Drama*' to '*Narrative in Drama*'.

Telephus

> *p. 25, line 6 of last para.* Change 'see Comm. on F 697...722–3' to 'see Jocelyn's commentary, especially on Enn. fr. 142 (cf. Eur. F 703), fr. 143 (F 697), fr. 146 (F 720)'.
>
> *p. 25, last line but 3.* Delete 'Schmitt 287,'.
>
> *p. 42, Comm. on F 696.1 at end.* Change '(5, 8...)' to '(5, 7...)'.
>
> *p. 43, Comm. on F 696.6.* Change '(8.54.7)' to '(8.54.6)'.
>
> *p. 44, line 8 of Comm. on F 699.* Change 'F 700' to 'F 705'.
>
> *p. 47, last line of Comm. on F 727.* Change '*Hec.* 276' to '*Hec.* 1276'.
>
> *p. 48, line 8 of Comm. on F 727b.* Change '(12)' to '(11)'.

Cretans

> *p. 61, F 472c, app. line 2.* Read '2nd C. A.D.'
>
> *p. 70, line 5.* Change 'xxvii Kambitsis' to 'xxxvii Kambitsis'.
>
> *p. 70, line 13 of Comm. on 16–20.* Change 'in 18' to 'in 17'.
>
> *p. 72, F 472bc.38.* Change 'F 448a.28' to 'F 448a.55'.
>
> *p. 77.* Change the lemma '40' to '40–1'.

Stheneboea.

> *p. 81, penultimate line.* Change 'I.(ii)' to 'I.(iv)'.
>
> *p. 84–5, Hypothesis 20 and App.* Read ἐπιβουλευθείς (3 times).

Bellerophon

> *p. 112, F 312a K.* Change 312a (Snell's number) to 286a.
>
> *p. 116 F 292.6* read just 'Stob.'s 'But I tell you...'
>
> *p. 117, F 293.2.* Change 'F 285.5–12 n.' to 'F 286 n.'
>
> *p. 118, last line but five,* Change 'see below' to 'see above'.
>
> *p. 118, penultimate line.* Change 'F 303 n.' to F 303.3 n.'

Cresphontes

> *p. 132, F 453.3.* Delete the colon-like mark after σέθεν.
>
> *p. 137, line 1 of Comm. on 43.* Change 'pp. 124–6' to 'pp. 123–4, 125'.
>
> *p. 143, last line of Comm. on F 450.* Change 'pp. 124–5' to 'pp. 123–4'.

p. 145, line 7 of Comm. on F 455. Change '*Mel.S.*' to '*Mel.D.*'.

Erectheus

p. 152, last line but six. Change 'F 360.40–9' to 'F 360.46–9'.

p. 163, App. for F 362.18–20. Change 'p. 124' to 'p. 123'.

p. 170, F 370.37. Insert a vertical line (= line-end in the papyrus) after φίλαν.

p. 177, line 1 of Comm. on F 358. Change '*Mel.D.*' to '*Mel.*'

p. 178, line 6. Change 'Kamerbeek [1992], 14' to 'Kamerbeek in Hofmann and Harder, *Fragmenta Dramatica* 114'.

p. 181, line 12 of Comm. on F 362. Change 'F 360.2' to 'F 362.2'.

p. 193, Comm. on F 370.93–94. Change 'Hom. *Il.* 550–1' to 'Hom. *Il.* 2.550–1'.

Phaethon

p. 200, line 5. Change 'F 472e.36–37' to 'F 472e.46–7'.

p. 203, § 7 line 4. Change 'adesp. 5f' to 'adesp. 5h'.

p. 211, transl. of line 96. Change 'the day which' to 'the celebration which'; the relative (article) refers to τέλει, not φάος.

p. 219, transl. of line 258. Change 'his anger' to 'some anger'.

p. 225, Comm. on 45–46, line 2. Change 'has hopes' to 'had hopes'.

p. 232, Comm. on 174. Change '*Cresph.* F 605.4 (n.)' to '*Mel.* F 506.4 (n.)'.

p. 233, Comm. on 178–213, lines 1–2. Delete '?208' (line 208 is not printed in the text), and change '191' to '181'.

p. 236, line 3. Change '(3rd Pers. Pl.)' to '(3rd Pers. Sing.)'.

Wise Melanippe, Captive Melanippe

p. 274, third line of Comm. on No. 660.23. Delete 'But'.

p. 280, line 4 of Comm. on F 511. Change '*Hel.* 830–1' to '*Hel.* 730–1'.

p. 280, line 8 of Comm. on F 513. Delete bracket after 'word'.

INDEXES

The Indexes cover (selectively) the Introductions and Commentaries in Volumes I and II (indicated in bold face with page-number, e.g. **I**.59, **II**.113). A superscript number (e.g. **I**.69^2) shows more than one reference on a page. Bold-faced page-numbers (e.g. **II.88–91**) show frequent references.

1. Ancient authors and texts

Accius, *Andromeda* **II**.143; *Minos*(?) **I**.59; *Philocteta* **II**.1, 3, 5 n. 3, 8, 26, 29, **30**; *Telephus* **I**.21, 25

Achaeus *Oedipus* **II**.113; *Philoctetes* **II**.12

Adespota: see 'Fragmenta adespota'

Aelian, *Var. Hist.* (2.8) **II**.93, 97

Aelius Aristides **I**.85ff., 149, 151, (*Or.* 2.934) **II**.300

Aeschylus, *Ag.* (104ff.) **I**.186, (717ff.) **II**.359; *Cho.* **I**.124, (385ff.) **I**.146; *Eum.* (273ff.) **I**.279, (977) **I**.145; *Pers.* (403f.) **I**.179; *PV* (1080ff.) **I**.189; *Sept.* **II**.106; *Suppl.* (204ff.) **I**.182, (212–3) **I**.234, (855) **I**.234.

Cretan Women **I**.59; *Danaides* (F 44) **I**.269; *Edonians* **I**.189; *Heliades* **I**.195, 198; *Laius* **II**.106; Lemnian tetralogy **II**.177; *Myrmidons* **I**.25; *Nemea* **II**.178, 183; *Oedipus* **II**.106; *Palamedes* **II**.92, 94; *Philoctetes* **II**.1f., 4f., 28; *Telephus* **I**.22, 24, 25; (F 281a) **I**.279

Alcaeus (Com.), *Pasiphae* **I**.59

Alcidamas, *Palamedes* **II**.97

Anaxagoras (A 8) **I**.232

Anaximander (A 27) **I**.232

Anthologia Palatina (3.5) **I**.121f.; (3.7) **II**.259, 261, 313–4; (3.10) **II**.169, 173–5, 256; (3.15) **I**.98f.; (3.16) **I**.240, 243

Antimachus, *Thebais* **II**.105, 177

Antiphanes, *Philoctetes* **II**.12, 143

Antiphon (B 44(b)) **II**.77

Apollodorus, *Library* (2.1.4) **II**.350, (2.2.1f.) **I**.90, (2.3.1f.) **I**.79, 90, 98f., (2.4.2ff.) **II**.133, 135ff., (2.8.4f.) **I**.121ff., **II**.334 (3.1.3f.) **I**.53f., 78, (3.5.5) **II**.259, 261f., (3.5.8f.) **II**.105, 107, 124, (3.6.4) **II**.133, (3.12.5) **II**.35, 36, 72, (3.15.1) **I**.150, 181, 193, (3.15.4) **I**.148ff., 176, (3.15.8) **I**.53, (*Epit.* 1.9) **II**.227, (*Epit.* 3.6f.) **II**.92, 94f., (*Epit.*

3.17ff.) **I**.17f., (*Epit.* 3.20) **I**.51, (*Epit.* 3.26f.) **II**.1ff. (*Epit.* 5.8.) **II**.1

Archelaus (A 4) **II**.77

Aristophanes, *Ach.* (204–625) **I**.18, (384) **I**.21, (395ff.) **I**.19, (411ff.) **I**.18, 23–4, 44, (423–4) **II**.3, (426ff.) **I**.98, (450, 456) **I**.21, (496ff.) **I**.45, (1190ff.) **I**.18, (1204ff.) **I**.18; *Birds* (202ff.) **I**.142, (508ff.) **II**.73, (1720ff.) **I**.234; *Clouds* (921ff.) **I**.18; *Eccl.* (441ff.) **II**.369, (465ff.) **I**.272; *Frogs* **I**.5, (52ff.) **II**.143, (64) 257, (840ff.) **I**.18, (849f.) **I**.53, 55, (1177ff.) **II**.350, (1206ff.) **II**.337, 351, (1309ff.) **I**.257f., **II**.231, (1315–6) **II**.231, (1320–8) **I**.257f., (1331ff.) **I**.66, (1356, 1359) **I**.53, (1451) **II**.93, (1482ff.) **II**.325; *Knights* **I**.46; *Lys.* (706f.) **I**.44, (853ff.) **I**.95, (865ff.) **I**.81, (1124ff.) **I**.269; *Peace* (58ff.) **I**.98, (126) **I**.96, (135) **I**.119, (146ff.) **I**.18, (560ff.) **I**.144, (974ff.) **I**.144, (1332ff.) **I**.234; *Thesm.* (23f.) **I**.18, (39ff.) **I**.19, (76f.) **I**.21–2, (120) **I**.185, (466–764) **I**.19, (547) **I**.247, (694f.) **I**.21f., (847–8) **II**.93, 97, (1009ff.) **II**.133ff., 137, 142f., 156ff.; *Wasps* (1074) **I**.94

Cocalus **I**.59; *Daedalus* **I**.59; *Georgoi* **I**.125; *Lemniai* **II**.177; (F 856) **II**.176

Aristophanes of Byzantium **I**.1

Aristotle, *Poetics* (1454a.22ff.) **I**.247

Asclepiades of Tragilos (F 12) **II**.35, (F 13) **I**.79, 98

Astydamas, *Bellerophon* **I**.83, 101; *Palamedes* **II**.97

Bacchylides (9.10ff.) **II**.177; (*Dithyr.* 26) **I**.53; (F 7) **II**.1f.

Callimachus (*Hymn* 3.190ff.) **I**.76

Callinus (F 1.6ff.) **I**.179

Carcinus (F 3) **I**.95

Cicero *De Diu.* (1.94) **II**.300, (I.115) **II**.89, (2.127) **II**.89

(F 745) **II**.333, 354; *Temenid.* **I**.123, 125, **II**.333, 337; *Theseus* **II**.141n.1
Fragments: (224 N) **II**.265, (846) **II**.333, (853) **II**.265, (867) **II**.42, (883, 885) **I**.21, (890) **II**.8, (896) **I**.197, (898) **I**.269f., (898a) **I**.21, (910) **I**.244, **II**.96, 262, 324, (911) **II**.264, (912) **I**.55, **II**.111, (918) **I**.21, **II**.265, (928) **I**.244, (929b) **I**.244, (937, 938) **II**.42, (950) **I**.244, (955h) **II**.137, 139, (958, 960) **II**.42, (969) **II**.333, 350, (971) **I**.197, (975) **I**.21, (976) **II**.42, (977) **II**.137, (981) **I**.152, (982) **I**.197, (985) **II**.137, (988) **I**.55, (1004) **I**.56, **I**.244, (1008) **II**.137, (1023) **I**.270, (1028) **II**.265, (1029) **II**.111, (1033) **I**.21, (1038) **II**.333, 361, (1047) **I**.231, (1052) **II**.333 (1058) **II**.265, (1060) **I**.138, (1062, 1064) **II**.137, (1066) **I**.21, (1068, 1082) **II**.42, (1083) **I**.123
Fragmenta adespota (PMG) (926e) **II**.137
Fragmenta adespota (TrGF) (5f) **I**.203, (8) **II**. 111, (10) **II**.8, (34) **I**.56, (37a) **II**.176, (44 N) **I**.21, (57) **I**.21, (60) **I**.56, 81, (71b) **II**.42, (88a) **II**.265, 303, (98 N) **I**.211, (284) **II**.111, (286, 289) **II**.42, (292) **I**.81, (356) **I**.72, (520) **I**.244, (537) **II**.137, (579) **II**.8, (591c) **II**.102, (634) **II**.176, (721b–c) **II**.42, (853) **II**.310
Genesis (4.16) **I**.100
Gorgias, *Palamedes* **II**.92, 97
Gregory of Corinth **I**.90
Herodotus (2.3.2) **I**.234, (5.4.2) **I**.143, (5.22) **II**.330, (7.61.3) **II**.133, (8.137ff.) **II**.330, 334f.
Hesiod, *Theog.* (154ff.) **I**.269, (984f.) **I**.198; *Works* (220ff.) **I**.278, (248ff.) **I**.278, (319ff.) **I**.79, (702f.) **I**.275; (984ff.) **I**.195, (F 10a. 20ff.) **I**.267; (F 43.81ff.) **I**.79, 82, (F 129. 16ff.) **I**.79; (F 135) **II**.133, 137; (F 145) **I**.53; (F 311) **I**.195, 198
Homer, *Iliad* (2.718ff.) **II**.1f., 6, (3.337ff.) **I**.44, (6.155ff.) **I**.79, 82ff., (6.192ff.) **I**.98f., (17.446f.) **I**.142, (18.478ff.) **I**.227, (22.347) **I**.77, (24.27ff.) **II**.43, (24.602ff.) **I**.145; *Odyssey* (8.266ff.) **I**.198, (11.260ff.) **II**.259, (11.271ff.) **II**.105f., (16.392) **I**.277, (20.13ff.) **I**.139
Homeric Hymns (2.150f.) **I**.193, (4.214f.) 146
Horace (*Ep.* 1.18.39ff.) **II**.259, 262, 300

Hyginus, *Astron.* (2.9–11) **II**.133, 136, (2.18) **I**.79, 82, 98; *Fab.* (7, 8) **II**.259, 261, 263, 311, (40) **I**.53ff., (46) **I**.148, (57) **I**.79, 82, 98f., (64) **II**.133, 138, (66, 67) **II**.105, 107f., 111, (74) **II**.169, 174, (91) **II**.35, 36, 39, 44 n. 5, 71, (101) **I**.17, (102) **II**.1, 4, (105) **II**.92, 94, (137) **I**.121, (152a, 154) **I**.195, (184b) **I**.121, (186) **I**.240, 242, (219) **II**.330, 335, (238.2) **I**.148, (252) **I**.267, (273.6) **II**.169, 175
Ioannes Logothetes **I**.90
Isocrates (6.22f.) **I**.121, (*Busir.* hyp.) **II**.93, 97
Libanius, *Decl.* (1.177), *Or.* (44.73) **I**.53
Life of Euripides **II**.333, 337
Little Iliad **II**.1f., (F 6, 7) **I**.22
Livius Andronicus, *Andromeda* **II**.143
Lucian (*Dial.Mar.* 14) **II**.133
Lycophron, *Andromeda* **II**.143
Lycurgus, *In Leocratem* (98ff.) **I**.148f., 155
Malalas, Ioannes **I**.53, **II**.105, 107, 259, 364
Manilius (*Astron.* 5.538ff.) **II**.133
Meletus, *Oedipodeia* **II**.113
Menander, *Epitrepontes* (1084ff.) **I**.279
Mimnermus (F 12.9 *IEG*) **I**.224
Nicolaus Damasc. (F 8) **II**.105, (F 31, 34) **I**.121
Nicomachus, *Alexandros* **II**.49
Nonnus, *Dionysiaca* (38.90ff.) **I**.195
Olympiodorus, *In Platonis Gorgiam* **II**.300
Orion (as source of frs.) **II**.166, 249, 331, 356, 360
Ovid, *Ars.Am.* (1.289ff.) **I**.53; *Met.* (1.747ff.) **I**.195, (2.210ff.) **I**.197, (4.668–5.238) **II**.133, 135–8, (6.110f.) **II**.259, 261
Pacuvius, *Antiopa* **II**.259f., **262f.**, 270, 298f., 303f., 309, 311, 314, 323
Papyri: P. Berl. (5514) **I**.240, 274ff., (9771) **I**.195f., (9772) **I**.240, 272ff., (9908) **I**.17, (13217) **I**.53f., 72, **II**.364, (21144) **I**.240; P. Derveni **II**.251; P. Hamb. (118) **II**.169, 227, 330, 351ff.; P. Fayum **I**.121; P. Leiden (145) **I**.240, P. Lit. Lond. (74) **II**.244, (86) **I**.244; P. Mich. (1319) **I**.123, (6973) **I**.121f., (6973) **I**.136, (unpubl., Hypoth. Eur. *Pal.*) **II**.92, 95, (unpubl., Hypoth. Eur. *Sthen.*) **II**.365; P. Milan (1) **I**.17, 42f.; P. Oxy. (419) **II**.330, 357f., (852) **II**.170, 228, 240ff., 244, 249f., 252f., (1176) **I**.240, (2455) **I**.17, 79, 104, 105f., 123, 169ff., 195f., 224, 240 **II**.1f., 226, (2458) **I**.121, 136, (2459) **II**.105f., (2460)

2. Language, style, metre

3. Names and Places

4. Topics